Making it tangible

Sascha Bernholt, Knut Neumann,
Peter Nentwig (Eds.)

Making it tangible
# Learning outcomes in science education

Waxmann 2012
Münster / New York / München / Berlin

**Bibliographic information published by die Deutsche Nationalbibliothek**
Die Deutsche Nationalbibliothek lists this publication in the
Deutsche Nationalbibliografie; detailed bibliographic data
are available in the internet at http://dnb.d-nb.de.

ISBN 978-3-8309-2644-3

© Waxmann Verlag GmbH, Münster 2012

www.waxmann.com
info@waxmann.com

Cover Design: Verena Hane, Kiel
Print: Hubert & Co., Göttingen
Printed on age-resistant paper, acid-free as per ISO 9706

Printed in Germany

All rights reserved. No part of this publication may be reproduced, stored in
a retrieval system or transmitted in any form or by any means, electronic,
electrostatic, magnetic tape, mechanical, photocopying, recording or
otherwise without permission in writing from the copyright holder.

**Preface**

The Leibniz Institute for Science and Mathematics Education (IPN) at the University of Kiel in Germany and the University of York Science Education Group (UYSEG) in the UK are major centres of research and development in science education. Both have many years' experience of research projects on different aspects of science education practice and policy, and of the development and evaluation of innovative approaches to science teaching and learning. In recent years, one focus of the work at both centres has been the drive to improve scientific literacy at all levels of school education, in particular through the development of context-based and context-led science courses.

As a means of exploring specific issues in some depth, the two Centres inaugurated a series of small conferences on selected themes. The idea was that each would involve a maximum of 30 participants, selected staff drawn from the two centres and invited experts on the chosen topic from a range of countries. In contrast to international conferences with hundreds of participants and dozens of parallel sessions, this setting allowed extensive and in-depth discussions and the opportunity to contrast in detail the different approaches and experiences contributed by leading international experts. This book presents some of the outcomes of the fifth of these conferences. The topic was learning outcomes in science education, how they might be defined and assessed – and how this might stimulate improved outcomes. This is a topic which is widely discussed and debated, as a common feature of today's educational reforms is the increasing focus on educational outcomes. However, despite this international trend, considerable differences can be found in the details.

The chapters of this book are based on the papers presented at the conference – revised in the light of the discussions. The expertise of the participants, their experience and the exchange of ideas and controversies during the symposiums are reflected in the quality of each individual contribution. The composition of the papers in this book therefore provides on the one hand an overview of different national approaches and developments concerning the topic of learning outcomes in science education; on the other hand, it provides a well-grounded compendium of challenges and open questions that need to be addressed by the international educational research community in the future, which makes this book of particular interest to the field.

December 2011                                      Olaf Köller (IPN, Kiel)
                                                   Robin Millar (UYSEG, York)

# Acknowledgements

We thank Professor Dr. Ilka Parchmann for contributing inspiring ideas and for her support in the process of planning and preparing this, the fifth IPN-UYSEG Conference in Science Education.

We are grateful to the staff of the Strandhotel Strande near Kiel who made our stay most effective as their aid allowed us to fully focus on the topic of the meeting. We moreover thank the student assistants who helped in organizing the symposium, planning arrivals and departures, organizing taxis or who just stepped into the breach whenever their help was needed.

We are much obliged to our patient and helpful authors. They wrote their papers prior to the symposium and read all contributions as preparation for the meeting. Subsequent to the symposium, we asked them for revisions in order to gain coherence and to reflect some of the major issues that emerged from the discussions. This was an iterative process and the authors were unfailingly cooperative.

We thank the German Research Foundation (DFG) for substantial funding without which it would not have been possible for the meeting to take place. In equal measure, we thank the Leibniz Institute for Science and Mathematics Education (IPN) for the financial and organisational support of the meeting.

Finally, we wish our readers to note that any mistakes that they find are our responsibility.

December 2011                                         Sascha Bernholt
                                                      Knut Neumann
                                                      Peter Nentwig

# Contents

**Part A** **Setting the Scene**

Chapter 1   Making it Tangible –
Specifying Learning Outcomes in Science Education
*Sascha Bernholt, Knut Neumann & Peter Nentwig*          13

**Part B** **The Big Picture**

Chapter 2   Moving Beyond Standards: How Can We Improve Elementary Science Learning? A German Perspective
*Kornelia Möller, Ilonca Hardy & Kim Lange*          31

Chapter 3   Developing a Framework for Diagnostic Assessment of Early Science
*Benő Csapó*          55

Chapter 4   The Design of an Assessment System Focused on Student Achievement: A Learning Sciences Perspective on Issues of Competence, Growth, and Measurement
*James W. Pellegrino*          79

Chapter 5   Learning Outcomes in Ireland –
Implications for the Science Classroom
*Declan Kennedy*          109

Chapter 6   Assessing Professional Competences and their Development in Vocational Education in Germany – State of Research and Perspectives
*Reinhold Nickolaus, Andreas Lazar & Kerstin Norwig*          129

## Part C    The Devil in the Details

**Chapter 7**  Competencies: The German Notion of Learning Outcomes
*Olaf Köller & Ilka Parchmann*    151

**Chapter 8**  Capturing the Diversity of Students' Competences in Science Classrooms: Differences and Commonalities of Three Complementary Approaches
*Sascha Bernholt, Sabina Eggert & Christoph Kulgemeyer*    173

**Chapter 9**  Assessment of Standards-based Learning Outcomes in Science Education: Perspectives from the German Project ESNaS
*Kerstin Kremer, Hans E. Fischer, Alexander Kauertz, Jürgen Mayer, Elke Sumfleth & Maik Walpuski*    201

**Chapter 10**  Standards, Competencies and Outcomes. A Critical View
*Horst Schecker*    219

**Chapter 11**  The Development, Validation, and Implementation of Standards in Science Education: Chances and Difficulties in the Swiss Project HarmoS
*Peter Labudde, Christian Nidegger, Marco Adamina & François Gingins*    235

**Chapter 12**  The Promise and Value of Learning Progression Research
*Joseph S. Krajcik, LeeAnn M. Sutherland, Kathryn Drago & Joi Merritt*    261

**Chapter 13**  Using Learning Progression to Organize Learning Outcomes: Implications for Assessment
*Xiufeng Liu*    285

**Chapter 14**  The Challenge of Alignment of Students' Learning Outcomes with Curriculum Guidelines, Instruction, and Assessment in Science Practice in Taiwan
*Mei-Hung Chiu & Hui-Jung Chen*    303

**Chapter 15**  Learning Outcomes for Science in Australia: How Are They Defined, Measured, and Implemented?
*Debra Panizzon*    341

**Part D        Perspectives from Different Countries**

Chapter 16   How Learning Outcomes in Science Are Specified and
             Measured in the English School System
             *Robin Millar, Mary Whitehouse & Ian Abrahams*          367

Chapter 17   An Examination of Turkish Science Curricula from a Historical
             Perspective with an Emphasis on Learning Outcomes
             *Alipaşa Ayas*                                          399

Chapter 18   Defining the Structure and the Content of a New Chemistry
             Curriculum in the Netherlands
             *Cris Bertona*                                          425

Chapter 19   Potential Learning Outcomes Inferred from French Curricula
             in Science Education
             *Patrice Venturini & Andrée Tiberghien*                 443

Chapter 20   Item Construction for Finnish National Level Assessment in
             School Physics Without Pre-Defined Learning Outcomes
             *Jari Lavonen, Heidi Krzywacki & Laura Koistinen*       477


**Part E        A Coda**

Chapter 21   Learning Outcomes in Science Education: A Synthesis of the
             International Views on Defining, Assessing and Fostering Science
             Learning
             *Knut Neumann, Sascha Bernholt & Peter Nentwig*         501

## Part A

# Setting the Scene

# Chapter 1
# Making it Tangible –
# Specifying Learning Outcomes in Science Education

*Sascha Bernholt[1], Knut Neumann[2] & Peter Nentwig[1]*
*IPN · Leibniz Institute for Science and Mathematics Education, Kiel, Germany*
*[1]Department of Chemistry Education, [2]Department of Physics Education*

## Abstract

Today, many countries have established educational standards. In addition, most of the recent educational reforms across the world are shifting away from traditional content-driven curricula. Instead, these reforms aim to provide clear, specific descriptions of the skills and knowledge that teachers are supposed to teach and students are expected to learn. The specification, however, what exactly students are expected to know and be able to do, varies widely between countries. In Germany for example, so called *competences* that students are expected to have acquired at a given stage in their school career (end of primary and end of lower secondary school, respectively) are specified. In other countries, learning outcomes are defined sometimes with a different notion, sometimes with just different terms. In March 2011, an international symposium brought renowned researchers together from countries with different notions of the nature and quality of learning outcomes for a conceptual clarification and better understanding among the international science education community.

## 1 Introduction

Triggered by international large-scale assessments, such as TIMSS (Beaton et al., 1996), PISA (OECD, 2001, 2004, 2007), or PIRLS (Mullis, Martin, Kennedy, & Foy, 2007), discussions about the achievement and effectiveness of the national school system have emerged in many countries. Several countries found themselves far behind their expectations with regard to the results of these international comparative studies. In response to these often disappointing findings, a debate about the aims of science education arose in many countries whether the current curricula are sufficiently prospective to provide a fruitful foundation for a successful and future-oriented science education in schools.

For a long time "the content of the science curriculum has largely been framed by scientists who see school science as a preparation for entry into university rather than as an education for everyone. No other curriculum subject serves such a strong dual mandate" (Osborne & Dillon, 2008, p. 21). However, with regard to the future needs of the students, the question pertained to what young adults need to learn in formal education in order to play a constructive role as a citizen in society (Tenorth, 2006). In the case of science education, the question arose regarding what is important to know, to value, and to be able to do in situations involving science and technology in a modern society (cf. deBoer, 2000).

In recent years and especially induced by the results of PISA, the idea of scientific literacy, albeit in different notions, received wide acceptance as the overall aim of science education (DeBoer, 2000; Gräber & Bolte, 1997; Gräber, Nentwig, Koballa, & Evans, 2002; Roberts, 2007). Although there is no general consensus about the exact meaning of or what constitutes scientific literacy, it is considered a functional educational concept which can provide both a basis for lifelong learning and a preparation for life in a modern society (e.g., Bybee, 1997; Millar & Osborne, 1998; Roberts, 2007).

Following the adoption of scientific literacy as the overarching aim of science education, a growing number of countries introduced science education standards in order to ensure that students in fact obtain scientific literacy (cf. Nentwig & Schanze, 2007). These standards intend to provide precise descriptions of the skills and knowledge that teachers are supposed to teach and students are expected to learn in order to become scientifically literate. Along with the introduction of standards assessment systems were developed to benchmark students' achievements in their struggle to obtain scientific literacy (Ravitch, 1995; Resnick & Resnick, 1983). The combination of clearly formulated learning outcomes and the assessment of students' achievement is a concept of educational governance and aims to enable a data-driven steering mechanism for the educational system towards a higher quality of teaching (Altrichter, Brüsemeister, & Wissinger, 2007; Amos, 2010).

In summary, the common feature of today's educational reforms is the increasing focus on educational outcomes. While some countries (e.g., the United States) traditionally maintained science education standards, others (e.g., Germany or France) relied on a different educational tradition. Due to students' mediocre science performance in large-scale assessments, attention shifts towards educational outcomes. The number of countries building on science education standards is growing. Countries that built on science education standards before initiated revisions of standards and assessment systems (e.g., Australia) (cf. Waddington, Nentwig, & Schanze, 2007). However, despite scientific literacy being the overarching aim of science education and the movement towards science education standards, the learning outcomes defined in these standards differ considerably amongst countries.

## 2 International Perspectives on Conceptualizing Educational Standards

### 2.1 Standards in Science Education

The country with the longest tradition in the use of science education standards probably is the United States with a history of standards that can be traced back to the 19th century – including a history of different conceptions, paradigms, debates, and controversies. In recent history the debate about standards in the United States was stirred up by the report "A Nation at Risk" (National Commission on Excellence in Education, 1983). This report evoked fundamental reforms of the American educational system. Since then, standards, standard-based curricula and subsequent assessments were considered a central shaping agent for what can be expected from students (Resnick, 1985). Standards for science education were published in the early 1990s by the American Association for the Advancement of Science [AAAS] (1993) and the National Research Council [NRC] (1996). Several other English-speaking countries developed science education standards around the same time, among them Canada (Council of Ministers of Education of Canada [CMEC], 1997) and the UK (Department for Education and Science [DES], 1989). About a decade later, Australia also followed the movement towards educational standards (Hafner, 2007).

European countries traditionally have not maintained educational standards (cf. Waddington, Nentwig, & Schanze, 2007). In response to the results of international large scale assessments, however, several countries introduced educational standards, among them Austria (Weiglhofer, 2007), Germany (Sekretariat der Ständigen Konferenz der Kultusminister der Länder in der Bundesrepublik Deutschland, 2005a, 2005b, 2005c), Luxembourg (Ministère de l'Éducation nationale et de la Formation professionnelle, 2009), and Switzerland (Wissenschaftliches Konsortium HarmoS Naturwissenschaften+, 2008).

Some Asian countries such as Japan and Korea maintain national science curricula (cf. Han, 1995; Ogawa, 1998), others such as China or Singapore build on something more closely related to what can be considered national science content standards (Liu & Ruiz, 2008). Interestingly, whereas countries/regions such as Korea or Taiwan have maintained cycles of curriculum revision ever since the introduction of national curricula (Chiu, 2007; Han, 1995), China and Singapore have only recently initiated major revisions of these standards (Curriculum Planning & Development Division [CPDD], 2000; Wei & Thomas, 2005; cf. Liu & Ruiz, 2008).

## 2.2 Different Concepts, Different Standards

Although science education standards in most countries are based on scientific literacy as the overarching aim of science education, in detail the standards differ considerably. In the **United States**, the Educate America Act (1994) dictates national and state standards on content, student performance, and opportunities to learn. Content standards refer to what is to be taught and learned, performance standards define degrees of mastery or levels of attainment, and opportunities-to-learn standards specify the availability of resources provided for learning (Ravitch, 1995). However, the national science education standards only contain content standards, teaching standards, and assessment standards (NRC, 2006). On state level, although all states have implemented content standards, many have not yet developed performance or opportunity-to-learn standards (Liu & Ruiz, 2008).

Currently, the Common Core State Standards Initiative is a state-led effort of 48 states, two territories and the District of Columbia to provide a clear and consistent framework of what students are expected to learn in English Language Arts and Mathematics. The standards are to provide appropriate benchmarks for all students, regardless of where they live. The draft standards were opened for public comment and are presently waiting to be adopted and implemented by the states.

Wilson (2006) lists several features of high-quality content standards including proficiency levels and performance expectations. Despite his demand for content standards to include proficiency levels, only few current content standards explicitly do so (cf. NRC, 2006). Instead, most content standards lack coherence and focus (Valverde & Schmidt, 2000). In a recent report, Duschl, Schweingruber, and Shouse (2007) criticize that in the current U.S. science content standards "little attention is given to how students' understanding of a topic can be supported and enhanced from grade to grade. As a result topics receive repeated shallow coverage with little consistency, which provides a fragile foundation for further knowledge growth" (p. 217). The report concludes that science standards need to be reorganized around core ideas of the respective domain and that learning progressions need to be developed which describe how students progress in developing a deeper understanding of the core ideas when proceeding from grade to grade (Duschl et al., 2007).

The idea of learning progressions became increasingly popular in the science subjects (Duncan & Hmelo-Silver, 2009). Learning progressions describe students' progression in understanding scientific phenomena (Steedle & Shavelson, 2009), i.e. "successively more sophisticated ways of reasoning within a content domain that follow one another as students learn" (Smith et al., 2006, p. 1). Learning progressions are not only about knowledge, but also about abilities and skills which allow successful solving of real-life problems (Schwarz et al., 2009; Smith, Wiser, Anderson, & Krajcik, 2006; Songer, Kelcey, & Gotwals, 2009).

As in the US in the early 1990s, a similar movement towards standards also took place around the same time in other countries such as **Canada** (CMEC, 1997) and the **UK** (DES, 1989). Based on a common framework of science learning outcomes (CMEC, 1997), the Canadian provinces have developed individual science education standards or curricula respectively. For example, the Ontario Science Curriculum (Ministry of Education, 2007, 2008a, 2008b) describes the knowledge and skills students are expected to acquire. Students' knowledge is organized around fundamental concepts, so-called big ideas. Students are expected to develop an increasing understanding of these concepts whilst proceeding from grade 1 to grade 12. Regarding scientific inquiry and experimentation skills, the Ontario Science Curriculum describes four categories of skills such as "Initiating" and "Planning" to operationalize the continuum of scientific inquiry and experimentation skills. The standards also define four performance levels which describe different levels of proficiency to be used for assessment.

**Australia** released national science education standards which were based on a first formulation of national goals for science education in 1989 and were revised in 1999 (cf. Hafner, 2007). Adapted to these goals, a measurement framework was developed (Ministerial Council on Education, Employment, Training and Youth Affairs [MCEETYA], 2003) that was heavily influenced by the framework used in PISA (e.g., OECD, 2001). Within this framework, a scientific literacy progress-map describes six proficiency levels with respect to three domains of scientific literacy (Hafner, 2007). On the level of the individual Australian states, science education standards take a similar approach. The New South Wales science education standards define content and outcomes in syllabi for K-6, 7-10, as well as for post-secondary education. The content is described in terms of what students learn about and what students learn to do while the outcomes describe the knowledge, the skills, and the understanding that are expected to be obtained by students (Hafner, 2007).

Asian countries like **China** and **Singapore** have traditionally maintained national science content standards (Liu & Ruiz, 2008). However, both countries have recently initiated major revisions of their national standards. Within the scope of these revisions, the idea of scientific literacy was integrated as the central purpose of science education (Curriculum Planning & Development Division [CPDD], 2000; Wei & Thomas, 2006). In most Asian countries/regions such as **Japan**, **Korea**, and **Taiwan**, the idea of scientific literacy worked its way into the formerly very content-oriented documents during the regular process of science curriculum revision (cf. Chiu, 2007; Han, 1995; Ogawa, 2001). In Taiwan for example, the recently revised science education curriculum includes so called guidelines of science education. Based on general goals for science education, these guidelines embrace eight core components of scientific literacy, so-called core competences, and five science content areas in which students are expected to develop the core competences (cf. Chiu, 2007). However, although the concept of competence obtains a central role in the PISA framework and made its way into revised versions of science education standards and curricula in Asian countries/regions, the concept of competence did not become as central as it did in Germany.

In the German-speaking countries, the concept of competence became widely used to specify the educational goals, to guide the designing of learning environments, and to direct the development of assessments (Ditton, 2002; Slavin, 2002). Turning away from previously used terms like knowledge, skills, ability, or qualification, the term competence is used to acknowledge the changed requirements of everyday- and working-life (Klieme & Leutner, 2006). This change was intended to be reflected in the formulation of the educational standards the development of which was highly influenced by the report of Klieme et al. (2003). With regard to educational settings, competences are mainly interpreted (at least in the German speaking countries) as clusters of cognitive prerequisites that must be available for an individual to perform well in a particular content area (Weinert, 1999). In summary, competences require long-term, cumulative learning opportunities, a broad experience, and a deep understanding of the topic (Weinert, 2001).

The concept of 'competence' is not only used in scope of research projects but was also chosen as the constitutive concept for educational standards in **Germany** (Sekretariat der Ständigen Konferenz der Kultusminister der Länder in der Bundesrepublik Deutschland, 2005a, 2005b, 2005c). The standards specify competences students are expected to have achieved by the end of secondary education. Because competences are considered domain-specific, standards were defined for each of the three science subjects (chemistry, physics, and biology). In an effort to show that science goes beyond factual knowledge, the standards for these subjects distinguish between four areas of competence (content knowledge, epistemological and methodological knowledge, communication, and socio-scientific reasoning), each of which embraces a list of specified competences. In order to grasp different degrees of achievement, three levels of cognitive complexity are proposed for all four areas as a rather rough measure: reproduction, application, and transfer. This conceptualization is intended to facilitate the measurement of learning outcomes as well as of students' progress across time of schooling.

To describe the structure, graduation, and development of competences, the formation and empirical examination of competence models have become a major research area in Germany (cf. Klieme, Leutner, & Kenk, 2010). Different domain-specific models have been published with the aim to describe competence in science subjects (e.g., Labudde & Adamina, 2008; Neumann, Kauertz, Lau, Notarp, & Fischer, 2007; Schecker & Parchmann, 2006). Additionally, national and international large-scale studies, e.g., PISA, use competence models as assessment frameworks (e.g., OECD, 2006).

**Austria** and **Switzerland** basically followed the German approach. Their standards describe competences students are expected to have obtained at certain points of time during their school career. In accord with the development in Germany, the same definition of competence is used and competence models are developed the structures of which even bear resemblance to the models discussed in the context of the German education system (cf. Labudde, Metzger, & Gut, 2009; Weiglhofer, 2007).

In the **UK**, the National Science Curriculum was first introduced in 1989 and has been revised several times since (Department for Education, 1995; Department for Education and Employment, 1999; DES, 1989). Science education and the science education curriculum in the UK are divided into several key stages. The original curriculum provided extensive lists of science content students should know, understand, or be able to do (DES, 1989). Each statement was assigned to one of ten levels of proficiency which were intended to span schooling grades K-12. In the recent revision, stages one to three embrace less extensive lists of what is to be taught (instead of to be learnt) and a series of eight performance levels which more generally describe what is expected from students on that particular level. As the National Science Curriculum considers the listed contents as to be taught, external examinations and school inspections are an integral part of the education system, to ensure that the achieved curriculum actually corresponds to the intended curriculum (cf. Millar, 2007). These external examinations fall back on the detailed definitions of performance levels that are provided in the curriculum material.

With regard to other European countries, the intended learning outcomes in science still demonstrates a wide variety. The **Danish** science curriculum in the Folkeskole (primary and lower secondary level school) for example describes core knowledge and skills for students to learn as well as guidelines for teachers to develop their teaching so students can reach these goals. Beyond formative assessment, there is no particular culture of standard-based assessments (cf. Dolin, 2007). **Finland** has a long tradition of decentralized assessments based on content-oriented curricula (as used to be the case in Germany). This led to disparities in how the goals specified in the curricula were assessed and consequentially to discrepancies in performance records between schools. Now, educational standards describe what students should know and be able to do at certain stages of schooling (cf. Lavonen, 2007).

# 3 Common Trends, Shared Issues

So far it seems that a consensus exists about the overarching aim of science education. Scientific literacy has developed into a common base of many national science education standards. As a consequence, by all standards students are expected to become scientifically literate in terms of being able to master everyday situations related to scientific phenomena. However, the exact understanding of the components of scientific literacy differs from country to country. In some countries, the components of scientific literacy are considered to be knowledge and skills; in other countries they are seen as competences (which embrace combinations of knowledge and skills); and then in some countries scientific literacy is understood to correspond to an understanding of scientific concepts and the ability to apply scientific inquiry skills.

Accordingly, there is no consensus with regard to clear, specific descriptions of the skills and knowledge that students are expected to learn. Nevertheless, most educational reforms currently tend to focus on educational outcomes as well as the development (or alignment) of assessment systems. In correspondence with the different national interpretations of scientific literacy, the focus of these assessments differs between countries. In some cases, however, the different perspectives and emphases are not as diverse as they seem at first sight. Albeit using a different notion, the recent development in the US is very similar to the movement towards models of competence in Germany. For instance, the idea of learning progressions in the US and Wilsons' (2006) conception of high-quality content standards including proficiency levels and performance expectations are similar to the German idea of competence development (cf. Schecker & Parchmann, 2006). The levels of understanding in a learning progression may be considered as levels of competency (Reiser, Krajcik, Moje, & Marx, 2003). However, only few researchers have established a connection (e.g., Liu, 2009) as the term 'competence' in the US is strongly limited to the vocational field (Melton, 1994). Similarly, the Australian national educational standards very much correspond to the German educational standards which were also strongly influenced by the PISA framework (Neumann, Kauertz, & Fischer, 2010). Similar to competence levels in Germany, the proficiency levels in the Australian national science education standards make frequent use of the idea of complexity (MCEETYA, 2002).

However, the assessment of learning prerequisites and outcomes is theoretically and methodically challenging. The measurement of learning outcomes must exhibit the differentiated internal structure of the knowledge base, i.e. the components as well as the level of proficiency. Furthermore, measurement should reveal changes and transformations in the process of learning and development (Klieme & Leutner, 2006). For this purpose, three major tasks can be identified: (1) the development of cognitive models of learning that can serve as the theoretical basis for assessment, (2) research on new measurement models and their applicability, (3) research on assessment designs. "Much hard work remains to focus psychometric model building on the critical features of models of cognition and learning and on observations that reveal meaningful cognitive processes in a particular domain" (Pellegrino, Chudowsky, & Glaser, 2001, p. 6). Without doubt, considerable expertise exists in the area of assessing students' knowledge or theorizing about educational goals; but the question of how to measure students' mastering of standards still remains largely unanswered (Fensham, 2009). Therefore, teachers in schools and science education reformers need additional detailed information about what students individually have already mastered and what their next level of development could be (Bernholt & Parchmann, 2011; Neumann, Fischer, & Kauertz, 2010). The use of theoretical constructs for the characterization of students' learning outcomes intends to align curricula, instruction, and assessment. The ambition to align different facets of the school system is a central feature of current developments in most educational reforms throughout the world.

With regard to the parallels and differences between the developments in many countries across the world, a discussion about the different national notions of what constitutes scientific literacy and how this superordinate goal can be specified and linked to student performance seems necessary. The comparison of different concepts of students' learning outcomes might also reveal misunderstandings due to different national traditions as well as to difficulties in the exact definition of concepts like 'knowledge', 'skills', and 'understanding' – especially with regard to translation issues. Additionally, a clarification of the central national conceptions could provide a constructive basis for further developments and scientific exchange.

## 4  The Symposium

Motivated by the controversy concerning the definition of learning outcomes, an international symposium in Kiel, Germany, brought renowned researchers together from countries/regions with different notions of the nature and quality of learning outcomes in March 2011. This is the fifth in a series of international symposia organized by the Leibniz Institute for Science and Mathematics Education at the University of Kiel (IPN) and the Science Education Group at the University of York (UYSEG) (cf. Bennett et al., 2005; Gräber, Nentwig, Koballa, & Evans, 2002; Nentwig & Waddington, 2005; Waddington, Nentwig, & Schanze, 2007). Twenty-seven science educators, psychologists, and educationalists were invited from 13 countries/regions. The participants produced papers about the situation in their countries/regions or about specific research programmes. These papers were made available well in advance of the meeting to all participants and served as basis for the detailed discussions at the symposium, which were held alternately in small groups and in the plenum. Some of the participants had been invited to the roles of chairs and discussants for particular sub-sections of the discussion. Their engagement and creativity in structuring their themes led to a variety of activities and proved to be crucial for the success of the event. After the meeting, the contributors were asked to revise their papers in the light of the discussions, and these revised versions became the core of this book.

The general structure of the book attempts to take advantage of the diversity and individuality of the 19 articles that were submitted by grouping them in three sections. Each of the individual contributions to this first section provides a broad overview about different approaches, challenges, and pitfalls on the road to the clarification of meaningful and fruitful learning outcomes. Additionally, the role and impact of different systemic factors and stakeholders are highlighted. This parts emphasizes how complex the endeavor of defining, assessing, and promoting of learning outcomes in science education is. The second set of papers provides deep insights into different, although comparable approaches which aim to frame, to assess, and to promote learning and learning outcomes in science education. Smaller projects are presented as well as broad, coordinated national programs. In addition, general and specific reproaches are included to reveal gaps and blind spots within current projects. The third set of papers reflects this ambition of striving for individual solutions in several countries. From different national perspectives, these papers outline the individual historical development, the deficits and problems that led to the current reforms, and finally what these reforms look like. Despite common trends, these national reports picture a diversity of school systems and educational traditions. These papers outline the problems and challenges in defining learning outcomes in science education and indicate that there will be probably no single solution that fits the needs of every country.

In summary, this book intends to provide an overview about different conceptions and different notions of the nature and quality of learning outcomes, about difficulties and challenges concerning research, school practice, and teacher education, as well as about different national perspectives and experiences. It intends to make tangible what in the literature sometimes remains blurred.

# References

Altrichter, H., Brusemeister, T., & Wissinger, J. (2007). *Educational Governance*. Wiesbaden: VS Verlag.

American Association for the Advancement of Science (AAAS) (1993). *Benchmarks for Scientific Literacy*. New York: Oxford University Press.

Amos, K. (2010). *International Educational Governance*. Bingeley, UK: Emerald Group Publishing.

Beaton, A. E., Martin, M. O., Mullis, I. V. S., Gonzalez, E. J., Smith, T. A., & Kelly, D. L. (1996). *Science Achievement in the Middle School Years: IEA's third International Mathematics and Science Study* (TIMSS). Chestnut Hill, MA: Center for the Study of Testing, Evaluation, and Educational Policy, Boston College.

Bennett, J., Holman, J., Millar, R., & Waddington, D. (2005). *Making a Difference. Evaluation as a Tool for Improving Science Education*. Münster: Waxmann.

Bernholt, S. & Parchmann, I. (2011). Assessing the complexity of students' knowledge in chemistry. *Chemistry Education Research and Practice, 12*, 167-173.

Bybee, R. W. (1997). Toward an understanding of scientific literacy. In W. Gräber & C. Bolte (Eds.), *Scientific Literacy* (pp. 37-68). Kiel: IPN.

Chiu, M.-H. (2007). Standards for science education in Taiwan. In D. Waddington, P. Nentwig, & S. Schanze (Eds.), *Making it Comparable – Standards in Science Education* (pp. 303-347). Münster: Waxmann.

Council of Ministers of Education of Canada. (1997). *Common Framework of Science Learning Outcomes*. Toronto: Council of Ministers of Education.

Curriculum Planning & Development Division [CPDD] (2000). *Science Syllabuses: GCE "O" & "N" level*. Singapore: CPDD.

DeBoer, G. E. (2000). Scientific literacy: Another look at its historical and contemporary meanings and its relationship to science education reform. *Journal of Research in Science Teaching, 37*(6), 582-601.

Department for Education. (1995). *Science in the National Curriculum*. London: Her Majesty's Stationary Office (HMSO).

Department for Education and Employment. (1999). *The national curriculum for England*. London: Her Majesty's Stationary Office (HMSO).

Department for Education and Science. (1989). *Science in the National Curriculum*. London: Her Majesty's Stationary Office (HMSO).

Ditton, H. (2002). Evaluation und Qualitätssicherung [Evaluation and Quality Control]. In R. Tippelt (Ed.), *Handbuch Bildungsforschung* (pp. 775-790). Opladen: Leske + Budrich.

Dolin, J. (2007). Science education standards and science assessment in Denmark. In D. Waddington, P. Nentwig, & S. Schanze (Eds.), *Making it Comparable – Standards in Science Education* (pp. 71-82). Münster: Waxmann.

Duncan, R. G. & Hmelo-Silver, C. E. (2009). Learning Progressions: Aligning Curriculum, Instruction, and Assessment. *Journal of Research in Science Teaching, 46*(6), 606-609.

Duschl, R. A., Schweinguber, H. A., & Shouse, A. W. (Eds.) (2007). *Taking Science to School: Learning and Teaching Science in Grades K-8*. Washington, DC: The National Academies Press.

Fensham, P. J. (2009). Real world contexts in PISA science: Implications for context-based science education. *Journal of Research in Science Teaching, 46*(8), 884-896.

Gräber, W. & Bolte, C. (1997). *Scientific Literacy – An International Symposium*. Kiel: IPN.

Gräber, W., Nentwig, P., Koballa, T., & Evans, R. (2002). *Scientific Literacy: Der Beitrag der Naturwissenschaften zur Allgemeinen Bildung* [Scientific Literacy: the contribution of the sciences to general education]. Opladen: Leske & Budrich.

Hafner, R. (2007). Standards in science education in Australia. In D. Waddington, P. Nentwig, & S. Schanze (Eds.), *Making it Comparable – Standards in Science Education* (pp. 23-59). Münster: Waxmann.

Han, J.-H. (1995). The Quest for National Standards in Science Education in Korea. *Studies in Science Education, 26*(1), 59 - 71.

Klieme, E., Avenarius, H., Blum, W., Döbrich, P., Gruber, H., Prenzel, M., et al. (2003). *Zur Entwicklung nationaler Bildungsstandards* [Regarding the development of National Education Standards]. Berlin: Bundesministerium für Bildung und Forschung.

Klieme, E. & Leutner, D. (2006). Kompetenzmodelle zur Erfassung individueller Lernergebnisse und zur Bilanzierung von Bildungsprozessen. Beschreibung eines neu eingerichteten Schwerpunktprogramms der DFG [Models of Competencies for Assessment of Individual Learning Outcomes and the Evaluation of Educational Processes. Description of a new DFG priority research program]. *Zeitschrift für Pädagogik, 52*(6), 876-903.

Labudde, P. & Adamina, M. (2008). HarmoS Naturwissenschaften: Impulse für den naturwissenschaftlichen Unterricht von morgen [HarmoS Science: impetuses for the science classes of tomorrow]. *Beiträge zur Lehrerbildung, 26*(3), 351-360.

Labudde, P., Metzger, S., & Gut, C. (2009). Bildungsstandards: Validierung des Schweizer Kompetenzmodells [Education standards: validation of the Swiss competence models]. In D. Höttecke (Ed.), *Chemie- und Physikdidaktik für die Lehramtsausbildung* (pp. 307-309). Münster: LIT Verlag.

Lavonen, J. (2007). National science education standards and assessment in Finland. In D. Waddington, P. Nentwig & S. Schanze (Eds.), *Making it Comparable – Standards in Science Education* (pp. 101-126). Münster: Waxmann.

Liu, X. & Ruiz, M. (2008). Using Data Mining to Predict K–12 Students' Performance on Large-Scale Assessment Items Related to Energy. *Journal for Research on Science Teaching, 45*(5), 554-573.

Melton, R. F. (2004). Competence in perspective. *Educational Research, 36*(3), 285-294.

Millar, R. (2007). How standards in science education are set and monitored in the English education system. In D. Waddington, P. Nentwig & S. Schanze (Eds.), *Making it comparable – Standards in science education* (pp. 83-100). Münster: Waxmann.

Millar, R. & Osborne, J (1998). *Beyond 2000: Science Education for the Future*. London: King's College London, School of Education.

Ministère de l'Éducation nationale et de la Formation professionnelle (2009). *Naturwissenschaften – Kompetenzorientierte Bildungsstandards – Niveau 8e* [Science: competence oriented education standards]. Luxembourg: Le Gouvernement du Grand-Duché de Luxembourg.

Ministerial Council on Education, Employment, Training and Youth Affairs [MCEETYA] (2002). *National Year 6 Primary Science Sample Assessment: Assessment Domain and Progress Map.* MCEETYA.

Ministerial Council on Education, Employment, Training and Youth Affairs [MCEETYA] (2003). *A Measurement Framework for National Key Performance Measures.* MCEETYA.

Ministry of Education. (2007). *The Ontario Curriculum, Grades 1–8: Science and Technology.* Toronto: Ontario Ministry of Education.

Ministry of Education. (2008a). *The Ontario Curriculum, Grades 9–10: Science.* Toronto: Ontario Ministry of Education.

Ministry of Education. (2008b). *The Ontario Curriculum, Grades 11–12: Science.* Toronto: Ontario Ministry of Education.

Mullis, I. V., Martin, M. O., Kennedy, A. M., & Foy, P. (2007). *PIRLS 2006 International Report: IEA's Progress in International Reading Literacy Study in Primary School in 40 Countries.* Boston, MA: TIMSS & PIRLS International Study Center.

National Commission on Excellence in Education (1983). *A Nation at Risk: The Imperative for Educational Reform.* Washington, DC: U.S. Government Printing Office.

Nentwig, P. & Schanze, S. (2007). Making it Comparable – Standards in Science Education. In D. Waddington, P. Nentwig & S. Schanze (Eds.), *Making it Comparable – Standards in Science Education* (pp. 11-19). Münster: Waxmann.

Nentwig, P. & Waddington, D. (2005). *Making it relevant. Context based learning of science.* Münster: Waxmann.

Neumann, K., Fischer, H. E., & Kauertz, A. (2010). From PISA to standards: The impact of large-scale assessments on science education in Germany. *International Journal of Science and Mathematics Education, 8*(3), 545-563.

Neumann, K., Kauertz, A., Lau, A., Notarp, H., & Fischer, H. E. (2007). Die Modellierung physikalischer Kompetenz und ihrer Entwicklung [Modelling structure and development of students' physics competence]. *Zeitschrift für Didaktik der Naturwissenschaften, 13*, 103-123.

OECD (2001). *Knowledge and Skills for Life – First Results from the OECD Programme for International Student Assessment (PISA) 2000.* Paris: OECD.

OECD (2004). *Learning for Tomorrow's World. First Results from PISA 2003.* Paris: OECD.

OECD (2006). *Assessing Scientific, Reading and Mathematical Literacy – A Framework for PISA 2006.* Paris: OECD Publishing.

OECD (2007). *PISA 2006: Science Competence for Tomorrow's world* (Vol. 1). Paris: OECD.

Ogawa, M. (1998). A cultural history of science education in Japan: an epic description. In W. W. Cobern (Ed.), *Socio-Cultural Perspectives on Science Education: An International Dialogue* (pp. 139-161). Dordrecht: Kluwer Academic Publishers.

Ogawa, M. (2001). Reform Japanese style: Voyage into an unknown and chaotic future. *Science Education, 85*(5), 586-606.

Osborne, J. & Dillon, J. (2008). *Science education in Europe: Critical Reflections*. Technical report, King's College London, London.

Pellegrino, J. W., Chudowsky, N., & Glaser, R. (2001). *Knowing What Students Know: The Science and Design of Educational Assessment*. Washington: National Academy Press.

Ravitch, D. (1995). *National Standards in American Education: A Citizen's Guide*. Washington, DC: Brookings Institution.

Reiser, B., Krajcik, J., Moje, E., & Marx, R. (2003). *Design strategies for developing science instructional materials*. Paper presented at the Annual Meeting of the National Association for Research in Science Teaching.

Resnick, D. P. & Resnick, L. B. (1983). Improving Educational Standards in American Schools. *Phi Delta Kappan, 65*, 178-180.

Resnick, L. B. (1985). Cognition and instruction: Recent theories of human competence and how it is acquired. In B. L. Hammonds (Ed.), *Psychology and Learning: The Master Lecture Series* (Vol. 4, pp. 123-186). Washington, DC: American Psychological Association.

Roberts, D. A. (2007). Scientific literacy / science literacy. In S. K. Abell & N. G. Lederman (Eds.), *Handbook of Research on Science Education* (pp. 729-780). Mahwah, NJ: Lawrence Erlbaum Associates.

Schecker, H. & Parchmann, I. (2006). Modellierung naturwissenschaftlicher Kompetenz [Modeling scientific competence]. *Zeitschrift für Didaktik der Naturwissenschaften, 12*, 45-66.

Schwarz, C. V., Reiser, B. J., Davis, E. A., Kenyon, L., Achér, A., Fortus, D., et al. (2009). Developing a learning progression for scientific modeling: Making scientific modeling accessible and meaningful for learners. *Journal of Research in Science Teaching, 46*(6), 632-654.

Sekretariat der Ständigen Konferenz der Kultusminister der Länder in der Bundesrepublik Deutschland (2005a). *Bildungsstandards im Fach Biologie für den Mittleren Schulabschluss*. München: Luchterhand.

Sekretariat der Ständigen Konferenz der Kultusminister der Länder in der Bundesrepublik Deutschland (2005b). *Bildungsstandards im Fach Chemie für den Mittleren Schulabschluss*. München: Luchterhand.

Sekretariat der Ständigen Konferenz der Kultusminister der Länder in der Bundesrepublik Deutschland (2005c). *Bildungsstandards im Fach Physik für den Mittleren Schulabschluss*. München: Luchterhand.

Slavin, R. E. (2002). Evidence-Based Education Policies: Transforming Educational Practice and Research. *Educational Researcher, 31*(7), 15-21.

Smith, C., Wiser, M., Anderson, C. W., & Krajcik, J. (2006). Implications for children's learning for assessment: A proposed learning progression for matter and the atomic molecular theory. *Measurement, 14*(1&2), 1-98.

Songer, N. B., Kelcey, B., & Gotwals, A. W. (2009). How and when does complex reasoning occur? Empirically driven development of a learning progression focused on complex reasoning about biodiversity. *Journal of Research in Science Teaching, 46*(6), 610 631.

Steedle, J. T. & Shavelson, R. J. (2009). Supporting Valid Interpretations of Learning Progression Level Diagnoses. *Journal of Research in Science Teaching, 46*(6), 699-715.

Tenorth, H.-E. (2006). Erziehung zur Persönlichkeit: Worauf zielt Bildung? [Education towards personality]. In H.-E. Tenorth, M. Hüther, & M. Heimbach-Steins (Eds.), *Erziehung und Bildung heute* (pp. 7-24). Berlin: Walter-Raymond-Stiftung der BDA, Kleine Reihe, H. 77.

Valverde, G. A. & Schmidt, W. H. (2000). Greater expectations: learning from other nations in the quest for 'world-class standards' in US school mathematics and science. *Journal of Curriculum Studies, 32*(5), 651-687.

Waddington, D., Nentwig, P., & Schanze, S. (2007). *Making it Comparable – Standards in Science Education*. Münster: Waxmann.

Wei, B. & Thomas, G. P. (2006). An examination of the change of the junior secondary school chemistry curriculum in the P. R. Chine: In the view of scientific literacy. *Research in Science Education, 36*(4), 403-418.

Weiglhofer, H. (2007). Austria at the beginning of the way to standards in science. In D. Waddington, P. Nentwig, & S. Schanze (Eds.), *Making it Comparable – Standards in Science Education* (pp. 61-70). Münster: Waxmann.

Weinert, F. E. (1999). *Concepts of Competence*. Contribution within the OECD-Project Definition and Selection of Competencies: Theoretical and Conceptual Foundations (DeSeCo). Neuchâtel: Bundesamt für Statistik (Ch).

Weinert, F. E. (2001). Concept of competence: A conceptual clarification. In D. S. Rychen & L. H. Salganik (Eds.), *Defining and Selecting Key Competencies* (pp. 45-65). Seattle, WA: Hogrefe & Huber.

Wilson, M. & Bertenthal, M. (Eds.) (2004). Systems for state science assessment. Board on Testing and Assessment, Center for Education. Division of Behavioral and Social Sciences and Education. Washington, D.C.: National Academy Press.Wissenschaftliches Konsortium HarmoS Naturwissenschaften+ (2008). *Harmos Naturwissenschaften+, Kompetenzmodell und Vorschläge für Bildungsstandards* [HarmoS Science+: competence model and proposals for educati ards]. Wissenschaftlicher Abschlussbericht. Ostermundingen: suterprint.

## Part B

# The Big Picture

# Chapter 2

## Moving Beyond Standards: How Can We Improve Elementary Science Learning? A German Perspective

*Kornelia Möller[1], Ilonca Hardy[2] & Kim Lange[1]*
[1]*Westfälische Wilhelms-Universität Münster,* [2]*Goethe-Universität Frankfurt am Main, Germany*

### Abstract

Results of recent research on school efficiency have renewed interest in early facilitation of science learning. Conceptions of science education in German elementary schools draw on the international notion of 'scientific literacy' (Bybee, 1997; Norris & Phillips 2003; OECD, 2006), and nowadays the aims of such early facilitation of 'scientific literacy' are largely consensual (Prenzel, Geiser, Langeheine, & Lobeheine 2003; Kleickmann, Hardy, Jonen, Blumberg, & Möller 2007). They encompass scientific knowledge, motivational orientation, scientific inquiry, and the nature of science.

Attempts to assess (TIMSS, PISA, IGLU-E) and standardize German elementary science education (GDSU, 2003) have revealed challenges, realities and gaps in the system, including that in Germany no standards are given for elementary science, the science syllabi differ among the 16 states, and curricula are not always implemented as claimed (TIMSS, 2007). As a consequence, a large number of studies have been conducted in the last decade to more deeply understand, and find ways to fix, these conditions. Thus German research in this field, including results from our own studies, will be examined in the following sections and related to a larger international discussion of science education. This includes research on the characterization of elementary students' scientific understanding and how it is best developed; on effective early science learning environments; and on the role teachers' professional knowledge plays in advancing elementary students' scientific understanding.

Lastly, research results will be discussed and conclusions for successful learning arrangements, for reaching multiple goals, and for supporting teachers' professional knowledge development will be given. Teacher education and teacher in-service trainings seem to be crucial to eventually improve students' learning progress in elementary school science education.

# 1 Introduction

In Germany, early learning in the natural sciences takes place within the elementary school subject, 'Sachunterricht', which includes topics from natural sciences, social sciences, history, and technology, and which covers grades one through four (children ages six through ten). The instructional aim of this subject is to enable children to orient themselves in their world, to acquire an adequate understanding of their environment, and to take an active part in shaping it. This subject should also lay the foundations for future learning processes in natural and social sciences as well as in history, geography, and technology.

There are two major goals set for children's natural science learning: Firstly, they should learn how to interpret natural phenomena; secondly, they should acquire knowledge of basic concepts within the respective sciences as well as methods of scientific inquiry.

In the past, the question of how to implement the above demands for natural science learning in the subject, 'Sachunterricht', was a source of controversy in Germany. During the 1970s, the early facilitation of scientific thinking had been an element of international and national curricula. However, misguided conceptions of science orientation and a lack of attention paid to how children think led to the elimination of physics, chemistry, and other technical topics from the existing syllabi, with biological and geographical topics largely replacing them. This shift occurred in Germany as well as in many other countries (Möller, 2004).

In the 1990s renewed interest in early science instruction in Germany resulted in the reintegration of natural science and technology topics back into school curricula (Möller, 2002). This renewed interest in a broad-based, early facilitation of science and technology learning was due to the results of current research on school effectiveness (TIMSS, PISA, IGLU-E), the growing demand for young people in scientific and technical professions, and findings from the areas of elementary school-related research on learning and instruction (Sodian, 1995; Bullock & Ziegler, 1999; Stern, 2002).

As a result, comprehensive science education for elementary school children is again fodder for intense debate. Questions like "What are the characteristic traits of learning outcomes in elementary science?", "How are elementary students coming to achieve these goals?", "What aspects of teaching strategies enhance students' learning?" (Appleton, 2007), and "What characteristics of teachers are crucial to student learning, and how can students studying to become teachers acquire appropriate knowledge in pre-service and in-service trainings?" (Abell, 2007) have generated an increasing amount of research on German elementary school science teaching and learning.

The following sections present (1) an overview of current elementary science education and (2) recent research in how to foster learning progress in elementary science education in Germany.

## 2 Objectives of Science Education in German Elementary Schools Today

Conceptions of science education in German elementary schools draw on the international notion of 'scientific literacy'; that is, a concept of a basic science education that allows for lifelong learning processes built on accessible, adaptable conceptual knowledge (Bybee, 1997; Norris & Phillips 2003; OECD, 2006).

More precisely put, the concept of 'scientific literacy' according to Prenzel, Rost, Senkbeil, Häußler and Klopp (2001) includes an understanding of central scientific concepts, methods of scientific inquiry, and scientific ways of thinking. It also includes epistemological views of the specific characteristics of scientific knowledge and inquiry (nature of science) as well as views of the relationship between science, technology and society. In addition, acquiring a certain readiness for- and interest in scientific questions count as part of a basic education in the sciences because these qualities are necessary for students to fully engage themselves in scientific problems and issues.

Today it is indisputable that this type of fundamental science education – drawing on the notion of scientific literacy – should be facilitated at the elementary school age. The aims of such early facilitation are also nowadays largely consensual (Prenzel et al., 2003; Kleickmann, Hardy, Jonen, Blumberg, & Möller 2007). They involve several criteria and refer to:

- the development of scientific knowledge, which includes conceptions that deal with content, general principles and rules *('scientific knowledge')*,

- the development of knowledge about science, which includes scientific ways of thinking and working as well as knowledge about the nature of science (*'understanding scientific inquiry' and 'the nature of science'*), and

- the development of a motivational orientation directed toward the sciences, which includes interest in thinking about natural phenomena and self-efficacy, namely the confidence in one's ability to discover and understand (*'motivational orientation'*).

*Scientific knowledge:* Elementary school students should develop basic and adaptable conceptions that enable them to interpret phenomena in the domains of optics, magnetism, electricity, air, sound, buoyancy, species, and the development of living organisms, among others. This does not mean the acquisition of mere factual knowledge, but rather the development of a conceptual framework that gives students the means to grasp physical regularities, material properties, chemical transformations, as well as attributes of living organisms. Such a foundation supports a better understanding of the natural world, with an additional positive influence on a learner's motivation and interest. Following up on Martin Wagenschein (1991) ('teaching to understand') and in accordance with principles of constructivist learning that emphasize students' cognitive activity (Gerstenmaier & Mandl, 1995; Bransford, Brown, & Cocking, 1999; Mayer, 2004), children's existing views and concepts should be taken up and gradually transformed into more adequate conceptions (Duschl & Hamilton, 1998; Vosniadou, Ioannides, Dimitrakopoulou &, Papademetriou, 2001; Duit & Treagust, 2003; Vosniadou, 2008).

*Understanding scientific inquiry* and *nature of science*: This includes aspects of epistemology, the nature of science, and the methodology of scientific research, which includes a basic understanding of the aims and methods of science, as well as insight into the process of constructing scientific knowledge. Developing theories, deducting and verifying hypotheses, interpreting data, and revising and enhancing theories are part of this dimension. For elementary school, this means that students should learn to ask questions, to make educated guesses, to realize that it is necessary to verify assumptions, to distinguish between evidence and assumption, to plan and conduct simple investigations, to justify an argument, to revise their assumptions based on evidence, and to exchange thoughts about their investigations and explanations. In doing so, they begin to learn techniques like observing, measuring, comparing and organizing, exploring and experimenting, assuming and verifying, discussing and interpreting, modeling and mathematizing, and researching and communicating (Sodian, Jonen, Thoermer, & Kircher, 2006; Sodian & Koerber, 2011; Flick & Lederman, 2006; Duit, Gropengießer, & Stäudel, 2004)

It is essential that the above-mentioned scientific methodologies and thought processes are not merely seen as skills to be rehearsed, but rather that they embody a deepened understanding of the processes of scientific research.

*Motivational orientation:* The motivational aims of such early learning in the sciences are in no way inferior to the two groups of aims described previously. A feeling of self-efficacy, of confidence in one's scientific abilities, should be promoted in order to foster interest and to prevent giving up on so-called 'hard' natural sciences in later years.

# 3 National and State-specific Standards, Studies of School Effectiveness, and Terms of Implementation

The 16 states in the Federal Republic of Germany are individually responsible for all matters of culture and education. Each of the 16 states establishes expected competencies, aims and agendas for the respective school subjects and for all grade levels. Therefore, 16 different curricula exist in Germany for science learning in elementary school; even the name of the school subject itself varies among the states. Unlike in secondary school science, there are no mandatory national standards for science education in elementary school.

In 2002, however, the Society for Teaching Natural and Social Sciences and Technology in Elementary School (Gesellschaft für Didaktik des Sachunterrichts, GDSU) in co-operation with school administrations and state ministries of education devised a framework with standards for the subject, 'Sachunterricht', in elementary school education, which also covers elementary school science education (Gesellschaft für Didaktik des Sachunterrichts, 2003). Those standards for science learning refer to scientific topics and scientific methods. This framework set in motion a restructuring of curricula in many German states, although it is not mandatory: Its implementation is only "recommended". Today, state-specific differences still exist, yet all curricula have amended topics for science education from the domains of biology, chemistry, and physics. Technical topics are included as well.

Almost all curricula include topics like sound, electricity, magnetism, air, optical phenomena, temperature, energy, weather phenomena, water supply and wastewater disposal, mixtures and solutions, states of matter and changes of state, as well as biological topics concerning plants, animals and the human body. Scientific methods (observing, asking questions, assuming, verifying assumptions, developing experiments, making deductions, documenting, reflecting, etc.) and scientific ways of thinking (arguing, communicating, etc.) are also part of almost all curricula. However, still most curricula fail to explicitly address the nature of science and the nature of scientific inquiry.

The standards of the German GDSU are only advisory in nature, not executive – a national implementation of standards has not been established in elementary schools. This may be due to the difference in syllabi in the 16 federal states with regard to their requirements and levels of competence as well as to the wide spectrum of content from the social and natural sciences within the subject 'Sachunterricht'. However, the comparative school achievement study, TIMSS 2007 (Martin, Mullis, & Foy, 2008) – the first international study in elementary school science education Germany took part in – shed some light on the scientific competencies of German elementary school students. Germany ranked 12th out of 36 countries, but did not differ significantly from the European average and only exceeded the OECD average by a very slim margin.

In addition, results suggest that gender and social background have a strong influence on the acquisition of scientific competencies. Evaluations by the interviewed teachers additionally suggested that only part of the assessed scientific competencies was actually acquired in classroom instruction. Referring to many of the chemistry and physics topics tested in TIMSS, teachers claimed that only one-third of the students actually studied the tested topics in class – although those topics are listed in most of the state curricula (Martin et al., 2008). As a result, in Germany the actual acquired scientific competencies seem to be strongly influenced by out-of-school learning situations.

Moreover, TIMSS examined the aspect of quality of instruction. In this specific area, Germany ranked below the international average. For example, only 14% of the tested students used experiments in more than half of their lessons (Martin et al., 2008). The results also showed a discrepancy between curricular claims and what is actually implemented in lessons. A reason for this may lie in the inadequate pre-service and in-service preparation of elementary school teachers: Referencing subjects in chemistry and physics, teachers of two-thirds of the tested students in TIMSS 2007 admitted that they felt insufficiently prepared for science instruction (Martin et al., 2008). These results illuminate some of the challenges facing the implementation of high-level elementary science instruction in Germany.

In sum, although elementary science education plays a major role in Germany's elementary education and although most of the present curricula in the different states include science topics, there are no mandatory standards for assessing the effectiveness of science learning in elementary schools, and there are many problems implementing high level science education in Germany's elementary schools.

Instead of assessing the implementation of national standards, research in Germany in the last decade has concentrated on how to facilitate learning progress in elementary school science education. Research has focused on children's preexisting knowledge, on how to diagnose this knowledge, how to foster conceptual understanding through adequate instruction in elementary school lessons and how to support children in restructuring their conceptual knowledge. Research has also focused on elementary school teachers' professional knowledge required for effective science teaching as well as on how to support teachers in the acquisition of competencies.

The following chapters will give an overview of the last decade of German research in this field, frame the collection of respective studies, and relate the results to a larger international discussion of science education.

## 4 Characterization of Science Understanding in Elementary School

Children enter instruction with specific prior beliefs and conceptions which are then changed and developed during science instruction. These processes of conceptual restructuring have long been investigated within the communities of developmental psychology, instructional psychology and science education. Within a constructivist view of learning, the nature and development of young children's naïve conceptions has been at the core of research for decades. Children construct these naïve conceptions based on experiences in their natural environment, such as interpretation of natural phenomena, the verbal explanations and terminology they hear in adult speech or the use of vocabulary in the media. Although plausible within the constrained interpretative framework of everyday life, these naïve conceptions are in most cases not compatible with scientific models and, thus, need to be fundamentally restructured into scientifically acceptable concepts and explanations. This restructuring process applies to both basic science concepts and meta-conceptual knowledge of scientific methods and beliefs (Vosniadou et al., 2008; Cepni & Cil, 2010).

Conceptual restructuring is thought of as a gradual process during which different forms of intermediate models and incoherent or fragmented knowledge structures are likely involved at different stages of development. For example, initial understanding of the concept of air usually involves the belief that air "is nothing" (i.e., is not part of the material world). It is only by evolving this initial belief into a concept of air that involves characteristics such as weight or deflation that new, scientifically valid concepts such as air pressure may be constructed. The degree to which even initial conceptions may be regarded as theory-like and involving coherent interpretative frameworks (Vosniadou, 2008) or as fragmented pieces of knowledge (p-prims; di Sessa, 2008) is still an issue of debate. While there is evidence for both views, our own findings on the coherence of elementary students' conceptions suggest that even the initial knowledge states are fragmented and disorganized (Schneider & Hardy, submitted). This means that incompatible explanations are used in parallel by students to explain science phenomena, as has been found in the topics of evaporation/condensation, chemical bonding, or force (e.g., DiSessa, Gillespie, & Esterly, 2004; Tytler & Prain, 2010). In our project on the assessment and development of conceptual understanding of science phenomena in elementary school, we found evidence of fragmented and domain-specific knowledge structures in the topics of floating and sinking and evaporation/condensation in a cross-sectional study with students in second, third, and fourth grade (Kleickmann et al., in press). Thus, conceptual restructuring may be considered to be a process in which initially disparate knowledge structures are integrated. Similarly, Larsson and Hallden (2010) conclude that conceptual change concerns the reorganization of already acquired knowledge involving either the integration of conceptions or the contextually dependent differentiation of conceptions, depending on the stage of conceptual development.

While research on conceptual change commonly focuses on the restructuring of basic science concepts, meta-conceptual knowledge, which is subsumed under the label of "scientific reasoning", also involves the restructuring of initial conceptions. With this in mind, we may differentiate between an understanding of the nature of science on the one hand and conceptual knowledge of science methods on the other as core components of successful science learning (e.g., Sandoval, 2003; Windschitl, Thompson, & Braaten, 2008).

For children to be able to draw a basic distinction between theory and evidence, three conditions need to be met (Kuhn & Siegler, 2006). Children need to realize that (a) a theoretical claim may be falsified, (b) evidence may be used as a means of falsification, and (c) evidence and hypotheses are different epistemological categories. Generally, young children have been shown to be epistemologically naïve; for example, data and observations are usually not related to theories or hypotheses, and epistemological beliefs consider scientific knowledge as accessible by simple mechanisms such as direct observation (Grygier, 2008; Carey, Evans, Honda, Jay, & Unger, 1989). Nevertheless, a basic understanding of strategies of experimentation, hypothesis testing and use of evidence has been observed even in pre-school and elementary school age groups (see Zimmerman, 2007, for a review). Even pre-schoolers, for example, are able to use diagrams as evidence supporting initial claims, and they are able to construct hypotheses with regard to covariation data (Koerber, Sodian, Thoermer, & Nett, 2005). A special challenge to young children is the concept that a certain form of evidence is inconclusive. According to Inhelder and Piaget (1958), children will be able to differentiate between conclusive and inconclusive evidence only in the realm of formal operations. In contrast, it has been shown that even six-year olds are able to do so in contextually rich domains (Sodian, Zaitchik, & Carey, 1991).

In a longitudinal study from elementary school to adulthood, stable individual differences were found with regard to both aspects of meta-conceptual science understanding. Specifically, an early understanding of the nature of science and early methodological competencies were found to be more important predictors of later argumentative skills than cognitive ability (Bullock et al., 2009). Apparently, the ability to use evidence in support of claims develops within the first years of school even without direct instruction (Sodian & Koerber, 2011). In addition, interventions on the nature of science and on methodological competencies have been shown to be effective at the elementary school age (e.g., Grygier, 2008; Quigley, Pongsanon, & Akerson, 2010; Strand-Cary & Klahr, 2008). Although empirical evidence of the *relation* between meta-conceptual knowledge and the acquisition and development of conceptual knowledge in different scientific domains is still scarce, one may assume that a naïve realistic or positivistic understanding of the nature of science will hamper the acquisition of science concepts because the conceptual frame for questioning one's own (mis)conceptions will be missing (see for example Wallace, Tsoi, Calkin, & Darley, 2003). For example, students with a naïve view of the nature of science will process instructional input that makes use of empirical evidence to support or falsify initial student claims differently than students with a more developed, constructivist view. However, a study by Stathopoulou and Vosniadou (2007) with tenth-graders also showed that a constructivist epistemology was a necessary, but insufficient precondition for grasping advanced science concepts. This points to the role of adequate instructional environments to induce conceptual restructuring – even in students with an advanced epistemology.

## 5    Effective Instructional Environments for Early Science Learning

In order to initiate and achieve conceptual restructuring in students, science instruction needs to allow students to integrate and differentiate their initially disconnected experiences and beliefs (Linn, 2006). This way, naïve conceptions may be discarded for more advanced concepts. However, traditional forms of instruction often fail in achieving students' long-term conceptual restructuring with regard to basic science concepts (Wandersee et al., 1994; Treagust & Duit, 1998). Apart from teachers' professional knowledge and epistemologies which are described in detail in the following section, it is the nature of the instructional environment that affects conceptual restructuring. Especially in elementary school, teachers need to balance aspects of inquiry-oriented classrooms with a focus on active learning and experimentation with elements of teacher-guided scaffolding. This allows students to productively process and relate evidence to prior conceptions and hypotheses. The design of learning environments in early science education has long been framed in the context of socio-constructivist theories of learning.

Recently, research pointing to the importance of instructional guidance within constructivist learning environments has revived a discussion about the elements of instructional scaffolding (e.g., Hardy et al., 2006; Kirschner, Sweller, & Clark, 2006; Mayer, 2004). For example, a comparison of two science learning environments revealed that third- and fourth graders showed higher achievement in a learning environment that incorporated feedback, examples and explanations than in an environment without these elements (Klahr & Nigam, 2004).

In our own research, we found that a learning environment in third grade on the topic of "floating and sinking" involving elements of instructional support in terms of content sequencing and cognitively activating teacher prompts, showed superior outcomes with respect to students' long-term conceptual restructuring compared to the same curriculum without these instructional support elements (open inquiry approach). A total of 161 third graders participated in this study, with three classrooms instructed within a curriculum with a high degree of instructional support, three classrooms instructed in the comparison group with a low degree of instructional support controlling for tasks, material, teacher and instructional time, and two classrooms serving as control groups without instruction on the topic of floating and sinking (Hardy et al., 2006). Students' conceptual understanding was assessed within a pre-post-follow-up design with a test assessing student explanations on the levels of misconception, explanations of everyday life as an intermediate state of conceptual understanding, and scientific explanations. Not only did students in the group with a high degree of instructional support show a more integrated understanding and abandon more of their misconceptions in the one-year follow-up, they also exhibited high levels of motivation and positive affective outcomes (Blumberg, Hardy, & Möller, 2008). This was true for both genders in the high-support group. Additionally, it was the group of low-achieving students that particularly benefited from the curriculum with instructional support. These results are also in line with conjectures put forward in a review by Shtulman (2009) pointing to the importance of long-term domain-specific instructional approaches for conceptual restructuring.

Similar to approaches concentrating on students' conceptual restructuring of basic science concepts, curricula focusing on the reconceptualization of the nature of science (i.e., students' epistemological beliefs) have been successful in long-term instructional approaches. For example, a comparison between a classroom instructed within a „nature of science" approach and a traditional classroom over a period of several years showed that students' understanding of the nature of science and of basic science concepts is affected over the long run (Smith, Maclin, Houghton, & Hennessey, 2000).

More short-term instructional approaches of five to ten 90-minute lessons have, however, also been shown to effectively raise elementary school students' understanding of the nature of science (Grygier, 2008, Sodian et al., 2006). Embedded into the topic of yeast formation, this curriculum explicitly addressed the formation of hypotheses according to theories, the design of experiments, and the interpretation of and reasoning with empirical evidence. A control classroom participated in a curriculum of similar topics without an explicit focus on the nature of science. After the unit, the students in the experimental class showed an implicit constructivist orientation of the nature of science, including superior methodological skills, while the progress of students in the control group was limited (see also Hardy, Kloetzer, Möller, & Sodian, 2010 for a comparison of scientific reasoning).

In sum, an effective learning environment needs to enable students to work on one topic or scientific issue intensively. This prolonged effort to grasp the underlying principles of scientific phenomena is especially important in elementary school, as it enables students to be familiarized with the nature of scientific thinking, testing, and argumentation, forming basic expectations and beliefs about the nature of science. Specifically, an effective learning environment incorporates elements of instructional scaffolding that allow learners to focus their cognitive activity on relevant concepts (see also Mayer, 2004, for a distinction between cognitive and behavioral activation). A teacher here may function as a moderator or coach who supports students' construction of insights and advanced strategies by employing adequate material, tasks, prompts and representations. Instructional support or scaffolding (based on Wood, Bruner, & Ross, 1976) then involves the process-oriented support of individual knowledge construction; this enables learners to solve on their own those elements of a task which are within their cognitive "reach", whereas instructional support serves as scaffolding for those elements of a task that are more advanced (see Puntambekar & Hübscher, 2005). According to Pea (2004), scaffolding serves the functions of (1) structuring a task, such as focusing a learner's attention on relevant elements or reducing the complexity of task, and (2) modeling solutions within a scientific context. This may encompass modeling more advanced ways of reasoning, argumentation, or the problematizing of student explanations (Reiser, 2004), thus leading to different ways of productively applying initial student conceptions to a broader scientific context. A common distinction between different kinds of scaffolding relates to process-oriented soft scaffolds and more static, hard scaffolds (Simons & Klein, 2007). While soft scaffolds have usually been investigated as types of teacher questions and prompts during instruction (e.g., Davis & Miyake, 2004), hard scaffolds include different forms of visualizations, tasks and materials (Hardy & Koerber, in press). In our own research, we investigated students' conceptual restructuring within the context of "floating and sinking" using different forms of representation. For example, in a classroom intervention, we varied whether students used a balance beam to represent density or whether they invented their own representations during instruction (Hardy et al., 2005). In a training study, we investigated the effects of a balance beam, a density matrix and numerical representations on students' conceptual understanding (Hardy & Stern, 2011). While we found that representations may be integrated effectively into science instruction in elementary school and were generally useful in supporting conceptual restructuring, we also found that their differential effects were quite dependent on student characteristics, sequencing of instructional tasks and teacher expertise.

The previous results convincingly show that students can obtain an understanding of the nature of science as well as general conceptual understanding as early as elementary school if conceptual change-oriented learning opportunities are provided that correspond to the basic principles of constructivist learning, and in which students can construct (more) adequate scientific explanations. These learning environments should (1) consider students' initial ideas about scientific phenomena, (2) support active learning that guides students towards the acquisition of self-regulated processes as well as applied and meaningful learning in collaborative learning situations and (3) support the development of students' conceptual understanding by supplying elements of instructional support. Creating such successful learning environments that are based on a well-balanced combination of these elements places difficult demands on teachers' instructional abilities. Understandably, this leads researchers to question which teacher competencies are necessary for promoting insightful learning that supports children's development of conceptual understanding in elementary science classrooms.

## 6 The Role of Teachers' Knowledge in Developing Elementary Students' Conceptual Understanding in Science Education

In order to answer this question, the focus of current research has now been broadened from identifying effective teaching strategies and behaviors and implementing these through 'teacher proof curricula' to studying the impact of teachers' professional competencies that underlie effective teaching. This shift in perspective was triggered by numerous studies that show how teachers' orientations towards science teaching and learning and teachers' inadequate knowledge about subject matter and learners, in fact, conflict with the conceptions that emphasize cognitively engaging science instruction (e.g., Berg & Brouwer, 1991; Cronin-Jones, 1991; Smith & Neale, 1989). These findings pointed out the importance of the influence and the complexity of teachers' knowledge and led to the investigation of teacher competencies such as knowledge, beliefs, and psychological functioning, and their role in successful teaching and learning outcomes, both generally and specific to science (e.g., Ball, 1988; Leinhardt & Greeno, 1986).

Within this broadened approach, most research on teachers' competencies has focused on teachers' knowledge and beliefs. The theoretical foundation was laid at the American Educational Research Association meeting in 1985, when Lee Shulman proposed a model for conceptualizing knowledge for teaching. There he introduced the constructs of generic pedagogical knowledge, content knowledge and pedagogical content knowledge as the core components of the specialized knowledge that is required for teaching. Although various researchers have added to or specified these sub-domains of teacher knowledge over the last decades, these three components have consistently appeared in literature and thus seem to be internationally accepted (Baumert & Kunter, 2006; Borko & Putnam, 1996; Bromme, 1997; Grossman, 1990; Munby, Russell, & Martin, 2001). Knowledge of generic pedagogy (PK) is described as general, subject-independent knowledge about classroom organization and management, general knowledge of learning theory and general methods of teaching. Content knowledge (CK) includes the knowledge of a subject or discipline per se and is not unique to teaching. It goes beyond the knowledge of facts, concepts, principles and theories to also include an understanding of how concepts and principles of a subject are organized and the rules of evidence and proof that are used to justify claims in a certain subject or discipline. Within this classification of teachers' knowledge, pedagogical content knowledge (PCK) is considered the central component of teachers' professional knowledge that distinguishes teachers from subject matter specialists (Grossman, 1990; Shulman, 1987). PCK is defined as a kind of "amalgam" of content knowledge with pedagogical and psychological knowledge as well as with the teachers' personal experiences, creating an understanding of how certain topics, problems or issues ought to be presented and adapted to the learners' different interests and abilities (Shulman, 1987). Magnusson, Krajcik, and Borko (1999) proposed a model of PCK in the domain of science education by defining five components to classify PCK for science teaching: (a) 'orientations towards science teaching', which represent overarching conceptions of viewing or approaching science teaching and learning; (b) 'knowledge of science curricula', including specific science curricula as well as mandated goals and objectives in science education; (c) 'knowledge of students' understanding of science', which includes common conceptions and areas of difficulties of particular topics; (d) 'knowledge of instructional strategies', including representations, activities, methods and other teaching strategies that apply to teaching particular topics within a domain of science; and (e) 'knowledge of assessment for science', which consists of knowledge of the dimensions of science learning that are important to assess, and knowledge of the methods by which that learning can be assessed. Within research groups in science education this model is internationally agreed upon and is seen as a useful conceptual framework for organizing research on science teacher knowledge (e.g., Abell, 2007; Henze, van Driel, & Verloop, 2008; Park & Oliver, 2008).

Today reviews of teacher education literature reveal a broad consensus that all facets of teachers' professional knowledge are important factors in instructional quality and student learning (e.g., Ball, Lubienski, & Mewborn, 2001; Baumert & Kunter, 2006; Munby et al., 2001). In the field of science education, this shared understanding is supported by findings of numerous qualitative studies that show how teachers' orientations towards science teaching and learning and teachers' knowledge about both subject matter and students affect the quality of instruction (for a review see Abell, 2007; Magnusson et al., 1999). Intentionally or not, teachers omit or weaken instructional elements that are critical for the development of students' conceptual understanding if, for example, they are not aware of students' typical misconceptions or the need to address them (e.g., Berg & Brouwer, 1991; Cronin-Jones, 1991; Smith & Neale, 1989). Other studies show that a lack of subject matter knowledge causes teachers to use scientifically inaccurate representations or explanations that can hinder students in achieving conceptual understanding in science classrooms (e.g., Sanders, Borko, & Lockard, 1993). While these qualitative studies provide detailed descriptions about the effects of teacher knowledge, the quantitative research base, by contrast, is rather poor, especially in the field of science. So far, quantitative studies mostly draw on distal indicators such as university courses taken or certification status achieved. Although findings tend to indicate a positive effect on student outcome (e.g., Goldhaber & Brewer, 2000), these indicators are today criticized as poor proxies of teachers' professional knowledge (Baumert & Kunter, 2006).

Contemporary empirical studies aim to develop theoretical frameworks and measurement instruments to directly assess the various domains of teachers' knowledge (e.g., Blömeke et al., 2008; Hill, Schilling, & Ball, 2004; Krauss et al., 2008). They also use these measures to predict the impact of the different components of teachers' knowledge on quality of instruction and conceptual understanding of learners. Up to today, these studies have mostly applied to mathematics teaching. Yet, they present the remarkable finding that teachers' mathematical knowledge, especially their PCK, is positively related to student gains in mathematical achievement (Baumert et al., 2010; Hill, Rowan, & Ball, 2005; Peterson, Fennema, Carpenter, & Loef, 1989). Comparable empirical research on the impact of domain-specific knowledge in science education is still rare (Abell, 2007), especially at the elementary school level.

Two different studies conducted by our own research group have examined the impact of teachers' PCK on students' conceptual understanding in science education (Kleickmann, 2008; Lange, 2010). The first study concerns elementary school science teachers' orientations towards science teaching and learning as part of PCK (Magnusson et al., 1999). Embedded in the DFG priority program, BiQua ("The Quality of Schools"), the research project investigated effects of teachers' orientations towards science teaching and learning that have been modified through in-service courses on students' learning achievement in elementary school science. After having participated in 16 all-day in-service courses, participants gave lessons on the topic of 'floating and sinking' in third and fourth grade classes. Before and after the instructional unit, students' conceptual understanding of 'floating and sinking' was measured by a questionnaire. In order to ensure similar conditions, all teachers were provided with boxes containing the material for instruction. Teachers' conceptions of teaching and learning were captured with Likert-scaled questionnaires (Kleickmann, Möller, & Jonen, 2005). The test on students' understanding of 'floating and sinking' included both multiple-choice and free-response items (Hardy et al., 2006). Data were collected from about 932 students in 46 classes. Effects of teachers' orientations towards science teaching and learning on students' gains in understanding were estimated using multilevel modeling. Results show that teachers' orientations towards science teaching and learning, modified through in-service courses, do indeed have an impact on students' achievement gains in elementary science lessons. Orientations which are in line with conceptual change approaches have a strong positive effect on students' gains in conceptual understanding of 'floating and sinking'. The so-called 'hands-on/minds-off' and the 'transmissive' orientation of teaching and learning have significantly negative effects on students' achievement gains. These effects remain significant after controlling for teachers' professional experience, for duration of instruction, teachers' physics-related interest and self-concept. Teachers' orientations that emphasize the necessity of students' motivation and everyday connections in elementary school science did not show any effect on students' gains in their understanding of 'floating and sinking' (Kleickmann, 2008).

The second study is part of the PLUS Project, which investigates conditions and outcomes of science teaching in the transition from elementary to secondary schools in Germany. This value-added study with a sample of 60 elementary school teachers and 1326 students (grades three and four) investigated whether and how elementary school science teachers' PCK in the content area 'states of matter and changes of state' influences students' understanding of this scientific concept. Teachers' PCK concerning the mentioned scientific topic was directly assessed using paper-and-pencil tests within two components: (a) 'knowledge of student understanding' (KSU) and 'knowledge of instructional strategies' (KIS). The developed items asked teachers, for example, to list as many alternative student conceptions as possible concerning an everyday situation, such as evaporation (KSU). Other items presented situations in which teachers were asked to detect comprehension difficulties or to describe behavior that promotes insightful student learning (KIS). The final test consisted of 14 items (11 free-response-, three multiple-choice items) and showed good psychometric qualities. Measures of students' achievement gains were drawn from a test that focused on the conceptual understanding of this topic in a pre-post design. Multilevel analyses revealed that the measured PCK has a substantial positive effect on students' learning gains in conceptual understanding of 'states of matter' after controlling for key student- and teacher-level covariates (Lange, 2010).

In sum, research on teachers' knowledge conducted in the field of science education provides empirical evidence in support of the assumption that teachers who know more about their subject and how this subject can be explained to students tend to provide higher-quality instruction and better learning outcomes. This seems to be true for both mathematical and science education, in secondary school grade levels as well as in elementary school science classrooms. Yet, some questions remain, especially in the field of science: Exactly how do PCK and CK regulate teaching behavior and student learning? Are they equally important? How do future and in-service teachers develop professional knowledge and how can pre-service and in-service education support the acquisition of this knowledge?

## 7 Beyond Standards: How Can We Improve Elementary Science Learning and Teaching?

In the article at hand, we have shown that insightful science teaching that leads to conceptual understanding is the aim of science education in Germany, starting as early as elementary school. In contrast to secondary schools in Germany and other countries, no educational standards at the elementary level have yet been established. Nevertheless, we believe it is important both to define clear, specific descriptions of the competencies that students are expected to learn, and to develop assessment tools that measure the outcomes of elementary school science education. However, the body of reviewed research leads us to further wonder: How exactly should science instruction at the elementary level be designed such that these aims can be reached? So far, we know that early science instruction should consider students' initial ideas about scientific phenomena, support active learning and provide instructional support that helps students to develop a more adequate conceptual understanding. Hands-on activities play an important role in corresponding learning arrangements. They provide the opportunity to experience phenomena, find answers to questions that arise in classroom discussions, and to verify or disprove ideas. However, research on scientific inquiry learning arrangement presents ample evidence that hands-on-elements are insufficient if not accompanied by students' active thinking and conclusion drawing (Minner et al., 2010). Therefore, the teacher's role in scaffolding students' thinking processes seems to be crucial. Exactly how to balance students' self-regulated processes and teachers' support of thinking processes, specifically for students with different learning prerequisites, still remains an area for further research.

Conceptual understanding is not the only aim of early science education. In agreement with the internationally accepted concept of scientific literacy, students' interest, self-efficacy, and self-esteem are just as important as cognitive competencies, especially in keeping students from dropping out of science. From recent research, we know that constructivist oriented learning environments with teachers' instructional support serve multiple goals (Blumberg et al. 2008), including motivational, cognitive, and self-related goals. For further research on "effective" learning environments, focusing on multiple outcomes seems to be important.

Additionally, the question, "What do teachers need to know to be able to implement the identified elements of good science teaching that would lead to meeting these standards?" needs to be dealt with. Research on teachers' competencies in science teaching in the elementary grades has shown a persistent problem: While secondary school science teachers are usually described as "subject specialists", elementary school teachers are usually characterized as "generalists" (Gess-Newsome, 1999). International and German research results confirm that elementary school science teachers often hold inadequate content knowledge (Summers & Kruger, 1994) and have low self-efficacy beliefs (Möller, 2004). There is still a lack of studies that directly examine deeper facets of elementary school science teachers' professional knowledge. However, since CK is considered to be a prerequisite of PCK development (van Driel, Verloop, & de Vos, 1998), one might argue that a lack of content knowledge leads to a lack of PCK. Qualitative research results underpin these theses (see section above).

With regard to orientations towards science teaching, it has been shown that elementary school teachers in the United States and in Germany hold "transmissive views" more than "conceptual change-oriented views" (Keys, 2005; Kleickmann, 2008). Considering the aforementioned finding that elementary school science teachers' PCK (and orientations that are in line with conceptual change approaches) positively predict student gains in science achievement, it seems to be of particular importance to support teachers in developing a higher level of professional knowledge, including conceptual change conceptions and views on teaching and learning in science.

Since research has shown that teachers' knowledge can be altered through courses (Kleickmann, Hardy, Jonen, Blumberg, & Möller, 2007; Richardson & Placier, 2001), initiatives designed to improve teacher education and in-service training must be supported. It might be possible to improve students' learning progress in science by improving teachers' professional knowledge through pre- and in-service educational programs that facilitate the acquisition of teachers' professional knowledge. We believe that research on the development of professional knowledge, including the knowledge of what comprises successful learning environments, could be a fruitful approach to eventually improving students' learning progress in elementary school science education.

# References

Abell, S. K. (2007). Research on science teacher knowledge. In S. K. Abell & N. G. Lederman (Eds.), *Handbook of Research on Science Education* (pp. 1105-1149). Mahwah, NJ: Erlbaum.

Appleton, K. (2008). Developing science pedagogical content knowledge through mentoring elementary teachers. *Journal of Science Teacher Education, 19*(6), 523-545.

Ball, D. L. (1988). Knowledge and Reasoning in Mathematical Pedagogy: Examining What Prospective Teachers Bring to Teacher Education. Unpublished doctoral dissertation. Michigan State University.

Ball, D. L., Lubienski, S., & Mewborn, D. (2001). Research on teaching mathematics: The unsolved problem of teachers' mathematical knowledge. In V. Richardson (Ed.), *Handbook of Research on Teaching* (4th ed., pp. 433-456). New York: Macmillan.

Baumert, J. & Kunter, M. (2006). Stichwort: Professionelle Kompetenz von Lehrkräften [Keyword: Professional competencies of teachers]. *Zeitschrift für Erziehungswissenschaft* (9), 469-520.

Baumert, J., Kunter, M., Blum, W., Brunner, M., Voss, T., Jordan, A., et al. (2010). Teachers' mathematical knowledge, cognitive activation in the classroom, and student progress. *American Educational Research Journal, 47*(1), 133-180.

Berg, T. & Brouwer, W. (1991). Teacher awareness of student alternate conceptions about rotational motion and gravity. *Journal of Research in Science Teaching, 28*(1), 3-18.

Blömeke, S., Seeber, S., Lehmann, R., Kaiser, G., Schwarz, B., Felbrich, A., et al. (2008). Messung des fachbezogenen Wissens angehender Mathematiklehrkräfte. In S. Blömeke, G. Kaiser & R. Lehmann (Eds.), *Professionelle Kompetenz angehender Lehrerinnen und Lehrer. Wissen, Überzeugungen und Lerngelegenheiten deutscher Mathematikstudierender und -referendare. Erste Ergebnisse zur Wirksamkeit der Lehrerausbildung* (pp. 49-88) *[Professional competencies of teachers-to-be. Knowledge, beliefs and learning opportunities of German mathematics students and teachers-in-training. First results about the efficacy of teacher training]*. Münster: Waxmann.

Blumberg, E., Hardy, I., & Möller, K. (2008). Anspruchsvolles naturwissenschaftsbezogenes Lernen im Sachunterricht der Grundschule – auch für Mädchen? [Challenging scientific learning in early science education in elementary school – for girls, too?]. *Zeitschrift für Grundschulforschung, 2*, 59-72.

Borko, H. & Putnam, R. T. (1996). Learning to teach. In D. C. Berliner & R. C. Calfee (Eds.), *Handbook of Educational Psychology* (pp. 673-708). Washington: MacMillan.

Bransford, J., Brown, A., & Cocking, R. (Eds.). (1999). *How People Learn*. Washington, DC: National Academy Press.

Bromme, R. (1992). *Der Lehrer als Experte. Zur Psychologie des professionellen Wissens [The teacher as an expert. The psychology of professional knowledge]*. Bern: Hans Huber.

Bromme, R. (1997). Kompetenzen, Funktionen und unterrichtliches Handeln des Lehrers [Teachers' competencies, functions and action in class]. In F. E. Weinert (Ed.), *Enzyklopädie der Psychologie: Psychologie des Unterrichts und der Schule* (Vol. 3, pp. 177-212). Göttingen: Hogrefe.

Bullock, M., Sodian, D., & Koerber, S. (2009). Doing experiments and understanding science: Development of scientific reasoning from childhood to adulthood. In W. Schneider & M. Bullock (Eds.), *Human Development From Early Childhood to Early Adulthood. Findings From the Munich Longitudinal Study* (pp. 173-197). Mahwah, NJ: Erlbaum.

Bybee, R. W. (1997). Toward an understanding of scientific literacy. In W. Gräber & C. Bolte (Eds.), *Scientific Literacy* (pp. 37-68). Kiel: IPN.

Carey, S., Evans, R., Honda, M., Jay, E., & Unger, C. (1989). An experiment is when you try it and see if it works. A study of junior high school students' understanding of the construction of scientific knowledge. *International Journal of Science Education, 11*, 514-529.

Cepni, S. & Cil, E. (2010). Using a conceptual change text as a tool to teach the nature of science in an explicit reflective approach. *Asia-Pacific Forum on Science Learning and Teaching, 11*(1), Article 11. Available at: http://www.ied.edu.hk/apfslt/v11_issue1/cepni/index.htm#con (Date of Access: 15.01.2011).

Cronin-Jones, L. L. (1991). Science teacher beliefs and their influence on curriculum implementation: Two case studies. *Journal of Research in Science Teaching, 28*(3), 235-250.

Davis, E. & Miyake, N. (2004). Explorations of scaffolding in complex classroom systems. *The Journal of the Learning Sciences, 13*(3), 265-272.

di Sessa, A. (2008). A "Theory bite" on the meaning of scientific inquiry: a companion to Kuhn and Pease. *Cognition and Instruction, 26*(4), 560-566.

di Sessa, A. A., Gillespie, N., & Esterly, J. (2004). Coherence vs. fragmentation in the development of the concept of force. *Cognitive Science, 28*, 843-900.

Duit, R., Gropengießer, H., & Stäudel, L. (Eds.) (2004). *Naturwissenschaftliches Arbeiten. Unterricht und Material 5-10 [Applied Science. Instruction and teaching material 5-10]*. Seelze: Friedrich Verlag.

Duit, R. & Treagust, D. F. (2003). Conceptual change: A powerful framework for improving science teaching and learning. *International Journal of Science Education, 25*, 671–688.

Duschl, R. & Hamilton, R. (1998). Conceptual change in science and in the learning of science. In B. Fraser, & K. Tobin (Eds.), *International Handbook of Science Education*. (pp. 1047-1065). Dordrecht: Kluwer Academic Publishers.

Flick, L.B. & Lederman, N.G. (2006). *Scientific inquiry and nature of science*. Dordrecht: Springer.

Gerstenmaier, J. & Mandl, H. (1995). Wissenserwerb unter konstruktivistischer Perspektive. [Knowledge aquisition from a constructivist perspective] *Zeitschrift für Pädagogik, 41*, 867-887.

Gesellschaft für Didaktik des Sachunterrichts (Society for Teaching Natural and Social Sciences and Technology in Elementary School) (2003). *Perspectives Framework for General Studies in Primary Education*. Bad Heilbrunn: Klinkhardt.

Gess-Newsome, J. (1999). Expanding questions and extending implications: A response to the paper set. *Science Education, 83*(3), 385-391.

Goldhaber, D. D. & Brewer, D. J. (2000). Does teacher certification matter? High school teacher certification status and student achievement. *Educational Evaluation and Policy Analysis, 22(2)*, 129-145.

Grossman, P. L. (1990). *The making of a teacher. Teacher knowledge and teacher education.* New York: Teachers College Press.

Grygier, P. (2008). *Wissenschaftsverständnis von Grundschülern im Sachunterricht [Elementary school students' understanding of the nature of science and scientific inquiry].* Bad Heilbrunn: Klinkhardt.

Hardy, I., Jonen, A., Möller, K., & Stern, E. (2006). Effects of instructional support within constructivist learning environments for elementary school students' understanding of "floating and sinking". *Journal of Educational Psychology, 98*(2), 307-326.

Hardy, I., Kloetzer, B., Möller, K., & Sodian, B. (2010). The analysis of classroom discourse: Elementary school science curricula advancing reasoning with Evidence. *Educational Assessment, 15*, 197-221.

Hardy, I. & Koerber, S. (in press). Scaffolding learning by the use of visual representations. *Encyclopedia of the Sciences of Learning.* Berlin: Springer.

Hardy, I., Schneider, M., Jonen, A., Möller, K., & Stern, E. (2005). Fostering Diagrammatic Reasoning in Science Education. *Swiss Journal of Psychology, 64*(3), 207-217.

Hardy, I. & Stern, E. (2011). Visuelle Repräsentationen der Dichte: Auswirkungen auf die konzeptuelle Umstrukturierung bei Grundschulkindern [Visual representation of density: Impacts on the conceptual reconstruction by elementary school students]. *Unterrichtswissenschaft, 39*(1), 35-48.

Henze, I., van Driel, J. H., & Verloop, N. (2008). Development of experienced science teachers' pedagogical content knowledge of models of the solar system and the universe. *International Journal of Science Education, 30*(10), 1321-1342.

Hill, H. C., Rowan, B., & Ball, D. L. (2005). Effects of teachers' mathematical knowledge for teaching on student achievement. *American Educational Research Journal, 42*(2), 371-406.

Hill, H. C., Schilling, S. G., & Ball, D. L. (2004). Developing measures of teachers' mathematics knowledge for teaching. *The Elementary School Journal, 105*, 11-30.

Inhelder, B. & Piaget, J. (1958). *The Growth of Logical Thinking From Childhood to Adolescence.* London: Routledge & Kegan Paul.

Keys, P. M. (2005). Are teachers walking the walk or just talking the talk in science education? *Teachers and Teaching: Theory and Practice, 11*(5), 499-516.

Kirschner, P.A., Sweller, J., & Clark, R.E. (2006). Why minimal guidance during instruction does not work: An analysis of the failure of constructivist, discovery, problem-based, experiential, and inquiry based teaching. *Educational Psychologist, 41*, 75-86.

Klahr, D. & Nigam, M. (2004). The equivalence of learning paths in early science instruction: Effects of direct instruction and discovery learning. *Psychological Science, 15*, 661–667.

Kleickmann, T. (2008). *Zusammenhänge fachspezifischer Vorstellungen von Grundschullehrkräften zum Lehren und Lernen mit Fortschritten von Schülerinnen und Schülern im konzeptuellen Verständnis [Elementary school teachers' subject-specific orientations towards teaching and learning science and elementary students' gains in understanding scientific concepts].* Münster: Inaugural-Dissertation.

Kleickmann, T., Hardy, I., Jonen, A., Blumberg, E., & Möller, K. (2007). Learning environments in primary school science – Scaffolding students' and teachers' processes of conceptual development. In M. Prenzel (Ed.), *Studies on the Educational Quality of Schools. The final Report on the DFG Priority Programme* (pp. 137-156). Münster: Waxmann.

Kleickmann, T., Möller, K., & Jonen, A. (2005). Effects of in-service teacher education courses on teachers' pedagogical content knowledge in primary science education. In H. Gruber, C. Harteis, R. Mulder & M. Rehrl (Eds.), *Bridging Individual, Organisational, and Cultural Aspects of Professional Learning* (pp. 51-58). Regensburg: Roderer.

Kleickmann, T., Pollmeier, J., Hardy, I., & Möller, K. (submitted). Die Struktur naturwissenschaftlichen Wissens von Grundschulkindern – eine person- und variablenzentrierte Analyse [The structure of scientific knowledge of elementary school children – a person- and variable-centered analysis]. *Zeitschrift für Entwicklungspsychologie und Pädagogische Psychologie*.

Koerber, S., Sodian, B., Thoermer, C., & Nett, U. (2005). Scientific reasoning in young children: Preschoolers' ability to evaluate covariation evidence. *Swiss Journal of Psychology, 64*(3), 141-152.

Krauss, S., Brunner, M., Kunter, M., Baumert, J., Blum, W., Neubrand, M., et al. (2008). Pedagogical content knowledge and content knowledge of secondary mathematics teachers. *Journal of Educational Psychology, 100*, 716-725.

Kuhn, D. & Siegler, R. S. (2006), *Handbook of Child Psychology: Volume 2: Cognition, Perception, and Language*. Hoboken, NJ: Wiley.

Lange, K. (2010). *Zusammenhänge zwischen naturwissenschaftsbezogenem fachspezifisch-pädagogischem Wissen von Grundschullehrkräften und Fortschritten im Verständnis naturwissenschaftlicher Konzepte bei Grundschülerinnen und -schülern [Elementary teachers' pedagogical content knowledge in science on elementary students' progress in understanding scientific concepts]*. Münster: Inaugural-Dissertation.

Larsson, A. & Hallden, O. (2010). A structural view on the emergence of a conception: conceptual change as radical reconstruction of contexts. *Science Education, 94*(4), 640-664.

Lee, E. & Luft, J. A. (2008). Experienced secondary science teachers' representation of pedagogical content knowledge. *International Journal of Science Education, 30*(10), 1343-1363.

Leinhardt, G. & Greeno, J. G. (1986). The cognitive skill of teaching. *Journal of Educational Psychology, 78*(2), 75-95.

Linn, M. (2006). The knowledge integration perspective on learning and instruction. In K. Sawyer (Ed.), *The Cambridge Handbook of the Learning Sciences* (pp. 243-264). Cambridge: Cambridge University Press.

Magnusson, S., Krajcik, J., & Borko, H. (1999). Nature, sources and development of pedagogical content knowledge for science teaching. In J. Gess-Newsome & N. G. Lederman (Eds.), *Examining Pedagogical Content Knowledge* (Vol. 6, pp. 95-132). Dordrecht: Kluwer.

Martin, M.O., Mullis, I.V.S., & Foy, P. (with Olson, J.F., Erberber, E., Preuschoff, C., & Galia, J.) (2008). *TIMSS 2007 International Science Report*. International Association for the evaluation of educational achievement (IAE).

Mayer, R. (2004). Should there be a three-strikes rule against pure discovery learning? The case for guided methods of instruction. *American Psychologist, 59*, 14-19

Minner, D.D., Levy, A.J. & Century, J. (2010). Inquiry-based science instruction –what is it and does it matter? Results from a research synthesis years 1984 to 2002. *Journal of Research in Science Teaching, 47(4)*, 474-496.

Möller, K. (2002). Anspruchsvolles Lernen in der Grundschule – am Beispiel naturwissenschaftlich-technischer Inhalte [Challenging learning in elementary school – taking the example of early science and technology content]. *Pädagogische Rundschau, 56*(4), 411-435.

Möller, K. (2004). Naturwissenschaftliches Lernen in der Grundschule – Welche Kompetenzen brauchen Grundschullehrkräfte? [Learning science in elementary school – Which competencies are necessary for elementary school teachers?] In H. Merkens (Ed.), *Lehrerbildung: IGLU und die Folgen* (pp. 65-84). Opladen: Leske + Budrich.

Munby, H., Russell, T., & Martin, A. K. (2001). Teachers' knowledge and how it develops. In V. Richardson (Ed.), *Handbook of Research on Teaching* (4th ed., pp. 877-904). Washington: American Educational Research Association.

Norris, S. & Philipps, L. (2003). How literacy in its fundamental sense is central to scientific literacy. *Science Education, 87*(2), 224-240.

Organisation for Economic Co-operation and Development (2006). *PISA 2006 Scientific Literacy Framework (Pisa Framework)*. Paris: OECD.

Park, S. & Oliver, J. S. (2008). Revisiting the conceptualisation of pedagogical content knowledge (PCK): PCK as a conceptual tool to understand teachers as professionals. *Research in Science Education, 38*(3), 261-284.

Pea, R. D. (2004). The social and technological dimensions of scaffolding and related theoretical concepts for learning, education, and human activity. *Journal of the Learning Sciences, 13*, 423–451.

Peterson, P. L., Fennema, E., Carpenter, T. P., & Loef, M. (1989). Teachers' pedagogical content beliefs in mathematics. *Cognition and Instruction, 6*(1), 1-40.

Prenzel, M., Geiser, H., Langeheine, R., & Lobemeier, K. (2003). Das naturwissenschaftliche Verständnis am Ende der Grundschule [Scientific understanding at the end of elementary school]. In W. Bos, E. Lankes, M. Prenzel, K. Schwippert, G. Walther, & R. Valtin (Eds.): *Erste Ergebnisse aus IGLU. Schülerleistungen am Ende der vierten Jahrgangsstufe im internationalen Vergleich* (pp. 143-187). Münster: Waxmann.

Prenzel, M., Rost, J., Senkbeil, M., Häußler, P., & Klopp, A. (2001). Naturwissenschaftliche Grundbildung: Testkonzeption und Ergebnisse [Basic education in science: Test designs and results]. In J. Baumert et al. (Eds.), *PISA 2000 – Basiskompetenzen von Schülerinnen und Schülern im internationalen Vergleich* (pp. 191-248). Opladen: Leske und Budrich.

Puntambekar, S. & Hübscher, R. (2005). Tools for scaffolding students in a complex environment: What have we gained and what have we missed? *Educational Psychologist, 40*, 1-12.

Quigley, C., Pongsanon, K., & Akerson, V. (2010). If we teach them, they can learn: Young students views of nature of science aspects to early elementary students during an informal science education program. *Journal of Science Teacher Education, 21*(7), 887-907.

Reiser, B. J. (2004). Scaffolding complex learning: The mechanisms of structuring and problematizing student work. *Journal of the Learning Sciences, 13*, 273–304.

Richardson, V. & Placier, P. (2001). Teacher change. In V. Richardson (Ed.), *Handbook of Research on Teaching* (4. ed., pp. 905-947). Washington, D. C.: American Educational Research Association.

Sanders, L. R., Borko, H., & Lockard, J. D. (1993). Secondary science teachers' knowledge base when teaching science courses in and out of their area of certification. *Journal of Research in Science Teaching, 30*(7), 723-736.

Sandoval, W.A. (2003). Conceptual and epistemic aspects of students' scientific explanations. *The Journal of the Learning Sciences, 12*, 5-51.

Schneider, M. & Hardy, I. (submitted). Pathways of conceptual restructuring of elementary school students'of floating and sinking.

Shtulman, A. (2009). Rethinking the role of resubsumption in conceptual change. *Educational Psychologist, 44*(1), 41-47.

Shulman, L. S. (1986). Those who understand: Knowledge growth in teaching. *Educational Researcher, 15*, 4-14.

Shulman, L. S. (1987). Knowledge and teaching: Foundations of the new reform. *Harvard Educational Review, 57*(1), 1-22.

Simons, K. D. & Klein, J. D. (2007). The impact of scaffolding and student achievement levels in a problem-based learning environment. *Instructional Science, 35*, 41-72.

Smith, C., Maclin, D., Houghton, C., & Hennessey, M. G. (2000). Sixth grade students' epistemologies of science: The impact of school science experiences on epistemological development. *Cognition and Instruction, 18*, 349-422.

Smith, D. C. & Neale, D. C. (1989). The construction of subject matter knowledge in primary science teaching. *Teaching and Teacher Education, 5*(1), 1-20.

Sodian, B. (1995). Entwicklung bereichsspezifischen Wissens [Development of domain-specific knowledge]. In R. Oerter & L. Montada (Eds.), *Entwicklungspsychologie* (pp. 622-653). Weinheim: Beltz.

Sodian, B. Jonen, A., Thoermer, C., & Kircher, E. (2006). Die Natur der Naturwissenschaften verstehen – Implementierung wissenschaftstheoretischen Unterrichts in der Grundschule [Understand the nature of science and scientific inquiry – Implementation of instruction in elementary school]. In M. Prenzel & L. Allolio-Näcke (Hrsg.), *Untersuchungen zur Bildungsqualität von Schule. Abschlussbericht des DFG-Schwerpunktprogramms*. Münster: Waxmann.

Sodian, B. & Koerber, S. (2011). Hypothesenprüfung und Evidenzevaluation im Grundschulalter [Testing hypotheses and evaluating evidence in elementary school]. *Unterrichtswissenschaft+, 39* (21-34).

Sodian, B., Zaitchik, D., & Carey, S. (1991). Young children's differentiation of hypothetical beliefs from evidence. *Child Development, 6*, 753-766.

Stathopoulou, C., & Vosniadou, S. (2007). Exploring the relationship between physics-related epistemological beliefs and physics understanding. *Contemporary Educational Psychology, 32*, 255–281.

Stern, E. (2002). Wie abstrakt lernt das Grundschulkind? Neuere Ergebnisse der entwicklungspsychologischen Forschung [How abstractly do elementary school students learn? Recent results in developmental psychology research]. In H. Petillon & B. Ofenbach (Eds.), *Jahrbuch Grundschulforschung* (Vol. 5, pp. 27-42). Opladen: Leske und Budrich.

Strand-Cary, M. & Klahr, D. (2008). Developing elementary science skills: Instructional effectiveness and independence. *Cognitive Development, 23*(4), 488-511.

Summers, M., & Kruger, C. (1994). A longitudinal study of a constructivist approach to improving primary school teachers' subject matter knowledge in science. *Teaching and Teacher Education, 10*(5), 499-519.

Treagust, D. F. & Duit, R. (1998). Learning in science: From behaviourism towards social constructivism and beyond. In B. J. Fraser & K. G. Tobin (Eds.), *International Handbook of Science Education* (pp. 3-25). Dordrecht: Kluwer Academic Publishers.

Tytler, R. & Prain, V. (2010). A framework for re-thinking learning in science from recent cognitive science perspectives. *International Journal of Science Education, 32*(15), 2055-2078.

van Driel, J. H., Verloop, N., & de Vos, W. (1998). Developing science teachers' pedagogical content knowledge. *Journal of Research in Science Teaching, 35*(6), 673-695.

Vosniadou, S. (2008). Science education for young children: A conceptual-change point of view. In O.A. Barbarin & B.H. Wasik (Eds.), *Handbook of Child Development and Early Education: Research to Practice* (pp. 544-557). New York: Guilford Press.

Vosniadou, S. (Ed.). (2008). *International Handbook of Research on Conceptual Change*. New York: Routledge.

Vosniadou, S., Ioannides, C., Dimitrakopoulou, A. & Papademetriou, E. (2001). Designing learning environments to promote conceptual change in science. *Learning and Instruction, 15*, 317-419.

Wagenschein, M. (1991). *Verstehen lehren [Teach understanding]* (2nd ed.). Weinheim: Beltz.

Wallace, C. S., Tsoi, M. Y., Calkin, J., & Darley, M. (2003). Learning from inquiry-based laboratories in nonmajor biology: An interpretive study of the relationships among inquiry experience, epistemologies, and conceptual growth. *Journal of Research in Science Teaching, 40*, 986-1024.

Wandersee, J., Mintzes, J., & Novak, J. (1994). Research on alternative conceptions in science. In D. Gabel (Ed.), *Handbook of Research on Science Teaching and Learning* (pp. 177-210). New York: Macmillan Publishing Company.

Windschitl, M., Thompson, J., & Braaten, M. (2008). Beyond the scientific method: Model-based inquiry as a new paradigm of preference for school science investigations. *Science Education, 92*(5), 941-967.

Wood, D., Bruner, J. S., & Ross, G. (1976). The role of tutoring in problem solving. *Journal of Child Psychology and Psychiatry and Allied Disciplines, 17*, 89-100.

Zimmerman, C. (2007). The development of scientific thinking skills in elementary and middle school. *Developmental Review, 27*(2), 172-223.

# Chapter 3

# Developing a Framework for Diagnostic Assessment of Early Science

*Benő Csapó*
*Institute of Education, University of Szeged, Hungary*

## Abstract

This chapter stems from the research of the past two decades on conceptualizing and assessing the quality of knowledge, especially knowledge as an outcome of science education. The findings that students performed well on some test types, whereas results were poor in other kinds of assessments, initiated a series of research projects. The results of these studies indicated that students' knowledge fell into several segments which may be independent form each other. The attempts for theoretical explanations and generalizations led to the conclusion that at least three different kinds of knowledge exist that are relevant to consider; different theoretical traditions may be mobilized to understand and describe the different aspects of students' knowledge, and, considering them simultaneously may result in a better framework for assessment. After an elaboration of the co-existence of the different theoretical directions, we applied this approach to the development of assessment frameworks for a diagnostic assessment project. The project aims at developing an online assessment system for the first six grades of primary school for reading, mathematics and science. Thus, the approach I present in this paper for science works well for mathematics and with some limitations for reading as well. However, this approach focuses on the initial stage of schooling; therefore, not all of its aspects can be generalized to later phases of education. In this chapter I present the empirical predecessor and theoretical resources of our current work on framework development. In order to enhance the diagnostic power of the assessments, we use three different types of test tasks for assessing the development of students' scientific reasoning, their scientific literacy and their scientific expert knowledge. Thus, for developing the framework for the tests we tap three different sets of theoretical resources. As will be shown, framework development for diagnostic assessment should be an analytic activity where goals should be carefully differentiated; on the other hand, teaching science should adopt a synthetic approach where the goals are seamlessly integrated.

# 1 Preliminary Considerations

Let me start this chapter with two not only theoretical, but rather philosophical considerations. Both emphasize the need for changing the way we used to approach the definition of outcomes of science education in the second half of the past century. The change I suggest may result in innovative taxonomies on the one hand, and may also bring us back to some old traditions, on the other.

The first consideration is related to the purpose of science education. It seems that science education is in crisis in a number of countries, which I argue, cannot be overcome without reconsidering its mission in modern societies. In the introduction of his famous book, Postman wrote over a decade and a half ago that '… without a transcendent and honorable purpose schooling must reach its finish and, the sooner we are done with it, the better. With such a purpose, schooling becomes the central institution, through which the young may find reasons for continuing to educate themselves' (Postman, 1995. x-xi). Let me specify the message of this citation to science education. Science education needs to find a new 'transcendent and honorable' purpose. With such a purpose we may have a chance to alter current trends and motivate young people to consider learning sciences as a mean for becoming more educated people.

The second consideration is related to the way we construct theoretical frameworks for defining outcomes of science education. There is still a strong temptation to look for a single theory which covers all aspects of learning and knowledge. If it fails to explain everything, it is thrown out and replaced with something else, based on entirely different, sometimes opposite assumptions to the previous one. One may recall a number of controversies, such as propositional knowledge or procedural skills, content or structure, Piaget or Vygotsky. I would argue for accepting several theoretical frameworks at the same time, acknowledging that none of them is able to describe all relevant aspects of the issue we are dealing with. To understand different features of the development of students' knowledge, we may need different theoretical approaches. I propose that as the controversy between wave or corpuscular properties of light cannot be resolved in a single theory, we have to construct different models when we try to explain different properties of knowledge. Instead of choosing one from the seemingly competing goals of science education, we must try to integrate them.

Furthermore, I challenge Lewin's claim that 'there is nothing more practical than a good theory' (1951, p. 169). There is something more useful: two good theories are more practical than one. In fact, I propose applying three good theories (or at least three different theoretical orientations) to set goals for science education and my aim is to show that this solution is more practical than using any one of them.

## 2 Research on Structure and Organization of Knowledge

### 2.1 Signals of Problems of Students' Science Knowledge

Traditionally, scientific research used to be a prestigious occupation in Hungary and scientist were highly regarded. This appraisal used to attract a number of bright young people to (natural) sciences in the past centuries until the late 1980s. This attraction resulted in not only renowned scientists, but also in talented and well prepared science teachers. Therefore, the results of the First International Mathematics and Science Study in 1972 were in line with expectations: Hungarian students ranked second in international survey, right after Japanese students. A decade later, in 1983, in the Second International Mathematics and Science Study, fourth graders exceeded all expectations as they ranked first, well ahead of their Japanese peers (Keeves, 1992). The first IEA assessments were based on Bloom's taxonomies, so the results of the application tasks could be separated from the rest of the tests, and more detailed analyses indicated that students performed relatively purely on the application items. Some other assessments in the late 1980s indicated that our students were good at the type of disciplinary knowledge IEA measured at the time. The explanation was quite obvious. The curriculum was demanding in terms of scientific content, the number of science lessons per week was relatively high, and science teachers were well selected and well trained.

This generally favorable picture was ruined by some findings of other types of assessments which indicated that students' general intellectual development was not as impressive as expected on the bases of the excellent science achievements and there were weak relationships between their reasoning skills and science achievements (Csapó, 1988). These findings questioned that the type of disciplinary science knowledge students possessed could be transferred easily to new contexts and situations. Some analyses of that time also indicated that the shortcomings of science knowledge were special cases of a more general problem. Hungarian schools focused on mastering expert-type knowledge in the particular disciplines but paid less attention on the application of knowledge outside the narrow disciplinary context. For example, a project comparing the Hungarian (matura) and Dutch school-leaving examinations pointed out that the Hungarian mathematics tests were mostly composed of pure, sterile mathematical tasks without referring to any practical contexts, whereas the Dutch mathematics tasks were more realistic and embedded in everyday contexts (Mátrai, 1997).

Based on these experiences, known within a smaller research community, but not among teachers or the general public, it was easily predictable that our students' results would not be as good as the early IEA assessments indicated, if their knowledge was assessed by different type of tests. This anticipation was confirmed by the 1995 TIMSS results: Hungarian students scored somewhere at the end of the first third of the countries (Beaton, Mullis, Martin, Gonzalez, Kelly, & Smith, 1996; Beaton, Martin, Mullis, Gonzalez, Smith, & Kelly, 1996). The results of PISA 2000 were even more revealing: science achievements were not significantly different from the OECD means (OECD, 2001). Being in the middle in the OECD ranking was not an issue in itself, but falling down from the top to the middle was shocking. The consecutive TIMSS assessments have indicated a decline in science and mathematics performances in the past decade, whereas science and mathematics results in PISA studies have not changed at all; they have been stable within the margin of error. The picture has got even more complex, as PISA 2009 indicated a significant (14 points) improvement in reading. This improvement prompts the question why no change has occurred in PISA in mathematics and science. As good reading is a tool for all further learning, its improvement is expected to transmit to other fields of study (OECD, 2010). This complex pattern of changes and unchanged achievements requires a more sophisticated tool to find a consistent explanation.

A further observation is students' negative attitudes towards science subjects. By the end of the 1990s, chemistry and physics were the two least liked school subjects. Students' attitudes towards mathematics were somewhere in the middle and they liked biology very much (Csapó, 2000). Furthermore, many students achieving well in science dislike learning sciences itself. As these facts indicate, science-related affective issues are not less complex than the cognitive ones.

A national core curriculum was accepted in 1997, which dealt with science only in brief as one of ten content areas. The content description was further shortened in 2003 and changed in 2007. The current legal version accepts the concept of key competencies, defining science competence as one of them. Nevertheless, the detailed content description details the ten content domains defined in the first version and devotes ca. 30 pages to science of 1–12 grades. Thus, textbook publishers as well as schools enjoy freedom in determining the actual content of teaching.

A national assessment system was established in 2001 and has been systematically carried out since 2003. The Assessment of Basic Competencies tests every student at grade 4, 6, 8, and 10 in reading and mathematics, but not in science. Hungarian students attending one of the academic tracks of high school, take a school-leaving examination (matura, Abitur) at the end of grade twelve. History, mother tongue and literature, and a foreign language are among the compulsory subjects, but science is not. This arrangement underlies the fact that makes the saying true: what is not tested is not taught. Science lost its leading role among the school subjects it used to have some decades ago.

As a consequence of several interacting causes, science education is in a critical situation. Several indicators signal this problem. The number of science and technology graduates is much lower than the economy would absorb. The number of applicants to science teacher training faculties is the lowest ever, fewer than the available places. The major problems related to science education were identified several years ago, but so far little has been done to tackle them. Although the problems became visible in the later phase of schooling they probably are rooted in the early school years. A contribution to the solution may be a systematic diagnostic assessment from the very beginning of formal education, followed by systematic intervention. The work reported in this chapter belongs to the foundation phase of developing such a system.

## 2.2 Empirical Projects on the Development of Skills and Organization of Knowledge

Since the beginning of the 1990s, a series of research projects have been carried out to examine the development of specific or general cognitive skills and different aspects of students' knowledge. A general observation was that students achieved well if their knowledge was tested in the same context where they mastered it. They were not only able to reproduce the teaching material, but also to demonstrate a certain kind of understanding of it. They were able to connect pieces of knowledge, draw conclusions from facts if everything remained within the boundaries of the given scientific topic; these are indicators of a kind of understanding what Gardner (1992) calls disciplinary understanding. On the other hand, students performed very poor if they were expected to apply their knowledge outside of the given context or discipline. In general, contradictions were observed between the high science achievements of students on disciplinary type tests and the poorer results in assessments measuring the application of knowledge and skills (Csapó, 1988, 1994, 1997; Csapó & B. Németh, 1995).

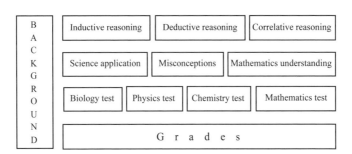

*Figure 1: The System of Variables in the School Knowledge Project (Csapó, 1998a)*

After several studies focusing only on a few variables, a systematic assessment project, called *School Knowledge Project* was designed that dealt with many relevant variables at the same time. Participants were 7th and 11th graders, and this way, development could be estimated from the cross-sectional design. The data collection was organized into a four-level model presented in Figure 1.

At the first level data characterizing students' school achievements were collected, such as grades given by the teachers. At the second level curriculum-based knowledge tests were used to measure how well students mastered what they were taught. These tests covered the teaching materials in four particular subjects: biology, physics, chemistry and mathematics.

At the third level three tests can be found. The science application test measured how students could apply their science knowledge outside of school, that is, in everyday situations. This test was constructed in a way that the tasks could be solved by utilizing the knowledge students were taught at school and what was measured by the tests at level two (B. Németh, 1998). As this test was based on authentic content placed in everyday situations, it was quite similar to the tests that PISA used some years later. The misconception test was built on some known, simple science misconceptions to examine if students used their scientific knowledge or their naive theories to interpret certain simple experiments or situations (Korom, 1997, 1998). The mathematics understanding test examined the depth of students' comprehension of some crucial mathematical concepts. It was composed of simple tasks which required deeper insight into certain mathematical issues, so they could not be solved mechanically by applying routine processes (Dobi, 1998).

The tests of the fourth level measured some general reasoning skills. The inductive reasoning test, used already in several other projects, contained tasks of verbal analogies, number analogies and number series (Csapó, 1997, 1998b). The deductive reasoning test covered the binary operations of propositional logic; the tasks mapped the truth functions of the logical operations (Vidákovich, 1998). The correlative reasoning tests examined students' reasoning about nondeterministic relationships (Bán, 1998).

The tests of the third and fourth level of the model were administered to both age groups in exactly the same form, so the difference between 7th and 11th graders could be directly assessed. Data collection took place in 1995, at the same time when the first TIMSS survey was administered.

The results of this project indicated again that students performed well at tests measuring their knowledge closely related to the curricular content, more precisely, close to the knowledge presented in the textbooks. On the other hand, they were unable to apply their knowledge beyond the context given in the textbooks. The most shocking results were found when comparing the 7th and 11th graders. The four years between these two ages are the most intensive period of schooling. students master an enormous amount of knowledge in this sensitive phase of development, but their general thinking abilities develop at a slower pace. Although they are presented complex scientific theories, science education has little impact on their misconceptions. In some areas 7th graders even outperformed their 11th grader peers. For example, the older students were less likely to accept probabilistic relationships indicating that science education presents them mostly deterministic relationships and confirms a simple mechanistic world view, what was confirmed by the analysis of textbook content as well. In sum, results indicated that students learn a lot, but partly in vain, as their knowledge cannot be applied outside of the narrow disciplinary area, and learning sciences does not contribute to their intellectual development as much as it would be desirable (For a summary of the empirical findings see Csapó, 2007). Results of several other projects confirmed the findings that students' knowledge fell into at least two different parts. One is school knowledge they are able to mobilize in school contexts and their applicable everyday knowledge that they mobilize when solving practical problems (Molnár, 2001, 2006).

As for the affective aspect, an increasing negative attitude towards chemistry and physics was found here as well. What was even more problematic was that many students who performed well at disciplinary knowledge tests and general reasoning tests alike (thus potential candidates for science related studies and professions) formed negative attitudes toward science subjects (so, probably will not pursue scientific studies).

One general conclusion of the project was that this unfavorable pattern of achievements can be attributed to the methods of teaching. Science education is focusing on the disciplinary aspects of content; teaching materials are organized according to the values and logic of the corresponding scientific research areas. General principles of cognitive development are not taken into account in the process of organizing teaching materials and designing textbooks, and students' actual preliminary knowledge is not considered during the actual teaching. A deeper understanding of the material is often not possible at the actual developmental level; therefore, reasoning is rarely encouraged. Teachers often expect their students to reproduce the content of textbooks. Precise definitions and close scientific argumentation are valued and considered as high achievement honored with good grades. Other research confirmed this interpretation. As the PISA 2000 highlighted, Hungarian students considered the reproduction of teaching material as the main goal of learning, and memorization was one of the main learning strategies (OECD, 2003). Students prefer reproductive learning strategies in the earlier phase of schooling as well (B. Németh & Habók, 2006).

The methods of teaching are mostly rooted in the way science teachers are trained and developed during their career. They receive high-level scientific training in the particular discipline, but learn very little of developmental psychology and teaching methods. Their pre-service training in teaching practice is limited to a few weeks or a dozen of lessons they are expected to teach. Their professional identity is strongly connected to the particular disciplines; their professional organizations are also formed according to the scientific disciplines (e.g., separate societies for mathematics teachers, physics teachers).

There were two further conclusions of these empirical projects. (1) For changing the current situation, two other goals of education should be elevated to the same level of importance what today the disciplinary orientation enjoys. Cultivating students' general intellectual abilities and enhancing their capabilities to apply their knowledge should receive equal attention, scientific and technical support as the disciplinary approach receives today. (2) The three main goals may be supported by different theoretical frameworks. The consequences of these conclusions were elaborated in the framework of the most recent projects.

## 3 A Three-Dimensional Conception of Knowledge as Goal of Education

Recent tendencies in science education may be considered as integrative or synthetic. A number of recently preferred approaches to teaching sciences such as integrated science, project-based methods, problem-based learning, and inquiry-based science education emphasize global approaches, aiming at connecting pieces of knowledge in a way that goes beyond the traditional disciplinary views and boundaries. The rapid career of the concept of competence fits very well into this trend: competency is a proper counterpart on the outcome side of the teaching and learning processes that I have just listed on the methods side.

Competence is a useful umbrella conception; it helps to cope with the compartmentalization or fragmentation of students' knowledge. Competence-based teaching may contribute to solving the problems I have described in the previous section. The concept of competence may inform teaching and may be functional for constructing summative tests, such as the PISA tests, or the Hungarian national reading and mathematical competency assessment tests. On the other hand, such a general conception has limited value if we intend to construct 'high resolution' formative or diagnostic tests aiming at analyzing the fine nuances of students' knowledge. Therefore, one of the most promising directions in recent educational research aims at identifying and describing the most important competencies (key competencies) and exploring their structure and function (see for example Schmid & Dinkelmann, 2007; Koeppen, Hartig, Klieme, & Leutner, 2008; Schott & Ghanbari, 2008; volume edited by Hartig, Klieme, & Rauch, 2008; and special issue of the *Zeitschrift für Pädagogik*, 2010).

If we aim at identifying different types of problems in students' learning, for example, insufficient mastery of the scientific concepts and domain specific skills, slowing or stagnating cognitive development or the difficulties in application of knowledge, we need different kinds of assessment instruments. These instruments should inform teachers about student's progress in several directions and should provide students with proper feedback on the strengths and weaknesses of their knowledge.

Inspired by the generalizable results of the empirical projects summarized in the previous section and by the needs of diagnostic assessments, I propose a three-dimensional model of the goals of school education. In this model I treat the goals separately that are related to (1) mastering the given curricular content, defined by the principles of the respective scientific disciplines; (2) the application of knowledge in relevant, authentic contexts, first of all in studying other subjects and in everyday life situations; and (3) the fostering students' general information processing capabilities, in short, developing their cognition. In this model, I consider each dimension of goals as equally important (for an elaboration if this model, see Csapó, 2004, 2010). Furthermore, I assume that they may be identified and defined separately at a conceptual-theoretical level, and different assessments scales may be constructed to measure them.

To pursue the different types of goals we need different underpinning theoretical resources. To understand the accumulation of disciplinary knowledge, a proper theoretical framework is based on the early approaches of cognitive science. This model distinguishes how novices and experts process information and represent knowledge. It explains the exceptional efficiency of expertise (expert knowledge): most of the time experts do not need to reason; they use their schemata which are ready for application. Expert knowledge is most efficient in familiar situations and cannot be easily applied in novel contexts. Thus, this model cannot explain a number of important characteristics of cognition and utilization of knowledge. One attempt to overcome the difficulties is to extend the 'novice-expert differences model' and to reformulate the conception of expertise. There are many successful applications of this approach or one of its derivatives in education as well. One of the most elaborated and most successful applications in education is the *How People Learn framework*, which has drawn from these theoretical resources as well (Bransford, Brown, & Cocking, 2000).

I agree with the critical remarks that the early information processing approach does not have a strong conception of development, and instead of sticking to it in every case, I propose to find a different theory for explaining the other aspects of knowledge.

Deanna Kuhn frames the following question in the title of the first chapter of her book: Why go to school? There may be several answers to this question; one is to master (a portion of the core) knowledge accumulated by sciences. This is the answer that relates to the disciplinary dimension of the goals of education. Nevertheless, she chooses another answer which then dominates her entire book: education for thinking (Kuhn, 2005).

The history of the goal of 'cultivating the mind' is as long as the history of education. However, scientifically established suggestions for doing it appeared only in the past century. This delay is quite understandable, if we consider that disciplinary knowledge is something that has an external representation (e.g., in textbooks). In contrast, constructs, such as intelligence, thinking, reasoning, creativity, and problem solving, do not have such a firm, visible external equivalent. When setting goals related to these constructs, we do not have external references; instead, we are dealing with the attributes of human mind. Therefore, we need scientific models of how the mind works to set goals for improving its working.

There are three main paradigms which accumulated relevant knowledge concerning this dimension of goals. The first one is intelligence research (psychometrics, individual differences approach) which by now has a century long history (see Carroll, 1993, for a synthesis of the findings of this approach, and for the reevaluation of the role of the concept intelligence can play in education: Adey, Csapó, Demetriou, Hautamäki, & Shayer, 2007). The second one is the work of Piaget and his school, especially useful for science education (Inhelder & Piaget, 1958). As they used science experiments for studying children's cognitive development, there are many direct hints in their results of how science education can be utilized for the enhancement of reasoning. The third paradigm is the most recent one, cognitive educational neuroscience, which has some specific messages for teaching reading and mathematics, and a very general one is relevant form the point of view of science education: the human brain is more plastic that psychologists have assumed. Therefore, by stimulating teaching even the biological structure may be modified (OECD, 2007; Stern, Grabner, Schumacher, Neuper, & Saalbach, 2005).

Improving thinking emerged as a research field and later as a scientifically established goal in the second part of the last century. Those approaches which aimed at direct teaching of thinking resulted in fewer usable solutions for the educational practice. Other approaches which use the teaching material as means of facilitating cognitive development (embedding, infusion, enrichment, content based methods etc.)

practically integrate the two dimensions discussed before (Glaser, 1984; Bransford, Arbitman-Sith, Stein, & Vye, 1985). The content based approaches fertilized curriculum development (see the conception of thinking curriculum) as well as teaching methods (Csapó, 1990, 1992, 1999).

The third dimension of goals is also at least two millennia old; as Seneca's famous saying indicates, *Non scolae sed vitae discimus*. Schools are expected to teach something that can be utilized in the real life. This type of knowledge is best conceptualized in the assessment frameworks of PISA. The experts of PISA introduced and elaborated a generalized conception of *literacy*. Reading literacy, mathematical literacy and scientific literacy denote the type of applicable knowledge that a young person needs to live a successful life in a modern society. As this literacy conception is well-known, I have only one comment on it: it cannot (or should not) be taught directly, only in itself. As the concrete contexts and situations are constantly changing, a better strategy is to help students to master well understood transferable disciplinary knowledge and the reasoning skill necessary to process and transfer it in order to make it applicable in novel contexts. Content based methods of improving thinking may help to cope with 'inert' knowledge (a type of knowledge which cannot be applied) and facilitate transfer as well (Bereiter & Scardamalia, 1985).

In sum, I propose to distinguish different types of knowledge, in our case, three types, and use the best theoretical frames available for each one. The theories may be based on different assumptions, their explanatory power may be limited in themselves, but together they are more useful than relying solely on one of them.

## 4 Theoretical Foundations for a Diagnostic Assessment Framework

### 4.1 The Context of Framework Development

The context and the purpose of the framework development determine how this work is performed; therefore, I summarize some of the characteristics of the entire project in which the present effort is embedded. A research and development project is in progress at the University of Szeged to develop an Online Diagnostic Assessment System (ODAS) for the first six grades of primary school in reading, mathematics and science. The project aims to establish an item bank containing several thousands of items. This task requires the development of assessment frameworks that describe in detail what should be assessed and what should serve as the basis of item development.

In the first phase of the project, the items (600 per domain as a minimum) were prepared for paper-and-pencil assessment. These items were administered to large representative samples to determine their difficulty levels in 2010. The results of the paper-and-pencil testing will be used to correct and improve the existing items and to create new items to cover the difficulty scale proportionally. Those items that fit into the online system have been migrated to the computerized platform and parallel online assessments have been carried out. The results are used to study the media effect and to establish the validity of the online assessment (Csapó, Molnár, & R. Tóth, 2009). Another round of paper-based assessment will be carried out in 2011, and the results will be used to establish developmental scales. Three separate scales will be established for the three dimensions described earlier. These scales span from grade one to grade six. For reading and mathematics, one of the three scales, the literacy dimension dealing with the application of knowledge, will be connected to the already existing national assessment scales. The two systems have a common measurement point at the end of grade six, so there is an opportunity to measure reading literacy and mathematical literacy on the same scale from grade one to twelve. (Unfortunately, science is not measured in the national assessment program.)

The results of paper-and-pencil assessments will be used as a reference point for further online assessments. The paper-based items then can be used for the purposes of several assessments, but this line of item development will end, and the focus of the work will shift to technology-based assessment.

At present, not every item type which exists on paper can be reproduced in the computerized platform. On the other hand, new types of items can be created on the computer with no equivalents on paper. Therefore, parallel item development takes place for creating computerized items. The assessment frameworks play a crucial role in this process, because the framework–item correspondence will be used as one of the means to control the validity of the online assessment. As different cognitive processes are activated when solving items on paper and on a computer, it has been clear from the beginning of this work that it is not possible to create measurement instruments for both media which are equivalent in every respect. Furthermore, utilizing newer features of technology-based assessment requires new types of cognitive skills, and ICT familiarity may moderate the results in different ways. However, the intention is to map the same framework when creating items for the different media. Therefore, framework development has to take into account these requirements as well.

## 4.2 Frameworks for Early Diagnostic Assessment

The recent tendency to shift to standard-based education has inspired the creation of assessment standards in several countries. This movement has been generating a massive literature which includes the revision of Bloom's taxonomy (Anderson & Krathwohl, 2001) and the creation of new taxonomies (e.g., Marzano & Kendall, 2007). A number of principles, guidelines, handbooks and manuals have been published on these issues (e.g., O'Neill & Stansbury, 2000; Ainsworth, 2003).

Although there are differences between standards and frameworks, the literature on standards proved to be instrumental in framework development as well. The common bases of standards and frameworks are that both seek to answer 'What ...' questions: 'What to teach?' and 'What to assess?'. This way, similar methods and techniques can be used to describe and represent the content of teaching and assessment. On the other hand, frameworks in themselves do not set criteria; they do not define what levels should be reached by a certain age or school year. These criteria are set in the National Core Curriculum, and the ODAS is expected to measure students' progress so that it can be compared to these criteria. Furthermore, ODAS provides two other points of reference for each assessment. One is the norms calculated from the results of the actually assessed population (or its subgroups), and another one (as the assessment results are longitudinally connected) is the individual student's result on the previous assessment.

A segment of the standards and assessment literature deals with formative or diagnostic assessments explicitly (Nichols, Chipman, & Brennan, 1995; Clarke, 2001, 2005; Black, Harrison, Lee, Marshall, & Wiliam, 2003; Ainsworth & Viegut, 2006; Leighton & Gierl, 2007; Marzano & Haystead, 2008). Some other works focus on science standards (National Research Council, 1996; Waddington, Nentwig, & Schanze, 2007) or assess the outcomes of science education (Brown, 1996; Harlen, 2006).

From the point of view of the age range covered by the ODAS, research on early science education also resulted in findings and ideas that were influential in the framework development process (Nentwig & Schanze, 2006; Harlen & Qualter, 2009). Recent research on assessment of young students is also relevant for the project (e.g., Snow & Van Hemel, 2008).

The assessment frameworks of the ODAS project will be published in three volumes, one volume will be devoted for each assessment domain. The volumes have a common structure. Each one comprises three opening theoretical chapters summarizing the scientific foundations of the three dimensions. The second parts of the volumes elaborate the content of assessment in detail.

## 4.3 Scientific Reasoning

The aim of diagnostic assessment of reasoning within science is to monitor students' cognitive development, to make sure they possess the reasoning skills necessary for them to understand and master the science learning material in a meaningful way on the one hand, and to check if science education stimulates students' cognitive development as much as can be expected, on the other hand. Science education (with mathematics) has been considered as one of the most important means of developing students' reasoning skills (Minstrell, 1989). The content-based methods of enhancing cognition by applying science material for stimulating development provide rich resources for identifying reasoning processes which can be relevant in learning science and which can be developed through science education (Adey, 1999; Adey, Bliss, Head, & Shayer, 1989; Adey & Shayer, 1994; Shayer & Adey 1981).

Several simple and complex reasoning skills have been identified for diagnostic assessment. For example, thinking operations, such as control of variables, seriation, class inclusion, classification, multiple classification, combinatorial reasoning, proportional reasoning, and probabilistic reasoning are all essential for understanding science and early science education offers excellent opportunities for developing the appropriate skills (Lawson, Adi, & Karplus, 1979; Schröder, Bödeker, Edelstein, & Teo, 2000). Analogical reasoning, inductive reasoning, hypothetical-deductive reasoning etc. are also processes which are applied in learning sciences as well as more complex procedures, such as pattern-making through analysing wholes/parts and similarities/differences, making predictions and justifying conclusions, reasoning about cause and effect, generating ideas and possibilities, weighing up pros and cons, etc. The assessment frameworks identify and describe these thinking processes in an operationalized form (Adey & Csapó, 2011). The diagnostic tasks embed these cognitive processes in appropriate science content. Similar thinking processes were identified and assessed in mathematics.

## 4.4 Scientific Literacy

The aim of diagnostic assessment of scientific literacy is to monitor how students are able to apply their knowledge mastered in a school subject (or outside school) in other school subjects or in authentic real-life contexts.

The concept of scientific literacy is older than the PISA assessments (see e.g., Das & Ray, 1989; Klopfer, 1991; Roberts, 2007), but it became broadly known after the first PISA results were published. Although there is no straightforward way to identify the relevant contexts of application of scientific knowledge, a large number of publications have dealt with the issues of authentic contexts of acquiring and applying science knowledge (e.g., Nentwig & Waddington, 2005).

For the diagnostic assessment of science similar resources can be utilized to the ones serving as resources for PISA. However, for the purpose of ODAS, these conceptions have to be transferred to the early years (B. Németh & Korom, 2011). The diagnostic assessment tasks designed for the assessment of scientific literacy are based on the disciplinary learning material taught at school or on knowledge that can be expected to be learned outside of school, and use authentic contexts that are different from the ones where the knowledge was acquired.

**4.5 Disciplinary Science Knowledge and Skills**

The purpose of the diagnostic assessment of disciplinary science knowledge and skills is to monitor how well students master the disciplinary content. Research scientists are invited to define the relevant areas.

The framework organizes the content of assessment according to the logic and principles of the relevant disciplines and also takes into account the psychological developmental principles (see Shayer & Adey, 1981). As science education has been dominated by the principles of the respective disciplines, a lot of resources are available for selecting and organizing the content (Korom & Szabó, 2011).

The tasks used for diagnostic assessment present the content in scientific contexts and intend to measure the depth of disciplinary understanding. There is a special emphasis on concept development and conceptual change. The assessment intends to monitor not only how successful science education is in enhancing students' scientific theories and explanations but also how well schools cope with misconceptions.

# 5 Organizing the Content of the Science Framework

As described in the previous section, the diagnostic assessment frameworks are based on a three-dimensional conception of knowledge. The detailed description of the knowledge to be assessed has an even more complex structure, as further aspects have to be taken into account. This approach is depicted in Figure 2.

The assessment system is developed for the first six grades of the primary school, and the progression of students in science will finally be assessed in three developmental scales. In the figure, these are represented as dimensions of learning. In accordance with the principles discussed earlier, these dimensions are the scientific thinking (which is informed mostly by the results of psychological studies), application of scientific knowledge (which can be identified as social needs and expectations concerning the quality of scientific knowledge), and scientific knowledge itself (derivates from the results of scientific disciplines).

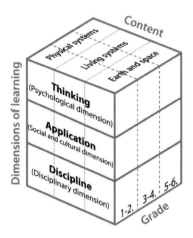

*Figure 2: Organization of the Assessment Content (Source: Korom, B. Németh, Nagy, & Csapó, 2011)*

The second aspect that has to be taken into account is the students' age. Although students' development will be measured on scales which overarch six grades, knowledge to be assessed could be arranged as a continuum. However, for practical reasons we followed the traditions of educational standards and curricula, and divided this continuum into three age groups (Grades 1–2, 3–4, and 5–6). Finally, the third aspect is the scientific content of the assessment where three areas are presented (Physical systems, Living systems, and Earth and space).

If the cube depicts the body of knowledge, the aspects discussed here identify 27 parts of it. If the frameworks are published in the form of a book, these blocks should be presented in a linear way. This means that the cube should be sliced up, and the blocks then should be systematically arranged. The way we arranged the materials is that first we separated the dimensions of learning, as they will constitute three different developmental scales. Second, the three age groups are considered whereby the scientific content of the assessment is elaborated.

The same approach has been applied in each assessment domain, thus the reading, and mathematics frameworks have a similar structure. Only the content dimensions are different, where the actual content of the particular domain is presented.

## 6 Conclusions and Further Research

The first phase of developing assessment frameworks has been completed. Not only the conceptual foundations have been laid down, but also the detailed descriptions of the content of assessment have been accomplished. This phase of the work has been guided by theoretical models and has been carried out on the bases of results of previous research. The conceptual underpinnings and the detailed frameworks are based on the best knowledge available. On the other hand, there are rapid developments in the related areas and the results of current research should be continuously integrated into the assessment frameworks. There are some further steps in devising the online assessment system which also have some immediate conclusions for the conceptual frameworks.

Based on the frameworks, guided by the detailed description of the content to be assessed a large number of items have to be constructed. Item writing has already started at an early phase parallel with the framework development and a few hundreds of items have been created. The teams responsible for framework development and for creating test items have been working in close cooperation. The items were first designed for paper-based assessments, piloted in paper-and-pencil tests, then migrated to the electronic platform and piloted again in an online environment. These piloting processes revealed some difficulties of item construction that can then be reflected in the process of framework development as well. It turned out again, that although the goals of science education related to application of knowledge and development of thinking are often emphasized in educational documents and policy recommendations, they are less known among the practitioners. Most items proposed by the team of item writers were clearly related to the traditional pure disciplinary content. Creating items for the assessment of application skills was a bit more difficult, but the recent works in competency based education and the impact the PISA frameworks made this job easier.

The most difficult dimension proved to be that of assessing scientific reasoning, creating items for assessing science-related thinking skills using the content of science teaching materials. The conclusions of these experiences for the framework development are that while items for the disciplinary dimension can be created more or less on routine bases, works in the other two dimensions require more attention and guidance. Especially, devising items in the reasoning dimension needs more support. As it is relatively novel and therefore more closely guided by the framework than by experience, more attention should be paid for the operationalization of the assessment content. The gap between research and practice should be bridged by extensive training of item writers.

Creating paper-based items and their migration to the electronic platform helped to reveal some characteristics of the knowledge to be assessed, for example, how the core issues remain unchanged while being represented in different ways. The first computer-based assessment of science (CBAS) in the PISA 2006 showed that there may be differences between the two media, and a study in the earlier phase of our current project has also indicated that some item types may prompt different cognitive processes if represented on paper or in computer (Csapó, Molnár, & R. Tóth, 2009). These findings call for further validity and media effect studies. More attention is needed when frameworks are mapped into electronic items, and the framework-item correspondence should be assured by careful analyses.

A further feedback for the revision of the framework is expected from the next phase of the field studies when the assessment scales will be established. Three separate science scales will be developed for the three dimensions discussed in this chapter. For this purpose, difficulty parameters of the items will be determined, and the item difficulty then may be compared with the position of the content measured by the item in the particular framework. The assumed hierarchy of the components of knowledge may also be verified on the bases of the empirical findings. These kinds of analyses can be carried out after a single assessment.

Additional analyses will be possible after several assessment cycles. As the data will be connected longitudinally, and students' development will be followed, the relationship between an earlier and a later assessment can be explored, even at the level of items. This way, the predictive power of the items can be studied, thus the diagnostic value of assessing certain components of knowledge can also be investigated. In general, detailed analyzes of the empirical data will serve rich sources for the revisions of the frameworks.

The ultimate reason of diagnostic assessment is to support teaching-learning processes. Its goals cannot be reached if teachers and students are not provided with training materials that can be used to fill the gaps indentified in students' knowledge. These materials can be practically delivered online by using the same network which is used for the assessment. As diagnostic assessment should focus on those components of knowledge that can be developed by the means available in school, training experiments, planned for the next stage of the project will also inform framework development. In sum, the frameworks are planned to be a component of a renewed teaching and learning system, in which the development of the other components may have an effect on the frameworks themselves.

References

Adey, P. (1999). Thinking science: Science as a gateway to general thinking ability. In J. H. M. Hamers, J. E. H. van Luit, & B. Csapó (Eds.), *Teaching and Learning Thinking Skills* (pp. 63-80). Lisse: Swets and Zeitlinger.

Adey, P., Bliss, J., Head, J. & Shayer, M. (1989) (Eds.). *Adolescent Development and School Science*. New York: The Falmer Press.

Adey, P., & Csapó, B. (2011). Developing and assessing scientific reasoning. In B. Csapó & G. Szabó (Eds.), *Framework for Diagnostic Assessment of Science*. Budapest: Nemzeti Tankönyvkiadó (in press).

Adey, P., Csapó, B., Demetriou, A., Hautamäki, J., & Shayer, M. (2007). Can we be intelligent about intelligence? Why education needs the concept of plastic general ability. *Educational Research Review, 2*(2), 75-97.

Adey, P., & Shayer, M. (1994). *Really Raising Standards: Cognitive Intervention and Academic Achievement*. London: Routledge.

Ainsworth, L. (2003). *Power Standards. Identifying the Standards that Matter the Most*. Englewood, CO: Advanced Learning Press.

Ainsworth, L. & Viegut, D. (2006). *Common Formative Assessments. How to Connect Standards-Based Instruction and Assessment*. Thousand Oaks, CA: Corwin Press.

Anderson, L. W. & Krathwohl, D. R. (2001). *A Taxonomy for Learning, Teaching and Assessing*. New York: Longman.

B. Németh, M. (1998). Iskolai és hasznosítható tudás. A természettudományos ismeretek alkalmazása [School knowledge and usable knowledge. Application of science knowledge]. In B. Csapó (Ed.), *Az iskolai tudás* [School knowledge] (pp. 115-138). Budapest: Osiris Kiadó.

B. Németh, M. & Habók, A. (2006). A 13 és 17 éves magyar tanulók viszonya a tanuláshoz. [13- and 17-year-old students' views on learning] *Magyar Pedagógia, 103*(2), 83-105.

B. Németh, M., & Korom, E. (2011). Science literacy and the application of scientific knowledge. In B. Csapó & G. Szabó (Eds.), *Framework for Diagnostic Assessment of Science*. Budapest: Nemzeti Tankönyvkiadó (in press).

Bán, S. (1998). Gondolkodás a bizonytalanról: valószínűségi és korrelatív gondolkodás [Reasoning about the uncertain: Probabilistic and correlational reasoning]. In B. Csapó (Ed.), *Az iskolai tudás* [School knowledge] (pp. 221-250). Budapest: Osiris Kiadó.

Beaton, A. E., Martin, M. O., Mullis, I. V. S., Gonzalez, E. J., Smith, T. A., & Kelly, D. L. (1996). *Science Achievement in the Middle School Years: IEA's Third International Mathematics and Science Study*. Chestnut Hill, MA: Boston College.

Beaton, A. E., Mullis, I. V. S., Martin, M. O., Gonzalez, E. J., Kelly, D. L., & Smith, T. A. (1996). *Mathematics Achievement in the Middle School Years: IEA's Third International Mathematics and Science Study*. Chestnut Hill, MA: Boston College.

Bereiter, C. & Scardamalia, M. (1985). Cognitive coping strategies and the problem of 'inert knowledge'. In S. F. Chipman, J. W. Segal & R. Glaser (Eds.), *Thinking and learning skills. Vol. 2. Research and Open Questions.* (pp. 65-80). Hillside NJ: LEA.

Black, P., Harrison, C., Lee, C., Marshall, B., & Wiliam, D. (2003). *Assessment for Learning. Putting it Into Practice*. Berkshire: Open University Press.

Bransford, J. D., Arbitman-Sith, R., Stein, B. S., & Vye, N. J. (1985). Improving thinking and learning skills: An analysis of three approaches. In J. W. Segal, S. F. Chipman, & R. Glaser (Eds.), *Thinking and Learning Skills* (pp. 133-206). Vol. 1. Hillsdale, NJ: Lawrence Erlbaum Associates.

Bransford, J. D., Brown, A. L., & Cocking, R. R. (2000). *How People Learn: Brain, Mind, Experience and School*. Washington, D. C.: National Academy Press.

Brown, J. H. (1996). *Assessing Hands-on Science*. Thousand Oaks, CA: Corwin Press.

Carroll, J. B. (1993). *Human Cognitive Abilities*. Cambridge UK: Cambridge University Press.

Clarke, S. (2001). *Unlocking Formative Assessment. Practical Strategies for Enhancing Pupils Learning in Primary Classroom*. London: Hodder Arnold.

Clarke, S. (2005). *Formative Assessment in Action. Weaving the Elements Together.* London: Hodder Murray.

Csapó, B. (1988). *A kombinatív képesség struktúrája és fejlődése* [Structure and development of combinative ability]. Budapest: Akadémiai Kiadó.

Csapó, B. (1990). Integrating the development of the operational abilities of thinking and the transmission of knowledge. In H. Mandl, E. De Corte, N. Bennett, & H. F. Friedrich (Eds.), *Learning and Instruction. European Research in an International Context. Vol. 2.2. Analysis of Complex Skills and Complex Knowledge Domains* (pp. 85-94). Oxford: Pergamon Press.

Csapó, B. (1992). Improving Operational Abilities in Children. In A. Demetriou, M. Shayer, & A. Efklides (Eds.), *Neo-Piagetian Theories of Cognitive Development. Implications and Applications for Education* (pp. 144-159). London: Routledge.

Csapó, B. (1994). Az induktív gondolkodás fejlődése. [The development of inductive reasoning] *Magyar Pedagógia, 94*(1-2), 53–80.

Csapó, B. (1997). The development of inductive reasoning: Cross-sectional assessments in an educational context. *International Journal of Behavioral Development, 20*(4), 609-626.

Csapó, B. (1998a). Az iskolai tudás vizsgálatának elméleti keretei és módszerei [Theoretical framework and methods of studying school knowledge]. In B. Csapó (Ed.), *Az iskolai tudás* [School knowledge] (pp.11-37). Budapest: Osiris Kiadó.

Csapó, B. (1998b). Az új tudás képződésének eszközei: az induktív gondolkodás. [Tools for creating new knowledge: Inductive reasoning]. In B. Csapó (Ed.), *Az iskolai tudás* [School knowledge] (pp. 251-280). Budapest: Osiris Kiadó.

Csapó, B. (1999). Improving thinking through the content of teaching. In J. H. M. Hamers, J. E. H. van Luit & B. Csapó (Eds.), *Teaching and Learning Thinking Skills* (pp. 37-62). Lisse: Swets and Zeitlinger.

Csapó, B. (2000). A tantárgyakkal kapcsolatos attitűdök összefüggései [Students' attitudes towards school subjects]. *Magyar Pedagógia, 100*(3), 343-366.

Csapó, B. (2004). Knowledge and competencies. In J. Letschert (Ed.), The integrated person. How curriculum development relates to new competencies (pp. 35-49). Enschede: CIDREE.

Csapó, B. (2007). Research into learning to learn through the assessment of quality and organization of learning outcomes. *The Curriculum Journal, 18*(2) 195-210.

Csapó, B. (2010). Goals of learning and the organization of knowledge. In E. Klieme, D. Leutner, & M. Kenk (Eds.). *Kompetenzmodellierung. Zwischenbilanz des DFG-Schwerpunktprogramms und Perspektiven des Forschungsansatzes. 56. Beiheft der Zeitschrift für Pädagogik* (pp. 12-27). Weinheim u.a.: Beltz.

Csapó, B. & B. Németh, M. (1995). A természettudományos ismeretek alkalmazása: mit tudnak tanulóink az általános és a középiskola végén? [The application of science knowledge: What do our students know at the end of primary and secondary schools?] *Új Pedagógiai Szemle, 8,* 3-11.

Csapó, B., Molnár, G. & R. Tóth, K. (2009). Comparing paper-and-pencil and online assessment of reasoning skills. A pilot study for introducing electronic testing in large-scale assessment in Hungary. In F. Scheuermann & J. Björnsson (Eds.). *The Transition to Computer-Based Assessment. New Approaches to Skills Assessment and Implications for Large-Scale Testing* (pp. 113-118). Luxemburg: Office for Official Publications of the European Communities.

Das, R. R. & Ray, B. (1989). *Teaching Home Science.* New Delhi: Sterling Publishers.

Dobi, J. (1998). Megtanult és megértett matematikatudás [Mathematics knowledge mastered and understood]. In B. Csapó (Ed.), *Az iskolai műveltség* (pp. 169-190). Budapest: Osiris Kiadó.

Gardner, H. (1992). *The Unschooled Mind. How Children Think and How Schools Should Teach.* New York: Basic Books.

Glaser, R. (1984). Education and thinking. The role of knowledge. *American Psychologist, 39*(2), 93-104.

Harlen, W. (2006). *Teaching, Learning and Assessing Science 5-12.* London: Sage.

Harlen, W. & Qualter, W. (2009). *The Teaching of Science in Primary Schools.* London: Routledge.

Hartig, J., Klieme, E., & Rauch, D. (Eds.) (2008). *Assessment of Competencies in Educational Context.* Göttingen: Hogrefe.

Inhelder, B., & Piaget, J. (1958). *The Growth of Logical Thinking from Childhood to Adolescence.* New York: Basic Books.

Keeves, J. P. (1992). *The IEA Study of Science III. Changes in Science Education and Achievement: 1970 to 1984.* Oxford: Pergamon Press.

Klopfer, L. E. (1991). Scientific literacy. In A. Lewy (Ed.), *The International Encyclopedia of Curriculum.* (pp. 947-948). Oxford: Pergamon Press.

Koeppen, K., Hartig, J., Klieme, E., & Leutner, D. (2008). Current issues in competence modeling and assessment. *Zeitschrift für Psychologie, 216*(2), 61-73.

Korom, E. (1997). Naiv elméletek és tévképzetek megjelenése a természettudományos fogalmak tanulása során [Naive theories and misconceptions in learning science]. *Magyar Pedagógia, 97*(1), 19-41.

Korom, E. (1998). Az iskolai tudás és a hétköznapi tapasztalat ellentmondásai: természettudományos tévképzetek [Contradictions of school knowledge and everyday experience: science misconceptions]. In B. Csapó (Ed.), *Az iskolai tudás* [School knowledge] (pp. 139-167). Budapest: Osiris Kiadó.

Korom, E. & Szabó, G. (2011). Scientific and curriculum aspects of teaching and assessing science. In B. Csapó & G. Szabó (Eds.), *Framework for Diagnostic Assessment of Science.* Budapest: Nemzeti Tankönyvkiadó (in press).

Korom, E., B. Németh, M., Nagy, L., & Csapó, B. (2011). Diagnostic assessment frameworks for science: Theoretical background and practical issues. In B. Csapó & G. Szabó (Eds.), *Framework for Diagnostic Assessment of Science.* Budapest: Nemzeti Tankönyvkiadó (in press).

Kuhn, D. (2005). *Education for Thinking.* Cambridge, MA: Harvard University Press.

Lawson, A. E., Adi, H. & Karplus, R. (1979). Development of correlational reasoning in secondary schools: Do biology courses make a difference? *American Biology Teacher, 41*(7), 420-425

Leighton, J. P. & Gierl, M. J. (2007) (Eds.). *Cognitive Diagnostic Assessment for Education. Theory and Applications.* Cambridge: Cambridge University Press.

Lewin, K. (1951). *Field Theory in Social Science. Selected Theoretical Papers.* D. Cartwright (Ed.). New York: Harper & Row.

Marzano, R. J. & Haystead, M. W. (2008). *Making Standards Useful in the Classroom.* Alexandria: Association for Supervision and Curriculum Development.

Marzano, R. J. & Kendall, J. S. (2007). *The New Taxonomy of Educational Objectives.* 2$^{nd}$ ed. Thousand Oaks, CA: Coewin Press.

Minstrell, J. A. (1989). Teaching science for understanding. In L. B. Resnick, & L. E. Klopfer (Eds.), *Toward the Thinking Curriculum: Current Cognitive Research* (pp. 129-149). Alexandria: Association for Supervision and Curriculum Development.

Mátrai, Z. (1997) (Ed.). Középiskolai tantárgyi feladatbankok I. Biológia – Matematika – Angol nyelv [Subject matter item banks for high schools I. Biology – Mathematics – English]. Budapest: Országos Közoktatási Intézet.

Molnár, Gy. (2001). Az életszerű feladat-helyzetekben történő problémamegoldás vizsgálata [Examination of problem solving in real life situations]. *Magyar Pedagógia, 101*(3), 347-373.

Molnár, Gy. (2006). *Tudástranszfer és komplex problémamegoldás* [Knowledge transfer and complex problem solving]. Budapest: Műszaki Kiadó.

National Research Council (1996). *National Science Education Standards.* Washington DC: National Academy Press.

Nentwig, P. & Schanze, S. (2006). *Es ist nie zu früh! Naturwissenschaftliche Bildung in jungen Jahren* [It is never too early! Science education in the early years]. Münster: Waxmann

Nentwig, P. & Waddington, D. (2005). *Making it Relevant. Context Based Learning of Science.* Münster: Waxmann.

Nichols, P. D., Chipman, S. F., & Brennan, R. L. (1995). *Cognitively Diagnostic Assessment.* Hillsdale, N. J.: Lawrence Erlbaum Associates Publishers.

O'Neill, K. & Stansbury, K. (2000). *Developing a Standards-Based Assessment System.* San Francisco: WestEd.

OECD (2000). *Measuring Student Knowledge and Skills. The PISA 2000 Assessment of Reading, Mamathematical and Scientific Literacy.* Paris: OECD.

OECD (2001). *Knowledge and Skills for Life. First Results from the OECD Programme for International Student Assessment (PISA) 2000.* Paris: OECD.

OECD (2003). *Learners for Life. Student Approaches to Learning. Results form PISA 2000.* Paris: OECD.

OECD (2007). *Understanding the Brain. The Birth of a Learning Science.* Paris: OECD.

OECD (2010). *PISA 2009 Results, Vol. I.: What Students Know and Can Do. Student Performance in Reading, Mathematics and Science.* Paris: OECD.

Postman, N. (1996). *The End of Education.* New York: Vintage Books.

Roberts, D. A. (2007). Scientific literacy/Science literacy. In S. K. Abell & N. G. Lederman (Eds.), *Handbook of Research on Science Education* (pp. 729-780). London: Routledge.

Roth, W. M. (1995). *Authentic School Science.* Dordrecht: Kluwer Academic Publishers.

Schmid, C. & Dinkelmann, I. (2007). *Bildungsstandards im nichtfachlichen Bereich: Probleme und Perspektiven am Beispiel der Lern- und Denkstrategien. Forschungsbericht*, Zürich: Pädagogische Hochschule Zürich, Departement Forschung und Entwicklung.

Schott, F. & Ghanbari, S., A. (2008). *Kompetenzdiagnostik, Kompetenzmodelle, Kompetenzorientierter Unterricht. Zur theorie und Praxis überprüfbarer Bildungsstandards.* Münster: Waxmann

Schröder, E., Bödeker, K., Edelstein, W., & Teo, T. (2000). *Proportional, Combinatorial, and Correlational Reasoning. A Manual Including Measurement Procedures and Descriptive Analyses.* Study "Individual Development and Social Structure". Data Handbooks Part 4. Berlin: Max Planck Institute for Human Development.

Shayer, M. & Adey, P. (1981). *Towards a Science of Science Teaching. Cognitive Development and Curriculum Demand.* London: Heinemann Educational Books.

Snow, C. E., & Van Hemel, S. (2008). *Early Childhood Assessment. Why, What and How.* Washington, DC: National Academies Press.

Stern, E., Grabner, R., Schumacher, R., Neuper, C., & Saalbach, H. (2005). Educational research and neurosciences – expectations, evidence and research prospects. Bonn/Berlin: Bundesministerium für Bildung und Forschung.

Waddington, D., Nentwig, P., & Schanze, S. (2007) (Eds.). *Making it Comparable. Standards in Science Education.* Münster: Waxmann.

Vidákovich, T. (1998). Tudományos és hétköznapi logika: a tanulók deduktív gondolkodása [Scientific and everyday logic: Students' deductive reasoning]. In B. Csapó (Ed.), *Az iskolai tudás* [School knowledge] (pp. 191-220). Budapest: Osiris Kiadó.

**Acknowledgement**

This chapter is based on the results of studies of the *Research Group on the Development of Competencies, Hungarian Academy of Sciences*.

## Chapter 4

# The Design of an Assessment System Focused on Student Achievement: A Learning Sciences Perspective on Issues of Competence, Growth, and Measurement

*James W. Pellegrino*
*Learning Sciences Research Institute, University of Illinois at Chicago, USA*

## Abstract

This paper discusses some of the most important conceptual, practical, and policy issues surrounding the *what* and *how* of assessment in K–12+ education. The general argument is that the learning sciences have made great strides in understanding the nature of learning and knowing, in ways that can and must inform the development of systems of assessments and the selection and use of models for measuring the status and growth of academic achievement in core areas of the curriculum. In developing this argument, the paper discusses a set of interconnected and critical issues regarding the nature and function of assessment in the larger educational enterprise. The first section of the paper is concerned with two critical issues in the development, implementation, and use of educational assessments. The first is that assessment should be integrated with curriculum and instruction, with all three guided by theories and research on the nature of learning and knowing in academic content domains. A second fundamental issue is that assessment is best conceptualized as a rigorous and carefully structured process of reasoning from evidence that should be driven by theories and data on student cognition and learning. The second section of the paper then elaborates a key aspect of the argument and focuses on some of what theory and research have to say about student knowledge and performance in subject matter domains. A discussion is provided of knowledge development in instructional domains with a particular emphasis on the concept of *learning progressions*. The latter should be used to shape the design of assessments of student learning and they have implications for contexts that span classrooms to state and national testing programs. Some of the broader implications of research and theory for assessment design and use are explored in the final section. Topics discussed include the functions and purposes of assessment and the timescales of learning which they are intended to represent. Specific attention is given to implications for the design of classroom assessments and large-scale assessments. Consideration is also given to why a coordinated and balanced system of assessments is needed to accomplish the goals of educational improvement.

# 1 Two Critical Issues in Conceptualizing Student Assessment

## 1.1 The Curriculum-Instruction-Assessment Triad

Assessment does not and should not stand alone in the educational system. Rather, it is one of three central components – curriculum, instruction, and assessment – as shown in Figure 1. The three elements of this triad are linked, although the nature of their linkages and reciprocal influence is often less explicit than it should be. Furthermore, the separate pairs of connections are often inconsistent in practice, which can lead to an overall incoherence in the educational enterprise.

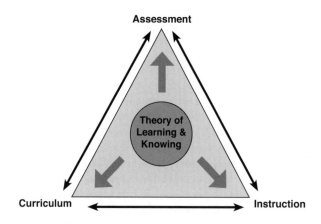

*Figure 1: Representation of the Interconnections Among Curriculum, Instruction, and Assessment and Pivotal Role of Theories of Learning*

*Curriculum* consists of the knowledge and skills in subject matter areas that teachers teach and students are supposed to learn. The curriculum generally consists of a scope or breadth of content in a given subject area and a sequence for learning. Content standards in a subject matter area typically outline the goals of learning, whereas curriculum sets forth the more specific means to be used to achieve those ends. Instruction refers to methods of teaching and the learning activities used to help students master the content and objectives specified by a curriculum. Instruction encompasses the activities of both teachers and students. It can be carried out by a variety of methods, sequences of activities, and topic orders. Assessment is the means used to measure the outcomes of education and the achievement of students with regard to important competencies. Assessment may include both formal methods, such as large-scale state assessments, or less formal classroom-based procedures, such as quizzes, class projects, and teacher questioning.

A precept of educational practice is the need for alignment among curriculum, instruction, and assessment (e.g., National Council of Teachers of Mathematics [NCTM], 1995, 2000; Webb, 1997). Alignment, in this sense, means that the three functions are directed toward the same ends and reinforce each other, rather than working at cross-purposes. Ideally, an assessment should measure what students are actually being taught, and what is actually being taught should parallel the curriculum one wants students to master. If any of the functions is not well synchronized, it will disrupt the balance and skew the educational process. Assessment results will be misleading, or instruction will be ineffective. Alignment is difficult to achieve, however. Often what is lacking is a central theory about the nature of learning and knowing, around which the three functions can be coordinated, as shown in Figure 1.

Most current approaches to curriculum, instruction, and assessment are based on theories and models that have not kept pace with modern knowledge of cognition and how people learn (e.g., Bransford, Brown, Cocking, Donovan, & Pellegrino, 2000; Donovan & Bransford, 2005; Donovan, Bransford, & Pellegrino, 1999; Pellegrino, Chudowsky, & Glaser, 2001; Pellegrino, Jones, & Mitchell, 1999; Shepard, 2000). They have been designed on the basis of implicit and highly limited conceptions of cognition and learning. Those conceptions tend to be fragmented, outdated, and poorly delineated for domains of subject matter knowledge. Alignment among curriculum, instruction, and assessment could be better achieved if all three are derived from a scientifically credible and shared knowledge base about cognition and learning in subject matter domains. The model of learning would provide the central bonding principle, serving as a nucleus around which the three functions would revolve. Without such a central core, and under pressure to prepare students for high-stakes accountability tests, teachers may feel compelled to move back and forth between instruction and external assessment and teach directly to the items on a state test. The latter approach, in which assessment serves as the tail wagging the educational dog, can result in an undesirable narrowing of the curriculum and a limiting of learning outcomes. Such problems can be ameliorated if, instead, decisions about both instruction and assessment are guided by models of learning in academic domains that represent the best available scientific understanding of how people learn (Bransford et al., 2000; Donovan & Bransford, 2005).

## 1.2 Assessment as a Process of Reasoning from Evidence

Educators assess students to learn about what they know and can do, but assessments do not offer a direct pipeline into a student's mind. Assessing educational outcomes is not as straightforward as measuring height or weight; the attributes to be measured are mental representations and processes that are not outwardly visible. Thus, an assessment is a tool designed to observe students' behavior and produce data that can be used to draw reasonable inferences about what students know. Deciding what to assess and how to do so is not as simple as it might appear.

The process of collecting evidence to support inferences about what students know represents a chain of reasoning from evidence about student learning that characterizes all assessments, from classroom quizzes and standardized achievement tests, to computerized tutoring programs, to the conversation a student has with her teacher as they work through a math problem or discuss the meaning of a text. In the 2001 report, *Knowing What Students Know: The Science and Design of Educational Assessment*, issued by the National Research Council, the process of reasoning from evidence was portrayed as a triad of three interconnected elements: the assessment triangle (Pellegrino et al., 2001). The vertices of the assessment triangle (see Figure 2) represent the three key elements underlying any assessment: a model of student *cognition and learning* in the domain of the assessment; a set of assumptions and principles about the kinds of *observations* that will provide evidence of students' competencies; and an *interpretation* process for making sense of the evidence. These three elements may be explicit or implicit, but an assessment cannot be designed and implemented without consideration of each. The three are represented as vertices of a triangle because each is connected to and dependent on the other two. A major tenet of the *Knowing What Students Know* report is that for an assessment to be effective and valid, the three elements must be in synchrony. The assessment triangle provides a useful framework for analyzing the underpinnings of current assessments to determine how well they accomplish the goals we have in mind, as well as for designing future assessments and establishing validity (e.g., see Marion & Pellegrino, 2006).

The *cognition* corner of the triangle refers to theory, data, and a set of assumptions about how students represent knowledge and develop competence in a subject matter domain (e.g., fractions). In any particular assessment application, a theory of learning in the domain is needed to identify the set of knowledge and skills that is important to measure for the context of use, whether that be characterizing the competencies students have acquired at some point in time to make a summative judgment, or for making a formative judgment to guide subsequent instruction so as to maximize learning. A central premise is that the cognitive theory should represent the most scientifically credible understanding of typical ways in which learners represent knowledge and develop expertise in a domain. More will be said in the next section about ways in which we currently think about cognition and the development of subject matter competence.

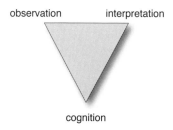

*Figure 2: The three elements involved in conceptualizing assessment as a process of reasoning from evidence*

Every assessment is also based on a set of assumptions and principles about the kinds of tasks or situations that will prompt students to say, do, or create something that demonstrates important knowledge and skills. The tasks to which students are asked to respond on an assessment are not arbitrary. They must be carefully designed to provide evidence that is linked to the cognitive model of learning and to support the kinds of inferences and decisions that will be made on the basis of the assessment results. The *observation* vertex of the assessment triangle represents a description or set of specifications for assessment tasks that will elicit illuminating responses from students. In assessment, one has the opportunity to structure some small corner of the world to make observations. The assessment designer can use this capability to maximize the value of the data collected, as seen through the lens of the underlying assumptions about how students learn in the domain.

Every assessment is also based on certain assumptions and models for interpreting the evidence collected from observations. The *interpretation* vertex of the triangle encompasses all the methods and tools used to reason from fallible observations. It expresses how the observations derived from a set of assessment tasks constitute evidence about the knowledge and skills being assessed. In the context of large-scale assessment, the interpretation method is usually a statistical model, which is a characterization or summarization of patterns one would expect to see in the data given varying levels of student competency. In the context of classroom assessment, the interpretation is often made less formally by the teacher, and is usually based on an intuitive or qualitative model rather than a formal statistical one.

A crucial point is that each of the three elements of the assessment triangle not only must make sense on its own, but also must connect to each of the other two elements in a meaningful way to lead to an effective assessment and sound inferences. Thus to have an effective assessment, all three vertices of the triangle must work together in synchrony. Central to this entire process, however, are theories and data on how students learn and what students know as they develop competence for important aspects of the curriculum.

## 2 Student Cognition and Domain Specific Learning

### 2.1 Acquisition of Competence

As part of studying the nature of knowledge and learning, researchers have probed deeply the nature of competence and how people acquire large bodies of knowledge over long periods of time. Studies have revealed much about the kinds of mental structures that support problem-solving and learning in various domains; what it means to develop competence in a domain; and how the thinking of high achievers differs from that of novices and low achievers (e.g., Bransford et al., 2000; Chi, Feltovich, & Glaser, 1981). What distinguishes high from low performers is not simply general mental abilities or general problem-solving strategies. High performers have acquired extensive stores of knowledge and skill in a particular domain. But perhaps most significant, their minds have organized this knowledge in ways that a make it highly retrievable and useful. Because their knowledge has been encoded in a way that closely links it with the contexts and conditions for its use, high achievers do not have to search through the vast repertoire of everything they know when confronted with a task or problem. Instead, they can readily activate and retrieve the subset of their knowledge that is relevant to the task at hand (Simon, 1980; Glaser, 1992). Such findings suggest that teachers should place more emphasis on the conditions for applying the facts or procedures being taught, and that assessment should address whether students know when, where, and how to use their knowledge.

Considerable effort has also been expended on understanding the characteristics of persons and of the learning situations they encounter that foster the development of expertise. Much of what we know about the development of expertise has come from studies of children as they acquire competence in many areas of intellectual endeavor, including the learning of school subject matter. From a cognitive standpoint, development and learning are not the same thing. Some types of knowledge are universally acquired in the course of typical development, while other types are learned only with the intervention of deliberate teaching (which includes teaching by any means, such as apprenticeship, formal schooling, or self-study). Infants and young children appear to be predisposed to learn rapidly and readily in some domains, including language, number, and notions of physical and biological causality. Infants who are only 3 or 4 months old, for example, have been shown to understand certain concepts about the physical world, such as the idea that inanimate objects need to be propelled in order to move (Massey & Gelman, 1988). By the time children are 3 or 4 years old, they have an implicit understanding of certain rudimentary principles for counting, adding, and subtracting cardinal numbers (Gelman, 1990; Gelman & Gallistel, 1978).

In math, the fundamentals of ordinality and cardinality appear to develop in all nondisabled human infants without instruction. In contrast, however, such concepts as mathematical notation, algebra, and Cartesian graphing representations must be taught. Similarly, the basics of speech and language comprehension emerge naturally from millions of years of evolution, whereas mastery of the alphabetic code necessary for reading typically requires explicit instruction and long periods of practice (Geary, 1995). Much of what we want to assess in educational contexts is the product of such deliberate learning in specific curricular and instructional domains. Accordingly, every domain of knowledge and skill needs to be understood in terms of the body of concepts, factual content, procedures, and other components that together constitute the knowledge that we intend for students to learn across a span of time such as single year, a cluster of grades such as middle school, or the entire K–12 grade range. In virtually every curricular and content domain this knowledge is complex and multifaceted, requiring sustained effort and focused instruction to master. Developing deep knowledge of a domain such as that exhibited by high achievers, along with conditions for its use, takes time and focus and requires opportunities for distributed practice with feedback.

Whether considering the acquisition of some highly specific piece of knowledge or skill such as the process of adding two numbers, or some larger schema for representing and solving a mathematics or physics problem or understanding a genre of literature, certain laws of knowledge acquisition always apply. The first of these is the power law of practice: acquiring knowledge takes time, often requiring hundreds or thousands of instances of practice in retrieving a piece of information or executing a procedure. This law operates across a broad range of tasks, from typing on a keyboard to solving geometry problems (Anderson, 1981; Rosenbloom & Newell, 1987). According to the *power law of practice*, the speed and accuracy of performing a simple or complex cognitive operation increase in a systematic non-linear fashion over successive attempts (see Figure 3 for an example of typical data). This pattern is characterized by an initial rapid improvement in performance as shown in Figure 3, followed by subsequent and continuous improvements that accrue at a slower and slower rate. Such nonlinear, monotonic changes, can be readily modeled quantitatively by power or exponential functions. Thus, as shown in the lower panel of Figure

3, the change is linear as a function of the log of attempts. Even so, these simple quantitative patterns are typically best explained by substantial qualitative changes in the nature of what is represented in long-term memory and how that knowledge is accessed and deployed.

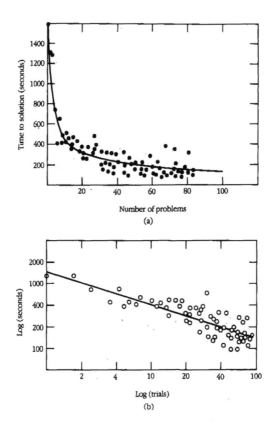

*Figure 3: An illustration of the power law of knowledge acquisition*

Consistent with the above, one of the most important findings from detailed observations of children's learning and performance is that children do not move simply and directly from a state of *not knowing* to one of *knowing* (Kaiser, Proffitt, & McCloskey, 1985). Instead, their performance may exhibit several different but locally or partially correct understandings and strategies (Fay & Klahr, 1996). They also may use less advanced strategies even after demonstrating that they know more advanced ones, and the process of acquiring and consolidating robust and efficient knowledge and strategies may be quite protracted, extending across many weeks and months and hundreds of problems and examples (Siegler, 1998). These studies have also found, moreover, that short-term transition strategies often precede more lasting approaches and that generalization of new approaches often occurs very slowly. Thus, it is useful to remember that growth and change in knowledge is seldom a simple matter and it does not often lend itself to simple linear scales with equal interval or ratio measurement properties. Rather, growth and change may often resemble a nominal or ordinal scale, both of which have very different implications for measurement and quantification.

We also know that repeated exposure to content and practice in performing tasks are not enough to ensure that knowledge and skill will be acquired appropriately and/or efficiently. The conditions of learning and practice are also important. The second major law of knowledge acquisition involves *knowledge of results*. Individuals acquire knowledge much more rapidly and appropriately if they receive feedback about the correctness of what they have done. If incorrect, they need to know the nature of their mistake (Thorndike, 1931). One of the persistent dilemmas in education is that students often spend time practicing incorrect skills with little or no feedback. Furthermore, the feedback they ultimately receive is often neither timely nor informative. Unguided practice (e.g., homework in math) can be for the less able student, practice in doing tasks incorrectly. One of the most important roles for assessment is the provision of timely and informative feedback to students (and their teachers) during instruction and learning so that the practice of a skill and its subsequent acquisition will be effective and efficient (Black & Wiliam, 1998; Sadler, 1989; Wiliam, 2007).

## 2.2 Domain-Specific Learning: The Concept of Learning Progressions

A central thesis of this paper is that the targets of inference for any given assessment should be largely determined by models of cognition and learning that describe how people represent knowledge and develop competence in the domain of interest (the *cognition* element of the assessment triangle). Starting with a model of learning is one of the main features that distinguishes the proposed approach to assessment design from typical current approaches. The model suggests the most important aspects of student achievement about which one would want to draw inferences, and provides clues about the types of assessment tasks that will elicit evidence to support those inferences (see also Pellegrino, 1988; Pellegrino, Baxter, & Glaser, 1999; Pellegrino et al., 2001).

A model of learning that informs assessment design should have as many as possible of the following key features:

1. Be based on empirical studies of learners in the domain of interest.
2. Identify performances that differentiate beginning and expert performance in the domain.
3. Provide a developmental perspective, laying out typical progressions from novice levels toward competence and then expertise, and noting landmark performances along the way.
4. Allow for a variety of typical ways in which children come to understand the subject matter.
5. Capture some, but not all, aspects of what is known about how students think and learn in the domain. Starting with a theory of how people learn the subject matter, the designers of an assessment will need to select a slice or subset of the larger theory as the targets of inference.
6. Lend itself to being aggregated at different grain sizes so that it can be used for different assessment purposes (e.g., to provide fine-grained diagnostic information as well as coarser-grained summary information).

Consistent with these ideas, there has been a recent spurt of interest in the topic of learning progressions (see Duschl, Schweingruber, & Shouse 2007; Wilson & Bertenthal, 2005). A variety of definitions of the learning progression (learning trajectory) construct now exist in the literature, with substantial differences in focus and intent (see e.g., Confrey, 2008; Confrey et al., 2009; Corcoran, Mosher, & Rogat, 2009; Duncan & Hmelo-Silver, 2009). Perhaps the most extensive discussion of the learning progression construct can be found in the 2009 Consortium for Policy Research in Education (CPRE) report *Learning Progressions in Science* (Corcoran et al., 2009). As described therein, learning progressions *(trajectories)* are empirically grounded and testable hypotheses about how students' understanding of, and ability to use, core concepts and explanations and related disciplinary practices grow and become more sophisticated over time, with appropriate instruction (Duschl et al., 2007). These hypotheses describe the pathways students are likely to follow to the mastery of core concepts. They are based on research about how students' learning actually progresses. The hypothesized learning trajectories are tested empirically to ensure their construct validity *(does the hypothesized sequence describe a path most students actually experience given appropriate instruction?)* and ultimately to assess their consequential validity *(does instruction based on the learning progression produce better results for most students?)*. The reliance on empirical evidence differentiates learning trajectories from traditional topical scope and sequence specification. Topical scope and sequence descriptions are typically based only on logical analysis of current disciplinary knowledge and on personal experiences in teaching.

The CPRE report (Corcoran et al., 2009) argued that learning progressions should contain at least the following elements:

1. *Target performances or learning goals* that are the end points of a learning progression and are defined by societal expectations, analysis of the discipline, and/or requirements for entry into the next level of education;
2. *Progress variables* that are the dimensions of understanding, application, and practice that are being developed and tracked over time. These may be core concepts in the discipline or practices central to literary, scientific or mathematical work;
3. *Levels of achievement* that are intermediate steps in the developmental pathway(s) traced by a learning progression. These levels may reflect levels of integration or common stages that characterize the development of student thinking. There may be intermediate steps that are non-canonical but are stepping stones to canonical ideas;
4. *Learning performances* that are the kinds of tasks students at a particular level of achievement would be capable of performing. They provide specifications for the development of assessments by which students would demonstrate their knowledge and understanding; and,
5. *Assessments* that are the specific measures used to track student development along the hypothesized progression. Learning progressions include an approach to assessment, as assessments are integral to their development, validation, and use.

In addition, the panelists contributing to the CPRE report (Corcoran et al., 2009) argued that learning progressions have some other common characteristics that seem especially relevant to the current discussion of developing more effective and useful measures of student achievement and growth. One of these characteristics is that they have internal conceptual coherence along several dimensions. For example, the progress variables capture important dimensions of understanding and practice and the achievement levels represent the successively more sophisticated levels of understanding and practice characterizing the development of student thinking over time. A progression may describe progress on a single progress variable or a cluster of related (and not just parallel) progress variables. It is also important that they can be empirically tested. The presumption is that they are not developmentally inevitable, but they may be developmentally constrained. Furthermore, they are crucially dependent on the instructional practices provided for the students whose development is studied in the processes of development and validation. Targeted instruction and curriculum will typically be required for students to progress along a trajectory; there may be multiple possible paths and progress is not necessarily linear. It may be more like ecological succession. A learning progression proposes and clarifies one or more possible paths and does not represent a complete list of all possible paths. At any given time, an individual may display thinking and/or practices characteristic of different points on the path, due to features of both the assessment context and the individual's cognition.

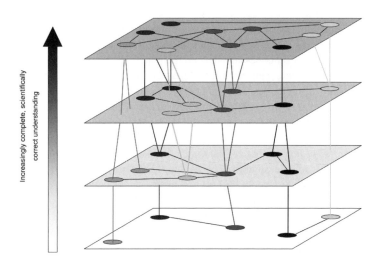

*Figure 4: A Representation of How Conceptual Elements May be Linked Within and Across Levels for a Learning Progression*

Figure 4 is an attempt to capture some of these ideas in a simple representation where it is assumed that there are core conceptual elements that are part of understanding a larger concept such as ratio and proportion, size and scale, or the atomic structure of matter. At each level in the system there are initial understandings of these core elements and they may be largely separate from one another. Some may be present in a person's knowledge structure and some may be absent. As one develops knowledge there is progress to the next level that implies a more sophisticated understanding of the core element. In addition, the elements within a level may become interconnected. Progress across levels involves assumptions in which there are increasing interconnections among the core elements and thus a much greater depth of understanding. We will try to illustrate this subsequently with some data from studies of the development of understanding for key concepts in science.

## 2.3 Examples from Science Learning

Investment in recent decades by federal agencies and private foundations has produced a wealth of knowledge about the development of students' science knowledge and understanding that, correspondingly, has led to the development of curricula that incorporate such knowledge. Much of contemporary research and theory is synthesized in a report on elementary science education by Duschl et al. (2007), *Taking Science to School*, which presented a view of what elementary school children should know and be able to do in science that drew on a solid research base in the learning sciences and science education. This view included mastery of facts as a critical element of science competence, but placed far more emphasis on understanding the process of science in explaining the natural world and the nature of scientific evidence and argument. It emphasized a deeper understanding of core science concepts and so-called big ideas and facility with the scientific reasoning process and the practices that scientists engage in when doing their work as part of a larger community that builds knowledge. Duschl et al. summarized this view in terms of four intertwining strands in which student proficiency in science is defined as being able to

- know, use, and interpret scientific explanations of the natural world;
- generate and evaluate scientific evidence and explanations;
- understand the nature and development of scientific knowledge; and
- participate productively in scientific practices and discourse.

These proficiencies share a great deal in common with those identified for mathematics (e.g., Kilpatrick et al., 2001) in the sense that they emphasize not just factual and procedural competence but the development of conceptual understanding that is connected to the doing of science. It is far beyond the scope of this paper to try to capture what is known empirically about the multiple aspects of science proficiency, including their development as a consequence of instruction. The literature on science cognition and its development covers a diversity of topics that span areas of science from the life sciences to physical sciences to the earth, space and environmental sciences (see Duschl et al., 2007). For our present purposes it is perhaps most useful to consider some of the ways in which the concept of learning progressions is being used to map out key aspects of science knowledge and understanding across the K–12+ spectrum.

The science education community has moved away from using a multitude of national, state and district standards to guide thinking about the science curriculum to a view that curriculum and instruction should be focused on helping students develop an understanding of core or big ideas ideas (Duschl et al., 2007). Big ideas of science involve concepts, principles, and models that help explain a broad range of phenomena and may encompass knowledge within a single or across multiple disciplines (Smith et al., 2006). Thus, big ideas are important for science literacy and should be considered the foundation for building a coherent science curriculum.

As part of the effort to identify big ideas that have implications for science and engineering education, four big ideas have been given special attention: structure of matter, forces and interactions, size and scale, and quantum effects. These four constitute foundational science content for nanoscale science and each of the big ideas informs and is informed by the others (see Figure 6; Stevens, Sutherland, & Krajcik, 2009). For example, the structure of matter and the way matter interacts are inextricably linked. The forces that generally dominate those interactions change with scale. Different physical models (i.e., classical mechanics, quantum mechanics, general relativity) are more appropriate to explain the behavior of matter at different scales. Therefore, building integrated understandings of these ideas requires connecting concepts across them.

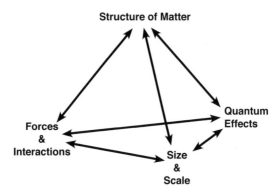

*Figure 5: Four of the Big Ideas Critical for Understanding Nanoscale Science*

Unfortunately, evidence shows that students have weak and underdeveloped understandings of these fundamental ideas and that includes the foundational concepts of size and scale (AAAS, 1993; Tretter, Jones, Andre, Negishi, & Minogue, 2006). Accordingly, efforts have been underway to develop an empirical learning progression for size and scale to better understand what students do know and understand and how we might design better instruction and assessment (Delgado, Stevens, Shin, & Krajcik, 2008). For present purposes we can represent possible understandings of size and scale in terms of four components that vary in sophistication. These four components have implications for the kinds of judgments and performances that individuals who posses each component understanding can demonstrate:

- *Qualitative relative:* A person can order objects by size:
  A > B > C > D > E > F > G > H > I > J.

- *Categorical:* A person can group objects of "similar" size and order groups by size:
  {A, B, C} > {D, E} > {F, G} > {H, I, J}.

- *Quantitative relative:* A person can designate that Object C is 1,000 times bigger than object E.

- *Absolute:* A person can specify absolute size such as Object E is 1 nm in length.

These components were used to generate a set of tasks suitable for probing the knowledge of students who spanned a range of grades from Grade 6 through college.

Figures 6 and 7 illustrate some of the results expressed in terms of the levels of sophistication of reasoning and understanding that students demonstrated across the full set of tasks. As shown in both figures, it was possible to order students along a continuum of levels of performance that reflect the components of size and scale that they understood as defined by the types of judgments they could make. As shown in Figure 6, some students were at the lowest level (Level 0) while others were at the highest level (Level 5) and there were students who fell into all of the levels in-between. In fact, it was possible to classify virtually all students into one of the six levels of knowledge and understanding. Figure 7 is an attempt to illustrate what this might mean using the visual representation of ordered levels shown earlier in Figure 4.

| No. students at the level | Order-group | Order-relative | Order-absolute | Absolute-relative (conceptual) | Absolute-relative (procedural) | Level |
|---|---|---|---|---|---|---|
| 6 | ✓ | ✓ | ✓ | ✓ | ✓ | 5 |
| 8 | ✓ | ✓ | ✓ | ✓ |   | 4 |
| 13 | ✓ | ✓ | ✓ |   |   | 3 |
| 3 | ✓ | ✓ |   |   |   | 2 |
| 5 | ✓ |   |   |   |   | 1 |
| 4 |   |   |   |   |   | 0 |
| # students | 35 | 30 | 27 | 14 | 6 |   |

*Figure 6: A Tabular Representation of Results Showing Levels of Student Understanding for Critical Components of Size and Scale*

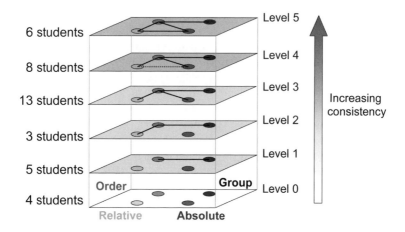

*Figure 7: A Graphical Representation of Results Showing Levels of Student Understanding for Critical Components of Size and Scale and Their Hypothetical Interconnections Within and Across Levels*

In general, while students in more advanced science courses have more sophisticated conceptions, there is wide variation between students in a given class. Most students cannot use the number of times bigger/smaller an unfamiliar object is compared to an object of known size to find the size of the unfamiliar object, and two thirds do not believe that the actual sizes and relative sizes are necessarily and logically related. Other connections, such as those between ordering and grouping, are much more widespread. As shown in Figures 6 and 7, it is possible to determine the order in which students tend to establish connections across facets of size and scale, and studies are underway to understand how this progression is related to the accumulation of accurate content knowledge about the size of specific objects.

Learning progressions of the type just illustrated have been delineated for other physical science concepts such as the structure of matter, as well as biological concepts like genetics, and earth and environmental science concepts (see e.g., Corcoran et al., 2009). Such progressions are based on various sources of evidence and much needs to be done to validate them. A part of the validation process includes using them productively for purposes of designing curriculum, instruction and assessment. The chapter by Krajcik et al. (*this volume*) provides an extensive discussion of the topic of learning progressions in science and their applicability to issues in the design of curriculum, instruction, and assessment.

## 2.4 Some Concluding Comments About Learning Progressions

There is considerable current interest in learning progressions but the field of practice and policy must be cautious in assuming that everything being espoused has a sound base and is ready for prime time. There is a danger in leaping too readily to embrace the construct without questioning the evidentiary base behind any given progression that is proposed. That said, there is much to potentially recommend learning progressions as ways to think about the assessment of student learning. One benefit of carefully described learning progressions is that they can be used to guide the specification of learning performances – statements of what students would be expected to know and be able to do. This was illustrated in the examples provided above for science. The learning performances can in turn guide the development of tasks that allow one to observe and infer students' levels of competence for major constructs that are the target of instruction and assessment within and across grade levels.

The potential relevance of any learning progression may vary with the purpose of the assessment and intended use of the information. This will be a function of the scope and specificity of the learning progression. The more detailed it is and the finer the grain size, the more useful it may be at levels close to classroom instruction. They have potential roles to play in supporting and monitoring development and growth and they may be especially relevant for aspects of diagnosis and instructional support. Finally, learning progressions can help us understand why working from a microto the macro-level understanding of student cognition and learning to generate assessments is more likely to lead to valid inferences about student achievement than the reverse. When we have detailed maps of the progress of student learning, at grain sizes that support instructional design and diagnostic assessment, we have a conceptual base that can be collapsed to make coarser judgments about aspects of growth and change appropriate to a broader timescale of learning. In doing so we preserve the validity of the assessment because we have a clear sense of the construct being measured and the level at which we can describe and understand student performance. Some of these issues are considered further in the next section.

# 3 Implications for Assessment Design

## 3.1 Assessment Purposes, Levels, and Timescales

Although assessments are currently used for many purposes in the educational system, a premise of the *Knowing What Students Know* report (Pellegrino et al., 2001) is that their effectiveness and utility must ultimately be judged by the extent to which they promote student learning. The aim of assessment should be "*to educate and improve* student performance, not merely to *audit* it" (Wiggins, 1998, p.7). Because assessments are developed for specific purposes, the nature of their design is very much constrained by their intended use. The reciprocal relationship between function and design leads to concerns about the inappropriate and ineffective use of assessments for purposes beyond their original intent. To clarify some of these issues of assessment purpose, design, and use, it is worth considering two pervasive dichotomies in the literature that are often misunderstood and conflated.

The first dichotomy is between *internal* classroom assessments administered by teachers, and *external* tests administered by districts, states or nations. Ruiz-Primo, Shavelson, Hamilton, and Klein (2002) showed that these two very different types of assessments are better understood as two points on a continuum that is defined by their distance from the enactment of specific instructional activities. They defined five discrete points on the continuum of assessment distance: *immediate* (e.g., observations or artifacts from the enactment of a specific activity), close (e.g., embedded assessments and semiformal quizzes of learning from one or more activities), *proximal* (e.g., formal classroom exams of learning from a specific curriculum), distal (e.g., criterion-referenced achievement tests such as required by the U.S. No Child Left Behind legislation), and remote (broader outcomes measured over time, including norm-referenced achievement tests and some national and international achievement measures. Different assessments should be understood as different points on this continuum if they are to be effectively aligned with each other and with curriculum and instruction.

A second pervasive dichotomy is the one between formative assessments used to advance learning and summative assessments used to provide evidence of prior learning. Often it is assumed that classroom assessment is synonymous with formative assessment, and that large-scale assessment is synonymous with summative assessment. What are now widely understood as different types of assessment practices are more productively understood as different functions of assessment practice, and summative *and* formative functions can be identified for most assessment activities, regardless of the level on which they function.

Drawing from the work of Lemke (2000), it is apparent that different assessment practices can be understood as operating at different *timescales*. The timescales for the five levels defined above can be characterized as *minutes, days, weeks, months,* and *years*. Timescale is important because the different competencies that various assessments aim to measure (and, therefore, the appropriate timing for being impacted by feedback) are *timescale-specific*. The cycles, or periodicity, of educational processes build from individual utterances into an individual's lifespan of educational development. What teachers and students say in class constitute verbal exchanges; these exchanges make up the lesson; a sequence of lessons makes up the unit; units form a curriculum, and the curricula form an education. Each of these elements operates on different cycles or timescales: second to second, day to day, month to month, and year to year.

The level at which an assessment is intended to function, which involves varying distance in "space and time" from the enactment of instruction and learning, has implications for how and how well it can fulfill various functions of assessment, be they formative, summative, or program evaluation (see National Research Council [NRC], 2003). As argued elsewhere (Hickey & Pellegrino, 2005; Pellegrino & Hickey, 2006), it is also the case that the different levels and functions of assessment can have varying degrees of match with theoretical stances about the nature of knowing and learning. With this in mind we now turn to the implications of cognitive theory and research for both classroom assessment practices and for large-scale assessment. These two contexts reflect some of the rich variation in assessment captured by the foregoing discussion of levels, functions, and timescales.

## 3.2   Implications for Design and Use of Classroom Assessment

Shepard (2000) discussed ways in which classroom assessment practices need to change to better support learning: the content and character of assessments need to be significantly improved to reflect contemporary understanding of learning; the gathering and use of assessment information and insights must become a part of the ongoing learning process; and assessment must become a central concern in methods courses in teacher preparation programs. Her messages are reflective of a growing belief among many educational assessment experts that if assessment, curriculum, and instruction were more integrally connected, as argued in Section 1, student learning would improve (e.g., Pellegrino et al., 1999; Stiggins, 1997).

Sadler (1989) provided a conceptual framework that places classroom assessment in the context of curriculum and instruction. According to this framework, three elements are required for assessment to promote learning:

1. A clear view of the learning goals (derived from the curriculum);
2. Information about the present state of the learner (derived from assessment);
3. Action to close the gap (taken through instruction).

Furthermore, there are ongoing, dynamic relationships among formative assessment, curriculum, and instruction. That is, there are important bidirectional interactions among the three elements, such that each informs the other. For instance, formulating assessment procedures for classroom use can spur a teacher to think more specifically about learning goals, thus leading to modification of curriculum and instruction. These modifications can, in turn, lead to refined assessment procedures, and so on. The mere existence of classroom assessment along the lines discussed here will not ensure effective learning. The clarity and appropriateness of the curriculum goals, the validity of the assessments in relationship to these goals, the interpretation of the assessment evidence, and the relevance and quality of the instruction that ensues are all critical determinants of the outcome. Starting with a model of cognition and learning in the domain can enhance each of these determinants.

For most teachers, the ultimate goals for learning are established by the curriculum, which is usually mandated externally (e.g., by state curriculum standards). However, teachers and others responsible for designing curriculum, instruction, and assessment must fashion intermediate goals that can serve as an effective route to achieving the ultimate goals, and to do so effectively, they must have an understanding of how students represent knowledge and develop competence in the domain. National and state curriculum standards set forth learning goals, but often not at a level of detail that is useful for operationalizing those goals in instruction and assessment. By dividing goal descriptions into sets appropriate for different age and grade ranges, current curriculum standards provide broad guidance about the nature of the progression to be expected in various subject domains. Whereas this kind of epistemological and conceptual analysis of the subject domain is an essential basis for guiding assessment, deeper cognitive analysis of how people learn the subject matter is also needed. Formative assessment should be based in cognitive theories about how people learn particular subject matter to ensure that instruction centers on what is most important for the next stage of learning, given a learner's current state of understanding.

It follows that teachers need training to develop their understanding of cognition and learning in the domains they teach. Preservice and professional development are needed to uncover teachers' existing understandings of how students learn and to help them formulate models of learning so they can identify students' naïve or initial sense-making strategies and build on those to move students toward more sophisticated understandings. The aim is to increase teachers' diagnostic expertise so they can make informed decisions about next steps for student learning. This has been a primary goal of cognitively based approaches to instruction and assessment that have been shown to have a positive impact on student learning, including the Cognitively Guided Instruction program (Carpenter, Fennema, & Franke, 1996) and others (Cobb et al., 1991; Griffin & Case, 1997). Such approaches rest on a bedrock of informed professional practice.

## 3.3 Implications for Design and Use of Large-Scale Assessment

Large-scale assessments are further removed from instruction but can still benefit learning if well designed and properly used. Substantially more valid, useful, and fair information could be gained from large-scale assessments if the principles of design set forth above earlier in Section 2 were applied. However, fully capitalizing on contemporary theory and research will require more substantial changes in the way large-scale assessment is approached, and relaxation of some of the constraints that currently drive large-scale assessment practices. Below we discuss some of the needed changes.

Large-scale summative assessments should focus on the most critical and central aspects of learning in a domain as identified by curriculum standards and informed by cognitive research and theory. Large-scale assessments typically will reflect aspects of the model of learning at a less detailed level than classroom assessments, which can go into more depth because they focus on a smaller slice of curriculum and instruction. For instance, one might need to know for summative purposes whether a student has mastered the more complex aspects of multicolumn subtraction, including borrowing from and across zero, rather than exactly which subtraction bugs lead to mistakes. At the same time, while policymakers and parents may not need all the diagnostic detail that would be useful to a teacher and student during the course of instruction, large-scale summative assessments should be based on a model of learning that is compatible with and derived from the same set of knowledge and assumptions about learning as classroom assessment.

As described in the *Student Cognition and Domain-Specific Learning* section, research on cognition and learning suggests a broad range of competencies that should be assessed when measuring student achievement, many of which are essentially untapped by current assessments. Examples are knowledge organization, problem representation, strategy use, metacognition, and participatory activities (e.g., formulating questions, constructing and evaluating arguments, contributing to group problem-solving). Furthermore, large-scale assessments should provide information about the nature of student understanding, rather than simply ranking students according to general proficiency estimates.

Large-scale assessments not only serve as a means for reporting on student achievement, but also reflect aspects of academic competence societies consider worthy of recognition and reward. Thus, large-scale assessments can signal worthwhile targets for educators and students to pursue. Whereas teaching directly to the items on a test is not desirable, teaching to the theory of cognition and learning that underlies an assessment can provide positive direction for instruction.

A major problem is that only limited improvements in large-scale assessments are possible under current constraints and typical standardized testing scenarios. Large-scale assessments are designed to meet certain purposes under constraints that often include providing reliable and comparable scores for individuals as well as groups; sampling a broad set of curriculum standards within a limited testing time per student; and offering cost-efficiency in terms of development, scoring, and administration. To meet these kinds of demands, designers typically create assessments that are given at a specified time, with all students being given the same (or parallel) tests under strictly standardized conditions (often referred to as *on-demand* assessment). Tasks are generally of the kind that can be presented in paper-and-pencil format, that students can respond to quickly, and that can be scored reliably and efficiently. In general, competencies that lend themselves to being assessed in these ways are tapped, while aspects of learning that cannot be observed under such constrained conditions are not addressed. To design new kinds of situations for capturing the complexity of cognition and learning will require examining the assumptions and values that currently drive assessment design choices and breaking out of the current paradigm to explore alternative approaches to large-scale assessment, including innovative uses of technology (see e.g., Quellmalz & Pellegrino, 2009).

### 3.4 Balanced Assessment Systems

Given that one form of assessment does not serve all purposes, it is inevitable that multiple assessments (or assessments consisting of multiple components) will be required to serve the varying educational assessment needs of different audiences. A multitude of different assessments are already being used in schools. It is not surprising that users are often frustrated when such assessments have conflicting achievement goals and results. Sometimes such discrepancies can be meaningful and useful, such as when assessments are explicitly aimed at measuring different school outcomes. More often, however, conflicting assessment goals and feedback cause much confusion for educators, students, and parents. In this section we describe a vision for coordinated systems of multiple assessments that work together, along with curriculum and instruction, to promote learning, but first we consider issues of balance and allocation of resources across classroom and large-scale assessment (see also NRC, 2003).

The current educational assessment environment in the United States clearly reflects the considerable value and credibility placed on external, large-scale assessments of individuals and programs relative to classroom assessment designed to assist learning. The resources invested in producing and using large-scale testing – in terms of money, instructional time, research, and development – far outweigh the investment in the design and use of effective classroom assessment. To better serve the goals of learning, the research, development, and training investment must be shifted toward the classroom where teaching and learning occurs.

Not only does large-scale assessment dominate over classroom assessment, but there is also ample evidence of accountability measures negatively impacting classroom instruction and assessment. For instance, as discussed earlier, teachers feel pressure to teach to the test, which results in a narrowing of instruction. They also model their own classroom tests after less-than-ideal standardized tests (Linn, 2000; Shepard, 2000). These kinds of problems suggest that beyond striking a better balance between classroom and large-scale assessment, what is needed are coordinated systems of assessments that collectively support a common set of learning goals, rather than work at cross-purposes.

To this end, an assessment system should exhibit three properties: comprehensiveness, coherence, and continuity. These notions of alignment are consistent with those set forth by various groups including the National Council of Teachers of Mathematics and the National Academy of Education.

By *comprehensiveness*, we mean that a range of measurement approaches should be used to provide a variety of evidence to support educational decision-making. Multiple measures take on particular importance when important, life-altering decisions (such as high school graduation) are being made about individuals. No single test score can be considered a definitive measure of a student's competence. Multiple measures enhance the validity and fairness of the inferences drawn by giving students various ways and opportunities to demonstrate their competence. Multiple measures can also be used to provide evidence that improvements in test scores represent real gains in learning, as opposed to score inflation due to teaching narrowly to one particular test (Heubert & Hauser, 1999).

For the system to support learning, it must also have a quality we refer to as *coherence*. One dimension of coherence is that the conceptual base or models of student learning underlying the various external and classroom assessments within a system should be compatible. While a large-scale assessment might be based on a model of learning that is coarser than that underlying the assessments used in classrooms, the conceptual base for the large-scale assessment should be a broader version of one that makes sense at the finer-grained level (Mislevy, 1996). In this way, the external assessment results will be consistent with the more detailed understanding of learning underlying classroom instruction and assessment. As one moves up and down the levels of the system, from the classroom through the school, district, and state, assessments along this vertical dimension should align. As long as the underlying models of learning are consistent, the assessments will complement each other rather than present conflicting goals for learning.

Finally, an ideal assessment system would be designed to be *continuous*. That is, assessments should measure student progress over time, akin more to a videotape record rather than to the snapshots provided by most current tests. To provide such pictures of progress, multiple sets of observations over time must be linked conceptually so that change can be observed and interpreted. Models of student progress in learning should underlie the assessment system, and tests should be designed to provide information that maps back to the progression. Thus, continuity calls for alignment along the third dimension of time.

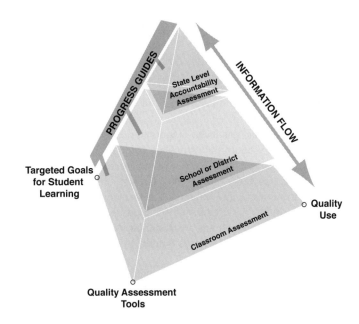

*Figure 8: Center for Assessment and Evaluation of Student Learning (CAESL) Representation of a Coordinated, Multilevel Assessment System*

Figure 8, developed by the Center for Assessment and Evaluation of Student Learning, provides a graphical illustration of what an assessment system might look and some of the factors that would serve to achieve balance and support the principles described above. The system illustrated in Figure 8 would be (a) coordinated across levels, (b) unified by common learning goals, and (c) synchronized by unifying progress variables. No existing system of assessments that we know of has these design features and meets all three criteria of comprehensiveness, coherence, and continuity, but there are examples of assessments that represent steps toward these goals. For instance, Australia's Developmental Assessment program (Masters & Forster, 1996) and the BEAR assessment system (Wilson & Sloane, 2000; Wilson, Draney & Kennedy, 2001) show how progress maps can be used to achieve coherence between formative and summative assessment, as well as among curriculum, instruction, and assessments. Progress maps also enable the measurement of growth (continuity). The Australian Council for Educational Research has produced an excellent set of resource materials for teachers to support their use of a wide range of assessment strategies – from written tests to portfolios to projects at the classroom level – that can all be designed to link back to the progress maps (comprehensiveness), however the underlying models of learning are not as strongly tied to research as they could be and should.

## 3.5  Some Final Thoughts

This is a heady time in education in the U.S. given the attempts to develop common core standards for major areas of the curriculum combined with an interest in developing quality assessment programs that can be used to measure student achievement and growth against those standards. All of this work is directed towards a more coherent approach to educational improvement and accountability than has been the case for the last decade. The U.S. Department of Education's *Race to the Top* initiative provides an opportunity to rethink how we design assessments to serve multiple purposes and how they can provide the types of information needed by the full range of actors and agents in the educational system from classroom teachers, to district leaders, to state superintendents, to federal policy makers. But with opportunity comes the peril of moving too quickly to implement systems without thinking through the complexity of the information needs of the various users and ways to insure compatibility and coherence across all levels of the system.

There are also serious issues regarding existing capacity to develop the full range of quality assessment materials and tools that are needed to get the job done, certainly if there is a short time horizon to accomplish everything. The policy community wants answers to design and implementation questions that the learning sciences and measurement sciences cannot fully answer. This is especially true for a complex topic like the most valid ways to measure the growth of knowledge and skill across time. It is not that the job can't be done but an investment must be made in research and development that runs the gamut from very basic science to highly applied design, and everything in between. One would hope that the *Race to the Top* initiative puts us on the right path even if it means that getting to the top takes a bit longer than is comfortable under typical political and legislative cycles. There no doubt will be tensions in working this all out. It is hoped that the conceptual framing of issues and the types of work on student learning described in this paper and can be helpful in steering the course. The education community needs to maintain focus on defining the progressions of knowledge and understanding that are both desirable and attainable and in so doing give substantive meaning to notions such as *fewer, clearer, higher*. And we need to make use of principled assessment design processes that start with careful deliberations about the evidence about student achievement we value and need rather than settling for the data we can most easily and cheaply collect.

## References

American Association for the Advancement of Science (1993). *Benchmarks for Science Literacy*. Washington, DC: AAAS.

American Association for the Advancement of Science (2001). *Atlas of Science Literacy*. Washington, DC: AAAS.

Anderson, J. R. (Ed.) (1981). *Cognitive skills and their acquisition*. Hillsdale, NJ: Lawrence Erlbaum Associates.

Black, P. & Wiliam, D. (1998). Assessment and classroom learning. *Assessment in Education, 5*(1), 7-73.

Bransford, J. D., Brown, A. L., Cocking, R. R., Donovan, M. S., & Pellegrino, J. W. (Eds.) (2000). *How People Learn: Brain, Mind, Experience, and School* (expanded ed.). Washington, DC: National Academies Press.

Carpenter, T., Fennema, E., & Franke, M. (1996). Cognitively guided instruction: A knowledge base for reform in primary mathematics instruction. *Elementary School Journal, 97*(1), 3-20.

Chi, M. T. H., Feltovich, P. J., & Glaser, R. (1981). Categorization and representation of physics problems by experts and novices. *Cognitive Science, 5,* 121-152.

Cobb, P., Wood, T., Yackel, E., Nicholls, J., Wheatley, G., Trigatti, B., & Perlwitz, M. (1991). Assessment of a problem-centered second-grade mathematics project. *Journal for Research in Mathematics Education, 22*(1), 3-29.

Confrey, J. (2008, July). *A Synthesis of the Research on Rational Number Reasoning: A Learning Progressions Trajectories Approach to Synthesis*. Paper presented at the 11th meeting of the International Congress of Mathematics Instruction, Monterrey, Mexico.

Confrey, J., Maloney, A. P., Nguyen, K. H., Mojica, G., & Myers, M. (2009, July). *Equipartitioning/Splitting as a Foundation of Rational Number Reasoning Using Learning Trajectories*. Paper presented at the 33rd Conference of the International Group for the Psychology of Mathematics Education, Thessaloniki, Greece.

Corcoran, T. B., Mosher, F. A., & Rogat, A. (2009). *Learning Progressions in Science: An Evidence-Based Approach to Reform.* New York, NY: Columbia University, Teachers College, Consortium for Policy Research in Education, Center on Continuous Instructional Improvement.

Delgado, C., Stevens, S., Shin, N., & Krajcik, J. (2008). Development of a learning progression for size and scale. In *Proceedings of 8th International Conference of the Learning Sciences (Vol. 3),* (pp. 317–318). Utrecht, Netherlands: ISLS.

Donovan, M. S. & Bransford, J. W. (Eds.) (2005). *How Students Learn History, Science and Mathematics in the Classroom.* Washington, DC: The National Academies Press.

Donovan, M. S., Bransford, J. D., & Pellegrino, J. W. (Eds.) (1999). *How People Learn: Bridging Research and Practice.* Committee on Learning Research and Educational Practice. Washington, DC: National Academies Press.

Duncan, R. G. & Hmelo-Silver, C. (2009). Learning progressions: Aligning curriculum, instruction, and assessment. *Journal for Research in Science Teaching, 46*(6), 606-609.

Duschl, R. A., Schweingruber, H. A., & Shouse, A. W. (Eds.) (2007). *Taking Science to School: Learning and Teaching Science in Grade K-8.* Washington, DC: The National Academies Press.

Fay, A. & Klahr, D. (1996). Knowing about guessing and guessing about knowing: Preschoolers' understanding of indeterminacy. *Child Development, 67,* 689-716.

Geary, D. (1995). Reflections of evolution and culture in children's cognition: Implications for mathematical development and instruction. *American Psychologist, 50*(1), 24-37.

Gelman, R. (1990). First principles organize attention to and learning about relevant data: Number and the animate-inanimate distinction as examples. *Cognitive Science, 14,* 79-106.

Gelman, R. & Gallistel, C.R. (1978). *The Child's Understanding of Number.* Cambridge, MA: Harvard University Press.

Glaser, R. (1992). Expert knowledge and processes of thinking. In D. F. Halpern (Ed.), *Enhancing Thinking Skills in the Sciences and Mathematics* (pp. 63-75). Hillsdale, NJ: Erlbaum.

Griffin, S. & Case, R., (1997). Re-thinking the primary school math curriculum: An approach based on cognitive science. *Issues in Education, 3*(1), 1-49.

Heubert, J. P. & Hauser, R. M. (Eds.) (1999). *High Stakes: Testing for Tracking, Promotion, and Graduation.* Washington, DC: National Academies Press.

Hickey, D. & Pellegrino, J.W. (2005). Theory, level, and function: Three dimensions for understanding transfer and student assessment. In J. P. Mestre (Ed.), *Transfer of Learning from a Modern Multidisciplinary Perspective* (pp. 251-293*).* Greenwich, CO: Information Age Publishing.

Kaiser, M. K., Proffitt, D. R., & McCloskey, M. (1985). The development of beliefs about falling objects. *Perception & Psychophysics, 38*(6), 533-539.

Kilpatrick, J., Swafford, J., & Findell, B. (Eds.) (2001). *Adding It Up: Helping Children Learn Mathematics.* Washington, DC: National Academies Press.

Lemke, J. J. (2000). Across the scale of time: Artifacts, activities, and meaning in ecosocial systems. *Mind, Culture, and Activity, 7*(4), 273-290.

Linn, R. (2000). Assessments and accountability. *Educational Researcher, 29*(2), 4-16.

Marion, S. & Pellegrino, J. W. (2006). A validity framework for evaluating the technical quality of alternate assessments. *Educational Measurement: Issues and Practice, Winter 2006,* 47-57.

Massey, C. M. & Gelman, R. (1988). Preschoolers decide whether pictured unfamiliar objects can move themselves. *Developmental Psychology, 24,* 307-317.

Masters, G. & Forster, M. (1996). *Progress maps. Assessment Resource Kit.* Victoria, Australia: Commonwealth of Australia.

Mislevy, R. J. (1996). Test theory reconceived. *Journal of Educational Measurement, 33*(4), 379-416.

National Council of Teachers of Mathematics (1995). *Assessment Standards for School Mathematics.* Reston, VA: NCTM.

National Council of Teachers of Mathematics (2000). *Principles and Standards for School Mathematics.* Reston, VA: NCTM.

National Research Council (2003). *Assessment in Support of Learning and Instruction: Bridging the Gap Between Large-Scale and Classroom Assessment.* Washington, DC: National Academies Press.

Pellegrino, J. W. (1988). Mental models and mental tests. In H. Wainer & H. I. Braun (Eds.), *Test validity* (pp. 49-60). Hillsdale, NJ: Erlbaum.

Pellegrino, J. W., Baxter, G. P., & Glaser, R. (1999). Addressing the "two disciplines" problem: Linking theories of cognition and learning with assessment and instructional practice. In A. Iran-Nejad & P. D. Pearson (Eds.), *Review of Research in Education* (Vol. 24), pp. 307-353). Washington, DC: American Educational Research Association.

Pellegrino, J. W., Chudowsky, N., & Glaser, R.(Eds.) (2001). *Knowing What Students Know: The Science and Design of Educational Assessment.* Washington, DC: National Academies Press.

Pellegrino, J. W. & Hickey, D. (2006). Educational assessment: Towards better alignment between theory and practice. In L. Verschaffel, F. Dochy, M. Boekaerts, & S. Vosniadou (Eds.), *Instructional Psychology: Past, Present and Future Trends. Sixteen Essays in Honour of Erik De Corte* (pp. 169-189). Oxford, England: Elsevier.

Pellegrino, J. W., Jones, L. R., & Mitchell, K. J. (Eds.) (1999). *Grading the Nation's Report Card: Evaluating NAEP and Transforming the Assessment of Educational Progress.* Washington, DC: National Academies Press.

Quellmalz, E. & Pellegrino, J. W. (2009). Technology and testing. *Science, 323,* 75-79.

Rosenbloom, P. & Newell, A. (1987). Learning by chunking: A production system model of practice. In D. Klahr & P. Langley (Eds.), *Production System Models of Learning and Development* (pp. 221-286). Cambridge, MA: MIT Press.

Ruiz Primo, M. A., Shavelson, R. J., Hamilton, L., & Klein, S. (2002). On the evaluation of systemic science education reform: Searching for instructional sensitivity. *Journal of Research in Science Teaching, 39,* 369-393.

Sadler, R. (1989). Formative assessment and the design of instructional systems. *Instructional Science, 18*, 119-144.

Shepard, L. A. (2000). The role of assessment in a learning culture. *Educational Researcher, 29*(7), 4-14.

Siegler, R. S. (1998). *Children's Thinking* (3rd ed.). Upper Saddle River, NJ: Prentice Hall.

Simon, H. A. (1980). Problem solving and education. In D.T. Tuma & F. Reif (Eds.), *Problem Solving and Education: Issues in Teaching and Research* (pp. 81-96). Hillsdale, NJ: Erlbaum.

Smith, C., Wiser, M., Anderson, C. W., & Krajcik, J. (2006). Implications of children's learning for assessment: A proposed learning progression for matter and the atomic molecular theory. *Measurement, 14*(1&2), 1-98.

Stevens, S. Y., Sutherland, L. M., & Krajcik, J. S. (2009). *The Big Ideas of Nanoscale Science and Engineering: A Guidebook for Secondary Teachers*. Arlington, VA: NSTA Press.

Stiggins, R. J. (1997). *Student-Centered Classroom Assessment*. Upper Saddle River, NJ: Prentice-Hall.

Thorndike, E .L. (1931). *Human Learning*. New York, NY: Century.

Tretter, T. R., Jones, M. G., Andre, T., Negishi, A., & Minogue, J. (2006). Conceptual boundaries and distances: Students' and experts' concepts of the scale of scientific phenomena. *Journal of Research in Science Teaching, 43*(3), 282-319.

Webb, N. L. (1997). *Criteria for Alignment of Expectations and Assessments in Mathematics and Science Education* (National Institute for Science Education and Council of Chief State School Officers Research Monograph No. 6.). Washington, DC: Council of Chief State School Officers.

Wiggins, G. (1998). *Educative Assessment: Designing Assessments to Inform and Improve Student Performance*. San Francisco, CA: Jossey-Bass.

Wiliam, D. (2007). Keeping learning on track: Formative assessment and the regulation of learning. In F. K. Lester Jr. (Ed.), *Second Handbook of Mathematics Teaching and Learning* (pp. 1053-1098). Greenwich, CT: Information Age Publishing.

Wilson, M., Draney, K., & Kennedy, C. (2001). *GradeMap* [computer program]. Berkeley, CA: BEAR Center, University of California, Berkeley.

Wilson, M. & Sloane, K. (2000). From principles to practice: An embedded assessment system. *Applied Measurement in Education, 13*(2), 181-208.

Wilson, M. R. & Bertenthal, M. W. (Eds.) (2005). *Systems for State Science Assessments*. Washington DC: National Academies Press.

# Chapter 5

# Learning Outcomes in Ireland – Implications for the Science Classroom

*Declan Kennedy*
*Department of Education, University College Cork (UCC), Ireland*

## Abstract

The signing of the Bologna Agreement in 1999 has major implications for all involved in third level education throughout the world. Since 2010 in the 45 countries that have signed up to the Bologna process, it is a requirement that all modules and programmes in third level institutions must be described in terms of learning outcomes. The effect of the Bologna Process is also being felt at high school level with new curricula being re-written in terms of learning outcomes.

This paper covers the background to the concept of Learning Outcomes, the use of Bloom's Taxonomy to write learning outcomes in science education, and the linking of learning outcomes to both teaching and learning activities as well as to assessment. In addition, the author discusses the effects of the introduction of learning outcomes into the teacher-training programme for student science teachers in his own university.

## 1 Why Has There Been a Focus on Learning Outcomes in Recent Years?

In June 1999, representatives of the Ministers of Education of EU member states convened in Bologna, Italy, to formulate the Bologna Agreement leading to the setting up of a common European Higher Education Area (EHEA). The overall aim of the Bologna Process is to improve the efficiency and effectiveness of higher education in Europe. One of the main features of this process is the need to improve the traditional ways of describing qualifications and qualification structures. As a step towards achieving greater clarity in the description of qualifications, it was specified that by 2010 all modules and programmes in third level institutions throughout the

European Higher Education Area had to be written in terms of learning outcomes. To date, most countries have achieved this target to varying extents. In an analysis of progress being made in the implementation of the Bologna Process in 48 countries, Rauhvargers et al. (2009) found that approximately 25% of the countries surveyed had fully implemented the learning outcomes approach in setting up a National Qualifications Framework (NQF), approximately 50% of countries were in the process of implementing NQF in their country, and approximately 25% of countries had not yet initiated this process. The authors of the report comment that steady progress has been made since 2007 and accept that the deadline to have completed the implementation of NQFs for higher education by 2010 appears to have been too ambitious.

The importance of learning outcomes has been clearly stated by the Council of Europe:

> *"Learning outcomes are important for recognition. [...] The principal question asked of the student or the graduate will therefore no longer be "what did you do to obtain your degree?" but rather "what can you do now that you have obtained your degree?". This approach is of relevance to the labour market and is certainly more flexible when taking into account issues of lifelong learning, non-traditional learning, and other forms of non-formal educational experiences."* (Council of Europe, 2002)

To date, all 27 countries of the EU and 18 other countries have signed up to the Bologna process. In addition to these 45 countries, many countries outside the Bologna process have aligning their third-level educational systems to be compatible with the Bologna process in order to facilitate description of qualifications, mutual recognition of degrees, and mobility of students.

A number of follow-up meetings were held after the meeting in Bologna to move the process of implementation forward. At the Berlin meeting in 2003, the Ministers for Education issued a communiqué on the position of the Bologna Process. They emphasised the creation of a common model for Higher Education in Europe and specified that degrees (Bachelor and Master) would be described in terms of learning outcomes, rather than simply number of credits and number of hours of study:

> *"Ministers encourage the member States to elaborate a framework of comparable and compatible qualifications for their higher education systems, which should seek to describe qualifications in terms of workload, level, learning outcomes, competences and profile. They also undertake to elaborate an overarching framework of qualifications for the European Higher Education Area."* (Berlin Communiqué, 2003)

Thus the Bologna Process has put the focus on learning outcomes in terms of this concept being a "common language" to describe the curricula in countries throughout the world.

## 2   How Are Learning Outcomes Defined?

The traditional way of designing modules and programmes in our universities was to start from the content of the course. A module is defined as a self contained fraction of student's programme workload for the year with a unique examination and a clear set of learning outcomes and appropriate assessment criteria (Kennedy, 2007). Traditionally, teachers decided on the content that they intended to teach, planned how to teach this content, and then assessed the content. This type of approach focussed on the teacher's input and on assessment in terms of how well the students absorbed the material taught. Course descriptions referred mainly to the content of the course that would be covered in the classroom and in lectures. This approach to teaching has been referred to as a "teacher-centred approach". Among the criticisms of this type of approach in the literature (Gosling & Moon, 2001) is that it can be difficult to identify precisely what the student has to be able to do in order to pass the examination.

International trends in education show a shift from the traditional teacher-centered approach to a student-centered approach, i.e. the focus is not only on teaching but also on what the students are expected to be able to do at the end of the module or programme (Kennedy et al., 2006). Hence, this approach is commonly referred to as an "outcome-based approach". Statements called intended learning outcomes, commonly shortened to learning outcomes, are used to express what it is expected that students should be able to do at the end of the learning period.

There are various definitions of learning outcomes in the literature (Jenkins & Unwin, 2001; Moon, 2002; Morss & Murray, 2005) but they do not differ significantly from each other. The following definition (ECTS Users' Guide, 2005, p. 47) of a learning outcome is considered a good working definition:

> *"Learning outcomes are statements of what a learner is expected to know, understand and/or be able to demonstrate after completion of a process of learning."*

The "process of learning" could be, for example, an individual lesson or lecture, a module, or an entire programme.

It is important to distinguish between the terms aims, objectives and, learning outcomes. The aim of a module or programme is a broad general statement of teaching intention, i.e. it indicates what the teacher intends to cover in a block of learning. Aims are usually written from the teacher's point of view to indicate the general content and direction of the module. For example, the aim of a module could be 'to introduce students to the basic principles of atomic structure'.

The objective of a module or programme is usually a specific statement of teaching intention, i.e. it indicates one of the specific areas that the teacher intends to cover. For example, one of the objectives of a lesson could be that "pupils would understand the concept of chemical bonding".

One of the problems caused by the use of objectives is that sometimes they are written in terms of teaching intention and other times they are written in terms of expected learning, i.e. there is confusion in the literature in terms of whether objectives belong to the teacher-centred approach or the outcome-based approach. The situation is nicely summarised by Moon (2002) as follows:

> *"Basically the term 'objective' tends to complicate the situation, because objectives may be written in terms of teaching intention or expected learning. [...] This means that some descriptions are of the teaching in the module and some are of the learning. [...] This general lack of agreement as to the format of objectives is a complication, and justifies the abandonment of the use of the term 'objective' in the description of modules or programmes."* (Moon, 2002)

Most teachers who have worked on the development of objectives for modules or programmes have encountered the above problem. One of the great advantages of learning outcomes is that they are clear statements of what the student is expected to achieve and how he or she is expected to demonstrate that achievement.

## 3   What Are the Guidelines for Writing Learning Outcomes?

The work of Benjamin Bloom (1913–1999) is a useful starting point when writing learning outcomes. Bloom identified three domains of learning – cognitive, affective and psychomotor – and within each of these domains he recognised that there was an ascending order of complexity. His work is most advanced in the cognitive domain where he drew up a classification (or taxonomy) of thinking behaviours from the simple recall of facts up to the process of analysis and evaluation. His publication *Taxonomy of Educational Objectives: Handbook 1, The Cognitive Domain* (Bloom et al., 1956) has become widely used throughout the world to assist in the preparation of curriculum and evaluation materials. The taxonomy provides a framework in which one can build upon prior learning to develop more complex levels of understanding.

In recent years, attempts have been made to revise Bloom's Taxonomy (Anderson & Krathwohl, 2001) but the original works of Bloom and his co-workers are still the most widely quoted in the literature.

Bloom proposed that the cognitive or knowing domain is composed of six successive levels arranged in a hierarchy as shown in Figure 1.

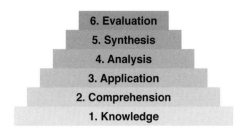

*Figure 1: The Levels in the Cognitive Domain of Bloom's Taxonomy*

Bloom's taxonomy is frequently used for writing learning outcomes as it provides a ready-made structure and list of verbs. Bloom's original list of verbs was limited and has been extended by various authors over the years. Whilst the list of verbs in a recent publication (Kennedy, 2007) is not exhaustive, it is hoped that the reader will find the lists in the above publication to be reasonably comprehensive.

In this short article, it is not possible to discuss the rules for writing learning outcomes but these rules and many examples are given elsewhere (Kennedy, 2007). Some examples of learning outcomes for various areas of Bloom's Taxonomy in the cognitive domain are given in Table 1. Note that each learning outcome begins with an action verb.

The affective domain deals with beliefs, attitudes, and values and the psychomotor domain covers the area of practical skills. Some examples of learning outcomes in the affective domain and psychomotor domains are shown in Table 2.

*Table 1: Examples of Learning Outcomes in the Cognitive Domain*

- Recall genetics terminology: homozygous, heterozygous, phenotype, genotype, homologous chromosome pair, etc.
- Relate energy changes to bond breaking and formation.
- Apply principles of classroom management to maintain an atmosphere of learning in the classroom.
- Debate the economic and environmental effects of energy conversion processes.
- Compare the classroom practice of a newly qualified teacher with that of a teacher of 20 years teaching experience.
- Summarise the main contributions of Michael Faraday to the field of electromagnetic induction.
- Evaluate the key areas contributing to the craft knowledge of experienced teachers.

*Table 2: Examples of Learning Outcomes in the Affective and Psychomotor Domain*

*Affective Domain*
- Accept the need for professional ethical standards.
- Display a willingness to communicate well with parents of your pupils
- Embrace a responsibility for pupils in your care.
- Participate in discussions about your progress with your mentor teacher.

*Psychomotor Domain*
- Operate the range of instrumentation safely and efficiently in the laboratory.
- Perform titrations accurately and safely in the laboratory.
- Construct simple scientific sketches of geological features in the field.
- Deliver an effective lecture demonstration to your fellow student science teachers.

In addition to writing module learning outcomes, we are also required by the Bologna Process to write programme learning outcomes. An example of the programme learning outcomes written for the Bachelor of Science Education degree in University College Cork are given in Table 3.

*Table 3: Programme Learning Outcomes for BSc(Ed) Degree Programme in University College Cork*

- Recognise and apply the basic principles of classroom management and discipline.
- Identify the key characteristics of excellent teaching in science.
- Develop comprehensive portfolios of lesson plans that are relevant to the science curricula in schools.
- Evaluate the various theories of Teaching and Learning and apply these theories to assist in the creation of effective and inspiring science lessons.
- Critically evaluate the effectiveness of their teaching of science in the second-level school system.
- Display a willingness to co-operate with members of the teaching staff in their assigned school.
- Foster an interest in science and a sense of enthusiasm for science subjects in their pupils.
- Synthesise the key components of laboratory organisation and management and perform laboratory work in a safe and efficient manner.
- Communicate effectively with the school community and with society at large in the area of science education.

Further examples of learning outcomes as well as a discussion on programme learning outcomes, are covered in more detail in a separate publication (Kennedy, 2007).

## 4 Learning Outcomes and Competences

In some papers in the literature, the term "competence" is used in association with learning outcomes. It is difficult to find a precise definition for the term competence. Adam (2004) comments that "some take a narrow view and associate competence just with skills acquired by training". The EU Tuning project *(Tuning Educational Structures in Europe)* which was initiated in 2000 (Tuning Project, URL 6) used the term competence to represent a combination of attributes in terms of knowledge and its application, skills, responsibilities, and attitudes and an attempt was made to describe the extent to which a person is capable of performing them.

The lack of clarity or agreement in terms of defining the term competence is apparent in the ECTS Users' Guide (2005), which describes competences as *"a dynamic combination of attributes, abilities, and attitudes"*. The Guide goes on to state that *"fostering these competences is the object of educational programmes. Competences are formed in various course units and assessed at different stages. They may be divided into subject-area related competences (specific to a field of study) and generic competences (common to any degree course)"*. The confusion regarding the term competence is nicely summarised by Winterton et al. (2005) as follows:

> *"There is such confusion and debate concerning the concept of 'competence' that it is impossible to identify or impute a coherent theory or to arrive at a definition capable of accommodating and reconciling all the different ways that the term is used."* (Winterton et al., 2005)

Since there does not appear to be a common understanding of the term competence in the literature, learning outcomes have become more commonly used than competences when describing what students are expected to know, understand, and/or be able to demonstrate at the end of a module or programme. In essence, learning outcomes bring clarity to what has been described as the "fuzzy concept" (Boon & van der Klink, 2002) of competence.

## 5 Linking Learning Outcomes to Teaching and Learning Activities and to Assessment

When writing learning outcomes, it is important to write them in such a way that they are capable of being assessed. Clearly, it is necessary to have some form of assessment tool or technique in order to determine the extent to which learning outcomes have been achieved by our students. Examples of direct assessment techniques are the use of written examinations, project work, portfolios, observation of teaching practice, etc. Examples of indirect assessment methods are surveys of employers, comparison with peer institutions, surveys of past graduates, retention rates, analysis of curriculum, etc.

The challenge for science teachers is to ensure that there is alignment between our teaching methods, assessment techniques, assessment criteria, and learning outcomes. Ramsden (2003) points out that evidence collected from student course evaluations shows that clear expectations on the part of students of what is required of them are a vitally important part of students' effective learning. Lack of clarity in this area is almost always associated with negative evaluations, learning difficulties, and poor student performance. Toohey (1999) recommends that the best way to help students understand how they must achieve learning outcomes is by clearly setting out the assessment techniques and the assessment criteria.

It is important that the assessment tasks mirror the learning outcomes since, as far as the students are concerned, the assessment is the curriculum: "From our students' point of view, assessment always defines the actual curriculum" (Ramsden, 2003). This situation is represented graphically by Biggs (2003b) as shown in Figure 2.

---

**Teacher**
**Perspectives:** Objectives → DLOs* → Teaching Activities → Assessment

**Student** ↓
**Perspectives:** Assessment → Learning activities → Outcomes

---

* Desired Learning Outcomes.

*Figure 2: The Different Perspectives of Teacher and Students (Biggs 2003b)*

In stressing this point, Biggs (2003a) emphasises the strong link between the curriculum and assessment as follows:

*"To the teacher, assessment is at the end of the teaching-learning sequence of events, but to the student it is at the beginning. If the curriculum is reflected in the assessment, as indicated by the downward arrow, the teaching activities of the teacher and the learner activities of the learner are both directed towards the same goal. In preparing for the assessment, students will be learning the curriculum."* (Biggs 2003a)

As already stated (Ramsden, 2003) as far as the students are concerned, the assessment **is** the curriculum. They will learn what they think will be assessed, not what may be on the curriculum or even what has been covered in lectures! The old adage that "assessment is the tail that wags the dog" is very true. Developing links between learning outcomes, teaching strategies, student activities and assessment tasks is very challenging for the teacher. Table 4 may be of help in developing these links.

*Table 4: Linking Learning Outcomes, Teaching and Learning Activities and Assessment*

| Learning Outcomes | | Teaching and Learning Activities | Assessment Techniques |
|---|---|---|---|
| Cognitive ↕ | Demonstrate knowledge, Comprehension, Application, Analysis, Synthesis, Evaluation | Lectures | End of module exam |
| | | Tutorials | Multiple choice tests |
| | | Discussions | Essays |
| | | Laboratory work | Practical assessment |
| Affective ↕ | Integration of beliefs, ideas, and attitudes. | Clinical work | Fieldwork |
| | | Group work | Clinical practice |
| | | Seminar | Presentation |
| Psycho-motor | Acquisition of physical skills. | Peer group presentation etc. | Project work etc. |

There may not be just one method of assessment to satisfy all learning outcomes and it may be necessary to choose a number of assessment methods.

The curriculum should be designed so that the teaching activities, learning activities and assessment tasks are co-ordinated with the learning outcomes. Biggs (2003a) refers to this type of process as involving **constructive alignment**. Biggs points out that in a good teaching system, the method of teaching, learning activities and method of assessment are all co-ordinated to support student learning.

> *"When there is alignment between what we want, how we teach and how we assess, teaching is likely to be much more effective than when it is not (aligned) ... Traditional transmission theories of teaching ignore alignment."* (Biggs 2003a)

# 6 Learning Outcomes in the Science Curriculum in Ireland

A revised Junior Certificate Science syllabus (age group 12–15) was introduced to schools in September 2003 (NCCA, 2003). Responsibility for new curricula in Ireland rests with the National Council for Curriculum and Assessment. This is a government organisation in which there is a committee with responsibility for each subject area. There is also a Board of Studied for Science which contains external experts and assessors to ensure uniformity of standards and quality assurance. Whilst science is not a compulsory subject in second level schools in Ireland, it is studied by over 90% of pupils. The curriculum has been written with a focus on learning outcomes and some examples of learning outcomes from the syllabus are shown in Table 5.

*Table 5: Examples of Learning Outcomes from the Junior Certificate Science Curriculum in Ireland*

| |
|---|
| • State the function of the urinary system; describe its structure, identifying the bladder, renal artery, renal vein, ureter, urethra and kidney. |
| • Locate the main parts of the eye on a model or diagram and describe the function of the cornea, iris, lens, pupil, retina, optic nerve and ciliary muscle |
| • Describe and discuss the impact of non-biodegradable plastics on the environment |
| • Investigate the ability of oxygen to support combustion in a glowing wooden splint and a lighted candle; |
| • Examine weather charts to observe variations in atmospheric pressure and relate these to weather conditions |
| • Identify good and bad conductors of heat and compare insulating ability of different materials |

Prior to the introduction of the syllabus, a series of inservice courses for science teachers were organised by the Professional Development Service for Teachers (PDST). This is a government organisation whose task is to provide high quality continuous professional development and support for teachers at primary and post-primary schools in Ireland. The continuing professional development courses for teachers emphasised an investigative approach to science teaching with particular emphasis on the achievement of the learning outcomes specified in the syllabus. These one-day inservice courses typically took place in local Education Centres and, over a two year period, each teacher attended four of these courses. The Irish Science Teachers' Association carried out a survey of its 1000 members to ascertain the views of teachers on the effectiveness of these inservice courses and also to gauge the views of teachers on the implementation of the new science syllabus (Higgins, 2009). Teachers liked the layout of the syllabus in terms of learning outcomes as it made it very clear what was expected of the pupils in terms of the knowledge, understanding, and skills required. However, it was felt that some of the learning outcomes were over ambitious in respect of the investigative approach incorporated in the practical activities. Surprisingly, of the 310 completed questionnaires, almost 70% of teachers reported problems in implementing an enquiry-led approach to teaching practical work investigations. Whilst the learning outcomes were clearly stated, there is still considerable work to be done at inservice level in order to assist teachers to improve practice by adopting an investigative approach to carrying out laboratory practical work in the secondary school.

One of the most immediate impacts of the introduction of learning outcomes has been the positive impact of the clarity of the learning outcomes in preparing students for examinations. Teachers reported a high level of satisfaction (Higgins, 2009) with the assessment of learning outcomes on the written examination paper. In Ireland, learning outcomes are assessed by means of both a written exam paper and by means of laboratory practical work. The written examination paper accounts for 65% of marks and the assessment of laboratory practical work accounts for 35% of marks. An examination of the Junior Certificate Science examination paper clearly shows that there is good alignment between the learning outcomes specified in the syllabus and the assessment of these learning outcomes on the written examination paper (Higgins, 2009). This is one of the key cornerstones of the learning outcomes approach discussed by Biggs (2003a) in his emphasis on the need for "constructive alignment", i.e. the linking of the learning outcomes to assessment and to teaching and learning activities.

The practical work undertaken in the syllabus consists of two parts referred to as Coursework A and Coursework B. Coursework A consists of 30 mandatory experiments equally divided into physics, chemistry and biology. In the introduction to the syllabus, the National Council for Curriculum and Assessment makes clear the purpose of the experiments in Coursework A.

*"In conducting an experiment, the student follows a prescribed procedure in order to test a theory, to confirm a hypothesis or to discover something that is unknown. Experiments can help to make scientific phenomena more real to students and provide them with opportunities to develop manipulative skills and safe work practices in a school laboratory."* (NCCA, 2003, p.7)

Over the three years of the Junior Certificate Science programme, each student is required to carry out each of these mandatory experiments and maintain a laboratory notebook in which a record of these experiments is kept according to certain criteria laid down by the State Examinations Commission. This organisation is the government agency with responsibility for the examinations system in Ireland. The practical notebooks must be available for inspection by the science inspectorate of the Department of Education and this coursework is allocated 10% of the overall marks.

In addition to the mandatory experiments in Coursework A, students are also required in the third year of the programme to undertake two investigations set by the State Examinations Commission. These investigations are referred to as Coursework B and the rationale for including these investigations is clearly outlined in the introduction to the syllabus:

> *"The term investigation is used to represent an experience in which the student seeks information about a particular object, process or event in a manner that is not pre-determined in either procedure or outcome. Such experiences can enable the student to observe phenomena, select and follow a line of enquiry, or conduct simple practical tests that may stimulate thought or discussion, thus leading to a clearer understanding of the facts or underlying principles. It should involve the student in following a logical pattern of questioning and decision-making that enables evidence to be gathered in a similar way to that used by scientists.*
> *Investigations can be used to develop skills of logical thinking and problem solving, and can give the student an insight into the scientific process. Thus, the student can appreciate the importance of using a fair test in order to arrive at valid deductions and conclusions, and the significance of making and recording measurements and observations accurately."* (NCCA, 2003, p.6)

In Ireland the State Examinations Commission distributes an annual circular to schools in which the three investigations for that year are listed. The investigations are changed each year and every student must carry out two of these three investigations. (It is also possible for students to substitute an investigation of their own choice but this is not a common choice in schools.) Coursework B investigations are written up by the students in booklets supplied by the State Examinations Commission and are externally marked by the same examiner who marks the terminal written examination of that student. Coursework B is worth 25% of the overall marks and the terminal written examination of two hours duration is worth 65% of the overall marks. As already mentioned, Coursework A is worth 10% of the overall marks and these marks are assigned by the pupils own science teacher. Some examples of investigations assigned to date by the State Examinations Commissions are listed in Table 6.

*Table 6: Some Examples of Coursework B Investigations Assigned by State Examinations Commission*

---

*Biology*
- A gardener suggests that the length of time taken for marrowfat peas to germinate is decreased if they are soaked in water in advance. Carry out a quantitative investigation of this suggestion.
- Carry out a quantitative survey of the plant species in a local habitat.
- Florists often supply a sachet of flower food/preservative with bunches of cut flowers. Carry out an investigation to compare the effectiveness of using a commercially supplied flower food/preservative with two other household substances as additives to prolong the life of cut flowers in a container of water.

*Chemistry*
- Investigate a range of plant pigments to evaluate their effectiveness as acid-base indicators.
- Investigate how the concentration of a hydrogen peroxide solution affects the speed at which it decomposes to produce oxygen gas.
- Compare by way of investigation the abilities of different indigestion remedies to neutralise excess stomach acid.

*Physics*
- Investigate the relationship between the temperature of a rubber squash ball and the height to which it bounces.
- Carry out an investigation of the relationship between the length of a metallic conductor (e.g., nichrome wire) and its resistance.
- Clothes made from certain fabrics, e.g., denim, are not suitable for hill walking or mountain climbing. Carry out an investigation to compare the thermal insulating properties of three different fabrics when they are dry and when they are wet. Denim must be included as one of the three fabrics.

---

In general, it is clear that the State Examinations Commission appear to be in agreement with the commonly used definition of an investigation, i.e. "a task for which the pupil cannot immediately see an answer or recall a routine method for finding it" (Gott & Duggan, 1995). It is also clear that the investigations set by the State Examinations Commission to date are a good mixture of the traditional variable-based type of investigation and the more exploratory type investigation

# 7 Introducing Learning Outcomes into Teacher-Training Programmes for Science Teachers

In 2005 learning outcomes were introduced into the teacher-training programmes for science teachers in University College Cork. This was carried out in response to the overall implementation of the Bologna Process in the university system in Ireland and also in response to the introduction of leaning outcomes into the curricula of secondary schools. An example of the type of work involved for one module of the Bachelor of Science Education programme in University College Cork is given in Table 7.

The level of detail shown in Table 6 is not required of staff when describing modules in the author's university but it has been found helpful by the author to set up such a table when designing or revising modules.

*Table 7: Linking Learning Outcomes, Teaching and Learning Activities and Assessment for Module ED2100 of BSc(Ed) Programme*

| Learning Outcomes | Teaching and Learning Activities | Assessment 10 credit module Mark = 200 |
|---|---|---|
| Cognitive<br>• Recognise and apply the basic principles of classroom management and discipline.<br>• Identify the key characteristics of high quality science teaching.<br>• Develop a comprehensive portfolio of lesson plans. | Lectures (12)<br><br>Tutorials (6)<br><br>Observation of classes (6) of experienced science teacher (mentor) | End of module exam.<br><br>Portfolio of lesson plans<br><br><br><br><br>**(100 marks)** |
| Affective<br>• Display a willingness to co-operate with members of teaching staff in their assigned school.<br>• Participate successfully in Peer Assisted Learning project. | Participation in mentoring feedback sessions in school (4)<br><br>Participation in 3 sessions of UCC Peer Assisted Learning (PAL) Programme.<br><br>Peer group presentation | Report from school mentor<br><br><br>End of project report.<br><br><br><br>**(50 marks)** |
| Psychomotor<br>• Demonstrate good classroom presentation skills<br>• Perform laboratory practical work in a safe and efficient manner. | Teaching practice<br>6 weeks @ 2 hours per week.<br><br>Laboratory work | Supervision of Teaching practice<br><br>Assessment of teaching skills<br><br>**(50 marks)** |

In addition to giving the detailed information shown in Table 7 to the student teachers, each student teacher is required to incorporate the learning outcomes for each lesson into the planning of each lesson. In the past, students simply listed the objectives of the lesson in their written lesson plan. An extract showing the aims, objectives and learning outcomes from one lesson plan is shown in Table 8.

*Table 8: Sample Extract from a Student's Lesson Plan*

---

**Objective:** The objective of this lesson is to give pupils an understanding of how sound waves are transmitted.

**Learning Outcomes**
At the end of this lesson students should be able to:
- Recognise that a wave carries energy from one place to another.
- Identify the different parts within a wave
- Associate the parts of a wave in a diagram to the compression and rarefaction of molecules in an actual physical wave.
- Explain why mechanical waves need a medium.
- Recognise that sound is a form of energy that causes the particles in a medium to vibrate.
- Explain how the amplitude of a sound wave determines the loudness of the sound.
- Distinguish between high frequency and low frequency sounds.

---

Whilst it is still too soon to draw definitive conclusions on the effect of introducing learning outcomes into the teacher-training programme for science teachers at UCC, a number of key points are emerging from reports of supervisors of teaching practice supervisors and the analysis of items such as student-feedback forms, students' portfolios, students' teaching practice files and examination results. These key points may be summarised as follows:

- Teaching practice supervisors find an improvement in the classroom performance of the student teachers with lessons more focused on the important outcomes as outlined by the student teachers in the lesson plans.

- In their written and oral reports the teaching practice supervisors comment on the fact there is enhanced preparation apparent in the students' lesson plans with students putting a lot of effort into selecting the appropriate teaching strategies matched to the intended learning outcomes.

- Student like the clarity of the learning outcomes given to them for each module of their programme. They feel that the transparency of the learning outcomes gives them direction and help them to understand what the they are expected to achieve in the module.

- Students liked the highlighting of the linking of the learning outcomes to the teaching and learning activities and to the assessment planned for them.

- In their reflective portfolios and lesson plan reflections, students have frequently commented on the fact that being required to write down the learning outcomes for each lesson prepared by them, helps them to focus on what they want to achieve in the lesson. This, in turn, helps them in assessing the lesson when reflecting on the lesson after they have taught it.

The above findings are consistent with some of the advantages of learning outcomes as discussed in the literature by Harden (2002) and Jenkins and Unwin (2001).

# 8   Some Concluding Points

International trends in education show a move away from the sole emphasis on a "teacher-centred" approach to a more "outcome-based" approach to education. This movement has gained increased momentum from the Bologna Process with its emphasis on student-centred learning and the need to have more precision and clarity in the design and content of programmes in our universities. This, in turn, is also affecting the design of science curricula in our schools which is reflected in our teacher training programmes for science teachers. From one perspective, learning outcomes can be considered as a sort of "common currency" that helps us to understand curricula at local, national and international levels.

In Ireland, the response from teachers suggests that the adoption of a learning outcomes approach has been successful in terms of the alignment of the learning outcomes to the assessment carried out by the written examination paper. However, problems have been encountered in linking the learning outcomes of practical work investigations to practice in the classroom, i.e. empowering teachers to adopt an inquiry-based approach to teaching practical work. The solution to this problem involves a more long term strategy of continuing professional development for teachers.

The requirement to make the teaching and learning process more transparent and more explicit presents a challenge to all of us involved in science education. In the short term, those of us teaching in Europe must prepare for the immediate challenge of expressing our teacher training programmes in terms of learning outcomes. In the longer term, the adoption of the learning outcomes approach has the potential to help us to embrace a more systematic approach to the design of teacher training programmes also to prepare our student teachers for the challenges of teaching science to their pupils.

## References

Adam, S. (2004). *Using Learning Outcomes: A Consideration of the Nature, Role, Application and Implications for European Education of Employing Learning Outcomes at the Local, National and International Levels.* Report on United Kingdom Bologna Seminar, July 2004, Herriot-Watt University.

Anderson, L.W. & Krathwohl, D. (Eds.) (2001). *A Taxonomy for Learning, Teaching and Assessing: A Revision of Bloom's Taxonomy of Educational Objectives.* New York: Longman.

Berlin Communiqué (2003). Available online at: http://www.bologna.ie/_fileupload/publications/BerlinCommunique.pdf

Biggs, J. (2003a). *Teaching for Quality Learning at University.* Buckingham: Open University Press.

Biggs J. (2003b). Aligning teaching and assessing to course objectives. *Teaching and Learning in Higher Education: New Trends and Innovations.* University of Aveiro, 13–17 April 2003.

Bloom, B. S., Engelhart, M. D., Furst, E.J, Hill, W. & Krathwohl, D. (1956). *Taxonomy of Educational Objectives. Volume I: The cognitive domain.* New York: McKay.

Boon, J. & van der Klink, M. (2002). *Competencies: The Triumph of a Fuzzy Concept.* Academy of Human Resource Development Annual Conference, Honolulu, HA, 27 Feb – 3 March, Proceedings Vol. 1, 327-334.

ECTS Users' Guide (2005). Brussels: Directorate-General for Education and Culture. Available online at: http://ec.europa.eu/education/programmes/socrates/ects/doc/guide_en.pdf

ECTS Users' Guide (2009). Brussels: Directorate-General for Education and Culture. Available online at: http://ec.europa.eu/education/lifelong-learning-policy/doc/ects/guide_en.pdf

Gosling, D. & Moon, J. (2001). *How to Use Learning Outcomes and Assessment Criteria.* London: SEEC Office.

Gott, R. & Duggan, S. (1995). *Investigative Work in the Science Curriculum.* Buckingham: Open University Press.

Harden, R. M. (2002a). *Developments in Outcome-Based Education.* Medical Teacher, 24(2), 117-120.

Higgins, Y. (2009). ISTA Questionnaire on Junior Certificate Science. *Science* 45(1), 17-19.

Jenkins, A. & Unwin, D. (2001). *How to Write Learning Outcomes*. Available online at: www.ncgia.ucsb.edu/education/curricula/giscc/units/format/outcomes.html

Kennedy, D., Hyland, A., & Ryan, N. (2006). Writing and using Learning Outcomes. *Bologna Handbook, Implementing Bologna in your Institution*, C3.4-1, 1-30.

Kennedy, D. (2007) *Writing and Using Learning Outcomes: A Practical Guide.*University College Cork: Quality Promotion Unit. (Available from www.NAIRTL.ie)

Moon, J. (2002). *The Module and Programme Development Handbook*. London: Kogan Page Limited.

Morss, K. & Murray, R. (2005). *Teaching at University.* London: Sage Publications

NCCA (2003). *Junior Certificate Science Syllabus*. Dublin: The Stationery Office. Available online at: http://jcscience.slss.ie/syllabus.html

Ramsden, P. (2003). *Learning to Teach in Higher Education*. London: Routledge.

Rauhvargers, A. et al., (2009) *Bologna Process Stocktaking Report*. Brussles: EU Education and Culture, Brussels. Available online at: http://www.ond.vlaanderen.be/hogeronderwijs/bologna/conference/documents/Stocktaking_report_2009_FINAL.pdf

Toohey, S. (1999). *Designing Courses for Higher Education*. Buckingham: SRHE and OU Press.

Winterton, J., Delamare-Le Deist, F., & Stringfellow, E. (2005). Typology of Knowledge, Skills and Competences: Clarification of the Concept and Prototype. CEDEFORP: Toulouse. Available online at: http://www.ecotec.com/europeaninventory/publications/method/CEDEFOP_typology.pdf

# Chapter 6

## Assessing Professional Competences and their Development in Vocational Education in Germany – State of Research and Perspectives

*Reinhold Nickolaus, Andreas Lazar & Kerstin Norwig*
University of Stuttgart, Institute of Educational Science and Psychology,
Department of Vocational Education, Germany

## 1 Point of Departure for Current Research Activities

In the second half of the last decade, the assessment of professional competences in vocational education received increased attention in Germany for various reasons: 1) the incipient reception of IRT-based statistical methods in educational science in the context of international comparative studies has reached vocational and business education by now. IRT-based competence models for (in total seventeen) professions from the fields of business and administration, health and hygiene and industrial-technical training were presented for the first time in the extensive ULME studies (Lehmann & Seeber, 2007). These models are applied to professional knowledge at the end of vocational education and training (VET) and were mainly unidimensional. Nevertheless, they have to be understood as first important steps of currently ongoing research activities aiming at the assessment of professional competences in vocational education. 2) Based on political initiatives first steps were taken to explore whether international comparative studies are feasible in the vocational field. Here the focus was, on the one hand, on general feasibility studies (Baethge et al., 2006; Baethge & Arends, 2009a, 2009b); and, on the other hand, on preliminary studies for the valid assessment of vocational competences (Abele et al., 2009; Gschwendtner, Abele, & Nickolaus 2009; Nickolaus, Gschwendtner, & Abele 2009; Winther & Achtenhagen, 2009). The main aim of the latter was to analyse whether computer simulations of work processes and systems provide valid data for competence assessments. These studies were of special interest not only because the requirements for validity are especially high in the field of vocational education, but also because the performance shown in professional practice was used as the validity criterion. 3) Stimuli were sent out by the debates in the run-up to the DFG (Deutsche Forschungsgemeinschaft, German Research Foundation) priority programme "Competence Models for Assessing Individual Learning Outcomes and Evaluating Educational Processes"[1]. Two projects from the field of vocational and business education are currently located within this program. 4) Various calls for proposals issued by the BMBF (Bundesministerium für Bildung und Forschung, Federal Ministry for Education and Research) have been and are being used to place pertinent project proposals. This applies to the BMBF programme "Hochschulforschung als Beitrag zur Professionalisierung der Hochschullehre – Zukunftswerkstatt Hochschullehre" (Higher Education Research as a Contribution to the Professionalisation of Higher Education – Higher Education as a Workshop for the Future) which deals with the question of how to model and measure teacher competences, for example. It also applies to the BMBF programme "Kompetenzmodellierung und Kompetenzmessung im Hochschulsektor" ("Modeling and Measurement of Competencies in Higher Education"), in which competence models and/or instruments for measuring competences are to be developed for eight different study subjects or fields. On top of that, the BMBF has called for proposals to model and measure competences in the area of "Bildung für eine nachhaltige Entwicklung (BNE)" ("Education for sustainable development (ESD)"). This call is also open for pertinent proposals from the field of vocational education. 5) European activities for the mutual recognition of certificates triggered many projects seeking to generate "practical" methods to measure and assess "professional competences". And 6) vocational qualification levels are to be included in the framework of NEPS ("National Educational Panel Study").

The common goal of all these activities is to provide instruments for assessing the outputs of educational programmes. They are required for comparisons but also for generating explanatory models and evaluating individual educational programmes. The lack of reliable instruments for the assessment of professional competences has been a substantial obstacle for both educational and evaluation research in the vocational field for a long time. Providing sustainable competence models and reliable and valid measuring instruments is made more difficult by the variety of professions and their dynamic developments, which require considerable efforts and constant updates. In the face of these problems, a possible alternative might be to develop competence models across the different professions instead of doing so within the individual professions. Such an attempt has been made in the field of engineering education in Australia (Coates & Radloff, 2008), for example. However, this does not seem to be very promising: recent findings (Abele et al., 2011) show that there are only moderate correlations between subject-specific and interdisciplinary problem-solving dispositions.

---

1  http://kompetenzmodelle.dipf.de/en?set_language=en

# 2 State of Research

Due to the various advantages of IRT-based competence assessments, current research efforts mainly focus on this approach.

## 2.1 Structural Modelling

The theoretical modelling underlying the assessment of professional competences is discussed controversially within the discipline. On the one hand, rather holistic approaches to "professional action competence" are favoured; on the other hand, the modelling process is restricted by practical limitations. In educational practice, it was the establishment of the concept of "action learning" (Handlungsorientierung) in the mid-1990s that paved the way for the construct of professional action competence (Sekretariat 2000), which came into frequent use at about the same time. This was concurrent with a greater emphasis on those dispositions that were assumed to be needed for keeping orientation in constantly changing environments and for being actively involved in their shaping (Seeber & Nickolaus, 2010, p. 249). Following the ideas of Heinrich Roth, who already made a distinction between professional, personal and social competence in the early 1970s, the construct of professional action competence was further differentiated. Currently the differentiation made by the Conference of the Ministers of Education (Sekretariat 2000) is especially popular. They distinguished professional, personal, and social competence and subsumed both performance-relevant cognitive dispositions and the willingness to apply these dispositions appropriately under these subdimensions (ibid.). Further differentiations were made, for instance, by Baethge et al. (2006) who, in reference to Reetz (1999), presented methodical competence as a separate competence dimension. These models are hypothetical but appear plausible, at least initially. Yet, studies on structural modelling at first did not attempt to research whether these differentiations can be confirmed empirically. The focus was rather on exploring whether further differentiations can be made within the aforementioned subdimensions. As a beginning, this question was easier to answer. On top of that, analysing the subdimensions and the measuring instruments that were developed in this context certainly is a precondition for research on the interplay between the different competence dimensions on a higher level. As to professional competence, to which we will limit ourselves hereafter, first analyses have confirmed two subdimensions across domains: a) professional knowledge and b) the ability to use this knowledge in different problem situations (Geißel, 2008; Gschwendtner, 2008, 2011; Gschwendtner, Abele, & Nickolaus, 2009; Nickolaus, Gschwendtner, & Geißel, 2008; Seeber & Nickolaus, 2010; Winther, 2010; Winther & Achtenhagen, 2009). Besides these, a separate subdimension for manual skills is assumed, especially in the field of industrial-technical training

(Nickolaus, Gschwendtner, & Abele, 2011), but no more recent studies are available yet[2]. What seems noteworthy about the previous findings and is quite known from other domains (Kintsch, 1998) is that procedural knowledge, i.e. profession-specific methodical knowledge, has not been confirmed empirically as a separate competence dimension (Geißel, 2008; Nickolaus, Gschwendtner, & Geißel, 2008). However, this might be due to the operationalisation of procedural knowledge which in the professional context always includes declarative knowledge components.

While the differentiation of professional competence into professional knowledge and the ability to apply this knowledge seems to be identifiable during the entire period of VET, both differentiation and fusion processes occur within these dimensions during VET. So far, such differentiation processes have been documented for professional knowledge in the professions of car mechatronics technicians and electrical/electronics technicians for energy and building technology (Geißel, 2008; Gschwendtner, 2008, 2011; Nickolaus et al., 2011). Curriculum-based learning processes seem to support these differentiation processes (Gschwendtner, 2011). Whether the differentiations of professional competence correspond with analogous differentiations of the application of knowledge is an unresolved, but in many ways important question for the assessment of competences. From a practical perspective, such differentiations are important insofar as the competence of individuals within the different subdimensions can vary considerably. Therefore, test versions giving specific weightings to test items in certain subdimensions can lead to false estimations of competence characteristics. From the perspective of measurement, multidimensionality is accompanied by reliability problems, as reliable competence estimates require a certain number of items. As more complex items (e.g., items requiring the application of knowledge) require a substantially longer test time[3], multidimensionality leads to conflicts between validity and reliability requirements which can only be resolved by a major extension of test time for all relevant subdimensions. So far, the multidimensional models of professional knowledge available in the field of industrial-technical training contain three (electrical/electronics technicians for energy and building technology) and five subdimensions (car mechatronics technicians) at the end of VET (Gschwendtner, 2011; Nickolaus et al., 2011), while in both professions unidimensional models show a better model fit for the end of the first year of training (Geißel, 2008; Gschwendtner, 2008; Nickolaus, Gschwendtner, & Geißel, 2008). In this context it is of central interest whether structural similarities can be

---

2   Teaching and assessing manual skills has been neglected in recent decades. This was probably because it was assumed that manual skills would become progressively unimportant for professional practice, a statement which in this generality is certainly not justifiable.
3   In order to gain reliable data on professional problem-solving abilities of car mechatronics technicians almost three hours of test time were needed in which the apprentices were working on complex and realistic tasks related to troubleshooting. The situation is very similar regarding electrical/electronics technicians, although constructive items have to be added for validity reasons here.

identified which provide insight into the causes of this differentiation process. If we include the field of business and administration, the following picture emerges:

| | Empirically confirmed subdimensions of professional competence at the end of vocational education and training | | |
|---|---|---|---|
| Electrical/ Electronics technicians for energy and building technology (Nickolaus et al., 2011) | Professional knowledge ←——→ Subject-specific problem-solving abilities<br>Traditional electro-technical installations    Electrotechnical basics    Control engineering/ modern electrotechnical installations | | |
| Car mechatronics technicians (Gschwendtner, 2011) | Professional knowledge ←——→ Subject-specific problem-solving abilities<br>Service    Engine    Engine management/ lighting    Transmission    Chassis | | |
| Industrial clerks (Winther & Achtenhagen, 2010; Winther & Achtenhagen 2009)* | Action-based competence ←——→ Comprehension-based competence<br>Value creation processes    Operational control processes | | |
| Office clerks (Seeber, 2008)** | Professional competence (Knowledge)<br>Accounting    Economics/ Business administration/ Law | | |
| Bank clerks (Rosendahl & Straka, 2011) | Professional competence<br>General economic competence    Banking competence<br>*or alternatively:*<br>5-dimensional following case situations | | |

\* In addition, Winther & Achtenhagen show economic literacy and economic numeracy as separate dimensions of profession-specific prior knowledge.
\*\* At the same time, Seeber presents indicators for further differentiation potentials within the subdimensions shown here, but the four-dimensional model has been discarded until now because of unsatisfying subtest reliabilities.

*Figure 1: Empirically Confirmed Subdimensions of Professional Competence at the End of VET*

What is striking about these structures is that in all studies the differentiations of subdimensions occur in relation to areas of activity, case situations or disciplines, with the latter dominating and at the same time showing close links to corresponding segments of activity. Differentiations are documented both for the subdimension of professional knowledge (electrical/electronics technicians, car mechatronics technicians, clerks) and for the application of knowledge (action-based competence – industrial clerks). In those cases in which the differentiations only relate to professional knowledge, it remains open whether the corresponding subdimensions can be empirically confirmed in respect to knowledge application, and vice versa. For instance, further studies are needed to check whether the professional problem-solving abilities of electrical/electronics technicians for energy and building technology – which so far have been modelled unidimensionally with regard to knowledge application – can be differentiated in a similar way than was shown for professional knowledge. So far we have exclusively used analytic types of items (troubleshooting) to operationalise the professional problem-solving abilities in our studies. The items were taken both from the field of traditional electrotechnical installations (e.g., troubleshooting an AC circuit) and control engineering (e.g., star delta reversing contactor circuit). However, dimensionality checks at this level require higher numbers of items when taking into account all identified knowledge dimensions and including both analytical and constructive items. Regarding the two industrial-technical professions two subdimensions become apparent that represent routine activities in the respective professions: traditional electrotechnical installations (electrical/electronics technicians) and service (car mechatronics technicians). In the case of electrical/electronics technicians, this subdimension is also remarkable because of its low correlation with the other two (rather cognition-based) subdimensions [4], a fact which can also be seen in the parameters of the structural equation model (Fig. 2).

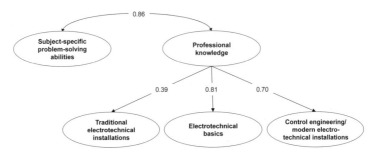

N = 382, X² = 226, df = 182, X²/df = 1.30, p = .01, CFI = .95, TLI = .96, RMSEA = .03

*Figure 2: The Relationship between Professional Knowledge and Professional Problem-Solving Abilities*

It might be possible that this is because traditional electrotechnical installations are mostly routine activities. Similar patterns, i.e. quite weak correlations between cognition-based performances and skill-based performances are also found when putting theoretical and practical exam performances in relation to each other (Abele, 2011).

---

4   0.24 (latent) with control engineering, 0.33 with electrotechnical basics.

In theory this can be explained by findings on skill acquisition, according to which cognitive abilities are primarily important in an early phase of acquisition while rather low correlations between performance and cognitive abilities appear in the automation phase at the latest (Ackerman, 1992). These findings are significant for further works on competence modelling: Despite the dynamics in the development of the respective qualification requirements, it can be assumed that the development of routines is important for many professional activities at a medium level of qualification. It should be checked whether performance continues to be substantially explained by the variance of cognitive abilities or whether willingness to give effort becomes the central predictor. It seems plausible that some competence aspects do not appear critical for performance in all areas of professional activity; this can also be confirmed empirically, e.g., concerning the troubleshooting abilities of car mechatronics technicians (Gschwendtner, Abele, & Nickolaus, 2009). Manual skills, for example, apparently do not explain any variance of cognition-based and very challenging activities such as troubleshooting.[5] However, these findings might also be a result of the limited variance of manual skills that were needed for the tasks and might additionally depend on the fact that almost all trainees have already reached the required skill level during their training.

Given the problems outlined above to simultaneously satisfy validity and reliability requirements within a limited test time, it seems appropriate, from a research strategic perspective, to systematically examine which activity segments allow the estimation of competence by only assessing some selected competence aspects.

Changing the perspective, the same phenomenon gives occasion to reflect upon the extent to which the existing competence models depend on test and item layouts. In the current state of research, certain basic structures appear across domains, but we are still far from being able to estimate the influence of specific test forms on modelling results. In order to do so, further validation studies are needed. Because of their complexity these studies will be restricted to parts of constructs, and have to follow a systematic structure in order to be able to relate them to each other.

---

5    It seems self-evident that routines can also develop in contexts like troubleshooting. However, these routines in troubleshooting often relate to the use of expert systems which are only of limited help when facing more complex problem situations.

## 2.2 Proficiency Scaling

Proficiency Scaling is used to analyse characteristics and distributions of ability levels (Hartig & Klieme, 2006). In vocational education research, two approaches are mainly used: the definition of critical thresholds following Beaton & Allen (1992) and the diagnosis of characteristics relevant for item difficulty using regression analytic methods following Hartig (2007). While Lehmann & Seeber (2007) in the ULME studies and Rosendahl & Straka (2011) worked with the method proposed by Beaton & Allen, Winther (2010), Winther & Achtenhagen (2009), Gschwendtner (2008) and Geißel (2008) used the method proposed by Hartig. This method is somewhat more demanding as it requires theoretical considerations on task characteristics that might be relevant for item difficulty. Ideally, this should already happen during test development, a fact which can not, or only partly, be assumed for the findings published until now. In most cases, estimates of the characteristics relevant for item difficulty were performed post hoc. Only recently attempts were made to systematically vary the characteristics influencing item difficulty during test development, albeit in a limited way. These restrictions not only occur because of the limitations regarding the number of test items, but also because our knowledge about the characteristics that potentially define difficulty is still quite limited, too. For instance, requirements of cognitive modelling appear to be relevant for item difficulty across domains and also beyond vocational education (Geißel, 2008; Gschwendtner, 2008; Nickolaus, Gschwendtner &, Geißel, 2008; Winther & Achtenhagen, 2009). Based on cognitive psychological reflections, some levels of Bloom's taxonomy were shown to be relevant for item difficulty across domains as well. On top of that, the degree of complexity has been confirmed empirically as being relevant for difficulty (although with different indicators). Operationalisations of complexity are the number of relevant elements and their linking (Gschwendtner, 2008), for example. In addition, there are numerous indications that other task characteristics are relevant for item difficulty: the degree of familiarity of a task or its curricular weighting (Geißel, 2008; Gschwendtner, 2008, 2011; Haolader, 2010), the number of solution steps, conceptual and procedural knowledge or mathematic requirements (Seeber, 2008; Nickolaus & Ziegler, 2005). In more recent works the item format turned out to be relevant for its difficulty as well. According to the findings, the presentation of images in addition to a textual representation can facilitate understanding of an item and increase the rate of correct solutions (Sass, 2010), or even decrease it, for example (e.g., Artelt et al., 2005). Apparently the fit between text and image information is important here.

This short overview of the present state of research illustrates the multitude of open questions that arise in this context. For example, it remains open whether the findings will be supported if item characteristics are systematically varied beforehand. Positioning effects and the influence of item formats also require further research in the field of vocational education. The latter seems especially interesting when taking into account validity aspects. Both the theoretical modelling of item difficulties and the systematic variation of the numerous characteristics that potentially define item difficulty pose a challenge for the research process, as they require quite high numbers of items and an extensive sample size. In the field of vocational education, a systematic variation of task characteristics is comparably more difficult because of the validity requirement which still has to be fulfilled. The problem is that the systematic variation of item characteristics sometimes reduces their authenticity. Despite the problems indicated here, currently on-going research activities give rise to the expectation that the state of knowledge can be successively broadened. Special interest might be directed at those characteristics related to item difficulty that were identified across domains as they point to similarities in the structure of cognitive processing.

## 2.3 Development Models

So far, no elaborate development models for professional competences exist. Against this background, the discussions in this section are intended as approximations which are based on the existing findings and try to bring the different approaches in relation to each other.

Statements that are based on empirical findings can, on the one hand, be made about relevant predictors (e.g., Lehmann & Seeber, 2007; Nickolaus et al., 2010, 2011; Seeber & Lehmann, 2011) and, on the other hand, about merging processes and differentiations within competence structures during VET (e.g., Gschwendtner, 2011; Nickolaus, Abele, & Gschwendtner, 2011; Rosendahl & Straka, 2011). On top of that, first longitudinal analyses show that not only progressive developments can occur during education, but that regression is also to be expected (Nickolaus & Ziegler, 2005; Rosendahl & Straka, 2011). Besides referring to studies on professional competence (development), basics of learning theories should also be considered in order to take further steps towards a broader knowledge about the development of professional competence.

*First Approximation*
Cognitive dispositions are central predictors of professional competence development, with particular significance attached to subject-specific prior knowledge, basic competences (mathematics, reading) and IQ (Geißel, 2007; Lehmann & Seeber, 2007; Nickolaus, Gschwendtner, & Geißel, 2008; Nickolaus et al., 2010). Aspects related to the quality of teaching and learning processes and motivational influences are also integrated into the explanatory models, but with considerably lower weightings (e.g., Nickolaus et al., 2010). Differential effects of teaching methods, if they can

be detected at all, remain modest in most cases as well (for an overview see Seifried & Sembill, 2010; Nickolaus, 2011). However, significant performance variances can be found within the respective teaching methods. So far, curricular foci and learning opportunities in the work process have been completely underestimated. According to analyses by Gschwendtner (2011) and Haolader (2010), (differing) curricular foci have a far-reaching impact on competence development. Gschwendtner shows that curricular foci also become relevant for emerging competence structures (ibid.) Even though professional knowledge is the main predictor of professional problem-solving abilities, significant proportions of variance are not explained. Other (more general) ability constructs like IQ and "general" or dynamic problem-solving abilities in the sense of Greiff & Funke (2009) also correlate positively, as can be expected (Abele et al., 2011), but considerably less. This demonstrates that (1) the knowledge required to cope with professional demands is of central importance for the actual problem-solving performance and that (2) problem-solving performance shares a great proportion of variance with general cognitive abilities. Even though professional knowledge and the ability to apply this knowledge in varying problem situations can, as shown above, be modelled as empirically independent competence dimensions across domains, they can also be interpreted from a developmental perspective as is already implied in Bloom's learning taxonomy. The central question is which additional competence aspects must be developed so the knowledge can really be applied.

*Second Approximation*
To answer this question, findings on skill acquisition could be helpful which suggest that three phases of skill acquisition can be distinguished (Ackerman, 1992): a) the cognitive phase, b) the associative phase and c) the automated phase. The cognitive phase is characterised by requirements with a high cognitive load such as the development of a thorough understanding for a task and the acquisition of knowledge, strategies and procedures that are necessary for its accomplishment. It is emphasised that consistent requirements are initially very helpful for this acquisition process (ibid., p. 599). This reduces complexity which is only increased in the later phases of skill acquisition. The associative stage is characterised by an increasing familiarity with requirements and task contexts. (Partial) performances are provided faster and with fewer errors. The individual perception of the task context becomes especially important for the quality of performance here. In the automation phase many activities are routine and can be accomplished with relatively low attention when the complexity of the requirements is low. Besides, the cognitive processes are automated, and psychomotoric abilities become dominant factors for manual performance.

The characteristics of the different phases correspond (partially) to the requirements characterising the different competence levels that have been identified up to now. Geißel (in the field of electrical/electronics technicians) and Gschwendtner (in the field of car mechatronics technicians), for example, include the familiarity and the complexity of the task context in their empirically based description of characteristics relevant for item difficulty. The higher the complexity, the lower is the probability of a correct solution, or the higher the competence level needs to be. The more familiar the requirement situation, the more likely it is that successful stimulus-response patterns are available. If the familiarity is higher (phase II), it might be expected that even more complex tasks can be mastered.

The parallels between the item characteristics identified in the scaling approaches and the characteristics of the skill acquisition phases might indicate that the process of cognitive and manual skill acquisition is influenced by similar factors as the process of acquiring professional knowledge or professional cognitive skills. When drawing a distinction between cognitive and manual skills, it can be assumed that cognitive skill acquisition is structurally similar to knowledge acquisition. As to manual skill acquisition, manual abilities and the individual potential for their development become additionally important. The relevance of general cognitive abilities like IQ for knowledge acquisition and a successful performance of professional problem solving is beyond doubt. Opposite to familiar requirements, which usually relate to skills that have already been developed, the aforementioned general cognitive abilities remain as or become even more important on higher performance levels in rather ill-structured situations such as problem solving. Against this background and following the model of Ackerman, it seems helpful to consider the possibility of relating varying requirements and competences for the assessment of competence developments. According to the model of Ackerman, the familiarity of a requirement is of central importance for the skills and efforts that an individual mobilises to accomplish the task. The more familiar the task, the higher the probability that more or less ingrained behaviour patterns are at least partially available and can be updated without a high level of cognitive load. If the complexity of a requirement increases because an increased number of elements needs to be considered, or because of a higher level of interconnection, or because of linear/nonlinear, continuous/discontinuous interactions between elements, for example, the number of degrees of freedom within the system (representing the respective requirement) increases at the same time. This, as a result, leads to a reduction/extension of the "predictability" (and familiarity) of the system. While the required level of cognitive skills rises when task complexity is increased, it can drop substantially in clearly defined contexts when the degree of familiarity rises. As this means that depending on the degree of familiarity (and the task complexity) different skills are used or have to be used in order to accomplish a task, the interpretation of performances as expressions of specific competence levels is not a trivial problem. Thus, it is conceivable that the same item can be solved by an individual who is familiar with the task, i.e. an individual that in respect to this requirement is in the third phase of skill acquisition and can draw on ingrained behaviour patterns, and by "novices" who still are in the first phase and therefore have to draw on "creative" and sometimes different solution patterns. In other words: solving the items alone does not provide reliable data about a person's position on the competence scale. On top of that, item characteristics are not sufficient to describe item difficulty, contrary to the assumption made in Hartig's model. The interaction between person and item is also relevant (cf. Alderson, 2000). If the level of competence can be described by the interaction between persons and items, it should be possible to describe competence development by the development of these interactions. As it seems unlikely that there is a possibility to document these interaction processes in assessments or in their longitudinal development with sufficient precision, the question arises to which extent it is possible to obtain (limited) information about competence development processes based on item solutions. Apart from the solution given, solution speed and, optionally, the quality of performance seem to be suitable indicators in situations that are related to typical professional activities and are characterised by a lower or higher degree of familiarity. Even if VET is taken as a phase of continuous knowledge development and competence acquisition, the consolidation of relevant knowledge and the development of necessary skills is intended and also expected to take place. In this context, it is of interest to know which phase of skill acquisition the test persons have reached. Metrological approaches to this question might focus on the speed and quality of solutions while varying the requirements, but probably only extensive qualitative analyses can provide deeper insight into the interaction between person and item. More accurate knowledge of the relationship between quantitative and qualitative data collected in this field would be desirable. As far as we know, such studies are still outstanding in the vocational field.

*Third Approximation*
The metrological assessment of competence developments requires suitable item layouts, i.e. sensitive items. As already indicated at the outset, not only progressive developments but also stagnation and regression can be expected. Regarding complex item layouts, it becomes apparent that a reliable assessment of competence developments on the basis of global indicators like "solved/unsolved" is impossible. In order to succeed, finer assessment systems are needed that are better able to reveal the quality of interaction between person and item. Another problem related to item sensitivity arises from one of the basic functions of VET, namely to initiate and support the development of relevant knowledge and skills for the respective profession. Consequently, completely new areas of (professional) knowledge may be addressed during education and training. It is rather difficult to create adequate items for such knowledge areas which can be used for testing at an early stage of education and competence development. One could also argue in this context that competence development in VET is linked to the development of specialised knowledge and skills. It seems futile to test the relevant professional knowledge before the corresponding teaching and learning processes or professional activities have taken place. This raises the question, which time span between tests is appropriate to assess compe-

tence developments. From a developmental perspective it seems to be of particular interest how knowledge which has been acquired in educational teaching and learning processes continues to develop under the impact of professional work.

Progressions of professional competences are probably only to be expected if the professional working environment (or other contexts) supports deeper reflections of knowledge. Regressions could be interpreted as a result of the fact that the relevant knowledge or competence facets have no or only little importance in the working environment. Stagnation would imply that the respective knowledge bears some importance but that there might be no need for any deeper reflections.

From a perspective of item sensitivity, it also seems relevant whether developments occur continuously or in jumps. When a discontinuous progress is assumed, the question of sensitivity could be reduced to identifying and representing the relevant development levels. When assuming a continuous progress, much more precise instruments might be needed. There are quite elaborate competence models such as the model of moral judgment, for example, where different competence levels are described that can be distinguished qualitatively by a number of indicators. However, contrary to Kohlberg's initial assumptions, these levels are by no means suitable to place an individual on the competence scale without regarding a specific situation.

In fact, it seems common that interactions between person and item vary according to the situation (Beck et al., 1996, 1998). Such inconsistencies could be interpreted as an expression of a yet unfinished development process towards a higher level. The hypothesis that such inconsistencies are reflecting situation- and group-specific differentiations is also plausible and empirically sustainable[6]. While the second interpretation can be brought in line with concepts of discontinuous development processes, the first interpretation could throw this assumption partially into doubt, as the transition phenomenon points to continuous developments. By drawing analogies to developments in natural systems, Minnameier (2005) argues for the hypothesis that understanding processes could also be described with the concept of discontinuous progress. He states that once the existing cognitive structure is unable to adequately reconstruct a given principle, it becomes necessary that the cognitive structure changes into the state of a higher order so as not to lose the ability of adapting (ibid., p. 71) or of being able to meet the respective challenge. Minnameier supports his assumption by pointing to analogous processes in the field of thermodynamics. However, what remains unconsidered is that nature provides a wide range of examples for continuous processes which could just as well be used to create analogies.

---

6   For more information on the discourse about this problem see papers by Beck (2003), Lempert (2003) and Zabeck (2002).

Doubts about Minnameier's hypothesis mainly arise when including knowledge acquisition into the considerations. Knowledge acquisition can be also described as taking place in small steps, i.e. as a process of assimilation. Concerning test design the question arises which "step sizes" are appropriate for a description of developments. It seems that this question can only be answered when having a more elaborate knowledge about development processes and their conditions and when taking into account aspects of the specific situations and the interaction between person and context.

## 3 Problems Concerning Reliability and Validity and Current Development Perspectives

As shown in section 2.1, recent research findings indicate that the competence structures of professional competence are multidimensional. Therefore, a valid assessment of competence levels requires test versions that provide reliable estimates in the different subdimensions. So far, it is unknown whether the multidimensionality found for professional knowledge has an equivalent when taking a closer look at the application of professional knowledge in problem situations. Should this be the case, professions like electrical/electronics technicians for energy and building technology would require test versions for three dimensions of professional knowledge and for three dimensions of knowledge application at the end of VET. Even with optimised test versions it can be assumed that at least two hours of test time per dimension are required for reliable and valid testing of knowledge application. The same applies for the reliable and valid assessment of professional knowledge which can also hardly be achieved in less than two hours. The central problem is then, how to gain robust data on competence levels while keeping test time and test motivation on an acceptable level. Of course, this problem is further exacerbated when manual skills are additionally taken into account.

For a valid and reliable competence assessment, the findings and reflections on the development of cognitive and manual skills have to be considered. On top of that, the acquired level of development has to be taken into account in order to get to know which skills need to be applied for accomplishing a specific task (both aspects were discussed under "Second Approximation"). Taking these aspects into consideration, it might be recommendable to use speed rather than power tests (controlling the quality of the given solutions) when testing competence areas for which it can be assumed that the third phase of knowledge or skill acquisition has already been reached. In the first phase of acquisition, speed tests would probably only provide limited validity and reliability.

From a strategic perspective, concerning further test development it seems advisable to: (1) optimise existing test versions with regard to reliability and test time, (2) explore which subdimensions can actually be assumed for knowledge application, (3) examine whether competence in the automated phase can be estimated by assessing the willingness to give effort and the relevant professional knowledge, and (4) carry out validity studies for the individual subdimensions, in which performances in real requirement situations are used as a reference for criteria-related validity.

On (1): Optimising the reliabilities of existing test versions is a challenge, especially in the area of problem solving[7]. This is because existing test versions in most cases have to struggle with reliability problems, which are caused by the fact that only a limited number of authentic and therefore valid items can be worked on during the given test time.

On (2): There is still a lack of differentiated test instruments on knowledge application. These are needed to decide about the question of subdimensions that need to be considered in this field. Concerning knowledge application in industrial-technical professions, tests were mainly based on analytical requirements (e.g., troubleshooting technical systems). Synthetic requirements have only been used sporadically (cf. Rauner et al., 2009) until now and still require rather extensive test times.

On (3): Given the quite numerous subdimensions, the question arises whether all these subdimensions are actually critical for performance and whether some dimensions can probably be estimated with less effort. This seems to be a promising path in skill segments like standard service of car mechatronics technicians, for example. Even though it can be assumed that this segment is very important in the whole spectrum of activities, it should not be critical for performance because of its high level of routine. It can be assumed for such segments that variance in performance can mainly be explained by the willingness to give effort and less by a variance in profession-specific skills. This is because the latter are usually sufficiently developed at an advanced stage of VET.

On (4): There are hardly any validity studies that include criteria-related validity. Without such validity studies, the explanatory power of the data generated with different test versions cannot be adequately estimated.

The challenges outlined here can be taken as a description of central development requirements and research desiderata. Overcoming these challenges will be a key factor for vocational education research and output assessment in the practical field. Besides, replication studies on structural and level modelling are urgently needed

---

7  For more details see Nickolaus, Gschwendtner, & Abele (2011).

to ensure reliable and, at the same time, valid competence estimates. On top of that, qualitative studies are needed which, dependent on the competence level that has been achieved, elucidate the interaction between person and item.

## References

Abele, S. (2011). Hängt die prognostische Validität eignungsdiagnostischer Verfahren von der Operationalisierung des Ausbildungserfolgs ab? In R. Nickolaus & G. Pätzold (Eds.), *Lehr-Lernforschung in der gewerblich-technischen Berufsbildung* (pp. 13-37). Stuttgart: Steiner (Zeitschrift für Berufs- und Wirtschaftspädagogik; Beiheft 25).

Abele, S., Achtenhagen, F., Gschwendtner, T., Nickolaus, R., & Winther, E. (2009). *Die Messung beruflicher Fachkompetenz im Rahmen eines Large ScaleAssessments im Bereich beruflicher Bildung (VET-LSA) – Vorstudien zur Validität von Simulationsaufgaben*. http://www.bmbf.de/pubRD/Kurzfassung_Abschlussbericht.pdf

Abele, S. et al. (2011). Fachspezifische und dynamische Problemlösefähigkeit (in preparation).

Ackerman, P. L. (1992). Predicting individual differences in complex skill acquisition: Dynamics of ability determinants. *Journal of Applied Psychology, 77*(1-6), 589-613.

Alderson, J. C. (2000). *Assessing Reading*. New York: Cambridge University Press.

Artelt, C., McElvany, N., Christmann, U., Richter, T., Groeben, N., Köster, J., Schneider, W., Stanat, P., Ostermeier, C., Schiefele, U., Valtin, R., & Ring, K. (2005). *Expertise – Förderung von Lesekompetenz*. Bonn & Berlin: Bundesministerium für Bildung und Forschung.

Baethge, M., Achtenhagen, F., Arends, L., Babic, E., Baethge-Kinsky, V., & Weber, S. (2006). *Berufsbildungs-PISA. Machbarkeitsstudie*. Stuttgart: Steiner.

Baethge, M. & Arends, L. (2009a). *Feasibility Study VET-LSA. A Comparative Analysis of Occupational Profiles and VET Programmes in 8 European Countries – International Report*. Bonn, Berlin: W. Bertelsmann (Vocational Training Research; Bd. 8).

Baethge, M. & Arends, L. (2009b). Die Machbarkeit eines internationalen Large-Scale-Assessment in der beruflichen Bildung: Feasibility Study VET-LSA. *Zeitschrift für Berufs- und Wirtschaftspädagogik, 105*(4), 492-520.

Beaton, A.E. & Allen, N.L. (1992). Interpreting scales through scale anchoring. *Journal of Educational Statistics, 17*(2), 191-204.

Beck, K. (2003). *Ethischer Universalismus als moralische Verunsicherung? Zur Diskussion um die Grundlegung der Moralerziehung*. Reihe: Arbeitspapiere, Heft 44, Lehrstuhl für Wirtschaftspädagogik, Johannes Gutenberg-Universität Mainz.

Beck, K., Bienengrüber, T., Heinrichs, K., Lang, B., Lüdecke-Plümer, S., Minnameier, G., Parche-Kawik, K., & Zirkel, A. (1998). Die moralische Urteils- und Handlungskompetenz von kaufmännischen Lehrlingen – Entwicklungsbedingungen und ihre pädagogische Gestaltung. In K. Beck & R. Dubs, *Kompetenzentwicklung in der Berufserziehung* (pp. 188-210). Stuttgart: Steiner (Zeitschrift für Berufs- und Wirtschaftspädagogik; Beiheft 14).

Beck, K., Brütting, B., Lüdecke-Plümer, S., Minnameier, G., Schirmer, U., & Schmid, S. N (1996), Zur Entwicklung moralischer Urteilskompetenz in der kaufmännischen Erstausbildung – empirische Befunde und praktische Probleme. In K. Beck & H. Heid, *Lehr-Lern-Prozesse in der kaufmännischen Erstausbildung* (pp. 188-207). Stuttgart: Steiner (Zeitschrift für Berufs- und Wirtschaftspädagogik; Beiheft 13).

Beck, K. & Krumm, V. (1999). *Wirtschaftskundlicher Bildungstest*. Göttingen: Hogrefe.

Geißel, B. (2007). *Differentielle Effekte von methodischen Entscheidungen und Organisationsformen beruflicher Grundbildung auf die Kompetenz- und Motivationsentwicklung in der gewerblich-technischen Erstausbildung*. Aachen: Shaker.

Geißel, B. (2008). Ein Kompetenzmodell für die elektrotechnische Grundbildung: Kriteriumsorientierte Interpretation von Leistungsdaten. In R. Nickolaus & H. Schanz (Eds.), *Didaktik der gewerblichen Berufsbildung. Konzeptionelle Entwürfe und empirische Befunde* (pp. 121-141). Baltmannsweiler: Schneider (Diskussion Berufsbildung; Bd. 9).

Greiff, S. & Funke, J. (2009). Measuring complex knowledge application – The Micro DYN approach. In F. Scheuermann & J. Björnsson (Eds.), *The Transition to Computer-Based Assessment – New Approaches to Skills Assessment and Implications for Large-Scale Testing*. Luxembourg: Office for Official Publications of the European Communities. http://www.psychologie.uni-heidelberg.de/ae/allg/mitarb/jf/Greiff&Funke_2009_LuxPaper.pdf (03.05.2010).

Gschwendtner, T. (2008). Ein Kompetenzmodell für die kraftfahrzeugtechnische Grundbildung. In R. Nickolaus & H. Schanz (Eds.), *Didaktik der gewerblichen Berufsbildung. Konzeptionelle Entwürfe und empirische Befunde* (pp. 103-109). Baltmannsweiler: Schneider (Diskussion Berufsbildung; Bd. 9).

Gschwendtner, T. (2011). Die Ausbildung zum Kraftfahrzeugmechatroniker im Längsschnitt. Analysen zur Struktur von Fachkompetenz am Ende der Ausbildung und Erklärung von Fachkompetenzentwicklungen über die Ausbildungszeit. In R. Nickolaus & G. Pätzold (Eds.), *Lehr- Lernforschung in der gewerblich-technischen Berufsbildung* (pp. 55-76). Stuttgart: Steiner (Zeitschrift für Berufs- und Wirtschaftspädagogik; Beiheft 25).

Gschwendtner, T., Abele, S., & Nickolaus, R. (2009). Computersimulierte Arbeitsproben: Eine Validierungsstudie am Beispiel der Fehlerdiagnoseleistung von Kfz-Mechatronikern. *Zeitschrift für Berufs- und Wirtschaftspädagogik, 105*(4), 556-578.

Haolader, F. (2010). *Technical and Vocational Education and Training – Curricula Reform Demand in Bangladesh. Qualification Requirements, Qualification Deficits and Reform Perspectives*. Promotion am Institut für Erziehungswissenschaft und Psychologie Abt. Berufs- Wirtschafts- und Technikpädagogik an der Universität Stuttgart.

Hartig, J. (2007). Skalierung und Definition von Kompetenzniveaus. In B. Beck & E. Klieme (Eds.), *Sprachliche Kompetenzen. Konzepte und Messung* (pp. 83-99). Weinheim: Beltz.

Hartig, J. & Klieme, E. (2006). Kompetenz und Kompetenzdiagnostik. In K. Schweizer (Eds.), *Leistung und Leistungsdiagnostik* (pp. 127-143). Berlin: Springer.

Kintsch, W. (1998). *Comprehension*. New York: Cambridge University Press.

Lehmann, R. & Seeber, S. (Eds.) (2007). *ULME 3. Untersuchungen von Leistungen, Motivation und Einstellungen der Schülerinnen und Schüler in den Abschlussklassen der Berufsschulen*. Hamburg: Behörde für Bildung und Sport.

Lempert, W. (2003). Modernisierung der Moral oder pseudomoralische Entmoralisierung? *Zeitschrift für Berufs- und Wirtschaftspädagogik, 99*(3), 436-452.

Minnamaier, G. (2005). *Wissen und inferentielles Denken. Zur Analyse und Gestaltung von Lehr-Lern-Prozessen.* Frankfurt: Lang.

Musekamp, F., Spöttl, G. & Becker, M. (2010). Schriftliche Arbeitsaufträge zur Erfassung von Differenzen in der Expertise von Facharbeitern und Auszubildenden. *Zeitschrift für Berufs- und Wirtschaftspädagogik, 106*(3), 336-360.

Nickolaus, R. (2010). Erklärungsmodelle für die Entwicklung der Fachkompetenz – Anmerkungen zu ihren Geltungsansprüchen und didaktischen Implikationen. *Zeitschrift für Berufs- und Wirtschaftspädagogik, 106*(4), 48-73.

Nickolaus, R. (2011). Didaktische Präferenzen in der beruflichen Bildung und ihre Tragfähigkeit. In R. Nickolaus & G. Pätzold (Eds.), *Lehr-Lernforschung in der gewerblich-technischen Berufsbildung* (pp. 159-176). Stuttgart: Steiner (Zeitschrift für Berufs- und Wirtschaftspädagogik; Beiheft 25).

Nickolaus, R., Geißel, B., Abele, S. & Nitzschke, A. (2011). Fachkompetenzmodellierung und Fachkompetenzentwicklung bei Elektronikern für Energie- und Gebäudetechnik im Verlauf der Ausbildung – Ausgewählte Ergebnisse einer Längsschnittstudie. In R. Nickolaus & G. Pätzold (Eds.), *Lehr-Lernforschung in der gewerblich-technischen Berufsbildung* (pp. 77-94). Stuttgart: Steiner (Zeitschrift für Berufs- und Wirtschaftspädagogik; Beiheft 25).

Nickolaus, R., Gschwendtner, T. & Abele, S. (2009). *Die Validität von Simulationsaufgaben am Beispiel der Diagnosekompetenz von Kfz-Mechatronikern. Vorstudie zur Validität von Simulationsaufgaben im Rahmen eines VET-LSA.* Abschlussbericht für das BMBF. Stuttgart

Nickolaus, R., Gschwendtner, T., & Abele, S. (2011). Valide Abschätzungen von Kompetenzen als eine notwendige Basis zur Effektbeurteilung pädagogischer Handlungsprogramme – Herausforderungen, Ansätze und Perspektiven. In M. Fischer, M. Becker & G. Spöttl (Eds.), *Kompetenzdiagnostik in der beruflichen Bildung – Probleme und Perspektiven* (pp. 57-74). 1. Aufl. Frankfurt: Lang.

Nickolaus, R., Gschwendtner, T., & Geißel, B. (2008). Entwicklung und Modellierung beruflicher Fachkompetenz in der gewerblich-technischen Grundbildung. *Zeitschrift für Berufs- und Wirtschaftspädagogik, 104*(1), 48-73.

Nickolaus, R., Rosendahl, J., Gschwendtner, T., Geißel, B., & Straka, G. A. (2010). Erklärungsmodelle zur Kompetenz- und Motivationsentwicklung bei Bankkaufleuten, Kfz-Mechatronikern und Elektronikern. In J. Seifried et al. (Eds.), *Lehr-Lern-Forschung in der kaufmännischen Berufsbildung – Ergebnisse und Gestaltungsaufgaben* (pp. 73-87). Stuttgart: Steiner (Zeitschrift für Berufs- und Wirtschaftspädagogik; Beiheft 23).

Nickolaus, R. & Ziegler, B. (2005). Der Lernerfolg schwächerer Schüler in der beruflichen Ausbildung im Kontext methodischer Entscheidungen. In P. Gonon et al. (Eds.), *Kompetenz, Kognition und neue Konzepte der beruflichen Bildung* (pp. 161-176). Wiesbaden: VS Verlag.

Rauner, F., Haasler, B., Heinemann, L., & Grollmann, P. (2009). *Messen beruflicher Kompetenzen. Band 1: Grundlagen und Konzeption des KOMET-Projekts.* Münster: LIT.

Reetz, L. (1999). Zum Zusammenhang von Schlüsselqualifikationen – Kompetenzen – Bildung. In T. Tramm, D. Sembill, F. Klauser & E. G. John (Eds.), *Professionalisierung kaufmännischer Berufsbildung* (pp. 32-51). Frankfurt: Lang.

Rosendahl, J. & Straka, G. A. (2011). Analysen zur wirtschaftlichen Fachkompetenz angehender Bankkaufleute. *Zeitschrift für Berufs – und Wirtschaftspädagogik* (in press).

Sass, S. (2010). *Computerbasierte Testverfahren – Einfluss des Aufgabenformats auf die Testleistung*. IPN BG 4/10, 5.

Seeber, S. (2008). Ansätze zur Modellierung beruflicher Fachkompetenz in kaufmännischen Ausbildungsberufen. *Zeitschrift für Berufs- und Wirtschaftspädagogik, 104*(1), 74-97.

Seeber, S. & Lehmann, R. (2011). Determinanten der Fachkompetenz in ausgewählten gewerblich-technischen Berufen. In R. Nickolaus & G. Pätzold (Eds.), *Lehr-Lernforschung in der gewerblich-technischen Berufsbildung* (pp. 95-112). Stuttgart: Steiner (Zeitschrift für Berufs- und Wirtschaftspädagogik; Beiheft 25).

Seeber, S. & Nickolaus, R. (2010). Kompetenz, Kompetenzmodelle und Kompetenzentwicklung in der beruflichen Bildung. In R. Nickolaus et al. (Eds.), *Handbuch der Berufs- und Wirtschaftspädagogik* (pp. 247-257). 1. Aufl. Bad Heilbrunn: Klinkhardt.

Seifried, J. & Sembill, D. (2010). Empirische Erkenntnisse zum handlungsorientierten Lernen in der kaufmännischen Bildung. *Lernen & Lehren. Elektrotechnik-Informatik und Metalltechnik, 98*, 61-67.

Sekretariat der ständigen Konferenz der Kultusminister der Länder in der Bundesrepublik Deutschland (Hrsg.) (2000). *Handreichungen für die Erarbeitung von Rahmenlehrplänen der Kultusministerkonferenz (KMK) für den berufsbezogenen Unterricht in der Berufsschule und ihre Abstimmung mit Ausbildungsordnungen des Bundes für anerkannte Ausbildungsberufe*. Berlin: BMBF.

Spöttl, G., Becker, M., & Musekamp, F. (2011). Anforderungen an Kfz-Mechatroniker und Implikationen für die Kompetenzerfassung. In R. Nickolaus & G. Pätzold (Eds.), *Lehr-Lernforschung in der gewerblich-technischen Berufsbildung* (pp. 37-53). Stuttgart: Steiner (Zeitschrift für Berufs- und Wirtschaftspädagogik; Beiheft 25).

Weber, S. & Achtenhagen, F. (2010). Molare didaktische Ansätze zur Förderung forschungs- und evidenzbasierter Lehr-Lern-Prozesse. In J. Seifried et al. (Eds.), *Lehr-Lern-Forschung in der kaufmännischen Berufsbildung – Ergebnisse und Gestaltungsaufgaben* (pp. 13-26). Stuttgart: Steiner (Zeitschrift für Berufs- und Wirtschaftspädagogik; Beiheft 23).

Winther, E. (2010). *Kompetenzmessung in der beruflichen Bildung*. 1. Aufl. Bielefeld: W. Bertelsmann.

Winther, E. & Achtenhagen, F. (2009). Skalen und Stufen kaufmännischer Kompetenz. *Zeitschrift für Berufs- und Wirtschaftspädagogik, 105*(4), 521-556.

Winther, E. & Achtenhagen, F. (2010). Berufsfachliche Kompetenz: Messinstrumente und empirische Befunde zur Mehrdimensionalität beruflicher Handlungskompetenz. *Berufsbildung in Wissen und Praxis, 1,* 18-21.

Zabeck, J. (2002). Moral im Dienste betrieblicher Zwecke? *Zeitschrift für Berufs- und Wirtschaftspädagogik, 98*(4), 486-503.

# Part C
# The Devil in the Details

# Chapter 7

# Competencies: The German Notion of Learning Outcomes

*Olaf Köller[1] & Ilka Parchmann[2]*
*Leibniz Institute for Science and Mathematics Education, Kiel, Germany*
*[1] Department of Education and Educational Assessment and Measurement*
*[2] Department of Chemistry Education*

## Abstract

The disappointing findings of the Third International Mathematics and Science Study (TIMSS) published in the 1990s (e.g., Beaton et al., 1996) sparked intense scientific and public debate about the educational goals of the German school system and the reforms necessary to improve students' academic achievement in science and mathematics. As a consequence of this discussion, the 16 federal states, in collaboration with the German Federal Ministry of Education and Research, established a program to improve the quality of teaching in science and mathematics (the SINUS program; see Fischer, Rieck, & Prenzel, 2010). Furthermore, they decided to participate in the OECD's Programme for International Student Assessment (PISA). However, Germany's performance in PISA 2000 was again disappointing, leading to a second wave of reforms. One substantial change was the introduction in 2003 and 2004 of educational standards to be attained in key subjects by the end of elementary education (grade 4) and lower secondary education (grade 9 or 10). These standards define core learning outcomes for seven subjects (biology, chemistry, English, French, German, mathematics, and physics). The Institute for Educational Progress (IQB) was founded in 2004 to monitor whether elementary and secondary school students in Germany were reaching these standards and to establish a system of national assessment. Since then, large item pools have been generated, providing hundreds of calibrated items measuring competencies in different subjects. In addition, major grant programs provided by the German Research Foundation (DFG) and the Federal Ministry of Education and Research (BMBF) have funded significant research programs on student competencies. These initiatives have not only assessed student competencies, but also addressed competence structures, their development, their domain specificity, and their relationship to constructs such as intelligence, social background, etc. This chapter provides an overview of educational standards in Germany, their assessment, and ongoing national research activities investigating the competencies of elementary and secondary students. Furthermore, it gives a short overview of projects on competencies conducted at the Leibniz Institute for Science and Mathematics Education (IPN).

# 1 Outcome Orientation, Standards, and Competencies in the German School System

In response to the findings of large-scale international assessment studies such as PIRLS, PISA, and TIMSS, many countries worldwide have introduced new concepts of educational governance, based on the idea that the quality of national educational systems is more effectively fostered by a focus on students' learning outcomes in core subjects (mathematics, mother tongue, science) than by an input-driven approach. Consequently, several national and international assessment programs have been initiated; the number of countries participating in international studies on student outcomes has increased steadily (e.g., PISA began with 31 participating countries in 2000, increasing to 71 by 2009; see Klieme et al., 2010); and educational standards have been established that define required learning outcomes in key school subjects as central goals of elementary and secondary education. For example, 48 of the 50 U.S. states have recently agreed on *Common Core State Standards* for English language arts and literacy in history / social studies, mathematics, science, and technical subjects.

In 2003 and 2004, based on an expertise by Klieme et al. (2003) and the recommendations of experts in teacher education, psychology, and educational research, the Standing Conference of Ministers of Education and Cultural Affairs of the Länder in the Federal Republic of Germany (KMK) agreed on common standards for elementary and secondary schools. These standards drew on Weinert's (2001) conceptual work on competencies and on subject-specific traditions regarding educational goals. They broadly describe the learning outcomes that are required in a domain at a certain grade level for students to achieve a certain school-leaving qualification. Although the German standards are based on the theoretical frameworks of international studies such as PIRLS, TIMSS, and PISA, and take national subject-specific traditions into account, there has been criticism that much more research is needed to verify the underlying competency models (see Schecker, *this volume*).

However, it has been argued elsewhere (see Köller, 2008a) that linking the standards to theory, educational models, and empirical research is a task for future research, which can help to refine both the models and the standards. Furthermore, Köller (2008a) has argued that the standards for mathematics, modern languages, and to some extent science have a firm theoretical grounding. The standards for modern languages are based on the Common European Framework of Reference for Languages (CEFR, e.g., Council of Europe, 2001). Those for mathematics are rooted in the work of the National Council of Teachers of Mathematics (NCTM, 2000), the PISA framework (e.g., OECD, 2003), Freudenthal's "Realistic Mathematics Education" (Freudenthal, 1983), and a key publication by Winter (1995). Finally, the standards for science draw on the large body of literature on scientific literacy (e.g., Bybee, 2008; OECD, 2006; Waddington, Nentwig, & Schanze, 2008) and the German tradition of science education at secondary level (see, for example, the expertise on core curricula for upper secondary school edited by Tenorth, 2004).

Table 1 provides an overview of the subjects and grade levels for which standards have been developed in Germany (indicated by bullet points). The standards for the end of upper secondary education are currently being developed and are due to be published in 2012.

*Table 1: Subjects and Grade Levels for Which Educational Standards Have Been Developed in Germany\**

| | Grade level | | | |
|---|---|---|---|---|
| | Elementary school | End of lower secondary school | | End of upper secondary school[1] |
| Subject | Grade 4 | Grade 9 | Grade 10 | Grades 12/13 |
| **German** (mother tongue) | • | • | • | • |
| **Mathematics** | • | • | • | • |
| Modern languages | | | | |
| **English** | | • | • | • |
| **French** | | | • | • |
| Science | | | | |
| **Biology** | | | • | • |
| **Chemistry** | | | • | • |
| **Physics** | | | • | • |

Note: *Empty cells indicate that no standards are available for the corresponding subject at the specific grade level; [1]The standards for the end of upper secondary school are currently under development and are due to be published in 2012.

In contrast to curricula, which differ substantially across the German states, the standards define the same goals for all 16 federal states. In elementary school (grade 4), the KMK standards are limited to the subjects of German and mathematics. No

standards have been developed for modern foreign languages at elementary level for several reasons:
- Curricula for English and French differ markedly across the 16 federal states.
- Some states start teaching a modern language in grade 1; others, in grade 3.
- There is no consensus across states on textbooks suitable for language teaching at elementary level.
- There is no tradition of elementary teacher education in modern languages.

Likewise, no standards have been developed for science education at elementary level. Possible reasons are that, again, there is no common science curriculum across the federal states; the volume of science education at elementary level differs across states; and science instruction is usually embedded in a subject called "Sachkunde", which is a mixture of civics education, geography, physics, and biology.

At lower secondary level, standards have been developed for the end of both grade 9 and grade 10. The grade 9 standards define outcomes for students taking the *Hauptschulabschluss* at the end of the vocational track; the grade 10 standards define goals for the more prestigious *Mittlerer Schulabschluss*. Science standards, which specify required outcomes in biology, chemistry, and physics, have been developed only for grade 10. The chapters by Schecker and Parchmann (2007) and Schecker (*this volume*) provide a comprehensive overview of the science standards. Note, however, that both the science and the mathematics standards are a mixture of content standards and performance standards. From the perspective of linking standards to competencies, a focus on performance standards would be preferable.

## 2 Research on Competencies

The publication of the PISA findings and the German educational standards sparked many research initiatives. Empirical studies are currently addressing:
- the structures of students' competencies,
- assessment and measurement models for competencies,
- the development of competencies, and
- the definition of proficiency levels.

A wealth of findings from this research have been published in recent years (Klieme, Leutner, & Kenk, 2010). Furthermore, the research scope has been extended to cover teachers' professional competence (e.g., Krauss et al., 2008) and teacher education. The following paragraphs report on these research activities.

## 2.1 Research on Competence Structures

A first step in assessing standards is the development and testing of theoretically informed structural models describing the facets of a given competence. For example, Figure 1 displays the facets of mathematics competence in elementary and secondary school as defined by the KMK standards (Köller, 2010).[1] As mentioned above, the mathematics standards represent a mixture of content and performance standards. Although the model is informed by the literature, it remains an open question whether it holds empirically. The next step is therefore to construct measurement models and to test the model structure on the basis of large student and item samples (for an overview, see Hartig, Klieme, & Leutner, 2008). Multidimensional IRT models (e.g., Adams, Wilson, & Wang, 1997) can be used to test such structural models, provided that they are not too complex.

Figure 1 proposes 11 facets of mathematics competence, indicating a high level of complexity. Winkelmann and Robitzsch (2009) have thus argued that the model can only be tested in two steps – examining, first, whether the contents can be distinguished and, second, whether the processes are separable in a multidimensional IRT analysis. Drawing on data obtained from a large sample of grade 3 and 4 students, the authors found convincing evidence for the validity of the model: the content facets as well as the process facets were strongly intercorrelated, but all correlation coefficients were substantially below 1, indicating multidimensionality. Furthermore, the intercorrelations suggested that collapsing all subscores to a total score in order to obtain a measure of general mathematics competence is appropriate in large-scale assessments, in particular. Analogous analyses have not yet been conducted for the science standards, but findings from the German extension to the PISA 2003 study (Rost et al., 2004) indicate that similar results can be expected. Rost and colleagues analyzed a national science test that consisted of items measuring seven facets of cognitive processes (decision-making, divergent reasoning, using graphical representations, convergent reasoning, mental models, verbalizing, and data interpretation). Statistical analyses revealed substantial correlations ranging from .58 to .88 among the facets, but all coefficients were below 1. Findings for both mathematics and science thus provide evidence that a priori structures hold in empirical tests, but there is also empirical support for a general competence factor. The same holds for other domains, such as foreign languages and the mother tongue: Leucht, Retelsdorf, Möller, and Köller (2010) recently analyzed tests on English reading and listening comprehension and found correlations of above .80 between the tests.

---

1   The model for science is reported in Schecker (*this volume*; for Switzerland, see the chapter by Labudde, *this volume*).

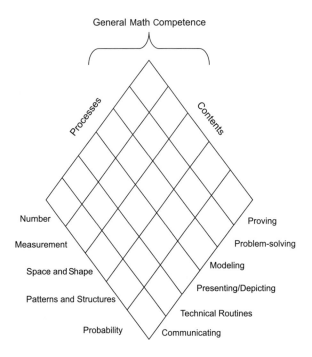

*Figure 1: Theoretical Structure of Mathematics Competence in the German Elementary and Secondary School Standards (see Köller, 2010)*

Studies in which data from national and international large-scale assessments were used to examine whether different instruments measure the same construct are also of particular interest in this context. Figure 2 shows two competing models. Rectangles indicate items or subtests; circles symbolize constructs (latent variables) such as mathematics or reading competence. In model A, the national and international test measure different but correlated constructs; in model B, both tests measure the same construct.

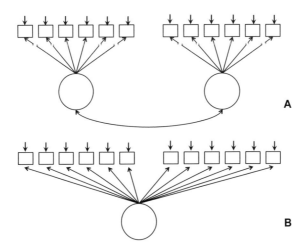

*Figure 2: Competing Competence Structure and Measurement Models from National and International Tests*

Two German studies have recently been published on this issue. Pietsch, Böhme, Robitzsch, and Stubbe (2009) analyzed data from $n = 4,728$ grade 4 students who were administered items from the Progress in International Reading Literacy Study (PIRLS) as well as items from the national test assessing the KMK standards in reading in 2006. A two-dimensional IRT analysis revealed a correlation of $r = .84$ indicating that, despite a strong overlap between the two constructs, the constructs measured were not the same (in model fit comparisons, the two-dimensional model outperformed the one-dimensional solution).

Of even more interest is a study conducted at the IPN (Frey, 2010). In this study, data from approximately 10,000 grade 9 students who worked on international PISA mathematics items as well as national mathematics items assessing the KMK mathematics standards were analyzed by means of confirmatory factor analysis. The analyses revealed a correlation of $r = .95$ between the two mathematics tests, indicating that both instruments measure more or less the same construct.

Overall, these two studies show that there is a strong overlap in the constructs measured by the international and national instruments. It may thus be possible to use national instruments to calibrate students on the international scale and vice versa.

## 2.2 Research on the Development of Competencies

From an educational perspective, it is interesting to investigate not only competence structures, but also how competencies and their structures change over time. To this end, three different types of developmental research have been established, the first investigating domain-specific achievement gains over time, the second examining how competence structures change over time, and the third addressing the robustness of measurement models over time. Figure 3 provides graphical representations of these three research lines.

Figure 3a shows two different growth trajectories (linear vs. nonlinear change) as a function of years of schooling. Studies investigating change in competencies usually use global measures and examine how much students learn in a certain domain per year. Recent U.S. studies by Lee (2010) and Hill, Bloom, Black, and Lipsey (2008) suggest that change over time is nonlinear (similar to the black line in figure 3a), at least for mathematics and reading. Specifically, learning rates are much higher in the earlier years (about 1 $SD$ in elementary school) than in the later years (about .10 $SD$ in grade 10) of schooling. German studies (for an overview, see Köller & Baumert, in press) have reported similar results. Findings by the Institute for Educational Progress (IQB) indicate substantial growth rates in elementary school (reading and math scores were about .70 $SD$ higher in grade 4 than in grade 3) that became much smaller by the end of lower secondary school (.10 $SD$ in reading and about .40 $SD$ in mathematics). Studies on longitudinal change in science competence are rare, but the available findings suggest that learning rates are generally smaller (on average .25 $SD$ per year; e.g., Köller & Baumert, in press). Viering, Fischer, and Neumann (2010) reported cross-sectional findings on change in content knowledge in physics. Based on the KMK standards for physics, the authors were interested in how students' basic concept of energy changes over time. Students from grades 6 to 10 were administered standardized tests. Statistical analyses revealed that their knowledge increased from grade to grade. However, the rates of change were relatively small (e.g., .24 $SD$ from grade 6 to grade 7).

Figure 3b shows how competence structures can change over time – i.e., become more complex as a result of the differentiation of cognitive abilities (Carlstedt, 2001). By way of example, the figure shows a competence structure with two correlated factors in earlier years (T1) that becomes more complex (three correlated factors) in later years (T2). Alternatively, differentiation of competencies can result in decreasing correlations among factors over time.

One explanation of this popular differentiation hypothesis is that competence acquisition is strongly influenced by general cognitive abilities in the early school years, but primarily affected by opportunities to learn in later years, thus resulting in more complex structures (e.g., Undheim, 1978). Empirical findings from research on academic achievement provide little evidence for such differentiation processes, however. More convincing evidence has been found for a de-differentiation, i.e., for correlations among factors increasing over time (e.g., Brunner, 2006). Indeed, the analyses of Winkelmann and Robitzsch (2009) for elementary school mathematics revealed lower correlations among factors than did Brunner's (2006) analyses of the PISA 2000 mathematics data at the end of lower secondary school. Because research on change in competence structures over time remains scarce, however, more studies in this area are needed in the future.

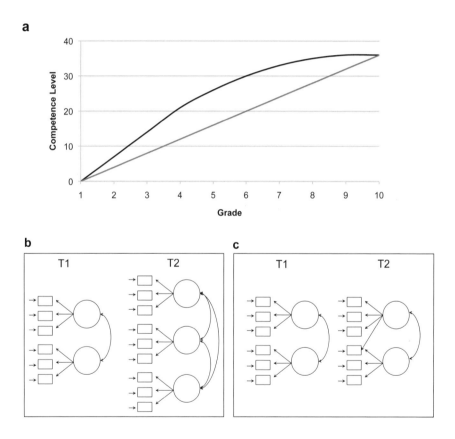

*Figure 3: Three Types of Research on the Development of Competencies: (a) Domain-specific Achievement Gains Over Time; (b) Change in Competence Structures Over Time (Differentiation); (c) Change in Measurement Models Over Time*

Invariance of measurement models is often an important issue in the investigation of developmental processes. Figure 3c illustrates a case in which invariance does not hold over time. At T1, all items have only one factor loading (between-item dimensionality), whereas at T2 at least one item has loadings on both factors (within-item dimensionality; see Zhang, 2004, 2005, on the distinction of between- and within-item dimensionality). Such changes in measurement models over time typically represent a serious problem, because they call the validity of the measures into question. If measures change their characteristics over time, it is often impossible to interpret mean-level changes in student outcomes (for a more detailed discussion of measurement invariance, see Marsh et al., 2010). The study by Viering et al. (2010) provides some evidence that measurement models can be robust over time – at least for content knowledge, in terms of the basic concept of energy. However, the discussion about linking errors in large-scale assessments (e.g., Mazzeo & von Davier, 2008; Xu & von Davier, 2010) clearly shows how changes in competencies can be biased when measurement models change over time.

## 2.3 Research on Standard Setting

The establishment of educational standards in Germany was associated with the introduction of a system of national assessment designed to test whether students are achieving the standards specified. The KMK described the German standards of 2003 and 2004 as *norm standards* (in German: "Regelstandards"). This approach was strongly criticized; it was argued that instead *minimum standards* should be defined (*basic standards* in the Swiss approach; see Labudde, *this volume*). However, closer inspection of the standards reveals that they define neither basic nor norm standards. Instead, they represent rather broad ideas of what students should achieve by the end of elementary and secondary education, with no substantial basis in empirical data regarding the proportions of students reaching the proposed achievement levels. Consequently, researchers argued (e.g., Klieme et al., 2003; Köller, 2008b; Schecker & Parchmann, 2007) that more theory building and empirical studies were necessary to reach a deeper understanding of standards and how they can be measured. Furthermore, it was argued that data from empirical studies should provide the basis for more concrete descriptions of norm and minimum standards (e.g., Köller, 2008b).

In 2005, the Institute for Educational Progress (IQB), in collaboration with many universities and research institutes, began to create large banks of calibrated items to assess student competencies (see Köller, 2008a and 2008b, for overviews) and to form a basis for national assessments of educational outcomes. Items have been calibrated on the basis of nationally representative samples of grade 3 and 4 students at elementary level and grade 8, 9, and 10 students at lower secondary level (Granzer, Köller, Bremerich-Vos, et al. 2009; Köller, Knigge, & Tesch, 2010). The calibration studies (for an overview, see www.iqb.hu-berlin.de) resulted in national competence scales with means of $M = 500$ and standard deviations of $SD = 100$. Standard-setting procedures (Cizek, 2001, 2006; Pant, Rupp, Tiffin-Richards, & Köller, 2009) were used to define proficiency levels (competence levels) and to link these proficiency levels to the KMK standards.

The term "standard setting" covers various consensual approaches in which panels of experts set discrete cutoff scores on continuous proficiency scales. These cutoff scores mark the boundaries of successive achievement levels (e.g., below minimum, minimum, proficient, and advanced) and are used to classify individuals. They are often used as a means to facilitate reporting on student achievement (e.g., in the PISA reports). It is believed that criterion-referenced interpretations of performance based on discrete proficiency levels can be communicated more easily to a wide variety of stakeholders than can norm-referenced interpretations based on continuous proficiency scales.

In the context of educational standards and their assessment, students can thus be assigned to proficiency levels, the simplest categorization being dichotomous: *proficient* or *not*. In the German debate about standards, the political expectations were that standard-setting procedures should provide cutoff scores for five competence levels:

Level 1: below the minimum standard
Level 2: minimum standard
Level 3: norm standard (proficient)
Level 4: norm standard plus (proficient plus)
Level 5: ideal standard

Minimum standards describe a competence level which, ideally, is attained by 100% of students (similarly to basic standards in Switzerland; see Labudde, *this volume*). Competence level 3 (proficient) corresponds to the expectations published by the KMK; level 4 (proficient plus) represents a competence level that most German students should achieve in the long run; and ideal standards describe expectations for high achievers under optimal instructional conditions. Documents have been published (see www.iqb.hu-berlin.de) describing all five proficiency levels and outlining the skills that students should possess from level 1 to level 5 in different subjects and grade levels. Figure 4 shows the distribution of grade 9 and 10 students on the *Mittlerer Schulabschluss* standards in mathematics, indicating that large proportions of students reach the expectations defined by the KMK standards (level 3 or higher; 78% in grade 10 and 58% in grade 9). The cutoff scores are the result of a standard-setting procedure based on the "bookmark" method (e.g., Cizek & Bunch, 2007), in which experts set cutoff scores by placing a marker between groups of items arranged by ascending difficulty in an *ordered item booklet* (OIB; Mitzel, Lewis, Patz, & Green, 2001). The item immediately following the bookmark is considered to be the first item of a proficiency level – and the last item in the booklet that a borderline examinee of that level is likely to answer correctly. The difficulty of this item (on an IRT scale with a mean of 500 and a standard deviation of 100) represents the cutoff score as presented in Figure 4.

There is much research questioning the validity of such standard-setting procedures, however (Pant et al., 2009). Moreover, it has been argued that different methods of standard setting lead to different cutoff scores and different proficiency level distributions of students. In a recent paper, Tiffin-Richards, Pant, and Köller (2011) compared the results of the *bookmark* and the *Angoff method*. The latter approach requires experts to read through a test and to evaluate each item in terms of whether a barely proficient or *borderline examinee* could answer it correctly. In the modified *Angoff method*, experts predict the *probability* that a borderline examinee will answer each item correctly. The borderline examinee is conceptualized as having an ability that places him or her at the lowest end of a proficiency level – i.e., just over the threshold between two adjacent levels.

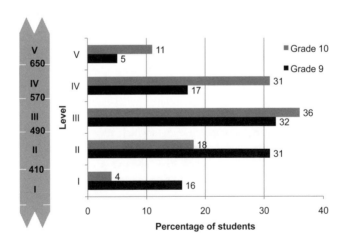

*Figure 4: Percentages of Grade 9 and 10 Students Reaching the Five Proficiency Levels in Mathematics (Basis: KMK Standards for the Mittlerer Schulabschluss)*

The findings of Tiffin-Richards et al. (2011) clearly showed that Angoff panelists placed cutoff scores higher than did bookmark panelists, resulting in larger proportions of students at lower proficiency levels when the Angoff method was used. These findings underline the arbitrariness of standard-setting methods. It is therefore important that researchers and policy makers report how cutoff scores were defined. From a scientific perspective, moreover, the findings highlight the need for more research on how the setting of cutoff scores is influenced by the methods used and by the composition of expert panels.

## 2.4 Research on Competencies at the IPN

The investigation of competencies, in terms of both their structures and development, is a major item on the IPN's research agenda. The institute's current projects (see Appendix 1) can be summarized under four categories:
- assessment of competencies, test development;
- analyses of models of competence structure and development in different school subjects;
- analyses of specific competence structures and factors influencing their development;
- application of competence models in (a) the design of learning tools and (b) panel and monitoring studies.

Assessment of competencies plays a particular role in the National Educational Panel Study (NEPS), in which the IPN is responsible for developing items assessing the mathematics and science competencies of different age groups (from kindergarten to adulthood). The institute is also involved in test development for PISA 2012. Finally, a large research project has recently been initiated to develop tests assessing teacher candidates' competencies at university.

As described above, different models have been developed with the aim of investigating the structures of competencies in a first step and their development at school in a second. These models are based on definitions of educational goals and their operationalization as standards for science and mathematics education. Research groups in all departments of the IPN are actively involved in this process. In mathematics, a special focus is placed on transitional phases between school types (e.g., the interface between elementary and secondary education). One question of interest uniting all projects is the robustness and transferability of models over time and school subjects. In addition to these broader perspectives, other projects investigate more specific competencies in school subjects. The Department of Biology Education is currently developing instruments to assess students' ability to understand biological systems, such as ecosystems. Another important competence in all science subjects is the development and execution of experiments. Finally, IPN scientists are investigating the use of subject-specific language and its association with (prospective) teachers' competencies (see Section 3 above).

Finally, based on the findings of its basic research and the models developed, the IPN conducts practice-oriented projects and monitoring surveys. In the first case, researchers and teachers cooperate in "learning communities" to develop teaching and learning material (e.g., learning tasks or feedback instruments) for use in science lessons. Existing textbooks, curricula, and classroom videos are analyzed and categorized according to models of competence structure and development.

Large-scale assessments and panel surveys are another highly relevant field of application; PISA and NEPS are two examples in which IPN is involved (see above).

# 3 Conclusion

As a consequence of large-scale international assessments such as PISA, PIRLS, and TIMSS, educational governance has recently seen a worldwide paradigm shift from input-driven to output-driven approaches. Despite much criticism, achievement and/or competence tests measuring students' educational outcomes have become increasingly popular. This paradigm change has prompted a wealth of international and national research on competence structures, their assessment, and their development in elementary and secondary education. In recent years, Germany has initiated systems of national assessment, and major grant programs have been put in place. A strong focus has been placed on psychometric models (e.g., the DFG priority program) with the aim of providing a better understanding of competencies and how they can be measured. Much of the IPN's research activity has been focused on this area (see Appendix 1). However, from the educational point of view, it seems important to extend this research program to projects on learning and instruction. The competencies approach requires student-oriented teaching in which students are cognitively activated by the instruction provided and self-regulate their work on demanding tasks and problems. However, there has been little research on how cognitively activating instruction can be implemented in German classes – or on the implications for teachers' professional development programs. Future research in the field of competencies should therefore place a stronger emphasis on relating the development of competencies to instruction.

# References

Adams, R. J., Wilson, M. R., & Wang, W. C. (1997). The multidimensional random coefficients multinomial logit. *Applied Psychological Measurement, 21*, 1-24.

Beaton, A., Martin, M. O., Mullis, I. V. S., Gonzales, E. J., Smith, T. A., & Kelly, D. L. (1996). *Science Achievement in the Middle School Years: IEA's Third International Mathematics and Science Study (TIMSS)*. Chestnut Hill, MA: Center for the Study of Testing, Evaluation, and Educational Policy, Boston College.

Brunner, M. (2006). *Mathematische Schülerleistung: Struktur, Schulformunterschiede und Validität*. [Academic achievement in mathematics, structure, differences among school types, and validity]. Doctoral Thesis. Berlin: Free University.

Bybee, R. (2008). Scientific literacy, environmental issues, and PISA 2006: The 2008 Paul F. Brandwein lecture. *Journal of Science Education and Technology, 17*, 566-585.

Carlstedt, B. (2001). Differentiation of cognitive abilities as a function of level of general intelligence: A latent variable approach. *Multivariate Behavioral Research, 36*, 589-609.

Cizek, G. (2001). Conjectures on the rise and fall of standard setting: An introduction to context and practice. In G. J. Cizek (Ed.), Setting Performance Standards: Concepts, Methods, and Perspectives (pp. 3-17). Mahwah, NJ: Erlbaum.

Cizek, G.J. (2006). Standard setting. In S. M. Downing & T. M. Haladyna (Eds.), *Handbook of Test Development* (pp. 225-258). Mahwah, NJ: Erlbaum.

Cizek, G. J. & Bunch, M. B. (2007). *Standard-Setting: A Guide to Establishing and Evaluating Performance Standards on Tests*. Thousand Oaks, CA: Sage.

Council of Europe (2001). *Common European Framework of Reference for Languages*. Cambridge: Cambridge University Press.

Fischer, C., Rieck, K., & Prenzel, M. (2010) (Eds.). *Naturwissenschaften in der Grundschule: Neue Zugänge entdecken* [Science in elementary school: Exploring new approaches]. Seelze: Klett, Kallmeyer.

Freudenthal, H. (1983). *Didactical Phenomenology of Mathematical Structures*. Dordrecht, The Netherlands: Reidel.

Frey, A. (2010). Konstruktvalidität des Tests zur Messung der Bildungsstandards in Mathematik für den Mittleren Schulabschluss [Construct validity of a test assessing the educational standards in mathematics at the end of lower secondary school]. In IPN (Ed.), *Research Report 2009/2010* (pp. 132-134). Kiel: Leibniz Institute for Science and Mathematics Education.

Granzer, D., Köller, O., Bremerich-Vos, A., et al. (Eds.) (2009). *Bildungsstandards Deutsch und Mathematik. Leistungsmessung in der Grundschule* [Educational standards for German and mathematics: Assessment in elementary school]. Weinheim, Germany: Beltz.

Hartig, J., Klieme, E., & Leutner, D. (Eds.) (2008). *Assessment of Competencies in Educational Contexts*. Göttingen: Hogrefe.

Hill, C. J., Bloom, H. S., Black, A. R., & Lipsey, M. W. (2008). Empirical benchmarks for interpreting effect sizes in research. *Child Development Perspectives, 2*, 172-177.

Klieme, E., Artelt, C., Hartig, J., Jude, N., Köller, O., Prenzel, M., Schneider, W., & Stanat, P. (Eds.) (2010). PISA 2009. *Bilanz nach einem Jahrzehnt* [PISA 2009: Conclusions after a decade]. Münster, Germany: Waxmann.

Klieme, E., Avenarius, H., Blum, W., Döbrich, P., Gruber, H., Prenzel, M., Reiss, K., Riquarts, K., Rost, J., Tenorth, H.-E., & Vollmer, H. J. (2003). *Zur Entwicklung nationaler Bildungsstandards: Eine Expertise.* [The development of national educational standards: An expertise]. Berlin, Germany: Federal Ministry of Education and Research.

Klieme, E., Leutner, D., & Kenk, M. (Eds.) (2010). Kompetenzmodellierung. Zwischenbilanz des DFG-Schwerpunktprogramms und Perspektiven des Forschungsansatzes. [Modeling competencies. Preliminary findings of the priority program of the German Research Foundation and perspectives for future research]. *Zeitschrift für Pädagogik, Supplement 56.*

Köller, O. (2008a). Bildungsstandards in Deutschland: Implikationen für die Qualitätssicherung und Unterrichtsqualität [Educational standards in Germany: Implications for assessment and teaching quality]. *Zeitschrift für Erziehungswissenschaft, 10, Sonderheft 9/2008*, 47-59.

Köller, O. (2008b). Bildungsstandards – Verfahren und Kriterien bei der Entwicklung von Messinstrumenten [Educational standards – Procedures and criteria for test development]. *Zeitschrift für Pädagogik, 54*, 163-173.

Köller, O. (2010). Bildungsstandards [Educational standards]. In D. H. Rost (Ed.), Handwörterbuch *Pädagogische Psychologie* (4th ed., pp. 77-83). Weinheim, Germany: Beltz/PVU.

Köller, O. & Baumert, J. (in press). Schulische Leistungen und ihre Messung [Academic achievement and its assessment]. In R. Oerter & L. Montada (Eds.), *Entwicklungspsychologie* (7th ed.). Weinheim, Germany: Beltz/PVU.

Köller, O., Knigge, M., & Tesch, B. (Eds.) (2010). Sprachliche Kompetenzen im Ländervergleich [Verbal competencies in cross-state comparison]. Münster, Germany: Waxmann.

Krauss, S., Brunner, M., Kunter, M., Baumert, J., Blum, W., Neubrand, M., & Jordan, A. (2008). Pedagogical content knowledge and content knowledge of secondary mathematics teachers. *Journal of Educational Psychology, 100*, 716-725.

Lee, J. (2010). Tripartite growth trajectories of reading and math achievement: Tracking national academic progress at elementary, middle, and high school levels. *American Educational Research Journal, 47*, 800-832.

Leucht, M., Retelsdorf, J., Möller, J., & Köller, O. (2010). Zur Dimensionalität rezeptiver englischsprachiger Kompetenzen [On the dimensionality of receptive English competencies]. *Zeitschrift für Pädagogische Psychologie, 24*, 123-138.

Marsh, H. W., Lüdtke, O., Muthén, B., Asparouhov, T., Morin, A. J. S., Trautwein, U., & Nagengast, B. (2010). A new look at the Big Five factor structure through exploratory structural equation modeling. *Psychological Assessment, 22*, 471-491.

Mazzeo, J. & von Davier, M. (2008). *Review of the Programme for International Student Assessment (PISA) Test Design: Recommendations for Fostering Stability in Assessment Results* (OECD Report EDU/PISA/GB(2008)28). Retrieved from http://www.oecd.org/dataoecd/44/49/41731967.pdf

Mitzel, H. C., Lewis, D. M., Patz, R. J., & Green, D. R. (2001). The Bookmark procedure: Psychological perspectives. In G. Cizek (Ed.), *Setting Performance Standards: Concepts, Methods and Perspectives* (pp. 249-281). Mahwah, NJ: Erlbaum.

NCTM (2000). *Pricinples and Standards for School Mathematics*. Reston, VA: NCTM.

OECD (2003). *The PISA 2003 Framework – Mathematics, Reading, Science and Problem Solving Knowledge and Skills*. Paris: OECD.

OECD (2006). *Assessing Scientific, Reading and Mathematical Literacy: A Framework for PISA 2006*. Paris: OECD.

OECD (2009). *PISA 2009 Assessment Framework – Key Competencies in Reading, Mathematics and Science*. Paris: OECD.

Pant, H. A., Rupp, A. A., Tiffin-Richards, S., & Köller, O. (2009). Validity issues in standard-setting studies. *Studies in Educational Evaluation, 15*, 95-101.

Pietsch, M., Böhme, K., Robitzsch, A., & Stubbe, T. (2009). Das Stufenmodell zur Lesekompetenz der länderübergreifenden Bildungsstandards im Vergleich zu IGLU 2006 [Comparison of the proficiency models of reading comprehension in national educational standards and PIRLS 2006]. In D. Granzer, O. Köller, A. Bremerich-Vos et al. (Eds.), *Bildungsstandards Deutsch und Mathematik. Leistungsmessung in der Grundschule* (pp. 401-425). Weinheim, Germany: Beltz.

Rost, J., Walter, O., Carstensen, C. H., Senkbeil, M., & Prenzel, M. (2004). Naturwissenschaftliche Kompetenz [Science literacy]. In PISA-Konsortium Deutschland (Ed.), *PISA 2003. Der Bildungsstand der Jugendlichen in Deutschland – Ergebnisse des zweiten internationalen Vergleichs* (pp. 111-146). Münster, Germany: Waxmann.

Schecker, H. & Parchmann, I. (2007). Standards and competence models: The German situation. In D. Waddington, P. Nentwig, & S. Schanze (Eds.), *Making it Comparable: Standards in Science Education* (pp. 147-164). Münster, Germany: Waxmann.

Tenorth, H. E. (Ed.) (2004). Kerncurriculum für die Oberstufe II: Biologie, Chemie, Physik, Geschichte, Politik. Expertisen im Auftrag der KMK [Core curriculum for upper secondary level: Biology, chemistry, physics, history, civics. Expert reports commissioned by the KMK]. Weinheim: Beltz.

Tiffin-Richards, S. P., Pant, H. A., & Köller, O. (2011): *Setting Standards for English Foreign Language Assessment: Methodology, Validation and a Degree of Arbitrariness*. Manuscript submitted for publication.

Undheim, J. O. (1978). Broad ability factors in 12- to 13-year-old children, the theory of fluid and crystallized intelligence, and the differentiation hypothesis. *Journal of Educational Psychology, 70*, 433-443.

Viering, T., Fischer, H. E., & Neumann, K. (2010). Die Entwicklung physikalischer Kompetenz in der Sekundarstufe I [The development of physics competence in lower secondary school]. *Zeitschrift für Pädagogik, Beiheft 56*, 92-103.

Waddington, D., Nentwig, P., & Schanze, S. (Eds.) (2008). *Making it Comparable. Standards in Science Education*. Münster, Germany: Waxmann.

Weinert, F. E. (2001). Concept of competence – A conceptual clarification. In D. S. Rychen & L. H. Salganik (Eds.), *Defining and Selecting Key Competencies* (pp. 45-65). Göttingen, Germany: Hogrefe.

Winkelmann, H. & Robitzsch, A. (2009). Modelle mathematischer Kompetenzen: Empirische Befunde zur Dimensionalität [Models of mathematics competence: Empirical findings on their dimensionality]. In D. Granzer, O. Köller, A. Bremerich-Vos et al. (Eds.), *Bildungsstandards Deutsch und Mathematik. Leistungsmessung in der Grundschule* (pp. 172-201). Weinheim, Germany: Beltz.

Winter, H. (1995). Mathematikunterricht und Allgemeinbildung [Mathematics instruction and general education]. *Mitteilungen der Gesellschaft für Didaktik der Mathematik, 61,* 37-46.

Xu, X. & von Davier, M. (2010). *Linking Errors in Trend Estimation in Large-Scale Surveys: A Case Study* (ETS Research Report RR10-10). Princeton, NJ: ETS.

Zhang, J. (2004): *Comparison of Unidimensional and Multidimensional Approaches to IRT Parameter Estimation* (ETS Research Report RR-04-44). Princeton, NJ: ETS.

Zhang, J. (2005): *Estimating Multidimensional Item Response Models With Mixed Structure* (ETS Research Report RR-05-04). Princeton, NJ: ETS.

## Appendix 1

Selection of Ongoing IPN Research Projects Concerning the Modeling and Investigation of Competencies in Different Domains

| Research Area/ Project Title | Central Goals, Approach, and Instruments | Key References |
|---|---|---|
| (1) *Educational assessment* Development of tests of mathematics, science, and computer literacy for the National Educational Panel Study (NEPS) | Development and validation of items measuring mathematics, science, and computer literacy in different age cohorts (from kindergarten to adulthood), IRT-based measures with (in some cases) common items, validation studies | Ehmke, T., Duchhardt, C., Geiser, H., Grüßing, M., & Heinze, A. (2009). Kompetenzentwicklung über die Lebensspanne. Erhebung von mathematischer Kompetenz im Nationalen Bildungspanel [Competence development across the lifespan. Assessment of mathematics competence in the National Educational Panel]. In A. Heinze & M. Grüßing (Eds.), *Mathematiklernen vom Kindergarten bis zum Studium. Kontinuität und Kohärenz als Herausforderung für den Mathematikunterricht* (pp. 313-327). Münster, Germany: Waxmann. |
| (1) *Educational assessment* Development of items assessing teacher candidates' competencies in university | Development of item pools to assess the content knowledge, pedagogical content knowledge, and pedagogical knowledge of teacher candidates in mathematics, biology, chemistry, and physics; IRT-based assessment models | |
| (1) *Educational assessment* Development of items for PISA 2012 | Development of mathematics items for the PISA 2012 study; IRT-based measures linked to items from previous PISA assessments; field trial in 2011 | |
| (2) *Models of competence structures and development* Examining the development of mathematics competence in transitional phases between kindergarten, school, and university | Development and validation of structural models of competencies; paper & pencil tests based on a normative models; analyses based on IRT models | Heinze, A., & Grüßing, M. (Eds.) (2009). *Mathematiklernen vom Kindergarten bis zum Studium; Kontinuität und Kohärenz als Herausforderung für den Mathematikunterricht* [Learning mathematics from kindergarten to university: Continuity and coherence as challenges for mathematics education]. Münster, Germany: Waxmann. |

| Research Area/ Project Title | Central Goals, Approach, and Instruments | Key References |
|---|---|---|
| (2) *Models of competence structures and development* <br><br> Examining the development of competence in physics | Extension of the "ESNaS" model to cover the development of student competence, with a special focus on the concept of energy; paper & pencil tests; analyses based on IRT models | Neumann, K., Viering T., & Fischer, H. E. (in press). Die Entwicklung physikalischer Kompetenz am Beispiel des Energie-Konzepts [The development of physics competence, drawing on the example of energy]. *Zeitschrift für Didaktik der Naturwissenschaften*. |
| (2) *Models of competence structures and development* <br><br> Modeling of competencies in chemistry | Application of the Model of Hierarchical Complexity to chemistry; paper & pencil tests; analyses based on IRT models | Bernholt, S., & Parchmann, I. (2011). Assessing the complexity of students' knowledge in chemistry. CERP, *Special Issue on Assessment, 12*, 167-173. |
| (2) *Models of competence structures and development* <br><br> Examining the development of competencies in secondary schools: individual and institutional determinants | Longitudinal multicohort studies to investigate effects of individual, instructional, and school characteristics on competencies and their change over time. Anchor-item designs, application of IRT equating methods to form common competence scales over time; longitudinal multi-level analyses | Köller, O., & Baumert, J. (in press). Schulische Leistungen und ihre Messung [Academic achievement and its assessment]. In R. Oerter, & L. Montada (Eds.), *Entwicklungspsychologie* (7th ed.). Weinheim, Germany: Beltz/PVU. |
| (3) *Models of specific competence structures and factors of influence* <br><br> System competence | Factors influencing the development of a "system competence"; analyses of teachers' and students' competencies at elementary level; paper & pencil tests and questionnaires; correlation analyses | Sommer, C., & Lücken, M. (2010). System competence – Are elementary students able to deal with a biological system? *Nordic Studies in Science Education – NorDiNa, 6*(2), 125-143. |
| (3) *Models of specific competence structures and factors of influence* <br><br> Individual factors influencing the development of mathematics competence | Correlations between knowledge, problem-solving competencies, and the mathematical competence of proof; paper & pencil tests and questionnaires; regression analyses | |

| Research Area/ Project Title | Central Goals, Approach, and Instruments | Key References |
|---|---|---|
| (3) *Models of specific competence structures and factors of influence*<br>Influence of instructional approaches in preschool science education | Learning outcomes across different instructional approaches in preschool science education, structured interviews, analyses based on IRT models | |
| (4) *Application of models and results to school practice*<br>Competence models as the basis for assessment-based instruction (komdif) | Application of competence models in real classroom situations, qualitative and quantitative studies, assessments based on IRT models | |
| 4) *Application of models and results to school practice*<br>"Chemie im Kontext," "NaWi_Transfer," "Emu" | Application of the Model of Hierarchical Complexity to analyses of chemistry textbooks and classroom videos and the design of learning tasks | |
| 4) *Application of models and results to school practice*<br>"SINUS in elementary schools" | Implementation of educational standards in elementary classrooms, helping teachers to understand the results of summative assessments, qualitative studies combined with (IRT-based) quantitative assessment of mathematics and science competencies | Fischer, C., & Rieck, K. (2010). Improving teaching in science and mathematics. In *Better: Evidence-based Education, 2*(3), 20-22. |

# Chapter 8

## Capturing the Diversity of Students' Competences in Science Classrooms: Differences and Commonalities of Three Complementary Approaches

*Sascha Bernholt[1], Sabina Eggert[2] & Christoph Kulgemeyer[3]*
[1]*IPN Kiel, Department of Chemistry Education;* [2]*University of Göttingen, Biology Education;*
[3]*University of Bremen, Institute of Science Education, Physics Education Group, Germany*

### Abstract

As a consequence of mediocre results in international large-scale assessments, Germany introduced national educational standards. For the science subjects, a normative structure of four competence areas and subordinate lists of specific competences were defined to describe the expected learning outcomes at the end of secondary school. As a consequence, a vast body of research projects address the modeling of competences.

The article provides detailed insights into three research projects that each aim to investigate a specific competence area of the German National Educational Standards (NES) and its respective affordances. For content knowledge in the domain of chemistry, a hierarchical model is proposed to predict the affordance level of knowledge-related items. Scientific communication in the domain of physics is explored by integrating psycholinguistic findings into a constructivist communication model. The result is a model that describes the specific requirements of science communication. Finally, socioscientific reasoning and decision making in the domain of biology is explored using a model from descriptive decision theory that was adapted for typical problem situations of applied science. All three sections describe the process of developing a theoretical outline and efforts for empirical investigations.

# 1 Introduction

With regard to social participation and citizenship in modern, industrial societies, the relevance of scientific understanding is widely acknowledged. However, it is difficult to describe in detail which specific knowledge and skills are necessary for public understanding and for the benefit of everyday life. These difficulties arise both from the specific nature of the sciences and from the changed requirements of everyday- and working-life.

On the one hand, science is not only a body of reliable knowledge that can be logically and rationally explained, as it is perceived in the Aristotelian tradition. In fact, science is a cultural phenomenon that is constituted, historically as factually, by a whole host of aspects, cultural and intellectual bases, and philosophical backgrounds. Therefore, science is a complex result of cognitive and technical efforts and constantly fluctuating communication processes (Brüggemann, 1967). In addition, it cannot offer any concluding results and the corpus of knowledge simultaneously expands and becomes antiquated faster and faster.

On the other hand, the requirements for modern citizens go far beyond factual scientific knowledge. „Citizens must be capable not only of knowing and learning, but also of opposing to science when the dependence on experts increases and general problems are no longer being discerned because of specialization and the jargon of specialists" (Oelkers, 1997, p. 97). Next to a basic scientific understanding, this requires knowledge about scientific methods and their limitations as well as a sense about the range of questions which can and cannot be answered by scientific inquiry (Boulding, 1961). „In the end, they [the citizens; note from the authors] should be able to deal with scientific predictions with the same sense of intelligent skepticism that might be used in dealing with other uncertain forecasts, such as those of economists or meteorologists" (Trefil, 2008, p. 174). This kind of intelligent skepticism is necessary to participate both in scientific discourse and societal debates related to scientific issues.

Accordingly, science teaching should provide the background and insights into scientific content and methods that are necessary for social participation. This overall aim of science education has received wide acceptance as part of the umbrella concept "scientific literacy" (DeBoer, 2000; Gräber & Bolte, 1997; Millar & Osborne, 1998), although there is no general consensus about its exact meaning or even the constituent parts (Roberts, 2007). This again makes it difficult to specify in detail what students are expected to learn during their school career.

One way to deal with this problem is by establishing educational standards. Standards intend "to crystallize goals and requirements of teaching and learning with reflected implementation and to make them measurable as clearly defined expected outcomes in performance surveys" (Oelkers & Reusser, 2008, p. 425). Educational standards aim to establish ties between the overarching aim of scientific literacy and detailed descriptions of students' achievements. They seek to close the gap between theoretical background and practical consequences. Furthermore, standards provide the basis for national assessments to decide whether preset standards have been reached by students. Several countries established educational standards (cf. Nentwig & Schanze, 2007), also as a result of international large-scale assessments like TIMSS (cf. Beaton et al., 1996) or PISA (OECD, 2001, 2004, 2007), among them Germany (KMK, 2004).

The German science standards specify competences students are expected to have achieved by the end of secondary school. The term competence is used to acknowledge the changed requirements of everyday- and working-life (Klieme & Leutner, 2006; cf. contribution by Köller & Parchmann, *this volume*).

Standards were defined for each of the three science subjects (biology, chemistry, and physics), as they are taught separately in Germany. In order to show that science goes beyond factual knowledge, the standards for these subjects equally distinguish between four areas of competence: content knowledge, scientific inquiry, communication, and socioscientific reasoning and decision making. Each of these four competence areas reflects a specific part of the scientific endeavor and embraces a list of competences that make specific demands on students' performance (cf. contribution by Kremer et al.).

The common structure of four competence areas in all science subjects as well as the subordinate lists of specific competences were defined normatively. As a consequence, a vast body of research projects and grant programs has been addressed to the modeling of competences (Klieme, Leutner & Kenk, 2010). The following three sections provide detailed insights into research projects that each aims to investigate a specific competence area and its respective affordances. The process of developing a theoretical outline and efforts for empirical investigations are described as well.

## 2 Content Knowledge

### 2.1 Theoretical Background

Research on expertise in different areas has shown that competences are largely domain-specific because they are acquired in specific situations and are linked to content-specific, task-specific, and/or demand-specific knowledge and experiences (Klieme et al., 2003). However, these domain-specific competences can be generalized in the course of cumulative learning opportunities and after a certain expertise is acquired (Wild et al., 2006). Similar to Bruner's (1977) conception of the spiral curriculum, dealing with several topics broadens the students' view and enhances their ability to more complex interdependencies and to understand key concepts.

To provide learning environments that foster this kind of cumulative learning processes, Duschl et al. (2008) advocate science standards that are organized around core ideas of the respective domain. This approach can also be found in research on learning progressions which intend to describe how students progress in developing a deeper understanding of particular core ideas when proceeding from grade to grade (cf. contribution by Krajcik, *this volume*; Corcoran et al., 2009; Duncan & Hmelo-Silver, 2009).

In order to bring cohesion to curriculum, instruction, and assessment, a model of cognition and learning that explains how students represent knowledge and develop competence in a domain could serve as a unifying element (Pellegrino et al., 2001). Currently, most cognitive theories use network models to describe the structure of declarative knowledge. These approaches describe the structure as a wide network in contrast to an accumulation of single elements (Anderson, 1984). Accordingly, the quality of knowledge rises with the degree of interconnectedness and every connection produces chunks as higher-order elements (Aebli, 1980; Laird et al., 1986).

## 2.2  Description of the Model

For rating the degree of cross-linking a theoretical cognitive network model (the Model of Hierarchical Complexity; Commons et al., 1998) was adapted and applied to the domain of chemistry. Its conceptual basis should provide a suitable foundation to assess the quality of students' knowledge. Incorporating facets of inquiry learning, the adapted model brings into focus the logical conjunction of facts and processes in order to establish causal and interdependent relations (Jonassen & Ionas, 2008). Hence, the complexity of a task depends on the explanatory power of the expected argumentation for a successful solution. Additionally, the structure of the model ties in with students' preconceptions as the starting point (see Tab. 1). Similar approaches were put forward by Shavelson et al. (2005) and Biggs & Collis (1982; Biggs, 1999).

*Table 1: Five Levels of Hierarchical Complexity for Task Development and the Analysis of Students' Achievement (Bernholt & Parchmann, 2011; Bernholt, 2010)*

| |
|---|
| **Level 1: Everyday Experiences** <br> Students describe everyday experiences and base their explanations on knowledge from daily life. They give examples for phenomena. They make and verbalize observations. |
| **Level 2: Facts** <br> Students provide isolated terms, definitions, and scientific regularities. Relations do not need to be explicated. The answers consist of reproduced facts without further explanations or argumentation patterns. |
| **Level 3: Processes** <br> Students describe phenomena and processes as a chronological sequence of distinct events or objects. Eventually, they use (mental) models for clarification purposes. The sequences do not only consist of before-after-descriptions but focus also on the process, e.g., in case of reaction mechanisms. |
| **Level 4: Linear Causality** <br> Students detect, describe, and explain linear cause-effect-relations. They give reasons for the kind and direction of the relation which go beyond simple if-then-descriptions. |
| **Level 5: Multivariate Interdependencies** <br> Students detect, describe, and explain relations beyond linear relations. They handle several variables, their interplay, and their contribution to complex cause-effect-relations. In case of a combination of several linear relations, students focus on the superposition and the reciprocal influence of the different relations. |

## 2.3 Empirical Evidence

In this particular project, the main focus lay on the quality of students' use and application of content knowledge within particular chemical topics. Several studies were conducted to analyse the usability of the model and its suitability to predict the difficulty of tasks. To control for the influence of different topics, the first investigations only covered one topic per test (e.g., combustion, acids and bases, etc.). The selection of particular topics within this content area was aligned with the state's curriculum and results from literature about learning pathways, difficulties and common misconceptions (Duit, 2009; Mulford & Robinson, 2002; Schmidt, 1997). The developed questions were used in problem-centred interviews to ensure their comprehensibility.

As a first example, the refined scheme of hierarchical complexity in the science domain was used to develop model-based tasks in the content area of combustion. A paper-and-pencil test was developed and set up in the school grades 6 to 11 to provide the quantitative data that is needed for a reliable classification of tasks. The test included both selected-response (n = 52) and constructed-response questions (n = 14). In order to take different prerequisites into account (especially expectable differences in reading and writing speed), the tests were adjusted to the different age groups by using a common-item non-equivalent groups design (Kolen & Brennan, 2004). The paper and pencil test was administered in 19 school classes from five schools in the German federal state of Lower Saxony (N = 460, 49% female). We hypothesized that the theoretical classification of the tasks according to the adopted model has a major impact on the difficulty of the test items. With regard to person characteristics we expected older students and those with better grades in chemistry courses to perform better on the test.

After ensuring a sufficiently high interrater-reliability, the coded results of the tests were Rasch-scaled using ConQuest (Wu et al., 2007). Sixty-four of sixty-six items show appropriate fit-parameters and the reliabilities of the different test forms were above common thresholds. A single-factor variance analysis indicates that about 57% of the item parameter variance is due to the model-based level of hierarchical complexity of the tasks ($F(4,59) = 17.10, p < .001, R^2 = .57$). This reveals the predictive power of the adopted model of hierarchical complexity with regard to the difficulty of the items. Comparing the two item formats, the selected-response items were significantly easier than the constructed-response items ($M_{SelecResp} = -0.77$, $M_{ConstrResp} = 2.33$, $t(62) = 6.22, p < .001, r = .62$). When in addition to the hierarchical complexity of the items, the item format is included as a second factor in an ANOVA, about 75% of the variance of the item parameter can be explained by both factors ($F(9,55) = 18.19, p < .001, R^2 = .75$; Bernholt, 2010).

Regarding the five levels of hierarchical complexity, the mean of the item parameters is increasing monotonically from the first to the fifth level of complexity. This indicates that all five levels of complexity are arranged in the correct order and the difficulty of the item is increasing from level to level. Despite this descriptive trend, only the first level of complexity can statistically be separated from the other four levels by an ANOVA with planed contrasts. Accordingly, the rank correlation (Spearman's Rho) is $\varrho = .53$ ($p < .01$), indicating an average tight relation between theoretical complexity and item parameter.

With regard to personal characteristics the analysis revealed significant correlations between the person parameter of the Rasch-scaling and the grade in chemistry (Pearson, bivariat: $.26 < r < .44, p < .01$; depending on age group) and between the person parameter and the age group (Pearson, bivariat: $r > 0.18, p < .001$). Both correlation coefficients are not very high, but are in line with the results of other studies investigating the relation of achievement tests and grades of school courses (Frenz et al., 1973) or school grades (Fraser et al., 1987). Combined, variance analysis showed that both factors have significant explanatory power to explain variance in the person parameter of the Rasch-analysis ($F(27,389) = 4.29$, $p < .01$, $R^2 = .24$).

These results were replicated in two further studies. Both studies used a similar design with a mixture of selected-response and constructed response-questions, dealing with the content areas of redox-reactions (N = 113, school grades 11 & 12) and acids and bases (N = 126, grade 10). The model-based classification of the 22 tasks concerning redox-reactions was able to predict their difficulty to a large extend ($F(4,17) = 6.13$, $p < .01$, $R^2 = .54$), as was the case for the 24 tasks concerning the topic acids and bases ($F(4,19) = 5.93$, $p < .01$, $R^2 = .57$). Similar to the first study on combustion, including the item format as second factor into the ANOVA increases the amount of explained variance up to 69% (redox-reactions, $F(5,16) = 7.11$, $p < .001$; $R^2 = .69$) and 72% (acids and bases, $F(8,15) = 4.77$, $p < .01$; $R^2 = .72$).

## 2.4 Conclusions

The main ambition of the studies was to analyze the hypothesis whether and to which extend the developed complexity scheme is able to predict item difficulty. With regard to item characteristics, the results of the quantitative study support the model's assumptions. The adopted model of hierarchical complexity explained large amounts of the variance in the data. This could improve the construction of tasks for central comparative tests because it allows a theory-based determination of task complexity. However, previous knowledge and experience concerning certain content would still influence the performance of different students attending different schools and classes, but the presented task-demand approach provides an objective and transparent indicator for the necessary affordances in tests.

Additionally, it was shown that the item format is a second factor with high explanatory power. Including the items' complexity and format in the ANOVA, both factors were able to explain 75% of the variance in the item parameter of the Rasch-scaling. The results of the main study are supported by the two studies on redox-reactions and acids and bases. The amount of explained variance is almost the same, both for the explanatory power of the hierarchical complexity alone and in combination with the item format (Bernholt, 2010). Both studies revealed that the construction manual using the five levels of complexity can be transferred to other topics without losing its predictive power with regard to the item difficulty. Further studies are intended to broaden this perspective and to take the influence of varying content and activities into account.

# 3 Communication

## 3.1 Theoretical Background

Learning the abilities necessary to communicate science content are crucial educational objectives in the science curricula of several countries. For example, the German NES (KMK, 2005), the American National Science Education Standards (CSMEE, 1996), and various Australian curricula (Hafner, 2007) explicitly specify the development of communication skills as an intended educational goal. Communication skills are crucial for both scientists and citizens to be able to participate in decision-making dialogues in an informed society. Even though there is agreement between curriculum developers about the importance of teaching communication skills in science, the concept of science communication is not very well researched. In contrast, research in the seemingly related area of argumentation is well documented in the science education research literature (Bricker & Bell, 2008; Driver, Newton & Osborne, 2000; Zeidler et al., 2006). Some aspects of the argumentation processes can be seen as communicative acts. However, argumentation has to do with reasoning, with logic, and with the ability to communicate the supporting claims of an assertion (Osborne, Erduran & Simon, 2004; Toulmin, 1958). Communication deals with preparing information adequately for a specific addressee, e.g., by choosing either everyday language or scientific terms. Argumentation therefore is a concept different to communication.

The German NES comprise science communication competence (SCC) as one of the four areas that form scientific competences. As mentioned above, the NES accord to Weinert's (2001) characterization of "specialized cognitive competences". In addition, Weinert points out that part of competence is also the individual's volition to use her/ his abilities in concrete situations (volitional aspect).

The NES for physics describe seven standards for communication students are expected to have acquired by the end of grade 10. Two examples are: "Students are able to ...

K1 ... share physics findings by using scientific language and scientific representation forms.
K2 ... distinguish between everyday language and scientific language when describing phenomena." (KMK, 2005, p. 12; translation by the authors).

However, these standards are not tested empirically. How to deal with them in an assessment situation is not described, also a theoretical background for the importance of these objectives respectively whether or not these objectives can be reached realistically is missing. The study of Kulgemeyer (2010) deals with this desideratum, his competence model for SCC comprises the standards described in the NES and will be described in the following

## 3.2 Description of the Model

Using a general constructivist communication model (Mehrten, 1995; Rusch, 1999) as a starting point, a model for science communication was developed (Kulgemeyer, 2010). The intention was to link general communication theory with science communication and to show the domain-specific elements of scientific communication.

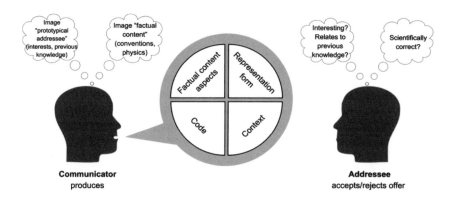

*Figure. 1: Constructivist Communication Model for Science Communication (Kulgemeyer, 2010)*

The model has – like most communication models – three important components: a communicator, who intends to communicate with an addressee about a factual content (Figure 1). The basic constructivist idea is that the communicator only partially knows which factual content he or she should select for the communication content and therefore merely speculates about the needs of the addressee. The communicator therefore neither knows about the pre-knowledge of the addressee whom he or she wants to communicate with, nor about the whole structure of the factual content that he or she intends to communicate. This is a parallel to the model of Clark (1996), who proposed a common ground in the knowledge of the communicator and the addressee as an important precondition for the understood information. The constructivist communication theory also focuses on the problem that the communicator cannot know whether there even is a common ground. In the communication, the communicator can try to fulfill the needs he or she thinks the addressee has or he or she can orientate him- or herself to the structure of the factual content. Both perspectives can lead to totally different results. A good example of language orientated towards the structure of a factual content would be the strict usage of scientific terms as the scientific language has a high density of defined terms and conventions that facilitate the communication between experts (e.g., 'wavelength' and 'frequency' in connection with light). However, a novice in this domain may need the vernacular to approach the same factual content (e.g., 'color'). The orientation to the needs of the addressee might result in using the vernacular. We distinguish between both these possible perspectives by referring to them as addressee-oriented communication and subject-adequate communication. The ability to find a proper balance between addressee-oriented and subject-adequate issues poses a challenge to scientific communication competence.

Another constructivist aspect of the model is the way the information is transferred from the communicator to the addressee. Information cannot be transported directly like in the model of Shannon and Weaver (cited in Shannon, 1948), as the addressee has to be active in the communication process. He or she perceives the communication content, as an offer of communication, which he or she is then free to accept or reject. The communicator has to construct a communication content that is attractive enough for the addressee to accept. He or she has mainly four options – called aspects of communication – that he or she can change to influence the attractiveness of the offer. These aspects are:

*Factual Content:* The scientific issues that the communicator chooses for the communication. In physics, this may be e.g., the phenomenon of dispersion of white light into the spectral colors.

*Context:* The factual connection in which the information is presented. In the example suggested above, the communicator could choose to present dispersion within the context of a rainbow. The importance of context for learning is a well-known issue in science education (Gilbert, 2006).

*Code:* The kind of language the communicator picks to communicate the information. He or she could for instance choose to communicate in scientific terms. The learning of scientific language is an important aim in science education that has been well researched (e.g., in mechanics by Rincke, 2007).

*Representation Form:* The communicator can choose between different means of presentation. In the example of light dispersion he or she could prefer a graphical representation of the optical path. The use of representation forms is part of current science education research (Chandrasegaran, Treagust, & Mocerino, 2008; Gilbert & Treagust, 2009).

This simple communication model (for details cf. Kulgemeyer & Schecker, 2009) provides a theoretical framework for the development of paper-and-pencil test items. Each item has to be linked to one of the perspectives (addressee-oriented communication and subject-adequate) and one of the aspects. The presented sample item from a paper-and-pencil-test about science communication (Figure 2; Kulgemeyer & Schecker, 2009) tests the *addressee-oriented* perspective of the model by dealing with the link between different articles about the same, correct scientific background to different addressees. However, as the articles differ in the *contexts* they use to describe heat transfer, this particular item covers the context aspect of the model.

---

You have found three articles in the internet explaining heat transfer. **All of the three articles are scientifically correct.**

**Article 1** explains heat transfer by giving details of a new type of combustion engine. Among other things, it describes how the motor must be cooled to avoid overheating and destruction.

**Article 2** explains heat transfer by showing the heat balance of the human body. Among other things, it describes why a coat keeps you warm from a physics point of view.

**Article 3** explains heat transfer regarding insulation of new buildings. Among other things, it describes which kinds of insulators conform to the new laws that house builders have to comply with.

**Decide which of these article is the most appropriate for ...**

|  | Art. 1 | Art. 2 | Art. 3 |
|---|---|---|---|
| ... tutoring your 12-year-old sister. | ○ | ● | ○ |
| ... an article in a daily newspaper. | ○ | ○ | ● |
| ... a talk to some engine builders. | ● | ○ | ○ |

---

*Figure 2: Sample Item from the Paper-and-Pencil Test (with Solution Included)*

According to Klieme et al. (2003), a competence model has to integrate a dimension that describes different levels of competence. The constructivist communication model describes the variables (aspects) a communicator may change to communicate successfully. For differentiating between levels of competence it is useful to integrate a psycholinguistic communication model (Dietrich, 2007). In such a model, the cognitive processes of the communicator in a particular communicative act are described. The first approach is to count the needed processes and to assume that the number of this processes (called "cognitive coefficient") is a measure for the difficulty of the situation – and therefore for the competence level. A standardized way to identify the number of needed processes is described in Kulgemeyer & Schecker (2009).

The theoretical competence model for SCC therefore integrates a constructivist and a psycholinguistic communication model and comprises three dimensions: perspective (with the two components addressee-oriented and subject-adequate), aspect (components: factual content, context, code, representation form) and cognitive coefficient (the number of cognitive processes needed to deal with a certain communication situation). Besides helping to construct test items the competence model is also useful for teachers to make the abstract educational objective of science communication skills more concrete. The model structure was validated empirically. In addition, two standardized ways to measure students' communication competence were developed (Kulgemeyer, 2010).

### 3.3 Empirical Evidence

As a quantitative instrument for the measurement of SCC, a paper-and-pencil-test was developed that covers the competence model (Kulgemeyer, 2010) – each test item could be linked to each one component of the three dimensions. The test was used in two pilot studies with overall 153 test persons and refined based on these results. In addition, stimulated-recall and think-aloud-methods were used to validate the test. In the main study the test was conducted with 241 students from 10$^{th}$-grade physics classes. It was finally Rasch-scaled and provides a sufficient reliability. As an additional qualitative instrument an expert-novice role-play was developed to cope with process-oriented communication competence. The basic idea of this role-play method is close to peer tutoring: grade ten students (communicators) have to explain simple physics phenomena to significantly younger students (addressees). The younger students had been trained with video feedback to respond in a specific way so that the older ones were prompted to vary their explanations in order to be successful. The younger students were asked to use unspecific prompts (e.g., "I just can't imagine that", or "Can you explain that a bit easier?") and request clarification whenever a scientific term was used. Thereby, the communicators were forced to simplify and exemplify their explanations step by step. The role-plays (overall N = 46) were videotaped, and the contents were analyzed by coding qualitative categories with qualitative content analysis (Mayring, 2000).

In the analysis of the quantitative data multidimensional Rasch-models were used to examine the relationship between the components of each dimension of the competence model (Einhaus, 2007). One main result is that the model can be used to describe competence in the area of science communication. With the dimension cognitive coefficient the model contains a dimension that describes competence levels. $R^2 = 65,2 \%$ of the item difficulty variance can be explained with this assumption of the cognitive coefficient forming three competence levels. The two aspects code and representation form were identified to be part of the same ability and can be integrated into one component of the dimension aspect, the two aspects factual content and context could each be differentiated from the other aspects. The components of the dimension perspective were found to be located on different competence levels: subject-adequate communication is the prerequisite for addressee-oriented communication. In the analysis of the qualitative data from the expert-novice role-play, the cognitive part of competence could be separated from the volitional part (Kulgemeyer & Schecker, 2010): the role-play is an assessment method for both important parts of Weinert's (2001) description of competence. Using these data as a part of a multitrait-multimethods-matrix (Campbell & Fiske, 1959), the paper-and-pencil-test could be confirmed as a valid instrument for the cognitive part of SCC but not for the volitional (Kulgemeyer, 2010).

Furthermore, the relationship between SCC and other competences or abilities was investigated, especially the relation to science content knowledge. An overlap of two aspects could be identified: content knowledge is needed to reach an average level of SCC, but seems to be an obstacle to reach highest values on the SCC-scale. Furthermore, using latent class analysis four different classes of students were found. The first group of students has high abilities both in content knowledge and subject-adequate communication but poor abilities in addressee-oriented communication. The second group forms the opposite: high abilities to communicate addressee-oriented but poor abilities in content knowledge and subject-adequate communication as well. The remaining two groups just separate students with high abilities overall from those with low abilities. These results could be confirmed with the qualitative data from the role-play: students with a high content knowledge had difficulties to communicate addressee-oriented, the best communicators had an average content knowledge.

### 3.4 Conclusions

The described competence model seems to be adequate to deal with SCC. In addition, two ways to measure SCC were developed. However, further research is needed. E.g., it has to be examined whether or not teaching communication strategies can prevent high content knowledge to be an obstacle for a high level of communication competence. In this context, the expert-novice role-play is currently adapted for teacher education to research the relationship between content knowledge, pedagogical content knowledge and communication competence. Furthermore, the finding that the paper-and-pencil-test is valid just for the cognitive part of Weinert's concept of competence has consequences for other competence areas as well. There is a need to research whether or not the volitional part of competence can be examined by using paper-and-pencil tests at all.

# 4 Socioscientific Reasoning and Decision Making

## 4.1 Theoretical Background

Socioscientific reasoning and decision making constitutes – alongside with content knowledge, scientific inquiry and science communication – one of the four competence areas within the German NES (KMK, 2005). In contrast to the areas of content knowledge and scientific inquiry, socioscientific reasoning and decision making constitutes a fairly new competence area for science education within the international but especially within the German context. Nevertheless, the importance of integrating socioscientific issues (SSI) into the science classroom to support students becoming literate citizens has been proposed by curriculum developers as well as researchers worldwide for more than two decades now (cf. AAAS, 1991; National Committee on Science Education Standards and Assessment, 1996; QCA, 1999; Ratcliffe & Grace, 2003; Sadler, Barab, & Scott, 2007). However, the implementation of socioscientific issues into the science classroom is still under way and faces many difficulties such as limited classroom time, dominance of teaching scientific content knowledge or teachers' reluctance to teach about issues that do not always correspond to their university education (Eggert & Bögeholz, 2010; Ratcliffe & Grace, 2003; Sadler et al., 2007).

In addition, the German NES only give a fairly general definition of what comprises socioscientific reasoning and decision making. There, socioscientific decision making is defined as the ability to evaluate and judge scientific evidence in different societal contexts (KMK, 2005, p. 7). The specific standards comprise a variety of different aspects that are considered to be relevant for this competence area. The focus is on different contexts that students should be able to work on such as sustainable development, bioethics, or personal and public health (ibid., p. 15). Although the national standards were developed to define students' learning outcomes at the end of grade 10, they were not primarily developed to serve as an assessment tool. To be able to assess students' competences with respect to the learning outcomes specified in the national standards, more research needs to be done concerning the theoretical foundations of socioscientific decision making, the development of adequate assessment tools, and the analysis of students' learning outcomes.

Using SSI in the science classroom is generally acknowledged as a means to foster students' abilities to support them becoming literate citizens (cf. Ratcliffe & Grace, 2003; Zeidler et al., 2006). SSI are typically real-world scenarios that are complex, ill-structured and lack an optimal solution (ibid.). Instead, several possible solutions or solution strategies exist that all have their limitations. Although SSI have their basis in science, they can no longer be solved by relying on scientific evidence only. Rather, they have to be solved by incorporating multiple scientific, economical and social perspectives as well as underlying value considerations (ibid.; Eggert & Bögeholz, 2010). In addition, SSI often represent issues of frontier science or "science in the making" (cf. Kolsto, 2001) that are characterized by a certain amount of uncertainty not only with respect to scientific evidence but also with respect to social and economic implications (cf. Sadler et al., 2007).

While working on SSI, students not only have to consider relevant content knowledge but also have to engage in various reasoning, argumentation and decision making processes in order to reach informed decisions. Existing research on socioscientific reasoning and decision making focuses primarily on the analysis of higher-order reasoning skills (cf. Erduran, Simon, & Osborne, 2004; Jimenez-Aleixandre, 2002; Kuhn, 1999; Zohar & Nemet, 2002), socioscientific reasoning (Sadler et al., 2007), or socioscientific decision making (Eggert & Bögeholz, 2010; Grace, 2009; Ratcliffe & Grace, 2003). Although these studies have different theoretical models such as Toulmin's argumentation model (Toulmin, 1958), the reflective judgment model (King & Kitchener, 2002), the developmental model of critical thinking (Kuhn, 1999), or models derived from decision theory (cf. Abelson & Levi, 1985; Betsch & Haberstroh, 2005), they all have central aspects in common. All models stress the importance of identifying or developing pros and cons with respect to possible solutions. Elaborate reasoning processes are characterized by the integration or synthesis of pros and cons as well as the ability to weigh arguments. In a similar vein, decision theory stresses the importance of evaluating the advantages and disadvantages of possible options (=solutions) as well as weighting their importance in order to reach an informed decision.

With respect to the research presented here, a meta-model from descriptive decision theory (Betsch & Haberstoh, 2005) was regarded as being most fruitful to explain central cognitive processes in decision situations. This model was adapted for the specific requirements of decisions with multiple legitimate solutions and applied to the context of SSI (cf. Bögeholz, 2011; Eggert & Bögeholz, 2006).

## 4.2 Model for Socioscientific Reasoning and Decision Making

According to Betsch and Haberstroh (2005), decision processes can be divided into three main phases: a preselectional, a selectional and a postselectional phase. In the preselectional phase, a problem situation is identified and possible solutions are generated. In the selectional phase, developed solutions are compared and evaluated. Finally, a choice for one solution or a combination of solutions is made. In the postselectional phase, the chosen solution will be implemented (ibid.).

On the basis of this model, the model for socioscientific decision making postulates two dimensions that take up central processes of the preselectional and the selectional phase (Bögeholz, 2011; Eggert & Bögeholz, 2006). The first dimension – "generating solutions" – describes students' abilities to comprehend and to describe a problem situation and to develop possible solutions. In addition, the dimension comprises the ability to reflect on possible solutions and the evidence on which these solutions are based. Thus, the focus within this dimension is on information search and integration processes. The second dimension – "evaluating solutions" – describes students' abilities to compare and evaluate multiple possible solutions and to reach an informed decision by using a decision making strategy. In contrast to spontaneous decision making behaviour, decision making strategies can generally be characterized by using "cut-offs" or "trade-offs" (cf. Jungermann, Pfister, & Fischer, 2004). When using cut-offs, individuals eliminate possible solutions if one aspect of a particular solution does not reach a certain level (ibid.). Thus, solutions are eliminated by using one piece of information at a time. When using trade-offs, individuals can trade-off advantages and disadvantages of possible solutions (ibid.). Solutions are evaluated by using and integrating several pieces of information at the same time. In addition, the dimension comprises the ability to reflect on and to monitor decision processes. Thus, this dimension focuses on students' reasoning and evaluation processes. Moreover, a third dimension – "understanding values and norms" – was postulated that especially acknowledges the ethical complexity of SSI. This third dimension describes students' abilities to comprehend and to reflect on values and norms that underlie and drive discussions about SSI as well as possible solutions to SSI (cf. Figure 3).

In line with existing research on socioscientific reasoning and decision making (cf. Science Education for Public Understanding Project (SEPUP), 1995; Seethaler & Linn, 2004; Wilson & Sloane, 2000) different levels of complexity were proposed for each dimension. In general, a base level competence (level 1) for all dimensions is characterized by using only one piece of information or evidence. An intermediate level (level 2) is characterized by using several pieces of information or evidence and/ or integrating some of the information/evidence given. An elaborate level (level 3) is characterized by integrating all relevant pieces of information/evidence. Besides, all levels are characterized by different qualities of reflection and monitoring processes. Figure 3 shows the proposed theoretical model and displays the assumption of different levels of complexity with respect to the dimension "evaluating solutions".

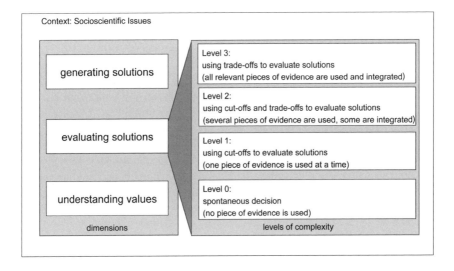

*Figure 3: Model for Socioscientific Reasoning and Decision Making (cf. adapted from Bögeholz, 2011)*

## 4.3 Empirical Evidence

Several studies were conducted to analyse whether the proposed theoretical framework could adequately explain students' socioscientific decision making processes while working on socioscientific issues with multiple possible solutions. The aim of these studies was to develop a reliable and valid test instrument. In order to measure socioscientific reasoning and decision making as proposed in the theoretical model, a between-item-multidimensionality approach was used (Wu, Adams, & Wilson, 1998). We assumed that performance on test items for each dimension can be traced back to only one latent trait.

First, a paper-and-pencil test was developed that covered students' competences with regard to the dimension "evaluating solutions". The test solely consisted of extended response questions. After having conducted qualitative studies, using think aloud protocols, the test was administered to 436 students from junior and senior high school as well as first year university undergraduates (cf. Eggert & Bögeholz, 2010). Students were confronted with two socioscientific decision making situations each with four different possible solutions. They were asked to compare all solutions as detailed as possible and to reach a decision for one solution or a combination of solutions. In addition, students were given a third situation, in which they were asked to monitor decision processes from other people. Students' answers were then scored using a scoring guide that accounted for students' ability to compare given options by using relevant pieces of evidence and applying cut-offs, trade-offs, or both. In addition, students' ability to monitor decision processes was also scored. Test scores on the different scoring rubrics were then Rasch-scaled using the Rasch Partial Credit Model (Masters, 1982). Preliminary analyses had shown that – in comparison to Latent Class Analyses and Mixed Rasch models – the Rasch Partial Credit model could explain the data best. WLE Person Separation reliability was found to be 0.66, EAP/PV reliability 0.70 (Eggert & Bögeholz, 2010). Item fit indices where in the acceptable range. Threshold analyses showed that some categories with respect to polytomous items had to be collapsed. Analyses also showed that the proposed increase in student ability with respect to "evaluating solutions" could be confirmed (cf. Fig. 3). In addition, linear regression could show that years of education had a strong effect on student ability ($r^2$=.28, p<.001). Correlations between student ability and grade in biology was not significant, while a correlation with grade in German as first language was $r = .23$ (p < .05). . These results were not unexpected in that test items were intended to trigger students' reasoning and argumentation processes.

Second, a paper-and-pencil test was developed that covered students' competences with respect to the dimension "generating solutions" (cf. Gausmann et al., 2011; Teschner et al., in prep.). The test again consisted of extended response questions. Think aloud protocols were used to optimize the developed test items. The final test instrument was administered to 580 students from junior and senior high school. Here, students were confronted with two socioscientific issues, in which they had to describe the socioscientific issue as a first step and as a second step to develop possible solutions. In addition, a third socioscientific issue was given in which students had to evaluate given solutions in terms of the presented information (Bögeholz, 2011). The scoring procedure was adapted from the procedure used with respect to the dimension "evaluating solutions".

Data analyses showed that student ability with respect to this dimension could again be analysed with the Rasch Partial Credit model (ibid.). WLE Person Separation reliability was found to be 0.62 (Teschner et al., in prep). Again fit indices were in the acceptable range (ibid.). Base level responses were characterized by using only one piece of information to describe a problem situation or to develop possible solutions. Intermediate level responses were characterized by using several single pieces of information, while elaborate level responses were characterized by integrating several pieces of information. Thus, there is evidence that the proposed increase in complexity – as described for the dimension "evaluating solutions" can also hold for this dimension.

## 4.4 Conclusions

The described studies showed that the two major dimensions – "generating solutions" and "evaluating solutions" – of the proposed model for socioscientific reasoning and decision making can each be explained using the Rasch Partial Credit model. Thus, there is evidence that students' performances on the two test instruments can be traced back to one latent trait. For the dimension "evaluating solutions", different competence levels were characterized by the use of different decision making strategies. These decision making strategies differed with respect to the amount of pieces of evidence that were used and the integration of evidence to reach a decision. In addition, different competence levels were also characterized by different qualities of monitoring processes. In a similar vein, competence levels for the dimension "generating solutions" were also characterized by an increase with respect to information integration.

However, more research needs to be done to replicate these findings. In addition, research is being conducted at the moment to develop a test instrument for the dimension "understanding values". The aim is to use all three test instruments in a quantitative study to use a multidimensional approach and to shed more light on the relations between all three dimensions.

# 5 Summary

The three approaches described in this article are embedded in the normative structure of four competence areas in the German NES. From this perspective, each of them provides complementary aspects of students' competences in the science subjects. This complementarity is reflected by a disjunctive conceptual basis (as can be seen in the cited literature) and methodological differences. As the presented research projects were planned independently of each other at different universities and in different research groups of different disciplines (biology, chemistry and physics education), this does not seem to be surprising. However, as all of the three approaches focus on modeling competence in the science subjects this separation raises different questions.

The use of competence models intends to provide a coherent framework for researchers and teachers to design learning environments and develop assessment systems. Different domain-specific models have been published in the German-speaking countries with the aim to describe competence in science subjects (e.g., Labudde & Adamina, 2008; Neumann, Kauertz, Lau, Notarp, & Fischer, 2007; Schecker & Parchmann, 2006). These models differ in the dimensions of competence, the graduation of each dimension, and in the methods used to develop the competence structure. Regarding the domain-specificity of the concept of competence (Weinert, 2001), an obvious problem is the definition of a "domain" and, accordingly, the level of analysis of a particular competence model (e.g., a model for chemistry competence or a model for conceptual understanding of acids and bases; cf. the contribution by Schecker, *this volume*) With respect to the level of analysis it is debatable where the dividing line between a competence (as a complex construct) and a simple ability lies.

While these questions might be answerable regarding content knowledge, it seems questionable whether an appropriate answer can be given for the other two presented competence areas of science communication on the one hand, and socioscientific reasoning and decision making on the other. Competent behavior in both areas makes use of scientific concepts or scientific evidence from a certain domain but broadens the perspective to incorporate economical and social perspectives as well as underlying value considerations. This broader concept of scientific competence calls the traditional compartmentation into question (e.g., biology, chemistry, and physics as separate disciplines as it is usual in Germany and several other countries). This is in line with the conceptual roots of these competence areas: Both the concept of competence and the overarching goal of scientific literacy focus on the mastery of everyday situations related to scientific phenomena and everyday situations are usually not limited to the perspective of a single discipline.

Situations that demand the application of science communication or socioscientific reasoning might require more or less content knowledge or conceptual understanding. Hence, the amount of necessary content knowledge varies across situations. The possibility of this continuum also induces the questions how the different competence areas are interrelated. Is content knowledge the basis for science communication and socioscientific decision making, i.e. is there a hierarchy within the competence areas? Or do the four competence areas describe qualitatively different skills and abilities (as the normative framework of the German NES envisions)? One might even say that both areas, science communication and socioscientific reasoning, are just special cases of dealing with science content knowledge and – even more – that this is basically what constitutes science competences. However, the role of content knowledge has to be further examined.

Another question is the influence of the situational context. Science communication competence relies on contextual factors (e.g., the individual's image of the addressee), which is also true for socioscientific reasoning. Explaining everyday phenomena (e.g., boiling of water or the electric circuit of a bicycle light) to your younger brother can be quite unelaborated, but can also be pretty challenging when your science teacher listens. A good explanation manages to balance between accuracy of the content and the abilities and knowledge of the addressee. In the given example, this balancing is complicated because of two diverse addressees but additionally by assuming that the teacher heavily attaches importance to factual accuracy. This is similar to socioscientific decision making situations involving personal value considerations where students' (but not only students') decisions are driven by a social desirability bias.

Currently, most competence models are normative, as in the case of the German NES. Therefore, strong efforts have and still are made to provide empirical evidence to the validity of the respective models. Further research is needed to shed light on the diverse open questions, of which some have been indicated above. In addition, there is also a need to develop effective ways to deal with competence orientation in classroom practice. Current research usually focuses on the modeling of competences, not on the way to teach them. As well as in central comparative tests, the model-based measurement method could help teachers to evaluate their classes, to discover problems and to reveal learning progress. In addition, it should be analyzed to what extent higher levels can be reached by specific impulses and supporting tools.

## References

Abelson, R. P. & Levi, A. (1985). Decision making and decision theory. In G. Lindzey & E. Aronson (Eds.), *Handbook of Social Psychology* (Vol. 1, pp. 231-309). Reading, MA: Addisson-Wesley.

Aebli H. (1980). *Denken: Das Ordnen des Tuns* [Thinking: Making order of action]. Band I. Stuttgart: Klett-Cotta.

Alves C. B., Gierl M. J., & Lai, H. (2010). Using automated item generation to promote principled test design and development. In S. Ferrara & K. Huff (Chairs), *Cognition and Valid Inferences About Student Achievement*. Cognition and Assessment SIG symposium at 2010 AERA Annual Conference, Denver.

American Association for the Advancement of Science (1991). *Science for All Americans, Project 2061*. New York: OUP.

Anderson, R. C. (1984). Some reflections on the acquisition of knowledge. *Educational Researcher, 13*(9), 5–10.

Beaton, A. E., Martin, M. O., Mullis, I. V. S., Gonzalez, E. J., Smith, T. A., & Kelly, D. L. (1996). *Science Achievement in the Middle School Years: IEA's third International Mathematics and Science Study* (TIMSS). Chestnut Hill, MA: Center for the Study of Testing, Evaluation, and Educational Policy, Boston College.

Bernholt, S. (2010). *Kompetenzmodellierung in der Chemie – Theoretische und empirische Reflexion am Beispiel des Modells hierarchischer Komplexität* [Modelling Competence in Chemistry – Theoretical and Empirical Reflections Using the Example of the Model of Hierarchical Complexity]. Berlin: Logos Verlag.

Bernholt, S. & Parchmann, I. (2011). Assessing the complexity of students' knowledge in chemistry. *Chemistry Education Research and Practice, 12*, 167-173.

Bernholt S., Parchmann I., & Commons M. L. (2009). Kompetenzmodellierung zwischen Forschung und Unterrichtspraxis [Modelling Scientific Competence between Research and Teaching Practice]. *Zeitschrift für Didaktik der Naturwissenschaften, 15*, 217-243.

Betsch, T. & Haberstoh, S. (2005). *The Routines of Decision Making*. Mahwah, NJ: Erlbaum Associates.

Biggs, J. B. (1999). *Teaching for Quality Learning at University*. Buckingham: SRHE and Open University Press.

Biggs, J. B. & Collis, K. F. (1982). *Evaluating the Quality of Learning – the SOLO Taxonomy* (1st Edition). New York: Academic Press.

Bögeholz, S. (2011). Bewertungskompetenz im Kontext Nachhaltiger Entwicklung: Ein Forschungsprogramm. In D. Höttecke (Ed.), *Naturwissenschaftliche Bildung als Beitrag zur Gestaltung partizipativer Demokratie* (pp. 32-46). Münster: LIT-Verlag.

Boulding, K. E. (1961). *The Image. Knowledge in Life and Society*. The University of Michigan Press.

Bricker, L. A. & Bell, P. (2008). Conceptualizations of argumentation from learning science studies and the learning sciences and their implications for the practices of science education. *Science Education, 92*, 437-498.

Brüggemann, O. (1967). *Naturwissenschaft und Bildung* [Science and Education]. Heidelberg: Quelle & Meyer.

Bruner, J. S. (1977). *The Process of Education*. Cambridge, MA: Harvard University Press.

Campbell, D. & Fiske, D. (1959). Convergent and discriminant validation by the multitrait multimethod matrix. *Psychological Bulletin, 56*(2), 81-105.

Chandrasegaran, A. L., Treagust, D. F., & Mocerino, M. (2008). An evaluation to promote students' ability to use multiple representation when describing and explaining chemical reactions. *Research in Science Education, 38*, 237-248.

Clark, H. (1996). *Using Language*. Cambridge: Cambridge University Press.

Commons, M. L., Trudeau, E. J., Stein, S. A., Richards, F. A., & Krause, S. R. (1998). Hierarchical complexity of tasks shows the existence of developmental stages. *Developmental Review, 18*, 237-278.

Corcoran, T., Mosher, F. A., & Rogat, A. (Eds.) (2009). *Learning Progressions in Science – an Evidence Based Approach to Reform*. Philadelphia, PA: CPRE – Consortium for Policy Research in Education. Available at: http://www.cpre.org/ccii/images/stories/ccii_pdfs/lp_science_rr63.pdf (Date of Access: January 2011).

CSMEE (Center for Science, Mathematics, and Engineering Education) (1996): *National Science Education Standards*. Washington: National Academy Press.

DeBoer, G. E. (2000). Scientific literacy: Another look at its historical and contemporary meanings and its relationship to science education reform. *Journal of Research in Science Teaching, 37*(6), 582-601.

Dewey, J. (2008). *John Dewey – The Middle Works (1899–1924)*, vol. 4: 1907-1909. Southern Illinois University Press.

DiBello, L. V. & Stout, W. S. (Eds.) (2008). Special issue: IRT-based cognitive diagnostic models and related methods. *Journal of Educational Measurement, 44*(4), 285-383.

Ditton, H. (2002). Evaluation und Qualitätssicherung [Evaluation and Quality Control]. In R. Tippelt (Ed.), Handbuch Bildungsforschung (pp. 775-790). Opladen: Leske + Budrich.

Driver, R., Newton, P., & Osborne, J. (2000). Establishing the norms of scientific argumentation in classroom. *Science Education, 84*(3), 287-312.

Duit, R. (2009). *STCSE – Bibliography: Students' and Teachers' Conceptions and Science Education*. Kiel, Germany: IPN (http://www.ipn.unikiel.de/aktuell/stcse/stcse.html) (January 2011).

Duncan, R.G. & Hmelo-Silver, C.E. (2009). Editorial – Learning progressions: Aligning curriculum, instruction, and assessment. *Journal of Research in Science Teaching, 46*, 606-609.

Duschl, R. A., Schweinguber, H. A., & Shouse, A. W. (Eds.) (2007). *Taking Science to School: Learning and Teaching Science in Grades K-8*. Washington, DC: The National Academies Press.

Eggert, S. & Bögeholz, S. (2006). Göttinger Modell der Bewertungskompetenz – Teilkompetenz „Bewerten, Entscheiden und Reflektieren" für Gestaltungsaufgaben Nachhaltiger Entwicklung. *Zeitschrift für Didaktik der Naturwissenschaften, 12*, 177-199.

Eggert, S. & Bögeholz, S. (2010). Students' use of decision making strategies with regard to socio-scientific-issues. An Application of the Partial Credit Model. *Science Education, 94*(2), 230-258.

Einhaus, E. (2007). *Schülerkompetenzen im Bereich Wärmelehre*. Berlin: Logos.

Erduran, S., Osborne, J. F., & Simon, S. (2004). Enhancing the Quality of Argument in School Science. *Journal of Research in Science Teaching, 41*(10), 994-1020.

Fraser, B. J., Walberg, H. J., Welch, W. W., & Hattie, J. A. (1987). Syntheses of educational productivity research. *International Journal of Educational Research, 11*(2), 145-252.

Frenz, H.-G., Krüger, K., & Tröger, H. (1973). Die Unangemessenheit der herkömmlichen Testdiagnostik für schulische Entscheidungen [The inadequacy of traditional diagnostics for decisions in school settings]. In H. Schiefele & R. Oerter (Eds.), *Diagnostik in der Schule* (pp. 53-93). München: Oldenbourg Verlag.

Gilbert, J. (2006). On the nature of "context" in chemical education. *International Journal of Science Education, 28*(9), 957-976.

Gilbert, J. & Treagust, D. F. (2009). Macro, submicro and symbolic representations and the relationship between them: Key models in chemical education. In J. Gilbert & D. Treagust (Eds.), *Multiple Representations in Chemical Education* (pp. 1-10). New York: Springer.

Gräber, W. & Bolte, C. (1997). *Scientific Literacy – An International Symposium*. Kiel: IPN.

Hafner, R. (2007). Standards in science education in Australia. In D. Waddington, P. Nentwig & S. Schanze (Eds.), *Making it Comparable. Standards in Science Education* (pp. 23-60). Münster: Waxmann.

Jimenez-Aleixandre, M. P. (2002). Knowledge Producers or Knowledge Consumers? Argumentation and Decision Making about environmental management. *International Journal of Science Education, 24*(11), 1171-1190.

Jonassen, D. H. & Ionas, I. G. (2008). Designing effective supports for causal reasoning. *Educational Technology Research and Development, 56*, 287-308.

Jungermann, H., Pfister, H. R., & Fischer, K. (2004). *Die Psychologie der Entscheidung* [The psychology of decision]. Heidelberg: Spektrum.

Klieme, E., Avenarius, H., Blum, W., Döbrich, P., Gruber, H., Prenzel, M., et al. (2003). *Zur Entwicklung nationaler Bildungsstandards – Expertise*. Berlin: Bundesministerium für Bildung und Forschung (BMBF).

Klieme, E. & Leutner, D. (2006). Kompetenzmodelle zur Erfassung individueller Lernergebnisse und zur Bilanzierung von Bildungsprozessen. Beschreibung eines neu eingerichteten Schwerpunktprogramms der DFG [Models of Competencies for Assessment of Individual Learning Outcomes and the Evaluation of Educational Processes. Description of a new DFG priority research program]. *Zeitschrift für Pädagogik, 52*(6), 876-903.

Klieme, E., Leutner, D., & Kenk, M. (Eds.) (2010). Kompetenzmodellierung. Zwischenbilanz des DFG-Schwerpunktprogramms und Perspektiven des Forschungsansatzes [Competence modeling]. *Zeitschrift für Pädagogik, Beiheft 56*. Weinheim: Beltz.

KMK (2005). Bildungsstandards im Fach Chemie für den Mittleren Schulabschluss. München: Luchterhand.

Koeppen, K., Hartig, J., Klieme, E., & Leutner, D. (2008). Current Issues in Competence Modeling and Assessment. *Zeitschrift für Psychologie/Journal of Psychology, 216*(2), 61-73.

Kolen M. J. & Brennan R. L. (2004), *Test Equating, Scaling, and Linking. Methods and Practices* (2. Edition). New York: Springer.

Kolstø, S. D. (2001). Scientific literacy for citizenship: Tools for dealing with the science dimension of controversial socioscientific issues. *Science Education, 85*, 291-310.

Kuhn, D. (1999). A Developmental Model of Critical Thinking. *Educational Researcher, 28*, 16-25.

Kulgemeyer, C. (2010). *Physikalische Kommunikationskompetenz. Modellierung und Diagnostik* [Physics communication competence: Modeling and Diagnosis]. Berlin: Logos.

Kulgemeyer, C. & Schecker, H. (2009). Kommunikationskompetenz in der Physik: Zur Entwicklung eines domänenspezifischen Kommunikationsbegriffs [Physics communication competence: on the development of a domain-specific concept of communication]. *Zeitschrift für Didaktik der Naturwissenschaften, 15*, 131-153.

Kulgemeyer, C. & Schecker, H. (2010). Kompetenzdiagnostik mit qualitativen Methoden am Beispiel eines Rollenspiels. Zum Verhältnis von Kognition und Volition bei Kommunikationskompetenz. PhyDid B – Didaktik der Physik –*Beiträge zur DPG-Frühjahrstagung* 1.

Labudde, P. & Adamina, M. (2008). HarmoS Naturwissenschaften: Impulse für den naturwissenschaftlichen Unterricht von morgen [HarmoS Science: impetuses for the science classes of tomorrow]. *Beiträge zur Lehrerbildung, 26*(3), 351-360.

Laird, J. E., Rosenbloom, P. S., & Newell, A. (1986). Chunking in soar: the anatomy of general learning mechanisms. *Machine Learning, 1*, 11-46.

Masters, G. N. (1982). A Rasch model for Partial Credit Scoring. *Psychometrika, 47,* 149-174.

Mayring, P. (2000). Qualitative content analysis. *Forum: Qualitative Social Research* [Online Journal], *1*(2). Available at: http://www.qualitative-research.net/fqs-texte/2-00/2-00mayring-e.htm [Date of Access: 21/09/2010].

McClelland, D. C. (1973). Testing for competence rather than for intelligence. *American Psychologist, 28*, 1-14.

MCEETYA (Ministerial Council on Education, Employment, Training and Youth Affairs) (2005). *National assessment: Program, science, year 6, 2003: Technical report.* Sidney: MCEETYA.

Merten, K. (1995). Konstruktivismus als Theorie für die Kommunikationswissenschaft. *MedienJournal, 4*, 3-21.

Millar, R. & Osborne, J. (1998). *Beyond 2000: Science Education for the Future.* London: King's College London, School of Education.

Mislevy, R. J. & Haertel, G. D. (2006). Implications of evidence-centered design in educational testing. *Educational Measurement: Issues and Practice, 25*(4), 6-20.

Mulford, D. R. & Robinson, W. R. (2002). An inventory for alternate conceptions among first-semester general chemistry students. *Journal of Chemical Education, 79*(6), 739-744.

National Committee on Science Standards and Assessment (1996). *National Science Education Standards.* Washington, DC: National Academy Press.

Nentwig, P. & Schanze, S. (2007). Making it comparable – Standards in science education. In D. Waddington, P. Nentwig, & S. Schanze (Eds.), *Making it Comparable – Standards in Science Education* (pp. 11-19). Münster: Waxmann.

Neumann, K., Kauertz, A., Lau, A., Notarp, H., & Fischer, H. E. (2007). Die Modellierung physikalischer Kompetenz und ihrer Entwicklung [Modelling structure and development of students' physics competence]. *Zeitschrift für Didaktik der Naturwissenschaften, 13*, 103-123.

OECD (2001). *Knowledge and Skills for Life – First Results from the OECD Programme for International Student Assessment (PISA) 2000.* Paris: OECD.

OECD (2004). *Learning for Tomorrow's World. First Results from PISA 2003.* Paris: OECD.

OECD (2007). *PISA 2006: Science Competence for Tomorrows world (Vol. 1).* Paris: OECD.

Oelkers, J. (1997). How to define and justify scientific literacy. In W. Gräber & C. Bolte (Eds.), *Scientific Literacy* (pp. 87-101). Kiel: IPN.

Oelkers, J. & Reusser, K. (2008). *Developing Quality – Safeguarding Standards – Handling Differentiation*. Berlin: BMBF.

Osborne, J., Erduran, S., & Simon, S. (2004). Enhancing the quality of argumentation in school science. *Journal of Research in Science Teaching, 41*(10), 994-1020.

Pellegrino, J. W., Chudowsky, N., & Glaser, R. (2001). *Knowing What Students Know: The Science and Design of Educational Assessment*. Washington, DC: National Academy Press.

Qualification and Curriculum Authority (1999). *The National Curriculum for England. Key Stages 1-4*. London: Crown.

Ratcliffe, M. & Grace, M. (2003). *Science Education for Citizenship*. Maidenhead: OUP.

Ravitch, D. (1995). *National Standards in American Education: A Citizen's Guide*. Washington, DC: Brookings Institution.

Rincke, K. (2007). *Sprachentwicklung und Fachlernen im Mechanikunterricht. Sprache und Kommunikation bei der Einführung in den Kraftbegriff* [Language development and subject learning in mechanic lessons]. Berlin: Logos.

Roberts, D. A. (2007). Scientific literacy / science literacy. In S. K. Abell & N. G. Lederman (Eds.), *Handbook of Research on Science Education* (pp. 729-780). Mahwah, NJ: Lawrence Erlbaum Associates.

Rusch, G. (1999). Eine Kommunikationstheorie für kognitive Systeme [A communication theory for cognitive systems]. In G. Rusch & S. Schmidt (Eds.), *Konstruktivismus in der Medien- und Kommunikationswissenschaft* (pp. 150-184). Frankfurt a. M.: Suhrkamp.

Sadler, T. D., Barab, S. A., & Scott, B. (2007). What do students gain by engaging in socioscientific inquiry? *Research in Science Education, 37*(4), 371-391.

Schecker, H. & Parchmann, I. (2006). Modellierung naturwissenschaftlicher Kompetenz [Modeling scientific competence]. *Zeitschrift für Didaktik der Naturwissenschaften, 12*, 45-66.

Schmidt, H.-J. (1997). Students' misconceptions – looking for a pattern. *Science Education, 81*(2), 123-135.

Science Education for Public Understanding Project (1995). *Issues, Evidence, and You: Teacher's Guide*. Berkeley: University Of California, Lawrence Hall of Science.

Seethaler, S. & Linn, M. (2004). Genetically modified food in perspective: An inquiry-based curriculum to help middle school students make sense of tradeoffs. *International Journal of Science Education, 26*(14), 1765-1785.

Sekretariat der Ständigen Konferenz der Kultusminister der Länder in der Bundesrepublik Deutschland (Ed.) (2005a). *Bildungsstandards im Fach Biologie für den Mittleren Schulabschluss* [Educational standards for Biology]. München: Luchterhand.

Sekretariat der Ständigen Konferenz der Kultusminister der Länder in der Bundesrepublik Deutschland (Ed.) (2005b). *Bildungsstandards im Fach Chemie für den Mittleren Schulabschluss* [Educational standards for Chemistry]. München: Luchterhand.

Sekretariat der Ständigen Konferenz der Kultusminister der Länder in der Bundesrepublik Deutschland (Ed.) (2005c). *Bildungsstandards im Fach Physik für den Mittleren Schulabschluss* [Educational standards for Physics]. München: Luchterhand.

Shannon, C. (1948). A mathematical theory of communication. *The Bell System Technical Journal, 27*, 379-423, 623-656.

Shavelson, R. J., Ruiz-Primo, M. A., & Wiley, E. W. (2005). Windows into the mind. *Higher Education, 49*, 413-430.

Slavin, R. E. (2002). Evidence-Based Education Policies: Transforming Educational Practice and Re-search. *Educational Researcher, 31*(7), 15-21.

Teschner, S., Ostermeyer, F., Eggert, S., Watermann, R., Hasselhorn, M., & Bögeholz, S. (in prep). *Analysing students' information integration processes while working on socioscientific issues*. Unpublished manuscript.

Toulmin, S. (1958). *The Uses of Argument*. Cambridge, UK: Cambridge University Press.

Trefil, J. S. (2008). *Why Science?* Arlington, VA: Teachers College Press & the National Science Teacher Association.

Waddington, D., Nentwig, P., & Schanze, S. (2007). *Making it Comparable – Standards in Science Education*. Münster: Waxmann.

Weinert, F. E. (1999). *Concepts of Competence*. Contribution within the OECD-Project Definition and Selection of Competencies: Theoretical and Conceptual Foundations (DeSeCo). Neuchâtel: Bundesamt für Statistik (Ch).

Weinert, F. E. (2001). Concept of competence: A conceptual clarification. In D. S. Rychen & L. H. Salganik (Eds.), *Defining and Selecting Key Competencies* (pp. 45-65). Seattle, WA: Hogrefe & Huber.

White, R. (1959). Motivation reconsidered: The concept of competence. *Psychological Review, 66*, 297-333.

Wild, E., Hofer, M., & Pekrun, R. (2006). Psychologie des Lernens [The psychology of learning]. In A. Krapp & B. Weidenmann (Eds.), *Pädagogische Psychologie* (pp. 203-267). Weinheim: Beltz PVU.

Wilson, M. & Sloane, K. (2000). From Principles to Practice: An Embedded Assessment System. *Applied Measurement in Education, 13*(2), 181-208.

Wu, M. L., Adams, R. J., Wilson, M. R., & Haldane, S. (2007). *ACER ConQuest. General Item Response Modelling Software*. Hawthorn, AUS: ACER Press.

Zeidler, D. L., Osborne, J., Erduran, S., Simon, S., & Monk, M. (2006). The role of argument during discourse about socioscientific issues. In D. L. Zeidler (Ed.), *The Role of Moral Reasoning on Socioscientific Issues and Discourse in Science Education* (pp. 97-116). Dordrecht: Kluwer Academic Publishers.

Zohar, A. & Nemet, F. (2002). Fostering Students' Knowledge and Argumentation Skills Through Dilemmas in Human Genetics. *Journal of Research in Science Teaching, 39*(1), 36-62.

# Chapter 9

## Assessment of Standards-based Learning Outcomes in Science Education: Perspectives from the German Project EsNaS

*Kerstin Kremer[1], Hans E. Fischer[2], Alexander Kauertz[3], Jürgen Mayer[1], Elke Sumfleth[4] & Maik Walpuski[4]*
[1]*Didaktik der Biologie, University of Kassel;* [2]*Didaktik der Physik, University of Duisburg-Essen;* [3]*Fakultät II – Physik, University of Education Weingarten;* [4]*Didaktik der Chemie, University of Duisburg-Essen, Germany*

### Abstract

The Standing Conference of German Ministers of Education released National Educational Standards (NES) to define expectations for regular learning outcomes in secondary schools for the three subjects of science: biology, chemistry, and physics. The NES in science explicitly focus on the development of students' competencies with respect to four areas of competence: *use of content knowledge, acquirement of knowledge, scientific communication, and evaluation and judgement.* Within the project ESNaS[1] (Evaluation of the National Educational Standards for Natural Sciences at the Lower Secondary Level), researchers first agreed on a competence model to describe hierarchical levels of competence based on the formulated expectations, and secondly, researchers and educators collaboratively developed test items according to this competence model for the task development of a national assessment. In a validation study, 998 test items were administered on 10th grade students from 160 schools in eight German federal states (N = 6845). Data were analyzed by one-parameter Rasch analyses to estimate difficulty, fit, and discrimination. The validation study provides evidence for the hierarchical graduation of item difficulty with respect to the test items' complexity and cognitive processes. Data based on the validation study are presented here, and future work and implications of the project are discussed.

---

1   Under the direction of the German Institute for Educational Progress (Institut für Qualitätsentwicklung im Bildungswesen, IQB.)

# 1 Introduction

In response to findings of international large-scale assessments such as the Programme for International Student Assessment (PISA) and the Third International Mathematics and Science Study (TIMSS), the Standing Conference of German Ministers of Education released the National Educational Standards (NES) as normative guidelines for secondary schools (Klieme et al., 2003; KMK, 2005a, 2005b, 2005c). The introduction of NES for grades 9 and 10, which are the last years of the secondary level of the German school system, aims to create the opportunity to make classroom teaching more efficient and comparable across the 16 federal states (Nentwig & Schanze, 2007). NES were developed for the subjects of mathematics, German, first foreign language (English, French) and sciences (biology, chemistry, physics).

German Science Educational Standards separately address each of the three subjects of science teaching (biology, chemistry, and physics) and aim to initiate profound changes for the teaching and assessment of the respective science subjects in school. First, the new standards explicitly focus on the development of competencies and define four areas of competence for science education: *use of content knowledge, acquirement of knowledge* (in an epistemological sense and through scientific inquiry), *scientific communication* and *evaluation and judgement*. Second, the NES initiate a shift from an input-oriented educational system to one that is output-oriented. National assessments based on these standards are expected to be central for assessing the quality development of the educational system – both as a whole and at the individual school level.

This article provides a short introduction to common features of the National Educational Standards (NES) for biology, chemistry and physics in Germany along with information concerning the initial preparation of the national level assessment for the science subjects within the project ESNaS. Described first are the development of a framework model for test item construction and the initial preparation of measurement scales for a national assessment. Second, results from a validation study and item examples are given, and lastly, the future status of assessment is discussed.

*National Educational Standards (NES) in Germany*

The discussion on educational standards for science began much earlier in many other countries than it did in Germany. Prior to the introduction of NES for secondary school (grade 9 or grade 10) graduation in Germany, a particular subject's content were outlined by written curricula for every school year. Each teacher was responsible for classroom instruction and the assessment of students' learning. The

German education system was input-oriented, what means that policymakers controlled curricula, teacher education, and school funding but policymakers neglected learning process outcomes, which would have helped monitor the educational system as a whole (Klieme et al., 2003). Many Anglo-American countries (e.g., the US and Canada), however, have a long tradition of standardization and standardized assessments (CMEC, 1997; NRC, 1996; Fischer, Kauertz, & Neumann, 2008). The US National Science Education Standards (NSES) focus on key content referring to scientific literacy by "specifying what facts, concepts and forms of inquiry should be learned and how they should be taught and evaluated" (Eisenhart, Finkel, & Marion, 1996, p. 266). In contrast, the German NES can be viewed as performance standards that specify competences. The term "competence" is based on Weinert's notion of competence as cognitive abilities and motivational, volitional, and social readiness to solve problems in variable situations (Weinert, 2001).

The conception of the NES as performance standards required that proficiency levels are established to refer to when measuring student performance. Similarly, the PISA framework describes proficiency levels with respect to the different components of scientific literacy. The description of these levels was obtained by grouping items within particular ranges of difficulty and describing these levels based on the items' content; that is, what area of scientific literacy they test. However, attempts to validate these proficiency levels failed (Prenzel et al., 2001). PISA 2000 was prior to the formation of the NES for science subjects, and no validated hierarchy of proficiency yet existed. Based on Blooms' taxonomy (Anderson & Krathwohl, 2001) the NES specify proficiency levels as reproduction, application, and transfer (Neumann, Kauertz, & Fischer, 2010).

*Evaluating science educational standards in Germany: The project ESNaS*

For the evaluation of the implemented NES in science, the German Institute for Educational Progress (German: Institut zur Qualitätsentwicklung im Bildungswesen, IQB) assembled the interdisciplinary project "Evaluation of the National Educational Standards for Natural Sciences at the Lower Secondary Level" (ESNaS) in 2007. The project aims to create a collection of standardized test items for the three science subjects in order to establish national performance scales based on the NES. Moreover, empirical research projects that build on these tasks or clarify subsidiary research problems are conducted to solve a number of research questions that occur during the process.

Within the project ESNaS, scientists from science education, linguistics, psychology, and psychometrics work together with educators and practitioners of schools and school administration from the 16 federal states. Item development was done separately for the three science subject of biology, chemistry, and physics by three groups of item developers (educators and practitioners) from all federal states. This process was coordinated and supervised by science education experts from four German universities. In advance of the item development process, the expert coordination teams developed a model of competence addressing the four areas of competence in the NES *(use of content knowledge, acquirement of knowledge, scientific communication, and evaluation* and *judgement)*. The model development was based on national and international research results from the three science subjects. During item development, experiences from different curricula of the federal states were equally taken into account due to close practitioner cooperation. All participating groups held numerous subject-specific and interdisciplinary meetings, and the entire development process was guided by advisory experts. The test items were evaluated by experts from science education, measurement, and linguistics, and revised by the item developers in an iterative feedback process. Pilot-studies with small samples were also carried out to ensure test items' comprehensibility and suitability for assessment.

Data collection for a nationwide validation of the model referring to the areas of competence *use of content knowledge* and *acquirement of knowledge* has been completed. The model will now be extended to cover the remaining two areas of competence *(scientific communication* and *evaluation and judgment)* and will be validated. Benchmarking for national performance scales of the NES with a representative sample of German students is intended for autumn 2011. A nationwide assessment will take place in 2012.

## 2   The Competency Model

*A three-dimensional model: Areas of competence, cognitive processes, and complexity*

Klieme and Leutner (2006, p. 876) propose a working definition of competencies as "context-specific cognitive dispositions that are acquired by learning and are needed to successfully cope with certain situations, problems, or tasks in specific domains". In order to assess students' competencies according to the demands of the NES, a framework is needed which allows for the description of both the required competencies and the levels of proficiency with respect to these competencies. Applying the concept of competence by Klieme and Leutner (2006) and Weinert (2001), the project ESNaS developed a competency model as a basis for test item development with reference to the German NES (Kauertz et al., 2010; Mayer et al., 2009; Wellnitz et al., in prep.; Walpuski et al., 2010).

As the three requirements of the NES ("reproduction", "application", and "transfer") are explicitly characterized as nonhierarchical, they are unable to operationalize item difficulty within an outcome-oriented competency model. Consequently, a variety of different models for biology (Mayer et al., 2009), chemistry (Bernholt et al., 2009) and physics (Kauertz & Fischer, 2006; Schecker & Parchmann, 2007) were suggested and have been empirically investigated since the publication of the NES. Commons et al. (2007) introduced a hierarchical order of complexity for the modeling of item difficulty (cf. Bernholt et al., *this volume*). Kauertz and Fischer (2006) provided first evidence that a system of six levels of complexity between factual knowledge and understanding of scientific concepts can be used to describe students' competency with respect to related content knowledge (cf. Kauertz, 2007). In addition to the complexity levels, cognitive processes that influence the difficulty of a task are used for modeling of competency (Atkinson & Shiffrin, 1968).

The ESNaS competency model adapted these findings and splits the requirement component from the NES into two axes – one referring to the complexity of a task and the other the cognitive processes of the students when dealing with the task. As a consequence, the ESNaS model results in a three-dimensional competency model, presented in Figure 1.

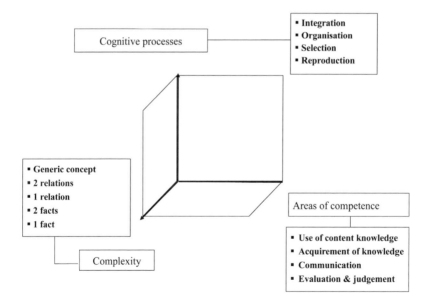

*Figure 1: Three-Dimensional ESNaS Competency Model*

The area of competence was set as a nonhierarchical axis into the ESNaS competency model. The areas of competence are described in more detail within the next section.

The axis of complexity describes the number of single scientific items and its interconnectedness that is needed to solve a task. This dimension includes five levels: 1 fact (I), 2 facts (II), 1 relation (III), 2 relations (IV), and generic concept (V), whereas facts are seen as the smallest possible units of knowledge in the respective area, relations indicate quantitative and qualitative functional connections between those facts, and concepts are seen as overarching scientific constructions. The level hierarchy is based on the assumption that individual facts are less complex than several facts and relations among them, and that relations are less complex than abstract generic concepts. For instance, to combine two relevant variables in an experiment, two facts and one relation are needed.

The axis for cognitive processes refers to cognitive activities that are necessary for solving a specific test item. The dimension refers to four levels of cognitive activities: reproduction, selection, organization, and integration. "Reproduction" refers to the recalling of facts, relations, or concepts from a given text, table, or figure. "Selection" requires applying certain criteria for finding specific scientific facts and relations, while "organizing" means to structure and categorize relevant facts, relations, and concepts. As the most sophisticated cognitive activity, "integrating" means to root relevant information in existing knowledge structures. Table 1 shows the criteria needed to operationalise the described four levels of cognitive activities for item construction.

*Table 1: Criteria for Item Development Addressing Cognitive Processes*

| Criteria<br>Cognitive processes | Similarity between presented and expected information | Conclusion on relationship | Similarity between presented and expected situation |
|---|---|---|---|
| Reproduction | identical | no | High |
| Selection | partially identical | no | High |
| Organisation | extended | yes | High |
| Integration | extended | yes | Low |

*Operationalization of the areas of competence: Use of content knowledge and acquirement of knowledge*

The content axis of the ESNaS competency model (Fig. 1) is nonhierarchical and differentiates between the areas of competence given by the NES and structuring sub-areas and aspects within the area of competence.

In the area of competence, *use of content knowledge*, the NES define basic concepts to structure the content knowledge of the three science subjects. By defining basic concepts, the NES intend to foster cumulative learning and to enable students to better organize their knowledge (KMK, 2004). The basic concepts in biology are: system, structure and function, and development and evolution; in chemistry: matter-particle relations, structure-property relations, chemical reactions, and energy; and in physics: matter, interaction, system, and energy.

The competence area, *acquirement of knowledge*, was not structured by the NES. The structuring elements of the ESNaS competence model were derived by assigning the standard statements to nationally and internationally accepted constructs in the field of scientific inquiry and reasoning (Abd-El-Khalick et al., 2004; Mayer, 2007; Lederman et al., 2002; Upmeier zu Belzen & Krüger, 2010). Furthermore, findings from the research-project "Biology in Context (bik)" (Bayrhuber et al., 2007) on an empirically validated competency model of scientific experimentation were taken into account (Mayer, 2007; Mayer et al., 2009). The assignment is shown in Figure 2 with selected standards from biology, chemistry, and physics.

Consequently, the following sub-areas were defined for the ESNaS competence model: *methods of scientific investigations, development of scientific models and theories*, and *nature of science*. The sub-areas are divided into aspects like *question, hypothesis, design*, and *data evaluation* for the sub-area *methods of scientific investigations* (Mayer et al., 2009). Figure 3 shows all sub-categories (sub-areas and aspects) that substitute the two areas of competence, *use of content knowledge*, and *acquirement of knowledge*.

*Subsidiary research studies*

As reported before, several subsidiary research studies were conducted to provide additional evidence for the validity of the model. In the following, research studies concerning the areas of competence, *use of content knowledge* and *acquirement of knowledge* are mentioned. Addressing *use of content knowledge*, content analyses of curricula and textbooks from the federal states were conducted to verify curricular validity of the contents used in test items (Härtig, 2010), and the influence of prior knowledge (whether present in the item stem or not) on item difficulty was investigated (Ropohl, 2010). Moreover, results from the validation study were used to examine whether the dimensions *use of content knowledge* and *acquirement of knowledge* can be discriminated empirically in terms of conceptual and procedural knowledge (Kampa, 2010). Addressing *acquirement of knowledge*, research projects analyzed the dimensionality of the sub-areas concerning nature of science (Neumann, 2010; Kremer & Mayer, 2009) and methods of scientific investigations (Wellnitz et al., 2010; Wellnitz & Mayer, 2011), as well as the construction and evaluation of competence test instruments for students of the primary level (Grade 5) (Mannel et al., 2010; Mannel, 2011).

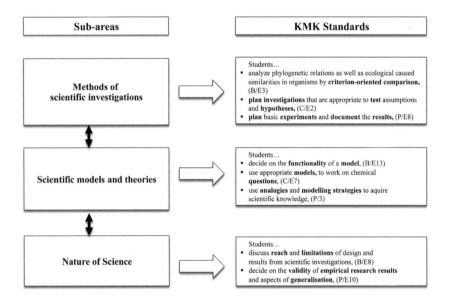

*Figure 2: Sub-Areas of Competence Referring to Acquirement of Knowledge and Relevant Standards*

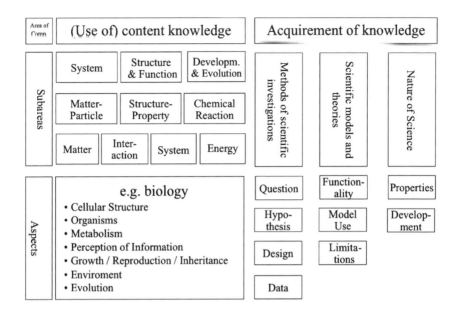

*Figure 3: Operationalisation of the Areas of Competence, Use of Content Knowledge and Acquirement of Knowledge According to Structuring Subareas and Aspects*

## 3 Validation Study: Methodology

Currently, data collection for a nationwide validation of the model referring to the areas of competence *use of content knowledge* and *acquirement of knowledge* has been completed. The main objective of this study is to ensure the validity and reliability of the test-items and to choose high quality test items for the subsequent benchmarking study planned for late 2011. Another goal is to evaluate the inner structure of the assessment and to compare this to the theoretical expectations of the competency model. The forthcoming benchmarking study is based on a representative nationwide sample and will calibrate national performance scales for the measurement of students' competencies in a national assessment in 2012. The assessment will coincide with PISA 2012.

*Design of the study*

Within the validation study, 998 test items from the three science subjects of biology, chemistry, physics were administered to n = 6845 students in the 10$^{th}$ grade (52% female, 48% male) from 160 schools in eight German federal states. Items and instruments were employed in test booklets in a multi-matrix design. In total, 393 open-ended items and 605 multiple-choice items were tested.

Additionally, test instruments were applied to subsamples for measuring known predictors of science competence (e.g., reading competence, cognitive ability, student interest in learning science, NOS understanding, parent competence, instructional quality, socio-cultural background, PISA items). The coding of open-ended items was trained in several coding test studies and subsequent coding workshops with ESNaS coordination team members. Coding schemes were improved iteratively in order to achieve an excellent interrater reliability among the five independent expert raters.

*Item formats and examples*

All items are included within a paper and pencil test addressing cognitive competencies (Klieme & Leutner, 2006). Performance assessment is not conducted. In general, a problem situation is given in a stem, followed by 3–6 items. The items can be assigned to three answering formats: multiple choice, long answer and short answer. Table 2 shows the number of test items addressing the areas of competence.

*Table 2: Number of Competence Test Items in the Validation Study*

| Area of competence | Number of items | | |
|---|---|---|---|
| | Biology | Chemistry | Physics |
| Use of content knowledge | 160 | 182 | 164 |
| Acquirement of knowledge | 189 | 120 | 183 |

Figure 4 shows an example of an open-ended (long answer) test item from biology referring to the *hypothesis* aspect from a sub-area of *acquirement of knowledge* on *methods of scientific investigations*. The item was designed to address the complexity of *1 relation (III)*, and the cognitive process *organization*. The item difficulty on the logit-scale for this item is -.811 logits.

Max wants to observe the growth conditions of plants. For an experiment he uses the "Busy Lizzie", a low maintenance and resistant houseplant.
He conducts the following experiment:

| Factors | Plant 1 | Plant 2 |
|---|---|---|
| Temperature | 25°C | 25°C |
| Placement | In a sunny window | In a dark closet |
| Watering | Once a week | Once a week |
| Fertilization | Twice a week | Twice a week |

Give the hypothesis (an educated guess) that underlies Max's experiment.

*Figure 4: Item Example from Biology*

Figure 5 shows an example of a multiple-choice test item from chemistry referring to the sub-area (basic concept) of *chemical reaction* from the area of competence, *use of content knowledge*. The item was designed to address the *1 relation (III)* complexity level and the cognitive process of *integration*.

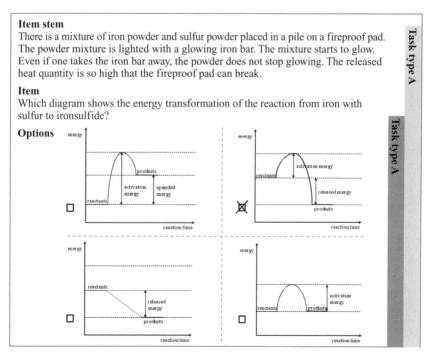

*Figure 5: Item Example from Chemistry*

Figure 6 shows an example of a multiple-choice test item from physics referring to the *question* aspect from a sub-area of *acquirement of knowledge* on *scientific investigations*. The item was designed to address the complexity of *1 relation (III)*, and the cognitive process, *organization*.

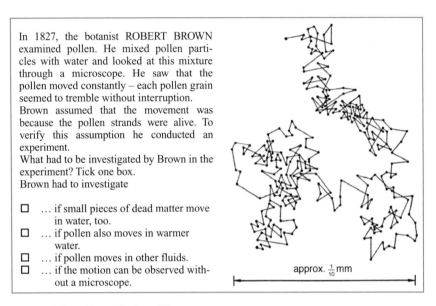

*Figure 6: Item Example from Physics*

*Data analyses*

One-parameter Rasch modeling for estimating item difficulty, fit and discrimination was performed separately for the three science subjects and for the two areas of competence, *use of content knowledge* and *acquirement of knowledge*.

Item difficulty estimates are expressed in logits, setting a logit value of 0 as the mean of the item difficulty estimate scale. The distribution of the difficulty estimates should range from -3 for low-difficulty items to 3 for the most difficult items. Item fit values provide information about which items can be used to increase the reliability of the test and, therefore, fit the construct to be measured. Satisfying infit values within the acceptable range should not exceed 1.10. Item discrimination indicates how well an item discriminates between high-performing and low-performing students. Satisfying discrimination should exceed .25.

# 5 Results

The validation study revealed that the entire range of personal ability could be covered with satisfying test items of acceptable fit and discrimination. The selection of items for further use was based on their quality parameters. Items with at least one of the test quality parameters (difficulty, fit, or discrimination) outside the acceptable range were labeled as critical. The critical items were either dropped or changed.

The distribution of the difficulty estimates, which should range from -3 for items of low difficulty to 3 for the most difficult items, was within the acceptable range for about 94 % of the tested items. About 82 % of test items resulted in satisfying infit values within the acceptable range (<1.10). About 91 % of the test items showed a satisfying discrimination (>.25). By this means, about 85 % of the test items were selected for further use within the upcoming benchmarking study.

The second goal in the validation study was to evaluate the inner structure of the assessment and compare it to the theoretical expectations outlined in the competence model. This especially concerns the hierarchical graduation of item difficulty with respect to complexity and cognitive processes. Therefore, test items with unsatisfying values in at least one parameter (difficulty, fit, or discrimination) were excluded. So, 944 test items remained. The assignment of these items to science subjects, areas of competence, complexity, and cognitive processes is specified in Table 3.

*Table 3: Distribution of satisfying items from the validation study*

| Complexity | I | | II | | III | | IV | | V | |
|---|---|---|---|---|---|---|---|---|---|---|
| Area of competence | CK | AK | CK | AK | CK | AK | CK | AK | CK | AK |
| Biology | 35 | 20 | 17 | 9 | 51 | 89 | 31 | 37 | 15 | 22 |
| Chemistry | 30 | 19 | 13 | 4 | 105 | 61 | 19 | 32 | 6 | 1 |
| Physics | 22 | 28 | 11 | 20 | 74 | 76 | 32 | 25 | 15 | 25 |

| Cognitive processes | Reproduction | | Selection | | Organization | | Integration | |
|---|---|---|---|---|---|---|---|---|
| Area of competence | CK | AK | CK | AK | CK | AK | CK | AK |
| Biology | 41 | 39 | 40 | 34 | 29 | 37 | 39 | 67 |
| Chemistry | 39 | 12 | 40 | 48 | 46 | 22 | 48 | 35 |
| Physics | 26 | 26 | 18 | 33 | 60 | 66 | 50 | 49 |

Note. CK: use of content knowledge; AK: acquirement of knowledge

Figure 7 and 8 show distributions of the item difficulty estimates for all of the according to the above mentioned criteria satisfying items from the validation study from all subjects and both areas of competence. Rasch analyses make clear that the difficulty distribution covers the whole range of the logit-scale. Moreover, it can be shown that item difficulty increases according to the requirement levels of the ESNaS competency model's dimensions of *complexity* and *cognitive processes*. Both requirement dimensions show significant correlations with item difficulty (complexity: $r = .36$, $p < .001$; cognitive processes: $r = .32$, $p < .001$). The results have to count as preliminary; additional sources of variance lead to partial overlapping of the levels.

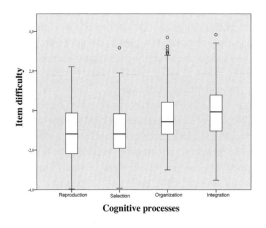

*Figure 7: Distribution of Item Difficulty Referring to Cognitive Processes*

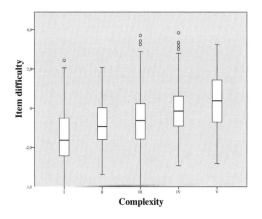

*Figure 8: Distribution of Item Difficulty Referring to Complexity*

The results replicate trends from earlier findings and show that the underlying competence model can serve as an adequate basis for hierarchically addressing competence requirements not only with respect to content knowledge, but also within the area of competence *acquirement of knowledge* (Kauertz et al., 2010; Kauertz & Fischer, 2006; Walpuski et al., 2010).

## 6 Implications and Future Perspectives

Coming from an input-oriented to an output-oriented view of teaching and learning processes leads to profound changes of evaluation and assessment strategies. In 2012, a representative national assessment will provide deepened empirical evidence about the competency status of German students. This data will be made accessible for the public and will surely be relevant for discussion about the future quality development to improve teaching and learning conditions.

To prevent the teaching-to-the-test phenomenon and to contribute to the implementation and acceptance of the NES, the item developers within the ESNaS project additionally create teaching materials, testing instruments, and reference examples addressing the competency model. The materials shall illustrate the differences between tasks to test and tasks to learn. They will be made accessible for schools and will provide opportunities for students to develop competencies within context-based and constructivist learning environments. They will also foster self-regulated evaluation of learning processes.

Assessment needs to become a central element for the advancement of students' learning in Germany. It can provide a framework in which educational objectives are set, students' progress is expressed and can provide a basis for planning future educational developments.

**References**

Abd-El-Khalick, F., BouJaoude, S., Duschl, R. A., Hofstein, A., Lederman, N. G., Mamlok, R., Niaz, M., Treagust, D., & Tuan, H. (2004). Inquiry in science education: International perspectives. *Science Education, 88*, 397-419.

Adkinson, R. C. & Shiffrin, R. M. (1968). *Human Memory: A Proposed System and its Control Processes.* New York: Academic Press.

Anderson, L. W. & Krathwohl, D. R. (2001). *A Taxonomy for Learning, Teaching, and Assessing: A Revision of Bloom's Taxonomy of Educational Objectives.* New York: Longman.

Bayrhuber, H., Bögeholz, S., Elster, D., Hammann, M., Hößle, C., Lücken, M., Mayer, J., Nerdel, C., Neuhaus, B., Prechtl, H., & Sandmann, A. (2007). Biologie im Kontext [Biology in context]. *MNU, 60*, 282-286.

Bernholt, S., Parchmann, I., & Commons, M. L. (2009). Kompetenzmodellierung zwischen Forschung und Unterrichtspraxis [Modelling competencies between research and instructional practice]. *Zeitschrift für Didaktik der Naturwissenschaften, 15*, 219–245.

Commons, M. L., Goodheart, E. A., Pekker, A., Dawson, T. L., Draney, K., & Adams, K. M. (2007). Using Rasch model scaled stage scores to validate orders of hierarchical complexity of balance beam task sequences. In E. V. Smith Jr. & R. M. Smith (Eds.), *Rasch measurement: Advanced and Specialized Applications* (pp. 121-147). Marple Grove, MN: JAM.

Council of Ministers of Education (CMEC) (1997). *K to 12: Common Framework of Science Outcomes*. Available at: http://204.225.6.243/science/framework.

Eisenhart, M., Finkel, E., & Marion, S. F. (1996). Creating the conditions for scientific literacy: A re-examination. *American Educational Research Journal, 33*, 261–295.

Fischer, H. E., Kauertz, A., & Neumann, K. (2008). Standards of science education. In S. Mikelskis-Seifert, U. Tingelband, & M. Brückmann (Eds.), *Four Decades of Research in Science Education – from Curriculum Development to Quality Improvement* (pp. 29-42). Münster: Waxmann.

Härtig, H. (2010). *Sachstrukturen in Physikschulbüchern als Grundlage zur Bestimmung der Inhaltsvalidität eines Tests* [Content structures in physics text books: content validity in large-scale assessments]. Berlin: Logos.

Kampa, N. (2010). *Dimensionality of Competence in Biology*. Poster presented at the JURE Conference in Frankfurt/Main, 19.07.-22.07.2010.

Kauertz, A. (2007): *Schwierigkeitserzeugende Merkmale physikalischer Testaufgaben*. Berlin: Logos.

Kauertz, A. & Fischer, H. E. (2006). Assessing students' level of knowledge and analysing the reasons for learning difficulties in physics by Rasch analysis. In X. Liu & W. J. Boone (Eds.), *Applications of Rasch Measurement in Science Education* (pp. 212-245). Maple Grove, MN: JAM.

Kauertz, A., Fischer, H. E., Mayer, J., Sumfleth, E., & Walpuski, M. (2010). Standardbezogene Kompetenzmodellierung in den Naturwissenschaften der Sekundarstufe I. [Modeling competence according to standards for science education in secondary schools.] *Zeitschrift für Didaktik der Naturwissenschaften, 16*, 135-153.

Klieme, E., Avenarius, H., Blum, W., Döbrich, P., Gruber, H., Prenzel, M., et al. (2003). *Zur Entwicklung nationaler Bildungsstandards* [Regarding the development of National Education Standards]. Berlin, Germany: Bundesministerium für Bildung und Forschung.

Klieme, E. & Leutner, D. (2006). Kompetenzmodelle zur Erfassung individueller Lernergebnisse und zur Bilanzierung von Bildungsprozessen. [Competence models for assessing individual learning outcomes and evaluating educational processes.]. *Zeitschrift für Pädagogik, 52*, 876-903.

Kremer, K. & Mayer, J. (2009). Wissenschaftstheoretische Reflexion als Kompetenz messen – Ein Beitrag zur Evaluation der Bildungsstandards im Fach Biologie. In U.

Harms et al. (Hrsg.), *Heterogenität erfassen – individuell fördern im Biologieunterricht* (pp. 102-103). Kiel: IPN.

Lederman, N. G., Abd-El-Khalick, F., Bell, R. L., & Schwartz, R. S. (2002). Views of nature of science questionnaire: Toward valid and meaningful assessment of learners' conceptions of nature of science. *Journal of Research in Science Teaching, 39*, 497-521.

Mannel, S. (2011). *Assessing Scientific Inquiry – Development and Evaluation of a Test for the Low-Performing Stage.* Berlin: Logos.

Mannel, S., Sumfleth, E., & Walpuski, M. (2010). Student assessment in the area of acquirement of knowledge. In M.F. Taşar & G. Çakmakcı (Eds.), *Contemporary Science Education Research: International Perspectives* (pp. 245-254). Ankara, Turkey: Pegem Akademi.

Mayer, J. (2007). Erkenntnisgewinnung als wissenschaftliches Problemlösen [Inquiry as scientific problem solving]. In D. Krüger & H. Vogt (Eds.), *Theorien in der biologiedidaktischen Forschung. Ein Handbuch für Lehramtsstudenten und Doktoranden* (pp. 177-186). Berlin: Springer.

Mayer, J., Grube, C., & Möller, A. (2009). Kompetenzmodell naturwissenschaftlicher Erkenntnisgewinnung [Modeling inquiry competence]. In U. Harms & A. Sandmann (Eds.), *Lehr- und Lernforschung in der Biologiedidaktik.* Innsbruck: Studienverlag.

National Research Council (NRC) (1996). *National Science Education Standards.* Washington, DC: National Academy Press.

Nentwig, P. & Schanze, S. (2007). Making it comparable – Standards in science education. In D. Waddington, P. Nentwig, & S. Schanze (Eds.), *Standards in Science Education* (pp. 11–19). Münster, Germany: Waxmann.

Neumann, I. (2010). *Beyond Physics Content Knowledge – Modeling Competence Regarding Nature of Scientific Inquiry and Nature of Scientific Knowledge.* (Unpublished doctoral dissertation). University Duisburg-Essen, Essen.

Neumann, K., Kauertz, A., & Fischer, H. E. (2010). From PISA to educational standards: The impact of large-scale assessments on science education in Germany. *International Journal of Science and Mathematics Education, 8*, 545-563.

Prenzel, M., Rost, J., Senkbeil, M., Häußler, P., & Klopp, A. (2001). Naturwissenschaftliche Grundbildung: Testkonzeption und Ergebnisse [Scientific literacy: Test conception and results]. In J. Baumert, E. Klieme, M. Neubrand, M. Prenzel, U. Schiefele, W. Schneider, et al. (Eds.) *PISA 2000. Basiskompetenzen von Schülerinnen und Schülern im internationalen Vergleich [PISA 2000: Basic competencies of students in international comparison]* (pp. 191-248). Opladen, Germany: Leske + Budrich.

Ropohl, M. (2010). *Modellierung von Schülerkompetenzen im Basiskonzept „Chemische Reaktion" – Entwicklung und Analyse von Testaufgaben.* Berlin: Logos Verlag.

Schecker, H. & Parchmann, I. (2007). Standards and competence models: The German situation. In D. Waddington, P. Nentwig, & S. Schanze (Eds.), *Standards inScience Education* (pp. 147–164). Münster, Germany: Waxmann.

Sekretariat der Ständigen Konferenz der Kultusminister der Länder der Bundesrepublik Deutschland (KMK) (Eds.) (2004). *Einheitliche Prüfungsanforderungen in der Abiturprüfung Physik.* Availabe at: http://www.kmk.org/fileadmin/veroeffentlichungen_beschluesse/1989/1989_12_01-EPA-Physik.pdf (Date of Access: 27.02.1011)

Sekretariat der Ständigen Konferenz der Kultusminister der Länder der Bundesrepublik Deutschland (KMK) (Eds.) (2005a). *Bildungsstandards im Fach Biologie für den mittleren Schulabschluss.* München: Luchterhand.

Sekretariat der Ständigen Konferenz der Kultusminister der Länder der Bundesrepublik Deutschland (KMK) (Eds.) (2005b). *Bildungsstandards im Fach Chemie für den mittleren Schulabschluss.* München: Luchterhand.

Sekretariat der Ständigen Konferenz der Kultusminister der Länder der Bundesrepublik Deutschland (KMK) (Eds.) (2005c). *Bildungsstandards im Fach Physik für den mittleren Schulabschluss.* München: Luchterhand.

Upmeier zu Belzen, A. & Krüger, D. (2010). Modellkompetenz im Biologieunterricht [Model competence in biology teaching]. *Zeitschrift für Didaktik der Naturwissenschaften, 16*, 59-75.

Walpuski, M., Kauertz, A., Fischer, H. E., Kampa, N., Mayer, J., Sumfleth, E., & Wellnitz, N. (2010). ESNaS: Evaluation der Standards für die Naturwissenschaften in der Sekundarstufe I [Evaluation of the National Educational Standards for Natural Sciences at the Lower Secondary Level]. In A. Gehrmann, U. Hericks, & M. Lüders (Eds.), *Bildungsstandards und Kompetenzmodelle: Eine Verbesserung der Qualität von Schule, Unterricht und Lehrerbildung* (pp. 171-184). Bad Heilbronn: Klinkhardt.

Weinert, F. E. (2001). Concept of competence: a conceptual clarification. In D. S. Rychen & L. H. Salganik (Eds.), *Defining and Selecting Key Competencies* (pp. 45-65). Seattle: Hogrefe & Huber.

Wellnitz, N., Fischer, H. E., Kauertz, A., Mayer, J., Neumann, I., Sumfleth, E., Walpuski, M. et al. (in prep.). Evaluation der Bildungsstandards – eine fächerübergreifende Testkonzeption für den Kompetenzbereich Erkenntnisgewinnung. *Zeitschrift für Didaktik der Naturwissenschaften.*

Wellnitz, N., Hartmann, S., & Mayer, J. (2010). Developing a paper-and-pencil-test to assess student's skills in scientific inquiry. In G. Cakmakci & M.F. Taşar (Eds.), *Contemporary Science Education Research: Learning and Assessment* (pp. 289-294). Ankara, Turkey: Pegem Akademi.

Wellnitz, N. & Mayer, J. (2011). *Modelling and Assessing Scientific Methods.* Paper presented at the Annual Meeting of the National Association for Research in Science Teaching (NARST), Orlando, FL, United States.

# Chapter 10
# Standards, Competencies and Outcomes. A Critical View

*Horst Schecker*
*Institute of Science Edcuation, University of Bremen, Germany*

**Abstract**

This paper reviews critically the potential of the German national physics education standards and their construct of 'competencies' for the specification and measurement of learning outcomes. Theoretical and empirical aspects are considered, focusing also on the relationship between process-oriented competencies and content knowledge. The scope of a competency is contrasted with knowledge and skills. German competence research has not worked out a common theoretical approach to the construct, which results in difficulties to measure competencies. The author concludes that in the current state, 'competence' or 'competency' does not provide a functional theoretical basis for the description of learning outcomes in science.

## 1 Introduction

In 2004, the German Standing Conference of the Ministers of Education (Kultusministerkonferenz; KMK) agreed upon national educational standards for physics, chemistry, and biology education (KMK, 2005). These Standards[1] describe the expected learning outcomes at the end of secondary school (grade 9 or 10; students about 15 years old). Achievement standards are presented on lists of competencies for four domains of science-related abilities[2]. The Standards support a paradigm shift from an input-driven approach towards curriculum development and teaching (description of content to be taught, allocation of resources for teaching) towards an outcome-oriented view on the development of competencies. Schecker and Parchmann (2007) explained the political background and the changes in the policies to initiate and supervise educational processes in schools.

---
1   "Standards" (with a capital "S") refer to the KMK-booklets.
2   "standards" (with a lower case "s") refer to the items of these lists.

The Standards have had a strong impact on curriculum development and teacher training. Science education researchers started modelling students' performances in science on the basis of competencies. section 2 introduces the notion of 'competencies' and the structure of the Standards. It also describes the Standards' influence on curriculum development and presents results from empirical studies on the structure of students' science competence.

However, the Standards and the construct of competencies have some shortcomings. Problems arise in a practical and empirical perspective regarding the specification of learning outcomes, the assessment of competencies, and the evaluation of the Standards. Theoretical questions concern the scope of a competency, the relationship between competence and performance, and the connection between process-competencies and content knowledge. Section 3 discusses these issues before a conclusion is drawn in section 4.

## 2 Standards and Competencies

### 2.1 Competencies

The idea of a competence-oriented development of educational standards was introduced in a basic document by Klieme et al. (2003). The authors refer to Franz Weinert's description of competencies as learnable cognitive abilities and skills to solve specific problems associated with motivational, volitional, and social dispositions for using these abilities and skills in variable situations (cf. Weinert 2001b, pp. 27). Weinert's frequently quoted definition, which combines cognitive dispositions to solve area-specific problems with motivational aspects, differs from generic competencies such as creativity, learning to learn, or working in teams. In contrast, Klieme and Leutner separate cognition from volition in a current research programme on modelling and measuring competencies. They define competencies as "learnable context-specific cognitive performance-dispositions, that functionally refer to situations and demands in specific areas" (Klieme & Leutner, 2006; translation and highlighting H.S.). Hartig (2008) argues that this restriction is useful for the description of the outcomes of formal educational processes because a student's motivation to make use of his or her cognitive competencies may vary considerably over time.[3]

---

[3] Another reason for excluding volition lies in the difficulties of an integrated measurement of cognition and volition. An example for an integrated approach is Kulgemeyer's (2010) study on science communication competencies. He examines the ability to explain physics phenomena combined with an interest of the explaining person in the addressee's understanding (cf. Bernholt, Eggert, & Kulgemeyer, *this volume*).

## 2.2 Structure of the Science Standards

The physics Standards consist of:
a) A preamble on the contribution of physics as a subject to the formation of students' personalities ("Allgemeine Bildung"; 1 page).
b) The description of four domains of scientific competencies (4 pages): 'application of content knowledge', 'science methods', 'science communication' and 'judgement'. The structure of content knowledge is classified by four so-called basic concepts: 'matter', 'interaction', 'system', and 'energy'. These concepts are further explained and described by facultative exemplifications (e.g., reflection and refraction for the concept of interaction).
c) A list of achievement standards (2 pages): 5 for 'content knowledge' (e.g., "use analogies to solve tasks and problems"), 10 for 'science methods' (e.g., "plan, carry out, and document simple experiments"), 7 for 'communication' (e.g., "distinguish between everyday language and scientific language"), and 4 for 'judgement' ("name implications of physics findings in historical or social contexts").
d) A table describing three demand profiles associated with the construction of tasks and problems for each domain of competencies. For content knowledge, these are 'reproduction', 'reorganisation/application', and 'transfer'.
e) 12 sample problems and their solutions (17 pages). Each item is classified into domain, demand, and basic concept. The classification can be represented as coordinates in the Standard's three-dimensional competence model (cf. Fig. 1).

Figure 1 shows the three dimensions of the normative model underlying the German standards for physics. The same dimensions with subject-specific basic concepts also apply to the Standards for biology and chemistry.

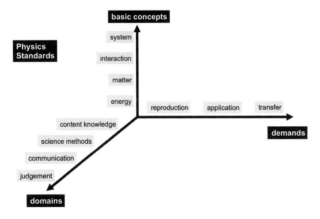

*Figure 1: Dimensions of the German Educational Standards for Physics*

## 2.3 Curriculum Development

In 2004, the 16 German federal states began to revise their science curricula in a competence-oriented perspective according to the Standards. Some of the states implemented far-reaching changes (e.g., Ministerium für Schule und Weiterbildung des Landes Nordrhein-Westfalen, 2007), others decided upon only moderate revisions (e.g., Niedersächsisches Kultusministerium, 2007). However, most of the textbooks had to be rewritten.

Following administrative directives that curricula must be competence-oriented as opposed to content-oriented, curriculum development teams had to balance between the description of generalised abilities and the teachers' needs for orientation on what exactly the abstract goals meant. In fact, several states differentiate between content-oriented competencies and process-oriented competencies (e.g., Niedersächsisches Kultusministerium, 2007), with process domains comprising 'methods', 'communication', and 'judgement'. One of the federal states considered only the three process-oriented domains as true competencies, while the application of content knowledge for solving content matter problems was not rated as a competency.

The counterpart to open curricula with very abstract competency descriptions are detailed curricula that state precisely which phenomena, experiments and concepts have to be dealt with. Competencies are formulated as narrowly as e. g. "students explain circular motion by a central force that changes direction" (Niedersächsisches Kultusministerium, 2007, p. 42) or "students explain the connection between a given energy-level diagram of hydrogen and spectral series" (SfBW, 2008, p. 15). Such descriptions are close to the approach of instructional objectives (Mager, 1984).

## 2.4 Research

The Standards triggered a number of empirical studies analysing the structure of science competence (e.g., Einhaus, 2007; Kauertz, 2008; Schmidt, 2008; Bernholt, 2010). Two central questions are:
- Can the four domains of science competencies (cf. Fig. 1) be distinguished empirically in students' test performances (construct validation)?
- What parameters provide adequate criteria for grading science competence?

Kauertz (2008) concentrated on the content-knowledge domain. He found that the four basic concepts for physics (see 2.2), supplemented by two further big ideas (formalism and science methods), explain a relevant amount of variance in students' performances. His main research interest lay in the question, which of the item properties make tasks difficult. Kauertz introduced a parameter for the "complexity" of a task and found that the difficulty of an item is connected to the number of facts and relations that have to be considered for its solution. The highest demands on the use of content knowledge were posed by tasks that needed a real conceptual understanding. Meanwhile, Kauertz' work has been used to develop tasks for the IQB-evaluation of the science Standards (Evaluation der Standards in den Naturwissenschaften der Sekundarstufe 1, ESNaS; Kauertz, Fischer, Mayer, Sumfleth & Walpuski, 2010). The ESNaS-model contains a second dimension for grading competencies, called "cognitive processes": reproduction, selection, re-organisation, and integration of the information given in a task or problem.

Bernholt, Parchmann and Commons (2009) proposed a different, five level-grading scale for the application of content-knowledge, called "hierarchical complexity". The five levels are: non-reflective use of everyday life knowledge, reproduction of scientific facts, description of processes, reasoning with causalities, and argumentation based on the integration of multiple interdependencies. Bernholt's (2010) scale integrates parts of Kauertz' separate dimensions 'complexity' and 'cognitive processes'. He validated his complexity scale in the content area of combustion and found that the hierarchical complexities of the test items explained more than 65% of the variance in item difficulties. Further applications of the scale in other content areas also yielded values for an explained variance of more than 50%.

Einhaus (2007) and Schmidt (2008) analysed the structure of students' physics abilities using the Bremen-Oldenburg model of science competence (cf. Schecker & Parchmann, 2006). The structure of this model is similar to the national science Standards' notion of competence. The analyses are based on empirical data about students' performances in the subject areas of heat and temperature, thermodynamics, and energy, and the test items covered the model-dimensions 'subject area', 'competence domain' and 'demands'[4]. It was statistically analysed whether competencies within these model-dimensions can be considered as graded, independent from each other, or existing parallel to one another. The analyses showed parallel levels of expertise in the domains of 'content knowledge', 'communication', and 'judgement'. According to Einhaus (2007), abilities to solve problems in thermodynamics are only loosely connected to expertise in the area of heat and temperature, although both subject areas refer to the same basic concept of 'energy'. Results from Einhaus and Schmidt's studies show that the abilities to meet the demand 'reproduction of knowledge' correlate strongly with the abilities for the 'application of knowledge' and can be considered as parallel manifestations of competencies. Thus, the model dimension 'demands' does not provide a proper grading scale for competencies. The results of

---

4   In this paper the dimensions are named according to the national Standards. The Bremen-Oldenburg model uses partly different terms.

Einhaus and Schmidt cast some doubt on the Standards' potential to describe the students' actual competence structures.

Other studies deal with specific issues of measuring competencies and/or selected domains of competence from the Standards model. Eggert (Eggert & Bögeholz, 2010) worked out a model for 'judgement' in the area of sustainable development. Her competence-scale has four ordinal levels, described by different elaborations of decision-making and reflection processes. Kulgemeyer (2010) validated an ordinal scale for science 'communication'. He defines this competency as the ability of students to provide scientific explanations for phenomena that are both, physically correct and addressee-oriented. The grading parameter, counting the number of subprocesses necessary for the production of an explanation, explains a variance of 65% regarding the items' level of difficulty.

Hammann (Hammann, 2004; Hammann, Phan, Ehmer & Grimm, 2008) did research on assessing pupils' experimental competencies. His model distinguishes three phases of experimenting: search hypotheses, test hypotheses and evaluate evidence. He identified four levels of competence for processes like forming hypotheses or controlling variables. Data were gathered with paper-and-pencil tests. Schreiber (Schreiber 2010; Schreiber, Theyßen & Schecker, 2009) focused on the aspects of the process to conduct real experiments, using inferential grading parameters for the different tasks (e. g. setting up apparatuses or gathering data). The assessment was done in the content area of electric circuits. Its results indicate that abilities to plan and conduct experiments or to evaluate experimental data do not form a coherent, uniform body of experimental competence. The attributed level of students' experimental expertise is influenced by content knowledge about current and electricity, and by practical experiences with handling multimeters. Obviously the time gap between dealing with electric circuits in their classes and the date of the test was crucial here.

## 3  Discussion

The model of the science Standards with its four competence-domains had not been discussed within the science education community before the Standards were enforced by the Kultusministerkonferenz. While in Switzerland, the HarmoS-project provided a research basis for the subsequent implementation of standards (see Labudde, Nidegger, Adaminac & Gingins, 2011), in Germany, empirical studies only followed after the introduction of the Standards. It remains an open question whether the normative model of the Standards is appropriate to describe students' actual cognitive structures (empirical model)[5]. There is an ongoing debate on how competencies differ from knowledge and skills – at least in precise, tangible formulations of competencies. This section discusses some of the practical, empirical, and theoretical problems arising from the structure of the standards and the somewhat fuzziness of the construct competency.

## 3.1 Practical and Empirical Aspects

### 3.1.1 Specification of expected learning outcomes

Expectations that the common framework given by the Standards would lead to more coherence between the 16 state curricula have only partially been fulfilled. The Standards' achievement goals are only vaguely formulated and thus open to different interpretations. This is a particular problem for the domain "content knowledge". Unfortunately, the Standards do not contain a syllabus stating the areas of physics where to develop the competencies. The achievement standards F1 to F3 (out of five standards) could be paraphrased as "Students use their structured basic knowledge of physics principles, magnitudes, measuring procedures, natural constants and simple physics laws to solve tasks and problems." (cf. KMK, 2005, p. 11). The question arises, "Which laws, principles, and measuring procedures?" This decision was left to the federal states which had to develop their own core curricula. These core curricula, however, often transfer the decision to the individual schools, which then would have to elaborate school-specific curricula (cf. Schecker, Bethge & Schottmayer, 2004). Only the understanding of the four higher order "basic concepts" is obligatory.

The lack of a national syllabus is due to the fact that the 16 German federal states had and still have different curricular traditions, disparate school systems, and different structures of teaching science (unequal numbers of lessons per year; separate subjects of physics, biology, chemistry versus integrated science). In Germany there has never been a real intention to harmonise the many different curricula (which is the explicit aim of the Swiss project "HarmoS", cf. Labudde et al., 2011). The four abstract basic concepts (see section 2.2) offered an easy way to avoid discussions in the Kultusministerkonferenz about obligatory content. This seemed to be possible because initially, it was not politically intended to evaluate the science achievement standards across the 16 states [6].

---

5 For the difference between normative and empirical models of competence, see Schecker & Parchmann (2007), and Schecker & Parchmann (2006).
6 This was only planned for the three main subjects of Mathematics, German and English.

3.1.2 Evaluation of the Standards

In 2003, the German federal states founded the Institute for Educational Progress (Institut für Qualitätssicherung im Bildungswesen, IQB, Berlin) to monitor the efficiency of the German school system and refine educational Standards. Problems arising from the absence of a national syllabus became virulent when the IQB decided eventually to prepare a national evaluation of the science standards. The survey will be carried out in 2012 with 14- and 15-year-olds to see whether the various German school systems reach the achievement goals. The test has to be valid for all 16 states with partly different curricula. In order to find out the overlap in the areas of content, Härtig (2010) analysed various textbooks with their state-specific editions.

Several items of the national test will only require to identify and reproduce pieces of factual information from the introductory text. This could be achieved in areas not even previously covered in a student's teaching. Therefore, the physics education experts who review the proposed units for the national evaluation have criticised such items as "reading literacy" (e.g., Schecker in Labudde et al., 2009). The steering group for the test development in turn argues that these items would be necessary to cover students in the lowest quartile of the competence spectrum (e.g., Fischer in Labudde et al., 2009).

It remains difficult to develop a test that is fair for all participants. This applies to content knowledge and methodological competencies as well as to science communication or judgement. Process competencies can only be tested by palpable, content-enriched tasks. In a test situation with strict time limits for the tasks, it is unrealistic to expect that students transfer their methodological competencies to or deliver judgements on unknown content areas.

3.1.3 Assessment of competencies

If we accept Weinert's description of competencies as performance dispositions for complex problems in the comprehensive sense of the construct, we have to assess competencies in complex problem situations. Competent problem solving demands the volitional integration of several facets of knowledge and skills.

As a practical example for physics, one may think of a student's ability to repair a broken bicycle light. This would require a number of systematic strategies to look for and localise the fault, some knowledge about parallel electric circuits, methods to test a bulb, and replacing the wire etc. (domains: content knowledge and methods). It would also presume the student's motivation to fix the problem him- or herself instead of calling for an expert. Another example for a complex problem situation could be the judgement whether it makes sense to grant subsidies for the purchase of battery-powered cars. In addition to political considerations and economic aspects, a personal point of view should be based on physics knowledge about the generation and storage of electrical energy, chains of energy transport and their efficiency factors. Such problems represent high-level demands for students. Looking at the results of PISA (OECD, 2007), we can safely assume that few students would be able to meet these demands under test conditions.

Hardly any of the sample tasks in the Standards or of the tasks for the evaluation of the standards come near the complexity of the two examples described above. Instead, sample tasks demand the extraction of factual content from given texts and tables, the application of Newton's third law, or the analysis of data (e.g., cf. IQB, 2010). Real experiments are not included (different from the Swiss HarmoS-Test; see Labudde et al. 2011). Restrictions in the scope of the tasks are due to the time boundaries and practical problems of a large-scale assessment. There are also tasks where judgements have to be made, e.g., in the context of imaging techniques in medical diagnoses. Most of the problems, however, are far from the complex demands students are confronted with in everyday-life situations. We should thus be cautious with using the term *competence*-test.

## 3.2 Theoretical Aspects

### 3.2.1 The scope of a competency

Hartig (2008) stresses that competencies should neither be formulated globally (like 'problem-solving competence') nor too content-specific (like speaking of a 'rule of three-competency'). This leads to the question: What is an appropriate scope of a science competency? In other words, referring to Klieme and Leutner: What is meant by "context", "situation", and "area"? "Area" can mean science in general or physics as a subject. Within physics, content areas like electromagnetism or mechanics could be named as areas. Further specifications of these areas are electrical energy or Newtonian dynamics. However, does a phrase like "Students are able to solve problems of force and motion" express an adequate level of accuracy for the description of a competency? Or is this too close to a "rule of three-competency"?

Hartig (2008, p. 21), one of the coordinators of the research cluster „Competence-modelling" funded by the German Research Foundation (Klieme & Leutner, 2006; Klieme, Leutner & Kenk, 2010), proposes the criterion that the specification of a competency should be related to "a set of reasonably similar, out-of-school situations, in which similar demands have to be surmounted". Road safety or electricity in the household might be the contexts (or situations) to fulfil this criterion. The achievement standards actually define a kind of safety competency: "Students use their physics knowledge to assess risks and safety measurements in experiments, in everyday-life and for modern technologies" (KMK, 2005, p. 12; domain 'judgement', standard B3). But is there really a set of reasonably similar situations in everyday-life that would make it useful and realistic to aim at such a general competency? Or should students rather develop specific knowledge about risks and precautions using electrical apparatuses? The focus of standard B3 would then lie on the willingness to apply this knowledge – which brings the aspect of volition in again (cf. Weinert, 2001b).

Typical situations in physics are to mathematise relationships between physics quantities and to do experimental investigations. Related methodological competencies can be found in the standards, e.g., "students plan, carry out and document simple experiments" (KMK, 2005, p. 11). Once again: Should the description of an outcome not be more precise, like "students control variables while investigating relationships between quantities in an experiment"?

A crucial challenge lies in Hartig's (2008) claim that competencies should be related to sets of "out-of-school situations". For physics, this restriction would considerably limit the number of adequate competencies. As a science, physics does not primarily aim at explanations for everyday-world phenomena. It is rather a body of advanced theoretical knowledge and methodological approaches to describe the very basic structures that underlie the touch and show-reality around us. Physics as a school subject must take this into account in order to find a balance between scientific within-subject and contextual out-of-school perspectives. At least in upper secondary education, most of the conceptual understanding and methodological abilities refer to academic applications within science and technology.

The questions above point at some fundamental issues of using competencies to describe learning outcomes. It is absolutely essential that the scope of the formulations of competencies will be discussed more thoroughly among science educators and under educational and disciplinary aspects.

3.2.2  Competence versus performance

'Competence' is the construct of a latent generic trait. The construct of 'competency' assumes that a student possesses generic structures in his or her cognitive system enabling him or her to generate solutions for classes of problem situations, e.g., to carry out experiments or to mathematise physics phenomena.

Competencies cannot be tested as such – they can only be investigated by analysing performances in specific situations. The description of situations where an assumed competency may become observable is called operationalisation of competencies. Competence tests first of all test performance. Performance in turn is nearly always connected to a specific application of knowledge and skills, i. e. to content-related problems – at least in science. This applies particularly for process-oriented competencies. If a student successfully conducts an experiment, this may either be an instance of an existing generic experimental competency or just an ability closely linked to a special experiment. Support for a generic trait could be gained, if we analysed a student's actions in a variety of settings posing similar experimental problems in different content areas of physics. This has hardly ever been done in empirical investigations with regard to individuals (cf. Weinert, 2001a, p. 59). Large-scale assessments like PISA or the evaluation of the German Standards avoid this problem because they do not aim at diagnosing individuals' competencies but at monitoring the success of a school system by accumulating data from different students who worked on different tasks in a proposed domain of competence.

### 3.2.3 Competencies versus content knowledge

The construction of compentency-based curricula assumes that process-competencies can be separated from content – an idea that originated in the subjects of arts and social science. Transferred to science this would mean that abilities to plan, carry out and document experiments can be developed and applied in varying content areas, so that the content becomes exchangeable. Fischler (2011) criticises such tendencies as "marginalization of content".

On the other hand, the need for precise content specifications in curricula is important for those states administering central exams in science. If the test poses sophisticated physics tasks, the description of general competencies does not really help either teachers or students to prepare for external final exams. Experimental strategies like controlling variables help young students to solve simple tasks, e.g., whether the time it takes for an effervescent tablet to dissolve in water depends on the water temperature (the amount of water has to be controlled). However, for older students doing the pre-university exams, such general strategies have only little meaning for sophisticated experimental tasks like determining the wavelength of a laser beam by diffraction and interference of light from a CD-ROM disk. They would rather need content specific experimental abilities in the area of wave optics. The more advanced the phenomena, concepts, and experimental methods become in the course of physics instruction, the more important are the content-related capabilities – and the more challenging it becomes to detach competencies from the content of instruction.

For the evaluation of the national science Standards, efforts have been made to diminish the effects of content knowledge for competence testing by presenting the factual background in the introductory texts of the test units (item stems). Many PISA-units follow a similar approach. Ropohl (2010) compared students' achievements in the domain 'application of content knowledge' within the area of chemical reactions for two different types of tasks. Type A tasks had an item-stem describing the content knowledge background while type B tasks did not include this information. Although the curricular validity of the test is given, there are no data as to whether and when the individual students had actually been taught the selected content in their classes before the test was written. The finding that type B items correlate higher with a separate test on content knowledge than type A items (cf. Ropohl, 2010, p. 98) is not surprising because most type B questions could also have been chosen for the content knowledge test. Type A items have a higher correlation with general cognitive abilities and reading comprehension than type B items. Ropohl concludes that type A items test the students' competence of dealing with content knowledge (given in the item-stem) as a general ability while type B items test content knowledge as such. Looking at the stems and questions in detail, one could alternatively conclude that type A items only test a general familiarity with scientific texts, helpful in deriving the pieces of information necessary to find the proper multiple choice answer, even if the topic itself is not known or understood. Students cannot be expected to fully grasp the ideas of an unknown topic simply by reading a short introductory text.

## 4 Conclusions

'Competency' is still an ambiguous construct, even if we exclude key competencies and focus on science-related dispositions instead.[7] Weinert (2001a) was striving for a "conceptual clarification" of the construct 'competence', but eventually he chose a pragmatic description of aspects: learnability, meeting of complex demands, cognitive and motivational components.

Meanwhile there is an inflationary use of the term "competency" both in curricula and in science education research, while we find a depreciation of the terms knowledge – in particular content knowledge – and skills. Often, however, the new label only replaces the old terms.[8]

---

7   On a larger scale the debate between researchers who promote a concept of competence relating to specific areas and others who emphasise the key competences is still going on (cf. Jude, Hartig & Klieme, 2008).

8   Lachmayer (2008) e.g., speaks of a "graphing competency", meaning the ability to work with diagrams in science (e.g., labelling axes, identifying trends of a graph).

An overview of German studies (see section 2.4) yields a multitude of approaches to the empirical investigation of science competencies. While the ESNaS-group applies Kauertz' (2008) complexity-scale to all four domains of competencies, other groups work with domain-specific grading parameters. The Swiss HarmoS-project (cf. Labudde et al. *this volume*) follows an own approach. So far, there is only little consensus between the research groups on proper sub-structures of science competencies, test methods, or graduation. Parchmann (2010) analysed the state of the science projects in the research cluster "competence-modelling" (German Research Foundation; cf. Klieme, 2010). She resumes that a coherent development towards a common meta-model of competence accompanied by area- and context-specifications is presently not discernible.

It is almost impossible to measure science competencies in Weinert's (2001b) comprehensive sense with paper-and-pencil multiple-choice tests. By subdividing a competency into facets and sub-facets to obtain more item clarity and validity, a large-scale assessment necessarily diverges from making complex demands. What we usually test are at best facets of competencies. We should thus be more careful with citing Weinert in the introductions of competence studies. It would be much easier to create learning environments and construct-valid assessments for students' competencies in a classroom situation, but it takes time to work out solutions for complex problems – more time than what is normally available in large-scale assessments.

In the current state of discussions, 'competence' does not provide a functional theoretical basis for the description of learning outcomes in science. The scope of a competency needs to be discussed more thoroughly. This discussion will have to be done for every group of school subjects. It should lead to a taxonomy of performance dispositions and a pragmatic consensual decision where to draw the line between what we call a competency in its true sense and what should be termed knowledge, skills and capabilities. Not only do we need a re-appreciation of content-related knowledge and skills as valid learning outcomes, we would also need a re-vitalisation of science education research and debate about the role of content (cf. Fischler, 2011). Competencies are useful as the descriptors of learning goals of a higher order. Yet, to provide a tangible orientation for teaching, curricula should be encouraged again to refer to knowledge, skills and capabilities as valid learning outcomes.

# References

Bernholt, S. (2010). *Kompetenzmodellierung in der Chemie – Theoretische und empirische Reflexion am Beispiel des Modells hierarchischer Komplexität* (doctoral thesis). Berlin: Logos.

Bernholt, S., Parchmann, I. & Commons, M. L. (2009). Kompetenzmodellierung zwischen Forschung und Unterrichtspraxis. *Zeitschrift für Didaktik der Naturwissenschaften 15*, 219-245.

Duit, R., Niedderer, H. & Schecker, H. (2007). Teaching Physics. In: S. K. Abell & N. G. Lederman (Eds.): *Handbook of Research on Science Education*, 599–629. Hillsdale, NJ: Lawrence Erlbaum.

Eggert, S. & Bögeholz, S. (2006). Göttinger Modell der Bewertungskompetenz – Teilkompetenz "Bewerten, Entscheiden und Reflektieren" für Gestaltungsaufgaben Nachhaltiger Entwicklung. *Zeitschrift für Didaktik der Naturwissenschaften 12*, 177–197.

Eggert, S. & Bögeholz, S. (2010). Students' use of decision making strategies with regard to socioscientific issues – an application of the Rasch partial credit model. *Science Education, 94*, 230–258.

Einhaus, E. (2007). *Schülerkompetenzen im Bereich Wärmelehre* (doctoral thesis). Berlin: Logos.

Fischler, H. (2011). Didaktik – an appropriate framework for the professional work of science teachers? In: R. Gunstone, D. Corrigan & J. Dillon (Eds.): *The Professional Knowledge Base of Science Teaching*. Springer.

Hammann, M. (2004). Kompetenzentwicklungsmodelle Merkmale und ihre Bedeutung – dargestellt anhand von Kompetenzen beim Experimentieren. *Der mathematische und naturwissenschaftliche Unterricht, 57*(4), 196–203.

Hammann, M., Phan, T. T. H., Ehmer, M. & Grimm, T. (2008). Assessing pupils' skills in experimentation. *Journal of Biological Education, 42*(2), 2–8.

Härtig, H. (2010). *Sachstrukturen von Physikschulbüchern als Grundlage zur Bestimmung der Inhaltsvalidität eines Tests* (doctoral thesis). Berlin: Logos.

Hartig, J. (2008). Kompetenzen als Ergebnisse von Bildungsprozessen. In: N. Jude, J. Hartig & E. Klieme (Eds.): *Kompetenzerfassung in pädagogischen Handlungsfeldern Theorien, Konzepte und Methoden* (pp. 15–25). Bonn: Bundesministerium für Bildung und Forschung.

IQB – Institut für die Qualitätsentwicklung im Bildungswesen (2010). *Sample Tasks of the Science Standards Evaluation*. Berlin: Institut für die Qualitätsentwicklung im Bildungswesen. Availabe at: http://www.iqb.hu-berlin.de/arbbereiche/testentw/projekte/projekte?pg=p_34&spg=r_7 (Date of Access: January 17, 2011).

Jude, N., Hartig, J. & Klieme, E. (2008). *Kompetenzerfassung in pädagogischen Handlungsfeldern Theorien, Konzepte und Methoden*, Bd. 26 von *Bildungsforschung*. Bonn: Bundesministerium für Bildung und Forschung.

Kauertz, A. (2008). *Schwierigkeitserzeugende Merkmale physikalischer Leistungstestaufgaben* (doctoral thesis). Berlin: Logos.

Kauertz, A., Fischer, H. E., Mayer, J., Sumfleth, E. & Walpuski, M. (2010). Standardbezogene Kompetenzmodellierung in den Naturwissenschaften der Sekundarstufe I. *Zeitschrift für Didaktik der Naturwissenschaften, 16,* 135–153.

Klieme, E., Avenarius, H., Blum, W., Döbrich, P., Gruber, H., Prenzel, M., Reiss, K., Riquarts, K., Tenorth, H.-E. & Vollmer, H. J. (2003). *Zur Entwicklung nationaler Bildungsstandards – Eine Expertise.* Bonn: Bundesministerium für Bildung und Forschung.

Klieme, E. & Leutner, D. (2006). *Kompetenzmodelle zur Erfassung individueller Lernergebnisse und zur Bilanzierung von Bildungsprozessen (Antrag an die DFG auf Einrichtung eines Schwerpunktprogramms).*

Klieme, E., Leutner, D. & Kenk, M. (Eds.) (2010). *Zeitschrift für Pädagogik, 56. Beiheft: Kompetenzmodellierung. Zwischenbilanz des DFG-Schwerpunktprogramms und Perspektiven des Forschungsansatzes.* Weinheim: Beltz.

KMK Sekretariat der Ständigen Konferenz der Kultusminister der Länder in der Bundesrepublik Deutschland (Ed.) (2005). *Bildungsstandards im Fach Physik für den Mittleren Schulabschluss.* München: Luchterhand.

Kulgemeyer, C. (2010). *Physikalische Kommunikationskompetenz – Modellierung und Diagnostik* (doctoral thesis). Berlin: Logos.

Labudde, P., Duit, R., Fischer, H. E., Harms, U., Mikelskis, H. F., Schecker, H., Schroeter, B., Wellensiek, A. & Weiglhofer, H. (2009). Schwerpunkttagung „Kompetenzmodelle und Bildungsstandards: Aufgaben für die naturwissenschaftsdidaktische Forschung". *Zeitschrift für Didaktik der Naturwissenschaften, 15,* 125–152.

Labudde, P., Nidegger, C., Adaminac, M. & Gingins, F. (2011). The development, validation, and implementation of standards in science education: chances and difficulties in the swiss project HarmoS. (see this volume)

Lachmayer, S. (2008). *Entwicklung und Überprüfung eines Strukturmodells der Diagrammkompetenz für den Biologieunterricht.* Doctoral thesis, Mathematisch-Naturwissenschaftliche Fakultät der Christian-Albrechts-Universität zu Kiel.

Mager, R. F. (1984). *Preparing Instructional Objectives.* Belmont, CA: Pitman Learning.

Ministerium für Schule und Weiterbildung des Landes Nordrhein-Westfalen (Ed.) (2007). *Kernlehrplan für das Fach Physik für die Jahrgangsstufen 5-9 in Gymnasien des Landes Nordrhein-Westfalen.* Düsseldorf.

Niedersächsisches Kultusministerium (Ed.) (2007). *Kerncurriculum für das Gymnasium, Schuljahrgänge 5-10.* Hannover.

OECD (2007). *PISA 2006. Science Competencies for Tomorrow's World. Volume 1 – Analysis.* Paris: Organisation for Economic Co-operation and Development.

Parchmann, I. (2010). Kompetenzmodellierung in den Naturwissenschaften – Vielfalt ist wertvoll, aber nicht ohne ein gemeinsames Fundament. In: E. Klieme, D. Leutner & M. Kenk (Eds.): *Zeitschrift für Pädagogik, 56. Beiheft*: *Kompetenzmodellierung. Zwischenbilanz des DFG-Schwerpunktprogramms und Perspektiven des Forschungsansatzes,* pp. 135–142. Weinheim: Beltz.

Ropohl, M. (2010). *Modellierung von Schülerkompetenzen im Basiskonzept Chemische Reaktion* (doctoral thesis). Berlin: Logos.

Schanze, S. & Nentwig, P. (2008). Standards im Naturwissenschaftlichen Unterricht – ein internationaler Vergleich. *Zeitschrift für Didaktik der Naturwissenschaften 14*, 125–143.

Schecker, H., Bethge, T. & Schottmayer, M. (2004). Schulinterne Curriculumentwicklung – Modell, Struktur und Entwicklungsprozess. In B. Brackhahn, R. Brockmeyer, T. Bethge & A. Hornsteiner (Eds.), *Standards und Kompetenzen und Evaluation* (pp. 61–101). München: Luchterhand.

Schecker, H. & Parchmann, I. (2006). Modellierung naturwissenschaftlicher Kompetenz. *Zeitschrift für Didaktik der Naturwissenschaften 12*, pp. 45–66.

Schecker, H. & Parchmann, I. (2007). Standards and Competence Models – The German Situation. In D. Waddington, P. Nentwig & S. Schanze (Eds.), *Making it Comparable – Standards in Science Education*, pp. 147–164. Münster: Waxmann.

Schmidt, M. (2008). *Kompetenzmodellierung und -diagnostik im Bereich Energie der Sekundarstufe I – Entwicklung und Überprüfung eines Testinventars* (doctoral thesis). Berlin: Logos.

Schreiber, N. (2010). Experimental skills in science: A comparison of assessment tools. In: *Proceedings of the ESERA Summerschool in Udine 2010*.

Schreiber, N., Theyßen, H. & Schecker, H. (2009). Experimentelle Kompetenz messen?! *Physik und Didaktik in Schule und Hochschule, 8*(3), 92–101.

SfBW – Die Senatorin für Bildung und Wissenschaft der Freien Hansestadt Bremen (Ed.) (2008). *Bildungsplan Physik für die Gymnasiale Oberstufe – Qualifikationsphase*. Bremen.

Weinert, F. (2001a). Vergleichende Leistungsmessung in Schulen – eine umstrittene Selbstverständlichkeit. In F. Weinert (Ed.), *Leistungsmessung in Schulen* (pp. 17–31). Weinheim: Beltz.

Weinert, F. E. (2001b). Concepts of competence – A conceptual clarification. In D. S. Rychen & L. H. Salyanik (Eds.), *Defining and Selecting Key Competencies*, (pp. 45–65). Göttingen: Hogrefe und Huber.

# Chapter 11

# The Development, Validation, and Implementation of Standards in Science Education: Chances and Difficulties in the Swiss Project HarmoS

*Peter Labudde [1], Christian Nidegger[2], Marco Adamina[3] & François Gingins[4]*
[1]*Centre for Science and Technology Education, University of Applied Sciences Northwestern Switzerland, Basel;* [2]*Service de la recherche en éducation, Geneva;* [3]*University of Teacher Education, Bern;* [4]*University of Teacher Education, Lausanne*

## Abstract

In order to improve the quality of science instruction in Switzerland, competencies and standards in science education for the end of grades 2, 6, and 9 have been developed and validated. This article focuses on the following question: By which process could empirical data be used to, firstly, develop and validate a competency model and secondly, to set standards in science education? The competency model consists of three axes: skills, domains, and levels. The skills include, among others, 'to ask questions and to investigate', 'to exploit information sources', and 'to organize, structure and model'. Four competency levels have been defined for each of the skills and for each of the three grades mentioned above. In order to validate the model and to evaluate the baseline performance of the pupils, different paper & pencil and performance tests have been undertaken with representative samples of about 10.000 students at the end of grade 2, 6, and 9. In total, more than 100 paper & pencil problems and 20 experiments have been developed and employed. At the beginning of each problem a situation is given, i.e. a stem, which is followed by 3–6 items. The results of the tests allowed the improvement of the competency model, proposing realistic standards, i.e. standards attainable for the pupils, and illustrating the standards by specific reference examples. Implications for further research in science education, the co-operation between researchers and policy makers, and teacher programmes will also be discussed.

# 1 Introduction

*Developing educational standards: One goal – different ways*

The national results published by international large-scale studies such as the Third International Mathematics and Science Study (TIMSS) and the Programme for International Student Assessment (PISA) have prompted the question: 'How can the outcomes of science education be improved?' and 'How can standards be set and/or be enhanced?' (for an overview see the contributions by Kremer et al. and Köller and Parchmann, *this volume*).

In nations with a federal structure, typical instruments for setting standards are publications and government documents such as a 'Common Framework' in Canada (CMEC, 1997), 'National Science Education Standards' in the USA (NRC, 1996) and 'Standards for the outcomes of the medium level of compulsory school' in Germany (*Standards für den mittleren Schulabschluss*, KMK, 2004a, 2004b, 2004c). Countries which have implemented centralised educational systems and nationwide tests, such as England and France, have the possibility to set standards for students by means of nationwide assessments. France, for example, has defined a new 'Common Socle' (*Le socle commun*, MEN, 2006, 2007) and has a long tradition of centralised testing at the end of lower secondary school and at the baccalaureate level.

In the documents mentioned above, and in most other similar documents of various other countries, terms such as goal, competency, standard, and curriculum have been applied. However, as Waddington, Nentwig, & Schanze (2007) have documented and pointed out, these terms are applied in different ways. A first approach for defining these terms, therefore, might be by using dictionary definitions where a goal is defined as *"the purpose towards which an endeavour is directed"*, competency as *"the ability to perform a task, a standard as an accepted or approved example of something against which others are judged or measured"*, and curriculum as a *"course of study"* (Collins English Dictionary, 2007).

The examples, which are mentioned in the different chapters of this volume, show that there are several ways to develop, validate, and implement nationwide standards in science education. Each of these includes several challenges and questions, such as: What are the main goals and competencies that should be pursued in science education in order to acquire scientific literacy, and, if at all, how can these competencies be measured? Are the standards realistic, e.g., are the majority of students able to achieve a basic level, also referred to as 'basic standards'? How can standards be illustrated by approved examples and what does 'approved' mean?

To answer these questions, empirical data can play an important role. Consequently, this article focuses on the following research question: *By which process can empirical data be used to validate a competency model and to set standards in science education?* The authors were obliged to address this question during the process of developing, validating, and proposing national standards in science education in Switzerland. Although a national project, many of its characteristics, procedures, questions, answers, and insights can be generalized and transferred to similar projects in other countries.

*Developing educational standards in Switzerland: The HarmoS project*

In Switzerland, the 'Swiss Conference of Cantonal Ministers of Education' (SCCME) initiated a large programme entitled 'Harmonisation of Compulsory School' (*Harmonisierung der obligatorischen Schule*, HarmoS, see EDK, 2009, 2011; Adamina et al., 2008; Labudde & Adamina, 2008) for two reasons. Firstly, in a country with 26 cantons (states) and each with its own educational system (Szlovak, 2005), a harmonization of all these systems and their structures was a necessity. Secondly, in order to set nationwide standards, the outcome of the 26 educational systems should thus be harmonized. Subsequently, in the setting of standards, science educators played a major role. Their tasks – as given to them by the SCCME – included the following (Labudde, 2008):
- Development of a first version of a competency model and standards;
- Validation of this first version and evaluation of the baseline performance of students' knowledge and capacities at the end of grades 2, 6, and 9;
- Revision of the competency model and the standards;
- Proposition of a competency model and of basic performance standards for the end of grades 2, 6, and 9 to the SCCME.

What is the overall purpose in developing a competency model and standards? The purpose is twofold: the competency model and standards should be the framework i) for the development of new curricula for each of the four Swiss language regions and ii) for a future continuous monitoring of the educational system as a whole. The latter will be on a national level with a representative sample of students. The competency model and standards are not meant as a highstakes assessment of national tests or a benchmarking of schools and teachers; these kinds of assessments are unknown in Switzerland and it is not the intention to introduce them.

As previously mentioned (Labudde, 2007a, 2007b), the development, implementation, and assessment of standards depend on the political frame (for an example see Klieme et al., 2004; Labudde, 2007a; Ravitch, 1995). The standards in the HarmoS project had to fulfil the following conditions which were specified by the politicians:

1) *Performance standards for students*, i.e. there is a focus on the learner, and on the outcome of instruction (for a more detailed discussion about standards see Klieme et al., 2004, and Ravitch, 1995).
2) *Standards for the end of grades 2, 6, and 9*, implying there should be a 'vertical coherence' during compulsory school. The decision to choose these grades is because the education system in most cantons is structured so that primary school includes grades 1–6, lower secondary school 7–9 (compulsory school ends at the end of grade 9). In the future, one wants to group two years of pre-school (kindergarten) and the first and second year of primary school into a so-called 1$^{st}$ cycle, followed by a second and third cycle (grades 3–6 and 7–9, respectively), i.e. grades 2, 6, and 9 will correspond to the end of these three cycles.
3) *Basic standards:* i.e. the large majority of students should be able to attain the requirements given by the standards; this condition may have been influenced by the idea of mastery learning and by the fact that too many students only reached the lowest level in the PISA science assessment.
4) *Standards for the subject 'science':* this corresponds to the tradition that in most of the cantons in Switzerland, biology, chemistry, and physics at compulsory school are taught as one subject, called 'science' whilst in some cantons STS (Science-Technology-Society).
5) *Validation of the competency model:* the competency model underlying the standards must be validated empirically.
6) *Description and illustration of the standards:* i.e. there should be a theoretical explanation of the standards as well as paradigmatic, 'approved' examples.
7) *Realistic standards:* it should be demonstrated that the large majority of the students are able to attain the basic standards, i.e. it should be shown that the standards are not only theoretical constructs but in fact verified empirically.

Figure 1 gives an overview of the various political and scientific phases involved in the project HarmoS. In this article we focus on the 'first scientific phase'[1].

As can be seen in Figure 1 the two overarching goals of the 'first scientific phase' of the HarmoS project were the development of a competency model and of basic performance standards. The development of the model comprised several steps, in particular the improvement from a first draft of the model over a second and third version to the final one; this process included a member check and an empirical validation, i.e. several paper & pencil and performance tests (see sections 2 and 3). Parallel to the competency model and including the same steps, basic standards were developed. By the end of the 'first scientific phase' the scientists proposed to politicians both the competency model and the basic standards.

---

1   For further publications about the project and for test items in German, French, and English, also see harmos.phbern.ch.

| | |
|---|---|
| 2002–2005 | *First political phase:*<br>1) Framing the HarmoS project by the SCCME<br>2) Submission of the project, i.e. call for proposals of research consortiums for the subjects first language, second language, mathematics, and science. Each of the consortiums had to fulfil several conditions, e.g., the core of the members of the consortiums had to be science educators<br>3) Allocation of the project to four consortiums, each of them responsible for one of the four subjects |
| 2005–2008 | *First scientific phase:*<br>4) Development of a first ($2^{nd}$, $3^{rd}$) version of a competency model and a $1^{st}$ and $2^{nd}$ version of basic standards<br>5) Validation of the $3^{rd}$ version and evaluation of the baseline performance of students' knowledge and skills at the end of grades 2, 6, and 9<br>6) Revision of the competency model<br>7) Proposition of a competency model and of basic performance standards for the end of grades 2, 6, and 9 to the SCCME |
| 2009–2011 | *Second political phase:*<br>8) Political determination and agreement on the competency model and the basic standards (see EDK, 2011) |
| From 2011 | *Further scientific and political phases:*<br>9) Development of a core curriculum for each of the Swiss language regions (German, French, Italian, Romansh); first steps are already being performed since 2008<br>10) Integration of the concept of competencies and standards in teacher programmes and in teacher professional development<br>11) Establishment of a national monitoring of the educational system<br>12) Establishment of a further support system for schools and teachers |

*Figure 1: The Political and Scientific Phases of the Project HarmoS*


The consortium HarmoS Science, which was responsible for the competency model and standards in science, included:
- Almost 20 science educators, five of them formed the board of the consortium (among them the authors of this article)
- More than 30 science teachers from primary and lower secondary schools
- An expert group of 14 individuals (researchers, members of the cantonal ministries of education, unionists, teachers)
- Half a dozen experts in psychometrics and more than 40 research assistants.

All in all there were more than 100 people involved. The staff came from different linguistic parts of Switzerland, ensuring that the various national cultures of Switzerland were fully represented. Everybody involved was initially informed of the political frame of HarmoS and the purpose of the future competency model and the standards.

## 2 The Competency Model: Skills, Domains and Levels

The Swiss consortium HarmoS Science has decided on a three-dimensional model including the following axes: skills, domains, and levels. In other competency models the term 'domains of competency' is used instead of the term 'skills'. We, however, prefer to use the term 'skill' (in the original languages, German and French, *'Handlungsaspekt'* and *'domaines d'action'*), in order to be able to distinguish between skill, domain, and competency. Figure 2 shows the model in its current version. In the past, the model underwent several changes, not in regard to the three dimensions, but the particular skills, domains, and levels.

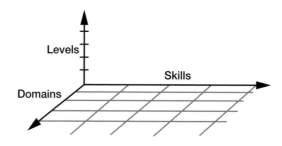

*Figure 2: The Three-Dimensional Competence Model for Science*

The axis of the skills was declared as the primary axis due to two reasons: on the one hand, the consortium wanted to focus on the skills and not on the domains in order to avoid a mere catalogue of concepts; on the other hand, the levels should be defined on the basis of this particular axis and not on the one of the domains. The first axis includes six skills[2]:1) to ask questions and to investigate, 2) to exploit information sources, 3) to organize, structure, and model, 4) to assess and judge, 5) to develop and realize, 6) to communicate and exchange views. Each of the skills is described in detail and consists of several subskills.

---

[2] The actual version from summer 2010 ('political phase' in Figure 1) includes the six skills as mentioned in the text. Two further 'skills' that had been part of the model in earlier versions have been deleted and transferred to an appendix of the description of the model, because they belong to different categories of 'skills'. One is 'to show interest and to be curious' and the other is 'to work self-reliantly and to reflect'.

The axis of the domains comprises 1) planet earth, 2) motion, force, energy, 3) perception and regulation, 4) structures and changes of matter, 5) organisms, 6) ecosystems, 7) human body, health, well-being, 8) nature, society, technology: perspectives. The axis of the domains as a whole is, although not explicitly mentioned, similar to the concept of STSE, which includes science, technology, society, and environment. Certain aspects of 'nature of science' have been integrated into different skills and domains, in particular into 'nature, society, technology: perspectives' and into 'to ask questions and to investigate'. Instead of using the term HarmoS Science we would prefer to talk about HarmoS Science+, in which case the 'plus' means: science plus technology, sustainable development, health education etc. We do not claim the list of domains to be final: a competency model is not the same as a corecurriculum or a curriculum that must include a final list of contents.

Only at the intersection of a skill and a domain is it possible for a student to achieve a competency, i.e. both axes are needed, the axis of the skills and the one of the domains. In other words, by changing the saying 'a theory without practice is empty, practice without a theory is blind' one could say: *'a skill without a domain is empty; a domain without a skill is blind'.* As defined by Weinert (2001), we use the term competencies as: *"cognitive abilities and skills possessed by or able to be learned by individuals that enable them to solve particular problems, as well as the motivational, volitional and social readiness and capacity to utilise the solutions successfully and responsibly in variable situations".*

The third axis includes four levels (I to IV) for each of the grades 2, 6, and 9. As Figure 3 shows, there is an overlap between the levels of the different grades. For example, the lowest level of grade 6, titled I/6, corresponds to the highest level of grade 2, titled IV/2. The model is progressive in the sense that a pupil can theoretically develop his or her competency from level I/2, the lowest at the end of grade 2, to level IV/9, the highest of grade 9. This means that a student, who is able to, for example, attain level I/6, cannot attain level II/6 or higher levels at that time, whilst a pupil who achieves I/9 can also achieve I/6.

We do not believe the progression to be a 'hard' one. That is to say, we do not expect the students to progress from one level to the next at the same pace, remaining at each level for an equal amount of time. Instead, the progression is a 'soft' one: each individual makes progress at his or her own pace; every pupil remains at different levels for different amounts of time (Labudde, 2008, p. 66).

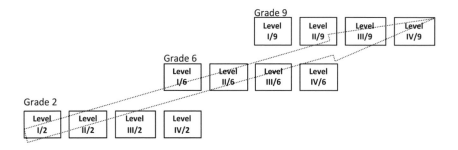

*Figure 3: The Development of a Skill, from the Lowest Level of Grade 2 to the Highest of Grade 9*

Each of the skills and their sub-skills corresponding to the different levels have been described in a sophisticated and meticulous way. In the plane that is given by the axis of the skills and that of the levels, hundreds of 'can-do-descriptions' have been formulated. For example, the skill 'to ask questions and to investigate' includes five sub-skills: 1) 'to look at phenomena more attentively, to explore more precisely, to observe, to describe, and to compare', 2) to raise questions, problems, and hypothesis', 3) 'to choose and apply suitable tools, instruments, and materials', 4) 'to conduct investigations, analyses, and experiments', 5) 'to reflect on results and examination methods. Table 1 gives an example of the sub-skill 'to look at phenomena more attentively, to explore more precisely, to observe, to describe and to compare'; the figure contains the lowest level of each of the grades 2, 6, and 9, i.e. I/2, I/6, and I/9.

*Table 1: The Lowest Levels of the Sub-Skill 'To Look at Phenomena More Attentively, to Explore More Precisely, to Observe, to Describe and to Compare' for Each of the Grades 2, 6, and 9 (Final Version)*

| **Level I/2:** Students can | **Level I/6:** Students can | **Level I/9:** Students can |
|---|---|---|
| • perceive and observe basic phenomena and describe them with everyday concepts. | • perceive and observe basic phenomena with more than one sense;<br>• conduct basic measurements, gather, rudimentarily arrange and compare data in order to describe basic phenomena. | • perceive and observe phenomena with more than one sense;<br>• conduct specific measurements, gather, arrange and compare data in order to describe phenomena. |

There is no comparable description of a progression in the domains. As already mentioned above, the axis of the skills has been declared to be the primary axis and not the axis of the domains. This is in order to avoid a mere catalogue of concepts which would become progressively more and more sophisticated. The competency model primarily refers to a progression in skills and not to a progression in understanding of concepts.

## 3   Validation of the Model and Evaluation of the Baseline Performance: Methodology

Our consortium had to fulfil two main tasks: firstly, the proposition of a competency model for science education at compulsory schools, and secondly, the proposition of basic standards for the end of grades 2, 6, and 9. The model and the standards should be validated and, in particular the standards, be realistic, i.e. the future standards should be connected to the baseline performance of the outcomes of science teaching. For the validation we chose a qualitative approach, i.e. a member check (in social studies also called informant feedback: see Morse et al., 2002), and a quantitative approach. It is this combination of qualitative and quantitative analyses – the latter one evaluating to what degree the standards that are aimed for are realistic and whether they correspond to the baseline performance – which is new in setting standards.

*Member check*

Mostly competency models and standards are developed and set without any empirical analyses, but only validated by a more or less broad member check. Though this type of validation is necessary, it is not a sufficient condition in the sense that a member check broadens the spectrum of ideas and helps to enroot the model and the standards in the communities of science teachers, science educators, key-stake holders in ministries, unions, and political parties, improving the acceptance of the future model and of the standards in those communities. We therefore performed a member check in a systematic way. It included:
- Regular meetings with the expert group, i.e. half a day every six months;
- The co-operation with 30 'ordinary' teachers, a collaboration which involved the discussion of the competency model as well as the problems and results of the tests;
- The organisation of specific HarmoS-workshops for teachers, each of them lasting half a day, in three different linguistic regions of Switzerland;
- Mostly by invitation, the presentation and discussion of the current version of the model in numerous conferences, workshops, and in-service training;

- A specific website (http://harmos.phbern.ch) showing the latest news about the project, the current versions of the competency model, and paradigmatic problems of the tests;
- Regular exchange with the three other consortiums, i.e. first language, second language, mathematics.

*Design of the paper & pencil and performance tests*

The consortium decided to validate all of the domains and five of the six skills: 'to ask questions and to investigate', 'to exploit information sources', 'to organise, structure, and model', 'to assess and judge', and – partly – 'to develop and realize'. However, the skill 'to communicate and exchange views' was not validated due to the lack of reliable and valid test instruments which could be used in a paper & pencil test.

In the paper & pencil tests, the problems and items were PISA-like (however the problems were not taken from PISA), i.e. at the beginning of the problem a situation was given, i.e. a stem, followed by 3 to 6 items. Almost all situations and items have been developed from scratch by teams of science educators and teachers. After piloting, almost one third of the items were deleted; the criteria for deleting them were bottom or ceiling effects, large differences between the results of the French and German speaking part of Switzerland, and difficulties with the marking.

The items had various formats: single choice, multiple choice, short answer, and long answer. The last two formats asked for specific words, a (short) description or explanation, a draft, drawing or a diagram. The time that was planned for answering one problem (with 3–6 items) was 15' for grade 2 and 10' for grades 6 and 9.

The performance tests consisted of short hands-on and/or lab-activities. Many of them were similar to those in the TIMSS-Performance-Test for 13-year old children; two of them were even used in our tests in a slightly changed manner, 'Solutions' and 'Batteries' (Harmon et al., 1997). The time that was given to work on one experiment and to answer the corresponding questions on the test sheet was 30' for all grades. The children worked individually, i.e. not in teams. About 20% of the problems and experiments were used in two grades, i.e. 2 and 6 or 6 and 9. This allowed us to compare the results of two age groups and to analyse the progression from 2 to 6 and 6 to 9, respectively. For a more detailed description of this performance test refer to Gut (2009, in preparation).

In all tests, a rotation plan was developed to ensure that each item was answered by at least 70 children of the same linguistic region of Switzerland. In general in the paper & pencil tests in grades 6 and 9 it was up to n=350 for each item, half of the students from the German, and half of them from the French speaking part of Switzerland. A main objective was to have a large number of items in order to cover different competencies. With a large sample, but only a small amount of test time, a data analysis on the basis of the item-response-theory and of Rasch scaling seemed to be an appropriate method to achieve the objective (see below section 'data analysis'). In all tests the students answered a short questionnaire that asked for their age, sex, mother tongue, parents, and interests in science. The given time to answer the questionnaire was about 10 minutes.

All test items, all hands-on activities, and the questionnaires have been piloted in at least two classes. The paper & pencil items, the marking schemes and the student questionnaires exist in French and German versions. The translation of these documents was done and controlled by the members of the consortium. The Italian speaking part of Switzerland was not included in the study because it represents only 4% of the Swiss population. What is more, building up a HarmoS-subgroup to be responsible for the Italian speaking part of Switzerland, translating the tests and marking schemes would have been too expensive.

*Grade 2:* The sample consisted of n=593 children in 30 classes of the German and French speaking parts of Switzerland (in Switzerland, the average size of a class is about 20). The classes were chosen randomly, but for logistic reasons classes were selected only from those cantons where members of the consortium came from. Since these cantons are the biggest and represent almost 50% of the Swiss population, one can argue that the sample is representative. The test consisted in total of 150 items in 16 paper & pencil problems and 8 experiments, i.e. the test was a combination of paper & pencil problems and hands-on activities. Each child worked on 4 paper & pencil problems (4 x 15') and 2 hands-on activities (2 x 30'). The test was performed in two sessions, each of those lasted one hour. During each test two test managers, who were members of the consortium, visited the class and supervised the test. The teacher of the class supervised one half of the class which answered the paper & pencil problems while the two managers each guided a quarter of the class during the performance tasks, i.e. the experimental ones.

*Grades 6 and 9:* In both grades a paper & pencil as well as a separate performance test were applied. In grade 6, the sample for the paper & pencil test consisted of n=4124 children in 255 classes, in grade 9 the sample was n=3888 adolescents in 273 classes. The classes were randomly drawn with the support of the Swiss Federal Institute of Statistics: A two-stage sample was used: 1) schools were sampled; 2) whole classes within a school were sampled (for details see Ramseier, 2008). The sample is representative of the German and French speaking part of Switzerland, which covers 96% of the Swiss population. The test for each of the grades consisted of 45 paper & pencil problems with a total of 229 items (grade 6) and 262 items (grade 9), respectively.

Each student answered 8 problems (in some cases only 4). The test was managed and supervised by the science teacher of the particular class.

The sample for the performance test differed from the one for the paper & pencil test. It consisted of n=663 in grade 6 (30 classes), and n=805 (44 classes) in grade 9. For this sample of 74 classes the representativeness is equal to the one in grade 2. Eight experiments had been developed for grade 6, and twelve for grade 9. Each student worked on 2 experiments (2 x 30'), and, in order to be able to compare these samples with the paper & pencil ones, 5 paper & pencil problems (5 x 10') were also included. Again, two test managers as well as the science teacher of the particular class guided and supervised these tests.

*Two typical test items*

Figure 4 shows a typical paper & pencil item for grade 6. The item belongs to the skill 'to exploit information sources' and to the domain 'planet earth'. 71% of the tested children answered at least three of the four questions correctly. In doing so, they fulfilled the basic standard that the consortium has proposed in regard to 'to exploit information sources' (see the next two chapters).

| **What will the weather be like in the next days?** ||||||
|---|---|---|---|---|---|
| In the schoolroom, two children display the weather forecast every week. For this purpose they cut out announcements out of newspapers and summarize them on a poster. This week the following details are on the poster: ||||||
| details | Monday | Tuesday | Wednesday | Thursday | Friday |
| sunshine | a lot | a lot | partly | little | partly |
| temperature lowest / highest value | 14 ° Celsius 28 ° Celsius | 15 ° Celsius 30 ° Celsius | 16 ° Celsius 32 ° Celsius | 17 ° Celsius 23 ° Celsius | 16 ° Celsius 26 ° Celsius |
| air humidity | low | low | middle to very high | high | middle to low |
| Always name two days (with the abbreviations Mo, Tue, We, Thu, Fr)! <br> 1. Which are the sunniest days? <br> 2. Which are the hottest days? <br> 3. Which are the most humid days? <br> 4. On which days could there be the most rainfall? ||||||

*Figure 4: A Typical Paper & Pencil Item for Grade 6 in Order to Assess the Skill 'to Exploit Information Sources'*

Figure 5 shows a typical hands-on activity for grade 2; the figure includes the marking scheme. The pupils examine a phenomenon under supervision and with given materials (in this case swimming and sinking). They describe their observation in words and with sketches and they explain their results. By doing so it becomes apparent how they understand the task, what they examine, how (exactly) they make their observations and how and with which elements and features they record their results. 57% of the children performed the activity and answered the question perfectly, i.e. got two marks. A further 16% acquired one mark. The consortium decided that one mark corresponds to the basic standard. Therefore, in this activity 73% of the sample had attained the basic standard (cf. the next two sections). For more typical test items see http://harmos.phbern.ch.

*Data analysis*

All paper & pencil problems and experiments were marked on the basis of a detailed marking scheme that exists in a German and French version. The markers, mostly research assistants, only marked tests in their mother tongue. The French and German speaking assistants marked the same problems at the same time in order to be able to discuss and solve specific marking problems.

For each of the tests a Rasch analysis was carried out; we used a one-parameter model (item difficulty). We made sure the items fitted the model and we selected items by using a discrimination index with a value of 0.3. Some of the items had to be cancelled due to inaccurate translations or to other complications during the testing. Other items could not be used for some of the analyses because the differences (item difficulty) between the results of the French and German speaking pupils were too large. For example, if one wanted to use an item later on as a paradigmatic example to illustrate a national basic standard, it would not be fair to use items with large differences between the regions to define national standards. As was the case in PISA, the mean and the standard deviation were fixed to 500 and 100 points, respectively. The Rasch analysis allows quantifying – on the same scale – both the difficulty of an item and the achievement of students (for a detailed description of our analyses see Ramseier, Labudde & Adamina, in press).

The task is introduced orally; the task text is commented by the test manager. Moreover, the following material is allocated: one cup filled to the half with water, as well as a little ship, two big and two small discs of metal (10g and 4g, respectively), and a candle.

*Your task*

1. Load your little ship as it has been shown.
2. Put the loaded little ship slowly onto the water.
3. Observe silently.
4. Describe and draw what has happened.

*Expected achievement*

1. The little ship is loaded with a small disc on the brim of the floor.
4. This happened:

The little ship swims inclined. (The side with the disc lies deeper in the water.)

*Examples of answers*[4]

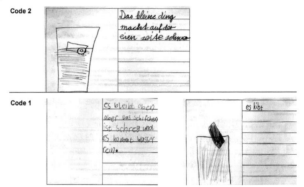

*Schema of correction*

**2 points (extended level):** The correct solution is fully recorded (see sketch); 3 of the 4 following elements are present: water surface visible, inclined little ship, little ship that is sinking, and disc at the lowest point in the little ship.
**1 point (level of the basic standard):** The correct solution is recorded in rudiments: the following two elements are present: water surface and inclined little ship. One error is tolerated.
**0 points (insufficient level):** All other answers.

*Figure 5: A Typical Hands-On Activity for Grade 2 in Order to Assess the Skill 'to Ask Questions and to Investigate'.*

---

4  The English translation of the three texts by German speaking children is the following one (the faults in grammar that the children made were translated one to one into English in order to have a translation as authentic as possible): 'The little thing makes heavy on the one side (at code 2)'; 'it remains on the top, but the little ship is inclined and water is coming in' (code 1, drawing on the left); 'it tilts over' (code 1, drawing on the right).

# 4 Results and Discussion

Given that the results of the tests in grade 2 and the results of the experimental tests in grade 6 and 9 are published elsewhere (Adamina et al., 2008; Gut, 2009, in preparation), in this article we focus on the paper & pencil tests in grades 6 and 9.

*Member check:* Almost all experts and teachers who were engaged in the member check strongly supported the competency model, its three dimensions, as well as the different skills and domains. They recognized the current curricula in the model and in its detailed description; at the same time they explained that the model offers numerous chances to develop science education in Switzerland. Experts in science education confirmed the model to be in good accordance with the current state of science education. The feedback of the experts and teachers led to some, mostly minor, changes in the model, i.e. their comments helped to develop a realistic model as well as realistic standards (see conditions 1 and 7 in the section 1).

The member check proved to be a valuable method for feedback, encouragement and criticism, and as a method to obtain suggestions for the development and improvement of the model. Furthermore, it helped avoid the development of a mere theoretical project with no relations to everyday instruction, but instead supported the development of a model that is not only rooted in the past but also opens new horizons. The member check and the empirical test complemented each other.

*Scores of the students:* As mentioned above, for each grade a scale is calculated. The scale is transformed so as to have an average of 500 points and a standard deviation of 100 points for the global science scale. If we observe the students' mean for the three skills, we notice significant differences between 'to assess and judge' and the two other skills in grade 6, as well as between 'to exploit information sources' and the two other skills in grade 9 (see Table 2). The scores of the students illustrate their actual performance which is invaluable help in getting an idea on which level basic standards can be defined. The scores also allow identifying paradigmatic problems, i.e. problems that both ask for specific skills as defined by the competency model and that can be solved by the large majority of students. Problems like these can be used to illustrate the basic standards (see conditions 3 and 6 in section 1).

The results of the Rasch analysis and the Gaussian-like distribution of the frequencies are no surprise. For example, the results in grade 9 are very similar to those obtained in PISA 2006 (Zahner, Rossier & Holzer, 2007) and a more detailed analysis, in which the HarmoS and the PISA data have been compared, confirmed this observation (Brühwiler et al., 2009).

*Characteristics of skills:* In the paper & pencil tests of grades 6 and 9, three skills were tested: 'to exploit information sources', 'to organize, structure and model', and 'to as-sess and judge'. Table 2 presents the number of items per skill, the average results of the students for each skill, and the standard error.

*Table 2: Characteristics of the Scales of Different Skills*

|  | to exploit information sources | to organize, structure and model | to assess and judge |
|---|---|---|---|
| **grade 6** | | | |
| N of items | 97 | 161 | 128 |
| mean | 506 | 502 | 495 |
| SE | 4.1 | 3.4 | 3.6 |
| **grade 9** | | | |
| N of items | 130 | 195 | 77 |
| mean | 511 | 495 | 497 |
| SE | 4.5 | 3.9 | 4.1 |

Table 2 shows the characteristics of the three skills for grade 6 and 9. The distribution is very large for all three skills as well as for both grades. This allows us to find paradigmatic examples which enable an illustration of what a basic standard (a regular or an excellence standard) can indicate. For example, the item illustrated in Figure 4 ('weather forecast') had a score of 485 (on the basis that 3 out of 4 questions had been answered correctly). This score is below the average of 500 (global science scale) and 506 (skill to exploit information source), respectively. Later on it was used as a paradigmatic example (see next section). In general, almost all items proved to be more difficult to the pupils than science teachers and science educators had predicted. Their prediction was either 'very easy', 'easy', 'medium' or 'difficult', i.e. a scale from level I to level IV. In many cases fewer pupils performed well on a 'very easy' or 'easy' item than had been expected; e.g., only 60 per cent of the pupils answered an item correctly that had been predicted to be 'very easy'. Nevertheless, the extensive tests and the Rasch analysis proved to be an extremely valuable instrument and methodology to get an idea of students' achievements (see conditions 3, 6, and 7).

*Correlations between skills:* How different are the particular skills that have been theoretically defined in the competency model? Table 3 presents the correlations between the three skills 'to exploit information sources' (eis), 'to organize, structure and model' (osm), and 'to assess and judge' (aj).

*Table 3: The Correlations Between the Skills for Grade 6 and Grade 9*

| Grade 6 (Grade 9) | | eis | osm | as |
|---|---|---|---|---|
| to exploit information sources | eis | 1.00 | | |
| to organize, structure and model | osm | 0.83 *(0.94)* | 1.00 | |
| to assess and judge | as | 0.85 *(0.82)* | 0.89 *(0.79)* | 1.00 |

The correlations between the different skills are relatively high, between 0.79 and 0.94. These correlations indicate that there are only small differences between the skills. Therefore, one could raise the question, if there should in fact only be one skill titled 'scientific literacy'. This would call into question a differentiated competency model as ours or others such as the Canadian, US, or German models.

*Correlations between domains:* How different are the eight domains that have been theoretically defined in the competence model? Since several items had to be deleted (cf. data analysis), the sample of some of the domains became too small to run a correlation analysis. We solved this problem by combining a) 'motion, force, energy' and 'perception and regulation', b) 'organisms' and 'ecosystems', c) 'human body, health, well-being' and 'nature, society, technology: perspectives'; the remaining domains, 'planet earth' and 'structure and properties of matter', stayed separate. In Table 4 the correlations between the domains are represented.

*Table 4: The Correlations between the Domains for Grade 6 and Grade 9*

| Grade 6 (Grade 9) | | mfe & pr | o & e | hhw & nstp | pe | scm |
|---|---|---|---|---|---|---|
| motion, force, energy; perception and regulation | mfe & pr | 1.00 | | | | |
| organisms; ecosystems | o & e | 0.70 *(0.65)* | 1.00 | | | |
| human body, health, well-being; nature, society, technology: perspectives | hhw & nstp | 0.60 *(0.59)* | 0.65 *(0.69)* | 1.00 | | |
| planet earth | pe | 0.72 *(0.62)* | 0.73 *(0.72)* | 0.68 *(0.72)* | 1.00 | |
| structures and changes of matter | scm | 0.71 *(0.73)* | 0.65 *(0.67)* | 0.74 *(0.68)* | 0.63 *(0.67)* | 1.00 |

The correlations between the domains vary between 0.59 and 0.74, i.e. they are still high. However, they are almost 0.2 lower than those between the skills; an explanation for this fact could be that the differences between certain domains – e.g., between domains that correspond more strongly to physical sciences and those that correlate more strongly to living systems – are larger than the differences between the different skills. From the perspective of psychometrics, one could raise the question as to whether the axis of the domains should be the primary axis of the model instead of the axis of the skills as done in our approach (see section 2).

*Comparison between students of different grades:* The items in the tests for the different grades, e.g., 2 and 6 or 6 and 9, showed an overlap of about 20%. For example, the paper & pencil tests for grades 6 and 9 had 46 common items. Analysing these 46 items, and performing a Rasch analysis which only includes these particular items, yields the possibility to compare the results of grades 6 and 9. The standard deviation (0.77) for this set of items in the two grades is the same. The standard error is also the same (0.11). The standard error between the two grades is 0.038. Figure 6 shows the comparison of the relative item difficulty in both grades. Each dot represents one of the 46 common items. The items that lie left of the diagonal (black line) are more difficult for students in grade 6 than for grade 9 students. The items to the right of the diagonal are more difficult for students in grade 9.

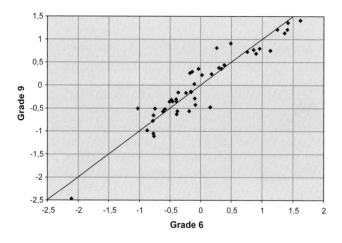

*Figure 6: Comparison of the Relative Item Difficulty between Grades 6 and 9 (46 items)*

The analysis shows a certain coherence of the data between the two grades. For example, the five most difficult items (above 1.0) are more difficult for grade 6 pupils. Most other items do not lie too far from the diagonal, indicating a fairly close difficulty level. Regarding the averages of grades 6 and 9 for this set of 46 items, the difference of 56 points is smaller than expected after three years of science teaching. Comparisons and analyses like these allow statements about the progression of skills and about the 'vertical coherence' of standards during compulsory school (see condition 2 in the section 1).

It seems that the pupils, at least partly, are not making much progression in lower secondary school. One interpretation could be the following: until the end of grade 6 all children, i.e. of different performance, are in the same class. At the beginning of grade 7, the Swiss school system is stratified, i.e. there are two or even three different tracks for low, medium and high performing pupils. The role and the type of science education can be different in the various tracks, and in some tracks Science teaching time has a greater importance.

*Further results:* Due to lack of space, other statistical results can only be mentioned briefly (for a more detailed analysis see Adamina et al., 2008, and Ramseier et al., in press). In grades 6 and 9, boys perform significantly better than girls. Furthermore, they show more interest in science and their self-concept in regard to science is higher. These gender differences are not unexpected, they are known from many national and international studies (for an overview see Murphy & Whitelegg, 2006). The results of the German speaking pupils are better than those of the French speaking pupils, an outcome that confirms the Swiss results in PISA (Zahner, Rossier, & Holzer, 2007). An empirical comparison between the categories, scores, and results of PISA 2006 and the HarmoS paper & pencil test in grade 9 showed a lot of similarities and statistical correlations. Details have been reported elsewhere (Nidegger, Moreau, & Gingins, 2009).

*Validity of the model and evaluation of the baseline performance:* For the following reasons we consider the HarmoS competency model as – more or less – valid: The empirical results of our tests which are based on this model confirm a broad spectrum of known results that have been gained by other methods and instruments, e.g.: progression from grade 6 to 9, differences between the German and French speaking parts of Switzerland, gender differences, and lower correlations between the domains than between the skills. The Rasch analysis shows a Gaussian-like distribution, both for the pupils as well as for the items; the spectrum of the difficulty of the items is very broad. Many of them, including the particular marking scheme and the empirical results of the paper & pencil tests, could be used to illustrate basic (regular or excellence) standards. The member check was positive; experts confirmed a good accordance of the model with existing curricula and with the present state of the art of science education.

# 5 From Empirical Results to the Proposition of Standards

The development and the validation of a competency model was one of the main tasks of the consortium, the other task was the proposition of basic standards. In the end, this proposition and the subsequent statutory definition of the standards by the ministry of education (in the case of Switzerland the SCCME) are normative decisions. This is how it is usually carried out in most of the countries worldwide. However, the HarmoS approach differs from this more common method because the proposition and definition of standards is supported by empirical results.

The science HarmoS consortium decided to propose the standards for all skills and grades in the same format: first comes the description of the basic standard followed by two to three illustrative problems or hands-on activities. For example, the basic standard for the skill 'to exploit information sources' is described for grade 6 in the following manner: 1) The theoretical description: *'Students can [...] read and highlight/mark information following an instruction (e.g., important words, designations in diagrams, symbols). Following an instruction they can identify the information that is needed to answer a given question. They are able to reproduce part of this information in their own words or by other means of representation [...]'* (see Table 1). 2) This theoretical description is illustrated by two or three paradigmatic examples, so-called reference examples. One of them is shown in Figure 5. Every example includes the problem, the marking scheme, and the empirical results of the test (the distribution of codes, the percentage of the students who had answered correctly, and the score on the Rasch scale). As the feedback of numerous teachers show, these examples are appreciated enormously by the colleagues in the schools.

For skills that had not been tested, e.g., 'to communicate and exchange ideas' or 'to work self-reliantly and to reflect', a theoretical description and an example were given as well. However, the example did not come from one of the tests, but from a so-called opportunity-to-learn, i.e. a short description of a learning unit that could serve in promoting the particular skill. For example, in order to illustrate the basic standard in regard to 'to communicate and exchange ideas' for grade 2, the suggestion is to visit and learn more about a gravel plant. During this teaching unit, children are asked to compare the gravel plant and the work performed there with their own experiences in a sandpit. We also presented a few opportunities-to-learn for some other skills as well. The reason for this is that in science education there are several skills, for example the continuous observation of a tree, meadow or creek during the whole year, that cannot be measured in (nationwide) tests and/or illustrated by paper & pencil items or short hands-on activities.

The development of a competency model, its validation, illustrative examples that can be used both in tests as well as in teaching units, and opportunities-to-learn are first steps in implementing standards in science education. They are a necessary, but not a sufficient condition for the successful implementation of standards. Other steps must follow, such as the development of new curricula, teaching units and materials, new education programmes and the professional development of teachers, a pilot project or programme, and an educational monitoring system.

# 6 Contributions, Limitations, and Future Work

What could be the contribution of the HarmoS science project to the development of the curriculum, the setting of standards, and the teaching of science? A competency model has been developed by the HarmoS project that can contribute to the discussion of the goals of science education, the meaning and contents of scientific literacy and the essential skills which students should acquire in science education. Concerning the skills and its fundamental concepts and contents, the competency model also provides a way to describe possibilities for cumulative science learning in the whole compulsory school system. As traditions, objectives, and contents of science education differ from country to country, a competency model of one country, e.g., Switzerland, can serve as a mirror to reflect on another country's model. With the globalization of science instruction, initiated – among other things – by PISA, comparisons of different competency models and curricula are essential for the further development of science instruction. Furthermore, this applies to setting standards: many countries have their own way of elaborating, defining, and implementing standards (Waddington, Nentwig, & Schanze, 2007). One of the interesting points about the HarmoS project is that we have tried to validate the standards and the corresponding reference examples before the standards enter into force. The references have been tested empirically in order to be able to propose realistic standards. These references, which can be used in daily instruction both for teaching and testing, and the underlying theory can contribute to the professional development of daily science instruction at school. Reference examples and opportunities-to-learn are warmly welcomed by the teachers.

What are the limitations of our project? There are some skills in the competency model that have neither been validated empirically nor described in detail, for example, the skill to work on a science 'research' project for a longer period of time. In HarmoS, we have focused on subject specific skills, but there are other skills that are important as well, such as the cross curricular competencies, for example. One should be aware of this omission when talking about school, science instruction, and its outcomes.

What remains on the research agenda? 1) There are several skills that are said to be important for science education and scientific literacy, but are only poorly described, defined, validated and implemented, such as 'to communicate and exchange views' or 'to work self-reliantly and to reflect'. 2) Another broad and important field for research and development is the formation and professional development of science teachers. In what way can we support them in teaching in a more competence-oriented approach? 3) Suitable instruments, which have yet to be developed, are required to measure specific competencies and outcomes of instruction. This also raises a broad spectrum of research questions, questions that need the co-operation of science education and psychometrics. 4) A systematic comparison – based on well-defined categories – between various competency models and standards from different countries and/or research groups could help to determine unintended priorities and/or omissions in one's own country. 5) What is the role of science education during the development, validation, and implementation of standards? How can the needs of science education and psychometrics be balanced? To what degree should science educators be engaged in modelling and evaluating competencies, rather than being engaged in scientifically based programmes for the professional development of teachers? These questions, and others, were among the most discussed issues at an international conference on 'Competencies and standards in science education: the role of science education' (Labudde et al., 2009).

What can we learn from this study, in particular from its empirical part? From the research point of view the study yields several insights: I) Tests and empirical data are an important basis when elaborating and proposing standards that should be realistic and should reflect both the actual performance of the students and the performance that is aimed for in the future. II) One should keep in mind, however, that proposing standards is still – also on the basis of empirical data – a normative process and decision. III) Empirical data can be used to adapt and to revise the underlying competency model. IV) Correlations of 0.8 or higher between various skills raise the question whether or not we can actually distinguish between different skills, or if instead, we should talk about one skill named 'scientific skill'. V) The lower correlations (0.59 to 0.74) between the different domains might suggest that the distinction between different domains, such as in tests, makes sense. VI) The progression from grade 6 to 9 is relatively small; therefore, the interesting question remains if this is the result of the stratified school-system in lower secondary school in Switzerland and if more progression could be observed in non-stratified school-systems in other countries.

Doing research in the area of standards does not just have a scientific dimension, but also a highly political one. As researchers, we send important signals to teachers, school administrators, and politicians when proposing standards, presenting reference examples, and suggesting test-instruments. As science educators, we should be aware of our political responsibilities when dealing with standards.

## Acknowledgements

The HarmoS science project and this article would not have been possible without the help of our collaborators of the HarmoS consortium. We gratefully acknowledge the efforts and the contributions of L. Bazzigher, B. Bringold, U. Frischknecht-Tobler, P. Gigon, C. Gut, B. Jaun-Holderegger, A. Jetzer, B. Knierim, S. Metzger, E. Ramseier, K. Raths, R. Stebler, P.-Y. Theurillat, M. Vetterli, U. Wagner, C. Weber, and A. Zeyer. Equally, our gratitude goes to all teachers, students, and research students who have participated in this project.

The project was supported by the SCCME, the Applied Universities of Bern, Luzern, Northwestern Switzerland, St. Gall, Vaud, Zürich, the University of Zürich, and the Service de la Recherche en Éducation in Geneva.

## References

Adamina, M., Labudde, P., Gingins, F., Nidegger, C., Bazzigher, L., Bringold, B., et al. (2008). *HarmoS Naturwissenschaften+: Kompetenzmodell und Vorschläge für Bildungsstandards – Wissenschaftlicher Schlussbericht (HarmoS Science+: A Competency Model and Propositions for Educational Standards – Scientific Report)*. Bern. Available at: http://harmos.phbern.ch.

Brühwiler, C., Nidegger, C., Domenico, A., Gingins, F., Buccheri, G., Moreau, J., et al. (2009). *PISA 2006: Analysen zum Kompetenzbereich Naturwissenschaften – Rolle des Unterrichts, Determinanten der Berufswahl, Vergleich von Kompetenzmodellen (PISA 2006: In-depth Analyses of Results in Science – The Role of Instruction, Factors Influencing a Career Choice, A Comparison of Competency Models)*. Neuchâtel: Bundesamt für Statistik.

CMEC, Council of Ministers of Education (1997). *K to 12: Common Framework of Science Outcomes*. Available at: http://204.225.6.243/science/framework.

*Collins English Dictionary* (2007). Glasgow: Harper Collins.

Driessen, H. (2007). Development and evaluation of science standards in the Netherlands. In D. Waddington, P. Nentwig & S. Schanze (Eds.), *Making it Comparable: Standards in Science Education* (pp. 221-236). Münster, New York, München, Berlin: Waxmann.

EDK (2009). *HarmoS – Zielsetzungen und Konzeption (HarmoS – Objectives and Conception)*. Bern: Schweizerische Konferenz der kantonalen Erziehungsdirektoren. Available at: http://www.edk.ch/dyn/11659.php (available in German, French, and Italian).

EDK (2011). *Grundkompetenzen für die Naturwissenschaften – Nationale Bildungsstandards (Basic skills in sciences – national standards)*. Bern: Schweizerische Konferenz der kantonalen Erziehungsdirektoren. Available at: http://www.edudoc.ch/static/web/arbeiten/harmos/grundkomp_nawi_d.pdf (available in German, French, and Italian).

Gut, C. (2009). Schweizer Bildungsstandards: Resultate der Experimentiertests (Standards in science education in Switzerland: results of the performance tests). In D. Höttecke (Ed.), *Chemie- und Physikdidaktik für die Lehramtsausbildung* (pp. 315-317). Berlin: Lit Verlag.

Gut, C. (in preparation): Experimentiertests als Instrument der Kompetenzbeurteilung von Schülerinnen und Schülern.

Harmon, M., Smith, T. A., Martin, M. O., Kelly, D. L., Beaton, A. E., Mullis, I. V., et al. (1997). *Performance Assessment in IEA's Third International Mathematics and Science Study*. Chestnut Hill, MA: TIMSS International Study Center, Boston College.

Klieme, E., Avenarius, H., Blum, W., Döbrich, P., Gruber, H., Prenzel, M., et al. (Eds.) (2004). *The Development of National Standards in Education: An Expertise (Zur Entwicklung nationaler Bildungsstandards: eine Expertise)*. Bonn: Bundesministerium für Bildung und Forschung.

KMK. (2004a). *Bildungsstandards in Biologie für den Mittleren Schulabschluss (Standards in Biology for The End of Grade 10)*. Bonn: Kulturministerkonferenz.

KMK. (2004b). *Bildungsstandards in Chemie für den Mittleren Schulabschluss (Standards in Chemistry for The End of Grade 10)*. Bonn: Kultusministerkonferenz.

KMK. (2004c). *Bildungsstandards in Physik für den Mittleren Schulabschluss (Standards in Physics for The End of Grade 10)*. Bonn: Kultusministerkonferenz.

Labudde, P. (2007a). *Bildungsstandards am Gymnasium: Korsett oder Katalysator? (Standards for the grammar school: corset or catalyst?)*. Bern: h.e.p. Verlag.

Labudde, P. (2007b). How to develop, implement and assess standards in science education? 12 challenges from a swiss perspective. In D. Waddington, P. Nentwig & S. Schanze (Eds.), *Making it Comparable: Standards in Science Education* (pp. 277-301). Münster: Waxmann.

Labudde, P. (2008). Developing and implementing new national standards in science education: The role of science educators. In B. Ralle & I. Eilks (Eds.), *Promoting Successful Science Education – The Worth of Science Education Research* (pp. 63-73). Aachen: Shaker.

Labudde, P., & Adamina, M. (2008). HarmoS Naturwissenschaften: Bildungsstandards für die Schule von morgen (HarmoS Science: Standards for The School of Tomorrow). *Beiträge zur Lehrerbildung, 26*(3), 351-360.

Labudde, P., Duit, R., Fickermann, D., Fischer, H., Harms, U., Mikelskis, H., et al. (2009). Schwerpunkttagung, Kompetenzmodelle und Bildungsstandards: Aufgaben für die naturwissenschaftsdidaktische Forschung' (Target Conference ‚Competence models and standards: Challenges for science education research'). *Zeitschrift für Didaktik der Naturwissenschaften, 15*, 125-152.

MEN, Ministère éducation nationale (2006). *Le socle commun des connaissances et des compétences – Décret du 11 juillet 2006 (A Common Framework of Knowledge and Skills – Decree of July 11ᵗʰ 2006)*. Paris: Ministère éducation nationale.

MEN, Ministère éducation nationale (2007). *Socle commun de connaissances et de compétences· Grille de référence – Les principaux éléments de mathématiques et la culture scientifique et technologique (A Common Framework of Knowledge and Skills: Reference Grid – The Main Elements of Mathematics and The Culture of Science and Technology)*. Paris: Ministère éducation nationale.

Morse, J. M., Barret, M., Mayan, M., Olson, K., & Spiers, J. (2002). Verification strategies for establishing reliability and validity in qualitative research. *International Journal of Qualitative Methods, 1*(2), 1-19.

Murphy, P. & Whitelegg, E. (2006). *Girls in the Physics Classroom. A Review of the Research on the Participation of Girls in Physics*. London: Institute of Physics.

Nidegger, C., Moreau, J., & Gingins, F. (2009). Kompetenzen der Schülerinnen und Schüler in den Naturwissenschaften: Erkenntnisse aus PISA und HarmoS (Students' competencies in science: insights from PISA and HarmoS). In C. Brühwiler, C. Nidegger, D. Angelone, F. Gingins, G. Buccheri, M. Mariotta, P. Kis-Fedi & U. Moser (Eds.), *PISA 2006: Analysen zum Kompetenzbereich Naturwissenschaften*. Neuchâtel: Bundesamt für Statistik.

NRC (1996). *National Science Education Standards*. Washington, D.C.: National Research Council NRC.

OECD (2007). *PISA 2006: Science Competencies for Tomorrow's World*. Paris: OECD.

Ramseier, E. (2008). Validation of competence models for developing education standards: Methodological choices and their consequences. *Mesure et évaluation en éducation, 31*(2), 35-53.

Ramseier, E., Labudde, P., & Adamina, M. (in press). Validierung des Kompetenzmodells HarmoS Naturwissenschaften: Fazite und Defizite (Validation of the HarmoS Science Competency Model: Results and Deficiencies). *Zeitschrift für Didaktik der Naturwissenschaften*.

Ravitch, D. (1995). *National Standards in American Education. A Citizen's Guide*. Washington, D.C.: Brookings Institution Press.

Schecker, H., & Parchmann, I. (2007). Standards and competence models: The German situation. In D. Waddington, P. Nentwig & S. Schanze (Eds.), *Making it Comparable: Standards in Science Education* (pp. 146-164). Münster, New York, München, Berlin: Waxmann.

Szlovak, B. (2005). *HarmoS – Lehrplanvergleich Naturwissenschaften (HarmoS – A Comparison of Science Curricula)*. Bern: Schweizerische Konferenz der kantonalen Erziehungsdirektoren.

Waddington, D., Nentwig, P., & Schanze, S. (Eds.). (2007). *Making it Comparable: Standards in Science Education*. Münster, New York, München, Berlin: Waxmann.

Weinert, F. E. (2001). Vergleichende Leistungsmessung in Schulen – eine umstrittene Selbstverständlichkeit (Comparing schools by evaluations: a controversial matter of course) (pp. 17-31). In: F. E. Weinert (Ed.), *Leistungsmessungen in Schulen*. Weinheim, Basel, Bonn: Beltz.

Zahner Rossier, C., & Holzer, T. (2007). *PISA 2006: Kompetenzen für das Leben – Schwerpunkt Naturwissenschaften (Nationaler Bericht) (PISA 2006: competencies for life – focus science (national report))*. Neuchâtel: Bundesamt für Statistik.

# Chapter 12

# The Promise and Value of Learning Progression Research

*Joseph S. Krajcik[1], LeeAnn M. Sutherland[2], Kathryn Drago[2] & Joi Merritt[1]*
[1]*Institute for Research on Mathematics and Science Education, Michigan State University, USA;* [2]*University of Michigan, USA*

## 1  What is the Problem?

All students are not learning as we, as educators and researchers, hope and expect, and as national and international test scores repeatedly reveal. Our premise is that in order for students to do so, and to fully participate in the world of the 21$^{st}$ century, they must develop deeper, integrated understanding of a small number of core science ideas rather than superficial knowledge of a broad range of discrete information. Core science ideas are those that thread across science disciplines and form the foundational building blocks for increasingly complex ideas (Stevens, Sutherland, & Krajcik, 2009; NRC, 2011). As learners link ideas together in web-like fashion, they develop integrated understanding that enables them to access information effectively and to use it to solve complex problems (Fortus & Krajcik, 2011; Sutherland, Shin & Krajcik, 2010). How can curriculum designers, educators and researchers help learners do this? Understanding how ideas develop across time and then purposefully supporting students in making connections is key. Developing and validating learning progressions (LPs) that demonstrate paths for linking core ideas and building understanding offers one potential route to inform science education, as LPs can then be used to guide curriculum development and assessment of student learning as Pellegrino *(this volume)* suggests.

## 2  What are Learning Progressions?

Learning Progressions may be thought of as a sequence of ways of reasoning about a set of ideas, a sequence successively more complex as learners move from less understanding to more sophisticated understanding about an idea as they engage in new learning experiences (Corcoran, Mosher, & Rogat, 2009). As such, learning progressions provide a developmental perspective on helping students learn. They move teaching and learning away from the single-page or single-paragraph description of content ideas so often presented in K-12 science textbooks, descriptions that may provide a complete model of a concept, but that do not help students or support teachers in helping students develop useable understandings. Learning progressions, by specifying how ideas develop over time, can provide curriculum designers with the tools to purposefully build upon and link students' current understandings to form richer and more connected ideas over time (Margel, Eylon & Scherz, 2008; Merritt, Krajcik & Shwartz, 2008). LPs not only build from the nature of the discipline but also from what is known about how students learn generally, how they learn particular science ideas, and how they reason about those ideas. Fortunately, materials are beginning to be built in this manner, including work by Margel and colleagues (Margel et al., 2008), Anderson and colleagues (Mohan, Chen, & Anderson, 2009), Duncan and colleagues (2008), and our own work (Krajcik, Reiser, Sutherland & Fortus, 2009; Merritt et al., 2008; Merritt, 2010). These materials were developed using a design-based research approach and were carefully researched in classrooms to examine how they support student learning and how the new ideas they introduce link to previous ideas in a coherent manner.

Although we do not believe that curriculum materials are an essential aspect of learning progression research, we contend that curriculum developers need to take advantage of LP research to design materials that take a developmental approach, and that provide opportunities for learners to build more connected and sophisticated understandings as they examine related ideas in new and more complex situations. However, curriculum materials that are based on LPs and what is known about student learning are needed to test learning progressions; otherwise, student learning and growth can only be tested using impoverished materials. Moreover, LP-based curriculum materials can help to inform learning progression developers about instructional components that help students to progress (discussed later).

Learning progressions need to build from solid research on how students initially learn an idea and then develop more advanced notions of the idea across time. Although we have some sense of how children learn core ideas about the particle nature of matter and force, for example, we know little about how they develop understanding of energy or evolution. Because LP work is in its infancy, systematic research needs to occur so that the science education and learning science communities can build and subsequently validate learning progressions.

Below, we highlight some important aspects of the design of and research on learning progressions. Learning progression work lies on a solid foundation of theory. In some ways, researchers are in a unique position with respect to science education, as the cognitive and learning sciences communities have provided key theoretical underpinnings from which learning progressions can be built. *Taking Science to School*

(Duschl, Schweingruber & Shouse, 2007) and *Knowing What Students Know* (Bransford, Brown & Cocking, 1999), for example, articulate well what is known about student learning. Never before has the science education community possessed more solid and robust understanding of how to promote learning from general principles, and we must capitalize on this knowledge and know-how. Two key learning principles on which learning progression research is built include the role of prior knowledge and the structure of expert knowledge. In many respects, learning progression research simply plays out these ideas in specific contexts. Below we briefly review both.

*Prior knowledge is key to building integrated understanding:* Learning occurs when new ideas are linked to prior knowledge and experiences, regardless of the "correctness" of the original ideas. That is, students enter school with thoughts about the world that are gleaned from their own experiences, and from what they have seen, heard, or experienced vicariously. Although their initial ideas might (and often do) differ from those of experts in the domain, they nonetheless serve as powerful resources on which to draw when building increasingly complex or in-depth understanding. Failure to draw upon initial ideas leads to knowledge that is fragmented and disconnected and that cannot be effectively used for problem solving or for future learning (Bransford, Brown & Cocking, 1999).

*Core ideas structure expert knowledge:* Expert/scientist knowledge is tightly connected around core ideas and conceptual frameworks that drive thinking, observations and problem solving, and that shape how they organize and structure new information (Bransford et al., 1999). The learning of experts also unfolds over time in a continuous process as they engage in new experiences and make connections among old and new ideas. Learning complex ideas takes time and often happens as individuals work on challenging tasks that require them to synthesize and to make connections. Therefore, learning is best facilitated when new and existing knowledge are structured around big ideas of a discipline so that concentrate on fewer ideas in depth – rather than a greater number of ideas at a superficial level – enabling more connections thus deeper understanding. The National Research Council has identified a small number of big/core ideas that drove their work in the design of the new conceptual framework for science education standards (NRC, 2011). The science education and learning science communities must come to build learning progressions around the big ideas of science so that all students are beter positioned to learn science.

What are big ideas? *Core* or *big ideas* are powerful in that they are central to the disciplines of science, provide explanations of phenomena, and are the building blocks for learning within a discipline (Stevens, Sutherland, & Krajcik, 2009). All big ideas (Stevens, Sutherland & Krajcik, 2009; NRC, 2012):

1. Have explanatory power within and across disciplines and/or scales, helping to explain a variety of phenomena.

2. Provide a powerful way of thinking about the world, providing insight into the development of a field, or having had key influence on a domain.

3. Are cognitively accessible to learners through age-appropriate experiences with phenomena and representations.

4. Provide building blocks by laying the foundation for future learning.

5. Help learners participate intellectually in making individual, social and political decisions regarding science and technology.

For example, one big idea that meets the above criteria might be: "The properties of matter can change with scale. In particular, as the size of a material transitions between the bulk material and individual atoms or molecules, it often exhibits unexpected properties that lead to new functionality. This transition generally occurs at the nanoscale" (Stevens et al., 2009).

To date, little empirical work has been available to guide the design of learning progressions around big ideas. Based on how experts structure their knowledge, only a small set of hypothetical LPs need careful development, further research, refinement and articulation. However, more than one trajectory for a single core idea might be possible, as learning is influenced by multiple factors including the quality and type of instruction. Thus, to help students develop specific and more refined ideas, a small number of LPs need to be developed first, and then classroom research using teaching experiments needs to occur in order to further refine and articulate each progression. As a global community of science educators, we must work together to identify and articulate the big ideas that all students need to learn, as this will advance our work in developing and testing learning progressions and associated curriculum and assessments.

Importantly, learning progressions are not linear. Students must revisit ideas under new conditions and in new contexts to refine and more strongly connect them, as ideas in one LP often link to ideas in another, and then lead toward different big ideas. For example, ideas related to force and interactions intersect with ideas related to transformations of matter and the structure of biological molecules. Without building certain key ideas related to forces and interactions, a learner could only proceed in a limited manner to understand transformations of matter and could only develop a descriptive model of transformation, rather than a mechanistic model.

## 3  What Must Be in a Learning Progression?

Learning progressions need to include five essential components: 1) big ideas, 2) levels that illustrate how students at each level reason with the content, 3) psychometrically valid assessments 4) instructional components to move students to the next level, and 5) rationales, boundaries and connections. Below we expand on each of these (see Table 1).

First, using the specified criteria for what makes a big idea, researchers need to identify and provide a clear explanation of the core constructs around which LPs could be developed. Unpacking the big idea (described in a later section herein) is part of this process.

Second, LPs need to clearly describe each level in the progression, including describing the reasoning expected at each level, prerequisite understandings necessary for succession to higher levels, and links to other ideas. Equally important is providing research-based articulations of why it is difficult for a learner to move to the next level, including the challenges many learners will experience in doing so. Levels need to build coherently, from one step to the next. However, levels are not necessarily based only the logic of the discipline but also need to take into consideration the learner's background (Anderson, 2008).

Third, each learning progression needs to include psychometrically validated assessment items that can identify students at a particular level. Assessments need to be written so that they engage students in cognitive activities so that LPs can be described in terms of how students should use the knowledge. (The next section describes how to develop learning performances.)

Fourth, each LP needs to include key instructional components that can move students from one level to the next. Instructional components might consist of analogies, tasks, or phenomena to observe or investigate that guide learners to the next level of understanding. Although other instructional strategies and sequences might support student learning of a particular idea, a researched set of instructional components that could help learners construct the understanding necessary to move to the next level is anessential features of learning progression work. For instance, in building a learning progression for the particle model of matter, learners need to know that gases are matter and, as such, have mass. Yet, it is well-documented that many middle school students do not think of gases as having mass. Learning progression research needs to suggest key experiences to help students develop this understanding. For example, students could determine the mass of a filled $CO_2$ cartridge, empty the cartridge, and then determine the mass of the empty container. Other examples might include students lifting empty and filled scuba tanks, or empty and filled tanks for a gas barbeque grill. The difference in mass between filled and empty tanks comes as a surprise to many. This type of key instructional component, linked to the corresponding level in the LP, illustrates how to support students moving to the next level.

We consider these instructional aspects critical components of LPs because without attention to the instructional supports that must be provided for student understanding to advance, a sequence of how ideas progress by itself does not support instruction that will facilitate student learning of big ideas. A difference of opinion exists in the learning science and science education communities about the value of these instructional components and whether they should be considered part of the learning progression or part of a teaching progression. We contend that research-based instructional components are necessary to validate a LP. When testing a learning progression, researchers need to examine how students progress when opportunities to learn exist; otherwise, researchers are only measuring the result of instruction not based on how students ideas develop across time, but based on curriculum materials that are not optimal for promoting learning (Roseman, Stern & Koppal, 2010).

Mohan, Chen, and Anderson's (2009) learning progression for environmental literacy provides a good illustration of the importance of conducting LP work in classrooms that target key ideas and use curriculum that provide opportunities for students to learn. In their work, high school students developed different understandings and did not reach upper levels of environmental literacy, given their current high school curriculum, because they did not have the opportunities to learn foundational ideas in the LP. However, students who took part in the project's teaching experiments and experienced coherent instruction, took a different path and reached higher levels of performance, as described in the learning progression. Hence, validating learning progressions needs to occur in authentic environments where the levels, assessments and instruction work together such that progress in each only happens with work on the other.

Although we do not address professional development herein, we agree with colleagues such as Lehrer and Schauble, who argue for the important role that professional development plays in helping teachers learn new practices, and that without appropriate professional development, it is unlikely that we will see implemented in classrooms the practices associated with LPs.

An argument in the work on LPs is the span of time that is necessary before referring to a sequence as a learning progression. The work that goes on through unit development is necessary to identify the assessments, the instructional activities, and learning tasks that can push students further in their understanding; however, the learning that occurs within a single unit is not to be considered a LP. Instead, a unit might address part of a learning progression, the whole of which would ultimately span several years.

Finally, each learning progression must provide rationale for considering an idea to be at a particular level, must provide connections to other learning progressions, and must provide boundaries for what is in and what is not in. Rationales provide a theory-based justification for why an idea is at a particular level. Rationales also point out how an idea builds from previous ones and how one idea will support the building of other, future ideas. Boundaries describe the ideas that lie beyond what students should learn at a particular level; they clarify the intent of the target content idea. For instance, introducing the concept of atoms and molecules is important for middle school students, as the particle model explains phenomena such as phase changes and gases; however, the structure of atoms is not appropriate before students have had experiences to build from. Research literature suggests that students are typically not able to grasp these ideas until later. Information about the structure of an atom is complicated, and ideas about electrical forces are not firmly developed. Boundary conditions might also suggest phenomena that would be too challenging for students to explore, or boundaries might describe non-productive or misleading phenomena to avoid. Connections include describing links to other big ideas and learning progressions.

*Table 1: Key Aspects of a Learning Progression*

| 1 | Big ideas |
|---|---|
| 2 | Levels of understanding |
| 3 | Psychometrically valid assessments |
| 4 | Instructional Components to move students forward |
| 5 | Boundaries, rationale and connections |

## 4 How to Develop Levels

*Unpacking:* The first step in developing a learning progression is to identify the big idea. Although this might seem like a simple task, the process leads to much debate among scholars involved in the process. Once the big idea is identified, a key aspect of learning progressions is thinking seriously about the idea, unpacking the big idea with respect to how it develops across time and identifying what cognition is necessary to demonstrate that understanding. In our own work, (Stevens, Sutherland & Krajcik, 2009; Krajcik, Reiser, Sutherland, & Fortus, 2009), we rigorously address content ideas by identifying and unpacking key science ideas. Unpacking refers to breaking apart and expanding concepts to elaborate the intended science content. When unpacking a science idea, we not only consider what content is important, but seriously consider how students can reason and use this knowledge by examining common student difficulties, prior understandings needed to build the target understanding, and aspects of prior conceptions that may pose challenges. Unpacking not only helps articulate the content, it also helps to identify what reasoning and use of knowledge is appropriate for learners. A key aspect of the unpacking process is consulting the learning literature to understand what students can and cannot do at a particular level. However, often the research needed to make decisions regarding what is challenging for students is not available; therefore, initial forays into developing levels may require revision when tested in classrooms. Unpacking is a critical aspect as it helps to decide what students can learn at a particular level. Table 2 summarizes the unpacking process.

*Table 2: Summary of Unpacking Process*

|  | |
|---|---|
| Step 1 | Identify a big idea using criteria for determining big ideas |
| Step 1a | Justify what makes it a big idea |
| Step 2 | Consider students' prior knowledge<br>• Consider developmental aspects of student learning<br>• Students' prior knowledge<br>• Possible non-normative ideas |
| Step 3 | Interpret the big idea<br>• Decompose into related concepts<br>• Break it down into smaller ideas<br>• What is important for students to know at the grade level of interest<br>• Clarify points<br>• What other ideas are needed<br>• Make links if needed to other core ideas and standards |

*Learning performances:* Once the key science ideas are identified and unpacked, we develop "learning performances" to articulate the cognitive tasks that students should accomplish with the content. The development of learning performances is a critical step, as declarative statements of content knowledge do not specify the type of reasoning students should engage in with ideas (Krajcik, McNeill, & Reiser, 2008; Shin, Stevens & Krajcik, 2010). Anderson and colleagues (Mohan, Chen, & Anderson, 2009) also take into consideration students' thinking about ecology and define levels for environmental literacy using learning performances (Mohan et al., 2009).

Learning performances combine content – initially stated as declarative knowledge – with scientific practices. Table 3 lists various scientific practices modified from several sources (NRC, 2011; College Board, 2009; CPRE, 2011). The sources from which each description is modified are provided in parentheses. This list is modified from the CPRE's Rapid Response Research Project (2011).

*Table 3: Scientific Practices*

| | |
|---|---|
| 1. Questioning | Asking and refining scientific questions that can be investigated empirically. (CBSCS #1, NRC) |
| 2. Find, evaluate, and communicate information | Finding, interpreting, evaluating, and communicating scientific information. (NRC, Common Core ELA) |
| 3. Designing investigations | Designing investigations, including hypothesizing, generating and selecting attributes and measures of these attributes, and data collection plans. (CBSCS #2, NRC) |
| 4. Collecting, representing, and analyzing data | Collecting, representing, analyzing and interpreting data; including searching for regularities and patterns in observations and measurements. (CBSCS #3, NRC) |
| 5. Explanation and prediction | Constructing predictions and explanatory accounts of phenomena, including evidence-based explanations. (CBSCS #4, NRC) |
| 6. Modeling | Developing, evaluating, and revising scientific models to explain and predict. (CBSCS #4, NRC) |
| 7. Argumentation | Engaging in argumentation to defend or critique scientific questions, designs of investigations, representations and analyses of data, evidence-based explanations, predictions, and scientific models. (NRC, missing from CBSCS) |

To develop a learning performance, a portion of each big idea is linked with a key practice. Table 4 shows an example of how to develop a learning performance. Table 5 shows the evidence necessary to meeting the learning performance.

*Table 4: Developing a Learning Performance*

| Big ideas | Practice | Learning performance |
|---|---|---|
| Atoms and molecules are perpetually in motion. In gases, the atoms or molecules have still more energy and are free of one another except during occasional collisions (From BSL 4D/M3.) | Models are often used to think about processes that happen ... too quickly, or on too small a scale to observe directly... (AAAS, 1993, 11B: 1, 6–8) | Students create models of a gas at the molecular level showing that a gas takes the shape of its container. |

*Table 5: Evidence for Student Meeting a Learning Performance*

| Learning performance | Evidence for the performance |
|---|---|
| Students create models of a gas at the molecular level showing how the gas takes the shape of its container. | Students construct models showing how a gas takes the shape of its container. Students will show that in the gaseous state gases are made up of particles that are free of one another except during occasional collisions and move in random straight lines until they have a collision. Because they are free of each other they can spread out in larger containers. |

The development of learning performances is critical because once they are developed, assessment tasks derive directly from them. See Figure 2 below for an assessment task matched to a learning performance and the evidence necessary to demonstrate that performance.

*Specifying levels of the learning progression:* Unpacking and identify learning performances play key roles in the process of identifying levels (Smith, Wiser, Anderson & Krajcik, 2006; Stevens, Delgado & Krajcik, 2009; Shin, Stevens & Krajcik; 2010). Identifying levels is accomplished by first describing the lower and upper anchoring points. These anchors are critical as they specify the range of content within the core idea that will need to be developed to specify levels of understanding (Smith et al., 2006; Stevens, Delgado, & Krajcik, 2010). Using the learning and cognitive research, the lower anchor explicitly describes the understanding that students must have before they can begin to develop understanding of ideas contained in the LP. If the starting point is at the early elementary level, then the lower anchor might be very basic. The upper anchor describes the knowledge and skills that students are ultimately expected to develop by the time they graduate from high school. Often this upper anchor is a description of the big idea and what students should do with this big idea.

Next the big idea needs to be unpacked by clarifying and elaborating it based on research findings about students' understanding of the big ideas and others associated with it. Following this, the development of learning performances for various levels needs to occur. Levels of the learning progression should not only contain the declarative content statements but also the cognitive tasks that describe how students should use the knowledge (Krajcik, McNeil, & Reiser, 2008). From this process, levels of how students can develop understanding of the big idea over time are developed that correspond to the experiences, knowledge and cognitive ability of students. Determining levels is an iterative process involving clarifications with experts in the field. However, it is only after testing with high quality curriculum materials that levels become more established.

Unfortunately, often the key learning research that is need to determine what learners are able to do or not, has not yet been conducted or published. Fortunately, researchers are beginning to carry out some of this fundamental research: Wiser and Smith for the particle model in the elementary grades, and Shin, Stevens and Krajcik for middle and high school; Golan for genomics at the middle and high school; Anderson and colleagues (Mohan, Chen, & Anderson, 2009) for environmental literacy and the carbon cycle; Wiser and colleagues, and Goldberg and Hammer for energy.

The unpacking process, designing learning performances, constructing assessment tasks and specifying levels, match nicely to the assessment triangle (Figure 1; also see Pellegrino, *this volume*; Pellegrino, Chudowsky, & Glaser, 2001, pp. 44-51). The unpacking process, the development of learning performances, and specifying levels match the cognition corner, and the development of the assessment task matches the observation corner. The cognition corner describes the specific understandings, the cognition to identify that understanding, and how that understanding develops across time (unpacking and learning performances). The observation corner describes the tasks students need to complete (assessment tasks). The interpretation corner specifies how far the student has moved along the learning performance based on its associated evidence.

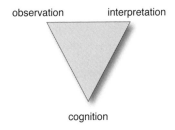

*Figure 1: Assessment Triangle*

Researchers from the Center for Policy and Research in Education (CPRE) with funding from the National Science Foundation in the United States developed a learning progression for the Structure, Properties and Transformation of Matter K-12 (CPRE's RAPID project[1], 2011). CPRE's RAPID project was led by Aaron Rogat (PI). Members of the project team who collaborated on the structure of matter's

---

1  To examine the CPRE learning progression go to
   https://mail.google.com/mail/html/compose/static_files/blank_quirks.html#_ftnref1.

hypothetical learning progression include: Jacob Foster, Massachusetts Department of Education; Fred Goldberg, San Diego State University; Joseph Krajcik, Michigan State University; Marianne Wiser, Clark University; Shawn Stevens, University of Michigan. This learning progression is an expansion of ideas presented in the K-12 Science Education Framework developed by the National Research Council (2011). Liu, this volume, also presents an example of a learning progression for the structure of matter described in the K-12 Science Education Framework (NRC 2011).

## 5 An Example Case: Student Learning Across Time in the IQWST Curriculum [2]

In this section, we present an example involving three units that build on each other across three years of middle school to help students develop integrated ideas related to the big idea: *Matter is made from atoms which are constantly in motion. Atoms themselves have substructure. The properties, states, and reactions of matter can be understood in terms of the interactions between and within atoms due to their substructure.* This big idea was modified from the draft version of the New Science Education Frameworks document. The three units are from the chemistry strand in the Investigating and Questioning our World through Science and Technology (IQWST) curriculum (Krajcik et al., 2009).

IQWST was built upon the notion of curriculum coherence, supporting students in building understanding of key ideas as they are revisited and expanded upon throughout a given year, as well as across the three years of middle school (Shwartz, Weizman, Fortus, Krajcik & Reiser, 2008). This was accomplished by using research literature to "identify clusters of science ideas that interrelate ... and build[ing] an instructional sequence to foster more complex understandings over time" (Krajcik, McNeill, & Reiser, 2008). This process included identifying big ideas from the literature, unpacking them, developing learning performances, and developing appropriate sequencing across time. Although IQWST was not developed based on a learning progression, as the curriculum was developed prior to discussions of LPs in the literature, a learning progression nonetheless emerged in the process of curriculum design.

Curriculum coherence, "presenting a complete set of interrelated ideas and making connections among them explicit" (Roseman, Linn, & Koppal, 2008), is considered the greatest predictor of student learning in the Trends in International Mathematics

---

2    This case study was modified from a paper presented at the 2010 NARST conference.

and Science Study (TIMSS) (Schmidt, Wang, & McKnight, 2005). However, most traditional science textbooks and instruction used in the USA do not support deep, integrated student learning due to their lack of coherence (Kesidou & Roseman, 2002; National Research Council, 2007). However, coherent curriculum would be best built if they emerged from learning progression, as the learning progression would guide the development.

This and similar literature provides the groundwork for improving curricular coherence and enhancing student learning in science education. However, the effect of coherent curriculum based on learning progressions on student achievement remains largely untested in the U.S. due to a lack of curricula incorporating LPs and measures to assess them.

Therefore, the IQWST curriculum can serve as a test for the effect of the proposed curricular sequencing of big ideas in science on student learning. Although IQWST units link multiple science content and process ideas within and across years, the focus of this study was the on the curriculum's coherence with regard to the structure of matter (Shwartz, Weizman, Krajcik, & Reiser, 2008).

In this work, we answer the following research questions: 1) What are students' learning gains (overall and for each target big idea) for the IQWST chemistry units? 2) In what ways do students' learning gains reflect the coherence of the IQWST chemistry curriculum? To answer these questions, we report pre- and posttest data highlighting the development of students' understanding of these big ideas as they progressed through IQWST from $6^{th}$ to $8^{th}$ grades during a large-scale National Field Trial. Answering these questions will allow us to discuss is linking ideas across time helps learners to build integrated understanding.

## 5.1 Study Design

*Participants:* This study reported findings from our National Field Trial, involving a cohort of approximately 3,000 students moving through middle school, and their 26 grade 6, 24 grade 7, and 18 grade 8 teachers[3]. Students attended schools in four states and represented a range of ethnic and socioeconomic backgrounds and academic abilities.

*The Curriculum Units*: The study focused on the $6^{th}$, $7^{th}$, and $8^{th}$ grade IQWST chemistry units. Each inquiry-oriented, project-based unit is 8–12 weeks in duration. The

---

[3] The number of teachers participating decreased due to attrition of schools over the course of the research.

6th grade unit supports students in developing a particle view of matter. Students also study the properties of matter and link those ideas to the composition of substances. The 7th grade unit continues to build upon these ideas by further developing students' understandings of the properties of matter and engaging them in carrying out and explaining chemical reactions at both the macroscopic and microscopic levels. The 8th grade unit requires students to use 6th and 7th grade understandings of the particle nature of matter, properties of matter, the composition of substances, and chemical reactions to explain the flow of energy and how matter is repeatedly transferred between organisms. Table 6 shows the big ideas explored in each chemistry unit.

*Table 6: Big Ideas Explored at Each Grade Level*

| Grade level | Big idea |
|---|---|
| 6th | particle nature of matter, properties of matter, composition of substances |
| 7th | particle nature of matter, properties of matter, composition of substances, chemical reactions |
| 8th | particle nature of matter, properties of matter, composition of substances, and chemical reactions now used to explain how the flow of energy and how matter is repeatedly transferred between organisms |

We designed each unit iteratively, following cycles of choosing standards, creating learning performances, and developing learning tasks. We developed learning performances by combining content standards with inquiry standards (see Table 4) to articulate what we expected students to know and be able to do. We created learning tasks to support students in meeting those learning performances. After each enactment cycle, we revised the materials based on student pre/post data and feedback from teachers and students (Krajcik et al., 2008). Additionally, during the feedback stage, we revised the materials to increase the coherence among the three units. Appendix 1 shows a portion of a learning progression (Merritt, 2010) that corresponds to the 6th grade materials from IQWST.

*Instruments:* We developed assessments for each unit based on the learning performances (Krajcik et al., 2008) thus the assessment items were closely aligned with our coherent curriculum design. Figure 2 shows an example of an assessment matched to the learning performance in Table 4 above. Each unit used a pre/posttest design that included 15 multiple-choice questions and 3 open-ended, constructed-response items. After we drafted items, we assessed each using the Project 2061 Item Analysis Procedure (DeBoer et al., 2007) to ensure that they aligned with the learning performances. As with the curriculum materials, we pilot tested assessments prior to their use in the National Field Trial.

*Procedure:* From the study population of approximately 3,000 students, we analyzed the learning gains of those who completed both the pre- and posttests for a given grade (n = 1,759 for 6$^{th}$ grade; n = 1,139 for 7$^{th}$ grade and n = 514 for 8$^{th}$ grade.) We examined the change in students' performance on multiple-choice items using a paired samples t-test. To assess the relationship of curriculum coherence to student learning, we used a general linear model for repeated measures to compare the 7$^{th}$ grade multiple choice test scores of students who participated in both 6$^{th}$ and 7$^{th}$ grade chemistry units (n = 1055) to those who only experienced the 7$^{th}$ grade unit (n = 486). We used a similar process for the analyzing the 8$^{th}$ grade.

---

Shayna had a small bottle of Bromine gas. The bottle was closed with a cork. She tied a string to the cork, and then placed the bottle inside a larger bottle. She sealed the large bottle shut. (See Figure 1). Next, Shayna opened the small bottle by pulling the string connected to the cork. Figure 2 shows what happened after the cork of the small bottle was opened.

First, draw a model that shows what is happening in this experiment. Second, explain in writing what is happening in your model.

Figure 1   Figure 2

---

*Figure 2: Example Assessment Item Aligned with the Example Learning Performance*

## 5.2 Findings and Analysis

*RQ1: Students' learning gains:* Students participating in the 6$^{th}$ grade chemistry curriculum experienced significant learning gains (Table 7). On average, students' overall test scores increased 5.44 points from pre- to posttest, and this gain corresponds to a significant effect size of 1.52 (p < 0.001) (Table 7). The majority of this gain is represented in students' increased understanding of particle nature of matter items.

Table 7: 6ᵗʰ Grade Student Learning Gains, 2007–2008 (25 Teachers, 1795 Students)

| Items (Max Score) | Pretest Mean (SD) | Posttest Mean (SD) | Gain (SD) | Effect Size[a] |
|---|---|---|---|---|
| Total (27) | 11.22 (3.59) | 16.67 (4.73) | 5.44 (4.02) | 1.52*** |
| Multiple Choice (15) | 5.95 (2.41) | 9.39 (3.14) | 3.45 (2.97) | 1.43*** |
| Written Response (12) | 5.27 (1.91) | 7.27 (2.10) | 2.00 (2.14) | 1.05*** |
| Particle Nature of Matter (23) | 9.32 (3.11) | 13.64 (3.83) | 4.32 (3.41) | 1.39*** |

[a] Effect size calculated by dividing gain score by standard deviation (SD) of the pretest. ***$p < 0.001$

Similarly, in 7ᵗʰ grade, students experienced significant learning gains (Table 8). Again, this gain represented a large effect size of 1.51 ($p<0.001$). The test contained items specific to the nature of chemical reactions, the target big idea in the 7ᵗʰ grade. Students' understanding of this big idea is dependent on their prior knowledge of the particle nature of matter and the rearrangement of atoms to form new substances in a chemical reaction. Again, their learning gains on chemical reaction related items represented a majority of the gain in the overall pre/posttest scores.

Similarly, in 8ᵗʰ grade, students experienced significant learning gains (Table 9). However, here this gain represented a small effect size of 0.59 ($p<0.001$). This lower effect size could be attributed to a number of experienced and proficient teachers who left the National Field Trial due to turnover, downsizing, or changes in school district leadership, the challenging content of this unit or both.

Table 8: 7ᵗʰ Grade Student Learning Gains, 2009–2010 (24 Teachers, 1139 Students)

| Items (Max Score) | Pretest Mean (SD) | Posttest Mean (SD) | Gain (SD) | Effect Size[a] |
|---|---|---|---|---|
| Total (25) | 7.79 (3.47) | 12.94 (5.10) | 5.24 (4.27) | 1.51*** |
| Multiple Choice (15) | 6.04 (2.42) | 9.45 (3.26) | 3.41 (2.84) | 1.41*** |
| Written Response (10) | 1.66 (1.79) | 3.49 (2.57) | 1.83 (2.63) | 1.02*** |
| Chemical Reactions (20) | 5.20 (2.77) | 9.42 (4.30) | 4.23 (3.96) | 1.53*** |

[a] Effect size calculated by dividing gain score by standard deviation (SD) of the pretest. ***$p < 0.001$

*Table 9: 8th Grade Student Learning Gains, 2008-2009 (9 Teachers, 514 Students)*

| Items (Max Score) | Pretest Mean (SD) | Posttest Mean (SD) | Gain (SD) | Effect Size [a] |
|---|---|---|---|---|
| Total (22) | 6.87 (2.65) | 8.44 (3.36) | 1.57 (3.33) | 0.59*** |
| Multiple Choice (14) | 5.08 (2.09) | 7.00 (2.68) | 1.92 (2.87) | 0.92*** |
| Written Response (8) | 1.07 (1.16) | 1.44 (1.38) | 0.37 (1.42) | 0.32*** |
| Chemical Reactions (18) | 4.85 (2.25) | 6.11 (2.80) | 1.26 (2.80) | 0.56*** |

[a] Effect size calculated by dividing gain score by standard deviation (SD) of the pretest. ***$p < 0.001$

*RQ2: Learning gains related to curricular coherence:* To investigate the relationship between student learning gains and curriculum coherence in the IQWST chemistry units, we compared the learning gains of students who participated in both 6th and 7th grade units to those of students who only participated in the 7th grade (Figure 3). First, it is interesting to note that students who had the 6th grade chemistry unit had higher pretest scores than those who did not. This finding suggests that students who had IQWST chemistry in 6th grade may have been able to leverage their prior knowledge of the particle nature of matter from 6th grade on the 7th grade chemistry pretest.

Second, regardless of whether they participated in both 6th and 7th grade chemistry units or only the 7th grade unit, all students had significant learning gains from pretest to posttest $F(1,1492)=2237.2$ $p<0.001$. Using Tukey HSD for repeated measures, all gains are significant $p<0.01$. Therefore, coherent curricula do not impede the learning of students who lack prior knowledge from a previous unit.

Third, we also found an interaction between the gain students experienced on their 7th grade pre/post test and number of years of IQWST curriculum they participated in. The 7th grade chemistry gain scores of students who participated in both 6th and 7th grade units were larger than their peers who did not experience the 6th grade chemistry unit, $F(1,1492)=21.8$ $p<0.001$. Therefore, the students who participated in the 6th grade IQWST chemistry unit were able to leverage their requisite knowledge to propel themselves further along a learning trajectory.

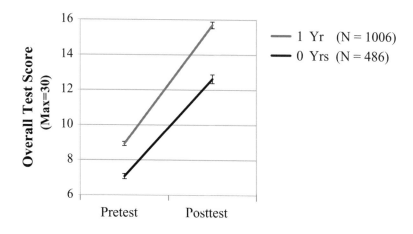

*Figure 3: Overall 7th Grade Chemistry Test Scores by Prior IQWST Experience*

We repeated these analyses for students completing the 8th grade chemistry IQWST curriculum. We compared four groups of students: those who participated in 1) only 8th grade chemistry, 2) only 6th and 8th grade chemistry, 3) only 7th and 8th chemistry, and 4) all IQWST chemistry units 6th through 8th grade. Again, the pretest scores of each group relate to the number of years the students participated in IQWST chemistry units. Similar to the 7th grade results, all four groups of students experienced significant gains from pretest to posttest $F(1, 772)=251.98$ $p<0.001$ during the eight grade (Figure 4). Using Tukey HSD for repeat measures, all gains are significant $p<0.01$. Finally, also like in the 7th grade, the interaction between pre/posttest gain in the 8th grade and number of years participating in IQWST is also significant $F(3, 772)=2.85$ $p<0.05$. Students who had three years of IQWST chemistry units had the highest pretest scores and the greatest learning gains of all groups.

In summary, these findings suggest that the understandings students built in the 6th grade chemistry curriculum may have provided them with a conceptual foundation for the 7th grade unit. The foundation students built by studying 6th and 7th grade chemistry may have provided them with a strong conceptual understanding to succeed in 8th grade chemistry. This foundation may have allowed them to achieve higher gain scores than peers without this prior knowledge. We cautiously advance these conclusions, as we realize that these two groups of students may have qualitative differences, which also affect their scores. For example, students may miss IQWST chemistry units because their teacher did not enact them or because of transience. We recognize that highly mobile student populations may have different resources than their less mobile peers, and these differences may, in part, account for differences in gain scores between the two groups.

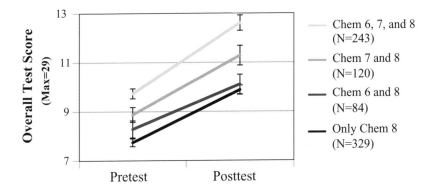

*Figure 4: Overall 8th Grade Chemistry Test Scores by Prior IQWST Experience*

## 6 Discussion and Concluding Comments

Our work focuses on coherence around big ideas of science that are important across IQWST units, but more importantly, these ideas are foundational across science disciplines (biology, Earth science, physics, and chemistry). Our findings suggest that curriculum coherence can help students develop more sophisticated understandings of core ideas than when ideas are not linked. Additionally, the findings support the notion that LPs offer a source for developing curriculum coherence that may increase student achievement and help them build integrated understandings. As such, this study supports the critical role that leveraging carefully constructed prior knowledge may play in facilitating learning (Bransford, Brown, & Cocking, 2000). Taken together, these data suggest that researchers' time would be well spent focusing on developing learning progressions on which curriculum can be built, and then testing LPs in authentic environments.

Learning progressions have been proposed as a means to help curriculum designers and teachers provide more finely grained coherence over time but much work still needs to be accomplished to capitalize on their potential power.

Future work on learning progressions includes 1) identifying and unpacking big ideas, 2) drawing on research to identify key instructional components, 3) designing and testing assessment items and instruments to measure the learning of big ideas; and 4) validating learning progressions in classroom contexts.

If the international community works together, we can make more substantial progress in this regard. Perhaps science education has landed on a theoretical and research paradigm for improving science learning that can drive its work for years to come and improve the education of children across the globe.

**Acknowledgements**

This research was conducted as part of the Investigating and Questioning Our World Through Science and Technology (IQWST) project and the Developing an Empirically-Tested Learning Progression for the Transformation of Matter to Inform Curriculum supported in part by the National Science Foundation Grants ESI 0101780 and DRL-0822038, respectively. Any opinions expressed in this work are those of the authors and do not necessarily represent either those of the funding agency or the University of Michigan and Michigan State University.

**References**

American Association for the Advancement of Science (AAAS). (1993). *Benchmarks for Science Literacy*. Washington, D. C.: American Association for the Advancement of Science and the National Science Teachers Association.

Anderson, C.W. (2008, March). Learning progressions for environmental science literacy. Paper presented at the meeting of the National Association for Research in Science Teaching, Baltimore, MD.

Bransford, J. D., Brown, A. L., & Cocking, R. R. (1999). *How People Learn: Brain, Mind, Experience and School*. Washington, D. C,: National Academy Press.

College Board, 2009. *College Board Standards for College Success – Science*. Available at: http://professionals.collegeboard.com/k-12/standards.

Corcoran, T., Mosher, F.A., & Rogat, A. (2009). *Learning Progressions in Science: An Evidence Based Approach to Reform* (CPRE Research Report #RR-63). New York: Center on Continuous Instructional Improvement, Teachers College – Columbia University.

CPRE's Rapid Response Research Project (RAPID), (2011). *Developing Hypothetical Learning Progressions in Support of the Implementation of New Science Standards*, funded by the National Science Foundation (award no. DRL-1051144). [1] Available at: https://mail.google.com/mail/html/compose/static_files/blank_quirks.html#_ftn1

DeBoer, G.E., Lee, H.S., & Husic, F. (2008b). Assessing integrated understanding of science. In Y. Kali, M.C. Linn, & J.E. Roseman, (Eds.), Coherent Science Education: Implications for Curriculum, Instruction, and Policy (pp. 153-182). New York, NY: Columbia University Teachers College Press.

Duschl, R. A., Schweingruber, H. A., & Shouse, A. (2007). *Taking science to school: Learning and Teaching Science in Grade K-8*. Washington, DC: The National Academies Press.

Fortus, D. & Krajcik, J. (2011). Curriculum Coherence and Learning Progressions. In B. J., Fraser, K. G., Tobin, & C. J. McRobbie, (Eds.), *The International Handbook of Research in Science Education* (2nd edition). Dordrecht: Springer.

Kesidou, S., & Roseman, J. E. (2002). How well do middle school science programs measure up? Findings from Project 2061's curriculum review. *Journal of Research in Science Teaching, 39*(6), 522-549.

Krajcik, J., McNeill, K. L., & Reiser, B. J. (2008). Learning-goals-driven design model: Developing curriculum materials that align with national standards and incorporate project-based pedagogy. *Science Education, 92*, 1-32.

Krajcik, J. S., Reiser, B. J., Sutherland, L.M., & Fortus, D. (2011). *Investigating Our World Through Science and Technology (IQWST)*. Sangari Global Education, New York, NY.

Liu, X. (2011). Using Learning Progression to Organize Learning Outcomes: Implications for Assessment. In S. Bernholt, K. Neumann, & P. Nentwig (Eds.), *Making it Tangible: Learning Outcomes in Science Education* (pp. 285-301). Münster: Waxmann.

Margel, H., Eylon, B., & Scherz, Z. (2008). A longitudinal study of junior high school students conceptions of the structure of materials. *Journal of Research in Science Teaching, 45*, 132-152.

Merritt, J. (2010). *Tracking students' understanding of the particle nature of matter*. Unpublished doctoral dissertation, Ann Arbor, MI: University of Michigan.

Merritt, J. D., Krajcik, J., & Shwartz, Y. (2008). Development of a learning progression for the particle model of matter. In *International Perspectives in the Learning Sciences: Cre8ing a Learning World. Proceedings of the Eight International Conference of the Learning Sciences – ICLS 2008* (pp. 75-81). Utrecht, the Netherlands: International Society of the Learning Sciences.

Mohan, L., Chen, J., & Anderson, C. W. (2009). Developing a multi-year learning progression for carbon cycling in socio-ecological systems. *Journal of Research in Science Teaching, 46*(6), 675-698.

National Research Council (2007). *Taking science to school*. Washington, D. C.: The National Academies Press.

National Research Council (2011). *Framework for K-12 Science Education: Practices, Cross-Cutting Concepts, and Core Ideas*. H. Quinn, H. Schweingruber, and T. Keller (Eds.), Washington, DC: National Academies Press.

Pellegrino, J. (2011). The Design of an Assessment System Focused on Student Achievement: A Learning Sciences Perspective on Issues of Competence, Growth, and Measurement. In S. Bernholt, K. Neumann, & P. Nentwig (Eds.), *Making it Tangible: Learning Outcomes in Science Education* (pp. 97-107). Münster: Waxmann.

Pellegrino, J.W., Chudowsky, N., & Glaser, R. (Eds.). (2001). *Knowing What Students Know: The Science and Design of Educational Assessment*. Washington, DC: National Academies Press.

Roseman, J. E., Linn, M. C., & Koppal, M. (2008). Characterizing curricular coherence. In Y. Kali, M. C. Linn & J. E. Roseman (Eds.), *Designing Coherent Science Education Curriculum: Implications for Curriculum, Instruction, and Policy*. New York: Teachers College Press.

Roseman, J.E., Stern, L., Koppal, M. (2010). A method for analyzing the coherence of high school biology textbooks. *Journal of Research in Science Teaching, 47*(1), 47-60.

Schmidt, W. H., Wang, H. C., & McKnight, C. C. (2005). Curriculum coherence: An examination of U.S. mathematics and science content standards from an international perspective. *Journal of Curriculum Studies, 37*(5), 525-559.

Shwartz, Y., Weizman, A., Krajcik, J., Fortus, D., & Reiser, B. (2008). The IQWST Experience: Using coherence as a design principle for a middle school science curriculum. *The Elementary School Journal, 109*(2), 199-219.

Smith, C. L., Wiser, M., Anderson, C. W., & Krajcik, J. (2006). Implications of research on children's learning for standards and assessment: A proposed learning progression for matter and the atomic-molecular theory. *Measurement: Interdisciplinary Research & Perspective, 4*(1), 1-98.

Stevens, S., Sutherland, L., & Krajcik, J.S., (2009). *The Big Ideas of Nanoscale Science and Engineering*. Arlington, VA: National Science Teachers Association Press.

Sutherland, L.M., Shin, N., & Krajcik, J.S. (2010). *Exploring the Relationship between 21$^{st}$ Century Competencies and Core Science Content*. Paper commissioned by the National Academies, National Research Council, Washington, DC. Available at: http://www7.nationalacademies.org/dbasse/Research_on_21st_Century_Competencies.html

# Appendix 1: Portion of a Learning Progression for the Structure of Matter: Particle Model of Matter (Merritt, 2010)

| Category | Description | Example | Progressing to Next Step |
|---|---|---|---|
| Complete Particle Model | Students use particles (molecules) to explain phenomena. There is empty space between the particles. The students are able to distinguish spacing AND motion relevant to the particular state they are in. Different substances have different properties because they are made of different atoms OR have different arrangements of same atoms. | Water vapor, liquid water, and ice are all made up of water molecules. The molecules in water vapor are far apart and move around freely. In a liquid, they are closer together, but move around each other. In a solid, they are close together and vibrate.<br><br>Sugar and water are not the same because they are made up of different molecules. | |
| Basic Particle Model | Students use particles (may use atoms and/or molecules) to explain phenomena. There is empty space between the particles. Students have difficulty in explaining the difference in spacing in different states and/or are unable to distinguish the difference in movement for all states. Different substances have different properties because they are made of different atoms or have different arrangements of same atoms. | Water vapor is made up of water molecules that are spaced far apart and move freely everywhere. Liquid water is made up of water molecules that are moving, but are closer together than in water vapor. In ice, the molecules are even closer together.<br><br>Sugar and water are not the same because they are made up of different molecules. | Students need to understand the difference in movement of a substance in different phases. For example, a simulation of the same substance as a solid, liquid and a gas should include the same representation for water molecules, but with different spacing and movement, including how movement changes as temperature changes. |
| Mixed Model | Students use particle and descriptive views when explaining everyday phenomena. When asked to describe what makes up a substance, students at this level often describe particles within a continuous medium. They do not understand that different substances have different properties because they are made of different atoms. Students describe solids, liquids, and gases as made up of smaller pieces of that same substance, which come together to form a whole. | Water is made up of water particles. The water particles exist within the liquid water. Thus, in between the particles is liquid water. | The idea that water is made up of the same atoms/molecules no matter the state should help students to realize that a substance's atoms/molecules do not change. For example, a model of ice, water and water vapor should include the same representation for water molecules, but with different spacing and movement. |
| Descriptive Model | Students at this level see objects as being a continuous medium. When asked to describe what makes up a common substance, they are described exactly as they appear. Thus, substances always have the same properties because the student has no concept that the substance may have a structure made up of smaller pieces. | Water is a clear, colorless liquid. Ice is a "clear" solid. They have different structures and are described differently. Therefore, they are not the same substances. | The ideas that objects are made up of parts could be a useful to help students realize that a pieces of a substance that looks continuous, can be broken down into smaller pieces. Student needs to realize that a substance is changeable (it can change phases), or in other cases, may be broken into smaller pieces. |

# Chapter 13

# Using Learning Progression to Organize Learning Outcomes: Implications for Assessment

*Xiufeng Liu*
*Department of Learning & Instruction, Graduate School of Education,*
*University at Buffalo, State University of New York, New York, USA*

## Abstract

There is a growing support in the US to use learning progression to organize science learning outcomes within and across grade levels from K-12. As a result, future science curriculum standards, curriculum materials development, assessment and classroom instruction will likely need to respond to learning progressions. This chapter discusses implications of learning progression for assessments. Using Item Response theory models, particularly Rasch models, it is possible to assess learning progression in both large-scale and classroom assessment. Assessment of a learning progression may start with deriving appropriate progress variables from the learning progression. A progress variable is a construct with an underlying unidimensional linear scale; it describes qualitatively different levels of performance students may demonstrate as they make progress in learning. Once progress variables are defined, assessment tasks and scoring rubrics may be created accordingly. For large-scale assessment, vertical and temporal linking item designs may be used to create linked tests so that measures from different tests for different grades and years may be equated to make them directly comparable. Students' measures from different tests may also be interpreted as performance levels on the progress variables. For classroom assessment, two approaches may be adopted. One is to use open-ended assessment tasks and a common scoring rubric corresponding to the defined progress variable. Another approach is to use linked tests developed externally. Students take different tests at the end of different units, and measures from different tests can be directly compared due to the temporal linking item design. Given that research on learning progressions in science is still in an early stage and well-developed learning progressions are rare, developing learning progression and measurement instruments will be iterative.

285

In July 2010, a committee of the National Research Council (NRC) on K-12 science education in the US released a document entitled *A Framework for Science Education: Preliminary Public Draft* (NRC, 2010). This document represents a nationally coordinated effort to develop a new generation of national science education standards in the US. It has been recognized that "many standards and curricula contain too many disconnected topics that are given equal priority. Too little attention is given to how students' understanding of a topic can be supported and enhanced from grade to grade" (NRC, 2007, p. 213). In order to address the above issue, the *framework* adopted learning progression as one of its guiding principles to organize learning outcomes from elementary through high school. Learning progression intends to "help children continually build on, and revise, their knowledge and abilities, starting from initial conceptions about how the world works and curiosity about what they see around them" (NRC, 2010, pp. 1-2). Because the *Framework* is intended to "act as a guide not only to Standards developers, but also curriculum designers, assessment developers, state and district science administrators, those responsible for science teacher education, and science educators working in informal settings" (NRC, 2010, p. 1), it will have significant impacts in all aspects of the US science education in the near future.

Krajcik, Merrit, Drago & Sutherland *(this volume)* provide a detailed explanation on the background for learning progression research, components of a learning progression, and approaches to developing a learning progression. Assuming that there is already an established learning progression or prototype learning progression, this chapter focuses on implications of the learning progression for assessment. Specifically, it discusses approaches to both large-scale and classroom assessment of learning progression.

In fact, a report by an earlier NRC Committee on Test Design for K-12 Science Achievement has already explicitly called for state science education standards to adopt a learning progression approach to organizing learning outcomes, and to state specific "learning performances" to elaborate content standards (NRC, 2006). The committee recommends some possible solutions to measure learning progression at the state level. Specifically, the committee recommends two designs to be used to measure learning progression. One is the evidenced-centered assessment design, and another construct modeling assessment design. The evidence-centered assessment design starts with the intended uses of assessment results (i.e. claims or inferences), then proceeds with identifying evidence or information to be collected to support the intended uses, and goes on to decide on the necessary tasks and how to assemble the tasks as a test in order to present to students (Mislevy, Steinberg, & Almond, 2002). This design is logically consistent with the backward design approach to instructional planning (Wiggins & McTighe, 2001). The construct modeling assessment design is similar to the conventional test design in that it starts with the clearly defined construct to measure, proceeds with designing measurement tasks and scoring keys/rubrics, and finally applies psychometric models (e.g., IRT) to help interpretation (Wilson, 2005). The approaches discussed in this chapter primarily follow this second design.

Since large-scale standardized tests and classroom based assessments differ significantly in their inferences from test results, this chapter will discuss separately implications of using learning progression to organize learning outcomes for large-scale assessment and for classroom assessment. This chapter is divided into three sections: the first section deals with large-scale assessment of learning progression; the second section deals with classroom-based assessment of learning progression; and the third section discusses the dynamic relationship between learning progression and assessment. The chapter concludes by making recommendations for future research and practices related to assessment of learning progression.

# 1 Large-scale Assessment of Learning Progression

In the US context, large-scale assessment of learning progression consistent with the *Framework* and the subsequent science educations standards will likely be in the form of state standardized tests as part of the state program evaluation, accountability, and high school graduation requirement systems. Before the current effort to develop a new generation of national science education standards, the *No Child Left Behind (NCLB)* law enacted in 2002 requires all states to develop rigorous state standards and implement state standardized tests to measure the attainment of the standards by students. Specifically, the law requires that measurement of proficiency of all students in science be conducted no less than one time during grades 3 through 5, 6 through 9, and 10 through 12. For example, the New York State currently administers state standardized tests in science at the end of grades 4, 8 and 12. The new generation of national science education standards to be developed based on the *Framework* will be assessed in accordance with the current NCLB.

One requirement, which is also a challenge, for measuring learning progression is comparability of measures across grades and years. Because it is desirable to administer different tests (i.e. sets of items) to students of different grades (e.g., grades 4, 8 and 12) and in different years, we need to convert measures from different tests to a common scale so that measures from different tests are directly comparable. This requirement may be called vertical and temporal equivalence.

In order to meet the above requirement, the first step in measuring a learning progression is to elaborate the learning progression into progress variables (NRC, 2007).

A progress variable is a construct with an underlying unidimensional linear scale. For example, the prototype learning progression on matter in the *Framework* consists of the intersection between a content dimension, e.g., atomic structure of matter and properties of matter, and a scientific and engineering practices dimension. A progress variable is a statement on the hypothetical or expected progressive performances of students on the above intersections from a lower grade to a higher grade that show distinct levels. Figure 1 shows a sample progress variable on energy and change from K-12. More than one progress variable may be derived from a learning progression. Underlying each progress variable is a linear scale along which student attainment of the learning progression may be quantitatively and qualitatively described.

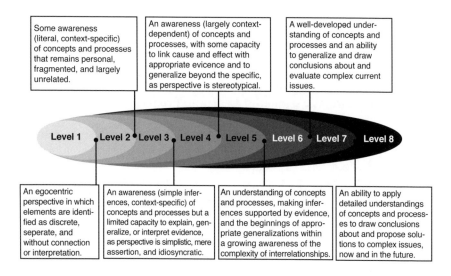

*Figure 1: A Sample Progress Variable for Energy and Change from K-12 (NRC, 2005, p. 82)*

Once a progress variable is defined, next steps in designing a measurement instrument or test of a learning progression involve selecting tasks and developing scoring criteria. Although selecting tasks and defining scoring criteria are routine procedures for any assessment design, special consideration is needed for measuring learning progression. In order to make later test equating possible, it is necessary to include a set of common items in different tests. These common items will act as a "bridge" to connect different tests into one "super test" so that measures from different tests can be equated onto a same scale. This test equating process is also called scaling.

Table 1 shows a sample vertical linking item test design that includes common items to connect three tests for grades 4, 8, and 12 respectively.

*Table 1: The Vertical Linking Item Design**

|  | Items of Test 1 | Linking Items between Test 1 and Test 2 | Items of Test 2 | Linking Items between Test 2 and Test 3 | Items of Test 3 |
|---|---|---|---|---|---|
| Grade 4 students | x | x |  |  |  |
| Grade 8 students |  | x | x | x |  |
| Grade 12 students |  |  |  | x | x |

*Cells with "x" indicate that those items are answered by students.

Similarly, in order to equate measures from tests for a same grade level but from administrations in different years, Table 2 shows a temporal linking item design for equating different tests given in different years.

*Table 2: The Temporal Linking Item Design**

|  | Items of Test 1 | Linking Items between Test 1 and Test 2 | Items of Test 2 | Linking Items between Test 2 and Test 3 | Items of Test 3 |
|---|---|---|---|---|---|
| Year 1 students | x | x |  |  |  |
| Year 2 students |  | x | x | x |  |
| Year 3 students |  |  |  | x | x |

*Cells with "x" indicate that those items are answered by students.

How many common items and what types of them should be included as linking items between two tests are critical decisions impacting the overall quality of achieving the vertical and temporal test equivalence. Too few common items included could undermine test equivalence, while too many items could substantially increase test cost. Also, high quality of common items could reduce the necessary number of common items and increase test equivalence, while low quality of common items could increase the necessary number of common items and decrease test equivalence. As a rule of thumb, a minimum of 20 items, or 20% of total items, are necessary (Wolfe, 2004). The quality and sufficiency of common items can later be empirically examined.

After items are constructed and scoring criteria are developed, pilot-testing and field-testing of items and tests will follow. Given the nature of data based on the above vertical and temporal linking item designs, i.e. a large number of missing values, Item Response Theory (IRT) models, such as Rasch models, are typically used for item and test analyses (for examples of applications of IRT, please refer to the chapter by Köller and Parchmann, *this volume*). In order to facilitate easy interpretation and comparison of test scores from different tests on a same progress variable, a conversion table may also be created. Table 3 shows a sample test conversion table for the progress variable called *Understanding of Matter* showing how scores from different tests may be directly compared. This direct comparison among the three tests for three different grade levels was made possible by Rasch modeling (see details in Liu, 2007).

Because a progress variable is usually defined in terms of a few qualitatively different performance levels (e.g., beginning, developing, proficient, and advanced), student measures on different tests may also be transformed into performance levels. In order to do so, we need to decide on what measure needs to be reached by a student for a performance level. This decision-making process is called standard-setting. Standard setting is a well-established field in psychometrics and large-scale standardized testing; various techniques are available (see Cizek & Bunch, 2007; Köller & Parchmann, *this volume*).

Once we have obtained measures of students on different progress variables and decided on how to transform measures into performance levels, we are ready to describe students in terms of learning progression. Because a learning progression typically consists of a number of progress variables, we could describe a student's learning progression in terms of combinations of performance levels on different progress variables over time. That is, at each time point (e.g., grade), we can describe a student's status of learning in terms of a set of performance levels. These performance levels can be conceptualized as a point in a space. As the student makes progress in learning along the learning progression, the student's status changes from one point to another in the space, and the trend line connecting various points in the space forms a learning trajectory. Figure 2 graphically shows how a student's learning trajectory may be defined as change across points in a space over time.

*Table 3: Conversion Table between Raw Scores and Rasch Scale Scores*

| Raw Score | Rasch Scale Score | | |
|---|---|---|---|
| | Elementary School Test | Middle School Test | High School Test |
| 0 | 31.94 | 34.31 | 35.84 |
| 1 | 34.72 | 35.67 | 37.64 |
| 2 | 37.13 | 36.94 | 39.30 |
| 3 | 39.21 | 38.13 | 40.83 |
| 4 | 41.00 | 39.23 | 42.26 |
| 5 | 42.53 | 40.26 | 43.58 |
| 6 | 43.85 | 41.22 | 44.82 |
| 7 | 44.98 | 42.12 | 45.98 |
| 8 | 45.96 | 42.97 | 47.08 |
| 9 | 46.83 | 43.76 | 48.12 |
| 10 | 47.62 | 44.51 | 49.13 |
| 11 | 48.38 | 45.22 | 50.11 |
| 12 | 49.13 | 45.90 | 51.07 |
| 13 | 49.91 | 46.56 | 52.02 |
| 14 | 50.76 | 47.19 | 52.99 |
| 15 | 51.71 | 47.81 | 53.97 |
| 16 | 52.81 | 48.42 | 54.99 |
| 17 | 54.08 | 49.03 | 56.05 |
| 18 | 55.56 | 49.65 | 57.17 |
| 19 | 57.29 | 50.27 | 58.35 |
| 20 | 59.30 | 50.91 | 59.62 |
| 21 | 61.64 | 51.57 | 60.98 |
| 22 | 64.33 | 52.26 | 62.44 |
| 23 | N/A | 52.99 | 64.01 |
| 24 | N/A | 53.75 | 65.72 |
| 25 | N/A | 54.56 | 67.56 |
| 26 | N/A | 55.42 | 69.56 |
| 27 | N/A | 56.34 | 71.72 |
| 28 | N/A | 57.33 | 74.06 |
| 29 | N/A | 58.38 | 76.58 |
| 30 | N/A | 59.51 | 79.31 |
| 31 | N/A | 60.72 | 82.25 |
| 32 | N/A | N/A | 85.41 |
| 33 | N/A | N/A | N/A |

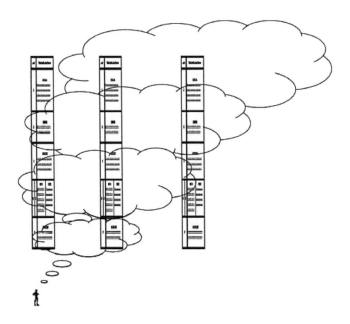

*Figure 2: A Learning Trajectory as Defined as Change Across Points in a Space (Wilson, 2009, p. 723)*

## 2 Classroom Assessment of Learning Progression

Classroom assessment of learning progression is conducted by a teacher and takes place during one academic year. The focus of classroom assessment of learning progression is to monitor individual students' learning trajectories along a learning progression during an academic year. Assessment for this purpose may be called formative assessment because identifying individual students' learning status at various time points during an academic year can inform planning more effective ongoing instruction.

First and foremost, a fine-grained learning progression for a course during an academic year must be developed. Often, learning progressions specified in the national and state curriculum standards are not specific for an academic year. If this is the case, when planning for the course, the teacher needs to develop a fine-grained learning progression on each of the big ideas of the course. These big ideas should transcend across all topics of the course, thus are foundational for developing understanding of specific concepts during the course. Figure 3 shows a fine-grained hypothetical learning progression on "perspectives of chemists" for a high school chemistry course.

In Figure 3, it was hypothesized that a general and foundational construct, perspectives of chemists, contributes to students' development of understanding of specific chemistry concepts during the course. This construct consists of three dimensions: matter, energy, and change. Each dimension corresponds to a progress variable. Along each progress variable, students may progress along a five-achievement-level trajectory.

**Outline of the Three Current Perspectives Variables**

| Levels (Low to High) | Matter | Change | Energy |
|---|---|---|---|
| 1. Notions | What do you know about matter? (initial ideas, logic, real-world knowledge) | What do you know about change? (initial ideas, logic, real-world knowledge) | What do you know about energy in relationship to chemistry? |
| 2. Recognition | How do chemists describe matter? | How do chemists describe change? | How do chemists explain energy transfer for chemical and physical changes? |
| 3. Formulation | How can we think about interactions between atoms? | How can we think about rearrangement of atoms? | How can chemists predict the extent of energy transfer and the resulting products of chemical and physical change? |
| 4. Construction | How can we understand composition, structure, properties, and amounts? | How can we understand type, progression, and extent of change? | How do different models explain the chemical and physical changes that may occur? |
| 5. Generation | What new experiments can we design to gain a deeper understanding of matter? | What new reactions can be designed to generate desired products? | How can we use these models to optimize this type of change? |

*Figure 3: A Hypothetical Learning Progression for a High School Chemistry Course (Claesgens, Scalise, Wilson, & Stacy, 2009, p. 69)*

There are at least two approaches to formative assessment of learning progression during an academic year: one is to use open-ended tasks and a global scoring rubric, and another is to use an externally developed formative assessment system specifically for a course. For the first approach, assessment tasks need to be open-ended so that they relate to all topics of the course. Examples of these tasks are concept mapping, open-ended inquiry projects, and portfolios. Carefully designed constructed-response questions (i.e. essay) may also be used. Figure 4 shows a sample scoring rubric for an open-ended constructed response question specifically targeting the progress variable of matter in Figure 3.

**Scoring for the Matter Variable**

*Level 0: Prestructural*
Student response is irrelevant to question (blank, "I don't know," doodle with no distinguishable words or diagrams).

*Level 1: Notions*
Describes materials or activity observed with senses; compares and contrasts, or generates logical patterns but without employing chemical concepts; using properties of matter as evidence for misconceptions of chemical explanations.

*Level 2: Recognition*
Explores meaning of words, symbols, and definitions to represent properties of matter; represents matter through arrangements of atoms as discrete particles; translates information represented in the periodic table to an atomic model that includes protons, neutrons, and electrons; and interprets simple patterns of the periodic table.

*Level 3: Formulation*
Recognizes that matter has characteristic properties due to the arrangement of atoms into molecules and compounds; describes chemical bonds as interaction of valence electrons in atoms; combines individual atoms to make molecules in patterns of bonding based on characteristic atomic properties; and interprets how electrons are shared, shifted, or transferred depending on atoms and types of chemical bonds formed.

*Level 4: Construction*
Explains molecular behavior and properties in terms of stability and energies involved in intra- and inter-molecular bonding; recognizes that changes in energy can change the condition/properties of matter; predicts effects of transfer of energy; relates energy to the motion and interaction of molecules; and explains changes in matter based on the energy required to break bonds.

*Figure 4: A Sample Constructed Response Question Scoring Rubric for Measurement of a Learning Progression (Claesgens, Scalise, Wilson, & Stacy, 2009, p. 73)*

Assessment of learning progression during a course usually takes place at the end of a unit. Although a same or different tasks may be used for different units, scoring will be conducted using a same scoring rubric, such as that in Figure 4. Feedback to students may be provided at the end of each unit and the assessment information is also used to inform planning and conducting instruction of subsequent units.

Another approach to measuring learning progression during a course is to apply a set of linked standardized measurement instruments or tests that are specifically developed to measure the constructs of a learning progression. This set of standardized instruments may be called a formative assessment system. Developing this system is usually beyond classroom teachers' resources and capability, thus usually conducted by external agencies or organizations. Developing such a system is based on a similar temporal linking item design shown in Table 2. Special considerations for this temporal linking item design are that different tests correspond to topics of different units of a course and a same sample of students takes all the tests in a sequence. Table 4 presents this temporal linking item design during a course.

*Table 4: Temporal Linking Item Design for Measurement of a Learning Progression During a Course\**

| Students | Formative Test 1 | Linking Item Set 1 | Formative Test 2 | Linking Item Set 2 | Formative Test 3 |
|---|---|---|---|---|---|
| S11 | x | x | missing | | |
| S21 | x | x | missing | | |
| ... | x | x | | | |
| S12 | missing | x | x | x | |
| S22 | | x | x | x | missing |
| .. | | x | x | x | |
| S13 | missing | missing | x | x | |
| S23 | | missing | x | x | |
| ... | | | | x | x |

\*Note: S11 denotes Student 1 at the end of unit 1, S12 Student 1 at the end of unit 2, S13 Student 1 at the end of unit 3, S21 denotes Student 2 at the end of unit 1, S22 Student 2 at the end of unit 2, S23 Student 2 at the end of unit 3; x denotes responses to items.

In the above temporal linking item design, a student takes different tests for different units as the course progresses. Students' performances on different tests are equated onto a same measurement scale so that students' performances can be directly compared. Students increase their overall achievement along the learning progression, and such growth may be plotted graphically as a learning trajectory. Figure 5 shows a hypothetical student's, Debbie Franks, learning trajectory during a course of study based on the 10 formative tests that are equated onto a same scale characterized by 5 performance levels. The student's learning trajectory is also compared to that of the entire class. We can see from Figure 5 that, although the student performance fluctuates somewhat from formative test 1 to formative test 8, the overall trend seems that the student is making progress in levels of understanding along the progress variable.

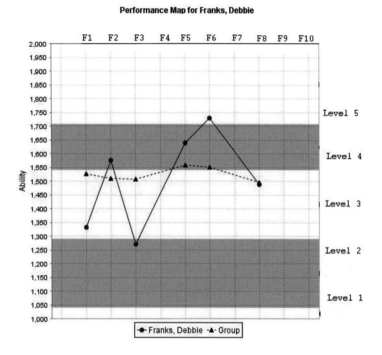

*Figure 5: Learning Trajectories During a Course (Adapted from Kennedy, 2005)*

The BEAR, *Berkeley Evaluation and Assessment Research (BEAR)*, assessment system (Wilson & Sloane, 2000) is a curriculum embedded assessment to measure students' learning progression during a course. The BEAR assessment system uses regular teaching and learning activities as assessment tasks distributed at various points during a course to assess students' learning progression. Although the assessment tasks are not standardized, the scoring is standardized by using a common categorization system (e.g., 4 for above the standard, 3 for meeting the standard, 2 for meeting some aspects of the standard, 1 for meeting one aspect of the standard, and 0 for meeting none aspect of the standard) for all assessment tasks. Further, estimation of students' learning progression based on various assessment tasks is also standardized using a common measurement scale obtained from multidimensional Rasch scaling. Thus, the BEAR assessment system can produce both individual and group student learning trajectories toward a defined learning goal – the learning standard. Teachers and students can use the assessment information to plan appropriate teaching and learning activities according to the learning trajectories, making the BEAR assessment system a formative assessment.

The BEAR assessment system has been implemented in various curriculums such as IEY (*Issues, Evidence and You* developed at the UC Berkeley's Lawrence Hall of Science). The validity of the BEAR assessment system has been argued from an approach called assessment net which is composed of (a) a framework for describing and reporting the level of student performance along achievement continua, (b) the gathering of information through the use of diverse indicators based on observational practices that are consistent both with the educational variables to be measured and with the context in which that measurement is taken place, and (c) a measurement model that provides the opportunity for appropriate forms of quality control. Evidence of validity for the BEAR assessment system comes from a variety of sources. The construct validity is claimed by developing assessment tasks and scoring rubrics as well as scaling learning progression along a hypothesized learning progression. The instructional validity is claimed by the match between instruction and assessment and teacher management and responsibility to conduct the assessment and interpret the assessment results. The criterion validity is demonstrated by comparing classes implementing the assessment system with classes not implementing the assessment system. The effect size for implementing the assessment system was found to be from 0.22 to 0.75. The reliability of the assessment system was primarily established by multidimensional Rasch modeling with reliability coefficients for different progress variables ranging from 0.65 to .90. Attention has also been given to fairness and absence of bias of the assessment system.

Another example of measurement of leaning progression is the Connected Chemistry as Formative Assessment (C2FA ) system being developed at the University at Buffalo, State University of New York. C2FA[1] measures student learning progression on chemical reasoning during a high school chemistry course. Chemical reasoning is a hypothetical construct underlying students' development of understanding of specific chemistry concepts, such as acids and bases, chemical equilibrium, etc. Chemical reasoning is conceptualized to consist of two dimensions: matter/energy and models. Two progress variables, one for each of the dimensions, are defined, with each progress variable having three performance levels.

---

1     Details about the project can be found at the project website at http://wings.buffalo.edu/research/ConnectedChemistry/

C2FA consists of 10 formative assessment tests, corresponding to 10 commonly taught chemistry units (i.e. atomic structure, state of matter, periodic table, stoichiometry, chemical equilibrium, acids-bases, gases, chemical bonding, solutions, and redox). All the tests are computer model-based. Each formative assessment test consists of about 25 ordered multiple-choice questions (Briggs et al., 2006). Students must manipulate the computer models to answer the questions. The 10 tests are linked according to the design shown in Table 4. Measures of students on the two progress variables are equated onto a same scale, thus directly comparable. Teachers conduct instruction according to their preferred sequences of units during a chemistry course, and administer one formative assessment test at the end of each unit. Levels of student performance on the two progress variables inform teachers in planning subsequent instruction of units (e.g., differentiated chemistry labs).

## 3 Dynamics between Learning Progression and Assessment of Learning Progression

Besides its theoretical foundation consistent with how students learn science (NRC, 2007), using learning progression to organize learning outcomes is a promising way to address a long-recognized problem associated with US science curriculums, i.e. "a mile wide and an inch deep". However, as Krajcik et al. discuss in their chapter in this volume, establishing a learning progression requires extensive empirical research over a long time, and new science education standards can not wait until all learning progressions are well-established empirically. In order to address this dilemma, we may treat a learning progression as a theory. As a theory, the validity of a learning progression can change depending on the accumulated evidence. At the beginning, a learning progression is mostly hypothetical. Gradually, as more and more evidence becomes available, a learning progression becomes more and more fine-tuned and eventually may be elevated into a sound theory.

Thus when developing a measurement instrument of a learning progression, it is necessary to start with a hypothetical learning progression. Once data are collected, appropriate data analysis is conducted to inform modification of the hypothetical learning progression. The revised learning progression will then be used to revise the measurement instrument and new data are collected again. The above iterative process terminates until there is a good agreement between the defined learning progression and the collected data based on the measurement instrument. This dynamic relationship between developing learning progressions and measuring learning progression is an important characteristic in research related to learning progression.

Stevens et al. (2010) differentiate hypothetical learning progression and empirical progression. A hypothetical learning progression is based synthesis of literature and expectations of student learning outcomes; it may not necessarily be bound by current curriculum and instruction. An empirical progression is the order of topics/concepts on which students develop understanding according to qualitative and quantitative assessment data; it is dependent on current curriculum and instruction. They suggest that a hypothetical leaning progression should be refined based on the empirical progression; and the ultimate goal is to achieve an alignment between the two. The above discussed dynamic relationship between learning progression and measurement of learning progression is consistent with Stevens et al.'s suggestion. The measured learning progression in the form of progress variables is the empirical progression.

Similarly, progress variables elaborated to measure a learning progression may initially be tentative, and validating the progress variables may also follow an iterative process. Köller and Parchmann *(this volume)* provide a few examples on validation of progress variables or constructs. Eventually, a well-developed measurement instrument of a learning progression must be grounded in a theoretically sound and empirically supported definition of progress variables.

# 4 Conclusion

The recently released and soon to be finalized conceptual framework for science education by a National Research Council committee is expected to drive science education reforms in the US in the near future. The *Framework* has adopted a guiding principle of learning progression to organize science learning outcomes. As a result, future science curriculum standards, curriculum materials development, assessment, and classroom instruction will need to address learning progressions. This chapter discusses implications of learning progression for assessments. It is possible to assess learning progression in both large-scale and classroom assessment. Assessment of a learning progression may start with deriving appropriate progress variables from the learning progression. A progress variable is a construct with an underlying unidimensional linear scale; it describes qualitatively different levels of performance students may demonstrate as they make progress in learning. A learning progression may consist of more than one progress variable depending on the dimensions of the learning progression. Once progress variables are defined, assessment tasks and scoring rubrics are then created accordingly. For large-scale assessment of learning progressions, vertical and temporal linking item designs may be used to create linked tests or measurement instruments so that measures from different tests for different grades and years may be equated to make them directly comparable. Students' measures from different tests may also be interpreted as performance levels on the progress variables. A student's learning trajectory from lower grades to higher grades can be described as changes in locations in a space defined by different performance levels on different progress variables. For classroom assessment of learning progressions, at least two approaches may be adopted. One is to use open-ended assessment tasks and a common scoring rubric corresponding to the defined progress variable. Another approach is to use a set of linked tests developed externally. Students take different tests at the end of different units, and measures from different tests can be directly compared due to the temporal linking item design. Classroom assessment of learning progression is a form of formative assessment; it has a potential to improve science teaching and student learning.

## References

Briggs, D. C., Alonzo, A. C., Schwab, C., & Wilson, M. (2006). Diagnostic assessment with ordered multiple-choice items. *Educational Assessment, 11*(1), 33-63.

Cizek, G. J. & Bunch, M. B. (2007). *Standard Setting: A Guide to Establishing and Evaluating Performance Standards of Tests.* Thousand Oaks, CA: Sage Publications.

Claesgens, J., Scalise, K., Wilson, M., & Stacy, A. (2009). Mapping student understanding in chemistry: The perspectives of chemists. *Science Education, 93*(1), 56-85.

Kennedy, C. A. (2005). *ConstructMap V4.2.* Berkely, CA: Berkeley Evaluation and Assessment Research (BEAR) Center, University of California, Berkeley.

Liu, X. (2007). Growth in students' understanding of matter during an academic year and from elementary through high school. *Journal of Chemical Education, 84*(11), 1853-1856.

Mislevy, R. J., Steinberg, L. S., & Almond, R. G. (2002). On the structure of educational assessments. *Measurement: Interdisciplinary Research and Perspectives, 1,* 3-67.

National Research Council [NRC] (2006). *Systems for State Science Assessment.* Washington, DC: The National Academies Press.

National Research Council [NRC] (2007). *Taking Science to School: Learning and Teaching Science in Grades K-8.* Committee on science learning, Kindergarten through eighth grade. Washington, DC: The National Academies Press.

National Research Council [NRC] (2010). *A Framework for Science Education: Preliminary Public Draft.* Washington, DC: National Academy Press.

Stevens, S. Y., Delgado, C., & Krajcik, J. (2010). Developing a hypothetical multi-dimensional learning progression for the nature of matter. *Journal of Research in Science Teaching, 47*(6), 687-715.

Wiggins, G. P. & McTighe, J. (2001). *Understanding by Design.* Upper Saddle River, NJ: Prentice Hall.

Wilson, M. (2005). *Constructing Measures: An Item Response Modeling Approach.* Mahwah, NJ: Lawrence Erlbaum Associates Publishers.

Wilson, M. (2009). Measuring progressions: Assessment structures underlying a learning progression. *Journal of Research in Science Teaching, 46*(6), 716-730.

Wilson, M. & Sloane, K. (2000). From principles to practice: An embedded assessment system. *Applied Measurement in Education, 13*(2), 181-208.

Wolfe, E. W. (2004). Equating and item banking with the Rasch model. In E. V. Smith, Jr., & R. M. Smith (Eds.), *Introduction to Rasch Measurement* (pp. 366-390). Maple Grove, MN: JAP Press.

# Chapter 14

# The Challenge of Alignment of Students' Learning Outcomes with Curriculum Guidelines, Instruction, and Assessment in Science Practice in Taiwan

*Mei-Hung Chiu & Hui-Jung Chen*
*National Taiwan Normal University, Graduate Institute of Science Education*

## Abstract

During the past two decades, the emphasis of educational research in Taiwan has followed several streams, including scientific literacy and competence in science learning. Based upon the needs and expectations of a given society, learning outcomes become more and more important when educational reforms are carried out. In Taiwan, learning outcomes are highly influenced by curriculum standards, in particular, school tests and national entrance examinations (e.g., high school and university entrance examination). They are mainly assessed via paper-and-pencil formats. While paper and pencil tests cannot be easily replaced by other formats (i.e., portfolios and performance assessment) and still play a dominate role in the Taiwanese school system, how to design more effective and meaningful test items to measure students' competence in science learning is a present-day challenge for school teachers and science educators. The purpose of this paper is to explore what definitions of learning outcomes exist, what methods can help us measure these learning outcomes, and how innovative instruction might show a new avenue to promote students' learning outcomes in science.

## 1 Introduction

In 1994 Executive Yuan (The highest executive branch of the government of Taiwan) established the "Committee on Educational Reform" in response to educational organizations' requests for educational reform and the recommendations from the 7th national education conference. This committee submitted a report on educational reform that outlined five educational reform objectives: un-authorizing education, taking good care of all students, smoothing channels for entering schools/universities, increasing teaching quality, and establishing a lifetime learning society. Over the past two decades, different approaches were taken to accomplish these goals. In science education, for instance, guidelines for the end of certain grades (such as $4^{th}$, $6^{th}$, and $9^{th}$), instead of standards for each grade were implemented, flexibility of teaching and assessment styles were promoted (such as multiple formats to assess students' learning outcomes in school practice), and multiple channels for screening students for high schools and universities were introduced. A report from the Ministry of Education (2003a, 2003b), revealed that although paper and pencil tests, in particular, multiple-choice format, still dominated school assessments, it recommended school that teachers consider various methods for assessing different perspectives of students' learning outcomes, such as performance assessment and written reports. However, at the national level, the entrance examinations measuring students' learning outcomes still used paper and pencil. In addition, due to a close relationship between curriculum guidelines and school assessment or national examinations, the learning outcomes for different grades were specified in the national curriculum guidelines announced by the Ministry of Education. Furthermore, in the *White Paper for Science Education* (Minister of Education and National Science Council, 2003), it is specifically pinpoted that the importance of structures and connections among curriculum, instruction, and assessment in science education practice in order to have high quality of educational outcomes.

Cheng (2005) found that there have been a few major changes made to the science curriculum in Taiwan over the past thirty years. They are as follows:
1. Curriculum goals shifting from national needs (e.g., educating students to be science, technology, and engineering majors) to societal and personal needs.
2. The basis of science curriculum design shifting from curriculum standards to curriculum guidelines; the policy of writing textbooks shifting from national versions to local versions (but still reviewed by government).
3. Rationale for science curriculum design shifting from elite education approach to scientific literacy for all approach.
4. Instructional strategies recommended by developmental science curriculum and standards (or guidelines) follow learning psychology theories.
5. Nature of curriculum contents shifting from subject-knowledge oriented to competence-based.
6. Curriculum development from an editor with few editorial board members to systematic experimental curriculum evaluated by external team.
7. Science instruction shifting from subject concept oriented to science-technology-society oriented; science instruction emphasizing integration of technological and societal issues.
8. Design of instructional activities shifting from teacher-centered to student-centered; and

9. Assessment of students' learning outcomes shifting from summative to formative, basic still, and multiple assessments.

However, some claims discussed above were not revealed as a consistent phenomenon in science practice. For instance, numbers 5, 7, 8, and 9 above might be considered as driving forces for educational reform in terms of learning environments and outcomes. But in reality, limited changes were observed from systemic studies. Currently, only limited studies (both national and international) specifically discuss the definitions and scope of learning outcomes anticipated in school science classrooms and assessments for learning outcomes to improve science education. The purpose of this article is to address learning outcomes from three perspectives: (1) the definitions of learning outcomes, (2) the methods of assessment at local and national levels, and (3) innovative instruction proposed to promote learning outcomes for the new needs in science education. Examples taken from research results and national examinations will be discussed in the following sections.

## 2 What Do We Mean by Learning Outcomes in Taiwan?

### 2.1 From National Perspectives

Due to the high stakes entrance examinations for high schools and universities, curriculum guidelines (or standards) in Taiwan play an important role in educational systems. The formation of the curriculum committees and rationale of the curriculum owned by the committee members in response to the society's needs are key elements in developing curriculum standards. This section will describe how the committee members are selected and how the standards guidelines are developed. First, the curriculum guidelines in science for Grades 1–12 were designed by two committees (namely one for Grades 1–9 as compulsory schools, and the other for Grades 10–12 as senior high schools)[1] including experts with background in science education and science (including physics, chemistry, biology, earth science, and technology). All the committee members were assigned by the Ministry of Education. Second, during the process of developing curriculum guidelines, various sources of curriculum standards (e.g., Australia, Hong Kong, Japan, United Kingdom, United States) and science education theories (e.g., constructivism, or student-centered approach, inquiry) were examined and then the committee members came to a consensus on the rationale for the curriculum. Then, the contents of the curriculum guidelines were specified and went before public hearings for

---

[1] In 2014, compulsory education will be from grades 1 to 12. The majority of high schools will take students' performance in school as a screening criterion for entering high schools.

further consensus among teachers, parents, or educational organizations. Third, once the guidelines were modified according to diverse sources of recommendations, they were announced by the Ministry of Education and all the textbook writers "had to" follow the guidelines to design textbooks which themselves had to be reviewed by the government before they could be sold to schools or students. Fourth, school science teachers asked book publishers to present their approved textbooks and related materials (such as CDs, teaching models, powerpoint materials, references) for them to select from.

In the past, the curriculum standards normally guided school instruction and textbook writing for about 10 years with minor changes during one wave of educational reform. However, recently, in response to rapid changes in societal, economic, and educational values, the duration time between reforms on curriculum guidelines has decreased (e.g., changes to the guidelines for lower secondary schools (grades 7–9) took place in 1994, 2001, and 2008; 1995, 2006, and 2010 for upper secondary schools (grades 10–12). These changes in policies influenced the revisions of textbooks and assessments to different degrees (Chiu & Liu, 2011).

Taking the integrated 9 year compulsory education announced in 2001 as an example, the major theme of the curriculum is to promote student "competency" that students could carry with them for a lifetime. The committee is responsible for identifying the key competencies that have to be developed during the 9 years or the 3 years in high school.

Currently, teachers follow the guidelines to design teaching materials and test items for assessing students' understanding of the contents learned in schools. In most cases, teachers teach content beyond what appears in the curriculum guidelines because teachers need to ensure that all content is covered in schools so that students could be well equipped for national examinations.

The science standards consist of eight competencies: (1) Process skills, (2) cognition in science and technology, (3) nature of science and technology, (4) development of technology, (5) scientific attitude, (6) habits of thinking, (7) applications of science, and (8) design and production. In each, indicators for the competencies are specified. For instance, at the lower secondary level (grades 7–9), the indicators for cognition are depicted as understanding atomic weight, molecular weight, and understanding chemical equilibrium and factors influencing chemical equilibrium. Both are relatively easy to assess in terms of competence. But to be specific, we still do not know the expected outcomes. It is in a vague format for textbooks writers to prepare the contents and for teachers to prepare teaching materials to match the goals of curriculum standards/guidelines.

So, the guidelines of each competency imply the learning outcomes expected at different stages in our system. On the one hand, this allows for some flexibility in textbook writing and instruction in schools by teachers. On the other hand, the anticipated outcomes of learning and teaching are not well perceived by all the educational agents (including students, teachers, textbook writers, parents, and school administrators).

As for Committee for high school curriculum guidelines, the process of recruiting members for the committee are quite similar to the one described above. In the latest version of the curriculum guidelines students' in chemistry must be able to understand the relationship between macroscopic phenomena and microscopic representations (such as models). Therefore, textbook writers are required to present more models (such as atomic or molecular models in representing chemical reactions). This expectation of students' understanding the role of models in science matches the trend of science education reform learning.

In sum, in our society, learning outcomes are defined in the national curriculum guidelines as the minimum requirements that school instruction and contents of textbooks are required to accomplish during school years (more complete indicators for Grades 1–9 but fewer for Grades 10–12). Learning outcomes are considered as students' performances on knowledge, skills, argumentations and other related competencies that can be observed, assessed, and measured in science practice after giving educational instruction over a period of time. Learning outcomes have to be in explicit form that can be precisely measured as opposed to competency that is relatively vague and implicit which needs to be more precisely defined as an output indicator for assessment. In other words, "competence" might be too abstract to grasp for assessment, but it can serve as a rationale for curriculum standards or reforms. If the "Learning Outcomes" are concrete and operationalized they can serve as explicit evidence of effectiveness of school instructions and policies on science education.

## 2.2 From International Perspectives

Learning outcomes are concerned with the achievements of the learner rather than the intentions of the teacher (expressed in the aims of a module or course). They can take many forms and can be broad or narrow in nature (Adam, 2004).

National Assessment of Educational Progress (NAEP, 2008) serves as a monitoring system to assess what U.S. students know and can do in science. It measures the science knowledge and skills of fourth-, eighth-, and twelfth-grade students. According to the NAEP science framework, developed by the National Assessment Governing Board, students are to be assessed in science in two areas: science content and science practice. Science content of NAEP (2009) is defined by a series of statements that describe key facts, concepts, principles, laws, and theories in three broad areas: physical science, life science, and earth and space sciences. As for the science practices, the second dimension of the framework, is defined by four science practices: identifying science principles, using science principles, using scientific inquiry, and using technological design (NAEP, 2009, p. 14). The new framework incorporates the following key features: it is intended to inform development of an assessment, not to advocate for a particular approach to instruction or to represent the entire range of science content and skills (NAEP, 2009, p. vi). The focus is on students' conceptual understanding, as well as their abilities to engage in some components of scientific inquiry and technological design (NAEP, 2009, p. vii). More importantly, science content is presented in detailed, grade-specific charts that also allow the reader to see the progression in complexity of ideas across grades (NAEP, 2009, p. vii). In line with the science content statements, the practices need to generate student performance expectations, and assessment items can then be developed based on these performance expectations.

As the National Research Council (NRC, 2007) pointed out, in the past research often treated aspects of scientific proficiency as discrete entities; however, current research indicates that proficiency in one aspect of science that is closely related to proficiency in others. NRC (2007) identified four strands for assessing students' outcomes: (1) to know, use, and interpret scientific explanations of the natural world; (2) to generate and evaluate scientific evidence and explanations; (3) to understand the nature and development of scientific knowledge; and (4) to participate productively in scientific practices and discourse. These four strands are intertwined. NRC identifies these four strands of scientific proficiency that lay out broad learning goals for students. These four strands could be considered a framework for designing programs for teaching materials as well as for teacher professional development. Also, the four strands reveal that students need to participate in learning science and become fluent with science in order to develop proficiency. In addition, it is important to be aware of the message that NRC tried to convey which was that the science-as-practice perspective invokes the notion that learning science involves learning a system of interconnected ways of thinking in a social context to accomplish the goal of working with and understanding scientific ideas (pp. 2-9). The focus is on how conceptual understanding of natural systems is linked to the ability to develop explanations of phenomena and to carry out empirical investigations in order to develop or evaluate knowledge claims. In short, a learning outcome is an expectation of what a student should learn as the result of a period of study.

More specifically, the UNESCO definition identifies student learning outcomes as follows and explicitly states that LOs are not concerned with the overall intentions of the teacher but the students' achievements. UNESCO states: "Statements of what a learner is expected to know, understand, and/or be able to demonstrate after completion of a process of learning as well as the specific intellectual and practical skills gained and demonstrated by the successful completion of a unit, course, or program. Learning outcomes, together with assessment criteria, specify the minimum requirements for the award of credit, while grading is based on attainment above or below the minimum requirements for the award of credit. *Learning outcomes are distinct from the aims of learning (emphasis added) in that they are concerned with the achievements of the learner rather than with the overall intentions of the teacher."* (Vlăsceanu, Grünberg, & Pârlea, 2004, pp. 41-42; emphasis added)

Apparently, we also see the impact of TIMSS and PISA on these educational reforms for measuring students' scientific literacy and their learning outcomes. For instance, TIMSS includes life Science (for $4^{th}$ graders) or biology (for $8^{th}$ graders), physical science (for $4^{th}$ graders) and chemistry and physics (for $8^{th}$ graders), and earth science (for both $4^{th}$ and $8^{th}$ graders). As for the Cognitive Domains in TIMSS, they were the same for both grades, encompassing a range of cognitive processes involved in knowing, applying, and reasoning that requires working scientifically and solving problems through the primary and middle school years. On the other hand, PISA tested 15 year olds about their scientific competencies which include identifying scientific issues, explaining phenomena scientifically, and using scientific evidence within a given context. The details of the competencies direct the expectations of students' learning at age 15. The recent literature on PISA (2009) results has been published in the Journal of Research in Science Teaching (see Bybee, Fensham, & Laurie, 2009) and International Journal of Science and Mathematics Education (see Anderson, Chiu, & Yore, 2010).

In this book, several chapters also discuss the definitions of learning outcomes. Whether the competency refers to the same content as the learning outcomes. In Germany, competencies are considered as the German notion of learning outcomes that include content and performance in a domain requiring long-term learning to gain deep understanding (Köller & Parchmann, *this volume*). Schecker *(this volume)* commented that the content knowledge standards are too vague to develop core curricula for schools across each state. In Finland, there are no predefined learning outcomes. Lavenon et al. *(this volume)* pointed out that pre-defined learning outcomes and national level assessment limit teachers' autonomy and neglect teachers expertise in planning teaching activities and assessments. The society trust teachers who are capable and be responsive for assuring the quality of students' outcomes of learning in education. This phenomenon is highly influenced by socio-cultural impacts, acting as a unique model. Kennedy *(this volume)* mentioned that learning outcomes defined by the ECTS users' Guide (2005, p. 74) might provide a good working definition: Learning outcomes are statements of what a learner is expected to know, understand and/or be able to demonstrate after completion of a process of learning. And then Kennedy took Bloom's taxonomy for describing the levels of students' learning outcomes in the cognitive domain in Ireland. In France, learning outcomes are concerned mainly with knowledge and abilities, and in a minor way, attitudes. Each grade is structured according to the hierarchical logic of domain (Venturini & Tiberghien, *this volume*). This is a more traditional manner but with consideration for individual differences in academic performance. In Switzerland, the competency model includes skills, domains, and levels as learning outcomes (Labudde, Nidegger, Adamina, & Gingins, *this volume*). The competencies share similar nature and merits with the German version. In Krajcik, Drago, Merrit, and Sutherland's *(this volume)* article, they referred to learning progression, instead of learning outcomes, to provide a developmental perspective on helping students learn core ideas and practices. It particularly emphasizes "core ideas" and their relation with practice that provides learners opportunities to build more connected and sophisticated understanding of related ideas over a period of time. In sum, all the definitions of learning outcomes share similar components, namely contents, practice, achievements over a long period of time, impact of instruction and assessment. Of course, due to the differences of cultures and societal expectations, variances exist between countries. Needless to say, the development of objectives of curriculum and standards need to be understood before they can be implemented in school practice.

Besides, the purposes of having learning outcomes are different from one culture to another. For instance, there are three uses of learning outcomes, namely, improving competency model (e.g., Labudde, et al., *this volume*; Bernholt, Eggert, & Kulgemeyer, *this volume*), proposing realistic standards (Labudde, et al., this volume), and preparation for the nationwide exams (e.g., Ayas, *this volume*; Millar et al., *this volume*; Panizzon, *this volume*). Although the functions of the use of learning outcomes are perceived and implemented differently, they are all designed to elicit students' scientific literacy for the 21$^{st}$ century according to national and global needs.

In sum, learning outcomes can be categorized according to three dimensions. First, the knowledge perspective, considered as fundamental competence, requires basic rote memory, practice and drill, and recall information. Second, the practice perspective, considered as application competence, requires application of knowledge components and their structure to contexts related to learning science. Third, the cognitive components, embedded in knowledge and practice, are defined as reasoning, argumentation, inquiry, and modeling abilities that are required to link pieces of knowledge together and to make learning content more meaningful for promoting higher levels of cognitive competence.

## 3 How to Assess Students Learning Outcomes?

Educational assessments may serve a variety of purposes, such as to inform students' learning outcomes in knowledge and skills in terms of proficiency, to provide school teachers with feedback on students' performance for improving their quality of instruction, and to provide recommendations for policy makers to promote excellence of education. Black and Wiliam (1998) defined assessment as including "all activities that teachers and students undertake to get information that can be used diagnostically to alter teaching and learning"

### 3.1 From National Perspectives

The following will introduce several programs and projects conducted in Taiwan and sponsored by the government.

3.1.1 National measurement of learning outcomes

In Taiwan, student learning achievements are measured by the national entrance examinations. Students attend the examination with teachers' and parents' expectations to get good scores in order to enter good schools. The Basic Competence Test (BCTEST), as the national entrance examination, is designed to assess learning outcomes of 14–15-year-olds (grade 9) in Taiwan. It launched in 2001 and is a high-stakes test to evaluate junior high school students' learning achievement and their developmental potential. It is and will still be a screening process of high school students in our system for deciding students' enrollment in senior high schools. It is also a standardized test, held twice a year, in May and July. It is scored under uniform conditions to make it possible to compare results across individuals or schools in Taiwan. In order to ensure the quality, reliability, and validity of the BCTEST, a series of standardized test construction procedures and evaluation criteria of the quailities of test items, scaling method, and scoring mechanism for operation of such a large-scale standardized testing system was established (Sung, Hsu, Tseng, Chiang, & Sun, 2007; also see BCTEST website).

About 300,000 students participate in the BCTEST every year. For example, the Committee of the Basic Competence Test for Junior High School Students reported that 303,744 students in total completed the BCTEST in 2010 with 3,832 students achieving the top 1% of test scores and 30,434 students achieving the top 10% (see Table 1). Students use BCTEST scores to apply for entering senior high schools (see Committee of BCTEST, 2011).

*Table 1: Distribution of Student Performance in BCTEST from 2007 to 2010*

| Distribution of student performance | Number of Students in 2007 | Number of Students in 2008 | Number of Students in 2009 | Number of Students in 2010 |
|---|---|---|---|---|
| Top 1% | 3,355 | 3,347 | 3,242 | 3,832 |
| Top 10% | 32,458 | 32,437 | 32,547 | 30,434 |
| Top 20% | 63,064 | 64,562 | 64,292 | 61,592 |
| Top 40% | 126,640 | 127,447 | 127,809 | 121,618 |
| Total | 314,974 | 317,928 | 315,408 | 303,744 |

Note: Data in this table was retrieved from the website of the Basic Competence Test (BCTEST) for Junior High School Students at http://www.bctest.ntnu.edu.tw and organized by the authors.

The BCTEST assesses both students' knowledge and competency in the natural sciences. Students' knowledge of natural science is assessed based on the National Curriculum Standards in Taiwan (1994) which include key concepts in five subject areas: biology, chemistry, earth science, health education, and physics (Minister of Education in Taiwan, 1994). Students' competencies are assessed according to the competency indicators developed by the Minister of Education in Taiwan (1994), and include knowledge of natural sciences, ability to use tables and figures, presence of higher-order thinking, and ability to integrate scientific knowledge. BCTEST assesses students' knowledge and competency via context-free and context-related questions. The context-related questions that assess the application of knowledge are especially focused on students' daily life and learning experiences. These questions stress the importance of students linking science studied in the classroom with science practices in the real world. This helps students see how the knowledge and skills they acquire in school can be applied in real life settings including research and industry.

The Committee of the Basic Competence Test for Junior High School Students reported the distribution of BCTEST questions according to the nation-defined competency indicators (See Table 2). From Table 2 it is evident that questions for assessing students' knowledge of natural science were the predominant type of questions on the BCTEST (average 33.8%). The second most common form of test question assessed students' higher-order thinking (average 16.4%). Questions for assessing students' ability to integrate scientific knowledge, which is at the high ability level and classified by Bloom as "synthesis," constituted only 11.4% of the BCTEST questions from 2007 to 2010 (see Committee of BCTEST, 2011).

Table 2: Distribution of Questions with Different Competences for BCTEST from 2007 to 2010

| Test  Competence | 2007 1st Test | 2007 2nd Test | 2008 1st Test | 2008 2nd Test | 2009 1st Test | 2009 2nd Test | 2010 1st Test | 2010 2nd Test | Average |
|---|---|---|---|---|---|---|---|---|---|
| Knowledge of natural science | 15 (25.9%) | 26 (44.8%) | 16 (27.6%) | 18 (31.0%) | 21 (36.2 %) | 15 (25.9 %) | 20 (34.5 %) | 26 (44.8 %) | 19.6 (33.8%) |
| Ability to use tables and figures | 22 (37.9%) | 14 (24.1%) | 16 (27.6%) | 16 (27.6%) | 12 (20.7 %) | 18 (31.0 %) | 14 (24.1 %) | 11 (19.0 %) | 15.4 (26.5%) |
| Ability of high order thinking | 20 (34.5%) | 15 (25.9%) | 17 (29.3%) | 16 (27.6%) | 17 (29.3 %) | 17 (9.3 %) | 16 (27.6 %) | 13 (22.4 %) | 16.4 (28.2%) |
| Ability of integrating scientific knowledge | 1 (1.7%) | 3 (5.2%) | 9 (15.5%) | 8 (13.8%) | 8 (13.8 %) | 8 (13.8 %) | 8 (13.8 %) | 8 (13.8 %) | 6.6 (11.4%) |

Note: Data in this table is retrieved from the website of the Basic Competence Test for Junior High School Students at http://www.bctest.ntnu.edu.tw and organized by the authors.

Table 3: Numbers and Percentages of Participants Answering Correctly on BCTEST from 2005 to 2007

| Test  Number of Students total Answered Correctly | 2005 1st Test | 2005 2nd Test | 2006 1st Test | 2006 2nd Test | 2007 1st Test | 2007 2nd Test |
|---|---|---|---|---|---|---|
|  | Male: 2627 Female: 2373 | Male: 2580 Female: 2420 | Male: 2627 Female:2373 | Male: 2580 Female: 2420 | Male: 2627 Female: 2373 | Male: 2580 Female: 2420 |
| MALE Students | 1642 (61.6%) | 1688 (64.2%) | 1608 (61.5%) | 1758 (69.1%) | 1537 (58.5%) | 1777 (68.9%) |
| FEMALE Students | 1429 (61.2%) | 1481 (62.5%) | 1462 (61.3%) | 1694 (69.0%) | 1375 (58.0%) | 1595 (65.9%) |
| ALL Students | 3071 (61.4%) | 3170 (63.4%) | 3070 (61.4%) | 3452 (69.0%) | 2912 (58.2%) | 3372 (67%) |

Note: The value in this table was calculated from the results of 5,000 student performances provided by the BCTEST committee.

Results for the BCTEST are released for research purposes. Researchers must complete an application form requesting access to the test results. Each year the BCTEST Committee randomly picks 5,000 students' scores and releases the average scores for these 5,000 students to researchers (no raw data is ever released). Table 3 is an example of the types of data released by the BCTEST Committee. From 2005 through 2007 the 5,000 BCTEST student sample maintained a correct response rate in the range of 58% to 69% (Chen, 2008). There was no difference between the correct response means of male and female students.

The following are examples of the two types of questions included in the BCTEST. In Box 1, titled *ACID-BASE TITRATION*, is an experiment-related question from the 1$^{st}$ test of the BCTEST in 2007. It consists of a figure and information on titration. In order to answer this question, students have to understand the apparatus presented and the chemical reactions involved during an acid-base titration process. The first component assesses whether students notice the used-looking container for solution being titrated. The second assesses whether students understand the chemical reaction in the process. Therefore, both students' knowledge of natural science and process skills for performing experiments are assessed in this question. According to the data provided by the BCTEST Committee (See Chen, 2008), this question was answered correctly by 53.0% of the student sample (of 5,000 students) in 2007 which is slightly below the average for correct responses for the whole test (58.2%). This result demonstrates the importance of teachers and students paying attention to experimental procedures and not just focusing on content knowledge from the textbook.

Box 2, titled *BUOYANCY*, is from the 2$^{nd}$ BCTEST in 2007. According to the report by the BCTEST Committee (see Website of BCTEST), students have to apply the principle of buoyancy to solve this question. Students' knowledge of natural science and higher-order thinking (reasoning and prediction) are both assessed in this question. In 2007, 38.8% of the selected student sample answered this question correctly, which was far below the average for the whole test (67.5%). As a result, students' higher-order thinking ability was called into question.

The different types of questions in the BCTEST represent a new trend in learning expectations from the educational system in Taiwan. Memorizing factual knowledge is no longer the goal of science education. As we can see the abilities being assessed by the questions in the BCTEST in Taiwan, are intended to help students develop inquiry, description, and prediction skills as the entire educational system shifts to a focus on real world application and life-long learning.

Box 1. *ACID-BASE TITRATION*: An Example of 1st TEST of BCTEST in 2007

A boy, named "A-Bin", would like to apply an experimental apparatus (as showed in the figure) to exam the acidity of an acid solution. He used Phenolphthalein as an indicator for titrating an acid solution with $NaOH_{(aq)}$, which was placed in a burette. Which of the following is correct?

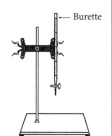

(A) The best choice of container for the acid solution is a BEAKER.
(B) During the titration process, the PH value is getting bigger.
(C) He had to mix Phenolphthalein with $NaOH_{(aq)}$ thoroughly before titration.
(D) At the equivalent point, the acid solution became colorless.

Box 2. *BUOYANCY*: An Example of 2nd TEST of BCTEST in 2007

"Xio-Hui" placed an object A on the top of another object B, and then put both of them into a beaker, which was filled with water. After a while, it reach a steady state that the surface for two objects contact with each other was with the same height of water in the beaker (see the figure). If object A and B were both cubes, with the same volume, but different density. If the density of object A is more than 0.5 g/cm³, which of the following is correct?

(A) The density of object B is more than 0.5 g/cm³ (B) The density of object B is equal to 0.5 g/cm³.
(C) If "Xio-Hui" slowly took object A away from the beaker, the height of object B submerged underwater became "h".
(D) If "Xio-Hui" slowly took object A away from the beaker, the height of object B submerged underwater is less than "h".

3.1.2 Longitudinal database for learning outcomes

Educational systems from different time spans may have different educational goals, which are developed according to the standards and curriculum unique to their time period. In order to monitor the effectiveness of a curriculum, various assessments are developed to explore student learning outcomes. Building a longitudinal database for exploring learning outcomes is especially helpful in educational reform in order to monitor students' change. The following cases discuss the need for a longitudinal database on learning outcomes.

*Case 1: National Database of Learning Outcomes of Taiwan Assessment of Student Achievement (TASA)*

The Taiwan Assessment of Student Achievement (TASA), launched in 2005, is a national assessment of Taiwanese students' knowledge in various subjects. The purpose of TASA is to create a longitudinal database about Taiwanese student achievement and provide a clearer picture of student academic progress over time. TASA is administered by the National Academic for Educational Research Preparatory Office, which has devoted great resources to building the TASA database. The results provide a reference for future curriculum reforms.

TASA has been conducted every year since 2005 to evaluate student achievement in five subjects: Chinese, English, Mathematics, Natural Science, and Social Science. It is administered at five educational levels: $4^{th}$, $6^{th}$, $8^{th}$, and $11^{th}$ grades in high schools, and $11^{th}$ grade in vocational high schools. Students were selected using a two-level sampling method, by the populations of the cities, and the number of schools and classes.

TASA continues to make efforts in adjusting the assessment framework. They developed a new assessment framework in 2008 and a pilot test was also conducted in that year. The new assessment of TASA was officially started in 2009, in which the selected participants and subjects for testing were changed. First, the selected participants were changed as follows: The students were divided into three groups: Elementary Students Group (Grades 4 and 6), Junior High School Students (Grade 8), and Senior High School Students (Grade 11 in Senior Schools, and Grade 2 in vocational high schools). Only one of these three groups receives TASA in a given year in the new assessment framework (Table 4). Therefore, the number of participant students was reduced (Table 5). For example, 78,008 students were assessed in 2006, and 3,4516 students were evaluated in 2009 (see TASA, 2011).

Second, the subjects for testing were changed as follows:
(1) Grade 4 Students: Every student is assessed in two subjects (which are selected from the three subjects: Chinese, Mathematics, or Natural Science).
(2) Grade 6, 8, and 11 Students, and $2^{nd}$ grade in vocational high schools: Every student is assessed in two subjects (which are selected from the five subjects: Chinese, English, Mathematics, Natural Science, and Social Science).
(3) Every year 200 to 320 students are selected to participate in a special test of each subject. The special tests include Chinese Writing Test, English Speaking and Writing Test, and Performance Test for Natural Science.

*Table 4: The Selected Participants and Subjects for Testing for TASA after 2008*

| Participants | Year | 2008 | 2009 | 2010 | 2011 | 2012 | 2013 | 2014 |
|---|---|---|---|---|---|---|---|---|
| Elementary School Group | Grade 4 | Pilot Test | Test | | Pilot Test | Test | | Pilot Test |
| | Grade 6 | Pilot Test | Test | | Pilot Test | Test | | Pilot Test |
| Junior High School Group | Grade 8 | | Pilot Test | Test | | Pilot Test | Test | |
| Senior High School Group | Grade 11 | | | | | | | |
| | Grade 2 in vocational high school | | | Pilot Test | Test | | Pilot Test | Test |

*Table 5: Numbers of Students Participating in TASA in 2005, 2006, 2007, and 2009*

| Year | Participants | Grade 4 | Grade 6 | Grade 8 | Grade 11 in Senior Schools, and Grade 2 in vocational high schools | Total |
|---|---|---|---|---|---|---|
| 2005 | | – | 15,983 | – | – | 15,983 |
| 2006 | | 17,428 | 21,499 | 19,484 | 19,597 | 78,008 |
| 2007 | | 17,154 | 21,227 | 20,031 | 38,140 | 96,552 |
| 2009 | | 12,969 | 21,547 | – | – | 34,516 |

Note: There were no TASA held in 2008 (only pilot test).

TASA assessed students' subject-area achievement from two aspects: knowledge and skills. Knowledge consists of the basic and important knowledge in the above subjects, whereas skills include process skills, scientific cognition skills, the nature of science, scientific thinking, scientific applications, and scientific attitudes. Both context-free and context-related questions are designed for TASA to assess student performance in natural science. For example, Box 3 titled *MAMMAL* is a context-free and single question for $4^{th}$ grade students. It includes four different kinds of animals in the answers. In order to answer this question, students have to understand the characteristics of mammals and apply those to the presented animals. It assesses $4^{th}$ graders' biology knowledge and process skills in classification. However, this question did not contain fruitful information in the stem to describe the characteristics of mammals. Students cannot make inferences from the provided information. The question can be answered correctly by memorizing the facts only, such as whale is a kind of mammal.

Another example in Box 4, titled *VAPOR*, shows context-related, multiple questions for assessing the 6th grade students' understanding about physical science. The questions are embedded in a daily life context. Students can observe the vapor phenomena in their lives. In question 1–1, students have to apply appropriate knowledge of science in this given situation and provide an appropriate explanation for the presented phenomena. Students' process skills in induction and inference are assessed in this question. Question 1–2 in Box 4 is embedded in a daily life context. However, due to the simplicity of the stem and answer of this question, students might answer the question correctly by memorizing the facts.

Besides assessing subject-area achievement TASA administers two types of questionnaires to students to collect information on the educational context for each student. This demographic information can help to relate student performance to other factors. Student questionnaires collect information about students' gender, socio-economic status, classroom experiences, and educational support. School questionnaires, completed by school principals, collect information about teaching practices, school resources, enrollment rates, and parental involvement.

---

**Box 3. *Mammal:* An example of TASA.**
Which one of the following is a mammal?
(A) Shark, (B) Whale, (C) Tilapia, (D) Paradise fish.

---

**Box 4. *Vapor:* An example of TASA**
Xio-Ming took out a bottle of soda from the refrigerator. He found that there were some water droplets outside the bottle after awhile.

1–1. According to your observation, where did the water come from?
(A) Soda evaporated and came out of the bottle.
(B) Water vapor in the air condensed outside the cold bottle and became water droplets.
(C) Cold soda evaporated to water droplets.
(D) Water droplets came out of the bottle.

1–2. Xio-Ming opened a refrigerator and saw white smoke coming out. What is the composition of the white smoke?
(A) Water Vapor, (B) Air, (C) Water Droplets, (D) Oxygen

Students' performance on TASA was investigated to depict students' learning progression. Lin, Hung, Lin, Lin, and Lin (2009) reported the relationships between student achievement in mathematics and student background characteristics. Two types of background measures were identified as variables: students' socioeconomic status and students' learning-goal orientation. According to the results of the TASA-Mathematic Part for 6$^{th}$ graders in 2006, students' better performance in mathematics tended to be associated with their higher socioeconomic status and stronger mastery goal orientation. Cheng and Chen (2009) analyzed students' performance in natural science of TASA in 2007, including process skills, scientific cognition skills, the nature of science, scientific thinking, scientific applications, and scientific attitudes. Results from the 8$^{th}$ graders showed they had good performance in induction and inference (57%), but their skills for organizing data and making correlations (33%) needed to be improved.

*Case 2: Database of Learning Outcomes Developed by Science Education Researchers*

Taiwan's educational reform has been ongoing for the past 10 years, including the Grade 1–9 Curriculum in 2001. Researchers were concerned about student learning outcomes of the educational system and students' achievement changed during this reform period. A research team led by Guo (Guo, Chiu, Huang, Chang, Chang, & Chou, 2009) was concerned about student learning outcomes in different educational systems as educational reform went on. They built a longitudinal database for monitoring students' outcomes.

Guo et al. (2009) suggested learning contents for learning science, including content topics and sub-topics be taught in each science discipline. Table 6 is an example of the key concepts that are expected to be learned in school science. Although details of each sub-topic are not listed here, the research project did develop specific content for each key sub-topic in order to form an outcome-based structure for future study. As for each scientific content area, expert validity was conducted. For instance, for the subject of chemistry, Guo et al. invited two university chemistry professors, three high school experienced chemistry teachers, and two graduate students (who are also experienced junior high school science teachers) to review the indicators and propositional statements of scientific concepts. Revisions were made according to the reviewers' comments.

Major topics and sub-topics in the subjects for science practice were developed and suggested for what should be learned for each assigned grade in the study. Four major topics were: understanding of scientific knowledge, application of scientific knowledge, competence in scientific inquiry, and quantitative reasoning skills. Sub-topics of each topic were also identified for the sake of developing test items. For example, the sub-topics of the first topic (Understanding of scientific knowledge, see the Appendix 1 for details) were:

1.1 Facts: scientific facts, terminology of science, and scientific laws

1.2 Relationship: knowledge of characteristics, structure, function, and relationships among science facts, concepts and laws.

Second, an assessment framework was developed for grade 4, 6, 9, and 12 students to categorize students' major learning outcomes. Two domains were included in the framework: content (subjects) and expected outcomes. Content domains included biology, chemistry, physics, earth science and inter-disciplinary subjects. Students' expected performance was organized in terms of their degree of proficiency in science practices, including understanding and applications of science concepts and principles, scientific inquiry skills, quantitative reasoning skills, the nature of science, and attitudes and other affective factors toward learning science. In order to document students' learning outcomes on a long-term basis, examples of students' expected performances, ranging from basic and proficient to advanced levels, were developed. In order to cover the appropriate and expected outcomes from the target students, science educators, researchers, scientists, school science teachers from different levels of educational systems were involved in developing the assessment framework and illustrative test items.

The topics, subtopics, and assessment framework were further developed for the test items to measure student outcomes. Table 6 is one part of the assessment framework that shows how learning outcomes for understanding of scientific knowledge was defined for different grades. With these specific definitions and expectations, the assessment items and instructional materials could be designed to achieve educational goals in the future (see a sample in Appendix 2).

Third, sample items for proficiency were designed to illustrate the content and competence that are expected of students (See Table 9). Based upon the framework we designed, as described above, a follow-up study was carried out by Chiu et al. (2011). In her project, a Web-based Hierarchical Assessment Technique with Concept Map (WHAT-CM) was developed in which she used concept maps to diagnose students' understanding of chemical concepts (Chiu, Wu, Chou, & Chen, 2011). The preliminary results from about 2000 participants showed that the immediate feedback of students' performance provided by the system aroused students' interest in knowing their level of understanding of the selected topics in the assessment. In addition, the outcome of learning path was identified for each individual student that allowed the researcher to further investigate the learning difficulties of specific students in chemistry.

*Table 6: Learning Outcomes of Understanding of Scientific Knowledge in Assessment Framework Designed for Grade 4, 6, 9, and 12 Students*

| Main Item | Definition | Sub Item | Definition | Grade 4 | Grade 6 | Grade 9 | Grade 12 |
|---|---|---|---|---|---|---|---|
| 1. Understanding of scientific knowledge | The foundation of scientific facts, information, and concepts help by students. | 1.1 Facts | Scientific facts, scientific terminologies and scientific laws. | 4.1.1 Simple scientific facts and definitions of simple scientific terminologies | 6.1.1 Scientific facts, definition of scientific terminologies and processes. | 9.1.1 Qualitative understanding of scientific facts, definition of scientific terminologies, processes and scientific laws. | 12.1.1 Quantitative understanding of scientific facts, definition of scientific terminologies, processes and scientific laws. |
| | | 1.2 Relationship | The knowledge of related attributes, structures, functions, and relations in scientific facts, concepts, and scientific laws. | 4.1.2 The relationship among simple scientific facts. | 6.1.2 The relationship among related attributes, structures, functions, in scientific laws. | 9.1.2. The attributes, structures, functions, and relations among similar scientific laws. | 12.1.2 The attributes, structures, functions, and relations in each different scientific laws representation. |

Due to our involvement in the Database research, the authors made Figure 1 to summarize major components and processes of the research. There were two systems in the framework: *Educational System* and *Researchers' System*. The Educational System included educational goals, standards, curriculum, learning, instruction, and learning outcomes. Among these components, alignment plays an essential role in the system The Researchers' System includes drawing from the existing literature (e.g., NAEP, 2009; NRC, 1996) and experiences from conducting both national and international large-scale assessments in science achievement (e.g., Chiu, Guo, & Treagust, 2007; PISA, 2006; TIMSS, 2003, 2007). The researchers in this system suggested contents for learning the sciences, developed an assessment frameworks and illustrative sample items as guidelines for designing test items to measure student achievement in the long run. The results of the Researchers' System provided feedback to the Educational System. This could cause the Educational System for making decisions on whether or not to change at the macro level (curriculum reform), or at the micro level (revising elements of the Educational System). This model could be applied to many research programs and educational reforms.

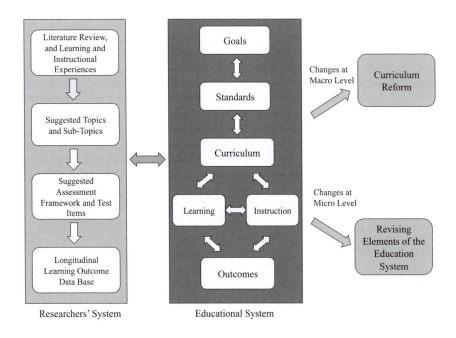

Figure 1: A Conceptual Framework of Database of Learning Outcomes Project

3.1.3 Learning performance in the international studies

Taking two examples from TIMSS 2003 (see Figures 2 and 3), we would not be surprised to see why our students in Taiwan performed so well on one problem but had difficulties in solving other problems related to daily life. The example shown in Figure 2 is quite consistent with the content taught in school science that needs relevant basic concepts about classification which could be learned by rote memory (Taiwan was ranked second place), whereas the example in Figure 3 taken from a famous science education research (McClosky, 1983) investigated physics concepts that are counter-intuitive to most learners (Taiwan barely scored above the international average). Put into a contextualized situation, our students lost their superior performance in science. What happens if the expected learning outcomes are to apply their scientific understanding to daily life events? Would the outcome of the assessment be different?

Example Item 3 (code: S032562)

Teresa is given a mixture of salt, sand, iron filings, and small pieces of cork. She separates the mixture using a 4-step procedure as shown in the diagram. The letters W, X, Y, and Z are used to stand for the four components but do not indicate which letter stands for which component.

Step 1: uses a magnet → W, X, Y, Z → X, Y, Z and W

Step 2: Adds water and removes the component that floats → X, Y, Z → Y, Z + water and X

Step 3: Filters → Y, Z + water → Z+water and Y

Step 4: Evaporates water → Z + water → water and Z

Identify what each component is by writing **Salt**, **sand**, **iron**, or **rock** in the correct spaces below.

Component W is : _____

Component X is : _____

Component Y is : _____

Component Z is : _____

| | Countries | Percent Full Credit (%) |
|---|---|---|
| 1 | Singapore | 68 (2.2) |
| 2 | Chinese Taipei | 67 (2.5) |
| 3 | Japan | 58 (2.5) |
| 4 | Hong Kong, SAR | 58 (2.3) |
| 5 | Estonia | 56 (2.8) |
| 6 | Korea, Rep. of | 54 (2.5) |
| 7 | Hungary | 51 (3.2) |
| 8 | Slovak Republic | 51 (3.0) |
| 9 | Latvia | 49 (3.4) |
| 10 | Scotland | 48 (2.9) |
| | International Avg. | 34 (0.4) |

*Figure 2: Students' Performance on TIMSS Item 3 (Code S036562)*

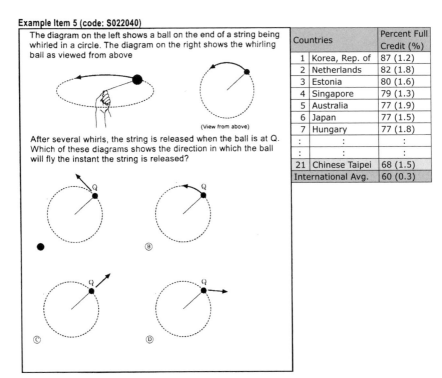

*Figure 3: Students' Performance on TIMSS Item 5 (Code S022040)*

3.1.4 Learning outcomes measurement of newly developed instructional strategies

Besides designing appropriate test items and building up a database to evaluate teaching effectiveness, researchers are also developing new instructional strategies to improve students' learning outcomes. These new instructional strategies need to be evaluated by alternative assessments to see whether students demonstrate better performance following exposure to these practices. Recently, both in Taiwan and the United States modeling ability has been considered to be one of the major competencies in learning science (Gilbert, Boulter, & Elmer, 2000). Considerable emphasis on models and modeling has been placed in the design of science curricula. It has been suggested that teachers' understanding of the nature of models is part of their understanding of the nature of science (Justi & Gilbert, 2002). For example, in Taiwan, the principles for the amendment of 99-course guidelines in chemistry at the level of general high school were justified in 2008. One of the educational goals of the guidelines is to develop students' ability to use models. Teachers are encouraged to apply models in their instructional practices. However, since this is a newly developed instructional strategy, assessments have to be developed to measure students' learning outcomes.

According to our systematic analysis of the previous studies on modeling (de Jong et al., 2002; Halloun, 1996; Hogan & Thomas, 2001; Justi & Gilbert, 2002; Lohner et al., 2005; Sins et al., 2005; Stratford &Soloway, 1998;), we identified several modeling stages for investigating students' modeling ability: (1) model selection, (2) model construction, (3) model validity, (4) model amplification, (5) model deployment, and (6) model reconstruction (Chang & Chiu, 2009). Of these modeling stages, the first five stages are mainly based on Halloun's (1996) viewpoint, and the sixth stage is a new one proposed by Chiu (2008). Because the modeling process is a dynamic and cyclic mechanism (Justi & Gilbert, 2002), the last stage of model reconstruction emphasizes the importance of conceptual change in understanding of a scientific model.

In order to assess students' level of modeling ability, Chang and Chiu (2009) adopted Biggs and Collis's (1982) "Structure of the Observed Learning Outcome (SOLO)" taxonomy to investigate students' learning outcome in terms of cognitive modeling ability. Six levels of modeling ability were identified: (1) No response – Level 0; (2) Uni-structure – Level 1; (3) Multi-structure – Level 2; (4) Relative structure – Level 3; (5) Extended abstract – Level 4; and (6) Multi extended abstract – Level 5. These can be used for measuring students' modeling ability and also serve as guidance for designing the instructional activities to promote students' modeling ability.

We applied the framework to an empirical study. Thirty 12th grade students were divided into three groups with 10 students randomly assigned to each group. They had not previously learned about the knowledge of electrochemistry. Of the three groups in this study, two experimental groups were respectively taught by Cognitive Apprenticeship Instruction (CA) and Modeling Instruction (MI), and one comparative group was taught by Conventional Instruction (CI). The results showed that the application and deployment abilities in the MI group did not improve easily, but for other modeling abilities, in particular, the model construction ability, the MI group made more progress than did the CA and MI groups after instruction; and the progression rank was: MI > CA > CI. In the study, we found that a successful approach with model-based instruction could elicit students' modeling ability. Modeling approach strategy was likely to be successful because the teacher's intentions behind the activity were to explicitly encourage the students to be actively involved in the modeling activity and explore the use of models in their own experimental work. Similar qualitative differences in learning outcomes with SOLO taxonomy were found by Trigwell and Prosser (1991). This study found strong relations between the surface approach and the quality of learning outcomes (Marton & Sälj, 1984; van Rossum & Schenk, 1984;). With the learning outcomes of modeling abilities specified by our design, we believe that the approach of explicit learning outcomes is not only to assess how well our students perform before/during/after instruction but also to facilitate teachers to design specific activities to promote better learning outcomes in terms of modeling ability.

## 3.2 From International Perspectives

There are various types of assessments that can measure students' learning outcomes. The following five types of assessment are the most commonly used methods to serve the purposes of education. The first type is called summative assessment that is made to show the learning outcome compared to curriculum standards of performance in order to provide information to administrators, policy makers, parents, and the public. The second type is called formative assessment that is used to provide teachers and students with feedback in order to improve teaching instruction or learning strategies. The third type is called accountability assessment that intends to drive changes in practice and policy by holding people accountable for achieving the desired reforms. This assessment is very much in the forefront as states and school districts design systems that attach strong incentives and sanctions to performance on state and local assessments. The first three were addressed by the National Research Council (1999, pp. 1-2).

The fourth type is called diagnostic assessment and is normally conducted before a treatment of instruction in order to provide teachers with information about students' prior knowledge or misconceptions that might influence their learning. In other words, this baseline information could be used to evaluate whether learning readiness occurs and how much learning is taking place that is attributed to a specified design of activities that promotes understanding. According to Treagust (1995), a two-tier test item has the first tier with options for content knowledge and the second tier with options about the reason or explanation of the first tier chosen by a learner. The two-tier test results could reveal the learner's naive conceptions of a particular specific phenomenon and how they are revised according to an instructor's expectations. Taiwan has adopted this method for a national survey on science concepts learning (See Chiu, Guo, & Treagust, 2007). This method has been widely used at the local level but not at a national or global level. The fifth type is called dynamic assessment and is based upon the idea of Vygotsky's Zone of Proximal Development (ZPD) for bridging the gap between what a learner could learn with and without scaffold or support from external sources. The dynamic assessment is an interactive approach to determine if a student has the potential to learn a new skill. It is also an interactive approach to psychological or psycho-educational assessment that embeds intervention within the assessment procedure. The last type is called performance assessment (Sweet, 1993). Kelly et al. (1998, p. 853) stated that performance assessments have been proposed as an important alternative to traditional paper-and-pencil tests in response to limitations of traditional measures of achievement. A science performance assessment puts students in a problem-solving context and allows them to pose a problem, devise procedures for carrying out an investigation, analyze data, draw inferences, and produce a solution. A performance assessment has been defined as consisting of: (a) a *task* using concrete materials that react to the actions taken by the student; (b) a format for the student's *response* (e.g., record procedures in a notebook, draw a graph, construct a table, write a conclusion); and (c) a *scoring* system that professionals (in this case researchers) can use to judge the reasonableness of procedures used to carry out the study. Performance assessment is still missing in national examinations and large scale research studies in Taiwan.

As the National Research Council (2003) has pointed out, the characteristics of an ideal assessment system according to a review of the relevant literature are comprehensive, coherent, continuous, integrated, and with high quality of assessments. Although various assessment systems are discussed, due to societal needs, high-stakes assessment still exists. There was also criticism of the impact of high-stakes, standardized testing on school learning (Black & William, 1998). Although many good ideas about assessments have been proposed by researchers and educators, some areas of assessment are still missing in dissemination into the school systems. For instance, inquiry is an important competence in science learning, however, few assessments at the national level have been developed to investigate students' achievement in the process of inquiry.

No matter what assessment the educators use, it is better to be an authentic assessment (Wiggins, 1989) in order to gain insights into students' learning outcomes in the science domain. As Bell and Cowie (2001) pinpointed, assessment must be a continuous process that facilitates "on-line" instructional decision making in the classroom (Gitomer & Duschl, 1995) and science classrooms should provide contexts for students to develop understanding of scientific explanations by assessing evidence, knowledge claims, and data (Duschl & Gitomer, 1991).

# 4 What Are the Factors Affecting Students' Learning Outcomes?

A large body of research data has been accumulated on the outstanding performance of Asian students in international science and mathematics assessments (i.e., TIMSS and PISA) (Anderson, Chiu, & Yore, 2010; Chiu, 2006). It is no longer new to learn that Asian countries/regions receive top rankings in TIMSS or PISA or win Olympiads in physics, chemistry, biology, and technology. Several similar factors impact the results of these phenomena, such as high-stakes entrance examinations for university and senior high school, and teachers' and parents' expectations (Stevenson & Stigler, 1992). However, data from international studies revealed that high performance and low motivation of students were a consistent finding among the Asian countries/regions. In other words, personal diligence a merit in learning by students to meet school teachers' and parents' high expectations has been cultivated in Asian cultures. This phenomenon was evident in Stevenson and Stigler's (1992) study. What educational goals do we, as science educators, intend to achieve? Are they cognition, process skills, attitudes, nature of science, inquiry, context-based learning, argumentation competence, metacognition, or others? If these are the components of competence that we anticipate our students to acquire, what outcome measures should we take to validate that the goals have been fulfilled? As for our experiences and observations of phenomenon in our society, three factors play crucial roles in our educational system, teachers' expectation, parents' expectation, and competitions among schools. In Taiwan, teacher professional development, certificate of levels of teachers' competence, and systemic evaluation of teachers' performance are raised for discussions and recommendations (Wu, Hwang, & Chang, 2011). It is a challenge for science educators, school teachers and administrators, and policy makers to shift their thinking about competitions to educating students to have vision and competence to live well and confront the challenges of the 21$^{st}$ century.

## 5  A Comprehensive Model for Alignment of Components in Learning Outcomes

Figure 4 shows that the measurement of students' learning outcomes is highly correlated with four dimensions: curriculum standards, competence to be achieved-curriculum, quality of instruction, and means of assessment. Each dimension includes elements that describe the nature of that dimension. All the dimensions influence the learning outcomes that we intend to measure. Curriculum standards include scientific content and practical skills (e.g., laboratory and contextualized work). Other competence includes cognition, skill, attitude, habit of minds, and modeling skills. Curriculum included various sources to achieve the intended goals of science education. For instance, epistemological designs and approaches in textbooks, learning environment, or the use of information technology as learning and teaching materials are considered. Assessment includes formative, dynamic, diagnostic, and summative assessments and alternative types for collecting learning outcomes. Instruction includes various teaching models, such as inquiry, context-based, and model-based models. From Figure 4, we could account for a learner's learning outcome as a product of curriculum standards, competence expected, contents and formats of various assessments, and instruction provided by school teachers in an educational system.

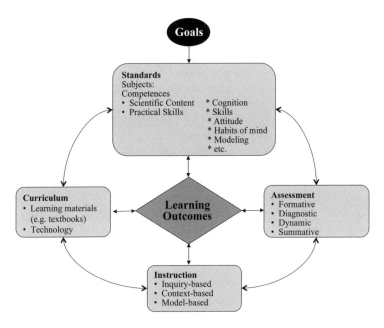

*Figure 4: Framework of Learning Outcomes Related to Science Competence, Assessment, Curriculum Standards, and Instruction*

In sum, Figure 5 depicts the relations and alignments among educational goals, curriculum standards, instruction, and learning outcomes in science learning over a period of time to further elaborate the comprehensive model addressed above. At one specific time, educational goals guide the development of curriculum standards (or guidelines), guidelines acting as the base of designing curriculum and then guiding the decisions for choosing appropriate instruction for school learning. The entire processes also needs to be evaluated through external experts or organizations in order to improve accountability of schools. The double arrows show the influences between two dimensions and also imply a back alignment is needed to provide feedback to the educational system. As Smith, Wiser, Anderson, Krajcik, & Coppola (2006) pointed out that actual learning is more like ecological succession, with changes taking place simultaneously in multiple interconnected ways.

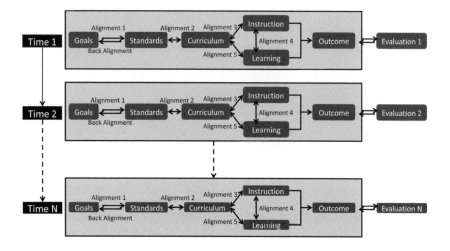

*Figure 5: Ideal Alignment of Curriculum Standards and Learning Outcomes*

## 6 Concluding Remarks

From the examples and discussions above, it might not be difficult to understand that improving students' ongoing learning and explicit expectations in science education from students, teachers, parents, school administrators, decision makers, curriculum standards designers, and policy makers should be clearly defined. What is the gap between reality and idealism? How do we bridge this gap? We make the following claims as concluding remarks:

*Claim 1: Learning outcomes (LOs) as indicators for learning progress*
  The shifting emphasis from general description of scientific literacy to explicit expectations of learning outcomes – in terms of proficiency as indicators of showing learners' learning progression – should be advocated in educational reform.

*Claim 2: Learning outcomes (LOs) as indicators for teaching efficiency*
  Classroom teaching plays an important role in changing students' conceptions about the scientific enterprise. Explicit expectations of students' learning outcome in cognition, attitudes, skills, and metacognition allow us to uncover the efficiency of science instruction in school practice.

*Claim 3: Learning outcomes (LOs) as indicators for policy making*
If our expected learning outcomes address the need in cognition of science content, performance skills in the laboratory, and motivation in learning sciences, then the outputs (e.g., assessment at different levels) of these learning outcomes can provide relevant information for policy makers to make appropriate judgments to improve science education and its impact on society.

With these claims in mind, we believe that there will be different impacts on science education at the following levels: classroom level, school system level, national level, international level, and global level.

1. At classroom level: For teachers professional development (including pre- and in-service teachers) as well as for students learning (including outstanding and ordinary students), explicit expectations of LOs could help teachers to shape their teaching agendas to bridge the gap between their anticipated performance and actual outcomes of their students.

2. At school system level: LOs could form the future infrastructure of a school to achieve and to understand the strengths and weaknesses of programs conducted in the school. That could deliver a win-win-win (winning for teacher-students-school) format.

3. At national level: For policy makers, parents, and the public, the expectations of LOs could help society understand the level that general civilians should reach with respect to a specific vision of education

4. At international level: Specifying the LOs in each society helps us understand the different scientific literacy anticipations and the levels of proficiency of performance in different countries. Beyond the outcomes of international studies (such as PISA and TIMSS), we could also compare the achievement scores across different countries.

5. At global level: If globalization literacy becomes an essential learning outcome, we need to move our curriculum from a conventional way of teaching to sociopolitical action and social responsibility (e.g., Hodson, 2003); therefore, we might change the world with different values of science education.

To summarize, learning enterprise is not a black or white world, where either one knows completely or does not know at all; and that not all students learn at the same pace, adopt the same learning style, and use the same mental representations of the concepts. We have to take individual differences into account while designing curriculum for cultivating students' scientific literacy. Therefore, learning outcomes with different degrees of proficiency and expectations for each individual, for example, those in Chang and Chiu's (2009) study with the SOLO taxonomy, should be carefully taken into account in science education practice. Particularly, definitions of learning outcomes should be operationalized and explicitly stated and understood by teachers, students, school administrators, test items designers, textbook writers, and policy makers.

Note:
Recently, the Ministry of Education in Taiwan (2011) announced that compulsory education will be 12 years in 2014. Therefore, how to design appropriate learning outcomes for assessing students' competence and how to select students and what should be counted as students' learning outcomes in schools became an important issue among parents, district superintendents, school teachers, and school principals. We suspect that school performance will be increase its percentages of selecting students for entering high schools. Therefore, in what ways, we could precisely assess students' competences and in what content, we should measure their levels of understanding and skills become challenges for schools and researchers.

## References

Adam, S. (2004). *Using learning outcomes – A consideration of the nature, role, application and implications for European education of employing learning outcomes at local, national and international levels.* Paper presented at the United Kingdom Bologna Seminar.

Anderson, J. O., Chiu, M. H., & Yore, L. (2010). First cycle of PISA (2000–2006) – International perspectives on successes and challenges: Research and policy directions. *International Journal of Science and Mathematics Education,* 8(3), 373-388.

BCTEST website (2011). Available at: http://www.rcpet.ntnu.edu.tw/eng/index.htm.

Bell, B. & Cowie, B. (2001). *Formative Assessment and Science Education.* Dordrecht: Kluwer Academic Publishers.

Biggs, J. & Collis, K. (1982) *Evaluating the Quality of Learning: the SOLO taxonomy.* New York: Academic Press

Black, P. & Wiliam, D. (1998). Assessment and classroom learning. *Assessment in Education,* 5(1), 7-74.

Bybee, R., Fensham, P. J., & Laurie, R. (Eds.) (2009). Special Issue: Scientific literacy and contexts in PISA science. *Journal of Research in Science Teaching,* 46(8), 861-960.

Chang, C. K. & Chiu, M. H. (2009). The development and application of modeling ability analytic index-take electrochemistry as an example. *Chinese Journal of Science Education,* 17(4), 319-342.

Chen, W. P. (2008). *Research on the Content Distributions of the Conceptions of "Acids, Bases, and Salts" in Textbooks and the Basic Competence Test for Junior High School in Taiwan.* Unpublished Master Thesis in Taiwan.

Cheng, C. M. & Chen, C. H. (2009). The analysis of Taiwan assessment of student achievement 2007. *Journal of Educational Research and Development, 5*(4), 2-38.

Cheng, Y. L. (2005). Review and perspectives of science educational reforms in Taiwan. *Science Education Monthly, 284,* 2-22.

Chiu, M. H. (2006). Science Performance and some related factors of Taiwan eighth-graders found in TIMSS 2003. In C. N. Chang (Ed.), *Report of Taiwan TIMSS 2003 – based on the Trends in International Mathematics and Science Study 2003* (pp. 5-44), Taipei: Science Education, National Taiwan Normal University.

Chiu, M. H. (2008). Theoretical framework for models and modeling. *Journal of Science Education* (Monthly, in Chinese), *306,* 2-9.

Chiu, M. H., Guo, C. J., & Treagust D. F. (2007). Assessing Students' Conceptual Understanding in Science: An introduction about a national project in Taiwan. *International Journal of Science Education, 29*(4), 379-390.

Chiu, M. H. & Liu, C. K. (2011). Review and perspective of the development of science education in Taiwan. In National Academy for Educational Research (Ed.), *Review and Perspective of the Development of Education in Taiwan* (pp. 181-198). Taipei: National Academy for Educational Research.

Chiu, M. H., Wu, W. L., Chou, C. C., & Chen, H. J. (2011, September). *Developing Web-Based Hierarchy Assessment Tools on Concept Map (What-Cm) for Students' Learning Outcomes in Chemistry.* Paper presented in the 4th Eurovariety in Chemistry Education Conference in Bremen, Germany.

Committee of the Basic Competence Test (BCTEST) for Junior High School Students. Available at: http://www.bctest.ntnu.edu.tw (Date of Access: March 24, 2011)

de Jong, T., van Joolingen, W. R., Lazonder, A., Ootes, S., Savelsbergh, E. R., & Wilhelm, P. (2002). *Co-Lab specifications; Part 1 Theoretical Background (Technical Report).* Netherlands: University of Twente.

Duschl, R. & Gitomer, D. (1991). Epistemological perspectives on conceptual change: implications for educational practice. *Journal of Research in Science Teaching, 28* (9), 839-858.

ECTS Users' Guide (2005). Brussels: Directorate-General for Education and Culture. Available at: http://ec.europa.eu/education/programmes/socrates/ects/doc/guide_en.pdf .

Gilbert, J., Boulter, C., & Elmer, R. (2000). Positioning Models in Science Education and in Design and Technology Education. In J. K. Gilbert & C. J. Boulter (Eds.), *Developing models in science education* (pp. 3-19). Dordrecht, The Netherlands: Kluwer.

Gitomer, D. & Duschl, R. (1995). Portfolio Culture Science. In S. Glynn & R. Duit, (Eds.), *Applying science education research to the classroom.* Hillsdale, NJ: Erlbaum Press.

Guo, C. J., Chiu, M. H., Huang, T. C., Chang, H. P., Chang, C. Y., Chou, C. Y., et al. (2009). Developing the assessment framework and illustrative Test items for science learning outcomes of elementary and high School students in Taiwan. *Journal of Science Education (in Chinese), 17*(6), 459-479.

Halloun, I. A. (1996). Schematic Modeling for Meaningful Learning of Physics. *Journal of Research in Science Teaching, 33*(9), 1019-1041.

Hodson, D. (2003). Time for action: Science education for an alternative future. *International Journal of Science Education, 25*(6), 645-670.

Hogan, K. & Thomas, D. (2001). Cognitive comparisons of students' systems modeling in ecology. *Journal of Science Education and Technology, 10*(4), 319-344.

Justi, R. S. & Gilbert, J. K. (2002). Modeling, teachers' views on the nature of modeling and implications for the education of modelers. *International Journal of Science Education, 24*(4), 369-387.

Kelly, G. J., Drukera, S., & Chena, C. (1998). Students' reasoning about electricity: Combining performance assessments with argumentation analysis. *International Journal of Science Education, 20*(7), 849-871.

Kennedy, D. (2011). Learning outcomes in Ireland – Implications for the science classroom. In S. Bernholt, K. Neumann, & P. Nentwig (Eds.), *Making it Tangible – Learning Outcomes in Science Education* (pp. 109-127). Münster: Waxmann.

Köller, O., & Parchmann, I. (2011). Competencies: The German Notion of learning outcomes. In S. Bernholt, K. Neumann, & P. Nentwig (Eds.), *Making it Tangible – Learning Outcomes in Science Education* (pp. 151-171). Münster: Waxmann.

Lavenon, J., Krzywacki, H., Koistinen, L. (2011). Construction of items for national level assessment in Finnish compulsory physics without pre-defined learning outcomes. In S. Bernholt, K. Neumann, & P. Nentwig (Eds.), *Making it Tangible – Learning Outcomes in Science Education* (pp. 477-497). Münster: Waxmann.

Lin, C. J., Hung, P. H., Lin, S. W., Lin, B. H., & Lin, F. L. (2009). The power of learning goal orientation in predicting student mathematics achievement. *International Journal of Science and Mathematics Education, 7,* 551-573.

Lohner, S., Van Joolingen, W. R., Savelsbergh, E. R., & van Hout-Wolters, B. H. A. M. (2005). Students' reasoning during modeling in an inquiry learning environment. *Computers in Human Behavior, 21*(3), 441-461.

Marton, F., & Säljö, R. (1984). Approaches to learning. In F. Marton, D. J. Hounsell, & N. J. Entwistle (Eds.), *The Experience of Learning* (pp. 36-55). Edinburgh: Scottish Academic Press.

McClosky, M. (1983) Naive theories of motion. In D. Gentner & A. L. Stevens (Eds.), *Mental Models*. Hillsdale, NJ: Erlbaum.

Minister of Education and National Science Council (2003). *White Paper for Science Education*. Taipei: Ministry of Education.

Minister of Education in Taiwan (1994). *National Curriculum Standards in Taiwan*. Taipei: Minister of Education in Taiwan.

Ministry of Education (2003a). *Effectiveness of 10 Year Compulsory Education Curriculum and Instruction for the 10 Year Education Reform*. Taipei, Taiwan: Ministry of Education.

Ministry of Education (2003b). *Report on Reflections of Currently Used Textbooks Review System and Upcoming Programs*. Taipei, Taiwan: Ministry of Education.

Ministry of Education in Taiwan (2011). *Revised High School Curriculum Guidelines* (99 Guidelines). Available at: http://www.edu.tw/HIGH-SCHOOL/content.aspx?site_content_sn=20674 (Date of Access: March 24, 2011).

NAEP (2008). *Science Framework for the 2009 National Assessment of Educational Progress*: National Assessment Governing Board, U.S. Department of Education.

NAEP (2009). Available at: http://nces.ed.gov/nationsreportcard/about/current.asp# naep2009

National Research Council (1996). *National Science Education Standards: Observe, Interact, Change, Learn*. Washington, D.C.: National Academy Press.

National Research Council (1999). *Children of Immigrants: Health, Adjustment, and Public Assistance*. Washington, DC: National Academy Press.

National Research Council. (2003). *Assessment in Support of Instruction and Learning: Bridging the Gap between Large-Scale and Classroom Assessment*. Washington, DC: The National Academies Press.

National Research Council (2007). *Taking Science to School: Learning and Teaching Science in Grades K-8*. Committee on Science Learning, Kindergarten Through Eighth Grade. In R.A. Duschl, H.A. Schweingruber, and A.W. Shouse (Eds.), Washington, DC: The National Academies Press.

Panizzon, D. (2011). Learning outcomes for science in Australia: how are they defined, measured and implemented? In S. Bernholt, K. Neumann, & P. Nentwig (Eds.), *Making it Tangible – Learning Outcomes in Science Education* (pp. 341-363). Münster: Waxmann.

Schecker, H. (2011). Standards, competencies and outcomes: A critical view. In S. Bernholt, K. Neumann, & P. Nentwig (Eds.), *Making it Tangible – Learning Outcomes in Science Education* (pp. 219-234). Münster: Waxmann.

Sins, P. H. M., Savelsbergh, E. R., & Joolingen, W. R. V. (2005). The Difficult Process of scientific modeling: An analysis of novices' reasoning during computer-based modeling. *International Journal of Science Education, 27*(14), 1695-1721.

Smith, C., Wiser, M., Anderson, C. W., Krajcik, J., & Coppola, B. (2006). Implications of research on children's learning for assessment: Matter and atomic molecular theory. *Measurement: Interdisciplinary Research and Perspectives, 14*(1 & 2), 1-98.

Stevenson, H. W. & Stigler, J. W. (1992). *The Learning Gap: Why Our Schools Are Failing and What We Can Learn from Japanese and Chinese Education*. New York: Simon and Schuster.

Stratford, S. J. & Soloway, E. (1998). Secondary students' dynamic modeling processes: Analyzing, reasoning about, synthesizing, and testing models of stream ecosystems. *Journal of Science Education and Technology, 7*(3), 215-234.

Sung, Y. T., Hsu, F. Y., Tseng, F. L., Chiang, L. P., & Sun, W. M. (2007). Basic competence test: A review and prospect. *Journal of Educational Research and Development (in Chinese), 3*(4), 29-50.

Sweet, D. (1993, September). *Performance Assessment*. Office of Research, Office of Educational Research and Improvement (OERI) of the U.S. Department of Education.)

Taiwan Assessment of Student Achievement (TASA). Available at: http://tasa.naer.edu.tw/15news-1.asp on March 20, 2011)

Treagust, D. F. (1995). Diagnostic assessment of student's science concepts. In S. Glynn & R. Duit (Eds.), *Learning Science in the Schools: Research Reforming Practice* (pp. 327-346). Hillsdale, NJ: Erlbaum.

Trigwell, K. & Prosser, M. (1991). Improving the quality of student learning: The influence of learning context and student approaches to learning on learning outcomes. *Higher Education, 22*, 251-266.

van Rossum, E. J., & Schenk, S. M. (1984). The relationship between learning conception, study strategy and learning outcome. *British Journal of Educational Psychology, 54*, 73-83.

Venturini, P., & Tiberghien, A. (2011). Potential learning outcomes inferred from French curricula in science education. In S. Bernholt, K. Neumann, & P. Nentwig (Eds.), *Making it Tangible – Learning Outcomes in Science Education* (pp. 443-476). Münster: Waxmann.

Vlăsceanu, L. Grünberg, L., & Pârlea, D. (2004). *Quality assurance and accreditation: A glossary of basic terms and definitions.* Bucharest: UNESCO-CEPES.

Wiggins, G. (1989). A true test: Toward more authentic and equitable. *Assessment Phi Delta Kappan, 70*(9) 703-713.

Wu, C. G., Hwang, C. L., & Chang, M. W. (2011). Review and perspective of the development of teacher education in Taiwan. In National Academy for Educational Research (Ed.), *Review and Perspective of the Development of Education in Taiwan* (pp. 1-20). Taipei: National Academy for Educational Research.

Appendix 1.

*Major Items and Sub-items for Science Practice*

| Topic | Subtopic |
|---|---|
| 1. Understanding of scientific knowledge: the basis of students' understanding of scientific facts, information, and concepts | 1.1 facts: scientific facts, terminology of science, and scientific laws |
| | 1.2 relationship: knowledge of characteristics, structure, function, and relationships among science facts, concepts and laws |
| 2. application of scientific knowledge | 2.1. Application in daily life the history of science and technology, the roles of science and technology to play in the human civilization, understanding of science and technology changing human's life |
| | 2.2. Application of technology the relationship between science and technology, and how to apply scientific principles in technology |
| 3. Competence in scientific inquiry<br><br>(1) scientific process skills: Scientists do research to get technique and strategy of scientific process skills<br><br><br><br><br>(2) Competence in scientific inquiry and problem-solving: problem-solving is a situation that students have to face and solve their unfamiliar and complex problems by using process of cognition. Due to the content of question is usually cross domains, students need to make inference and to analyze the content deeply in order to decide relations and concepts that are related to the questions. | 3.1 Observation: to get the information of objects and events by using motor sense organs |
| | 3.2 Classification: to gather or arrange different classifications which are based on the characteristics or standard of objects or events |
| | 3.3 Measuring and recording data: to describe the size of objects and events by using both standard or nonstandard measurement or estimation |
| | 3.4 Differentiating and controlling variables: to identify the variables which can influence the result of experiment and to control the single variable while others remain constant |
| | 3.5 Question understanding, raising questions or assumption to see if students understand sources for texts, diagrams, or formulas, and attract appropriate information from their existing background knowledge |
| | 3.6 Representation: including how students construct representations, transfer representations, or to solve problems via the use of external representations |
| | 3.7 Analyzing and finding properties: including how students analyze and define variables of questions and relationship among variables |
| | 3.8 Submitting and evaluating solutions (including explanation and predicting): to predict the trends, to generate inferences, and to provide explanations. Supporting the ideas by evaluating strategies of different explanations and solving problems. |

| Topic | Subtopic |
|---|---|
| 4. Quantitative reasoning skills | 4.1 Inductive reasoning being able to observe laws or characteristics of data, and to predict or infer the results from the law |
| | 4.2 Deductive reasoning being able to infer the result from logical reasons while analyzing data, and to convince people of rationality of the holistic reasoning |
| | 4.3 Proportion reasoning being able to infer results from the relationship among variables' proportions |
| | 4.4 Combination and decomposition being able to combine and decompose scientific data appropriately |
| | 4.5 Unit transformation being able to transfer the units to help inferring the result with units |
| 5. Nature of science: ways, values, and beliefs which are from knowledge and development of sceince | 5.1 World view of science scientist's belief and attitude toward what he has down and results, including the ideas of world is interpretable scientific thoughts are alterable knowledge of science is permanent and science is not the solution for all problems |
| | 5.2 Scientific inquiry: Characteristics of inquiry are embedded in features of science: including evidence is necessary for science; logic and imagination are combined for science; explanation and prediction can be proceed by science; scientists attempt to realize and avoid prejudices; and science is not the authority |
| | 5.3 Scientific enterprises: science is an enterprise with different features, including individual, social, and organizational features. It also means that science is a complicated social activity: science is not only divided into different subjects, but also enforced by different organizations; the standard ethical principles should be followed while enforcing science; and scientists participant in some specific or standard public affairs |
| 6. Factors of attitude and affection: the major issues of several factors of attitude and affection are motivation, and personality for science | 6.1 Anxiety: anxiety means a secondary or conditional inner driving force of learning theory and propels individuals to make avoidance reaction; anxiety includes feelings of tensed, agitation, anxious, worry, and fear. There are two types of anxiety, that is, trait anxiety and situational anxiety. |
| | 6.2 Motivation: the inner process which can evoke or remain individual's activity and stimulate the activity to reach a goal the major motivations are achievement motivation, affiliation motivation, cooperation motivation, incentive motivation, and goal orientation motivation. |
| | 6.3 Personality: the unique personality which shows the individual's attitude toward other people, events, himself/herself, and environment; the personality consists of personal needs, motivations, interests, ability, attitude and values;in terms of the situational approach and interaction, there is different explanations to describe the relationship between personality and behavior. |

## Appendix 2.

*Demonstration of Chemistry Examination*

| Topic | Matter changes | Sub-topic | Chemical Reactions |
|---|---|---|---|
| Category | understanding of scientific knowledge | Sub-category | Science relations |
| Grade | 9th grade | Test designer | |

Content statements

P9.24: The reaction rate indicates the speed of chemical reaction. The factors of influencing reaction rate are: the property of the reactants, temperature, surface area and catalyst. For instance, increasing the surface area, that reactant molecules move faster and are more likely to collide and then to increase the reaction rate.

Illustrative Item

**Basic**
1. The figure shows the experiment of hydrogen peroxide produces oxygen. Which of the following statement of this experiment is true?
(A) The hydrogen peroxide can be added a lot at once, itl increases the reaction rate.
(B) $MnO_2$ is a catalyst; it does not decrease its amount after the reaction.
(C) The higher the concentration of hydrogen peroxide is, the slower the reaction is.
(D) $MnO_2$ is a catalyst; it decreases its amount after the reaction.

Key: (B)

**Proficient**
2. John uses same concentration of Hydrogen peroxide for an experiments. According to the following table, compare the reaction rate in different conditions and answer the questions.

| Experiment | Reaction rate | Temperature | Adding Manganese dioxide ($MnO_2$) |
|---|---|---|---|
| A | X | 20°C | No |
| B | Y | 30°C | Yes |
| C | Z | 40°C | Yes |

Which has the larger reaction rate? X, Y or Z? Why?
(A) X is larger, because the temperature is lower.
(B) Y is larger, because the temperature is moderate and the adding of $MnO_2$.
(C) Z is larger, because the temperature is the highest and the adding of $MnO_2$.
(D) Y and Z have the same rate, because they both add $MnO_2$.

Key: C

**Advanced**

3. For knowing the relationship of reaction rate, John uses sea shells to react with hydrochloric acid, which produces carbon dioxide ($CO_2$)?. Besides, he measures the production rate of $CO_2$ separately by the following table.

| Experiment | Sea shells | Hydrochloric acid | Temperature |
|---|---|---|---|
| A | 1g, entire piece | 40 20mL | 30 |
| B | 1g, fragments | 40 20mL | 30 |
| C | 1g, powder | 40 20mL | 40 |
| D | 1g, powder | 40 20mL | 60 |

According to the experiments A, B, C and D, please arrange the $CO_2$ production rate from large to small:
(A) A B C D  (B) B A D C
(C) D B A C  (D) D C B A

Key: D

# Chapter 15

## Learning Outcomes for Science in Australia: How Are They Defined, Measured, and Implemented?

*Debra Panizzon*
*Flinders Centre for Science Education in the 21$^{st}$ Century, Flinders University, Australia*

### Abstract

Consideration of learning outcomes in Australia is somewhat challenging given our move over the last two decades to embrace a *science for all focus* to ensure that science has greater meaning to a wider audience of students while ensuring that our more capable students remain challenged, motivated, and stimulated by the sciences. Addressing this array of students in secondary science education requires greater diversification of the curriculum, teaching via meaningful contexts, and the use of authentic assessment tasks. However, this change in pedagogy and focus is difficult for teachers when simultaneously confronted with increasing accountability from government authorities and widespread implementation of national testing. The result is that in such a climate many science teachers retain their traditional assessment practices with a focus around specific learning outcomes – often those measured in the national tests or credentialing examinations. This chapter explores Australia's current *state of play* regarding learning outcomes in science and where it sits in relation to educational research. Initially, the Australian context is described including our present transition from state-based science curricula to our first national curriculum (Australian Curriculum Science). Following this is a theoretical discussion about the way in which learning outcomes are conceptualized, developed, and measured within Australia's current science curricula documents. The final section of the chapter has a more practical focus around student achievement in relation to learning outcomes. Here the purpose and role of assessment as a means of determining *what students know* and *can do* is explored along with the complexity that exists as teachers navigate their own classroom practices and the expectations of systems of education.

# 1   The Australian Context

Until recently, education in Australia was left to the jurisdiction of six individual states and two territories with complete independence operating around the development and implementation of curricula. As such, there were many different versions of curricula operating in a country with approximately 22,522,000 people. To the present date, the only document agreed to by all Ministers of Education for each of these jurisdictions was the *Melbourne Declaration on Educational Goals for Young Australians* that specifies the broad overarching goals of schooling along with a commitment for action. The main goals of this document include:

- Developing stronger partnerships between students, parents (carers), and broader providers for education in the community including schools and business;
- Supporting quality teaching and school leadership;
- Strengthening early childhood education;
- Enhancing middle years development;
- Supporting senior years of schooling and youth transitions;
- Promoting world-class curriculum and assessment;
- Improving educational outcomes for Indigenous youth and disadvantaged young Australians, especially those from low socioeconomic backgrounds; and
- Strengthening accountability and transparency by ensuring that quality information on schooling is accessible (Ministerial Council on Education, Employment, Training and Youth Affairs [MCEETYA], 2008).

Within this framework, individual jurisdictions were able to design curricula to meet the needs of their own contexts with commonality in science across the curricula more likely in the senior years of schooling (i.e., Years 11 and 12) (Matters & Masters, 2007). Aligned with curriculum, assessment too has been determined by individual states and territories. The only exceptions to this process is the National Assessment Program Literacy and Numeracy (NAPLAN) tests that are conducted in Years 3, 5, 7 and 9, and the National Assessment Program Scientific Literacy in Year 6. Australian students also participate in international tests such as the Program for International Student Assessment (PISA) and Trends in Mathematics and Science Study (TIMSS).

Given this context, there is often considerable diversity across Australia in terms of the degree of detail provided for teachers regarding the depth of conceptual coverage in science. For example, the New South Wales Board of Studies (2010) provides a specific science syllabus from Kindergarten through to Year 12 with teachers having minimal flexibility about what to include or exclude in their science classrooms. This differs greatly to South Australia where teachers from Reception to Year 10 are guided by a broad framework that is driven by learning outcomes. Essentially, this science framework articulates to teachers what students need to know on a year-by-year basis while providing guidance about the pedagogies that might support students in achieving these learning outcomes. Hence, it is this diversity along with alleged student movement between jurisdictions that prompted the national government to produce a single national curriculum in science (in addition to other subjects).

While a national curriculum for science (termed Australian Curriculum Science) from Reception to Year 12 was attempted in the early 1990s, it will actually eventuate in 2012. Importantly, an assessment and reporting regime will be aligned to this curriculum but as yet scant details are available. However, the critical point to accentuate here is that although this science curriculum is being developed at a national level – its implementation including the necessary professional development for teachers is squarely the responsibility of the individual states and territories. Subsequently, from the outset there is the potential for huge gaps to develop between what can be referred to as the intended (i.e., formally written) and implemented (i.e., what is actually taught) curriculum.

## 2 Conceptualising Learning Outcomes

Over the last two decades, Australia as with most other countries moved from an emphasis on learning objectives (i.e., inputs) to student learning outcomes (i.e., outputs) as part of the global shift to outcomes-based education. Importantly, this required a major change from teachers' thinking about their own aims or goals towards monitoring what their students had learnt and/or could demonstrate after a teaching sequence.

Learning outcomes are broadly conceived as indicators of what students have learnt; what they are able to demonstrate cognitively, attitudinally, and/or behaviourally (ACACA, 2008). In Australian they are a central focus for curriculum documents with greater detail provided for the senior years of schooling (i.e., Years 11 and 12 in Australia). While these learning outcomes should exemplify what is valued in science education, it is often assessment (which is not necessarily aligned to curriculum and learning outcomes) that ultimately determines the focus for teachers in their classrooms (Cole, 1990; Hamilton, 2003). Unfortunately, increased accountability in the senior years of schooling in Australia has further exacerbated this issue with a top-down effect evident in the junior years of schooling.

In the Australian Curriculum Science there is no mention of learning outcomes per se with a move towards achievement standards. These are conceived as a hierarchy of described levels of achievement against which students' school assessments and examination performances can be mapped and reported. The assumption underpinning this standards-based approach is that an A or B or C will have a defined meaning that is constant over time (ACACA, 2008). For the classroom teacher they describe levels of achievement of the content, skills, and understanding expected *following a course* of study (ACACA, 2008; Chudowsky & Pellegrino, 2003). So, the achievement standard indicates the degree to which the student meets or demonstrates learning for a particular sequence of study at a point in time (ACACA, 2008) (although learning outcomes are not actually specified).

As with many other components of education, the success of these standards in providing the clarity required for teachers to make the necessary judgements about students' learning is highly questionable. In states in Australia where students' performances are already measured against achievement standards, too often these are written within restricted timelines and in the absence of any kind of theoretical framework to guide construction so that they are hierarchical in structure. More often, differentiation between levels of standards becomes merely a play on verbs or adverbs for teachers. It is clear from the research that the issues discussed here are not isolated to Australia and are evident in a number of countries e.g., the US (see Wilson & Berthenthal, 2005).

## 3 Modelling Learning Outcomes

In science, learning outcomes exist as categories often appearing to fall within Bloom's original taxonomy including the cognitive, affective, and psychomotor domains (ACACA, 2008). Within the existing state and territory science curricula learning outcomes are reasonably broad embracing:

1. *Content knowledge and/or understanding* with reference to the discipline knowledge and the essential 'stuff' of science, such as scientific facts, concepts, or ideas.
2. *Scientific inquiry skills and processes* that attempt to encapsulate the way in which scientists work including ways of questioning, observing, predicting, conducting investigations, collecting data and analysis, evaluating and communicating.
3. *Attitudinal* components that encourage students to behave ethically; develop responsible views around the environment and their role in its future; and support students to recognise the need for a balance between what is possible scientifically and what should be actualised.
4. *Values* that embrace the importance of science in helping us understand the world in which we live with the goal of scientific literacy (i.e., students able to use their scientific insights and understanding to make informed decisions about global issues and their impact). Importantly, these outcomes enable students to recognise that science is not value-free.

5. *Nature of science* and the way in which scientific knowledge is socially constructed through peer review and debate over time; the history and cultural significance underpinning science.

However, while all of the categories of learning outcomes may exist, much of the discussion and emphasis in science tends to be around content (i.e., facts and knowledge) with those outside the educational sphere not recognising that content is *only part* of learning. What they miss is that understanding the process of knowledge construction is fundamental if students are to develop a deeper understanding of science as a way of thinking and knowing (Goodrum, Hackling & Rennie, 2001; Pellegrino, Chudowsky & Glaser, 2001). Central to developing this type of understanding is that while scientific learning outcomes may be presented as discrete units, there is considerable interdependency given that it is not possible to grasp the nature of science without understanding the process by which scientific knowledge is validated socially within the scientific community. For example, in the new Australian Curriculum Science there is a strand entitled *Science as a Human Endeavour*, which addresses the personalisation of science in helping students develop an awareness of the historical, cultural, social, and environmental significance and relevance of science (ACARA, 2010). However, teaching this strand in isolation from the other two strands – *Science inquiry skills* and *Science understanding* – is likely to inhibit students from developing the rich understanding of the nature of science intended in the new curriculum.

Critically, science-learning outcomes do not appear to be of equal quality with some seemingly valued more highly than others. For example, in Year 12 in Australia there is a high degree of accountability given that the final grade awarded to a student (termed the Australian Tertiary Admission Rank [ATAR]) is the chief discriminator for entrance into university (with the exception of Queensland). Most jurisdictions for this level require teachers' assessment plans to be submitted to an external authority for critique. Anecdotal evidence indicates that in these plans, science teachers tend to weight some learning outcomes more highly (e.g., understanding of scientific concepts) than others. This weighting is usually influenced by their prior experiences so that assessment of learning outcomes becomes an exercise in optimising the benefit for students so as to ensure the highest possible ATAR. However, even in junior years teachers are likely to make a judgement about the degree to which they will focus on scientific attitudes and values compared with content learning outcomes given the influence of parents and other stakeholder groups. This is clearly evident in the type of items used to assess their students informally or as part of classroom assessment (Panizzon & Pegg, 2008).

In addition to these extrinsic factors impacting student learning, there is ample evidence that the quality and/or degree of learning engagement in science is impacted by factors that lie within the affective domain (e.g., motivation, identity) so that it becomes a complex interplay operating within any science classroom (OECD Global Science Forum, 2006). Several recent studies (e.g., Schreiner & Sjøberg, 2007; Sjøberg & Schreiner, 2005) and syntheses of literature around the declining participation rates of students in the science, technology, engineering, and mathematics (STEM) related fields explore the contribution of these factors (Panizzon, 2009; Tytler, Osborne, Williams, Tytler & Clark, 2008).

## 4 Developing Learning Outcomes

For some time in Australia there has been a view that science is not for just the elite few who may become research scientists. In the last two decades or so a science for all agenda (Fensham, 1985) has become a high priority, which in recent years has been encapsulated as scientific literacy.

> *All students can achieve science literacy if they are given the opportunity to learn. Students will achieve understanding of science concepts in different ways and at different depths of understanding and at different rates of progress, but opportunity to learn implies that all students have the chance to the maximum extent possible* (Wilson & Bertenthal, 2005, p. 7).

However, one of the issues to emerge in striving for this goal is to ensure that we also meet the needs of our high-achieving students who may be interested in pursuing careers in science. Clearly, if we are to cater for this diversity of students we require a differentiated curriculum with appropriate learning outcomes (Rennie & Goodrum, 2007), which is not an easy task. For example, while outcomes based upon a criterion-based framework may be more relevant and meaningful for less-engaged students, these outcomes are often very specific and minimalistic in nature. What do we do for the more able students? How then do we help science teachers equate this differentiation in their classrooms for reporting purposes?

Raising these questions assumes that there are degrees of achievement demonstrable in relation to learning outcomes. This view is certainly supported by the extensive research evidence pertaining to students' conceptual growth for scientific concepts along with their alternative conceptions (see Pfundt & Duit, 2009, for a bibliography). For example, research around learning progressions in the US suggests that it is possible to provide a developmental perspective of students' understandings of key scientific concepts in a way that helps students develop richer and greater connections with time (Corcoron, Mosher & Rogat, 2009; Krajcik, Merrit, Drago & Sutherland, *this volume*; NRC, 2007). Similarly, the Cognitive Acceleration through Science

Education (CASE) work by Michael Shayer and Phillip Adey from Kings College in the UK uses Piaget and Vygotski for their theoretical underpinning. Over the years they have developed 30 science-related activities that encourage students' cognitive development based on a stage-developmental perspective. Results from their studies suggest that many students perform significantly better than their colleagues on nationally set examinations in science, mathematics, and English even though students were not specifically taught for these tests (Shayer & Adey, 2002).

Other work using neo-Piagetian frameworks conceive of learning as being developmental to a certain extent with students progressing through levels or along a continuum of understanding. However, unlike Piaget this is not age-related and not indicative of students being at a particular stage for all scientific concepts. These models then recognise that students demonstrate greater understanding for some concepts than others based upon their own prior experiences and knowledge thereby supporting constructivism. One such example used in Australia is the Structure of the Observed Learning Outcome (SOLO) model developed by Biggs and Collis (1982). Incorporated in the SOLO model are two important features. The first concerns the nature or abstractness of the response and is referred to as the *mode of thinking* because it refers to the type of intellectual functioning required to address a particular stimulus. There are 5 modes of thinking including sensorimotor, ikonic, concrete symbolic, formal, and post formal with each mode having its own identity, its own specific idiosyncratic character. The important consideration here is that all modes are available and continue to develop throughout life in response to experiential, social, cultural, educational, or genetic factors (Collis, Jones, Sprod, Watson & Fraser, 1998).

The second feature of the SOLO model depends on an individual's ability to handle, with increased sophistication, relevant cues. This feature is referred to as *levels of response*, which are seen to reside within cycles of learning that provide a hierarchical description of the nature of the structure of a student response. While these three levels occur within each mode, the specific nature of these levels is dependent on the particular mode targeted by the stimulus item. A *unistructural (U)* response is one that includes only one relevant piece of information from the stimulus item; a *multistructural (M)* response contains two or more relevant pieces of data with no integration demonstrated; and a *relational (R)* response is one that integrates all relevant pieces of information from a stimulus (Panizzon & Pegg, 2008; Pegg, 2010). As the model provides a developmental and hierarchical component it has been used successfully with Rasch modelling (Panizzon & Bond, 2006; Watson, Kelly & Izard, 2006).

Within Australia the SOLO model 1982 version has been used extensively in the higher education sector (Boulton-Lewis, 1995). However, what is missing from much of this work is the evolution of the model based on further research over time identifying two-cycles of learning (i.e., $U_1$-$M_1$-$R_1$ and $U_2$-$M_2$-$R_2$) evident in the concrete symbolic and formal modes of functioning (Biggs & Collis, 1991; Collis et al., 1998; Panizzon, 2003). Within science education it has provided a theoretical framework for a number of conceptual understanding studies (Panizzon, 2003; Quinn, Pegg & Panizzon, 2009; Tytler 1993) while being used as a framework for assessing students' understanding in science and mathematics (Panizzon & Pegg, 2008). Nationally, the model underpins the Scientific Literacy Progress Map (MCEETYA, 2003) used in the National Assessment Program Scientific Literacy test for Year 6 students and with the Primary Connections materials produced by the Australian Academy of Science.

More recently, the Department of Education and Training in New South Wales has used the SOLO model as framework for developing science items for their state-based *Essential Secondary Science Assessment* (ESSA) test, which is conducted annually with Year 8 students in government schools. The test consists of 75 multiple-choice questions that are focused at a particular level of the model (i.e., unistructural, multistructural), three extended-response questions, and an online practical item. ESSA items are linked to four main strands identified in the Year 8 science syllabus.

- *Strand 1: Knowledge and Understanding* outcomes that embrace the history, processes, applications and interactions between science, technology, society, and the environment along with real-world issues arising from these interactions. Additional, outcomes describe knowledge and understanding of the physical world, matter, the living world, and the Earth and space.
- *Strand 2: Planning and Conducting Investigations* covers outcomes relating to the planning of investigations, the gathering and recording of valid and reliable first-hand data.
- *Stand 3: Communicating* embraces outcomes involving the gathering of data and transforming it for a particular purpose and audience.
- *Strand 4: Critical Thinking* includes outcomes requiring students to make and justify predictions, generalisations, inferences; identify cause and effect relationships; use models to explain phenomenon; and, evaluate problem-solving strategies (NSW Department of Education and Training [DET], 2005).

Importantly, all items are trialed and psychometrically validated using Rasch modelling before inclusion in the test each year with data from the test being similarly analysed. Once completed, each school receives detailed diagnostic analyses of the achievements of individual students, various groups within the school, and the school's performance as a whole. This feedback is provided by an innovative, web-based, centralized software system called School Measurement, Assessment and Reporting Toolkit (SMART). Additionally, reports are also generated and printed for each student. Hence, science teachers are able to use the results to monitor individual student progress while reflecting upon possible gaps in teaching that may be hindering students' learning in science.

## 5 Measuring Learning Outcomes

Much of the difficulties in education exist around the measurement of student learning outcomes with teachers experiencing great angst in this regard. Within the traditional norm-based framework, teachers use criteria to judge student performance to determine mark allocation. Over the last few years in Australia, assessment rubrics have been implemented as a means of addressing the needs of teachers in this regard. However, the bottom line is that the validity of the single-score student result depends solely upon the relevance, accuracy, and reliability of the actual criteria applied within the rubric along with the teacher's interpretation. Too often, these rubrics are developed around anecdotal information or based upon teacher expectation rather than being guided by research or other substantive evidence.

As a means of addressing the inadequacies of norm-based assessment there was a shift towards a criterion-based framework as a means of identifying more qualitatively *what students could do and understand.* A criterion is defined as a threshold between levels of increasing competence that marks a change in the quality of a performance. The thresholds become standards against which a student's performance is judged, so that an individual's level of performance is judged independently from that of other students. Given that this is an interpretive approach, it requires judgments to be made on the basis of a comparison with defined standards of performance. However, in many instances in Australia this has led to a tendency towards a minimum level of learning achievement or the development of standards that do not represent a developmental or hierarchical sequence of learning.

In the current climate there is much that the education field could learn from psychology in relation to measurement. For example, what is often missing from discussions of learning outcomes in science education in Australia is a lack of clarity about the *construct* actually being measured (Wilson & Bertenthal, 2005). A construct is defined as "the competency, or aspect of thinking or learning, that one is aiming to assess" *(i.e., an area of knowledge, skill or ability)* (Chudowsky & Pelegrino, 2003, p. 76). Following on from this is often a lack of rigor in measuring human variables in relation to learning.

Models do exist that provide the means for actually measuring achievement of learning. In Australia, as in other places around the world, the Rasch models provide a mechanism for dealing with interval level data (e.g., student scores on a test) and, equally important, they are able to transform raw data (such as those produced by Likert scales) into abstract, equal-interval scales for further statistical analyses (Bond & Fox, 2006). The output of this type of analysis is an estimate of the item difficulty and the respondent ability for polychotomously scored items (Wright & Masters, 1982). This is very useful in checking that items within tests or on assessment tasks are measuring *what they are supposed to measure*.

Within Australia, Rasch modelling is used nationally with the NAPLAN testing (literacy and numeracy) and with the Year 8 ESSA test used in NSW (Tognolini, 2005). However, this level of measurement is only available with large-scale tests or in some states where they have specific group to focus on assessment within schools. An example here is the *Educational Measurement and School Accountability Directorate*, which is a section of the Department of Education and Training in NSW.

## 6 Differences Between Formal and Informal Assessment of Learning Outcomes

Assessment is the process of gathering and interpreting information about the progress of students' learning (Hackling, 2004; Pellegrino, 2002). Importantly, there are many different terms associated with assessment including formal and informal, formative and summative, classroom or high-stakes. To really appreciate these differences it is valuable to consider the purposes of assessment that have become increasingly prevalent in Australia over the last decade or so in response to changing political and educational imperatives (Cowie, 2009). For example, NAPLAN tests were originally implemented to inform schools and educational systems about their progress. However, in 2010 the *My School* website was developed to share these results with parents and other interested parties in a totally open forum. While schools are not actually listed in order as with a League Table it is possible for comparisons to be made about a range of aspects in relation to the school. Already there is evidence that some secondary schools are using NAPLAN results to accept or refuse primary students thereby raising the accountability of this testing to a higher level than originally intended. As a consequence of these types of changes, teachers are now in a tricky position where they are often expected to adapt their practices to meet the needs of a number of stakeholders including students, parents, administrators, policy makers and government authorities (NRC, 2003) with data being used for a range of purposes.

Wiliam (2000) categorised the major purposes of assessment into the four broad categories.

1. *Evaluative:* refers to assessment used to evaluate curricula and institutions (e.g., schools, systems) and in so doing serve the purpose of accountability. Examples include the Australian national benchmarking tests in numeracy and literacy, TIMSS, and the PISA programs whereby the performance of schools or systems is monitored against specified standards.
2. *Summative:* incorporates assessment that monitors the degree to which students have achieved learning outcomes with results used to inform grading and reporting. Subsequently, these grades are used to identify those students ready to progress to the next year level of education.
3. *Formative:* includes assessment that provides feedback to students about their learning progress while informing teachers about where teaching might be directed to support and enhance student learning.
4. *Diagnostic:* refers to assessment to gauge a student's conceptions, understandings, and alternative conceptions *prior* to teaching a particular topic so that the student's difficulties can be addressed specifically through the teaching process (Matters, 2006).

The broad criteria for all these forms of assessment should be the same in that they are all attempting to gauge and monitor the degree to which students have achieved learning outcomes in science. However, what ultimately determines the nature, structure, and the emphasis of the assessments used by teachers to inform their own teaching practices is summative and evaluative assessment or *formal* assessment (Parker & Rennie, 1998). Research evidence both in Australia and globally clearly indicates that what is assessed formally and/or externally will highlight for teachers what is valued by the system and where best to focus their attention. Of course this is not explicitly stated but is the prevailing underlying message that is quickly perceived by science teachers (Eltis, 2003; Hamilton, 2003; Panizzon & Pegg, 2008).

## 7  Systematically Enhancing Student Achievement

Learning in science is conceived as the development of competency in a particular area with new information linked to existing knowledge to build deeper understandings not as the accretion of facts and skills (Goodrum, Hackling, & Rennie, 2001; Treagust, Jacobowitz, Gallagher, & Parker, 2001). If the focus remains on the learning outcomes for a particular year level in science then all of those outcomes should be assessed appropriately throughout the year so that students know in an ongoing manner *what they understand* and *where* they need to concentrate their efforts (Pellegrino, *this volume*). Hence, there is movement or growth in student achievement of these specified outcomes. Equally important in this process is that teachers use this information to decide *where best to target* the next teaching sequence to address the needs of their students to enhance their learning.

Considered in this way, assessment moves away from being an activity that occurs at the end of a teaching sequence (which is how it is conceptualised for summative purposes involving high-stakes testing) to become an important and highly informative component of the teaching and learning cycle. Biggs (1996) referred to this as constructive alignment with a linking between the three arms of any curriculum – content/skills/values/attitudes, pedagogy, and assessment.

The emphasis on teaching in relation to student achievement has become a higher priority in Australia given emerging evidence from large-scale tests, such as PISA and TIMSS. For example, work by Cresswell (2004) identified that around 10–18% of the variation in Australian student achievement in PISA related to differences between schools, with an additional 50% of variation attributable to differences between classrooms in the same school. So, while there is often much consternation about across-school comparisons, PISA analyses indicate that there is actually greater variation in student achievement between classrooms in the same school than across schools (OECD, 2004). Hence, focusing on teacher practice around assessment is critical for our students.

Central to the impact of teachers is feedback. In a meta-analysis of 500 research projects, Hattie and Timperley (2007) found the effect size for feedback was 0.79 placing it in the top 10 greatest influences on student achievement. Importantly, they identified differences in the type of feedback provided by teachers, which they conceptualised around four distinct levels. The two levels with the highest effect sizes included when teachers (i) provided information about the process underlying students' understandings of the task (i.e., Level 2); and (ii) helped students develop their skills around self-regulation (i.e., Level 3). Not surprisingly, teachers appear to find providing feedback quite difficult in that while they may be able to assess the standard of student work when the purpose is summative, they often struggle to suggest how the work could be improved i.e., what is needed for a student to enhance their grade from a B to an A (Wiliam, 2000).

Given this discussion, there are two critical points to make around assessment regardless of its purpose. The first point is that ultimately it is the quality of the assessment items that matter – whether they be produced by the science teacher and used informally to assess students; or part of a test developed by a system as a final examination of student learning in science. Yet, the quality of items used by teachers is strongly influenced by those used in state or national tests (e.g., NAPLAN in Australia, or the Scholastic Aptitude Test [SAT] in the US). Unfortunately, as alluded to by the Commission on Instructionally Supportive Assessment (2001) in the US tests developed too hurriedly neither support instruction nor supply accurate evaluative information for accountability programs, and there is a widespread misunderstanding that high-quality achievement tests can be developed in two years or less (p. 12).

Similar statements could also be made in relation to teacher-produced items that tend to focus on learning outcomes that teachers consider are more important or valued (e.g., content) to the detriment of other higher-order thinking skills (e.g., critical reasoning, complex problem-solving) (Shepard, 2000). Linked to this is the need for teachers to select tasks that are appropriate in allowing students to demonstrate particular learning outcomes. For example, not all practical skill outcomes in secondary science can be assessed using traditional pen and paper items. However, working with science teachers to change these practices even though they understand the significance is difficult in Australia (Panizzon, Callingham, Wright, & Pegg, 2008) with teachers tending to rely upon the traditional practical report (aim, materials, method, etc.) or the occasional practical test.

The second critical point to make about assessment is that if teachers are to make valid and reliable judgements about student achievement, the rubrics, standards or whatever other criteria are used for guiding their decisions must be suitably organised and structured.

*Standards must be clear, detailed and complete; reasonable in scope; rigorous and scientifically correct; and built upon a conceptual framework that reflects sound models of student learning. They should also describe examples of performance expectations for students in clear and specific terms so that all concerned will know what is expected of them (Wilson & Bertenthal, 2005).*

Unfortunately, most standards do not meet all of these criteria. As Australia moves towards the development of national achievement standards around the Australian Curriculum Science, there is much to learn from other countries.

## 8 Role of Assessment in the Classrooms

Changes to traditional summative or formal assessment methods over the last decade (Morgan & Watson, 2002) with the introduction of assessment of learning (Black & Wiliam, 1998) have encouraged teachers to make major shifts in relation to their notions of assessment. Rather than a focus around the collection of marks for accountability and reporting purposes, teachers have needed to think about assessment as being embedded (Wilson & Sloane, 2000) into the teaching and learning process.

*Classroom assessment informs teachers how effectively they are teaching and students how effectively they are learning. Through classroom assessment, teachers get continual feedback on whether and how well students are learning what teachers hope they are teaching. And students are required, through a variety of classroom assessment exercises, to monitor their learning, to reflect on it, and to take corrective action while there is still time left (Cross, 1998, p. 6).*

When science teachers in Australia generally are asked about the ways in which they assess their students, the majority mention tasks that clearly meet a summative or formal assessment agenda. For example, in a national study by Goodrum et al. (2001) the main tasks identified by secondary science teachers included tests, examinations, research assignments, and traditional practical reports. Research suggests that a predominance of these types of tasks used solely for summative purposes has the potential of

- reducing a discipline (e.g., science) to learning about facts,
- lowering the level of cognition required by the student,
- inhibiting student questioning as they maintain focus on the topic being taught,
- ensuring that most teachers 'teach to the test',
- restricting teaching to aspects that are assessable in this manner, and
- ensuring that creative and innovative teaching methods are omitted as teachers 'violate their own standards of good teaching' (Black, 1993, p. 52; Goodrum et al., 2001).

There is an important point to be made here and that is that each of these traditional science assessment tasks has the potential of being used formatively (informally) or in a diagnostic manner to enhance student learning in an ongoing manner. The critical aspect is around how the teacher *uses the results from these tasks*. Instead of focusing solely on marks or the most correct answer, encouraging students to reflect upon their responses and consider how their answers could be improved provides valuable feedback that allows students to build their scientific understandings (Atkin & Coffey, 2003; Black & Wiliam, 1998; Hattie & Timperley, 2007).

In a recently completed project funded by the South Australian Certificate of Education (SACE) Board, we set out to explore the use of ICTs and e-assessment in *Contemporary Issues and Science* with Years 11 and 12 students in South Australia (Panizzon, Elliott & Westwell, 2011). The two-year pilot project was focused around designing, implementing, and reporting upon new types of electronic assessment items that assess the learning outcomes for the subject *Contemporary Issues and Science*. The particular emphasis was around those outcomes and scientific processes difficult to assess authentically with pen and paper. For example, students were assessed in relation to their ability to design investigations, make observations, classify data, formulate hypotheses, interpret data and make inferences, problem-solve, think critically, and analyse and draw conclusions from results. As these items were developed using electronic tools, computer-generated and completed by the students on computers, critical aspects of science such as replication and time-bound processes (e.g., rates of change) could be incorporated into the tasks.

Each item was scaffolded in that it allowed students to move through each section of the item with feedback provided immediately. Hence, students could continue to move through and finish the item even though they may have provided incorrect responses at particular points. An example of this is provided in Figure 1 showing an initial screen for an item entitled *Grey Water* with students having to select appropriate washing detergents to undertake an investigation. Once selections of detergents were made it was possible for students to follow three possible pathways through this section of the item depending on the scientific accuracy of their responses (see Figure 2).

*Figure 1: Example of screen capture for item around Grey water*

In this way, whether students were initially correct or required a second attempt they eventually moved back to the same position of the item again, which in this example was screen 3 and the identification of variables. As all students' responses to all items were captured in this manner, we were able to track the different pathways used by students in working through an item in relation to time.

Subsequently, the focus with these items was about identifying what the students actually understood and how they could apply their understanding to a range of scientific contexts. This overcame much of the emphasis on memorisation with the result being that many of the science teachers commented upon the increased participation and achievement of their less-engaged or supposedly less-able students. On the other hand, some of their more able students appeared to struggle with aspects of the items highlighting for teachers areas to target so as to enhance their learning. For example, while these students may have been able to define a dependent variable, they were not able to select it from a range of possible options provided in the item.

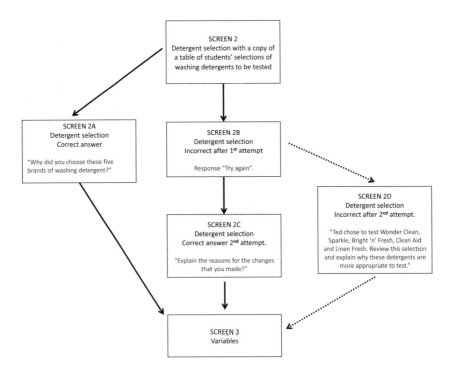

*Figure 2: Possible pathways for students' responses*

*You think – a lot of these things you've taught really well and they have done it since Year 8 – so why didn't they do very well? Because of the working knowledge compared to what the expected answer is and there is a difference in the thinking ... one of the advantages of these items is that you can actually see the processes and how they think through a problem rather than given the expected answer. The questions are different!* (Teacher from project)

Importantly, this project was not about taking multiple-choice or extended response items and placing them in an electronic forum (i.e., on the computer) – it required major reconceptualization for the science teachers and the researchers involved. While the results are still being analysed, the pilot e-assessment project appears to have addressed a number of the gaps evident in many science assessment tasks.

## 9   Impact on Teachers of Measuring Student Learning

The increasing demands for measuring student learning for different purposes has led to a number of identifiable impacts on teachers and the classroom. One of the most obvious impacts of the high-stakes assessment regime on classroom assessment has been a *teaching-to-the-test* mentality in countries like the Australia, the UK, and the US (Linn, 2000; McNeil, 2000). In Australia, so strong is this growing culture that teachers have been reprimanded even dismissed from their positions for actually *coaching* their students in the primary (elementary) years for pending NAPLAN tests but even worse, for altering answers while the test is being conducted. This demonstrates the increasing pressure being placed on teachers to attain acceptable results for their students. However, what is overlooked is that even if students attain high results are these tests simply measuring basic skills and disregarding higher level thinking skills? Are we actually striving for mediocrity? Shepard (2002–2003) found exactly this result in the US by comparing the performance of students between two different standardised tests conducted in one district. Essentially, although the tests were matched and statistically equated, there was an 8-month drop in student performance in mathematics on the alternative test. Hence, it is critical that educators continue to question the reliability and integrity of what these externally-prepared tests are ultimately measuring (Pellegrino et al., 2001).

Equally important is the subsidiary impact of this test focus. Again there is evidence that it leads to a reduction in the breadth of the curriculum addressed resulting in further narrowing of the type of assessment tasks and/or the style of items teachers implement in their own classroom assessment practices (Shepard, 2002–2003). Unfortunately, the high degree of accountability in the senior years of schools has a top-down effect driving assessment practices in the junior years of secondary schooling, which is now beginning to affect even the primary or elementary years (Goodrum et al., 2001; Shepard, 2000).

Fortunately though, teachers are incredibly resourceful. McNeil (2000) found that more competent teachers practiced "double-entry bookkeeping" – teaching what was needed by students for standardised tests along with what they considered was the real knowledge necessary for conceptual understanding. This same strategy for dealing with conflicting assessment requirements was identified also with highly accomplished/experienced science teachers in New South Wales (Australia) who kept two assessment records. The first was for formal assessment and consisted of only five annual assessment results for students in Years 11 and 12 (as specified by the educational authority). The second was an informal gathering of information from these same students based upon classroom assessment tasks completed over the course of each year. Teachers justified the need for both entries because they felt the five required tasks simply did not provide the information necessary over a substantive period of time for making judgements about student achievement and ability in relation to the learning outcomes (Panizzon et al., 2008).

## 10    Conclusion

Teachers are ultimately responsible for making judgements about the quality of students' understandings (Linn, 2000) because "teachers are in the best position to ensure that assessment is equitable" (Morgan & Watson, 2002, p. 80).

> *Quality assessment requires clear and valued goals for student learning as the assessment targets, quality tools for gathering evidence of student learning, sound interpretations of the evidence, and quality uses of the information to guide instruction and provide students with useful feedback ... Teachers must also recognize that all components of assessment must be aligned, and that any one assessment is embedded in a system of assessments to provide coordinated information* (Gearhart, Nagashima, Pfotenhauer, Clark, Schwab, Vendlinski, et al., 2006, p. 5).

Unfortunately, science teachers in Australia are increasingly being asked to undertake classroom assessment for many different purposes: (i) to inform students and themselves; (ii) to report to parents, principles, and school governing bodies; and, (ii) for educational and political accountability processes (Cowie, 2009). It is clear from the research evidence that this has created conflict and confusion leading to a de-skilling and/or de-professionalization of many teachers (McNeil, 2000; Shepard, 2000). Caught in the middle, teachers are attempting to juggle an *assessment for learning agenda* while still attaining the highest results possible for students on any external examination that the school participates in – whether at a national or international level. Ultimately, each teacher will decide where best to focus their attention and this may not necessarily be based around ensuring the highest quality learning outcomes in science.

## References

Atkin, J. M. & Coffey, J. E. (2003). *Everyday Assessment in the Science Classroom*. Arlington, Virginia: National Science Teachers Association Press.

Australasian Curriculum, Assessment and Certification Authorities. (ACACA) (2008). *Changing Secondary Schools in Australia Years 7–10 – State by State*. Available at: http://acaca.bos.nsw.edu.au/go/changing-schools/ (Date of Access: November 3rd 2010).

Australian Curriculum, Assessment and Reporting Authority (ACARA) (2010). *Shape of the Australian Curriculum: Science*. Available at: http://www.acara.edu.au/curriculum/phase_1_-_the_australian_curriculum. html (Date of Access: November 17th 2010).

Biggs, J. (1996). Enhancing teaching through constructive alignment. *Higher Education, 32*, 347-364.

Biggs, J. & Collis, K. (1982). *Evaluating the Quality of Learning: The SOLO Taxonomy*. Ithaca, NY: Academic Press.

Biggs, J. & Collis, K. (1991). Multimodal learning and the quality of intelligent behaviour. In H. Rowe (Ed.), *Intelligence, Reconceptualisation and Environment* (pp. 57-76). New Jersey: Lawrence Erlbaum Associates.

Black, P. (1993). Formative and summative assessment by teachers. *Studies in Science Education, 21*, 49-91.

Black, P. & Wiliam, D. (1998). Inside the black box: Raising standards through classroom assessment. *Phi Delta Kappan, 80*(2), 139-148.

Bond, T. G., & Fox, C. M. (2006). *Applying the Rasch Model: Fundamental Measurement in the Human Sciences, 2nd Edition*. New Jersey: Lawrence Erlbaum Associates.

Boulton-Lewis, G. M. (1995). The SOLO taxonomy as a means of shaping and assessing learning in higher education. *Higher Education Research and Development, 14*(2), 143–154.

Chudowsky, N. & Pellegrino, J. W. (2003). Large-scale assessments that support learning: What will it take? *Theory into Practice, 42*(1), 75-83.

Cole, N.S. (1990). Conceptions of educational achievement. *Educational Researcher, 19*(3), 2-7.

Collis, K. F., Jones, B. L., Sprod, T., Watson, J. M., & Fraser, S. P. (1998). Mapping development in students' understandings of vision using a cognitive structural model. *International Journal of Science Education, 20*(1), 45-66.

Commission on Instructively Supportive Assessment (2001, October). *Building Tests to Support Instruction and Accountability: A Guide for Policy Makers.* Available at: www.aasa.org/issues_and_insights/assessment/building_tests.pdf (Date of Access: December 14th 2010).

Corcoran, T. B., Mosher, F. A., & Rogat, A. (2009). *Learning Progressions in Science: An Evidence-Based Approach to Reform.* New York, NY: Columbia University, Teachers College, Consortium for Policy Research in Education, Center on Continuous Instructional Improvement.

Cowie, B. (2009). The evolution of assessment purposes and practices. In S. Richie (Ed.), *The world of science education: Handbook of research in Australasia* (pp. 235-248). Netherlands: Sense Publishers.

Cresswell, J. (2004). School Effectiveness. Schooling Issues Digest, 1, 1–8. Available at: www.dest.gov.au/sectors/school_education/publications_resources/profiles/schooling_issues_digest_school_effectiveness.htm (Date of Access: January 13th 2011).

Cross, P. K. (1998). Classroom research: Implementing the scholarship of teaching. *New Directions for Teaching and Learning, 75,* 5-12.

Eltis, K. J. & Crump, S. (2003). *Time to Teach, Time to Learn: Report on the Evaluation of Outcomes Assessment and Reporting in NSW Government Schools.* Sydney, Australia: NSW Department of Education and Training.

Fensham, P. (1985). Science for all. *Journal of Curriculum Studies, 17,* 415-435.

Gearhart, M., Nagashima, S., Pfotenhauer, J., Clark, S., Schwab, C., Vendlinski, T., Osmundson, E., Herman, J., & Bernbaum, D. J. (2006). *Developing Expertise With Classroom Assessment in K-12 Science: Learning to Interpret Student Work – Interim Findings from a 2-Year study.* CSE Technical Report 704. Available at: www.cse.ucla.edu/products/reports/R704.pdf (date of Access: March 3rd 2008).

Goodrum, D., Hackling, M., & Rennie, L. (2001). *Research Report: The Status and Quality of Teaching and Learning of Science in Australian Schools.* Canberra: Department of Education, Training and Youth Affairs (DETYA).

Hackling, M. W. (2004). Assessment in science. In G. Venville & V. Dawson (Eds.), *The Art of Teaching Science* (pp. 126-144). Crows Nest, NSW: Allen & Unwin.

Hamilton, L. (2003). Assessment as a policy tool. *Review of Research in Education, 27,* 25-68.

Hattie, J. & Timperley, H. (2007). The power of feedback. *Review of Educational Research, 77*(1), 81-112.

Linn, R. L. (2000). Assessments and accountability. *Educational Researcher, 29*(2), 4-16.

Matters, G. (2006). Using data to support learning in schools: Students, teachers, systems. *Australian Education Review, 49.* Available at: http://www.acer.edu.au/resdev/15_Data.html (Date of Access: August 5th, 2008).

Matters, G. & Masters, G. (2007). *Year 12 Curriculum Content and Achievement Standards.* Available at: www.cse.ucla.edu/products/reports/R704.pdf http://www.dest.gov.au/sectors/school_ education/publications_resources/profiles/y12_curriculum_standards.htm (Date of Access: March 20th, 2008).

McNeil, L. M. (2000). *Contradictions of reform: The Educational Costs of Standardization.* New York: Routledge.

Ministerial Council on Education, Employment, Training and Youth Affairs (MCEETYA) (2003). *National Year 6 Science Assessment Report.* Available at: http://www.mceetya.edu.au/mceetya/defaultasp?id=12107 (date of Access: March 10th, 2006).

Ministerial Council on Education, Employment, Training and Youth Affairs (MCEETYA) (2008). *The Adelaide Declaration on National Goals for Schooling in the Twenty-first Century.* Available at: http://www.mceecdya.edu.au/mceecdya/melbourne_declaration, 25979.html (Date of Access: July 7th, 2010).

Morgan, C. & Watson, A. (2002). The interpretative nature of teachers' assessment of students' mathematics: Issues for equity. *Journal of Research in Mathematics Education,* 33(2), 78-107.

National Research Council [NRC] (2003). *Assessment in support of instruction and learning: Bridging the Gap between Large-Scale and Classroom Assessment.* Washington, DC: National Academies Press.

National Research Council [NRC] (2007). *Taking Science to School: Learning and Teaching Science in Grades K-8.* Committee on Science Learning, Kindergarten through Eighth Grade. Washington, DC: National Academy Press.

New South Wales Board of Studies (2010). Science Years 7–10 Syllabus. Available at: http://www.boardofstudies.nsw.edu.au/syllabus_sc/science.html (Date of Access: December 10th, 2010).

New South Wales Department of Education and Training (2005). *Essential Secondary Science Assessment: Writing Task Marking Procedures.* Sydney: NSW DET.

OECD. (2004). *What Makes School Systems Perform: Seeing School Systems Through the Prism of PISA.* Available at: http://www.oecd.org/document/33/0,3343,en_32252351_32236159_33858849_1_1_1_1,00.html (Date of Access: January 12th, 2011).

OECD Global Science Forum. (2006). *Evolution of Student Interest in Science and Technology Studies: Policy Report.* Available at: http://www.oecd.org/dataoecd/16/30/36645825.pdf (Date of Access: September 3rd, 2006).

Panizzon, D. (2003). Using a cognitive structural model to provide new insights into students' understandings of diffusion. *International Journal of Science Education,* 25(12), 1427-1450.

Panizzon, D. (2009). Enhancing student participation and engagement in science: Lessons from research. *South Australian Science Teachers' Association Journal,* 2, 4-7.

Panizzon, D. & Bond, T. (2006). Exploring Conceptual Understandings of Diffusion and Osmosis by Senior High School and Undergraduate University Science Students. In X. Liu & W. J. Boone (Eds.), *Applications of Rasch Measurement in Science Education* (pp. 137-164). Maple Grove, MN: JAM Press.

Panizzon, D., Callingham, R., Wright, T., & Pegg, J. (2008). *Shifting Sands: Using SOLO to Promote Assessment for Learning With Secondary Mathematics and Science Teachers.* Refereed paper presented at the Australasian Association for Research in Education (AARE) conference in Fremantle, Western Australia, 25–29th November 2007.

Panizzon, D., Elliott, K., & Westwell, M. (2011). Paper presented at the Australasian Science Educators Research Association Conference (ASERA) in Adelaide, South Australia, 29th June to 2nd July 2011.

Panizzon, D. & Pegg, J. (2008). Assessment practices: Empowering mathematics and science teachers in rural secondary schools to enhance student learning. *International Journal of Science and Mathematics Education, 6*, 417-436.

Parker, L.H. & Rennie, L.J. (1998). Equitable assessment strategies. In B. J. Fraser & K. G. Tobin (Eds.), *International Handbook of Science Education* (pp. 897-910). Dordrecht: Kluwer Academic Publishers.

Pegg, J. (2010). *Promoting the Acquisition of Higher-Order Skills and Understandings in Primary and Secondary Mathematics.* Available at: http://research.acer.edu.au/research_conference/RC2010/16august/ (Date of Access: Retrieved January 7th 2011).

Pellegrino, J. W. (2002). Knowing what students know. *Issues in Science and Technology, 19*(2), 48-52.

Pellegrino, J. W., Chudowsky, N., & Glaser, R. (Eds.) (2001). *Knowing What Students Know: The Science and Design of Education Assessment: Executive Summary.* Available at: http://www.nap.edu/catalog/10010.html (Date of Access: Retrieved October 1st, 2010).

Pfundt, H. & Duit, R. (2009). Bibliography of students and teachers' conceptions and science education. Retrieved December 20th 2010, from http://www.ipn.uni-kiel.de/aktuell/stcse/stcse.html

Quinn, F., Pegg, J., & Panizzon, D. (2009). First-year biology students' understandings of meiosis: An investigation using a structural theoretical framework. *International Journal of Science Education, 31*(10), 1279-1305.

Rennie, L. J. & Goodrum, D. (2007). *Australian school science education national action plan 2008–2012: Background research and mapping.* Available at: http://www.dest.gov.au/NR/rdonlyres/94684C4C-7997-4970-ACAC-5E46F87118D3/18317/Volume1final_28August2008.pdf (Date of Access: July 29th, 2009).

Schreiner, C. & Sjøberg, S. (2007). Science education and youth's identity construction – two incompatible projects? In D. Corrigan, J. Dillon, & R, Gunstone (Eds.), *The Re-emergence of Values in the Science Curriculum* (pp. 231-248). Rotterdam: Sense Publishers.

Shayer, M. & Adey, P. (2002). *Learning Intelligence: Cognitive Acceleration Across the Curriculum from 5 to 15 Years.* UK: Open University Press.

Shepard, L. A. (2000). The role of assessment in a learning culture. *Educational Researcher, 29*(7), 4-14.

Shepard, L. A. (2002–2003). The hazards of high stakes testing. *Issues in Science and Technology, 19*(2), 53-58.

Sjøberg, S. & Schreiner, C. (2005). How do learners in different countries relate to science and technology? Results and perspectives from the project Rose. *Asia Pacific Forum on Science Learning and Teaching, 6*(2), 1-17. Available at: http://www.ied.edu.hk/apfslt (Date of Access: September 5th, 2006,).

Tognolini, J. (2005). *Using Online Assessment to Inform Teaching and Learning in Primary and Secondary Classrooms.* Available at: http://research.acer.edu.au/research_conference_2005/3 (Date of Access: December 17th, 2010).

Treagust, D., Jacobowitz, R., Gallagher, J. L., & Parker, J. (2001). Using assessment as a guide in teaching for understanding: A case study of a middle school science class learning about sound. *Science Education, 85,* 137-157.

Tytler, R. (1993). Developmental aspects of primary school children's construction of explanations of air pressure: the nature of conceptual change. *Research in Science Education, 23,* 308-316.

Tytler, R., Osborne, J., Williams, G., Tytler, K., & Clark, J. C. (2008). *Opening Up Pathways: Engagement in STEM Across the Primary-Secondary School Transition.* Available at: http://www.dest.gov.au/sectors/career_development/publications_resources/profiles/Opening_Up_Pathways.htm (Date of Access: July 4th, 2008).

Watson, J., Kelly, B., & Izard, J. (2006). A longitudinal study of student understanding of chance and data. *Mathematics Education Research Journal, 18*(2), 40-45.

Wiliam, D. (2000). *Integrating Formative and Summative Functions of Assessment.* Paper presented to the WGA 10 for the International Congress on Mathematics Education 9, Makuhari, Tokyo. Available at: http://www.dylanwiliam.net/ (Date of Access: August 18th, 2007).

Wilson, M. & Bertenthal (Eds.) (2005). *Systems for State Science Assessment: Executive summary.* Available at: http://www.nap.edu/catalog/11312.html (Date of Access: November 12th, 2010).

Wilson, M. & Sloane, K. (2000). From principles to practice: An embedded assessment system. *Applied Measurement in Education, 13*(2), 181-208.

Wright, B., & Masters, G. (1982). *Rating Scale Analysis.* Chicago, IL: Mesa Press.

# Part D

# Perspectives from Different Countries

# Chapter 16

# How Learning Outcomes in Science Are Specified and Measured in the English School System

*Robin Millar, Mary Whitehouse & Ian Abrahams*
*Department of Education, University of York, UK*

## 1    Context and Background

### 1.1    Assessment in the English Education System: A Historical Perspective

According to Richards (2000), students in England have historically been subjected to more national external examinations as the principal means of assessing and certifying students' attainment than in any other country in the world. By 'external examinations', we mean examinations that are set and marked by someone other than a teacher in the student's own school. Most of these are written pencil-and-paper instruments, though for some subjects oral and practical instruments are also used (or have in the past also been used).

Alderson (2003) refers to the bodies that operate this assessment process as an industry that has developed for the primary purpose of testing and statistically classifying children. It may be useful to look briefly at this history of this 'industry', and the influences that have shaped it. External examinations were first introduced in England in the 1850s for the purpose of selecting candidates for admission to the major universities. The University of Oxford Delegacy of Local Examinations was founded in 1857, followed a year later by the University of Cambridge Local Examinations Syndicate, and a similar body at the University of Durham. As Black (1998) notes, the abandonment of oral tests in favour of written ones had only become widespread in the universities around the 1830s. Some people saw them as "a necessary evil, their bad effects on learning being acknowledged by many who also judged that the universities in the new situation of growing demand for entry and the need to reassure the public of their standards, could not do without them" (Black, 1998, p. 10). On the other hand, MacLeod (1982) quotes the view of one commentator that "Public examinations were one of the great discoveries of nineteenth century Englishmen" (p. 1), and comments that "written examinations would eventually remove the undesirable consequences of unregulated favouritism, and would, if universally extended, have a salutary influence on society generally" (MacLeod, 1982, p. 1).

Examinations were seen by many as a significant improvement on other means of gaining entry to desirable courses, institutions, and positions – based on family background, connections, patronage. The drivers of change were a concern for social justice, and a desire to identify able students from less privileged backgrounds who could contribute to economic and commercial development.

Over the second half of the 19th century, other universities established similar bodies for assessing students for admission to their courses. Among them were two which, together with the Oxford and Cambridge boards, were the forerunners of the three Awarding Bodies we have today: the University of London Extension Board and the Northern Universities Joint Matriculation Board (JMB), founded by the Universities of Manchester, Liverpool, and Leeds (joined later by Birmingham).

When, in 1918, the first national educational qualifications for England were introduced (the School Certificate, taken at 16, and the Higher School Certificate, taken at 18), the universities' examination boards took on the role of providing these, offering the new qualifications in place of their own qualifications. This practice continued, with little change, until 1951, when the General Certificate of Education (GCE) examination was introduced to replace the School Certificate. This, too, was taken at age 16 (at Ordinary, or O-level) and age 18 (at Advanced, or A-level). Initially, seven examination boards in England offered GCE examinations, with two more being established shortly afterwards, one by another consortium of universities and the other by the City and Guilds of London Institute, a body with a background in assessment of vocational courses. In order to set examinations for school students, examination boards had to publish documents that were known as 'syllabuses', which set out the content that could be examined, and therefore acted as a guide to both teachers and question writers. The latter group included, for most examining boards, university academics and experienced school teachers.

In the 1950s, England had a tripartite secondary education system, established by the 1944 Education Act, consisting of Grammar Schools, Technical Schools and Secondary Modern Schools [1]. Selection was by an examination at the end of primary school (age 11) known as the 11-plus. This was an external written examination in English and mathematics, supported by psychometric tests based on IQ testing. GCE O-level syllabuses and examinations were designed primarily for grammar school students and were increasingly seen as unsuited to many of the students in the other types of secondary school. So, in 1965, the Certificate of Secondary Education (CSE) was

---

[1] This had many similarities with the German system of Gymnasium, Realschule, and Hauptschule.

introduced. This was aimed at the 80% of 16-year-old students who did not take O-levels and, prior to 1966, left school largely without formal qualifications. CSEs were administered by several newly established regional examinations boards which did not have direct university involvement.

Following the widespread introduction of comprehensive schools in many (though not all) local authority regions in England from 1986, the tensions caused by having two assessment systems for 16-year-olds (GCE and CSE) became more apparent. The two examinations had very different status in the eyes of employers and the public in general, and led to very different educational and career paths beyond age 16. Schools had to allocate students to the GCE or CSE route at the age of 14, and this was widely seen by many educationalists as a self-fulfilling prediction for many of the students assigned to the CSE route. To create a more equal system, GCE O-level and CSE were merged in 1986 to form the General Certificate of Secondary Education (GCSE). Mergers and rationalisation of the existing GCE and CSE examining boards led to four consortia in England offering syllabuses and examinations for the new GCSEs in a range of subjects.

Soon, however, it became apparent to those involved that closer links between the organisations responsible for examining at GCSE level and at GCE A-level were both sensible and desirable. Mergers followed, forming organisations which offered examinations at both levels. These new organisations also began to merge with the bodies offering vocational qualifications, which were becoming more common in schools. These moves were largely encouraged by successive governments, wishing to simplify the system and improve consistency by having fewer examining boards. The outcome is the three Awarding Bodies we have in England today: the Assessment and Qualifications Alliance (AQA), Oxford, Cambridge and RSA[2] Examinations (OCR), and Edexcel. The first of these is based on a university campus and has links going back to the Joint Matriculation Board (JMB) but is run as an educational charity; the second is owned and run by the University of Cambridge as a non-profit making organisation; the third has its origins in the University of London Examinations and Assessment Council and was initially run as an educational charity before being taken over by Pearson in 2003, becoming the first (and still the only) British examination board to be run by a profit-making company. The income of Awarding Bodies comes largely from the fees charged to schools and individuals to enter for one of their examinations.

Finally, it is worth noting that schools have, at all times, been free to choose to base their teaching programme for any given subject on the syllabus or specification offered by any one of the Examining Boards (or Awarding Bodies). In practice, there has been some regional preference in the board chosen for many subjects, and a

---

2  RSA stands for Royal Society of Arts.

certain loyalty to the board a school has adopted in the past, though this has weakened over time, with other factors playing a larger role in these decisions. Chief among these has been teachers' perception of the workload associated with implementing a specification, in particular its teacher assessed elements (discussed below).

We have outlined this history in some detail, in order to give a sense of how long established the English approach to assessing educational outcomes at school level is. As a result, it is deeply ingrained in the thinking and perceptions of all the main stakeholders in education: teachers at school and university level, students, parents, employers, and policymakers (including government ministers). It would be difficult to change substantially, for example, by giving a larger role in high-stakes summative assessment to teacher assessment of their own students. In general, the reliability and predictive validity of examination results is not seriously questioned by most stakeholders [3] – and the use of external examinations is widely seen to guarantee a level of 'fairness' to students that might be compromised by teacher assessment.

As has been mentioned already, intended learning outcomes are specified by a syllabus, which indicates the topics on which examiners can set questions, and may also give a general indication of the balance in the examination between knowledge (recall) and understanding. Older syllabuses for GCE O-level and A-level were largely a list of topics and sub-topics, with the expected level of student performance more clearly indicated in practice, and in the eyes of teachers, by the questions asked in previous years. The introduction of GCSE in 1986 did not materially alter this. Over time, however, the style of syllabuses evolved towards fuller and clearer specification of learning outcomes (what students should know, understand, etc.). Also in the 1990s, these documents came to be known as 'specifications' rather than as 'syllabuses'.

In this context, the introduction of the first National Curriculum in England in 1989 did not represent a 'quantum leap' in the extent to which the content of the curriculum was specified. At Key Stage 4 (students aged 15–16), the situation was quite the reverse; the national curriculum outlined subject content in less detail than many of the GCSE specifications current at the time. Required content was set out in 10 levels of increasing demand. An example, from the curriculum strand on Electricity and magnetism is shown in Figure 1. Teachers were very familiar with having course content specified in at least this detail. What was new was having the content of the science programme for primary school, and for the first three years of secondary school set out in similar detail – and, of course, having new national tests for students at ages 11 and 14 [4].

---

[3] Despite research evidence (Black & Wiliam, 2006) that this confidence might not be justified.
[4] These have now been discontinued.

Pupils should:
*Level 4*
- be able to construct simple electrical circuits.

*Level 5*
- be able to describe and record diagrammatically simple electric circuits that they have made.
- be able to vary the flow of electricity in a simple circuit and observe the effect.

*Level 6*
- understand the term voltage and be able to measure the potential difference across a conductor, such as a bulb, buzzer or heating element.
- understand how electrostatic charge generated in everyday contexts can be safely discharged.
- be able to recognise and explain simple electromagnetic effects in a range of common devices.

*Figure 1: Extract from the 1989 National Curriculum for Science (DES/WO, 1989, p. 56)*

Pupils should be taught:
a how to measure current in series and parallel circuits.
b that energy is transferred from batteries and other sources to other components in electrical circuits.
c that resistors are heated when charge flows through them.
d the qualitative effect of changing resistance on the current in a circuit.
e how to make simple measurements of voltage.
f the quantitative relationship between resistance, voltage and current.
g how current varies with voltage in a range of devices (for example, resistors, filament bulbs, diodes, LDRs and thermistors).
h that voltage is energy transferred per unit charge.
i the quantitative relationship between power, voltage and current.

*Figure 2: An Extract from the 1995 Version of the National Curriculum for Science (DfE/WO, 1995, p. 34)*

The first version of the English national curriculum, as Figure 1 shows, listed things that 'students should know', 'understand', and 'be able to do'. This language was maintained in its first revision in 1991, but changed when it was subsequently revised in 1995 to statements of what 'pupils should be taught'. Figure 2 illustrates this with an extract from the Physical Processes strand for Key Stage 3 (students aged 11–14). The reason for the change of wording was a growing recognition that a document that was legally binding could specify what schools and teachers had to teach, but could not state what pupils had to learn. The language of learning outcomes is, however, used throughout Awarding Bodies' specifications for GCSE and GCE A-level.

Assessment in science at GCSE and GCE A-level (and the assessments at ages 11 and 14 introduced with the national curriculum) have never been wholly based on written tests. From the start of GCE in 1951, science subjects have included a practical examination. In GCE, this often took the form of a test taken on a specified day, and with a specified time limit, in which students carried out a practical activity they had not previously seen or done, and wrote a short report on this, which was then marked externally. This was not without its logistic demands for the relatively small number of students taking GCE O-level and A-level, but was seen as impossible to implement with the much larger numbers taking GCSE from 1986. So students' practical capability came to be assessed in GCSE through coursework tasks carried out in their normal classroom, supervised by their normal teacher, and marked by him or her according to a set of criteria which were the same for all Awarding Bodies. The teacher's marking was then moderated by an examiner (often a teacher at another school, or a former teacher) who read a sample of students' reports and checked that the teacher's marking was to the agreed standards. A significant influence on the form this assessment took was the tasks developed by the Assessment of Performance Unit (APU) for their surveys of students' performance from 1980–84. These took the ability to design and carry out a practical investigation as the pinnacle of science performance; many of their examples of investigations were explorations of the effect of one or more independent variables on a dependent variable. This, under the vernacular label, 'fair testing', came to dominate national curriculum assessment of practical capability (Watson, Goldsworthy, & Wood-Robinson, 1999). A detailed account and discussion of this is provided by Donnelly, Buchan, Jenkins, Laws, and Welford (1996).

## 1.2 Assessment in the English National Curriculum

This has been already outlined in the previous section, so only a little more need be said about it here. The English national curriculum specified for the first time the science content that should be taught at each of four 'Key Stages'. Student attainment at the end of Key Stage 4 was to be assessed by the GCSE examination. As discussed above, intended learning outcomes at this stage are set out in more detail than the national curriculum provides in the specifications published by the Awarding Bodies. The examination papers produced by these bodies become public documents after they have been used once; there is no item banking. So past papers become an important resource for teachers in preparing their teaching, and preparing students for their examinations. These past questions are in effect operationalisations of the statements of the specification, though teachers would not describe them in these terms. They are, perhaps, the most significant influence on teaching at Key Stage 4, particularly in the year leading up to the GCSE examination.

A major innovation introduced by the national curriculum was assessment of students at ages 7, 11 and 14. At age 7, this was based entirely on teacher assessment. At 11 and 14, it involved a national test, plus teacher assessment. The first two versions of the National Curriculum (1989, 1991) set out the subject content for each science topic in a series of 10 levels of increasing demand. This also provided some guidance for those who wrote the national tests for the ends of Key Stages 2 and 3 (age 11 and 14). From the 1995 version of the National Curriculum onwards, subject content was prescribed for each Key Stage, and students' performance was to be assessed against a set of level descriptions. For each of the four main strands of the curriculum (scientific enquiry, biology, chemistry, physics), a hierarchy of eight levels of performance, plus a description of 'exceptional performance' beyond level 8, were set out. An extract from the 1999 version of the National Curriculum is shown in Figure 3. The national curriculum (QCA, 2004) explains that:

*"In deciding on a pupil's level of attainment [...], teachers should judge which description best fits the pupil's performance. When doing so, each description should be considered alongside descriptions for adjacent levels."* (p. 54)

Other official guidance (QCDA, 2009) tells teachers they should

*"... use their knowledge of a pupil's work over time to judge which level description is closest to the pupil's performance. In reaching a judgement, they should take into account written, practical and oral work, as well as classroom work, homework and the evidence from any tasks or tests."* (p. 10)

> **Attainment Target 3: Materials and their properties**
> *Level 4*
> Pupils demonstrate knowledge and understanding of materials and their properties drawn from the Key Stage 2 or Key Stage 3 programme of study. They describe differences between the properties of different materials and explain how these differences are used to classify substances [for example, as solids, liquids, gases at Key Stage 2, as acids, alkalis at Key Stage 3]. They describe some methods [for example, filtration, distillation] that are used to separate simple mixtures. They use scientific terms [for example, evaporation, condensation] to describe changes. They use knowledge about some reversible and irreversible changes to make simple predictions about whether other changes are reversible or not.
>
> *Level 5*
> Pupils demonstrate an increasing knowledge and understanding of materials and their properties drawn from the Key Stage 2 or Key Stage 3 programme of study. They describe some metallic properties [for example, good electrical conductivity] and use these properties to distinguish metals from other solids. They identify a range of contexts in which changes [for example, evaporation, condensation] take place. They use of knowledge of how a specific mixture [for example, salt and water, sand and water] can be separated to suggest ways in which other similar mixtures might be separated.

*Figure 3: Extract from Science Level Descriptions in the 1999 Version of the National Curriculum (DfEE/QCA, 1999)*

This approach has its origins in the recommendations of the Task Group on Assessment and Testing (TGAT), chaired by Paul Black, which was set up to advise on the assessment of the first national curriculum. This in turn drew on the experience of the Graded Assessment in Science Project (GASP) (Swain, 1989). The ways in which national curriculum assessment fall short of the ideas and ideals of the TGAT are discussed by Black (1994).

The key point to note here is that the use of level descriptions of the sort shown in Figure 3, to underpin teacher assessment grades, is rather different from the way in which curriculum content is specified. Consequently those charged with writing test items for the national tests at age 11 and 14 had to rely on professional judgment and experience to judge the level to which a given question corresponded. Over time, the rather vague (and under-theorised) view of progression in understanding which is implicit in the level descriptions was reified by teachers and other educational professional into a notion of 'levelness', which became an accepted and unquestioned part of teachers' discourse, and presumably of their thinking. Many teachers came quite quickly to believe that they could recognise, say, level 5 work when they saw it. At no point was there any serious challenge by teachers, or anyone else involved, of the many assumptions implicit in the level descriptions. In practice the levels appropriate to a given Key Stage (for example, levels 3, 4, 5 and 6 at Key Stage 3) became little more than labels for well below average, slightly below average, average, and above average. One final observation is worth making; students' levels, as assessed by their teachers on the basis of classwork, were consistently lower, at both age 11 and 14, than the grades given for the external national tests (DfE, 2010) – which rather undermines the popular view that teacher assessment cannot be trusted because it is likely to be too lenient.

Mandatory national tests at 11 in science, and at 14 in all subjects, were discontinued from 2007, after several years of pressure from teachers and others. Tests for age 14 are still produced and made available for schools to use if they choose, but the assessment of pupils at these ages is now based entirely on teacher assessment, using the level descriptions, and expansions of them (such as those produced by the National Strategies for Assessment of Pupil Progress (APP) described later).

### 1.3  Assessment for Learning

Both the Education Reform Act of 1988 which established the National Curriculum, and the Task Group on Assessment and Testing (TGAT) report (DES, 1988), emphasised the importance of formative assessment by teachers. Despite this, the introduction and implementation of formative assessment was relatively slow moving. Russell, Qualter, and McGuigan (1995), for example, commented that "the classroom reality of formative and diagnostic teacher assessment [was] seriously in need of development" (p. 489).

Influential work by Black and Wiliam in the late 1990s was to put formative assessment more firmly on to the agendas of both teachers and policymakers. This began with the publication of a review of research on the impact on learning outcomes of formative assessment, which concluded that this had a very significant impact on raising students' attainment across subjects and ages (Black & Wiliam, 1998a). To disseminate the findings and implications of this review more effectively to practitioners, Black and Wiliam also published a short report aimed at teachers, entitled Inside the Black Box (Black & Wiliam, 1998b). This was a 20-page, A5 sized booklet, with a striking black cover. It was widely read by teachers – and was followed up by Black and Wiliam with a project in three local authority regions in England to work with teachers to try to implement formative assessment. This has been reported in several journal articles and a book (Black et al., 2003).

The evidence of the impact of formative assessment on learning, and the strategies suggested in Inside the Black Box, were picked up by policymakers. From around 2004, formative assessment, under the label 'Assessment for Learning' (AfL), became a key component of the UK government's strategy for improving teaching and learning. A government minister described it as being at the 'very heart of good teaching and learning' (Miliband, cited in Smith & Gorard, 2005a). The Assessment for Learning Strategy (DCSF, 2008) outlined a joint project between the Department for Children, Schools and Families, the National Strategies (discussed below), the Qualifications and Curriculum Development Authority, and the Chartered Institute of Education Assessors, with substantial financial backing, to embed 'Assessment for Learning' (AfL) in schools.

The idea of Assessment for Learning has seemed to resonate well with many teachers' views on assessment, and so has become quickly and widely accepted as 'a good thing' to which teachers aspire. Even its advocates, however, recognise that implementation may be more challenging than many teachers suppose. A small-scale study by Smith and Gorard (2005b) of an attempt to introduce formative assessment in one school found that the progress of a treatment group receiving only formative feedback (but no summative marks or grades) was less than that of three other control groups. They suggest that this may be partly due to the fact that teachers in their study school had not been given the extended training and support offered to those in the implementation study by Black, Harrison, Lee, Marshall, and Wiliam (2003). The study raises questions about the quality of implementation of methods and approaches advocated by policymakers when minimal training and support are provided.

More recently, Black (2008) has also suggested that the widespread dissemination of AfL has resulted, in many places, in a diluted version of formative assessment which involves little more than continuous monitoring of student performance, often with little, if any, impact on subsequent teaching and/or learning practices. Despite these concerns about implementation, there is no doubt that the idea of 'Assessment for Learning' has become part of science teachers discourse over the past decade, and is an important part of the climate within which educational assessment currently takes place.

## 1.4 The National Strategies

Finally, in this overview of influences on the assessment of science education in England today, it is necessary to describe briefly the role of the National Strategies. Following the 1997 general election in the United Kingdom, the newly elected Government set a target that 80 percent of 11 year-olds should achieve, by 2002, specified standards in English in the National Curriculum tests. In order to reach these targets, a National Literacy Strategy was developed, proposing lessons that teachers should use and providing training in implementing them. Although this was not mandatory, it was widely adopted from September 1998 in most English primary (pupil age 4–11) schools. This was followed shortly afterwards by a National Numeracy Strategy – and in 2003 the two were combined under a single Primary National Strategy. This had become, in effect, a separate unit within the Department for Education and Employment. At the same time, the teaching approaches advocated by the National Strategy were extended into lower secondary school, as the National Key Stage 3 Strategy, with a small central team of people with a science teaching background co-ordinating of the work of Strategy Consultants in the local authority regions throughout England, who provided direct support and training for science teachers in their schools. Its homepage described the National Strategies (2010) as:

*"professional development programmes for early years, primary and secondary school teachers, practitioners and managers. They are one of the Government's principal vehicles for improving the quality of learning and teaching in schools and early years settings and raising standards of attainment."*

One of several strands of the Strategy focused on developing and promoting Assessment for Learning (see section 1.3 above).

With the ending of mandatory national tests at 11 and 14 in 2007, the National Strategy has been instrumental in developing an approach called Assessing Pupil Progress (APP) as a framework for teacher assessment. APP is a structured approach to pupil assessment in Key Stage 3 based on five Assessment Foci (AF) that are said to underpin National Curriculum assessment: (1) Thinking scientifically; (2) Understanding the applications and implication of science; (3) Communicating and collaborating in science; (4) Using investigative approaches, and (5) Working critically with evidence.

For each of these foci, eight levels of performance are described, with the aim of supporting teachers in:

1. making judgements about their pupils' attainment, keyed into national standards.
2. developing and refining their understanding of progression in science.
3. gathering diagnostic information about the strengths and areas of development of individual pupils and groups of pupils.
4. tracking pupils' progress over time to inform the planning of teaching.
5. planning teaching that is matched to pupils' needs.
6. supporting the transfer of meaningful information at key transitional points, e.g., from Key Stage 2 to Key Stage 3.
7. facilitating the setting of meaningful curricular targets that can be shared with pupils and parents.

As a means of attempting to standardise teacher assessment, in relation to national standards, teachers' judgments are guided by Assessment Guidelines that provide the criteria for achieving each of the eight levels for each assessment focus. In addition, teachers are able to access examples of assessed student work that is illustrative of performance at each of the eight levels (National Strategies, 2010). This builds on work that has already been undertaken in some local authority regions to support teachers in achieving greater consistency in teacher assessment while this was required alongside external national tests.

## 2    How Are Learning Outcomes Specified?

We now turn to the question of how learning outcomes in science are specified in the English education system. We approach this 'how' question from two angles. First, we will outline the form which the specification of outcomes takes. Then we will explain briefly the process by which these documents are developed and written, and who actually writes them.

### 2.1    How Science Learning Outcomes Are Specified in England: Format

As described above, a National Curriculum for science, alongside other subjects, was first introduced in England in 1989. There have been a number of reviews since that date, although there have been fewer changes for pupils in primary education (ages 5–11) than in secondary education. Primary schools still use the National Curriculum from 1999 (DFEE/QCA, 1999). This gives an outline of the subject content that should be taught (as in the example shown in Figure 1 earlier), together with descriptions of the sort of skills, knowledge, and understanding they will be expected to achieve, and a set of descriptors of levels of attainment (see Figure 3 earlier).

The National Curriculum for Key Stage 4 (ages 15–16) was revised in 2004 for teaching from 2006. The content that must be taught is described in a programme of study (QCA, 2007a) which is much briefer than previous versions. There is also a change in emphasis, with the requirement that:
"Teachers should ensure that the Knowledge, skills and understanding of how science works are integrated into the teaching of the Breadth of study."
The 'How science works' aspect of the national curriculum covered four aspects:
- Data, evidence, theories, and explanations
- Practical and enquiry skills
- Communication skills
- Applications and implications of science

The 'Breadth of study' lists in outline the areas of science that should be used to develop students' knowledge, skills, and understanding. This was described in much briefer terms than in earlier versions of the curriculum. Figure 4 shows the headings used and the required content for biology. Note that this is a minimum requirement for all students at this age.

---

**Breadth of study**
During the Key Stage, pupils should be taught the **Knowledge, skills and understanding** of how science works through the study of organisms and health, chemical and material behaviour, energy, electricity and radiations, and the environment, Earth and universe.
**Organisms and health**
In their study of science, the following should be covered:
a   organisms are interdependent and adapted to their environments
b   variation within species can lead to evolutionary changes and similarities and differences between species can be measured and classified
c   the ways in which organisms function are related to the genes in their cells
d   chemical and electrical signals enable body systems to respond to internal and external changes, in order to maintain the body in an optimal state
e   human health is affected by a range of environmental and inherited factors, by the use and misuse of drugs and by medical treatments.

---

*Figure 4: How Required Content is Specified in the 2007 Science National Curriculum (QCA, 2007a)*

A similar revision followed for Key Stage 3 (ages 11–14) for teaching from September 2008 (QCA, 2007b). Again the programme of study was specified more briefly than before, with a structure similar to the Key Stage 4 document. At Key Stage 3, this much briefer specification of curriculum content coincided with the ending of statutory tests for students aged 14. Thus teachers had more freedom to teach a curriculum they thought appropriate for their students.

*GCSE Science*
The assessment of the National Curriculum at Key Stage 4 (age 15–16) is operationalised through the GCSE examinations. The Awarding Bodies (ABs) each have one, or two, suites of GCSE Science specifications. Ofqual, the government regulator, produces GCSE criteria, both general criteria covering all GCSE assessments (Ofqual, 2007) and specific criteria for each subject (Ofqual, 2009). The GCSE Science criteria are a statutory document which determines the knowledge, under-

standing, skills objectives common to all GCSE specifications in Science. These criteria are intended to ensure comparability between the various Science GCSE qualifications developed by the ABs.

In developing a scheme of assessment of a Science specification, an AB must describe the learning outcomes in terms of:
- **subject content** – a list of the required science knowledge, understanding and skills
- **assessment objectives** – descriptions of the abilities students will be required to demonstrate through the assessment tasks

The GCSE Science subject content is based on the requirements of the National Curriculum. For example at Key Stage 4, the National Curriculum includes a section *Energy, electricity and radiations* (Figure 5).

---

In their study of science, the following should be covered:
a   energy transfers can be measured and their efficiency calculated, which is important in considering the economic costs and environmental effects of energy use
b   electrical power is readily transferred and controlled, and can be used in a range of different situations

---

*Figure 5: An Example of How Required Subject Content is Specified in the National Curriculum (QCA, 2007a)*

The GCSE Science criteria develop these statements further to make it clear which aspects of the topic must be included (Figure 6).

---

GCSE specifications in science must require learners to demonstrate knowledge and understanding of:
- the generation and control of electrical power and the relationship between power, current and voltage.
- the distribution and uses of electricity.
- the relationship between power, energy and time.
- energy conservation, the efficiency of energy transfer and the associated economic and environmental implications.

---

*Figure 6: An Example of How Required Subject Content is Specified in the GCSE Science Criteria (Ofqual, 2009)*

Awarding bodies then spell out in much more detail what they expect students to know and understand – and what will be tested in the examinations they set. For example, in a specification designed to meet these criteria (the OCR Science A. Twenty First Century Science specification), part of the first bullet point and the third bullet point above are addressed in module P3 Sustainable energy. Figure 7 shows part of that module.

---

**P3.1 How much energy do we use?**

5. understand that when electric current passes through a component (or device), energy is transferred from the power supply to the component and/or to the environment
6. recall that the power (in watts, W) of an appliance or device is a measure of the amount of energy it transfers each second, i.e. **the rate at which it transfers energy**
7. use the following equation to calculate the amount of energy transferred in a process, in joules and in kilowatt hours:
energy transferred    =    power         ×    time
(joules, J)                       (watts, W)         (seconds, s)
(kilowatt hours, kWh)    (kilowatts, kW)    (hours, h)
8. use the following equation to calculate the rate at which an electrical device transfers energy:
power               =    voltage        ×    current
(watts, W)               (volts, V)            (amperes, A)
9. understand that a joule is a very small amount of energy, so a domestic electricity meter measures the energy transfer in kilowatt hours
10. calculate the cost of energy supplied by electricity given the power, the time and the cost per kilowatt hour

---

*Figure 7: An Example of How Subject Content is Specified in a GCSE Science Specification (OCR, 2011a)*

The **bold** part of statement 6 above will only be assessed in higher tier examination papers, taken by the higher attaining candidates entered for the examination.

Note that, for progression to GCE A-level studies in Physics, a student will be expected also to have studied GCSE Additional Science, which includes further study of electricity and magnetism, beyond that which is specified by the National Curriculum (but also set out in national subject criteria for Additional Science).

There are five different GCSE Science specifications available to schools in England. Another way of ensuring comparability between specifications is to require the assessments to apply similar weightings to the different assessment objectives. The GCSE criteria specify the weighting between assessment objectives (Table 1).

*Table 1: Weighting of Assessment Objectives in GCSE Science Examinations (OfQual, 2009)*

| Assessment objectives | | Weighting (%) |
| --- | --- | --- |
| AO1 | Recall, select and communicate their knowledge and understanding of science | 30 – 40 |
| AO2 | Apply skills, knowledge and understanding of science in practical and other contexts | 30 – 40 |
| AO3 | Analyse and evaluate evidence, make reasoned judgements and draw conclusions based on evidence | 25 – 35 |

When writing assessment tasks – both examination papers and the assessment criteria for practical and investigational skills tasks – the Awarding Body must ensure that the overall weighting for the different assessment objectives is in the range specified.

In addition to the specific subject content there are some overarching ideas about science that must be included in all specifications. These are usually described under the heading 'How science works' (Figure 9).

---

GCSE specifications in science must require learners to demonstrate knowledge and understanding of:
- science as an evidence-based discipline.
- the collaborative nature of science as a subject discipline and the way new scientific knowledge is validated.
- how scientific understanding and theories develop and the limitations of science.
- the importance of scale in terms of time, size and space.
- how and why decisions about science and technology are made.
- hazard identification and the nature of risk.
- risk factors and risk assessment including potential benefit.
- the importance of working accurately and safely.
- ethical implications of science and its applications.

---

*Figure 9: GCSE Criteria for 'How Science Works' (Ofqual, 2009)*

Some of the statements above were introduced for the first time in 2006, and some of the specifications implemented them more fully than others. As the emphasis on this aspect of science learning was new, many teachers did not understand fully what was required and have found (and continue to find) it difficult to prepare students for assessment.

GCSE specifications in science must also encourage students to develop their skills in applying their knowledge and understanding. These skills are also set out in the GCSE subject criteria (Figure 10).

GCSE specifications in science must require learners to develop the ability to:
- plan practical ways to answer scientific questions and test hypotheses; devise appropriate methods for the collection of numerical and other data; assess and manage risks when carrying out practical work; collect, process, analyse and interpret primary and secondary data including the use of appropriate technology; draw evidence-based conclusions; evaluate methods of data collection and the quality of the resulting data.
- use models to explain systems and processes; develop arguments and explanations, and draw conclusions using scientific ideas and evidence.
- communicate scientific information or ideas and scientific, technical and mathematical language, conventions and symbols.

*Figure 10: Abilities Which GCSE Subject Criteria Require Specifications to Develop (Ofqual, 2009)*

The first of these statements is partly assessed through school-based assessment of students' work in planning and carrying out practical investigations to test a hypothesis. Until 2006, all specifications used the same framework and criteria for assessment of these abilities. Since then, however, a variety of approaches have been adopted. In some of the 2006 GCSE specifications, a small proportion of the marks were provided by teacher assessment of practical capability – whilst most of the marks were awarded for answers to written questions about a practical task. One set of specifications, OCR Science A Twenty First Century Science (OCR, 2005), used practical investigations, a data analysis task and a case study of a science-related issue to assess the abilities listed in Figure 10.

*Advanced Level Sciences*

For students studying science beyond GCSE (age 16–18), there is a wide range of qualifications available. Here we concentrate on the GCE A-level which is the most commonly used qualification to gain entry to university courses. There are currently four different A-level specifications for each of Chemistry and Physics and three for Biology.

Again, to ensure some comparability between specifications in terms of both the body of knowledge students are expected to learn, and the way in which grades are awarded, there are national subject criteria for each subject, which set out the body of knowledge that must be included, including How Science Works. For example, Figure 11 shows the criteria for one chemistry topic. Most of these statements will be assessed in the first year of the two year course; the bold statement (g) is assessed in the second year examination papers.

---

2.2 Formulae, equations and amounts of substance
  a) Empirical and molecular formulae.
  b) Balanced chemical equations (full and ionic).
  c) The Avogadro constant and the amount of substance (mole).
  d) Relative atomic mass and relative isotopic mass.
  e) Calculation of reacting masses, mole concentrations, volumes of gases, per cent yields and atom economies.
  f) Simple acid–base titrations.
  g) **Non-structured titration calculations, based solely on experimental results ...**

---

*Figure 11: Extract from A-level National Criteria for Chemistry (QCA, 2006)*

As at GCSE level, there is again a set of assessment objectives, which are spelled out in rather more detail than in the 2009 GCSE equivalents (Figure 8 above). These are shown in Figure 12. Of these, AO3 is largely assessed through school-based assessment, with the different specifications choosing different ways of assessing the skills.

**AO1: Knowledge and understanding of science and of How science works**
Candidates should be able to:
a) recognise, recall and show understanding of scientific knowledge.
b) select, organise and communicate relevant information in a variety of forms.

**AO2: Application of knowledge and understanding of science and of How science works**
Candidates should be able to:
a) analyse and evaluate scientific knowledge and processes.
b) apply scientific knowledge and processes to unfamiliar situations including those related to issues.
c) assess the validity, reliability and credibility of scientific information.

**AO3: How science works**
Candidates should be able to:
a) demonstrate and describe ethical, safe and skilful practical techniques and processes, selecting appropriate qualitative and quantitative methods.
b) make, record and communicate reliable and valid observations and measurements with appropriate precision and accuracy.
c) analyse, interpret, explain and evaluate the methodology, results and impact of their own and others' experimental and investigative activities in a variety of ways.

*Figure 12: Assessment Objectives for GCE A-Level Science Examinations (QCA, 2006)*

## 2.2 How Science Learning Outcomes Are Specified in England: The Process

Having outlined the format and level of detail in documents that specify science learning outcomes in England, we now turn to the process by which these documents, and other documents that influence the specification of learning outcomes, are generated.

*National Curriculum*
The first version of the National Curriculum, taught from 1989, was an element of the 1988 Education Reform Act. The government Department for Education and Science asked an expert group of science educators to write a consultation document with proposals for a science curriculum. After wider consultation, the National Curriculum was published. At the same time a new body was set up to administer aspects of the National Curriculum – the National Curriculum Council (NCC).

Subsequent reviews of the curriculum have been administered by the NCC and its successors. Each review has taken the form of a public consultation (more recently using the internet) alongside the opportunity for stakeholders, including the learned bodies, teachers, business, and industry to also make representations. However the final documents have been the work of civil servants. The most recent body responsible for curriculum matters – the Qualifications and Curriculum Development Authority (QCDA) was disbanded by the new government in 2010.

In 2011, the Secretary of State for Education announced a complete review of the whole National Curriculum. The review will be managed by the Department for Education. The evidence base for the review will be provided by an Expert Panel. One of the declared drivers for the review is the position of the UK in international comparisons such as PISA.

*Subject criteria*
The regulator (until recently QCDA) is responsible for developing the Subject Criteria which Awarding Bodies (ABs) follow to develop both GCSEs and A-levels. They consult with both the public and stake holders, before publishing the final criteria. The final decisions are made by the regulator, though the documents are approved by the Secretary of State for Education.

*GCSE and A-level specifications*
The Awarding Bodies develop the specifications to match the criteria. The work is largely done by professional examiners, who will be either practising teachers or former teachers. The AB needs to produce a specification and assessment that are acceptable both to the regulator – the Office of Qualifications and Examinations Regulation (Ofqual) – and attractive to the teachers who will choose the specifications to be taught in their schools. There is some flexibility in the criteria to allow some variety of content and assessment. This leaves some space for curriculum development and innovation. ABs will invite focus groups of teachers to comment on their plans, particularly if innovative modes of assessment are to be used. The development period is usually too short for any real trialling of new ideas. Specifications and sample examination papers must be approved before the qualification can be accredited.

## 3 How Are Learning Outcomes Assessed?

Having looked at how intended learning outcomes are specified, we now turn to the methods and instruments used to assess learning outcomes. Many of the key features of this have already been discussed and explained in earlier sections of this paper.

*Key Stages 1–3*
Currently, in Key Stages 1–3 (age 5–14), students' progress in science is assessed by their teachers. Teachers are required to assess the 'level' their students are working at, using a series of level descriptors as discussed above (see Figure 3). To help them carry out their assessment role, teachers can use test papers supplied by the government and also their observations of the students' written work and practical work. Exemplar material is provided through official websites (such as the QCA and National Strategies websites) to help teachers make their judgements.

*Key Stage 4 – GCSE Sciences*
At Key Stage 4 (age 14–16), there is a variety of qualifications available to students, including some vocational qualifications which we do not discuss here.

There are decisions about curriculum pathways for students and schools to make. Most students take one, two or three GCSEs in the sciences. There are common content elements between some of these. Figure 13 shows the relationship between the content taught in Science, Additional Science and Physics, Chemistry, and Biology. To satisfy National Curriculum requirements students must study the material in Science – that is B1, C1, and P1. To progress to A-level, students must also study B2, C2, and P2. Some may choose, or be encouraged, to study B3, C3, and P3 in addition, making a total of three GCSEs. Although we do not have space here to discuss applied science curriculum options fully, we have included GCSE Additional Applied Science, as this option enables schools to offer a different science course pattern for some students that also leads to two GCSEs.

All the GCSEs in the sciences, except the Additional Applied Science specifications, have the same assessment rules: 25% of the assessment is school-based assessment and the remaining 75% can be assessed in a maximum of three papers. All the specifications for 2011 use two or three papers for this assessment. The assessment is currently modular, with the possibility of the examinations being taken at stages through the course. The new government has expressed a wish to return to a linear approach with all the examinations being taken at the end.

Senior examiners writing papers must ensure that they assess material on the specification and that the paper has the correct balance between the assessment objectives. Questions are written by a team of examiners, many of whom are former or practising teachers. Examiners are paid by the Awarding Body for this work. After a paper has been drafted, it is scrutinised by a committee to ensure that it meets the specification requirements. Amendments are made and a further level of scrutiny is carried out before the paper is printed and sent to schools for use. To ensure security, all candidates take the paper at the same time. The papers are then sent back to the Awarding Body for marking by examiners, who are usually active teachers or retired teachers. Many teachers regard marking examination papers as useful experience to ensure they prepare their students as well as possible. They are also paid for this work by the Awarding Body.

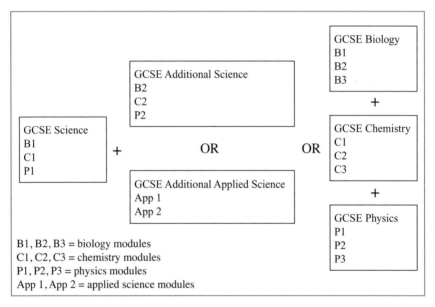

Figure 13: Science Course Pathways at Key Stage 4

A range of question styles are used in examination questions, including objective questions and short answer questions (Figure 14).

---

Many diseases are caused by viruses. Children are given vaccines to protect them against viral disease.

Complete the following sentences.

It is difficult to kill viruses inside the body because viruses ..........................................................................

................................................................................................................................................................

The vaccine stimulates the white blood cells to produce ...........................................................................

---

The Earth's oceans and atmosphere are sources of useful substances.

Chlorine can be obtained from seawater.

(i) Describe a test to show that a gas is chlorine.

................................................................................................................................................................

................................................................................................................................................................

................................................................................................................................................................

................................................................................................................................................................

(ii) State, with a reason, a safety precaution you should take when testing for chlorine gas.

................................................................................................................................................................

................................................................................................................................................................

................................................................................................................................................................

................................................................................................................................................................

*Figure 14: Examples of GCSE Science Short Answer Questions (AQA, 2011; Edexcel, 2010)*

For the new 2011 specifications there will be, for the first time in science, questions requiring extended answers worth up to 6 marks with a 'level of response' mark scheme (see Figure 16 below). The question shown in Figure 15 is written to address some of the following GCSE Subject criteria statements:

GCSE specifications in science must require learners to demonstrate knowledge and understanding of:
- the generation and control of electrical power and the relationship between power, current and voltage.
- the distribution and uses of electricity.
- energy conservation, the efficiency of energy transfer and the associated economic and environmental implications,

as well as an understanding of:
- science as an evidence-based discipline.
- how scientific understanding and theories develop and the limitations of science.
- how and why decisions about science and technology are made.
- hazard identification and the nature of risk.
- risk factors and risk assessment including potential benefit.

and demonstrate skills:
- develop arguments and explanations, and draw conclusions using scientific ideas and evidence.
- communicate scientific information or ideas and scientific, technical and mathematical language, conventions and symbols.

(Ofqual, 2009)


The question in Figure 15 is taken from sample assessment material. The mark scheme for the question is shown in Figure 16. For a 'real' paper, the mark scheme written when the paper itself is written is considered a 'first draft'. Once the Principal Examiner and other senior examiners for the paper have read a wide range of responses from students, they amend the mark scheme to ensure that all valid responses are covered by the marking scheme. This is essential to ensure that the team of markers, who will mark up to 600 papers each, are consistent in the criteria they use and the judgments they make.

The in-school assessment of practical and investigation skills varies across the specifications. To ensure that the work assessed is that of the student, the regulator is introducing from 2011 tighter controls than previously. The Awarding Body must set the tasks – for instance the hypothesis to be tested; some previous specifications allowed students or teachers to choose their own tasks. The students must write their final report or answer questions about the task under controlled conditions, similar to those required for examinations. However they do not have to carry out the research and practical work under such controlled conditions. Teachers will mark students' work and a sample will be sent to the Awarding Body for moderation, as described earlier.

> One way of supplying electricity to the country is with nuclear power stations.
>
> Some people are very concerned about the risk to the public from the waste produced in these power stations, while other people think the risk is very low.
>
> The Government will have to make decisions on this, but these decisions may be controversial.
>
> Explain why people have different views on the risk from nuclear waste, and why any decision made by the Government may be controversial.
>
> *The quality of written communication will be assessed in your answer to this question.*
>
> ...........................................................................................................................................
> ...........................................................................................................................................
> ...........................................................................................................................................
> ...........................................................................................................................................
> ...........................................................................................................................................
> ...........................................................................................................................................
> ...........................................................................................................................................
> ...........................................................................................................................................
> ...........................................................................................................................................
> ...........................................................................................................................................

*Figure 15: An Example of a GCSE Science Extended Answer Question (OCR, 2011b)*

| Expected answers | Additional guidance |
|---|---|
| **[Level 3]**<br>Most relevant points are present. A balanced argument is provided recognising the different points of view of local people, environmentalists and energy providers. The difference between real risk and perceived risk is discussed. All information in answer is relevant, clear, organised and presented in a structured and coherent format. Specialist terms are used appropriately. Few, if any, errors in grammar, punctuation and spelling.<br>(5 – 6 marks)<br>**[Level 2]**<br>A balanced discussion is attempted, but significant aspects of the 'pros' or 'cons' in the views of different groups, and the difference between real and perceived risk, may be omitted. May confuse chemical and radioactive poisoning. For the most part the information is relevant and presented in a structured and coherent format. Specialist terms are used for the most part appropriately. There are occasional errors in grammar, punctuation and spelling.<br>(3 – 4 marks)<br>**[Level 1]**<br>Recognises that waste is hazardous, but does not explain why. A balanced answer is not attempted. Answer may be simplistic. There may be limited use of specialist terms. Errors of grammar, punctuation and spelling prevent communication of the science.<br>(1 – 2 marks)<br>**[Level 0]**<br>Insufficient or irrelevant science. Answer not worthy of credit.<br>(0 marks) | **relevant points include:**<br>• uranium/nuclear fuel is a non-renewable energy source<br>• waste is radioactive<br>• radiation can cause cell damage/cancer<br>• remains radioactive for a very long time<br>• large amounts of energy from little fuel<br>• little $CO_2$ produced<br>• small environmental impact (compared to coal/oil etc)<br>• Government responsible for regulation<br>• perceived risk may seem high to people near waste sites<br>• real risk may seem low to people far away<br>• radiation is 'invisible'<br><br>**accept :**<br>• hazards of terrorist attack<br>• waste can contaminate water supplies, soil etc.<br>• must be must be kept securely for a long time in eg deep secure sites<br><br>**ignore:** arguments based on safety of power stations (Chernobyl, Japan etc)<br><br>**reject** explosion or other confusion with nuclear bomb |

*Figure 16: Mark Scheme for the Question Shown in Figure 16 (OCR, 2011b)*

## Key Stage 5 (16+) A-level sciences

Many of the instruments and procedures for assessing science at A-level are very similar to those at GCSE.

A-level assessment is also modular, with the opportunity to take examinations throughout the course. A-levels are a two year course, with the first half of the assessment leading to a lower qualification, GCE AS-level. Most students will take the AS assessment during the first year of the course and some will stop at that stage and collect their qualification, not continuing to the second year. For each year of the course, there are two examinations and one module of in-school Controlled Assessment which again assesses practical and investigation skills, though some courses also use part of it to assess aspects of How Science Works.

# 4 What Are the Implications for Classroom Practice of the Ways in Which Learning Outcomes Are Specified and Assessed?

Summative assessment in England of science learning outcomes is mainly by externally set and marked paper-and-pencil tests. At A-level and GCSE, these tests are based on published course specifications which list the content that may be assessed in greater detail than the national curriculum, or the national subject criteria which the course specifications are required to meet. These are high stakes examinations for students, as they determine access to more advanced courses, and jobs. They are also high stakes for schools, as data on the GCSE and A-level performance of students in every school is published annually, in the form of 'league tables' which place schools in order of their students' attainment.

Not surprisingly, this leads to considerable pressure on teachers to maximise the results that their students achieve. Whilst the use of external examinations means that teachers have no control over the specific questions set on a year by year basis, experienced teachers develop a familiarity with the sort of questions that are likely to be set for a particular specification and use this to 'teach to the test'. Pragmatically speaking, teaching to the test has the advantage that past questions operationalise the learning outcomes in a way that is far more succinct and useful to teachers than the learning outcomes in the syllabus statements themselves. However, increasing accountability of schools on the basis of their students' examination grades has led to teaching that is more narrowly focused on course specifications, using textbooks that are increasingly closely matched to a specific, named course specification. It has also increased the amount of teaching time used to familiarise students with the style of examination questions, and the amount of coaching in examination technique.

The national tests at age 11 and 14, introduced by the national curriculum (until they were discontinued in 2007), were not high stakes for students, but were decidedly high stakes for schools, as comparative league tables of schools (as outlined above) are also published for these Key Stages. Also, there is no equivalent at this level of the Awarding Bodies' specifications to articulate the course content more fully. Hence the national tests played a very large part in operationalising the expected standards – and much class time in the year leading up to the tests was spent on revision, test practice, and coaching in test-taking technique.

Turning then to the teacher-assessed aspects of the curriculum. At A-level and GCSE, students' capability in planning and carrying out a practical investigation is assessed in almost all courses, and this is done by teacher assessment, following criteria set out in the Awarding Bodies' specifications, with external moderation to ensure adequate consistency and uniformity. This, particularly at GCSE level, has not encouraged the kind of practice that it was intended to promote. In response to pressure on teachers to maximise students' marks, assessed practical work became formulaic (Donnelly, 2000) with teachers' primary concern no longer being the development of understanding of the scientific approach but simply the achievement of good marks. The Ofsted (2002) subject report on science noted that many teachers saw these 'investigations' in a very different light from 'normal' practical work. In a study on practical work by Abrahams (2006), one teacher made the distinction between assessed practical work and 'normal' practical work particularly clear:

> *„When we do investigations, I'm perfectly honest with the kids. I'll say to them that, as a piece of science, I think this is garbage, in terms of getting coursework marks it's superb. So we'll just play the game, we'll spend two or three weeks playing the game, getting some good marks, and then we can move on and do some science again. That's intellectual honesty." (p. 318)*

It could be argued that part of the underlying problem here is a lack of clarity within the science education community quite generally about what, exactly, students are supposed to learn about the processes of scientific enquiry – and how their level of understanding of this can best be assessed. As a result there are no well-established traditions and methods for assessing students' practical capability. What the English experience shows is that this can easily lead, in a high stakes assessment context, to teaching, learning and assessment practices that are a very long way from those that were intended (Donnelly et al., 1996).

At Key Stages 2 and 3, the national curriculum required teacher assessment alongside external national tests. Both were reported in terms of the 'level' the student had attained (see Figure 3 above). Teacher assessment and national tests were said to have equal weight – though external audiences tended to place more confidence in the national tests. However, the data, as we have commented earlier, in fact show that teachers' judgments were consistently more severe than national tests. The impact on practice of teacher assessment at these Key Stages has been primarily in terms of teacher workload. Also, in some local authority regions, procedures have been introduced to help teachers to standardise their judgements of students' levels. Teachers are required to assemble portfolios of examples of students' work that they judge to be at each level, then meet with other teachers to share and review these – leading towards a shared understanding of the characteristics of work at each level. This is widely seen as valuable for the professional development of the teachers involved.

# 5 The Relationship of Assessment Practices to Research and Theory

It should be clear from the complexity of the account above that assessment practices in science in England have evolved in response to events, rather than being the product of sustained rational planning towards a clearly defined and consensually agreed goal. There is no obvious model of progression in learning underpinning the way in which subject content is specified by the national curriculum. Content seems more often to be placed at different levels on the basis of past practice, and practitioner wisdom. In only a few places in the earlier version of the national curriculum was there any evidence that research on concept learning in science has influenced the way content was specified. Those instances disappeared with the move from 2004 to briefer statements of the national curriculum.

It would also be difficult to discern anything that could be termed a 'theoretical model' or 'perspective' on assessment underpinning the assessment practices that have been used. Practices are based on established practices, and on tacit views and ideas rather than explicit ones. In the past decade, the work of Black and Wiliam on formative assessment, supported by related work on assessment by a group of academics (Assessment Reform Group, 2005), have greatly raised the profile of formative assessment, and its recognition by teachers and policymakers under the label of 'Assessment for Learning'. It is still unclear whether the aspirations of this group can be implemented in schools in a manner that is reasonably faithful to their intentions (as discussed earlier). There are still significant questions about how formative and summative purposes of assessment might be reconciled and integrated.

Finally, it has been, and continues to be, commoner to criticise examinations and tests for emphasising outcomes that are easiest to assess rather than those that are of greatest value, and to bemoan the pressures on teachers to 'teach to the test' because these are high-stakes for students and for schools, than to consider and explore ways of harnessing assessment as a lever for modifying and improving practices, through its key role in operationalising objectives, and encouraging teaching towards specific performances that we would like to see students demonstrating.

## References

Abrahams, I. Z. (2006). *Between Rhetoric and Reality: The Use and Effectiveness of Practical Work in Secondary School Science.* Unpublished PhD thesis, University of York, UK.

Alderson, P. (2003). *Institutional Rites and Rights: A Century of Childhood.* London: Institute of Education, University of London.

AQA (2011). *GCSE Science A Unit Biology B1* [online] Manchester: AQA available at http://www.sciencelab.org.uk/resourcezone/sciencea.php (Date of Access: 27 January, 2011).

Assessment Reform Group (2005). *The Role of Teachers in the Assessment of Learning*. London: Institute of Education.

Black, P. (1994). Performance assessment and accountability: The experience in England and Wales. *Educational Evaluation and Policy Analysis, 16*(2), 191-203.

Black, P. (1998). *Testing: Friend or Foe? Theory and Practice of Assessment and Testing*. London: Falmer.

Black, P. (2008). Strategic decisions: Ambitions, feasibility and context. *Educational Designer, 1*(1), 1-26.

Black, P. & Wiliam, D. (1998a). Assessment and Classroom Learning. *Assessment in Education: Principles, Policy and Practice, 5*(1), 7-74.

Black, P. & Wiliam, D. (1998b). *Inside the Black Box*. London: School of Education, King's College London.

Black, P. & Wiliam, D. (2006). The reliability of examinations. In J. Gardner (Ed.), *Assessment and Learning* (pp. 119-131). London: SAGE Publications.

Black, P., Harrison, C., Lee, C., Marshall, B., & Wiliam, D. (2003). *Assessment for Learning. Putting it Into Practice*. Maidenhead: Open University Press.

DCSF (Department for Children, Schools and Families) (2008). *The Assessment for Learning Strategy*. Available at: http://publications.education.gov.uk/eOrderingDownload/DCSF-00341-2008.pdf

DES (Department for Education and Science) (1988). *National Curriculum: Task Group on Assessment and Testing*. London: Department for Education and Science.

DES/WO (Department for Education and Science/Welsh Offfice) (1989). *Science in the National Curriculum*. London: HMSO.

DfE (Department for Education) (2010). Presentation at DfE seminar; *Science, State of the Nation*, 29 November. Based on published data for 2000-2010.

DfE/WO (Department for Education/Welsh Office) (1995). *Science in the National Curriculum for England*. London: HMSO.

DfEE/QCA (Department of Education and Employment/Qualifications and Curriculum Authority). (1999). *Science. The National Curriculum for England*. London: HMSO.

Donnelly, J. (2000). Secondary science teaching under the national curriculum. *School Science Review*, 81(296), 27-35.

Donnelly, J., Buchan, A., Jenkins, E., Laws, P., & Welford, G. (1996). *Investigations by Order. Policy, Curriculum and Science Teachers' Work Under the Education Reform Act*. Nafferton: Studies in Education Ltd.

Edexcel (2010). *GCSE Chemistry Unit C1* [online] London: EdExcel available at http://www.edexcel.com/quals/gcse/GCSE-science-2011/Pages/The-exams.aspx [Date of Access 27 January 2011].

MacLeod, R. (Ed.) (1982). *Days of judgement: Science, Examinations and the Organisation of Knowledge in Late Victorian England*. Driffield: Nafferton Books.

National Strategies (2010). Archived National Strategies material can be found at http://webarchive.nationalarchives.gov.uk/20110809101133/http://www.nsonline.org.uk/ (Date of Access: 22 September 2011).

OCR (2005). *GCSE Science A: Twenty First Century Science Suite 2007* Cambridge: OCR available at http://www.ocr.org.uk/qualifications/type/gcse_2006/tfcss/index.html (Date of Access: 27 January 2011).

OCR (2011). *GCSE Science A: Twenty First Century Science Suite* Cambridge: OCR available at http://www.ocr.org.uk/download/kd/ocr_40691_kd_gcse_spec.pdf (Date of Access: 21 June 2011).

OCR (2011b). *GCSE Science A: Twenty First Century Science A181/02 Unit 1: Modules P1, P2, P3 December 2010* Cambridge: OCR available at www.ocr.org.uk/qualifications/type/gcse_2011/tfcs/science_a/index.html (Date of Access: 19 September 2011).

Ofqual (Office of Qualifications and Examinations Regulation) (2007). *GCSE Qualification Criteria.* London: QCA.

Ofqual (Office of Qualifications and Examinations Regulation) (2009). *GCSE Subject Criteria for Science.* London: Ofqual.

Ofsted (Office for Standards in Education) (2002). *Secondary Subject Reports 2000/01: Science.* A report from Her Majesty's Chief Inspector of Schools in England. Reference number: HMI 371. www.ofsted.gov.uk (Date of Access: January 2011).

QCA (Qualifications and Curriculum Authority) (2004). *National Curriculum. Science.* London: HMSO.

QCA (Qualifications and Curriculum Authority) (2006). *GCE AS and A-level Subject Criteria for Science.* London: QCA.

QCA (Qualifications and Curriculum Authority) (2007a). *Science, Programme of Study for Key Stage 4.* London: QCA.

QCA (Qualifications and Curriculum Authority) (2007b). *Science, Programme of Study for Key Stage 3.* London: QCA.

QCDA (Qualifications and Curriculum Development Authority) (2009). *Teacher Assessment and Reporting Arrangements. Key Stage 3.* London: QCDA.

Richards, C. (2000). Testing, testing, testing. *Education Journal,* June, *46,* 19.

Russell, T. A., Qualter, A., & McGuigan, L. (1995). Reflections on the implementation of national curriculum science policy for the 5-14 age range: Findings and interpretations from a national evaluation study in England. *International Journal of Science Education, 17*(4), 481-492.

Smith, E. & Gorard, S. (2005a). Putting research into practice: An example from the 'Black box'. *Research Intelligence, 91,* 4-5.

Smith, E. & Gorard, S. (2005b). They don't give us our marks': The role of formative feedback in student progress. *Assessment in Education, 12*(1), 21-38.

Swain, J. R. L. (1989). The development of a framework for the assessment of process skills in a graded assessments in science project. *International Journal of Science Education, 11*(3), 251-259.

Watson, R., Goldsworthy, A., & Wood-Robinson, V. (1999). What is not fair with investigations? *School Science Review, 80*(292), 101-106.

# Chapter 17

## An Examination of Turkish Science Curricula from a Historical Perspective with an Emphasis on Learning Outcomes

*Alipaşa Ayas*
*Faculty of Education, Bilkent University, Ankara, Turkey*

**Abstract**

Learning outcomes are steps for children in classrooms to climb up the stairs of science and feel how knowledge comes into existence in different science disciplines. Science education concentrates on several aspects from the nature of science to science process skills at one end of the continuum to developing basic concepts at the other end. This includes understanding the relationship among concepts to build principles, theories, and laws of science as well as its relation to the environment and technological developments based on scientific inventions. Any science curriculum to some extent has to deal with these issues in different countries around the world. Such is true for Turkey as well. The Turkish science curricula from elementary up to the end of secondary education have been under renovation from 2004. With the new changes, not only have the curricula changed but also the philosophy behind the curricula, together with methods of assessment. Also, it was the first time that a University-National Ministry of Education (NME) cooperation was established and that development was planned from a holistic way by developing supplementary materials to help better implementation in schools. In this paper, the changes will be dealt with by giving a particular focus on learning outcomes, on how they are perceived, how they are assessed and what implications they have for science classrooms. Also considered are teachers' reactions to the changes, parents' views, and how the exams (OKS, an exam for selecting students for high schools and YGS, an exam selecting students for different departments of higher education) are affecting the changes.

# 1  Introduction

Readers will see that there appear to be different approaches to define and assess learning outcomes in countries around the globe. It is intriguing that there appears to be no single way in defining and assessing learning outcomes in different countries. This becomes very clear by looking into the previous and following chapters in this book, Part C. The British has extensive experiences in assessment, and their experiences go back to mid eighteenth century (see Millar, Whitehouse, & Abrahams, *this volume*), some other countries, including Turkey, seemed to have their own trajectory of experiences. For example, it is interesting to see that Finnish assessment in science is not based on pre-defined learning outcomes (see Lavonen, Krzwacki, & Koinstinen, *this volume*). The Turkish experiences on the issue will be the topic of this paper with a historical perspective in science education.

Turkey has a population of more than 70 million. About 14.5 million are students at primary and secondary schools. Turkey is a bridge between Asia and Europe. It is also an associate candidate to the European Union. Turkey is a rapidly developing country, which has been affected very little by the recent recession or economic crisis which widely affected almost all countries (World Bank, 2010). Turkey is currently the seventeenth most developed industry in the world (Akkoyunlu-Wingley & Wingly, 2008).

From an official point of view, education is seen as one of the most important factors influencing the nation's development. Every citizen deserves a full education in respect to his/her abilities and desires; no one should deprive them of this fundamental right. In the 1982 Constitution of the Turkish Republic it is stated that "... the determination to safeguard the everlasting existence, prosperity, and material and spiritual well-being of the Republic of Turkey, and to ensure that it attains the standards of contemporary civilisation, as a full and honourable member of the world family of nation" (OECD, 1989, p. 97). To achieve this ultimate aim, the National Ministry of Education (NME) has been undertaking major developments in the school system and curricula, particularly in recent years. Beside the state's efforts to improve the quality of education, citizens also have a view that they should spend effort, including extra money, to support the education of their children. The majority of them send their children to private organizations called *dershane* (cramming schools) during weekends and evenings to prepare them for OKS and YGS exams (Students from high schools have to take a National Entrance Examination called YGS for admission to university).

Although the education system has undergone several changes, starting from the early days of Republican times, the basic framework has remained essentially the same. It consists of three main components: These are basic education, secondary education, and higher education.

Families, as it is probably the case in many other countries, want their children as a result of formal education to gain a high standard of living. They expect that secondary education will prepare their children for higher education institutions, which make their desire possible. It is thus understandable that students' first choices for further education at the University Entrance Examination are generally prestigious ones such as medical schools and some engineering departments. Second choices include departments such as teacher education, business, and administration. Unfortunately, the basic science departments such as chemistry, physics, and mathematics as well as some of the engineering departments are not popular with many students. Even though the places available at universities are fewer than the number of applicants, some of these science and engineering programs cannot fill up their available places (ÖSYM, 2009). The problem is that the graduates of these departments have difficulty finding a good and well-paid job.

Turkey is a rapidly developing country, especially since 2004. For a new phase of education, reform was possible because the country had an improving economy, greater governmental continuity, and a more stable political environment. Also, Turkey's candidacy for EU accession provides an unprecedented opportunity in many ways including a clear target for the future. The ultimate aim of the country is to be fully industrialized and be a full member of the European Community.

The educational system, as indicated above, basically consists of three main components that are briefly dealt with in the section below. Although some changes have taken place within the system, the general structure is almost the same as that during the Republican history (NME, 2005; OECD, 2007). Compulsory education within this system increased from 5 to 8 years in 1997, by Act number 4306 (Akyüz, 2009).

**Basic education** is eight years beginning at the age of 6 and is compulsory for every citizen. However, pre-schools, which serve 3–6 year-old children, aim earlier. There are several kinds of pre-schools, such as day-care centres, pre-primary classes and kindergartens. Also, the NME has decided to include the last year of pre-school within elementary education in some cities, in a pilot program. However, due to economic reasons, the inclusion of all children in pre-school education will take some time.

**Secondary education** covers vocational, technical, and general high schools *(lycees)* and gives four years schooling for pupils aged 15–18. Until 2008 it was only three years. Every student who graduates from elementary school is eligible to continue his/her education in these schools. In public schools it is free of charge. However, there is a nation-wide competitive exam to enrol in these secondary schools called OKS. The most successful students in the exam choose to be enrolled in the best schools in science, called science and social science *lycees*. The next group is enrolled in Anatolian high schools, and the rest to other types of school.

Normally, all students with a high school *(lycee)* diploma have the right to continue their education at **Higher Education** institutions. However, since the numbers of places available at higher education institutions are less than the number of applicants, there is a central examination system (called YGS) in Turkey. About 1,500,000 students took the 2010 YGS exam, but fewer than half were placed in the universities including the Open Education in the Anatolia University which does not have face-to-face instruction. However, as mentioned above about 70,000 of the places available are not filled because of their unpopularity in leading to a job.

## 2 Historical Developments in Science Education

In this paper, the historical developments of science education in Turkey will be examined with emphasis on the following questions:

- What are students expected to learn and what is actually learned?
- What is seen as learning outcomes? And, how are they assessed?
- What implication does that have for science classrooms?

To answer these questions fully may not be possible because there is very limited empirical research on the new curricula, which came into existence in 2004 and are not yet completed.

When the Republic of Turkey was founded in 1923 after the First World War, several innovations were introduced. One was changing the alphabet from Arabic letters to Latin. When the Latin characters were accepted as the Turkish alphabet in 1928, there were no written sources with these letters. There was a need to write books including science textbooks for physics, chemistry, and botany. Since the educational system was centralized in 1924 (Act 430), the writing of textbooks was done by a group of science teachers assigned by the NME. The textbooks were ready for the 1929–1930 academic year. According to Özinönü (1976), the process of instruction and content organization of textbooks were didactic. The main target of learning objectives was to teach at knowledge and comprehension levels rather than higher levels.

## 2.1 Effects on Science Education from the Western World

Science education in Turkish schools has been influenced by the curricular developments in the west after the 1930s at four particular times (Ayas, Çepni & Akdeniz, 1993). The first began in 1932 and continued up to the late 1940s. Western textbooks were translated into Turkish, but only the textbooks and no supplementary material. Besides helping students to acquire the facts and principles of science, the main features of this trend in terms of learning outcomes were to give impetus to the acceptance of individual development through social adaptation. However, since the supplementary materials for the textbooks were not translated into Turkish, it was difficult for teachers to learn about the philosophy, teaching processes, learning outcomes, and assessment techniques of these programs. Teachers had to take care of everything themselves as well as they could. The possible role of in-service training for a better implementation of the curriculum was not seen (Özinönü, 1976). In fact, there was no official body founded at that time for this purpose.

## 2.2 The Second Impact

The second impact from the West was experienced by the beginning of the 1950s. It resulted in the development of a few curriculum experiments. It was not particularly significant because only a few sporadic curricular experiments were developed with the help of American educators and supported by the Ford Foundation. Examples are the *Istanbul Girls Lycee* experiment and the *Ankara Trial (Deneme) Lycee* experiment (Soylu, 1984).

However, within this framework, there was another attempt through cooperation between the NME and the Ford Foundation. A National Committee on Education was established. The committee prepared a list of problems which were then considered in developed countries in order to find possible answers. The committee members visited several countries including Japan, USA, Britain, Germany, France, and Italy. They concluded in their report that it was impossible to completely copy one country or another, saying that if it were tried it would be a disappointment (The Report, 1961). The committee also noted that, in terms of science education, Turkish secondary schools provide too little opportunity in comparison with the visited countries in terms of practical or hands-on activities. Therefore, the students were not able to develop the intended learning outcomes as much as they should.

## 2.3 The Third Impact

While Turkey was still searching for a way to overcome her educational problems, the developed world was already in another stage of development, commonly known as post-1950s curricula. Sputnik, the first Russian Space Ship in 1957, caught the west by surprise. In response, the USA developed a number of curriculum programs, namely PSSC, CHEM Study, and BSCS, which later affected many other countries, including Turkey.

This was the third time, and maybe the most important, that Turkish science education was influenced by outside curricular developments. This time, the changes were directed at first only to secondary schools, *lycees*; later to elementary schools (Ayas, 1993). This time the move was more organized and led to the establishment of the Science *Lycee* in Ankara in 1964.

It was intended that the Science *Lycee* would use modern curricular materials (in science; CHEM Study, PSSC, and BSCS) with selected outstanding students. The teachers too would be selected carefully from amongst qualified science teachers. After two years of planning, with the help of educators from Florida State University, the school was opened in 1964 with 100 students (Ayas, Çepni, & Akdeniz, 1993).

Since science subjects have some similarities, it is not necessary to look at all three but take one of them as an example. In the case of chemistry, CHEM Study (Chemical Education Material Study) was adapted. There is no doubt that the CHEM Study project was an inquiry-oriented curriculum. The general characteristics of it were summarized by Berkem (1980) as follows:

- "Chemistry is taught as an experimental science; it is based on students laboratory work.
- It is aimed to show that forces among atoms and molecules determine the characteristics of material.
- Concepts of chemical energy and equilibrium are emphasized.
- Atomic structure is approached from the view of quantum mechanics.
- Traditional approaches such as dealing with the subjects according to their historical developments or including the important elements of periodic system has been given up.
- Examples of practical application of chemistry have been kept to a minimum" (p. 253).

At the start, the chemistry programme, like physics and biology, was covered in the three-year of *lycee*. After 1974, it was taught only in the last year – by increasing the weekly period from three to six hours. In order to prepare students for this chemistry course, the students were offered four hours of general science per week in the first year of *lycee* which concentrated mainly on chemistry topics (Berkem, 1980).

With regard to this pilot, the programs were redesigned to further adjust them to the Turkish context and to again pilot and disseminate them to a wider school setting all around the country, possibly to all *lycees*. During the second pilot about 100 general *lycees* and 89 teacher-training *lycees* were involved (Turgut & Pekgöz, 1976). As a result of this implementation, the Eighth Supreme Council of Education took the decision that the projects be implemented for a wider study (Turgut, 1981). The programmes were then finally disseminated to about 900 *lycees*, about 37% of the total in 1983 (Durusoy, 1984). This low percentage shows that, even after more than fifteen years, the curricula had still not reached many high schools. Throughout this period all other schools were implementing the traditional curriculum that had remained unchanged since the 1950s (Turgut, 1981). This created inequality within the centralized educational system, even though one of the main aims of the system is to provide equal opportunities for every individual.

The reason for lack of dissemination to a wider extent was financial. The support provided by the Ford Foundation ended in 1981. In addition, the Science Education Development Commission was abolished. It therefore became very difficult for NME to continue with such foreign projects. Thus, they were abolished in 1984 (Turgut, 1990).

In fact, a national conference held in Ankara in 1984 found that the projects as a whole were not sufficiently successful. The reasons given included lack of adaptation of the projects to pre-service teacher education, not enough in-service training, crowded classrooms, and lack of materials such as chemicals and equipments (TED *Bilimsel Toplantisi*, 1984). However, the saddest thing was that the experiences were that this implementation could not lead Turkey to design its own, original curricular programmes which might suit the national needs and conditions better (Ayas, Çepni & Akdeniz, 1993).

At the same time, although the projects were evaluated in order to improve them, the traditional programmes that were implemented parallel to the modern curricula in the majority of *lycees* were not touched. The main features of the traditional curriculum were:
- The learning objectives were stated in very general terms, there was no specific one for each topic which could easily be understood by the teachers;
- Most of the topics were out of date;
- The textbooks were insufficient in terms of quality and quantity;

- The suggested teaching methods were mainly unknown because there was no accompanying teacher's guide nor laboratory manual, unlike the foreign curricula;
- The topic headings and general learning objectives were the teachers' main source of information (Turgut, 1981).

Additionally, according to a survey carried out among the countries in the Council of Europe, it was found that in this traditional Turkish curriculum, practical work was hardly ever done due to lack of facilities (Thompson, 1972). It is not surprising that learning outcomes related to science process skills and practical abilities were not achieved.

In 1984 when the foreign curricula were abandoned, the parallel-running traditional curricula were also stopped. To develop a new curriculum, individual subject groups were established by the Board of Education in the NME. The group members were composed of subject teachers, inspectors from the NME, and a few academics from university science departments. The groups were asked to write textbooks in a short time.

For these new textbooks, teacher's guides and laboratory manuals that normally accompany textbooks in modern curricula were not produced. The objectives and some of the content headings were taken from the abolished foreign curricula, but not the teaching approach. According to some Turkish educators such as Turgut (1990), this was going back to the traditional way of curriculum development and implementation. Therefore, the science (physics, chemistry and biology) groups, as well as other subject groups, prepared a new curriculum.

The aims, objectives, and the syllabus of this new curriculum (chemistry) were published in 1985 (MEB, 1985). The course objectives are stated in very general terms. Teachers had to prepare their own specific topic objectives "if they can". The new curriculum mainly considered the development of:

- students' understanding of basic principles and concepts,
- students' scientific skills,
- students' critical thinking skills,
- positive attitudes towards laboratory and science,
- students' manipulative skills.

In addition, a more specific objective was:
- to stimulate and prepare high school *(lycee)* students to continue the study of science at post-secondary level.

The guidelines also indicated that most lessons should be carried out in laboratories, as individual work or group work. If this was not possible, at least demonstrations or films should be included, and there should be teacher-led classroom discussions.

These aims and learning objectives are in fact similar to those of modern curricula as stated by Alpaut (1984) at a national conference on the problems of education and instruction in secondary schools. However, they still lack specificity.

Elementary schools also had a curriculum change. In 2000-1 the new science curriculum began to be implemented. It emphasized active learning and student-centred learning in science. More specific descriptions of learning objectives were made for each science topic (Çalık & Ayas 2008). The curriculum gives more responsibility to students in their learning. However, science teachers were not fully equipped with the skills required to implement the curriculum adequately and to give more opportunities to students in their learning. The reason was a lack of in-service training in the new methods of student-centred activities. Moreover, although pre-service teacher education programs began to train new teachers for student-centred activities, the number of new teachers in the schools is few in comparison with current teaching staff. Thus, teacher-centred activities in classrooms were still dominant.

## 2.4 The Fourth Impact

The Turkish education system, therefore, was slowly adjusting itself to the developed world from 1990. However, the West had already shifted to another stage, (possibly due to breakdown of USSR and the Eastern Block) in which constructivist ideas became dominant (Çalık & Ayas, 2008). This was the fourth time that Turkey had felt moved to do something to renovate the school curricula, and the strongest. It applied from elementary up to the end of secondary education. In the case of science, which formally starts at grade 4 (age 9–10 years) of elementary education and goes to the 12$^{th}$ grade, the curriculum has been developed step by step. It began with grade 4 in 2003, and each year new curricula per grade have been added.

In summary, we have seen that until the millennium the innovations introduced into Turkey, driven from the West, were not successful in incorporating the desired curricula and learning outcomes, even with foreign advisors. Classroom implementation, even with the modern curricula (PSSC, CHEM Study and BSCS), was still traditional. In all these curricula only general objectives with a behaviourist approach were stated.

It seems that the difference between Western countries and Turkey with regard to the economical, social, and cultural contexts limited the effects of the curricula (Ayas,

Çepni, & Akdeniz, 1993). Also, having different types of school using different curricula was not justifiable because NME should provide equal opportunities to all students. The new curricula developed for all school subjects also included only general objectives, and there was no specific consideration of specific topic learning outcomes. That means there was still a need for updating the curricula to Western standards.

## 3 Developments in Science Education after 2000

### 3.1 How the New Developments Differed

The new developments were different from the previous ones, because all the Commissions established included Turkish Educators and teachers. There was a more organized effort on how to develop the new curricula in all subjects. Some general meetings were held with university academics, experienced school teachers, and key staff from the NME. They decided on the philosophy, psychology, and general approaches to teaching and learning, parallel to the developments in the West. They set up basic rules to be followed in the process of developing a new curriculum for each subject area (OECD, 2005; MEB, 2005).

In this new initiative the curricula are revised by considering innovations in technology, the subject field, educational sciences, and European Union standards. A needs analysis was conducted by a specialized commission for each subject, from elementary up to the end of secondary level, in line with opinions obtained in a democratic way from non-governmental organizations, universities, inspectors, administrators, and teachers.

The subject commissions worked on basic competencies that every student should have in the subject field, conducting a skills analysis for each course, and forming concept maps and connections across courses. Materials needed for the effective implementation of the programs, and information technology and guidebooks for teachers, were prepared following the examples of other countries.

In the case of the science curriculum, grades 4–8 (ages 10–14) are considered as a whole. Before developing the science curricular materials in detail a general framework was identified (MEB, 2005). It includes the topics, learning objectives, teaching-learning methods, and a hierarchical development of concepts, skills and attitudes. The new curriculum not only includes the titles of topics and general objectives, as in the traditional curriculum, but also students' specific learning outcomes. They are called "students' gained skills and abilities" in the curricular documents. In addition, teacher's guides, student workbooks, and suggested ideas for performance-based assessments are provided. It is worth mentioning at this stage that Turkey also decided, from 2003, to take part in international studies such as PISA and TIMSS to see how our students rank among OECD and other countries around the globe.

## 3.2 General Learning Objectives

In order to see how **general learning objectives** were phrased in the new curriculum some examples are given in the following (MEB, 2005):

- To enable students develop themselves so they become scientifically literate.
- To equip students to learn and understand the natural world, and to enjoy living with its richness.
- To encourage students to develop curiosity in the scientific and technological developments and events around us.
- To associate and understand the relationship between science, technology, society and the environment.
- To enable students to structure new knowledge by reading, searching and discussion.
- To help students develop knowledge, curiosity, attitudes and experience about science and science-related professions or jobs.
- To enable students to learn how to learn and follow the changing nature of knowledge and jobs, so as to update their knowledge and skills by themselves in their profession.

When we look at these general objectives we see that they are phrased similar to that of many western countries.

These are only the main objectives of the science subjects from elementary up to the end of secondary education. The curriculum development teams in each subject area state specific subject and topic objectives also. The specific learning outcomes for each topic are stated in terms of "students' gains" as a result of learning. This is in fact quite new for school teachers because they used to decide and write down students learning outcomes by themselves. However most teachers had difficulty in writing them, so there was copying from each other because of inspection rules. Inspectors visit schools from time to time and check whether teachers prepare their lesson, unit and yearly plans, including learning outcomes. Now it is possible, with the new science curricula for teachers to find the information via supplementary materials beside textbooks.

# 4 Learning Outcomes

## 4.1 The new Vision

In this section, I give a more specific examination of learning outcomes, focussing on the questions given in the last paragraph of the introduction section. To answer these questions there is a need for research into the current science curricula for elementary schools, and physics, chemistry and biology curricula for secondary education.

The Grade 4–8 science curriculum strongly emphasizing scientific literacy as the underlying vision of science curricula (MEB, 2005), and presents a number of issues. These are:

- teaching less but deep is more important,
- teaching the nature of science is a key idea,
- constructivist learning is the main focus to consider individual differences,
- measurement and assessment vision is renewed,
- developmental stags and individual differences are considered,
- the order of presenting concepts and knowledge should be coherent,
- fitting other subject areas and interdisciplinary topics are carefully considered.

By looking at the main ideas we can easily say that the science curriculum considers what students should learn in science classrooms. There is a reduction in content in comparison with the old science curriculum. There are fewer topics than the previous curriculum because many teachers and inspectors' reports indicated that it was impossible to cover all the topics in the old curriculum (MEB, 2005; MEB, 2006). Therefore, elimination of some topics could make it possible for students to learn more deeply, and for teachers to cover all the topics.

However, for the questions, "is it possible now to cover the topics? And, do the students learn the intended knowledge and skills?" The answer is clearly no. This is in spite of the fact that, since the late 1990s, there has been a considerable change in initial teacher education with programs and courses renewed, and with an increased emphasis on methodology and work in schools (Grossman & Sands, 2008; Grossman, Onkol & Sands 2007). However, the newly produced teachers (Akşit, 2007) are greatly outnumbered by those still in the system, and they have not received enough in-service training to cope with the new curricula. The teachers who need in-service training are many, because the total number of teachers is over 600 000. Many of these, in all subject areas, still need some type of training related to the new curricula. This new curricular change represents, in fact, the most comprehensive effort in Republican history in many respects. That means teachers from all subject areas need in-service training. It is costly, and therefore sometimes becomes unaffordable in terms of both finance and finding professional teaching staff on the new curricula, either from the universities or from the NME.

Another important difference with the old science curriculum is in the way learning outcomes are phrased. In the old science curriculum (for elementary schools grade 4–8) a behavioral approach was used: goals, aims and behavioral objectives were stated for each topic. In the new curriculum they referred to as "students' gains". That seem to be more student-centered and constructivist than the old curriculum (ERG, 2005).

The same is true for *lycee* physics, chemistry and biology curricula. The change for the *lycee* curricula is in fact a real shift from traditional to constructivist ideas. Because in the old curricula only general objectives for each science subject were given. The rest was up to the teachers. In the new science curricula, besides general aims and objectives, specific learning outcomes for each topic are now given (MEB, 2007 a, b, c; MEB, 2008 a,b,c,d,e,f; MEB 2009 a, b, c). This is a desirable development in science teaching in Turkey but, because of lack of in-service training on the implementation of new curriculum, there are severe problems in implementation. Teaching still therefore tends to be traditional in many cases: teachers use lecturing and question-answer methods, followed by paper-pencil-based traditional assessment. This was what they used to do in the old curricula. In fact, resistance to change is a common problem in education as argued by Fullan (2001). Akyüz (2009) also indicates that there are always very bright ideas on paper in education but the implementation is often problematic in Turkish classroom.

## 4.2 The New Curricula

Looking more closely at the science curricula at both elementary and secondary levels, we can easily see that the new curricula are parallel to the USA, Canada (especially British Columbia), Ireland and Singapore. This was also indicated by the science curriculum development committee of the NME (MEB, 2005; MEB, 2006, MEB 2007a). In terms of content and spiral approach it is similar to that of the Irish and Canadian science curricula (ERG, 2005). It also emphasizes science-technology-society and environment (STSE), as is the case in Canada. Even the suggestions to teachers, parents and students are similar to that of these countries.

Figure 1 shows the relationship between key topics of the science and technology curriculum and how science process skills (SPS), science-technology-society and environment (STSE), and attitudes and values (AV) are inter-related. This figure is also used for *lycee* (secondary) physics curriculum. The physics curriculum development committee indicated that they have examined the physics curricula of more than 30 countries before developing the current one (MEB, 2007a). In the case of chemistry and biology the committees indicated only that they have also examined other countries curricula without indicating the number and names of countries.

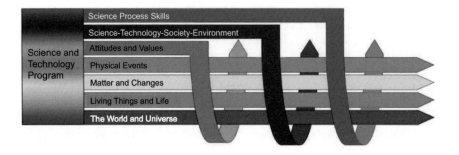

*Figure 1: The Relationship Among Science-Technology-Society and Environment (STSE); Science Process Skills; and Attitudes and Values in 2004 Science Curriculum (Taken and Translated from MEB, 2005, p. 29)*

In examining the learning outcomes, we see that they are clearly stated and expressed in measurable and observable terms for both elementary and secondary science curricula. Learning outcomes are parallel to general aims and goals of science education and stated in terms of "students' gains" in STSE, SPS and AV areas.

The wording of each learning outcome completes the stem: "It is expected that in the related topic the students ....". The stem is followed with a verb, i.e. explain, prepare, indicate, perform an experiment, search and present, give examples, show with an experiment etc. The lists are not necessarily exhaustive, however, and teachers may choose to address additional items that also fall under the general requirement set out by the outcome in the curriculum. Table 1 gives examples from Science Curricula at different grades and subjects.

If we look at the learning outcomes from the perspective of Bloom's *Taxonomy*, it can be easily observed that they are in the three domains: cognitive, affective and psychomotor. As normally expected, these domains mainly include the following:
- The cognitive domain includes *knowledge, understanding and application, and higher mental processes*.
- The affective domain specifies attitudes, beliefs, and the spectrum of values and value systems.

- The psychomotor domain concerns those aspects of learning associated with movement and skill demonstration, and integrates the cognitive and affective consequences with physical performances (Bloom, 1956).

Table 1: Examples of Learning Outcomes in Science Curricula at Different Grades and Subjects (Taken and Translated from MEB, 2005, 2006, 2007 & 2008)

| Subject and Level | Learning outcomes | Sample activity | Explanations |
|---|---|---|---|
| Science and Technology Grade 5 Unit 3 | 3. It is expected that in relation to organs in the excretory system, the student: 3.1 shows the places of excretory system organs and structure on human body model and explain their roles briefly. | Students identify excretory system organs on a human body diagram or human body model (3.1). | 3.1 Organs of excretory system including kidney, ureter, urethra and bladder are taught but details are omitted at this stage |
| Physics Grade 9 Unit 1 | 1. It is expected that in relation to classification of matter, the student: 1.1 explains that mass and volume are common features of matter. 1.2 classifies matter based on its state. | Kinds of matter: can you classify the substances you see in the near environment? | 1.1 This learning outcome should be dealt with at macro level, for example photon should not be mentioned at this stage 1.2 Remind students, solid, liquid and gas as the states of matter, then explain plasma with examples from daily life. |
| Chemistry Grade 10 Unit 1 | 1. It is expected that in relation to chemical entities, the student: 1.1 differentiates among atom, molecule, ion and radicals. | Examples of atom, molecule, ion and radical could be examined. There could be a reaction between these different entities and each of them looses their properties after the reaction (1.1). | 1.1 It is important to emphasize that atoms, molecules, ions and radicals are known as 'chemical entities'. Radicals are introduced as simple examples like •NO, •NO2, •ClO2 and these entities are similar to molecules by definition. Also, atoms like •H, •O•, •Cl could be considered as radicals with incomplete orbits. |
| Biology Grade 11 Unit 1 | 1. It is expected that in relation to structure of plants, the student: 1.3 shows the basic structure of a fanerogam on a diagram. 1.6 states the functions of a body and gives examples of main types of plant body. | Investigation of body and roots of different plants on microscope (1.3, 1.5, 1.6). | 1.6 Gramineous and ligneous types of bodies are exemplified. Also, structure of plant barks should be mentioned. |

## 4.3 Assessment in the New Science Curricula

The curricula for all levels of education have to guide teachers in assessing students. Sample questions, problem-solving exercises, checklists, sample rubrics for assessment, concept maps, self-peer appraisal techniques, report preparation, are all provided (i.e. MEB, 2005, 2007a, b, c). However, we must ask if teachers have the knowledge and skills to make use of some of these examples, and we come again to the issue of training teachers in in-service programs. Even the quality of existing in-service training is questionable to teach skills required for the new curricula (Elmas & Geban, 2010; Güneş, Ateş, Eryılmaz, Kanlı, Serin, Arslan & Gülyurdu, 2010; Şenel Çoruhlu, Er Nas & Çepni, 2009; Akşit & Sands, 2006a). There is therefore a discrepancy between what students are expected to learn and what they actually learn.

In addition, teaching and learning is not only affected by the teachers' teaching habits, or lack of in-service training, or resistance to change, but also from a number of other issues. These include student learning habits and nation-wide competitive exams (SBS and YGS). Learning outcomes may be clearly set out in the curriculum, but learning is not happening as intended. Although a deeper or higher level of learning is planned beside low level of learning, it is mostly the low level which is attained.

The PISA 2009 Report, recently published, indicates that Turkish students scored in science (in terms of scientific literacy) in the last three countries among OECD countries (OECD, 2010). There were no students who scored at level 6 among the Turkish science sample. The majority of students are at level two and below of the six categories (MEB-EARGED, 2010b). Even though the major emphasis in the new science curriculum (grades 4–8 ages, 10-14) has been to develop scientific literacy, still Turkish students scored poorly in the PISA test.

However, there was a 30-point increase from the 2006 PISA test, in which the average of the Turkish sample was 424 (MEB-EARGED, 2010a; Alacacı & Erbaş, 2010). The average score for scientific literacy among all OECD countries was raised 3 points (from 498 in 2006 to 501 in 2009) while Turkish students' score was raised ten times more.

It seems that the results presented in the 2009 PISA report should be carefully interpreted to answer the question whether the new curricula have had an effect on the 30 points average increase in the Turkish sample.

## 4.4 Research with the New Curricula

Since the curricula are new, only limited empirical studies have been done so far. Some new research is just coming out for publication in journals, and presentations are being made in the conferences. However, my own and my research teams' experiences during the implementation of the science curricula in elementary and secondary schools; and our ongoing research in schools with teachers, students, school administrators, curriculum developers in some subjects, and staff in the central units of the NME; and our contacts with parents, show some other problems besides the ones mentioned above.

Although at first it seems that there are impressive developments in the system in comparison with earlier curricula, the problems in implementation cast a shadow over the new developments. For example, a recently-published report based on a survey conducted by the Research and Development office of the NME (EARGED) into the elementary science curriculum (grades 4–8) with teachers and students shows that 73 % of teachers are still using lecturing, 38.8% indicate that students are copying what the teacher has written on the board, and they sometimes do group work (EARGED, 2009). There is no evidence from the report that students carry out practical activities or have opportunities to take responsibility for their own learning.

In some cases, we know that parents do their children's assignments, because some of the performance assignments are difficult for students. This is actually given as a reason why parents do the assignments! The issue was even raised in Parliament between MPs of the ruling party and main opposition party during the budget discussion of 2011. There may also be cultural reasons for this, as children possibly do not trust themselves to perform the assignment.

Culturally and traditionally, many students and teachers are not used to student-centered approaches. The traditional Turkish family has an authoritarian character, although it is changing fast. Therefore, the teacher is the respected person in the classroom and students believe that he/she knows "everything" and is able to transfer knowledge from his/her head directly to theirs, – unlike Bodner's (1990) argument that there is no way that knowledge can be transferred from teacher to student without any change. Hence, classrooms stay as they always have been – authoritative unit in teaching/learning activities. Both teacher-pupil relationships and the quality of learning continue to be affected.

## 4.5 Impediments to the New Curricula

Because of the nature of the examinations, SBS and YGS, which are mostly based on academic knowledge with most questions testing students' skills of remembering and recalling, they are the most important obstacles to the new curricula (Şahin, 2010). Although some questions in these exams are intended to assess higher level thinking skills, the culture of preparation for them in *dershanes* (cram schools) have a damping down affect on chilren's learning of the subject matter. Most *dershane* teachers emphasize remembering and recalling of subject matter in order to prepare for the exams. In schools, teachers also concentrate on solving numerical problems after a short lecture on the topic in the lesson, parallel to *dershanes*. Learning outcomes are put aside, as preparation for the nationwide exams takes over. Thus, methods of teaching in science classrooms are limited to almost full lecturing, with limited question and answer and discussion. There is very little, if any, of real-life implementation of learned concepts and topics, student-led question-answer sections, hands-on laboratory activities, carrying out projects as required by the new curricula in all science subjects in elementary and secondary *(lycee)* levels. It also limits assessment methods to paper and pencil tests, in most cases, at the expense of performance-based assessment procedures.

Parents do not have to buy school books because they are provided by the state to all students, but teachers in many cases tend not to follow them. Rather, they use free-of-charge books prepared for the SBS and YGS exams normally used in private *dershanes*. We can estimate the high cost of providing textbooks free of charge by the government (about 100 million books are provided free).

We can also return to the lack of sufficient in-service training to enable teachers to better implement the new curricula and use the state-provided textbooks. Many teachers clearly indicate that they did not have in-service training. Those who did, had only about three days which they thought was insufficient to cope with the current changes in teaching-learning methods and assessment techniques (Elmas & Geban, 2010; Güneş, Ateş, Eryılmaz, Kanlı, Serin, Arslan & Gülyurdu, 2010). In an evaluation of in-service training on the new curricula it was found that many of the participants were not happy with the training provided (Ayas, Akdeniz, Çepni, Baki, Çimer & Odabaşı Çimer, 2007).

Black and Wiliam (1998) indicate that "learning is driven by what teachers and students do in the classrooms". Therefore, as a key person in helping children in organizing their learning the quality of teachers, and their initial and later training, are very important. Black and Wiliam also advised using formative assessment in the classroom to better develop students' knowledge and skills. To learn what is happening inside the classroom is, in fact, a necessity if one hopes to follow a new change.

It has not been done extensively in schools of Turkey yet. For a change to happen, classroom activities should concentrate on at least four activities: questioning, feedback through marking, peer- and self-assessment, and formative use of summative tests (Black, Harrison, Lee, Marshall & Wiliam, 2002). Unfortunately, the formative use of assessment, although it is required by the new curricula, is one of the least performed activities by teachers (MEB, 2005; EARGED, 2009).

Learning objectives are stated in clear, measurable and observable terms but teachers do not use them to design lessons in the classrooms (MEB, 2005; MEB 2007a, b, c). Therefore, traditional teaching and assessment are still going on in the system. So, learning outcomes are not driven by classroom implementation or assessment of the new curricula as intended, old traditions and habits are still used.

The new curricula provide to teachers lesson, unit and yearly plans as a guide. Before, they had to prepare them for themselves. However, teachers' use of them is not very satisfactory because, according to the results of limited research done on the topic, they still use the traditional way of teaching (EARGED, 2009; Elmas & Geban, 2010). In addition, the quality of teachers limits the implementation (Güneş, Ateş, Eryılmaz, Kanlı, Serin, Arslan & Gülyurdu, 2010; Şahin, 2010; Akşit & Sands, 2006b).

A further issue affecting implementation is crowded classrooms. In some cases, the number of students makes it impossible to use new ideas as advised by the current curricula in assessment, based on students' work and effort (Şahin, 2010). Class size ise being reduced yearly by the efforts of NME, by establishing new schools and by improving infrastructure. However, in many cases their may still be around 40 or more students. Teachers have difficulty coping with such a crowded group in performance-based assessment, as following each student with their individual differences is too time consuming to assess the performance of each. Therefore, teachers tend to use tradational paper-pencil teacher-made tests, either short answer or multiple choice, or other types of objective questions.

## 5 Conclusions and Suggestions

The new science curricula represent a much better program than the old, from many perspectives. As an example, we may consider its emphasis on developing scientific literacy. Since some of those who take science will not continue their education in a science-related area, they need to make their decisions accurately in a scientific society. For that, they need skills such as critical and creative thinking, problem-solving, using information technology and caring about social life (MEB, 2005), all of which are main issues considered in the new science curricula.

The most problematic part in the new curricula is related to its implementation as planned. As discussed above, the key person is the teacher. The quality or training of teachers is definitely a major limitation to the implementation. Since the new curricula have changed teaching methods, types of activities, students' roles in learning, and assessment methods, there is much for the teacher to learn. A teacher-centered approach is replaced by a student centered one. However, changing things on paper does not guarantee the hoped-for result. To return to the issue of classroom assessment where the teacher has to use not only paper-pencil tests but now also performance-based strategies. Performance-based assessment requires different data collection techniques such as observation, student self-assessment and peer-assessment, quizzes and tests (written, oral, practical), samples of student work, projects, oral and written reports, performance reviews, and portfolio assessments. These are all new for most Turkish science teachers and they need training, not yet done properly. The *European Commission Report on Science Education* (EC, 2007) indicates that: "Teachers are key players in the renewal of science education. Among other methods, being part of a network allows them to improve the quality of their teaching and supports their motivation". This notion is particularly critical if in-service training cannot be provided for teachers.

NME has planned and conducted studies at elementary and secondary levels, every three years starting from 2002, to determine students' achievements and related factors on achievement. The results for the 2008 study at elementary level (EARGED, 2009), as briefly indicated above, are not very pleasing. The report related to secondary subjects is not published yet. However, it is not expected that the results will be much different from those for the elementary level. Teachers are predominantly using teacher-centered instruction and not the student-centered activities suggested by the new curricula. Also, students' achievement level with respect to target grade level learning objectives decreases over the years. It is highest at grade 4 and lowest at grade 8 (elementary). In the EARGED (2009) report, it was also indicated that they expected about 70% of learning outcomes should be met. However, the average is 64% at grade 4 and 48% at grade 8. Moreover, in terms of the students' attitudes, the sample responses for the item "I like science" showed that the degree of "liking" science drops steadily from grade 4 to 8 (EARGED, 2009).

There was, interestingly, no mention of assessment and its relation to students' learning in the report. That might mean that although the science curriculum developers emphasized changing attitudes of teachers in assessing their students during the learning process, there may be no change in teachers as well as curriculum evaluators. This is clearly based on anecdotal evidence, informal observations and the limited empirical research done so far. It is a crucial issue which needs to be considered to better implement the new curricula as planned.

The new curricula include formative assessment in teaching (i.e. MEB, 2005, 2006a, b, c, 2007a, b, c) and forces teachers to use it. This is due to the review of western countries curricula by curriculum developers. In the science curricula of British Columbia, Canada, there is a clear explanation of the relation between assessment and learning (British Columbia MoE, 2008). It was stated and explained that *'Assessment for Learning', 'Assessment as Learning' and 'Assessment of Learning'* are very important parts of the curriculum and teachers need to be aware of what it all means. In Turkey, for the reasons argued above, the school and teaching culture do not yet seem to be at an appropriate stage for plans to be fully implemented. The change will take time/ Teachers, students, parents, school administrators, inspectors and others related to school should all be part of the change (Fullan, 2001). Otherwise, it will be hard to see if and when the changes will fully take place.

### Acknowledgement

I would like to thank Prof. Dr. Margaret Sands and Assoc. Prof. Dr. Cengiz Alacacı from Faculty of Education, Bilkent University for their valuable comments on this paper.

### References

Akkoyunlu-Wingley, A. & Wingly, S. (2008). Basic Education and Capability Development in Turkey. Available at: http://www.bilkent.edu.tr/~wigley/akkoyunluwigleyturkeyeducationcapabilities.pdf (Date of Access: December 16th, 2010).

Akşit, N. (2007). Educational reform in Turkey. *International Journal of Educational Development, 27*(2), 129-137.

Akşit, N. & Sands, M. (2006a). Issues and Challenges Facing Education in Turkey. In J. Arnest & D. Treagust (Eds.), *Education Reform in Societies in Trasition: International Perspectives* (pp. 13-28). Rotterdam: Sense Publishers.

Akşit, N. & Sands, M. (2006b). Turkey: Paradigme Change in Education. In C.S. Sunal & K. Mutua (Eds.), *Research on Education in Africa, Caribbean and the Middle East: Book III, Crosscurrents and Crosscutting Themes* (pp. 253-271). Charlotte, NC: Information Age Pub Inc.

Akyüz, Y. (1989). *Türk Eğitim Tarihi: MÖ 1000-MS 2009'a*. Gözden Geçirilmiş 15. Baskı. Ankara, Turkey: Pegem Akademi.

Alacacı, C. & Erbaş, A.K. (2010). Unpacking the inequality among Turkish schools: Findings from PISA 2006. *International Journal of Educational Development, 30*, 182-192.

Alpaut, O. (1984). *Fen öğretiminin verimli ve işlevsel hale getirilmesi*. A paper presented in orta öğretim kurumlarında fen öğretimi ve sorunları, Türk Eğitim Derneği Bilimsel Toplantısı, Ankara, Turkey, 12–13 June.

Ayas, A. (1993). *A Study of Teachers' and Students' View of the Upper Secondary Chemistry Curriculum and Students' Understanding of Introductory Chemistry Concepts in the East Black-Sea Region of Turkey*. Unpublished PhD Thesis, University of Sothampton, UK.

Ayas, A., Akdeniz, A., Çepni, S., Baki, A., Çimer, A., & Odabaşı Çimer, S. (2007). *Baseline Study on Efficiency of In-Service Training*. (BEP 2/04-CQ). Republic of Turkey Ministry of National Education Projects Coordination Centre Basic Education Project Directorate.

Ayas, A., Çepni, S., & Akdeniz, A.R. (1993). Development of the Turkish secondary science curriculum. *Science Education, 77*(4), 433-440.

Berkem, A.R. (1980). Turkey: Secondary School Education. In A. Kornhauser et al. (Eds.), *Chemical Education in the Seventies*. IUPAC CTC. Oxford, UK: Pergamon Press.

Binay, H. (1982). *Turkey: Socio-cultural information*. Strasbourg: Council for cultural cooperation.

Black, P., Harrison, C., Lee, C., Marshall, B., & Wiliam, D. (2002). *Working Inside the Black Box: Assessment for Learning in the Classroom*. Department of Education & Professional Studies. King's College, London.

Black, P. & Wiliam, D. (1998). *The Black Box: Formative Assessment*. London, UK: King's College.

Bloom, B. S. (1956). *Taxonomy of Educational Objectives: The Classification of Educational Goals By a Committee of College and University Examiners*. New York: McKay.

Bodner, G. M. (1990). Why good teaching fails and hard-working students don't always succeed. *Spectrum, 28*(1), 27-32.

British Columbia MoE. (2008). *Science grade 10: integrated resource package 2008*. Ministry of Education, Province of British Columbia.

Çalık, M. & Ayas, A. (2008). A critical review of the development of the Turkish Secondary Science Curriculum. In R. K. Coll & N. Taylor (Eds.) *Science Education in Context: An International Examination of the Influence of Context on Science Curricula Development and Implementation* (pp. 161-174). Rotterdam: Sense Publishers.

Durusoy, M. (1984). *Fen öğretiminde karşılaşılan başlıca sorunlar ve nedenleri*. A paper presented in ortaöğretim kurumlarında fen öğretimi ve sorunları, panel I, Türk Eğitim Derneği Bilimsel Toplantısı, Ankara, Turkey, 12-13 June.

EARGED (2009). *ÖBBS 2008 İlköğretim Öğrencilerinin Başarılarının Belirlenmesi* (Türkçe, Matematik, Fen ve Tecnology, Sosyal Bilgiler, İngilizce) Raporu. MEB Eğitim Öğretim Dairesi Başkanlığı: Ankara.

EC (2007). *Science Education Now: A Renewed Pedagogy for the Future of Europe*. Expert Group (High Level Group on Science Education; Michel Rocard (Chair), Peter Csermely, Doris Jorde, Dieter Lenzen, Harriet Walberg-Henriksson, Valerie Hemmo (Rapporteur)). Brussels: EU.

Elmas, R. & Geban, Ö. (2010). *High School Chemistry Teachers' Views Related to the New Chemistry Curriculum*. Paper presented in World Council of Comparative Education Societies (WCCES) conference, June 14-18, Istanbul, Turkey.

ERG (2005). *Yeni ogretim programlarını inceleme ve değerlendirme raporu*. Eğitim Reformu Girişimi, Sabancı Üniversitesi: İstanbul.

Fullan, M. (2001). *The New Meaning of Educational Change*. Third Edition. London: Routledge Falmer.

Grossman, G. & Sands, M. K. (2007). Curriculum Reforms in Turkish Teacher Education: Attitudes of Teacher Educators towards Change in an EU Candidate Nation. *International Journal of Educational Development, 27*(1), 138-150.

Grossman, G. & Sands, M. K. (2008). Restructuring Reforms in Turkish Teacher Education: Modernization and Development in a Dynamic Environment. *International Journal of Educational Development, 28*(1), 70-80.

Güneş, B., Ateş, S., Eryılmaz, A., Kanlı, U., Serin, G., Arslan, A., & Gülyurdu, T. (2010). *Yenilenen fizik dersi öğretim programının uygulanma süreci ve yaşanan sıkıntılar üzerine bir araştırma*. Paper presented at the biannual meeting of IX. Ulusal Fen Bilimleri ve Matematik Eğitimi Kongresi. Dokuz Eylül Üniversitesi Buca Eğitim Fakültesi, 23-25 Eylül, İzmir, Turkey.

Holmes, B. (1983). *International Handbook of Educational Systems*. Volume 1. Oxford, UK: Wiley.

MEB (1939). *Birinci maarif şurası: çalışma programı, konuşmalar lahikalar*. Istanbul Maarif Vekaleti.

MEB (1962). *Yedinci milli eğitim şurası kararları*. Milli Eğitim Basimevi, Ankara, Turkey.

MEB (1971). *Sekizinci milli eğitim şurası; esaslar, kararlar ve raporlar*. Milli Eğitim Basimevi, Ankara, Turkey.

MEB (1985). Lise kimya müfredat programı. *Tebliğler Dergisi*, Sayı: 2197.

MEB (2005). *İlköğretim fen ve teknoloji dersi (4 ve 5. sınıflar ) öğretim programı*. Millî Eğitim Bakanlığı Talim Ve Terbiye Kurulu Başkanlığı: Ankara.

MEB (2006). *İlköğretim fen ve teknoloji dersi (6, 7 ve 8. Sınıflar ) öğretim programı*. Millî Eğitim Bakanlığı Talim Ve Terbiye Kurulu Başkanlığı: Ankara.

MEB (2007a,b,c). *Ortaöğretim 9. sınıf fizik, kimya ve biyoloji öğretim programları*. Millî Eğitim Bakanlığı Talim Ve Terbiye Kurulu Başkanlığı: Ankara.

MEB (2008 a,b,c,d,e,f). *Ortaöğretim 10. ve 11. sınıflar fizik, kimya ve biyoloji öğretim programları*. Millî Eğitim Bakanlığı Talim Ve Terbiye Kurulu Başkanlığı: Ankara.

MEB (2009 a,b,c). *Ortaöğretim 12. sınıf fizik, kimya ve biyoloji öğretim programları*. Millî Eğitim Bakanlığı Talim Ve Terbiye Kurulu Başkanlığı: Ankara.

MEB-EARGED. (2010a). *PISA 2006 projesi ulusal nihai raporu (pisa 2006 national final-report)*. TC Milli Eğitim Bakanlığı EARGED: Ankara.

MEB-EARGED (2010b). *PISA 2009 projesi ulusal ön raporu (PISA 2009 national pre-report)*. TC Milli Eğitim Bakanlığı EARGED: Ankara.

NME (2005). *Basic Education in Turkey: Background Report.* Available at http://dx/doi.org/10.1787/10482440705 and on the OECD website at: www.oecd.org/edu/reviews/nationalpolicies.

OECD (1989). *Review of Educational Policies for Education: Turkey.* Paris: OECD.

OECD (2005). *National Education Policy Review Background Report: Republic of Turkey Ministry of National Education.* Paris: OECD.

OECD (2007). *Reviews of National Policies for Education – Basic Education in Turkey.* Paris: OECD. Available at: http://www.oecd-ilibrary.org/education/reviews-of-national-policies-for-education-basic-education-in-turkey-2007_9789264030206-en (Date of Access: December 2$^{nd}$, 2010).

OECD (2010). *PISA 2009 Results: What Students Know and Can Do: Student Performance in Reading, Mathematics and Science Volume I.* Available at: http://dx.doi.org/10.1787/9789264091450-en.

Oğuzkan, A. F. (1985). *Orta dereceli okullarda öğretim: amaç, ilke, yöntem ve teknikler.* Emel matbaacilik, Ankara. Turkey.

Oğuzkan, T. (1981). *Türkiye'de ortaöğretim ve sorunlari.* Hisar Eğitim Vakfı, Yayin No: 1. Istanbul, Turkey.

ÖSYM (2009). *2009-ÖSYS: Üniversiteler ile ilgili istatistiksel bilgiler: alanlara göre yerleşen ve boş sayıları (Lisans).* Available at: http://www.osym.gov.tr/belge/1-11525/eski2yeni.html. (Date of Access: December 20$^{th}$, 2010).

Özinönü, A.K. (1976). *Innovation and Changes in Secondary Science Curriculum.* Faculty of Arts and Sciences Publication Number 30. Middle East Technical University, Ankara, Turkey.

Şahin, İ. (2010). Curriculum Assessment: Constructivist Primary Mathematics Curriculum in Turkey. *International Journal of Science and Mathematics Education 8*, 51-72.

Şenel Coruhlu, T., Er Nas, S., & Çepni, S. (2009). Fen Ve Teknoloji Öğretmenlerinin Alternatif Ölçmedeğerlendirme Tekniklerini Kullanmada Karşilaştiklari Problemler: Trabzon Örneği. *Yüzüncü Yıl Üniversitesi, Eğitim Fakültesi Dergisi.VI*(I), 122-141. Available at: http://efdergi.yyu.edu.tr

Soylu, H. (1984). *Fen öğretiminde yeni yaklaşımlar.* A paper presented in orta öğretim kurumlarında fen öğretimi ve sorunlari. Türk Eğitim Derneği bilimsel toplatısı, Ankara, Türkiye, 12-13 June.

TED Bilimsel Toplantısı (1984). *Orta öğretim kurumlarında fen öğretimi ve sorunları*, Proceeding of Türk Eğitim Derneği Bilimsel Toplantısı, Ankara, Turkey, 12-13 June.

The Report (1961). *The Report of the National Commission on Education,* Translated to English by M. Austin. American Board Publication Department. Istanbul, Turkey.

Thompson, J. J. (1972). *European Curriculum Studies* (in the academic secondary school). No: 4-Chemistry. Council for cultural cooperation. Strasbourg: Council of Europe.

Turgut, M. F. (1981). Fen ve Matematik Öğretimi. In T. Oğuzkan (Ed.) *Türkiye'de ortaöğretim ve sorunları.* Hisar Vakfı Yayin no.1. Istanbul, Turkey.

Turgut, M.F. (1990). Turkiye'de fen ve matematik programlarini yenileme çalımaları. *Hacettepe Üniversitesi Eğitim Fakültesi Dergisi*, 5, 1-14.

Turgut, M. F. & Pekgöz, M. (1976). *Yeni ortaöğretim sisteminde modern matematik ve fen programlarinin denenmesi ve teşmili üzerine araştırmalar projesi kesin değerlendirme raporu*. Ankara, Fen Öğretimini Geliştirme Bilimsel Komisyonu.

Turkish Review (1989). The educational tradition of the Ottoman Empire and development of the Turkish educational system of Republican era. *Turkish Review Quarterly Digest*, 3(16), 13.

World Bank (2010). *Financial Crisis: What the World Bank is Doing*. Available at: http://www.worldbank.org/financialcrisis/bankinitiatives.htm (Date of Access: December 20th, 2010).

# Chapter 18

## Defining the Structure and the Content of a New Chemistry Curriculum in the Netherlands

*Cris Bertona*
*ICLON (Leiden University Graduate School of Teaching)*
*Leiden University, The Netherlands*

**Abstract**

In this paper we analyse the process of the definition of intended learning outcomes in an innovative curriculum in Dutch chemistry education. The paper starts with the description of curricular and examination responsibilities in the Netherlands and the context of the Dutch situation concerning the innovative process of the chemistry curriculum in secondary education. Motive and aims of this new curriculum are distinguished from earlier curriculum innovations over the last three decades. Furthermore, we will focus on specific characteristics of the new curriculum that are of importance for the choices regarding the specifications of the attainment targets. The characteristics concern the context concept approach, the organisation of the concepts (structure of the new curriculum) and issues of assessment. Problems and challenges will be described in relation to the outcomes of the evaluations of the curriculum and the process of innovation. Conclusions will be related to the difficulties to escape from a traditional structure.

## 1 Introduction

The aim of this paper is to contribute to the discussion concerning the definition of intended learning outcomes in an innovative curriculum in Dutch chemistry education. The paper is based on a variety of reports and curriculum evaluations regarding the innovation of the Dutch chemistry curriculum from 2002 until 2010. In addition this article is based on author's experiences as chair of the Syllabus Committee Chemistry in 2006–2007 and in 2010–2011. The Syllabus Committee is charged with the assignment to provide the attainment targets of the curriculum with specific descriptions of the skills and knowledge of students at the end of secondary school education, to meet requirements of examination.

Dissatisfaction with the current curriculum led to an investigation, ordered by the Dutch Ministry of Education, on the necessity for curriculum innovation. The present curriculum is seen as overload, build on isolated facts rather than a coherent entity and is strongly content oriented. Also does this curriculum not meet the demands of modern society on science education, in particular chemistry education.

A new curriculum must contribute to scientific literacy, illuminate the relevance of chemistry for society and improve the motivation for chemistry as a school subject as well as for further educational choices. A process of approximately ten years of development has led to a new curriculum based on the context concept approach. This new curriculum will be introduced nationwide in 2013.

According to Goodlad (1979) and Van den Akker (1998) the process of implementation of a new curriculum can be described in different curricular representations. From an ideal curriculum, based on the original vision, through a formal, perceived, operational and experienced curriculum, to an attained curriculum. The attained curriculum displays the learning outcomes achieved by the students.

The new program for chemistry education, as laid down in the syllabus, can be seen as the formal curriculum and consists of generally formulated attainment targets, including the specifications of these targets, regarding knowledge and skills. Examination will show to what extent students learned what they were supposed to learn (attained curriculum). However, besides the expected learning outcomes concerning knowledge and skills, there are also expectations regarding issues of perception of chemistry, relevance and motivation that underlay the new program as these were part of the problems the new program should take in account.

In general, assessment has a considerable influence on what is taught and how learning is organised in classroom practice. In the Netherlands national assessment determines half the grade for a particular school subject. Because of this importance of the national examination teachers are very eager to prepare students properly for these exams. Therefore national exams determine for a substantial part what happens in the classroom. In the Netherlands the specifications of the skills and knowledge as described in the syllabus are restrictive for the constructions of the exams. Adequate description of the skills and knowledge that meets the recommendations as described in visionary documents can therefore contribute to diminish incongruence between the ideal curriculum and the experienced and attained curriculum. The Syllabus Committee is thus challenged to provide the new curriculum for specifications on skills and knowledge that meet the innovative aspects and expectations of the new program.

To identify some of the difficulties encountered in the process of defining specifications of a new curriculum, it is important to understand the historical background and to have an idea how the process of innovation of the chemistry curriculum in the Netherlands has been undertaken. In addition it is useful to have some notion how responsibility for curriculum and examination is organised in the Netherlands to understand the occurring bottlenecks and recommendations.

This paper starts with the description of curricular and examination responsibilities in the Netherlands and the context of the Dutch situation concerning the innovative process of the chemistry curriculum in secondary education. Next we will focus on specific characteristics of the new curriculum that are of importance for the choices the Syllabus Committee makes regarding the specifications and addressing the specifications to certain items. Problems and challenges the Syllabus Committee has met will be described in relation to the outcomes of the evaluations of the curriculum and the process of innovation. In the last section conclusions will be drawn.

At this moment the process of defining the specifications of the curriculum for a new version of the syllabus is still ongoing. Until the delivery of this new syllabus the exact content of the syllabus has to remain confidential. Therefore, explicit examples of the specifications of the attainment targets can not be given yet.

## 2 Context and Historical Background

### 2.1 Responsibilities for Curriculum and Examination

To understand some of the difficulties met in the process of defining specifications for a new curriculum it is important to have some notion how responsibility for curriculum and examination is organised in the Netherlands.

Acting on development in society or education, the government can install a committee to elaborate on a new curriculum. Subsequently the new curriculum has to be established by the government. The curriculum is written in more general terms and needs to be specified in specific descriptions to meet the requirements of national examination.

The College of Examination is the national institute which is responsible to install a Syllabus Committee to formulate the specifications. To ascertain a maximal support the committee must consist of representatives of different stakeholders, such as teachers, exam constructors etc.

The syllabus describes the specific skills and knowledge students are supposed to have acquired at the end of the secondary school chemistry education. The syllabus only describes what students are supposed to know and do with this knowledge. The syllabus does not describe how students are supposed to gather this knowledge and skills. Put in other words, there is no prescription of pedagogical choices. Furthermore another institute, the CITO, is responsible for the construction of the exams.

Until 2006 the Netherlands had a comprehensive national curriculum for all students in a distinctive level of education. At the end of secondary school education the national curriculum was assessed as a whole in a national exam.

Starting from 2007 one part of the curriculum is designated for assessment in the national exam and another part is only assessed in exams under the responsibility of the school board. To support teachers the SLO (Netherlands National Institute for Curriculum Development) developed a handbook with suggestions for specification regarding the attainment targets of the curriculum that are not specified in the syllabus. However, these suggestions are not compulsory.

## 2.2 Curriculum Changes: An Overview from 1968 until 2011

In February 2002 the Dutch Minister of Education installed a committee, the Exploratory Committee for Chemistry, with the assignment to investigate on the problems concerning chemistry education in secondary schools in the Netherlands. The motive is the growing gap between chemistry as a school subject and the academic, technological, and societal position of chemistry.

This resembles the situation in 1968 as at that time the motive for a reflection on the current curriculum was similar. The Committee Curriculum Renewal for Chemistry had been asked to develop a new curriculum that fitted better to the demands society made to chemistry education. The current curriculum was perceived as outdated and prepared students primarily for a study in the field of chemistry. Characteristics of this new curriculum were that it not only prepared students for a study in chemistry, but also as participants of a continuously changing society.

As a result of this curriculum renewal a national updated curriculum was introduced in 1985. Since then no major adjustments have been made to this program, nor has this program been completely evaluated. This process took such a long time because all the course material has been developed in collaboration with teachers and has been evaluated through consecutive cycles. All this resembles the approach of the current innovation.

Although the assignments for a new curriculum are similar, the expectations and demands on education have changed and therefore ask for a new approach. Due to the evolution of chemical knowledge on the one hand and the decreased time available for chemistry education in the total school curriculum, caused by a nation-wide general curriculum change in 1999, on the other hand, the gap between school chemistry and chemistry as an academic discipline became even bigger. In addition, the importance of chemistry for the society is not being recognised. Van Berkel mentions in his dissertation that "the structure of dominant school chemistry as a whole suffers from a sevenfold isolation: from common sense, every day life and society, history and philosophy of science, technology, school physics and from chemical research" (Van Berkel, 2005, p. 68). In an earlier publication de Vos et. al. state that students are even "alienated from chemistry since the chemical theories presented in chemistry lessons have little in common with products and experiences in their everyday life" (De Vos, Bulte, & Pilot, 2002, p.109).

In June 2002, the Exploratory Committee for Chemistry presented her analysis and recommendations in the publication "Building Chemistry" (SLO, June 2002). In this publication it is pointed out that there is a broad consensus on the necessity for a curriculum renewal.

The major outcomes of this analysis are the following:

- in society there is a negative image of (the role of) chemistry.
- the importance of chemical industry for society is not visible and chemical industry has concerns about chemical education.
- chemistry in school diverges from modern chemistry in the real world.
- there is a lack of motivation for chemistry as a school subject.
- there is also a gap between chemistry in the third year of secondary education and following years.
- the examination requirements of the chemistry program are perceived as restrictive and leave little space for personal preferences.

The Exploratory Committee advises to set up a new committee to outline a plan for a renewal of the chemistry curriculum in secondary school that solves the problems mentioned above. In October 2002, the Committee for the Renewal of Chemistry Education starts off to elaborate the conditions for a new curriculum. In the report "Chemistry between Context and Concept, designing for Renewal" (SLO, 2003) the committee advises to develop a curriculum that:

- focuses on the understanding of the chemistry behind products and processes,
- relates to current and future questions, and
- is described in less restrictive examination programs and therefore provides possibilities for differentiation and new developments.

The committee suggests to design a program based on the context concept approach. The choice for this approach is based on developments of curriculum innovation in Germany (ChiK), England (Salter's Advanced Chemistry, 21st Century Science), and United States (ChemCom, Chemistry in Contexts) concerning the changing perspectives on subject content, pedagogies, and aims of science education.
The report also addresses issues concerning consequences of this context concept approach for examination and for successful introduction and implementation of the new curriculum.

The Steering Committee New Chemistry takes up the responsibility to determine and implement a framework for a new curriculum based on the work of the former committees. The task of the Steering Committee is to design a "renewed, innovative, renewable" curriculum, to develop course material that meets the requirements of a context concept approach, in collaboration with secondary school teachers, and to investigate if the new curriculum is feasible, teachable, and can be assessed in the Dutch educational system.

To accomplish her task the Steering Committee takes up the following activities from spring 2004 to December 2010:

1. Student learning material has been developed, starting from the third year of secondary school education. In the Netherlands this is the first year of chemistry education. The course material consists of modules based on the context concept approach. The material is developed by teams of teachers with a coach (often a researcher or a teacher educator) working together in so called learning communities. According to the recommendations of the Committee for the Renewal of Chemistry Education this bottom up approach will contribute to the ownership of the teachers for the course material and therefore the curriculum. For an adequate implementation of the new curriculum it is important the learning material being recognisable by other teachers that did not participate in the process of development.

2. The developing of learning materials also served to identify features concerning the important chemical concepts and inspiring contexts. The demands on the material are that it:

- contributes to scientific literacy,
- makes enthusiastic for further education in natural or engineering sciences,
- gives insight in the daily practice of chemists, and
- gives to all students an impression of the meaning of chemistry for Dutch society.

Based on the experiences, four different curricular outlines emerged, based on different preferences regarding the type of context, the opinions concerning how chemistry knowledge is acquired and beliefs about classroom practice. Comparison of the different outlines and the experiences in school practice with the new course material led to a list of concepts resulting in a draft for a new curriculum for chemistry ("Adviesexamenprogramma"). Several times during the process different stakeholders (teachers, representatives of third education, chemical industry etc.) were asked to give feedback on the new curriculum.

3. To determine whether the new curriculum is feasible, teachable, and can be assessed in the Dutch educational system, the new curriculum has been taught in 20 secondary schools, using exclusively the new developed course material, and is assessed accordingly. For this purpose separate pilot exams have been constructed ("Examen Experiment").

Parallel with the process of innovation a formal examination program with specifications of the specific skills and knowledge is produced under the responsibility of the College of Examination. The Syllabus Committee provided the detailed descriptions of the attainment targets of the new curriculum for the assessment of this curriculum during the pilot period (Syllabus 2007). At this very moment a new Syllabus Committee is working on the specification of the definitive version of the new curriculum as it is presented for approval to the minister of education. Although the new curriculum is not approved by the minister yet, expectations are positive.

Meanwhile similar curriculum innovations are ongoing in biology, physics, and mathematics. Therefore, the Ministry of Education ordered an evaluation of the innovative process as a whole. This evaluation is carried out by the SLO and ascertains whether the innovation coincides with the baselines and recommendations as formulated by the various committees and resulted in a program that is feasible and can be assessed adequately.

Additional research by DUO Market Research on the appreciation by teachers of the new developments in chemical education has been commissioned by the chemical industry. Unlike the research carried out by the SLO teachers that did not participate in the innovation process were also asked to give their opinion.

All these here above mentioned activities should contribute to an *evidence based* development of chemistry education in secondary schools.

On the 1st of February 2011 the conclusions of the Steering Committee concerning the process developing a new chemistry curriculum that meets requirements of feasibility, 'teachability' and assessment were presented to the Dutch Minister of Education in the report "Chemistry in dynamics of the future" (SLO, 2010). In the report the new chemistry curriculum ("Adviesexamenprogramma") is described in general terms and needs to be further specified to meet the requirements of examination.

Based on the recommendations in the report and the different evaluations the minister will decide on a nationwide introduction and implementation of the new program in 2013.

# 3 Characteristics of the New Program in Relation to the Development of the Syllabus and Outcomes of the Evaluations of the Curriculum

The Syllabus serves a dual purpose. On one hand the specifications provide parameters for the construction of assessment and examination. On the other hand teachers can use the specifications to make choices concerning the content of the teaching materials and arrange classroom practice accordingly. Furthermore publishers can use the syllabus for the development of teaching materials.

As mentioned before, an additional feature of the syllabus is that it can support the introduction and implementation of the new curriculum if the innovative features of the new curriculum are reflected sufficiently. We will discuss how the following three characteristics of the new curriculum relate to the development of the syllabus:

- context concept approach in relation to assessment;
- organisation of the concepts into domains;
- national exams in relation to school exams.

## 3.1 Context Concept Approach, a Pedagogical Choice?

The Committee for the Renewal of Chemistry Education suggested to develop a new curriculum based on the context concept approach and made up a model for this approach. Two central concepts, the molecule concept and the micro macro concept, form the fundament of the model. According to the Committee these concepts represent the core features of chemistry. These concepts need to be specified with chemical knowledge as it is assessed in the examination program. The new program is based on a continuous interaction between contexts and concepts. The contexts are the starting point for exploration and applications of chemistry and relate to one of the features of the new curriculum ("focus on the understanding of the chemistry behind products and processes"). They are the bridge between reality and the chemical concepts. Contexts are chosen in the theoretical, experimental, social, or vocational field to meet features like development of knowledge and skills, the experimental nature of chemistry, scientific literacy, the position of chemistry in the Dutch society, and the meaning of chemistry for different professions.

The syllabus describes the specific skills and knowledge students are supposed to have acquired. The syllabus does not describe *how* students are supposed to gather this knowledge and skills. In the Netherlands state prescribed pedagogies do not exist. Teachers are therefore free to choose their own methods. On the level of the operational curriculum this means that teachers can choose to use the new course material while implementing the curriculum. However they can also choose to use more traditional books and methods, and anything in between. In the end all students must be able to take the same exams of the new national curriculum regardless how the education has taken place.

To foster the introduction and implementation of the new curriculum the syllabus should in one way or another reflect this context concept approach as it is one of the essential features of the innovation of the program. This seems to be contradictory with the fact that there is no prescription of the pedagogical choices. This has important implications for the construction of the syllabus as the specifications are used for the construction of exams. One of the challenges for the syllabus committee is to produce a syllabus that reflects the innovative approach on one hand without prescribing pedagogies on the other end.

The different committees for innovation of the science curricula became aware of this problem and addressed this issue in a policy letter ("Didactiek, examenprogramma's en vakvernieuwing", Stuurgroep vakvernieuwing β5). In this policy letter it is stated that the formulation of the attainment targets do determine to a certain extent what happens in the classroom. For example, to attain a specific skill it will be necessary to practice this skill in classroom practice. In this way there is a certain relation between classroom practice and the attainment targets. However, the committees for innovation contest that the context concept approach consists of a pedagogical prescription: the elaboration of the context concept approach by the different science committees has in common that the acquired knowledge must be applied in contemporary contexts. This approach on how knowledge is supposed to be used relates to issues of transfer of knowledge. The following attainment target is an example of how this works out:

*The candidate is able to explain "selectivity" and "specificity" in relation to chemical reactions, and if appropriate knowledge concerning catalysis, at least in the context of production of food, pharmaceuticals or transport of substances in the human body.* (translation of attainment target VWO no. 35; Apotheker, Bulte, De Kleijn, Van Koten, Meinema, & Seller, 2010)

The new curriculum has been constructed accordingly to this way of thinking about context. The context concept approach is not an imposed pedagogical choice but it is used as a guideline for organising the attainment targets into domains. In addition the attainment targets focus on the application of knowledge. The new curriculum shifted away from a content oriented perspective to a curriculum in which it is more important to be able to use knowledge in different contexts. The question arises to which extent teachers are really free to make their own pedagogical choices.

Later we will discuss the implications of a different organisation of the attainment targets into domains on the construction of the syllabus. First we will focus on some aspects of context concept approach as it is perceived by different stakeholders.

The curriculum evaluation made by SLO shows that teachers do not agree upon the difference concerning the new curriculum with the respect to the current curriculum. Some think the content has changed, others are convinced that the pedagogical approach is the core change. Furthermore, the DUO-Market research, in which not only teachers involved in the innovation process are questioned, makes clear that, although a majority of the teachers is in favour of a new curriculum, there is no majority in favour of the context content approach. The question arises if it is sufficiently clear what the innovation consists of, and what the context concept approach means.

The construction of the syllabus 2007 suffered because of this confusion on the interpretation of context in relation to pedagogical choices. The Syllabus Committee itself lacked sufficient know-how concerning the vision on the new curriculum. At that time no examples of how examination of the new curriculum could look like were available yet.

As a result the Syllabus Committee did not succeed in producing a syllabus that reflected the ideas of innovation.

The curriculum evaluation conducted by SLO confirms this image. The writers of the report remark that the development of the course material and the construction of the syllabus seemed to be separate trajectories. More interaction between the content of the syllabus and the school practice would have been more fruitful.

Regarding the second version of the syllabus, it is too early yet to make sensible remarks concerning the aspects of context. However the expectations are positive. The Steering Committee reports that consultations of teachers reveals that the proposed curriculum ("Adviesexamenprogramma") reflects the innovation of the curriculum. As this is the backbone of the curriculum it is to be expected that the new syllabus shall reflect the innovation.

Also possible difficulties regarding the lack of know-how are likely to be overcome. The new Syllabus committee consists also of teachers that were involved in the process of innovation as developers of course materials or because they tested some of the new course material. This will facilitate the translation of the ideal curriculum in the formal curriculum hopefully leading to a syllabus in which the innovation of the curriculum is recognisable.

## 3.2 Organisation of Concepts into Domains

One of the main characteristics of the present curriculum is that it focuses on the acquirement of a thorough knowledge base of chemical concepts. As mentioned earlier, the program consists of isolated facts rather than a coherent entity. The present curriculum consists of a list of attainment targets organised in domains. The domains represent a traditional view of the curriculum based on a historical perspective (substances, structure and bonding, organic chemistry, biochemistry, acid and bases, etc.). According to De Vos et. al. the chemistry curriculum has a sedimentary structure with "different incoherent layers being even inconsistent in several cases" (De Vos, Bulte, & Pilot, 2002, p.107).

The Dutch model of the context concept approach is the base for a new structure of the curriculum. The re-structuring took place in two steps, a proposed program in 2006, "Ontwerpprogramma 2006" (Table 1), and a revised version in 2010, "Adviesexamenprogramma" (Table 2). In this version of the proposed curriculum the concepts are organised in seven domains. According to the Steering Committee this way of regrouping the concepts not only creates more coherence but it also illustrates how the central concepts (the molecule concept and the micro/macro concept) that characterises the new chemistry curriculum relate to the contexts. It is a challenge for the Syllabus committee to clarify this in the specification of the attainment targets.

Table 1: Domains of the Proposed Program in 2006

| Ontwerpprogramma 2006 |
|---|
| *Skills*<br>A1 General skills<br>A2 Scientific skills<br>A3 Chemical skills |
| *Content*<br>B Research methods<br>C Structures<br>D Synthesis<br>E Chemistry of life<br>D Materials E Sustainable development |

Table 2: Domains of the Proposed Program in 2010

| Adviesexamenprogramma |
|---|
| *Skills*<br>A1 General skills<br>A2 Scientific skills<br>A3 Chemical skills |
| *Chemical concepts*<br>B Chemical substances and materials<br>C Chemical processes and laws<br>D Development of chemical knowledge |
| *Context fields*<br>E Innovation and chemical research<br>F Industrial (chemical) processes<br>G Society, chemistry and technology |

Domain A describes the different skills (general skills, scientific skills, and specific chemical skills). The chemical skills deals with understanding of the chemical concepts and chemical reasoning using these concepts.

Domains B, C, and D consists of the "robust chemical concepts" and form the theoretical backbone of the curriculum. This is the knowledge that student are supposed to acquire and use in different contexts. Domains E, F, and G describe the context fields, in which this knowledge can be applied. Important features of chemistry and chemical engineering, like innovation, the role of chemistry regarding health, prosperity and sustainability, and societal issues are dealt with.

It is important to notice that the development of the syllabus took place simultaneously with the development and testing of the new learning materials. The first Syllabus Committee started off with a baseline ("Ontwerpprogramma 2006") for the new curriculum that still leaned upon a traditional organisation of the concepts. The seven domains did not foster an innovative description of the sub-domains and the specification of the sub-domains. In addition the Committee used the content of the regular program for the formulation of the specifications because it was not yet clear from the process of developing course materials which conceptual content the new chemistry program would consist and how the acquired knowledge was supposed to be applied in contexts. At that time the first course material for the new program just started to become available.

Furthermore the Syllabus Committee struggled at one hand to what extent detailed description was needed for examinational requirements to avoid misunderstandings and at the other hand the recommendation of the Committee for the Renewal of Chemistry Education advocating more generally described specifications. The conflicting interests regarding the degree of detailing led to a syllabus for a program that did not solve the issue of overload and did not reflect the character of the new curriculum.

These difficulties seem to be overcome for the process of the construction of a new version of the syllabus. Accurate description of the concepts will always be indispensable for examination purposes. However, to deal with the issue of overload it can be useful to look at it from a different angle. It may not be the degree of detail, but the number of concepts that are felt to be indispensable for the new curriculum, to cause overload.

Starting off with a more old-fashioned organisation of the concepts and the list of traditional concepts did not facilitate the process of choosing the concepts that could be left out of the new curriculum. Considerations with respect to the selection of concepts regarded mainly issues concerning the construction of the exams. It seemed difficult to leave behind some of the familiar concepts. Not only this was an issue for the Syllabus Committee. Teachers involved in the experimental curriculum were forced to make choices themselves, because of the overload of the first syllabus, and encountered the same problem.

Using the latest version of the proposed new curriculum ("Adviesexamenprogramma"), based on the experiences with the new course material, questions like "what does this specific concept add to the specific sub-domain", and even more important "how does this relate to the context" seem to be more appropriate. Furthermore a list of relevant concepts ("Overzichten van concepten en vakbegrippen") that emerged from the course materials is now available. In other words, the choices are more likely to be made on a need to know basis.

### 3.3 National Examination (Central Exams) in Relation to School Examination

In the Netherlands the definitive grade of a specific subject in secondary school education is based for 50% on internal school exams and for 50% on external central exams. The central exams are constructed by CITO and take place at the end of the last year of secondary school education. The school is responsible for the internal school examination. These exams are constructed by the teachers and there is a variety of possibilities when these assessments take place.

Until 2007 the chemistry curriculum was assessed as a whole, both in the school exams and in the central exams. Starting from the exams in 2007, some sub-domains of the program are addressed to be assessed in the school exams only. Regarding the new curriculum only 60% of the curriculum will be assessed in the central examination.

For the syllabus this means only the items that are assigned to the central exams will be provided with a specification. Although the SLO will supply a description for the part of the program that is not centrally assessed schools can make their own choices regarding the depth or broadness of these specific items of the curriculum.

It is important to notice this means that undoubtedly there will be differences between schools regarding the broadness and depth of the curriculum that is not specified in the syllabus. As a consequence the constructors of the exam are not allowed to explicitly ask questions about knowledge that is not specified in the syllabus or implicitly expect this knowledge to be present.

This also has implications for the construction of the syllabus. In the proposed curriculum the attainment targets are no longer grouped in domains consisting of similar concepts. As a consequence it is possible that, for example, concepts concerning electrochemistry are spread over different domains. For example: in context field F, industrial (chemical) processes, one of the attainment targets deals with the issue of energy in relation to sustainability.

*The candidate is able to describe chemical technological processes regarding the conversion of energy in sustainability contexts and is able to use knowledge regarding production of energy to describe processes, to define conditions for these processes, and to be able to judge proposals for adjustment.* (translation of attainment target VWO no. 41; Apotheker, Bulte, De Kleijn, Van Koten, Meinema, & Seller, 2010)

Electrochemical cells, fuel cells, batteries are topics which fit into this attainment target. However to be able to make judgements regarding these topics some knowledge of electrochemistry is necessary. This knowledge should be specified in one of the domains B, C, or D on a need to know basis.

Attention must be paid to the way knowledge is assessed in the national exams in comparison to the school exams. Initially the Committee for the Renewal of Chemistry Education advised to assess conceptual knowledge in the national exams en assess the interaction between contexts and concepts and the application of knowledge in the school exams. In this way an innovation of the methods of examination could also be accomplished. A condition for this innovation was a guarantee for the quality of the school exams. During the process of innovation this vision seemed to have changed.

Building on the idea that assessment is directional for teaching practice, to foster innovation it is more likely to assess the innovational aspects of the curriculum in the national exams.

In the curriculum evaluation by SLO, teachers themselves suggested that, after the implementation of the new curriculum, education based on more traditional approaches is supposed to produce worse results for the national exams. In the syllabus special attention should be paid to the specifications with respect to the description of the application of the knowledge in order to reflect the innovative aspect and therefore give directions for assessment. The SLO evaluation displays that as long as there are not enough examples of new exams available teachers tend to make (traditional) assessments based on conceptual knowledge instead of application of knowledge and interactions between contexts and concepts.

# 4 Conclusions

Already in 1994, De Vos et. al. mentioned in their analysis of the structure of chemistry curricula a tension "between the traditional content and the modern aim of school chemistry" (De Vos, Van Berkel, & Verdonk, 1994). In 2002, De Vos et. al. state that "re-designing a chemistry curriculum for general education has become a serious problem involving the difficult task to escape from a tradition that has become self-evident over the years" (De Vos, Bulte, & Pilot, 2002).

In this paper we described recent developments in the change of the chemistry curriculum in the Netherlands. We put this development in a historical perspective to illustrate the background of the recent developments. Difficulties concerning the specification of the new curriculum were described regarding three characteristics of the new curriculum. Now we will describe some conclusions that can be drawn regarding these recent developments.

- If in the process of innovation in a curriculum the development of the attainment targets and the development of course material is a parallel process it is crucial that there is some degree of mutual agreement on the directions of both processes in order to avoid diverging paths for either processes. In the light of the outcomes of the different researches, from which we can conclude that there is no agreement on the nature of the innovation and there are doubts about the context concept approach, it is important to pay attention not only to adequate information towards the teacher community but also to teacher professionalisation.

- It seems like innovation of a curriculum needs a rupture from the old structures. The overload of the first version of the syllabus can be explained from the fact that no real choices have been made. This is consistent with the findings of Van Berkel (2005). Innovation and old traditions were integrated leading to on overload in conceptual knowledge. A complete different structure is more likely to foster innovation.

- Differences between national exams and school exams regarding the content of the curriculum can create a certain tension. If the curriculum is not assessed as a whole in both exams it is important to pay attention how to address attainment targets to different domains and how to specify them, to make adequate assessment possible.

- The formulation of the specification of the attainment targets is determinative for the way knowledge is assessed in national exams and school exams. It differs whether knowledge is assessed, or application of knowledge is assessed. To foster an adequate formulation in order to provide sufficient resemblance between the ideal curriculum and the attained curriculum, examples of the innovative aspects of exams must be available. This will also be beneficial for teachers to implement the new curriculum.

# References

Apotheker, J., Bulte, A., de Kleijn, E., van Koten, G., Meinema, H., & Seller, F. (2010). *Scheikunde in de dynamiek van de toekomst ("Chemistry in dynamics of the future")*. SLO, Stichting Leerplanontwikkeling, Enschede.

De Vos, W., Van Berkel, B., & Verdonk, A.H. (1994). A coherent structure of the chemistry curriculum. *Journal of Chemical Education, 71*, 743-746.

De Vos, W., Bulte, A.M.W., & Pilot, A. (2002). Chemistry curricula for general education: Analysis and elements of a design. In J. K. Gilbert, O. De Jong, R. Justi, D.F. Treagust, & J. H. Van Driel (Eds.), *Chemical Education: Towards Research-Based Practice* (pp. 101-124). Dordrecht, The Netherlands: Kluwer Academic Publishers.

Driessen, H. P. W. & Meinema, H. A. (2003). *Chemie tussen context en concept ("Chemistry between Context and Concept, designing for Renewal")*. SLO, Stichting Leerplanontwikkeling, Enschede.

Goodlad, J. (1979). *Curriculum Enquiry: The Study of Curriculum Practice*. New York: McGraw-Hill.

Ottevanger, W., Folmer, E., Bruning, L., & Kuiper, W. (2010). *Curriculumevaluatie Bètaonderwijs Tweede Fase Deelrapport: Evaluatie Examenpilot Nieuwe Scheikunde havo/vwo 2007–2010*. SLO, Stichting Leerplanontwikkeling, Enschede.

Stuurgroep vakvernieuwing β5 (2008). *Didactiek, Examenprogramma's en Vakvernieuwing*. Available at: http://www.betanova.nl.

Van Berkel, B. (2005). *The Structure of Current School Chemistry*. Thesis Universiteit Utrecht.

Van den Akker, J. (1998). The science curriculum: Between ideals and outcomes. In B. Fraser & K. Tobin (Eds.), *International Handbook of Science Education* (Vol. 1, pp. 421-447). Dordrecht, The Netherlands: Kluwer.

Van der Woud, L., & van Grinsven, V. (2010). *Rapportage Onderzoek Nieuwe Scheikunde*. DUO Market Research, Utrecht.

Van Koten, G., De Kruijf, B., Driessen, H. P. W., Kerkstra, A., & Meinema, H. A. (2002). *Bouwen aan Scheikunde ("Building Chemistry")*. SLO, Stichting Leerplanontwikkeling, Enschede.

# Chapter 19

## Potential Learning Outcomes Inferred from French Curricula in Science Education

*Patrice Venturini*[1] *& Andrée Tiberghien*[2]
[1]*University of Toulouse, France*
[2]*University of Lyon, France*

## Abstract

This paper analyses the new French curricula in physics and chemistry education from grade 7 to grade 12 that is to say in the secondary schools. It aims at envisaging their potential learning outcomes and for this, it characterises the structure, the coherence and the epistemological status of the content to be taught, the students' expected performances in terms of cognitive demand, and the recommended process for teaching science which is related to inquiry based teaching. Our analysis shows that the curriculum of grades 7 to 9 (lower secondary schools) possesses continuity, unity, and coherence. We claim that this gives stability and sense to the learning outcomes. At the end of grade 9, the totality of the learning outcomes constitutes a general physics and chemistry culture, in which memorised knowledge holds a preponderant place. The construction of a specialised scientific culture begins in grade 11 and continues in grade 12: activities dealing with interpretative thinking play at this moment a predominant part. Grade 10 has an intermediate status. These three curricula are structured by themes. The themes of grades 10 and 11 gather together concepts that belong to very different scientific domains while the themes of grade 12 present more unity and are associated to few indications to teach their content. Thus, particularly in grades 10 and 11, teachers have to invent the continuity of knowledge, to structure concepts beyond the different themes, and to clear up the epistemological status of the different sub-topics. Otherwise, we hypothesise that outcomes will be factual, disjointed, and meaningless. As for the particular inquiry process described in the curricula, it lacks of a moment for reflection and criticism about the process itself. Thus it will be difficult for the students to internalize its different steps, their role, and their status, in relation with the nature of science. Lastly, these curricula are implemented in a particular context, characterized by teachers' habits of very detailed and guiding indications given by the institution, teachers' personal and professional inexperience of inquiry processes, teachers' lack of knowledge about the nature of science, and teachers' lack of in-service training. These elements lead us to fear a deterioration of the learning outcomes mentioned in the different curricula, particularly in higher secondary schools (grade 10 and 11), at least in the near future.

**Potential learning outcomes inferred from French curricula in science education**

Like many countries, France recently established new standards in science education and thus modified the totality of its national curricula. The curriculum for lower secondary schools changed in 2006, and the change occurred in higher secondary schools in 2010[1]. The aim of these new curricula is, of course, to generate new learning outcomes.

The IEA[2] tri-partite model defines a curriculum at three levels (Houang & Schmidt, 2008, p. 2; Schmidt et al., 1997, p. 176):

- The intended curriculum, that is to say what a system intends students to study and learn. The curriculum announces or lists intentions, aims, and goals;
- The implemented curriculum, that is to say what is taught in classrooms;
- The attained curriculum, that is to say what students are able to demonstrate that they know.

Moreover, Schmidt et al. (1997, p. 178) add a "potentially implemented curriculum" comprising textbooks and other organized resource materials. These materials help make possible one or more potential implementations of curricular intentions.

French curricula come under the category of "curricula as intended learning outcomes" which focus on "ends, with lesser consideration of the means of reaching them. Purpose is specified by the intended outcomes" (Anderson, 2006, p. 812[3]; citing Shubert, 1986) (see extracts of curricula Appendices 1 and 2). Thus in this paper, to analyse the learning outcomes, we only consider the intended curriculum at different secondary grades. Of course, we are particularly aware that there are many differences between expected learning outcomes as defined in the intended curricula

---

[1] The previous change took place in 1996 in lower secondary schools and 1998 in higher secondary schools.
[2] International Association for the Evaluation of Educational Achievement.
[3] Anderson (2006, p. 811-814) presents a set of categories for describing different conceptions of a curriculum: curriculum as content or subject matter, curriculum as a programme of planned activities, curriculum as intended learning outcomes, curriculum as a cultural reproduction, curriculum as experience, curriculum as discrete tasks and concepts, curriculum as an agenda for social reconstruction, curriculum as "currere".

and real learning outcomes. However, we consider that the intended curriculum gives characteristic shape and direction to instruction because it is the content target for the implemented curriculum (Porter, 2004, p. 141). Thus we assume that the analysis of the potential learning outcomes will give us a first insight into what real learning outcomes could be. We will discuss the potential learning outcomes with regard to the context they are implemented in to give ideas on what they could really be in the class.

First, we give an outline of the French educational system, including science education, to describe the context in which the different curricula are developed in general terms. Afterwards, we point out the general structure of the successive curricula. To go into the analysis in depth, a theoretical framework is presented in the third part of this paper. Its use provides information about the potential learning outcomes that is discussed in the course of its presentation in the forth section. Lastly, we conclude by characterising the potential learning outcomes and making assumptions on what they could really be in the coming years.

# 1 Insights into the French Educational System Focusing on Science Education

French instruction is divided into three official "levels": 1) primary level (eight years, including three years in nursery school and the first five years of compulsory primary school – grades 1 to 5); 2) secondary level (seven years including four years in lower secondary school – grades 6 to 9 – and three years in higher secondary schools – grades 10 to 12); 3) higher education level. At the end of the lower secondary school, students choose between vocational and general/technological higher secondary school. Thus, until grade 9, all the students are subject to the same syllabuses and, at the end of the lower secondary school, all students are supposed to have acquired the knowledge and competences listed in the "Common Base of Knowledge and Competences". However, this is not compulsory for moving to the upper grade. At the end of the first year in the general higher secondary school (grade 10), students select general or technological training, in which they choose a particular orientation. For example, in general higher secondary schools, students choose among humanities, economics and science and take the corresponding courses from grade 11 to grade 12. In this paper, we choose to analyse the science education outcomes related to the secondary level, from which we exclude vocational and technological schools and only consider the course of scientific studies in general higher secondary schools.

French curricula are national; they are published in the "Official Journal of the French Republic" and are thus considered as texts of law: every teacher has to abide by them. Schooling is compulsory for children aged between six and sixteen.

From the secondary level, science education concerns biology and geology (taught by the same teacher) on the one hand, and physics and chemistry (taught by another teacher) on the other. Each group has a specific curriculum even though, in the lower secondary level, the two curricula have a common preamble. We focus here on the physics and chemistry curriculum. Physics and chemistry start to be taught as such at grade 7 and continue through to grade 12 in secondary schools [4].

To sum up, in the following we analyze the physics and chemistry learning outcomes derived from intended curricula from grade 7 to grade 12. Sometimes we focus more particularly on its physics part. We consider it useful to sketch the curricular structure for each of these lower and higher secondary levels. At the same time, we point out the main changes that have occurred during recent years.

## 2 Structure of the Curricula in Physics and Chemistry

### 2.1 Curriculum of Lower Secondary School (Grades 7 to 9)

This curriculum has changed progressively grade by grade since 2006 and now chemistry and physics teaching in lower secondary schools depends on one global curriculum concerning all grades. The curriculum guide governing physics and chemistry teaching comprises four parts:

- The first part is the "common introduction" to science, technology and mathematical education. It mainly details:
    - the scientific elements belonging to the Common Base of Knowledge and Competences (CBKC), that is to say "what it is indispensable to have mastered at the end of compulsory schooling";
    - the different steps of the investigative process;
    - the "convergence themes", which are themes each taught discipline should contribute to (see 4.3 and note 8).
- The second part is a preamble dedicated to physics and chemistry teaching. It completes the common introduction and specifies how these academic disciplines contribute to the scientific and technological culture of students. It also specifies the links the teacher has to implement with other academic disciplines and ICT. Lastly, it gives general information about assessment and about contents.

---

[4] However, science is also taught in nursery and primary schools.

- The third part concerns all the physics and chemistry contents the teacher must teach. Contents are presented grade by grade and structured by scientific themes (like Electrical circuits working in continuous current; Light sources and rectilinear propagation of light, Water in our environment etc.). For each theme, expected knowledge and abilities are defined, completed with some comments for the teacher (see Appendix 1 for an extract of this part of curriculum).
- The fourth part is the chapter of the CBKC dedicated to "scientific and technological culture". Knowledge, abilities, and attitudes are successively listed, some of them being related to physics and chemistry.

Compared to the previous curriculum, three major changes have taken place:
- The curriculum strongly emphasises the use of an investigative process (the same change occurred before at the primary level) while neither contents nor time allotted to teach them have changed.
- The CBKC lists, in particular, the elements that constitute "the scientific and technological culture" of each student.
- Science, technology, and mathematics curricula come under a "common introduction".

## 2.2 Curricula of Higher Secondary Schools (Grades 10 to 12)

Each grade is governed by an independent curriculum. The curriculum of grade 10 changed in 2010 and the curriculum of grades 11 and 12 will respectively change in 2011 and 2012. Each curriculum comprises two parts. The first one, named "preamble" gives some general indications about the aims of the curriculum and the methods to reach them (scientific process, experimental approach, historical perspective, links with other academic disciplines, the use of ICT), and presents the three structuring themes or phases. The second part presents "notions and contents" (that is to say "concepts to study") and "expected competences" in greater detail (see Appendix 2 for an extract of this part of curriculum in grade 10).

Compared to the previous syllabuses, five major changes have been introduced in grades 10 to 12:

- The contents to be taught were previously structured by physics or chemistry themes (mechanics, optics, organic chemistry, etc.). They are now structured by societal themes (sport, health, and universe in grade 10) or by "major phases of the scientific process: observation, understanding, action" (grades 11 and 12).

- The three curricula explicitly develop a set of "expected competences" associated to particular contents.
- The three curricula mention the investigative process as a pedagogical method the teacher has to use in his/her class.
- The duration of chemistry and physics teaching has been decreased from four hours a week to three hours since 2010 in grades 10 and 11, but has been maintained at five hours a week in grade 12.
- Curricula no longer provide examples of classroom activities or detailed comments about how to teach the various subjects. However, these comments are more developed in the grade 12 curriculum.

## 2.3 Discussion

Two of these new orientations seem to have particular consequences:
- Great importance is now given to the investigative process: its use is nearly compulsory in lower secondary schools and is strongly suggested in higher secondary schools. However, we consider that the students' investigations cannot concern really open questions due to time constraints: the content to be taught in grade 10 and 11 is indeed approximately the same as it was in the previous curricula which were taught in a transmissive way and time allotted to teach it has even been reduced; moreover, if the weekly duration of teaching has been maintained in grade 12, teachers have to prepare students to the final examination of the secondary school held at the end of the grade. Thus, the investigative process has to be developed in the class under time pressure.
- Expected outcomes are expressed in terms of "competences". In the "potentially implemented curriculum" of lower secondary schools, competences have been well specified and they are part of the core of school common outcomes (Common Base of Knowledge and Competences). On the other hand, in higher schools' curricula, the culture of competence is new, and the institutional definition of "competence" is not very clear (see section 4.3).

Implementing the investigative process in class (moreover under time constraints) and reasoning in terms of competence constitute an important qualitative jump compared with teachers' current professional habits. We must keep this in the back of our minds while characterising the learning outcomes from the analysis in depth of the intended curriculum.

# 3 Elements on which to Base the Analysis of the Intended Curriculum

According to the different papers quoted below, there are different and complementary ways to provide the reader with information about a curriculum and thus about its potential outcomes:
- Characterising the structure of the content to be taught (mapping topics over different grades and analysing the global "coherence" of the whole) and its epistemological status.
- Characterising the expected performance in terms of the corresponding cognitive demand.
- Characterising the process recommended to teach content as it often refers implicitly or explicitly to the scientific process.

These different points are successively addressed below. Applied to the different French curricula of science education, they will allow us to answer the questions related to conceptualisation, modelling, and development of learning outcomes.

## 3.1 Characterisation of the Structure, Coherence and Epistemological Status of the Content to Be Taught

### 3.1.1 Structure and coherence of the content to be taught

On the occasion of the "Survey of Mathematics and Science Opportunities" (SMSO), a TIMSS international curriculum analysis (Schmidt et al., 1997), researchers designed a tool to provide a broad multigrade map of content coverage for all topics: *"Topic Trace Mapping"* (TTM). Experts of each country had to use their knowledge of their country's curriculum guides to report:

- at what age each topic was intended to be introduced to students;
- the range of ages during which instruction was intended to take place;
- any age for which the topic was to be a focus (that is to receive special curricular emphasis)" (Schmidt et al., 1997, p. 193).

Moreover, they also had to specify how the sub-topics fit together in the coverage of the topic as a whole. However, this *In-depth Topic Trace Mapping (ITTM)* is not feasible for all the topics; it focused on only some of them. The combination of TTM and ITTM gives both breadth and depth to the points of view about the intended curriculum and thus on its macro and micro-structure. These tools allow analyses to be made on the "coherence" of the successive curricula or parts of curricula considered as a whole.

According to Schmidt, Wang, & Mc Knight (2005, p. 528), content standards are coherent when taken together if "they are articulated over time as a sequence of topics and performances consistent with the logical and, if appropriate, hierarchical nature of the disciplinary content from which the subject matter derives. [...]. This implies that, for a set of content standards 'to be coherent', they must evolve from particular [...] to deeper structures [5]. It is these deeper structures by which the particulars are connected [...]. This evolution should occur both over time within a particular grade level and as the student progresses across grades." When content standards are not based on a progressive structure that reflects the discipline, they "seem to appear arbitrary and look like a 'laundry list' of topics *(ibid.)*.

3.1.2 Epistemological status of content to be taught

The coherence of knowledge concerns not only the conceptual content but also its relation to reality. As Koponen & Pehkonen (2010) propose:

*"The idea of a special role of coherence in the context of giving explanations has been elaborated further by Thagard (1988, 1992, 2000, 2007), who on this basis introduces the idea of explanatory coherence, which is concerned with giving coherent explanations of real phenomena." (p. 262).*

To analyse the epistemological status of the knowledge to be taught, we focus on the modelling process in science that implies explanatory coherence. Moreover, in physics teaching, most of "the constructed models are [...] validated by matching them with experimental results" (Koponen & Pehkonen, 2010, p. 264). The associated processes will be analysed according to our development of a theoretical approach called "the two worlds" developed to design physics teaching resources and analyse teaching/learning activities in the classroom (Tiberghien, Vince, & Gaidioz, 2009). The main components that we distinguish are: (1) Theoretical physics statements/relations between physics concepts; (2) Selecting and processing the theoretical elements that fit the selected events and measurements; (3) Model built from components 2 and 4; (4) Selecting and treating events and measuring; (5) Observation of and experimenting on objects and events.

At secondary school level, we consider that modelling consists of going back and forth between these components: the given order does not mean that modelling im-

---

5 Failure to increase in sophistication and complexity across the grades would indicate a lack of coherence (Houang & Schmidt, 2008 p. 11).

plies all components or that only successive components can be related; all relations are possible. In physics teaching, the relations are often between the observations of the selected events and/or the actions of measurements on the one hand, and their formal treatments on the other (Tiberghien, Veillard, Le Maréchal, Buty, & Millar, 2001). The relations between theory and observation are a way to understand physics; they are not the aim of modelling. This analysis leads us to group the four components into two sets: first, the world of objects and events, including observations and measurements which, due to the physics teaching level, can be done directly; and second, the world of theories and models which involve theoretical statements and modelling components, including treatments of measurements and/or of selected events. Such a distinction allows us to analyse to what extent the concepts in the knowledge to be taught explain the material situations to be investigated without needing implicit knowledge or "ad hoc" theoretical knowledge that has to be given by the teacher.

## 3.2 Characterisation of Curriculum Elements with Expected Performance in Terms of Cognitive Demand

Defining curriculum content only in terms of topics is insufficient as reported by Porter (2004, p. 142). For him, content can further be defined by associating each topic with the types of cognitive demands that it makes. Porter (2002, p. 4; p.13) uses a five-level scale to characterise the cognitive demands. They are specified by the nature of corresponding tasks (and language frequently associated [6]):

- *Memorise facts, definitions, formulas* (recognise, identify, recall, recite, name, tell);
- *Perform procedures / solve routine problems* (do computation, make observation, take measurements, compare, develop fluency);
- *Communicate understanding of concepts* (communicate scientific ideas, use representations to model scientific ideas, explain findings and results, explain reasoning, describe, select);
- *Solve non-routine problems / make connections* (apply and adapt a variety of appropriate strategies to solve non-routine problems, analyse data, recognise patterns, explore, judge);
- *Hypothesise, generalise, prove* (complete proofs, make and investigate scientific hypothesis, infer from data and predict, determine the validity of scientific proposition).

---

6 Porter's proposition concerns mathematics, it has been slightly adapted for use in science.

In other respects, Dagget (2005) proposes the relevance of knowledge as another dimension to characterise curricula. The relevance is assessed with a five-level scale according to the extent of the domain the knowledge works on: 1) just knowing in one discipline; 2) Applying knowledge in one discipline; 3) Applying knowledge across disciplines; 4) Applying knowledge to real-world predictable situations; 5) Applying knowledge to real-world unpredictable situations.

Lastly, Newberry & Kueker (2008) have built a method for analyzing curricula based upon the principles of both Porter and Daggett. They propose four levels of Depth-Of-Knowledge (DOK) to characterise the performance expectations (*ibid.*, p. 23-24). Each objective of the curriculum concerning one topic is related to one level of DOK. A histogram representing the number of topics for each level is built and averages, median, etc. are given. Results can concern units or global science content. Webb (2002, p. 5-7) documents each level of DOK for a science curriculum:

- *Recall and reproduction of information and procedures;* Level 1 only requires students to demonstrate a rote response, use a well-known formula, follow a set procedure (like a recipe), or perform a clearly defined series of steps. A "simple" procedure is well-defined and typically involves only one step. Verbs such as "identify," "recall," "recognize," "use," "calculate," and "measure" distinguish Level 1;
- *Working with skill and concepts;* the content knowledge or process involved requires students to make some decisions about how to approach the question or problem and these actions imply more than one step. Keywords that generally distinguish a Level 2 item include "classify," "organize," "estimate," "make observations," "collect and display data," and "compare data";
- *Strategic thinking;* activities have more than one possible answer and require students to justify the response they give; experimental designs involve more than one dependent variable. Level 3 requires reasoning, planning, using evidence, developing a logical argument for concepts, explaining phenomena in terms of concepts, and using concepts to solve non-routine problems in science. The cognitive demands are complex and abstract and concern non-routine problems;
- *Extended thinking;* students are required to relate ideas within the content area or among content areas, have to select one approach among many alternatives or devise them to solve the situation, develop generalizations of the results obtained and the strategies used and apply them to new problem situations. Cognitive demands are very high and tasks are very complex. They need an extended period of time and often concern real-world situations.

As Newberry & Kueker's work takes account of both Porter's and Daggett's proposals, this method seems to be the most appropriate. However, with regard to the French context and to describe its lower levels more accurately, we propose slight modifications of this scale. In French curricula, many expected performances are related to simple recall of knowledge and to simple procedures and computation. For this reason, we decompose the first level *"Recall and reproduction of information and procedures"* into two parts: in our scale, we dedicate Level 1 to simple memorisation of knowledge and Level 2 to simple implementation of procedures and computation. As for the three upper levels of Newberry & Kueker's scale, on the one hand, we enrich them with elements taken from the same levels in Porter's scale[7] and, on the other hand, we clarify the title "working with concepts and skills" because it could also be applied to the levels "strategic thinking" and "extended thinking". We propose to call it "Start interpretative thinking", insofar as it refers to the use (in a modest way compared to what happens in the upper levels) of some concepts and skills that students have to choose to approach the question at stake. Thus, the five levels of our scale are:

1) Recall information;
2) Simple implementation of procedures and computations;
3) Start interpretative thinking;
4) Strategic thinking;
5) Extended Thinking.

An extended description of each of these levels is given in Appendix 3.

## 3.3 Characterisation of the Process Recommended for Teaching Science

The curricular guides recommend the use of an "investigative process" that we can relate to inquiry based teaching[8]. Generally speaking, it calls for defining and solving scientific problems by carrying out experiments. That is why we refer first to scientists' work to characterise this process.

Following Bybee (2002), Etkina et al. (2010, p. 55) use the term of *"scientific abilities"* to describe "some of the most important procedures, processes, and methods that scientists use when constructing knowledge and solving experimental problems." According to them *(ibid.)*, "scientific abilities include but are not limited to collecting and analyzing data from experiments; devising hypotheses and explanations and building theories; assessing, testing, and validating hypotheses and theories;

---
7   In our opinion, they are very close regarding the nature of cognitive demand.
8   When we speak of French curricula, we use "investigative process" instead of the international denomination "inquiry process" 1) to adopt the name used in French curricula "démarche d'investigation"; 2) because "inquiry based teaching" often refers to more open questions than the "investigative process" does in French classes.

and using specialized ways of representing phenomena and of communicating ideas (Duschl, Schweingruber, & Shouse, 2007; Ford & Forman, 2006).

Furthermore, Ford and Forman (2006, pp. 12-16), who based their work on a literature review, point out the social dimension of scientific activities, which is not really emphasised by Etkina et al. According to Ford and Forman, science practices include social, material and rhetorical dimensions. Actually, science's rationality and development are based on debates occurring in scientific communities. These debates are ultimately arbitrated by material aspects which also characterize what the discussions are about and why; scientific communities can be considered as involving the two roles of "constructor" and "critiquer" of claims regarding matters of fact, methods and values, working in interplay, and needing the mastery of a particular way of interacting. Thus, debating claims may be considered as a scientific ability.

Tiberghien (2011) completes these characterisations by borrowing elements from Hacking's point of view about scientific activities because "he associates modelling and processes" (which makes sense considering the two worlds theory). Hacking (1983, p. 213) makes a "tripartite division of activities: [...] speculation[9], calculation[10] and experimentation. By speculation I shall mean the intellectual world open to experimental verification". In other words, speculation concerns "the intellectual representation of something of interest, a playing with and restructuring of ideas to give at least a qualitative understanding of some general feature of the world". Hacking enhances the speculative part of scientific activities here.

We claim that this set of scientific abilities corresponds to the main part of scientists' work. But as pointed out by Etkina et al. (2010, p. 55),
*"for scientists, these abilities are internalized and become habits of mind used to approach new problems; they are scientists' cognitive tools. For the students who have not internalized these processes and procedures, scientific abilities are processes that they need to use reflectively and critically (Salomon & Perkins, 1989). After students internalize them, these abilities become their habits of mind as well".*

According to Tiberghien (2011), inquiry processes cannot be taught and learned by imitation (there is no scientist working in the classroom); doing alone will not allow students to give scientific meaning to their actions. Thus, it is necessary "to make explicit and put into words these abilities" in order that students build knowledge about science working.

---

9  "A dictionary says that the word 'theory' etymologically is derived from a Greek word which, in one connotation, is a speculation" (Hacking, 1983, p. 213).

10  "I do not mean mere computation, but the mathematical alteration of a given speculation, so that one brings into closer resonance with the world" (Hacking, 1983, p. 214).

*"Teaching science as an enquiry into enquiry must address epistemic goals that focus on how we know what we know, and why we believe the beliefs of science to be superior or more fruitful than competing viewpoints. Osborne (2001) has argued, if science and scientists are epistemically privileged, then it is a major shortcoming of our educational programs that we offer so little to justify the accord that the scientists would wish us to render unto scientific knowledge"* (Duschl & Grandy, 2008, p. 32).

Taking account of the whole of the previous analysis[11], we propose the following set of abilities (considered as processes, methods, and procedures) to characterise inquiry processes in science:

- Devising hypotheses/speculations and explanations;
- Developing, improving experiments and measures;
- Collecting and analyzing data from experiments;
- Using specialised ways of representing phenomena;
- Using specialised ways of communicating ideas;
- Building theories (theoretical elements);
- Assessing, testing, and validating hypotheses and theories;
- Debating claims related to matters of fact, methods, speculations, values ...
- Using the previous abilities reflectively and critically.

Now, we make use of this set of references on French intended curricula.

## 4 Potential Learning Outcomes Inferred from the Analysis of Intended Curricula

We first present the different topics to be taught, analysing their structure, their coherence and their epistemological status. We claim that these characteristics are important for knowledge to be available and efficient when required. In a second step, this leads us to examine the expected performances linked to the different topics mentioned in the different curricula (knowledge, abilities, and competences to master). These performances are analysed in terms of cognitive demand. Particular performances concern the scientific (or experimental) process. Thus, we analyse these potential outcomes separately in relation with the investigative process. We discuss the different analyses at the end of each section.

---

11  Particularly the analyses of Etkina et al. and Tiberghien.

## 4.1 Structure, Coherence, and Epistemological Status of the Content to Be Taught

Curricula are successively analysed at macro, intermediate, and micro levels.

### 4.1.1 Global structuring

At a macro level of analysis, annual contents to be taught are always divided into three parts[12]. Each of them is associated to a general theme.

*Table 1: General Themes of the Different Curricula*

| | | | |
|---|---|---|---|
| Grade 7 | Water in our environment – Mixtures and pure bodies | Continuous current circuits – Qualitative study | Light: sources and rectilinear propagation |
| Grade 8 | From the surrounding air to the molecule | Continuous current laws | Light: colours, images, speed |
| Grade 9 | Chemistry, science of matter transformation | Electrical energy and alternating current circuits | From gravitation to mechanical energy |
| Grade 10 | Health | Sport practice | The universe |
| Grade 11 | Observing: colours and images | Understanding: laws and models (fundamental interactions; conservation of energy) | Action: challenges of the 21st century (Energy; Synthesis of new molecules and materials) |
| Grade 12 | Observing: waves and matter | Understanding: laws and models (time and movement; matter structure and transformation; energy, matter and radiation) | Action: challenges of the 21st century (Resources saving and environmental protection; synthesis of new molecules; information transmission and storage) |

In lower secondary schools (grades 7, 8, and 9) physics and chemistry domains structure the contents to be taught. Moreover, a part of the knowledge linked to each theme contributes to "convergence themes" with other academic disciplines (energy, environment, sustainable development, meteorology and climatology, health, security, statistical way of thinking about the world). However, these "convergence themes"

---

12 There are three parts surely because there are three terms in a school year.

are not taught directly and, consequently, relating knowledge coming from different disciplines is under the students' responsibility.

Grade 10 is the first common year[13] of higher secondary school. Learning outcomes are presented within two social themes (health and sport practice). The third theme (the Universe) is more ambiguous insofar as it has both social and scientific status. Grade 11 is the first year of specialised scientific studies for students who choose a science orientation until the end of grade 12. The three themes of both curricula are related to the three steps (or phases) of initiation to the scientific process: "observing, understanding, and acting". These thematic organisations are probably linked to the purposes of the different curricula: grade 10 aims to make students want to study science in grade 11, and grade 11 and 12 aim to enhance the scientific process.

4.1.2 Structuring of topics and sub-topics in physics

The following Topic Trace Mapping over the six grades (Table 2) indicates, at an intermediate level, the content coverage for all physics topics from grade 7 to grade 12. Relating to Schmidt et al.'s proposals (1997) to obtain breadth and depth points of view of the intended curriculum and check its coherence, two In-depth Topic Trace Mappings on the electrokinetics and optics sub-topics have been built. However, they are not given here due to the paper space constraints. Since relations between the general themes (Table 1) and some topics (Table 2) are not evident, they are indicated in Appendix 4.

The analysis of Table 2 reveals that during grades 7 to 9, students are supposed to acquire knowledge and competences about different topics. The general properties of matter and its particular structure (molecules, atoms) are broached. The students work on the basic laws and properties of electric circuits and are given a general view of domestic electricity, particularly in relation to safety and energy. Colour vision and lens elements, notions connected to gravitation, weight and mass, and links between mechanical energy and car safety complete this comprehensive view. Grade 7 is characterised by a phenomenological approach and focuses on the physical properties of matter[14], while models and electricity[15] are more concerned in grade 8. Grade 9 puts the emphasis on domestic electricity[16] and energy aspects, drawing on what has already been said about energy in the previous grades. Mechanics, which can be considered as more abstract, is only tackled slightly in grade 9 while Electricity and Properties of Matter progressively unfurl from grade 7 to grade 9 (see Table 2).

---

13  Common for all general and technological schools.
14  39% of expected knowledge and abilities concern physical properties of matter in grade 7.
15  38% of expected knowledge and abilities concern electricity in grade 8.
16  37% of expected knowledge and abilities concern electricity and magnetism in grade 9.

*Table 2: Topic Trace Mapping over Six Grades in Physics*

| Topics | Grade 7 | Grade 8 | Grade 9 | Grade 10 | Grade 11 | Grade 12 |
|---|---|---|---|---|---|---|
| **Physical properties of matter** | | | | | | |
| Mixtures and pure bodies | X | | | | | |
| Physical quantities linked to matter | X | | | X | | |
| State changes | X | | | | X | |
| Gas properties | | X | | X | | |
| Structure of matter | | X | X | X | X | |
| Nuclear reactions | | | | | X | |
| Energy | | | | | X | X |
| **Electricity – Magnetism** | | | | | | |
| Electric circuit | X | | | | | |
| Electric conduction | X | | X | | | |
| Current strength – Voltage | | X | X | X | | |
| Series circuit – Parallel circuit | X | X | | | | |
| Resistance | | X | | | X | |
| Current and voltage laws | | X | | | | |
| Energy (Power – sources) | X | X | X | | X | |
| Safety | X | X | X | | | |
| Electrostatics | | | | | X | |
| Magnetic field – Force of Laplace | | | X | | X | |
| **Optics** | | | | | | |
| Light sources – Vision | X | X | | | X | |
| Light propagation | X | X | | X | | |
| Lenses | | X | | | X | |
| Colours of objects | | X | | | X | |
| Energy | | X | | | X | |
| **Waves and modern physics** | | | | | | |
| Waves properties | | | | | | X |
| Undulatory properties of light | | | | X | X | X |
| Quantization of energy – Case of light | | | | | X | X |
| Spectral analysis | | | | X | X | X |
| Electromagnetic waves | | | | | X | X |
| Mechanical waves | | | | | | X |
| Wave particle duality | | | | | | X |
| Limited relativity | | | | | | X |
| Information transmission & storage | | | | | | X |
| **Mechanics** | | | | | | |
| Gravitational interactions | | | X | X | X | |
| Weight mass | | | X | X | X | |
| Frame of reference – Kinematics | | | | X | | X |
| Actions – Forces | | | | X | X | X |
| Newton's laws – Momentum | | | | X | | X |
| Oscillators | | | | | | X |
| Work | | | | | | X |
| Energy | | | X | | X | X |

As for grade 10, two trends appear. On the one hand, this grade again brings up elements of the CBKC (e.g., alternative voltage and its properties, weight and mass, gravitational interactions, light propagation) or just completes them (e.g., temperature and pressure added to physical quantities). On the other hand, this grade goes further into elements related to properties of matter (electronic layers, structure of nucleus, and microscopic model of gas), optics (wavelength, spectroscopy) and mechanics (forces, Newton's law, and kinematics). Most of them will be studied thoroughly in grades 11 and 12 (Table 2). Grade 11 tackles the structure of matter, electricity, optics, waves, modern physics, and mechanics together. The majority of its topics has already been broached (12 out of 20 in lower secondary schools, 3 out of 20 in grade 10 – see Table 2) and the curriculum now goes into them in depth. Lastly in grade 12, new topics are introduced (7 out of 16) and are related to more complex concepts (e.g., limited relativity or waves properties); the curriculum focuses on mechanics, waves, and modern physics. To complete this global view, we point out twice a year's break in two physics domains: optics (grades 9 and 12) and electricity (grades 10 and 12).

Although the last three curricula are different regarding the nature of learning outcomes, they are structured by themes which are not linked to physics domains as they were in grades 5 to 7. In particular in grade 10, two themes come from society activity: sport practice and health whereas in grades 11 and 12 the themes are related to science functioning. Thus, we have to take into consideration not only the nature of the topics to be taught, but also how they appear in the different themes. For that, we can give a brief glimpse into the "notions and contents" related to the different themes. For example, the theme "sport practice" (grade 10) comprises, among other things, forces, principle of inertia, dissolving, dilution, chemical reaction, pressure, molecular models, chemical formulae, chromatography etc., and the theme "understanding: laws and models" (grade 11) comprises radioactivity, electrostatics, dissolving, state change, alcohol nomenclature, energy of chemical reaction, magnetic field, gravitation, and kinetic and potential energy. Therefore, each theme or sub-theme gathers together very heterogeneous topics and sub-topics. However, this trend is less marked in grade 12. If the themes gather together sub-themes that are only juxtaposed (e.g., the theme "Understanding: laws and models" gathers the three sub-themes "time movement and evolution; matter structure and transformation; energy, matter, and radiation"), the sub-themes contents are generally more consistent.

4.1.3   Epistemological status of the "notions and contents" to be taught (grades 10 to 12)

The curriculum of grades 7 to 9 specifies the expected knowledge and abilities while the curricula of grades 10 to 12 specify both the "notions and contents" to be taught and the associated "expected competences" (see Appendices 1 and 2). At the previous intermediate level of analysis of the "notions and contents", we have already pointed out that the topics are not grouped together according to the logic of physics domains. At a micro level of analysis, we observe elements with different epistemological status (objects and events, concepts and models) at the same level of presentation and without any differentiation. For example, in grade 11, the sub-theme "colour vision and image" brings together elements that are related to

- Objects and events, comprising objects (eye, thin converging lenses, real and virtual image), properties and physical quantities (colours of objects, vergence of lenses), and phenomena and events (eye accommodation, colour blindness);
- Models and theories, comprising concepts (absorption, diffusion, transmission), models (model of the reduced eye, lens equation, additive and negative synthesis of colour), or comparison of models (working comparison of eye and camera).

Moreover, sometimes concepts or models are missing to explain the events in question. For example, (grade 10) to investigate the principles underlying scanning and radiography, the set of concepts including "sound and electromagnetic waves", "rectilinear propagation of light", "velocity of light and sound", "refraction and total reflection" are insufficient. The knowledge to be taught does not fully match the material situation the curriculum proposes to explain, which needs elements about the phenomena of absorption, transmission, reflection when waves go through matter. Thus, in this case, relations between the world of models and theories and the world of phenomena and events are partial. Furthermore, in this example, physics concepts are just placed side by side: therefore, students cannot link electromagnetic waves characterized by their frequency and rectilinear propagation of light or refraction even though they both belong to the same world of models and theories, while they will perhaps inappropriately link properties of sound waves and light waves.

4.1.4 Discussion

In our opinion, the description above shows that the themes of grades 7 to 9 possess continuity and unity: they belong to three domains of physics and are developed over two or three years. Their topics are articulated over time according the hierarchical structure of physics. In each domain, complexity increases steadily inside a particular grade and also from grade 7 to grade 9. Thus, we claim that this curriculum is coherent regarding Schmidt, Wang & Mc Knight's definition (2005, p. 528). This coherence favours relations between different learning outcomes, giving them stability and sense. Moreover, these learning outcomes really deal with knowledge of the Common Base of Knowledge and Competences (CBKC) that all students must have at the end of grade 9 (for example: "Knowing that the energy perceptible in motion can have different forms and can be transformed from one to another; knowing electric energy and its importance; knowing the resources of fossil energy and renewable energies"). To sum up, this curriculum seems to be coherent and to reach its main aim regarding the topics in question.

Concerning grade 10, we have pointed out the existence of two trends, one related to the extension of the CBKC, and the other to the deepening of scientific knowledge. Thus, we claim that this grade and its learning outcomes have an ambiguous status: partially linked to the common culture and not fully linked to the specialised scientific culture. As for grade 11, it goes further into topics and all domains of physics are addressed, while grade 12 broaches concepts that are much more complex and focuses only on mechanics, waves, and modern physics. Therefore, the nature of learning outcomes of grades 11 and 12 clearly changes: they now contribute to a specialised scientific culture and make a break with learning outcomes from grades 7 to 9. Moreover, in grades 11 and 12, it is difficult to structure teaching on the basis of theme structuring insofar as it is impossible to learn and teach physics by only focusing on observation (theme 1) or only on focusing on modelling (theme 2). In the same perspective, it is difficult, in grade 10, to relate the expected competences (expressed in physics and chemistry terms) to the corresponding social themes (see the discussion section 4.2.4). Lastly, the previous description also points out that: 1) themes of grades 10 to 12 make a break with themes of grades 7 to 9 in that they concern social life or the scientific process[17] and no longer domains of physics or chemistry; 2) these themes of grades 10 and 11 gather together different topics and look like a "laundry list" while the contents tackled within a sub-theme in grade 12 are generally more coherent ; 3) these themes bring together sub-topics with very different epistemological status and sometimes a lack of epistemological coherence.

To sum up, grades 10 and 11 are sorely lacking in coherence on several levels. Thus the teacher has first to build the content coherence: he/she has to invent the continuity of knowledge[18], to structure concepts beyond the different themes, and to clear up the epistemological status of the different sub-topics. Moreover, he/she has to give more thematic coherence to the different set of topics and also takes account of what is known about physics and chemistry learning (Tiberghien, Vince & Gaidoz, 2009). In our opinion, without these actions, which need time in class[19] and are not specified in the two curricula, learning outcomes will be sparse, factual, local, and meaningless. Now, the coherence of learning outcomes, their meaning, and their efficiency are completely under the teacher's responsibility. This situation is not alarming from the absolute point of view but the French context makes it worrying. In the previous

---

17  According to the curriculum.
18  This is all the more necessary as the two curricula do not give any indications about teaching content as was previously the case.
19  Teaching time has been reduced but without reducing the content to be taught.

curricula (which are still valid in grade 12 until 2012), teachers had indications about what to teach in what order and for what duration, when to lecture and when to work in the laboratory; they also had precise comments on what to say and what not to say when teaching a particular topic. They have been strongly guided if not strongly constrained for many years. Thus, we think that they are totally unprepared for the liberty and responsibility attributed by these two new curricula. As for the curriculum of grade 12, the gap is less important for teachers: six pages of teaching instructions are proposed in relation with each theme, and the continuity of knowledge is easier to invent, at least within each sub-theme because their contents are more coherent. However, the necessity to clear up the epistemological status of different contents remains. Lastly, our analysis shows that the three curricula of grades 10 to 12 taken as a whole lack of homogeneity. Each of them seems to be built by a different team having its own priorities and only sharing with others the same general orientations: investigative process as pedagogical method; outcomes described in terms of expected competences; contents structured within themes.

## 4.2 Expected Performances and Associated Cognitive Demand

According to curricula, different types of expected outcomes are linked to physics topics. After this first specification, these expected outcomes are analysed in relation to the corresponding cognitive demand. Moreover, some outcomes are more general and are mentioned in preambles. We note them afterwards. Due to their important role in the pedagogical process, those that are related to the investigative process are analysed in the next section.

### 4.2.1 Expected outcome related to physics topics: knowledge, abilities, attitudes, competences

The Common Base of Knowledge and Competences (end of grade 9) distinguishes knowledge, abilities, and attitudes, the whole making up "scientific culture", and the curriculum preamble of grades 6 to 9 mentions the acquisition of "specific disciplinary knowledge and abilities to make use of them in different situations, developing formative and responsible attitudes". The curriculum guide distinguishes "knowledge" (like "the laser is dangerous for eyes") from abilities (like "Practicing an experimental process with light sources, diffusing objects, and opaque obstacles". Moreover, a document completing the curriculum guide details the different abilities and proposes different levels for them according to the different grades. For example the general ability "practicing an experimental process" comprises the particular ability "hypothesizing" among other things. At the end of grade 6, the student has to "choose a hypothesis in a list"; at the end of grade 8, he/she has to "propose a hypothesis corresponding to the problem defined"; lastly, at the end of grade 9, he/she has to "propose one or more hypotheses corresponding to a given situation".

In the higher secondary schools, the curricula specify only "expected competences" for example "Knowing the value of the speed of sound in air"; "Extracting and exploiting information related to the wave nature and wave frequency". Thus, the list of "expected competences" (that is to say "knowledge to summon up, abilities to make use of and attitude to acquire") juxtaposes knowledge items and various abilities, and mastering one of them may, in fact, be considered as a competence[20]. This definition and the list of "expected competences" are the sole elements given in both curricula to help teachers implement them. Moreover, competences are often formulated in a general way and thus can lead to different levels of formalization or activities. For example:

- "Qualitatively interpreting the dispersion of white light by a prism" (grade 10) can lead to various interpretations while remaining qualitative.
- "Describing the model of the eye" (Grade 11) can lead to an elementary model or to a more complex one.
- "Practicing an experimental process" can be reduced to carrying out a defined protocol, or can concern the experimental study of a phenomenon using few concepts and variables (this situation occurs in most cases), and even the solving of an open question.

These examples are not isolated cases, and most of the other items remain ambiguous.

### 4.2.2 Characterisation of expected outcomes by the nature of the associated cognitive demand

This characterisation is founded on the five level scale presented in Appendix 3 which is applied to each different expected knowledge and ability (grades 7 to 9) and to each different expected competence (grades 10 to 12) listed in the various curricula. As general abilities are often mentioned (e.g., practicing an experimental process) we have counted them as many times as they deal with different contents. Furthermore, some formulations are ambiguous; thus the classification also depends on the knowledge researchers have about what is most likely to happen in a classroom from a given expected knowledge, ability or competence. However, we claim that this does

---

20 Furthermore, we can see that this view of competence is different from the common one, according which competences refer to a potentially successful action in a particular context, including the cognitive resources and the schemes allowing their efficient activation on time (Perrenoud, 1998).

not cast doubt on the general trends shown by the Table 3, even though the given percentages could be debated and vary a little according to different researchers.

*Table 3: Distribution of the Expected Outcomes According to Different Grades and Different Levels of Cognitive Demand (Number and Percentage). These Percentages are Indicative*

| Level | Grade 7 | Grade 8 | Grade 9 | Grade 10 | Grade 11 | Grade 12 |
|---|---|---|---|---|---|---|
| 1 Recall information | 90 – 64 % | 73 – 56 % | 78 – 61 % | 43 – 40 % | 53 – 33 % | 65 – 34 % |
| 2 Simple implementation of procedures and computations | 32 – 23 % | 24 – 18 % | 28 – 22 % | 32 – 30 % | 43 – 26 % | 45 – 24 % |
| 3 Start of interpretative thinking | 18 – 13 % | 34 – 26 % | 22 – 17 % | 33 – 31 % | 65 – 40 % | 74 – 39 % |
| 4 Strategic thinking | 0 | 0 | 0 | 0 | 2 – 1 % | 5 – 3% |
| 5 Extended Thinking | 0 | 0 | 0 | 0 | 0 | 0 |
| Total of expected knowledge, abilities and competences | 140 – 100 % | 131 – 100 % | 128 – 100 % | 108 – 100 % | 163 – 100 % | 189 – 100 % |

From grades 7 to 9, we observe that priority is given to knowledge memorisation while "interpretative thinking" is nearly marginal. The balance of expected outcomes is partially restored in grade 10, although the number of items linked with interpretative thinking does not exceed one out of three. A reversal logically occurs in grades 11 and 12, in which priority is given to interpretative thinking.

Students have very few opportunities to exercise "strategic thinking" in grades 11 and 12. More surely, they can exercise "strategic thinking" and "extended thinking" outside of the regular curriculum. Actually, grade 10 offers courses to enable students to choose their orientation at the end of the year. Among them, "Scientific Methods and Practices" allows a minority of students to deal with projects related to mathematics, biology, geology, physics, and chemistry for three hours a week. Besides, in grade 11, students have to carry out "Personal tutored work" for two hours a week, dealing with an open scientific question they choose and solve in groups using two academic disciplines. One of them can be physics. But these opportunities do not concern all students.

### 4.2.3 Expected outcomes mentioned in preambles

Preambles mention other outcomes related to

- Attitudes: besides the usual "sense of observation, curiosity, critical mind etc.", each curriculum lays particular stress on "liking for science";
- Vocational projects: outcomes of grades 10 to 12 now include knowledge about scientific professions;
- Culture: relations between science, art and technology must now be taught in each grade while students have to know elements linked to the history of scientific knowledge in grades 10 to 12;
- Mastery of language: progress is expected (in French but as well in English in grade 12);
- ICT: ICT must be used in a suitable way (doing science, looking for information, working with others...);
- Measures and uncertainty in grade 12.

### 4.2.4 Discussion

Thanks to the structuring of general abilities according the different grades, teachers in lower secondary schools have tools to help them to work on these elements. Thus, we think that learning outcomes at this level can soon include abilities like "practicing a scientific (or experimental) process", "looking for, extracting, and structuring information" or "communicating a process and results". We think that this could happen even though we are aware that the importance of the number of expected outcomes related to memorization and simple implementation could be an obstacle. On the other hand, for the moment, teachers of higher secondary schools have no help in implementing progressive work on abilities linked to the previous grades. Thus, we think that there is very little chance of seeing more general scientific abilities in learning outcomes than with the previous curriculum, at least for the next few years. Besides, bearing in mind that "competences" in grades 10 to 12 comprise punctual knowledge, elementary procedures and general abilities, teachers have to organize these elements for students to be aware of the different levels (both for content, epistemology and also for relations to technical uses) of what they learn.

The nature of the cognitive demand associated with expected competences changes strongly at the start of grade 11 and learning outcomes will change considerably in nature insofar as the majority of activities deal with "interpretative thinking". This change is borne out in grade 12, and moreover the concepts at stake are more complex (see Table 2). This important break may be an obstacle for many students, particularly for those who are not interested in physics, even if they choose a scientific orientation. Thus, the quality of the learning outcomes could be affected and these students could be as disengaged as they were with the previous curriculum in the same grade for the same reasons (Venturini, 2007a, p. 1075). This break also signifies that, before grade 11, spaces for arguing and debate, challenging activities, collaborative works, and moments of autonomy under the students' responsibility have not the same importance, at least if we base our judgement on the number of expected outcomes linked to them. Now, these spaces, activities, works, moments etc. are liable to engage students in studying physics (Venturini, 2007b, pp. 227-234). Therefore, we are not at all sure that "liking for physics" will be a learning outcome shared by a majority of students. This hypothesis is enhanced by the nature of expected competences of grade 10; they are formulated in physics and chemistry words and thus have little chance to develop the scientific interest of teenagers, whereas scientific topics are included in a social perspective precisely to give rise to scientific vocations.

Lastly, as for knowledge about scientific professions, the history of science or links between the arts, science and technology, inventing the topics to be considered and their distribution over grades is the teachers' responsibility. We hypothesize that, in the coming years, these learning outcomes will be absent because of teachers' lack of mastery of these points and even more of how to teach them.

### 4.3 Characterisation of the French Investigative Process Recommended for the Teaching of Science

According to the curriculum preamble for lower secondary schools, "physics and chemistry teaching allows students to be able (1) "to practice a scientific process"; (2) "to handle and experiment"; (3) "to express and exploit the results provided by measurements or documents. [...] The investigative process helps to develop these abilities". This pedagogical process comprises seven stages ("seven moments") and the order of their presentation does not imply that they have to be implemented linearly in the lesson: (1) "choice of a situation embodying a problem"; (2) "Students' appropriation of the problem"; (3) "Formulation of conjectures, explanative hypotheses and possible protocols"; (4) "Investigation or problem solving carried out by students"; (5) "argumentative exchanges dealing with the proposals put forward"; (6) "acquiring and structuring new knowledge"; (7) "making knowledge operational".

We discuss these two sets of definitions, first by comparing them with our characterisation of investigative processes and, second, by hypothesising on what could effectively happen in the classrooms, taking the context into account.

4.3.1 Discussion on the characterization of the French investigative process

To begin this discussion, we recall the list of "processes, procedures and methods" characterising inquiry processes (see section 1.3): Devising hypotheses/speculations and explanations; Developing, improving experiments and measures; Collecting and analyzing data from experiments; Using specialized ways of representing phenomena; Using specialized ways of communicating ideas; Building theoretical elements; Assessing, testing, and validating hypotheses and theories; Debating claims related to matters of fact, methods, speculations, values; Using the previous abilities reflectively and critically.

Comparing the different stages of the French investigative process to the elements of this list, we observe the absence of moments for reflection and criticism about the process itself so that students internalize its different steps and their role and status. Besides, we claim that the French process lacks in "devising speculations and explanation". If students have to formulate "explanative hypotheses" (stage 3), the speculative models (often naïve) leading to these hypothesis are not emphasized. Following Hacking's analysis, we think that "speculation" is an important part of scientific work and we agree with Windschitl, Thompson and Braaten (2008, p. 941) when they propose "a model based inquiry as a new paradigm of preferences for school investigations". As for the other elements of the list, we claim that the different stages of the French investigative process include them to a greater or lesser degree, at least in their description if not directly in their title. For example, we find in stage 7 "making knowledge operational" "exercises aimed at mastering ways of expression linked to knowledge: natural and symbolic language, graphic representations ..." This can be related to "using specialised ways of representation" and "using specialised ways of communication".

Thus, we can expect several learning outcomes linked to the scientific process provided that teachers include moments in their lessons for reflection on and criticism of the process.

4.3.2 Discussion on the implementation of the French investigative process

However, this conclusion has to be strongly tempered regarding the context in which the French investigative process is implemented. To our mind, it is characterised 1) by lack of teachers' mastery of scientific or investigative processes; 2) by lack of time to conduct the process and the obligation to teach contents in a given time (see section 3.3).

Insofar as teachers (or at least a very large majority of them) have never experienced this process themselves as active participants and, moreover, do not master science epistemology (Abd-El-Khalick & Lederman, 2000; Roletto, 1998), we hypothesise that many of them will naturalise the process following all the given stages formally and linearly. This will lead to a stereotyped process associated with a considerable loss of meaning. We consider that time pressure will encourage such developments. Some (rare) experienced teachers of lower secondary schools stand back slightly and deal with the time pressure in two ways: some of them focus on the pedagogical dimension of the investigative process; others focus on its scientific dimension.

- The former build lessons where moments of students' activity and moments of structuring alternate regularly (Calmettes, 2010). During students' activity, they identify elements they will draw on afterwards and watch over students' use of the components of the learning environment provided. During the moments of structuring they recall previous knowledge, draw on writings or utterances of good students, preventively eliminate disruptive phenomena, lead students to use scientific vocabulary and draw only on results allowing them to argue in favour of the knowledge at stake. In this case, we assume that learning outcomes concerning the scientific process will be rare.
- The latter build lessons working on a part of the investigative process at each lesson[21]. For example, in one lesson, they work on hypothesising with students, who devise speculations and explanations, and they implement themselves the protocol to assess each hypothesis without calling on the students while, in another lesson, they will propose three or four hypotheses themselves and will ask the students to build a protocol to assess each of them. During the remaining time, they teach contents in a conventional way. In this case, we expect some learning outcomes related to the scientific process, particularly if, at the end of the term or the year, students have the opportunity to conduct a project involving all the scientific abilities previously identified. However, in our opinion, teachers have to be careful not to focus only on the process at the expense of scientific content.

---

21  We base this assertion on the knowledge we have on what happens in French science classrooms, and on two teachers' interviews.

## 5 Conclusion: Characterisation of French Learning Outcomes in Physics Education

Based on this long analysis of French intended curricula, we are now able to characterise the potential learning outcomes in physics education from grade 7 to grade 12 (we recall that grades 7 to 9 take place in lower secondary schools). In the second part of this conclusion, we make assumptions about what they could really become in the near future.

### 5.1 Potential Learning Outcomes in Physics Education

Outcomes concern mainly knowledge and abilities and, in a minor way, attitudes. These three categories of outcomes are distinguished in grades 7 to 9 but they are not explicitly mentioned in grades 10 and 11, where they are considered as "competences". Abilities can have a local scope like procedures or know-how; they also can have a general and more powerful scope when they are linked to the unfolding of the scientific process.

Learning outcomes from grades 7 to 9 are structured according to the hierarchical logic of domains of physics, their complexity increases steadily over grades and they constitute a coherent whole. This concerns knowledge as well as abilities. On the other hand, learning outcomes from grades 10 to 12 are structured according to themes and not according to the logic of physical domains. Moreover, they include objects belonging to different epistemological categories without any differentiation. The list of the themes' outcomes lacks both content and epistemological coherence. Lastly, general abilities linked to the scientific process are likewise defined over grades. Thus, if the two intended curricula of grades 10 to 12 are interpreted narrowly and without considerable structuring work from the teacher, outcomes will be factual, disjointed and meaningless, even if for grade 12 the continuity of knowledge in each theme is easier to grasp. Moreover, in all the cases, the quality of ability outcomes related to the scientific processes is governed by the teacher's introduction of moments of reflection and criticism during the investigative process for students to internalise the process. This teacher's introduction added to moments of students' "speculation" governs the existence of outcomes related to the nature of science. However, all curricula being very dense, the teachers, who have little or no training on the nature of science, are not inclined to deal with it.

At the end of grade 9 (i.e. the end of the lower secondary school), the totality of the learning outcomes constitutes a general physics and chemistry culture, as defined in "the Common Base of Knowledge and Competences". Memorised knowledge holds a preponderant place in this general culture. In contrast to this situation, grades 11 and 12 starts with a specialised physics culture: it goes thoroughly into the outcomes provided by the lower secondary school, it deals with all main domains of physics and activities dealing with interpretative thinking play a predominant part. Their learning outcomes may be characterised by an important qualitative jump compared to the previous ones. Lastly, learning outcomes provided by grade 10 have an intermediate status: some of them come under a general physics and chemistry culture while others already participate in a specialised culture. Besides, they concern recall of knowledge, simple implementation of procedures and calculation, and interpretative thinking in a more or less similar way.

To complete this overview, we must point out particular expected learning outcomes: knowledge about scientific professions, about the history of science and about relations between art and science. We have already drawn attention to the importance of the teacher's work to implement activities related to these points for the first time in his/her professional life. Lastly, a desire to study science is another important outcome which may be considered only as a result of school activities.

## 5.2 Probable Learning Outcomes in the Near Future

On several occasions, we have pointed out how much the French context in science education poses a great threat to the quality of learning outcomes. Teachers now have to deal with: teaching under time pressure; personal and professional inexperience of investigative processes; lack of knowledge about the nature of science; strong and totally new responsibilities for knowledge structuring in higher secondary schools; teaching new topics not related to their professional culture; lack of in-service training. Thus, for the next few years, we hypothesise (and have already observed in some classes) a serious deterioration of the previous potential outcomes, particularly in higher schools (the implementation of the new curriculum is now in progress in grade 10): naturalisation of the investigative process, hence lack of outputs related to a desire to study science and to contemporary knowledge of the scientific process; deterioration of the quality of knowledge outcomes (disjointed and meaningless); sham activities concerning scientific professions, history of science and relations between art and science; etc. However, we think things will go a little better in lower secondary schools due to the structuring and the indications of the curriculum.

To sum up, we consider that major changes have occurred in French science curricula for which French science teachers are not prepared at present, particularly in higher secondary schools, where teachers are in a state of confusion. Without a serious effort in favour of in-service training and clarification and structuring of higher schools' curricula, physics teaching will probably become critical.

# References

Abd-El-Khalick, F. & Lederman, N. (2000). Improving science teachers' conceptions of nature of science: a critical review of the literature. *International Journal of Science Education*, *22*(7), 665-701.

Anderson, R. D. (2006). Inquiry as an organizing theme for science curricula. In S.K. Abell & N.G. Lederman (Eds.), *Handbook of Research in Science Education* (pp. 807-830). Mahwah (NJ): Laurence Erlbaum Associates Inc.

Bybee, R. W. (2000). Teaching science as inquiry. In J. Minstrell & E. van Zee (Eds.), *Inquiring in Inquiry Learning and Teaching in Science* (pp. 20–46). Washington, DC: American Academy for the Advancement of Science.

Calmettes, B. (2010). Analyse praxéologique ascendante et pragmatique de pratiques ordinaires. Rapport pragmatique à l'enseigner. Étude de cas: Des enseignants experts en démarche d'investigation en physique [Pragmatic relation to teaching. Case study: expert teachers in physics investigative processes]. *Revue Didactique des Sciences et des Techniques*, 2, 235-272.

Daggett, W. (2005). Achieving academic excellence through rigor and relevance. *International Center for Leadership in Education*. Available at: http://www.leadered.com/white_papers.html (Date of Access: January 1$^{st}$, 2010).

Duschl, R. A. & Grandy, R. (2008). Reconsidering the character and role of inquiry in school science: framing the debates. In R. A. Duschl & R. Grandy (Eds.), *Teaching Scientific Inquiry* (pp. 1-37). Rotterdam: Sense Publishers.

Duschl, R. A., Schweingruber, H. A., & Shouse, A. W. (2007). *Taking Science to School: Learning and Teaching Science in Grades K-8*. Washington, DC: National Academies Press.

Etkina, E., Karelina, A., Ruibal-Villasenor, M., David, R., Jordan, R., & Hmelo-Silver, C. E. (2010). Design and Reflection Help Students Develop Scientific Abilities: Learning in Introductory Physics Laboratories. *Journal of Learning Sciences*, *19*(1), 54-98.

Ford, M. J. & Forman, E. A. (2006). Redefining disciplinary learning in classroom contexts. In J. Green & A. Luke (Eds.), *Review of Research in Education*, 30, 1-32.

Hacking, I. (1983). *Representing and Intervening. Introductory Topics in the Philosophy of Natural Science*. Cambridge: Cambridge University Press.

Houang, R. D. & Schmidt, W. H. (2008). *TIMSS International Curriculum Analysis and Measuring Educational Opportunities*. Communication at the 3$^{rd}$ IEA International Research Conference (IRC-2008). Taipei, September 2008.

Koponen, I. T. & Pehkonen, M. (2010). Coherent Knowledge Structures of Physics Represented as Concept Networks in Teacher Education. *Science & Education, 19*(3), 259-282.

Newberry, P. B. & Kueker, D. (2008). *How Do You Recognise a Rigorous and Relevant Curriculum: A Method for Analysing Rigor and Relevance in Science and Mathematics Curricula*. Available at: http://www.vivayic.com/whitepapers/curricula_analysis.pdf (Date of Access: January 1$^{st}$, 2011).

Perrenoud, P. (1998). La transposition didactique à partir de pratiques : des savoirs aux compétences [Didactic transposition from practices: from knowledge to competences]. *Revue des sciences de l'éducation, 24*(3), 487-514.

Porter, A. (2002). Measuring the content of instruction: Uses in research and practice. *Educational Researcher,* 31, 3-14.

Porter, A. (2004). Curriculum assessment. In J. Green, G. Camilli, & P. Elmore (Eds.), *Complementary Methods for Research in Education* (pp. 141-159). Washington DC: AERA.

Roletto, E. (1998). La science et les connaissances scientifiques [Science and scientific knoweledge]. *Aster,* 26, 11-30.

Salomon, G., & Perkins, D. N. (1989). Rocky roads to transfer: Rethinking mechanisms of a neglected phenomenon. *Educational Psychologist, 24*(2), 113-142.

Schmidt, W. H., Raizen, S. A., Britton, E. D., Bianchi, L. J. & Wolfe, R. G. (1997). *Many Visions, Many Aims: A Cross-National Investigation of Curricular Intentions in School Science.* Dordrecht, The Netherlands: Kluwer.

Schmidt, W. H., Wang, H. A., & McKnight, C. C. (2005). Curriculum Coherence: An Examination of US Mathematics and Science Content Standards from an International Perspective. *Journal of Curriculum Studies, 37*(5), 525-559.

Schubert, W. H. (1986). *Curriculum: Perspective Paradigm and Possibility.* New York: Macmillan.

Thagard, P. (1988). *Computational Philosophy of Science.* Cambridge, MA: MIT Press/ Bradford Books.

Thagard, P. (1992). *Conceptual Revolutions.* Princeton: Princeton University Press.

Thagard, P. (2000). *Coherence in Thought and Action.* Cambridge, MA: MIT Press.

Thagard, P. (2007). Coherence, truth, and the development of scientific knowledge. *Philosophy of Science,* 74, 28-47.

Tiberghien, A. (2011). Conception et analyse de ressources d'enseignement: le cas des démarches d'investigation. [Design and analysis of teaching resources: the case of investigative processes] In M. Grangeat (Ed.), *Les démarches d'investigation dans l'enseignement scientifique. Pratiques de classe, travail collectif enseignant, acquisitions des élèves.* Lyon: INRP.

Tiberghien, A., Veillard, L., Le Maréchal, J.-F., Buty, C., & Millar, R. (2001). An analysis of labwork tasks used in science teaching at upper secondary school and university levels in several European countries. *Science Education,* 85, 483-508.

Tiberghien, A., Vince, J., & Gaidioz, P. (2009). Design-based Research: Case of a teaching sequence on mechanics. *International Journal of Science Education, 31*(17), 2275-2314.

Venturini, P. (2007a). The Contribution of the Theory of Relation to Knowledge to Understanding Students' Engagement in Learning Physics. *International Journal of Science Education, 29*(9), 1065-1088.

Venturini, P. (2007b). *L'envie d'apprendre les sciences. Motivation, attitudes, rapport au savoirs scientifiques* [The desire to study science. Motivation, attitudes, relation to scientific knowledge]. Paris: Fabert.

Webb, N. L. (2002). *Depth of Knowledge Levels for Four Content Areas.* Available at: http://facstaff.wcer.wisc.edu/normw/All%20content%20areas%20%20DOK%20levels%20 32802.doc (Date of Access: January 1st, 2010).

Windshitl, M., Thompson J., & Braaten, M. (2008). Beyond the scientific method: model based inquiry as a new paradigm of preferences for school investigations. *Science Education 92*(5), 941-967.

## Appendix 1: Extract from the curriculum guide (grade 7)

## B- Electric circuits in continuous current – qualitative study

This part of the curriculum guide is based on observation and practice, without measurements. It introduces the elementary properties of series or parallel circuits and the first notions of energy conversion and transfer. It arouses strong interest due to the importance of electricity in daily life. It is related to convergence themes: energy, safety

| Knowledge | Abilities | Comments |
|---|---|---|
| ELECTRIC CIRCUIT Experiments must not be done with the domestic supply voltage for safety reasons | | |
| A generator is necessary for a lamp to give light, for a motor turn. A generator transfers electric energy to a lamp or a motor. A solar cell converts light energy into electric energy. | Implementing a simple circuit to switch on a lamp or to turn over a motor. Following a given protocol. | Convergence theme: energy |
| In the presence of a generator, a circuit must be closed so that the energy transfer occurs. Then, there is a flow of current. | | |
| Danger when short-circuiting a generator | Identifying a generator short-circuit and the corresponding danger. Obeying safety rules | The teacher mentions danger of electric plugs. Their pins are considered as terminals of a generator. Convergence theme: safety |

## Appendix 2: Extract from the curriculum guide (grade 10)

## Health

Citizens must acquire a scientific culture so that they are able to make rational choices about health. The theme aims to illustrate and to explain the role of physics and chemistry in the domains of medical diagnosis and medicaments

| Notions and contents | Expected competences |
|---|---|
| The analysis of periodic signals, the use of medical imaging and analyses allow a diagnosis to be made. Examples will be chosen in the domain of health (electrocardiogram, electroencephalogram, X-ray, and scan). The observation of the results provided by medical analyses allows the notions of concentration, chemical species and matter structuring to be introduced. ||
| ... <br> Sound waves, electromagnetic waves – Frequency domains <br> Rectilinear propagation of light <br> Velocity of light in vacuum and in air <br> Refraction and total reflection | ... <br> Extracting and exploiting information related to the wave nature and wave frequency <br> Knowing the value of the speed of sound in air <br> Knowing the value of the speed of light in vacuum or in air <br> Practising an experimental process on refraction and total reflection <br> Practising an experimental process to understand the principle of exploring methods and the influence of properties of the propagation media. |
| Chemical species, pure body and mixtures <br> A model of the atom <br> ... | Extracting and exploiting information related to the nature of chemical species mentioned in various contexts <br> Knowing the composition of an atom and its nucleus <br> Knowing the atom is eclectically neutral <br> Knowing the symbols of some elements |

## Appendix 3: Our five level scale for analyzing expected performance

(based on Newberry & Kueker's scale, illustrated by Webb for science, and completed by elements of Porter's scale)

| Level | Definition | Keywords representing the cognitive demand |
|---|---|---|
| 1 Recall information | Students give a rote response. | Identify, recall, recognise, recite, name, tell etc. |
| 2 Simple implementation of procedures and computations | Students use a well-known formula, follow a set procedure (like a recipe), or perform a clearly defined series of steps. | Do computation, calculate, use, measure etc. |
| 3 Start of interpretative thinking | The content knowledge or process involved requires students to work with some concepts, to make use of some skills and, for both, to make some decisions as to how to approach the question or problem. | Explain, communicate scientific ideas, make observations, classify, organise, estimate, collect select and display data, use representations to model scientific ideas, explain findings and results, compare data etc. |
| 4 Strategic thinking | Activities have more than one possible answer and require students to justify the response they give; experimental designs involve more than one dependent variable. The cognitive demands are complex and abstract. | Explore, plan, analyse data, recognise patterns, judge, use evidence, use concepts and apply or adapt a variety of strategies to solve non-routine problems in science, etc. |
| 5 Extended Thinking | Students are required to make several connections, relate ideas within the content area or among different content areas, have to select one approach or strategy among many alternatives or devise them to solve the situation. Cognitive demands are very high, tasks are very complex, need an extended period of time and concern real-world situations. | Conduct an investigation, from specifying a problem to designing and carrying out an experiment, to analyzing its data and forming conclusions; Hypothesise, generalise, prove |

# Appendix 4: Relations between physics topics and the general themes of the different curricula

| Topics | Related general themes |
|---|---|
| Physical properties of matter | Water in our environment – Mixtures and pure bodies; From the surrounding air to the molecule; Health; Sport practice; The universe; Understanding: laws and models (fundamental interactions; conservation of energy; energy, matter and radiation) |
| Electricity Magnetism | Continuous current circuits – Qualitative study; Continuous current laws; Electrical energy and alternating current circuits; Health; Understanding: laws and model (fundamental interactions; conservation of energy); Action: challenges of the 21st century (Energy) |
| Optics | Light: sources and rectilinear propagation; Light: colours, images, speed; The universe; Observing: colours and images |
| Waves – Modern physics | Observing: waves and matter ; Understanding: laws and models (energy, matter and radiation); Action: challenges of the 21st century (Resources saving and environmental protection; information transmission and storage) |
| Mechanics | From gravitation to mechanical energy; Sport practice; the Universe; Understanding: laws and model (fundamental interactions; conservation of energy; time and movement) |

# Chapter 20

# Item Construction for Finnish National Level Assessment in School Physics Without Pre-Defined Learning Outcomes

*Jari Lavonen, Heidi Krzywacki & Laura Koistinen*
*Department of Teacher Education, University of Helsinki, Finland*

## Abstract

In Finland, there are no pre-defined learning outcomes in the national-level curriculum, but the outline of school education is grounded on the description of the aims and goals set for teaching and learning. This particularly increases teachers' autonomy and power over decision-making that seems to be related to increasing the quality of teaching and learning in physics. On a national level, the Finnish National Board of Education (FNBE) has organized infrequent monitoring of learning outcomes in mathematics and the Finnish language at the compulsory education level based on a representative sample. The monitoring is used for evaluating the educational policy and improving school education as well as allocating resources for in-service teacher education. At the end of 2010, FNBE decided to organize a national-level assessment of students' knowledge and skills in physics based on a representative sample in 2011. The intention is to assess how well students have acquired the knowledge and skills indicated in the aims set for teaching. Since the learning outcomes are not defined in the national-level curriculum and the education system is decentralized, designing the test was a challenge. Therefore, a framework was constructed for designing the testing and analyzing the assessment data based on a two-dimensional cross-classification following the revised model of Bloom's taxonomy. It is argued that pre-defined learning outcomes are not the only way to assure quality at the national level, and it is noteworthy that the quality assurance of education can be approached from different perspectives. In this paper, we analyse how the items of the national level assessment can be constructed without the description of pre-defined learning outcomes in the curriculum. Also some examples of the field-trial test questions are given.

# 1   Introduction

In Finland, teachers are responsible for monitoring the quality of teaching and learning in their classrooms. In addition to this, local authorities monitor student learning based on samples. Moreover, on a national level, the Finnish National Board of Education (FNBE) has organized infrequent monitoring of learning outcomes in mathematics and the Finnish language at the compulsory education level based on a representative sample. The monitoring was done with the aim of evaluating educational policy and improving schooling in general.

At the end of 2010, the FNBE decided to organize a national-level assessment of students' knowledge and skills in physics based on a representative sample from May 2011. The intention was to assess how well students have acquired the knowledge and skills indicated in the aims and goals set for teaching in the *National Core Curriculum for Basic Education* (NCCBE) (FNBE, 2004). The assessment data was collected through a paper-and-pencil test and it will be used as a basis for designing the national-level curriculum reform in 2013. Designing the test was particularly challenging for two reasons: the learning outcomes are not defined in the NCCBE, and the education system is decentralised. Each municipality and even schools implement teaching in their own way based on the local level curriculum. Consequently, since no clear national-level statements about the expected learning outcomes exist, i.e. what students should know and how they should be able to demonstrate their skills, a framework for designing the national-level assessment in physics needed to be established. The test items were designed in cooperation with teachers and researchers.

In this paper, we analyse how items for the national-level assessment in compulsory school physics were constructed in Finland without the aid of pre-defined learning outcomes in the national-level curriculum. We elaborate on assessment and the quality of teaching and learning in a specific context such as the Finnish educational system. In Finnish school education, the aims and goals in the national-level curriculum provide an outline for teaching but no description of pre-defined learning outcomes. The Finnish tradition fosters various ways of teaching and carrying out assessment practices at the school level. To conclude, some examples and discussion of the field-trial test items are given to provide a practical perspective for designing the test. The final test items were selected based on the students' responses to the trial test items and appropriate statistical analysis of the data.

## 2 Pre-defined Learning Outcomes and the Quality of Learning

There is a long history of using pre-defined learning outcomes for indicating aims in the national-level curriculum and using them as the basis for monitoring the quality of teaching and learning through testing. Learning outcomes are defined as statements of what a learner is expected to know, understand or be able to do at the end of a learning sequence. Learning outcomes have been classified into various categories in different settings, for example, the division into three categories: knowledge (facts, principles and concepts), skills (cognitive and practical skills) and competences (e.g., an ability to take responsibility and act autonomously) (Kennedy, Hyland, & Ryan, 2006).

The general idea behind transforming the educational aims stated in the national curriculum into the form of learning outcomes is enhancing transparency and accountability of learning outcomes, and increasing the quality of learning. Moreover, the description of the learning outcomes of a learning sequence is assumed to enable learners to have an active role in the learning process alongside their teachers (Spady, 2003). Learning outcomes are increasingly used and have been considered as an important basis for the quality of education in European educational policy. However, there are some countries, like Finland, where the intended learning outcomes have not been used to express the aims of education and consequently, to increase the quality of school teaching and learning.

The roots of describing learning outcomes can be argued to be close to the behaviouristic tradition of teaching and learning of the 1970's in the US. One developer of this approach was Robert Mager, who proposed the idea of writing specific statements about observable outcomes, *instructional objectives* (Mager, 1984). The main idea was to define the 'end behaviour' in precise terms in order to create a basis for optimal instructional treatment. This kind of simplistic idea of teaching and learning could lead to an approach that does not consider learning as a process. For example, the support for individual learning processes could be overlooked. Furthermore, defining intended learning outcomes and having testing consolidate the phenomenon of 'teaching to the test' refers to the unwanted and largely unintended consequences of testing (Popham, 2004). Selecting particular content areas or skills to be trained, having bias towards the aims of the curriculum, and teaching skills that are easy to test are among the unwanted outcomes (Sturman, 2003). This approach is especially claimed to decrease the amount of science inquiry in science education.

In order to improve the quality of teaching and learning, it is important to consider the different aspects behind the concept. The term 'quality' is complex depending on the perspective, and here, we approach this question with a broad understanding of the phenomenon, i.e., a kind of teaching which leads to the intended learning outcomes either indicated in the national-level documents or, like in the Finnish system, defined by an individual teacher in a particular learning situation. High quality teaching and learning supports the acquiring of competence for life-long learning and improving qualifications to match labour market expectations. The quality of education is also related to the transparency of educational systems and, moreover, adding to the flexibility and accountability of education.

Pre-defined learning outcomes are not the only way to assure quality at the national level, and it is noteworthy that the quality assurance of education can be approached from different perspectives. There is a general international interest in using the information from classroom-based assessment not only for improving teaching and learning but also for the purposes of educational decision-making and maintaining the quality of education. Recent research has focused on the shift towards teacher-conducted procedures such as alternative and formative forms of assessment (e.g., Black & Wiliam, 2003; Inbar-Lourie & Donitsa-Schmidt, 2009).

# 3 Finnish Education Context

*General context*

Our review is based on several sources: official Finnish education policy documents such as the *Education and Research 2003–2008: Development Plan* (2004), *Teacher Education Development Programme* (2001), and articles written by workers of the Finnish Ministry of Education (FME) and Finnish National Board of Education (FNBE), such as Halinen (2008), Jakku-Sihvonen and Niemi (2006), and Laukkanen (2008). Education policy is controlled by FME and FNBE. These bodies are responsible for developing school education, preparing the *National Core Curriculum for Basic Education* (NCCBE) (FNBE, 2004), and organizing national-level assessment based on samples. Raising the quality of education, promoting educational equality, and offering broad literacy to all Finnish citizens have been the central aims of the Finnish education policy. Key decisions in this direction were made in the 1970's along with other Nordic countries: a comprehensive school system was established (Committee report, 1970). According to this policy, all students with different starting-points should attend a common and free comprehensive school and learn together with others as long as possible.

The Finnish educational system is characterised by the devolution of decision power and responsibility at the local level: the local municipalities have to plan the local curriculum with teachers in accordance with the NCCBE (FNBE, 2004) and collect assessment data for evaluating education. In the NCCBE, the general and subject specific aims as well as core contents of each school subject (syllabus) are described on a general level. All school subjects are seen as having equal value regarding an individual's growth associated with personality, moral, creativity, knowledge, and skills. Furthermore, the themes related to integration beyond separate school subjects are also described in the NCCBE. Thus, the outline of Finnish school education is grounded on the description of the aims set for teaching. From the point of view of legislation, municipalities and teachers are obliged to follow these guidelines. Assessment in the Finnish educational system is based on monitoring, i.e. how well the aims have been reached. In accordance to this, it is stated in the NCCBE that *"The assessment is to address the pupil's learning and progress in the different areas of learning"* (FNBE, 2004).

The purpose of the local-level curriculum is to outline schooling and implementation in more detail. Teachers have an active role in designing the local-level curriculum. The curriculum work is meaningful primarily because of the emphasis on the design process rather than the end product, the written form of the curriculum: this process promotes teachers' awareness of and commitment to the development of schooling. Therefore, the curriculum work has a central role in school improvement.

Schools and teachers are responsible for choosing learning and assessment materials as well as teaching methods to be used in their teaching in accordance with the requirements of the curriculum. In the 1990's, the national level inspection of learning materials was terminated. Moreover, neither school inspections nor national exams have taken place since the 1980's. According to the PISA 2006 school questionnaire, the participating Finnish schools reported that school principals together with teachers are heavily responsible for disciplinary and assessment policies at the school level such as selecting the textbooks (100%, OECD average 83.5%), determining the course content (70.1%, OECD average 65.9%), and deciding which courses will be offered (90.1%, OECD average 69.9%) (Lavonen & Laaksonen, 2009). In Finland, assessment is concentrated at the school level and primarily implemented by teachers. This 'decentralisation' allows a teacher to reflect on teaching and learning in their classroom: they can choose how to use different forms of assessment suitable for each situation, such as formative assessment of students' experimental work as well as summative assessment. In general, teachers are valued as experts in curriculum development, teaching, and assessment at all school levels (FNBE, 2004).

In addition to the school-based assessment, local authorities need assessment data for distributing educational resources and especially for allocating support for low achieving schools. For this purpose, they need to monitor learning outcomes through sample-based testing as a basis for decision-making. On the national level, educational policy and schooling is improved through infrequent monitoring of learning outcomes based on a representative sample. However, Finnish teachers and schools are not heavily controlled by external evaluation. Education authorities and national-level education policy-makers trust teachers and their professionalism: teachers are enabled to decide how to provide good education to all kinds of children and young people. Furthermore, mutual trust also exists between teachers and parents (Lavonen & Laaksonen, 2009).

*Science in Finnish school context*

Guidelines, i.e. goals and contents, for the science subjects of physics, chemistry, and biology are presented in the national level curriculum (FNBE, 1994, 2004). According to content analysis, the goals are relatively similar to the competencies described in the PISA 2006 framework (Lavonen, 2007; Lavonen & Laaksonen, 2009; OECD, 2006). The curriculum emphasizes activities, where the students can identify scientific phenomena, explain and interpret data related to scientific phenomena, as well as draw conclusions based on evidence. In Finland, practical work and demonstrations are an integral part of teaching and learning science subjects. According to the PISA scientific literacy assessment, Finnish student performance is the highest and at the same time, the variation of the performance is the smallest among all OECD countries (Lavonen & Laaksonen, 2009).

In Finnish primary school at grades 1–4, science is an integrated school subject and at grades 5–6, it is taught as the combined subjects of physics and chemistry as well as biology and geography. In primary school, on average, 2.5 lesson hours per week is allocated for science taught by primary school teachers. Primary school teachers have a Masters' level degree including a major in education and a minor in multidisciplinary pedagogical studies of all school subjects, such as physics and chemistry education.

In lower secondary school at grades 7–9, science is divided into the separate subjects of physics, chemistry, biology, and health education. Science is taught by subject teachers, who have a Masters' level degree in the respective subject, such as in physics or chemistry. Altogether, 6 lesson hours per week is allocated for science on average. This number of weekly lesson hours is relatively high when compared internationally (Waddington, Nentwig, & Schanze, 2007).

## 4 The Framework for National Level Assessment

At the end of 2010, the FNBE decided to organize national-level assessment of students' knowledge and skills also in physics based on a representative sample. The intention was to assess how well the students have acquired the knowledge and skills indicated in the aims set for teaching in the NCCBE (FNBE, 2004). Affective aspects were also considered in monitoring educational outcomes. The assessment data was collected in May 2011 using a paper-and-pencil test and it will be used as a basis for designing the national-level curriculum reform in 2013.

However, designing the test was a challenge particularly for two reasons: the learning outcomes are not defined in the NCCBE and the education system is decentralised as described above. Each municipality and even schools implement teaching in their own way based on the local level curriculum. Consequently, establishing a framework for designing the national-level assessment in physics was needed. Here, we first describe in more detail the way science teaching is outlined in the curriculum aims. Secondly, we elaborate on the structure of the two-dimensional framework. In the following section, we will discuss the construction of the test and the test items suitable for the framework. Moreover, we will offer examples of items.

*The curricular aims as the basis for design*

The general goals of compulsory school physics are written from the teacher's point of view to indicate the general content and direction of teaching physics. The aims are descriptions of teacher instruction. A good example is the description of core task of physics teaching:

> *"In grades 7–9, the core task of physics instruction in the seventh through ninth grades is to broaden the pupils' conception of the nature of physics. The instruction guides the pupil in thinking in a manner characteristic of science, in acquiring and using knowledge, and in evaluating the reliability and importance of knowledge in different life situations. The purpose of the experimental orientation is to help the pupils to perceive the nature of science."*

In addition to the general goals, specific aims are described as statements of teaching intention, indicating specific areas that should be addressed in a learning sequence. Actually it is not easy to decide whether these more specific aims are written in terms of outlining the teaching intention or in terms of expected learning outcomes. For example, specific aims for learning science inquiry skills are described as following:

"The pupils will learn in physics in grades 7–9
- scientific skills, such as the formulation of questions and the perception of problems,
- to make, compare, and classify observations, measurements, and conclusions; to present and test a hypothesis; and to process, present, and interpret results, at the same time putting information and communication technology to good use,
- to plan and carry out a scientific investigation in which variables affecting natural phenomena are held constant and varied, and correlations among the variables are uncovered,
- to formulate simple models, to use them in explaining phenomena, to make generalizations, and to evaluate the reliability of the research process and results,
- to use various graphs and algebraic models in explaining natural phenomena, making predictions, and solving problems."

Aims for learning science subject matter are also described:
- In grades 7–9 the pupils will learn in physics to use appropriate concepts, quantities, and units in describing physical phenomena and technological questions.

Specific physics contents are also listed in the curriculum. The contents of physical systems are for example:
- natural structures and proportions (grades 7–9);
- motion and forces, models of uniform and uniformly accelerating motion (grades 7–9);
- various basic phenomena of vibrations and wave motion; production, detection; observation, reflection, and refraction of wave motion (grades 7 – 9).

In addition to focusing on learning knowledge and skills, there are also goals for developing students' affective domain. Pupils' interest in studying science subjects is considered:
- In grades 7–9 the purpose of the experimental orientation is to stimulate the pupils to study physics and chemistry.

Finally, there are also aims for learning sustainable development principles, the role of science in the society and history of science. Pupils should become familiar with societal issues and decision making:
- In grades 7–9 the instruction in physics helps pupils' understand the importance of physics and technology in everyday life, the living environment, and society. It also provides capabilities for making everyday choices, especially in matters related to environmental protection and the use of energy resources.

*The two-dimensional framework: knowledge and cognitive processes*

Taxonomies developed for knowledge and cognitive processes are typically used for writing learning outcomes, designing test items and planning teaching. These taxonomies provide a ready-made structure and collection of verbs (Kennedy, Hyland & Ryan, 2006). The framework for designing the test items for the national physics test was based on the analysis of both knowledge areas and cognitive processes activated either in science learning or in testing.

This two-dimensional cross-classification followed the revised model of Bloom's taxonomy introduced by Anderson and Krathwohl (2001). In this taxonomy, firstly, science knowledge is composed of four types of knowledge: (1) factual knowledge; (2) conceptual knowledge which constitutes *knowledge of science*, i.e., concepts, phenomena, and processes, and *knowledge about science*, i.e., scientific inquiry and scientific explanations; (3) procedural knowledge, which is related to science process skills, for example, formulating questions, recognising problems as well as applying simple models to explain phenomena, and integrated science process skills such as using reference sources in order to obtain information, using graphs in explaining phenomena, making predictions, and solving problems; and (4) meta-cognitive knowledge and skills. Specific contents mentioned in the national curriculum, for example motion and force, vibrations and wave motion, heat, electricity, and natural structures, needed to be placed in the framework within the first three knowledge areas that were tested.

Furthermore, the items have been framed within a wide variety of life situations involving science and technology, like *health, natural resources, environmental quality, and the history of science and technology*. In item design, these situations were related to three major contexts: *personal* (self), *social* (community), and *global* (life across the world). Consequently, the contexts were chosen considering their relevance to students' interests and lives.

*The knowledge dimension*

Conceptual knowledge: Knowledge of physics and knowledge about physics

Conceptual knowledge means understanding physics' concepts, laws and theories (Gott & Duggan, 1995). In the national level curriculum (FNBE, 2004), two categories of knowledge of physics are described: concepts (concepts, quantities, and units for describing physical and technological phenomena) and phenomena and processes (e.g., transformations of energy). The concepts are needed in describing structures and interactions in nature and discussing phenomena related to energy. Relationships and causality are important aspects of phenomena and processes.

Scientific inquiry and scientific explanations form the two categories of knowledge about physics that are introduced in the NCCBE (FNBE, 2004). Scientific enquiry centres on inquiry as the central process of science and the various components of that process. Scientific explanations are the results of scientific inquiry.

Specific knowledge of physics has been introduced related to motion and force, vibrations and wave motion, heat, electricity, and natural structures as follows:

Concepts and processes related to motion and force
- interactions and the forces (e.g., gravitation, friction, buoyancy force);
- motion, models of uniform and uniformly accelerating motion;
- work done by a force, mechanical energy and power;
- equilibrium phenomena;
- pressure.

Concepts and processes related to vibrations and wave motion
- vibrations and wave motion, production, detection, observation, reflection, and refraction;
- light (importance and applications, properties, quantities, and laws);
- sound (importance and applications, properties, quantities, and laws);
- optical instruments.

Concepts and processes related to heat, i.e. phenomena associated with the heating and cooling of objects and substances, description of those phenomena with appropriate concepts and laws, importance and applications of thermal phenomena and energy
- temperature, heat expansion;
- heating and cooling of objects, heat capacity;
- phase transitions, fusion heat, heat of evaporation;
- conservation and degradation of energy, heat as a form of energy and heat transfer.

Concepts and processes related to electricity
- electric and magnetic forces between objects;
- direct-current circuits; voltage, electric current, measuring current and voltage (= 'basic phenomena of electric circuits');
- resistors, resistance, coupling of resistors:
- electric energy, power and price of energy; transfer of energy in a circuit;
- safe application of electric phenomena in everyday life and technology;
- electromagnetic induction and its use in energy transmission; use of electricity at home.

Concepts and processes related to natural structures
- structures in nature (e.g., atom, solar system);
- interactions that keep structural components together; binding and release of energy in processes occurring between components;
- radioactive decay; fission and fusion; ionizing radiation and its effect on nature; radiation protection.

Procedural knowledge

Procedural knowledge is needed in thinking-behind-doing, and it does not for instance refer to measuring itself, but to the decisions that must be made about what to measure, how often and over what period to measure as well as how to present the data and analyse it. Warwick, Linfield and Stephenson (1999) draw clear distinctions between the concepts of 'process skills' and 'procedural knowledge', and, for example, relate the latter to the critical nature of dialogue about evidence. According to the NCCBE (FNBE, 2004), procedural knowledge can be classified into two categories:

Procedural knowledge related to science process skills
- formulation of questions and recognising of problems;
- observation and measurement;
- comparison and classification;
- process, present, and interpret the data;
- conclusions (estimations and predications) based on the data;
- present and test a hypothesis;
- plan and carry out investigation (control of variables, looking for correlations);
- formulation of simple models;
- use of models to explain phenomena;
- the reliability of the research process and results.

Procedural knowledge related to integrated science process skills
- use reference sources to obtain information;
- reliability of the information of different sources;
- use of graphs in explaining phenomena, making predictions, and solving problems;
- use of algebraic models in explaining phenomena, making predictions, and solving problems.

## The dimension of cognitive processes

In the framework, the dimension of cognitive processes was structured through three levels instead of six levels presented in the original taxonomy. These levels were used as the basis for designing the items. The use of the taxonomy is complicated and not necessary as reliable as aimed. Especially the classification of the desired skills has been found to vary with individuals. Therefore, the dimension of cognitive processes has been reduced to three levels (Remember, Understand, Apply and create) as described in Table 1.

*Table 1: Three-Level Cognitive Processes Dimension (Remember, Understand, Apply and Create) and the Aim of the Item*

| Scale | Aim of the item |
| --- | --- |
| Remember | Remembering<br>• recognise, list, describe, identify retrieve, name ...<br>• can the student recall information? |
| Understand | Understanding<br>• interpret, exemplify, summarise, infer, paraphrase ...<br>• can the students demonstrate understanding the meaning of a concept?<br>• can the student explain ideas or concepts? |
| Apply and create | Applying<br>• implement, carry out, use ...<br>• can the student use the new knowledge in another familiar situation? analysing- compare, attribute, organise, deconstruct ...<br>• can the student differentiate between constituent parts?<br>Evaluating<br>• check, critique, judge, hypothesise ...<br>• can the student justify a decision or course of action? creating<br>• design, construct, plan, produce ...<br>• can the student generate new products, ideas or ways of viewing things? |

# 5  Design of the Test and Item Types

*Construction of the test*

The paper-pencil test is a typical form used in national level assessment. The test used in the field-trial consisted of 33 questions, each of which was worth 3 points. Each question contained 2 to 4 items. The scoring of the questions is described in the coding manual and examples of the coding are given below.

The test was designed to measure students' knowledge and skills in physics based on the aims indicated in the *National Core Curriculum for Basic Education* (FNBE, 2004). Therefore, the items were designed in accordance with the curriculum. While creating the test, several other issues, such as reliability, validity, educational impact, cost effectiveness, and acceptability of the items, were taken into account (Jacobs & Chase, 1992).

Reliability pertains to the accuracy with which a score on a test is determined. A crucial aspect in reliability is that the test should indicate the score that a student would obtain in any other equally difficult test in the same field. In addition, the test should cover the entire content area and comprise of a range of possible questions. Consequently, passing the test should not depend on a particular test but have the same result with any given test.

Validity refers to whether the questions test what they are intended to test. One way to increase validity is to assure that experts score higher in the test than students. Alternative approaches include (a) an analysis of the distribution of course topics within test elements and (b) an assessment of the soundness of individual test items.

Cost effectiveness and acceptability are also of importance. The costs of examinations have to be taken into account. Furthermore even a well-designed examination will not be successful if it is not accepted by teachers and students.

*About test item types*

The item types in the test were: multiple choice, true/false, matching, short answer, essay/long answer, graphical, and computational questions (Cunningham, 1998). There were several demands for the items to be designed from the point of view of item type. The National Board of Education recommended the use of multiple choice, true/false and matching items at least in 70% of the all items due to this increasing the high reliability in the coding. Budget limitations also demanded types of items that are easily coded by optical scanners and appropriate software.

Multiple choice items were composed of one item (stem) with multiple possible answers (choices), including the correct answer(s) and incorrect answer(s) (distractors). The students selected the correct answer by ticking the box as presented in Figure 1.

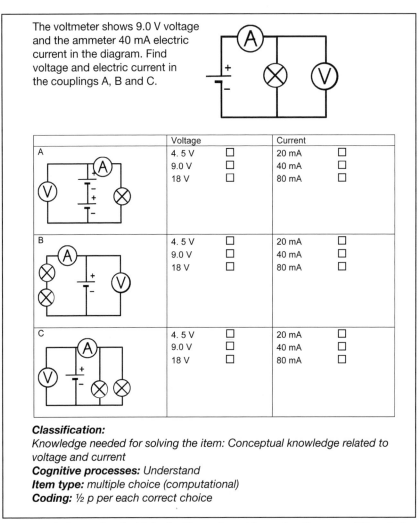

*Figure 1: An Example of a Multiple Choice Item, Measuring Conceptual Knowledge Related to Voltage and Current*

True/false items are composed of a statement. Students respond to the items by indicating whether the statement is true or false. However, since the statements have to be defensibly true or absolutely false, constructing the statements flawlessly is a challenge. When students indicate a false statement correctly, it is possible only to conclude that they knew the statement was false, not that the correct answer was known. True/false items provide students with a 50% chance of guessing the right answer. For this reason, a series of four true false items are used in the test and credit is not given when only one correct answer is indicated as described in Figures 2 and 3.

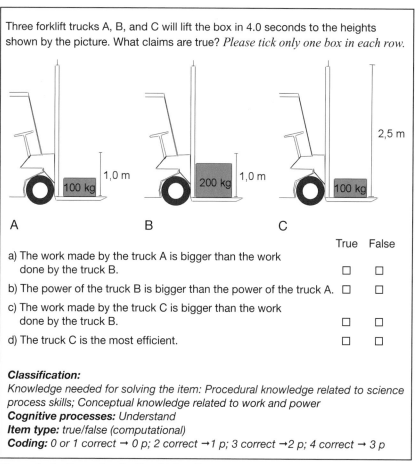

*Figure 2: An Example of a True/False Choice Item, Measuring Conceptual Knowledge Related to Work and Power*

In the laboratory a wooden block' was drawn along the surface of the table. In the test the force *(F)* and the distance *(s)* were measured. The results were presented in a table. The calculated work *(W)* made by the force is also shown in the table.

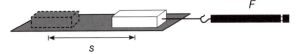

| *s* (m) | *F* (N) | *W* (J) |
|---|---|---|
| 0.10 | 2.0 | 0.20 |
| 0.20 | 2.0 | 0.40 |
| 0.30 | 2.0 | 0.60 |
| 0.30 | 2.0 | 0.80 |
| 0.50 | 2.0 | 1.0 |

What conclusions are you able to make on the basis of the test?
*Please tick only one box in each row.*

|  | True | False |
|---|---|---|
| a) The force is constant in all the tests. | ☐ | ☐ |
| b) When the force increases, the work done by the force will increase. | ☐ | ☐ |
| c) When distance increases, the work done by the force will increase. | ☐ | ☐ |
| d) The work done by the force is constant. | ☐ | ☐ |

***Classification:***
*Knowledge needed for solving the item: Procedural knowledge related to science process skills; Conceptual knowledge related to motion and force*
***Cognitive processes:*** *Understand*
***Item type:*** *true/false*
***Coding:*** *0 or 1 correct → 0 p; 2 correct →1 p; 3 correct →2 p; 4 correct → 3 p*

What is your opinion about the item?
*Please tick only one box in each row.*

|  | Totally disagree | | | | Totally agree |
|---|---|---|---|---|---|
| The content of the question was interesting. | ☐ | ☐ | ☐ | ☐ | ☐ |
| I am sure I can solve this question. | ☐ | ☐ | ☐ | ☐ | ☐ |
| I will benefit from this type of topic in my further studies. | ☐ | ☐ | ☐ | ☐ | ☐ |
| I will benefit from this type of topic in my everyday life. | ☐ | ☐ | ☐ | ☐ | ☐ |

*Figure 3: An Example of a True/False Choice Item, Measuring Conceptual Knowledge Related to Motion and Force Followed by an Affective Domain Item*

Matching items are answered through pairing each of a set of stems, e.g., definitions, with one of the choices provided, such as concepts or values. These items are used to assess recognition and recall as well as understanding as described in Figure 4.

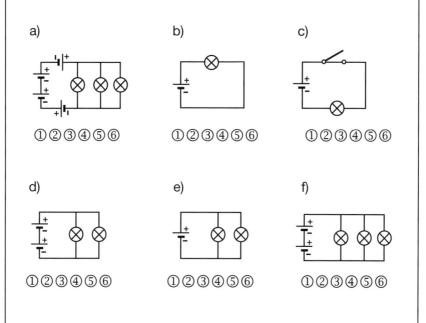

Figure 4: An Example of a Matching Item, Measuring Conceptual Knowledge Related to Electric Energy

These three item types are used in testing student's factual and conceptual knowledge of a broad range of content. Students can respond to these items relatively quickly and a broad domain can be covered. Therefore, their main advantage is their high reliability.

Multiple-choice and a combination of true and false questions are often found to be unsuitable for activating higher cognitive processes. However, our challenge was also to use these items for measuring understanding and applying, and moreover, procedural knowledge. Therefore, creating multiple choice, true/false, and matching items has been time consuming due to these challenges.

Short answer questions are typically composed of a brief prompt that demands a written answer that varies in length from a couple of words to a few sentences. Although, they are often used to test factual and conceptual knowledge, we used these items also for measuring procedural knowledge as described in Figure 5. Essay questions provide a complex prompt that requires written responses, which can vary in length from a couple of paragraphs to many pages. Unfortunately, we were not able to have these types of items that would assess how well students can summarise, hypothesise, find relations, and apply known procedures to new situations.

---

Even up to the 1850 it was believed that the heat is made of material, flogistonia. In practice it was recognised that the temperature of metal objects increases when they were bent or, for example, the metal was sawn. The phenomenon was explained by the mass of the object increasing as the object warms. Joule conducted the study that changed our understanding of heat. He sawed a cannonball into two parts and was able to show that heat is not a material.

What did Joule measure in the test?
What did he conclude on the basis of the measurements?

***Classification:***
*Knowledge needed for solving the item: Procedural knowledge related to integrated science process skills; Conceptual knowledge related to energy*
***Cognitive processes:*** *Apply and create*
***Item type:*** *Short answer question*
***Coding:*** *Measurement of mass before and after → 1 p.; Small pieces mentioned → 1 p.; Comparison of masses → 1 p.*

*Figure 5: An Example of a Short Answer Item Measuring Procedural Knowledge Related to Integrated Science Process Skills and Conceptual Knowledge Related to Energy*

# 6 Discussion

In this paper, a short review on pre-defined learning outcomes and quality of learning was given. The Finnish context of science teaching and learning was also discussed from the point of view of quality. We elaborated on how science learning outcomes at the national level could be measured without having a basis of definitions of intended learning outcomes. Consequently, this paper describes how quality is strived for in Finland without having pre-defined learning outcomes in the national level curriculum. According to PISA scientific literacy assessment, the quality of science teaching and learning in Finnish compulsory school has been relatively high.

Our paper elaborates on the reasons why Finnish educational authorities are hesitating to form a description of learning outcomes at a national level. The most important reason for not having any pre-defined learning outcomes is the education policy principle according to which the devolution of decision power and responsibilities are allocated at the local level. Teachers are regarded as experts who are able to plan, implement and assess student learning outcomes. The teachers are the ones to define the intended learning outcomes while they are planning the lessons or in the teaching situation. Actually, pre-defined learning outcomes are not the only way to assure the quality of science education: the quality assurance of education can be approached from different perspectives. There is no empirical evidence, which could justify the Finnish tradition but there are convictions on which the education policy is based.

The Finnish approach does allow for sample-based national level testing and monitoring. For this purpose, the learning outcomes are created based on the aims indicated in the NCCBE by researchers, not by administrative personnel. The researchers have to construct learning outcomes, which are only based on national level goal setting. However, this approach offers novel possibilities to describe learning outcomes grounded on the goals for higher abstract knowledge structures and skills and design the items for this purpose. Moreover, this type of approach guides teachers to analyse goals in a versatile way while they are planning the learning activities. The assessment is not restricted or biased by the planning process.

Recent discussions on European educational policy have emphasised the shift from teaching aims to learning outcomes as a strategy to improve the quality of education (Kennedy, Hyland & Ryan, 2006). However, the learning outcomes approach does not replace from the point of view of educational quality assurance the quality assurance of educational arrangements, e.g., quality of teachers and teaching. Strictly pre-defined learning outcomes as well as national level assessment limit teachers' autonomy and neglect their expertise in planning, teaching and assessment (cf. Inbar-Lourie & Donitsa-Schmidt, 2009).

# References

Anderson, L. W. & Krathwohl, D. R. (Eds.) (2001). *A Taxonomy for Learning, Teaching, and Assessing: A Revision of Bloom's Taxonomy of Educational Objectives.* New York: Addison Wesley Longman Inc.

Black, P. & Wiliam, D. (2003). In Praise of Educational Research: Formative Assessment. *British Educational Research Journal, 29*(5), 623-637.

Committee report (1970: A4). *Peruskoulun opetussuunnitelmakomitean mietintö I* [Report of the Committee of Comprehensive School Curriculum I]. Helsinki: Valtion painatuskeskus.

Cunningham, G.K. (1998). *Assessment in the Classroom.* Bristol, PA: Falmer Press.

*Education and Research 2003–2008; Development Plan* (2004). Publications of the Ministry of Education, Finland 2004:8.

FNBE (1994). *Framework Curriculum for the Comprehensive School* (in Finland). Helsinki: State Printing Press and National Board of Education.

FNBE (2004). *National Core Curriculum for Basic Education 2004.* Helsinki: National Board of Education.

Gott, R. & Duggan, S. (1995). *Investigative Work in the Science Curriculum.* Buckingham: Open University Press.

Halinen, I. (2008). *Keys to Success in Finland.* Talk given at the World Education Congress: The Best Among the Best. Valencia, 19.04.2008.

Inbar-Lourie, O. & Donitsa-Schmidt, S. (2009). Exploring Classroom Assessment Practices: The Case of Teachers of English as a Foreign Language. *Assessment in Education: Principles, Policy & Practice, 16*(2), 185-204.

Jacobs, L. C. & Chase, C. I. (1992). *Developing and Using Tests Effectively: A Guide for Faculty.* San Francisco: Jossey-Bass.

Jakku-Sihvonen, R. & Niemi, H. (Eds.) (2006). *Research-based Teacher Education in Finland – Reflections by Finnish Teacher Educators.* Research in Educational Sciences 25. Turku: Finnish Educational Research Association.

Kennedy, D., Hyland A., & Ryan, N. (2006). *Writing and Using Learning Outcomes: a Practical Guide.* Available at: http://www.bologna-handbook.com/index.php?option=com_docman&task=doc_details&gid=127 (Date of Access: January 10th, 2011).

Laukkanen, R. (2008). Finnish Strategy for High-Level Education for All. In N. Soguel & P. Jaccard (Eds.), *Governance and Performance of Education Systems* (pp. 305-324). The Netherlands: Springer.

Lavonen, J. (2007). National Science Education Standards and Assessment in Finland. In D. Waddington, P. Nentwig, & S. Schanze (Eds.), *Making it Comparable* (pp. 101-112). Münster: Waxmann.

Lavonen, J. & Laaksonen, S. (2009). Context of Teaching and Learning School Science in Finland: Reflections on PISA 2006 Results. *Journal of Research in Science Teaching, 46*(8), 922-944.

Mager, R. F. (1984). *Preparing instructional objectives* (2nd edition). Belmont, CA: Pitman Learning.

OECD (2006). *Assessing Scientific, Reading and Mathematical Literacy: A Framework for PISA 2006*. Paris: OECD.

Popham, W. J. (2004). "Teaching to the Test" – An Expression to Eliminate. *Educational Leadership, 62*(3), 82-83.

Spady, W. G. (2003). Outcome Based Education. In J. W. Guthrie (Ed.), *Encyclopedia of Education* (2nd edition, pp. 1827-1831). New York: Macmillan Reference.

Sturman, L. (2003). Teaching to the Test: Science or Intuition? *Educational Research, 45*(3), 261-273.

*Teacher Education Development programme* (2001). Publications of Ministry of Education, Finland 2001.

Waddington, D., Nentwig, P. & Schanze, S. (Eds.) (2007). *Making it Comparable*. Münster: Waxmann.

Warwick, P., Linfield, R. S., & Stephenson, P. (1999). A Comparison of Primary Pupils' Ability to Express Procedural Understanding in Science Through Speech and Writing. *International Journal of Science Education, 21*(8), 823-838.

# Part E

# A Coda

# Chapter 21
# Learning Outcomes in Science Education: A Synthesis of the International Views on Defining, Assessing and Fostering Science Learning

*Knut Neumann*[1], *Sascha Bernholt*[2] *& Peter Nentwig*[2]
*IPN · Leibniz Institute for Science and Mathematics Education, Kiel, Germany*
[1]*Department of Physics Education,* [2]*Department of Chemistry Education*

## 1 Introduction

Globalization has changed the world – and with it the world of education. With the distance between national markets shrinking, a small advantage concerning natural or human resources today can become the basis for becoming a leading country in the world of tomorrow. The competition between national economies has reached the area of education, and countries need their educational system to provide their economy with more qualified people. Consequently, assessment programs comparing countries' educational systems such as the Trends in Mathematics and Science Study (TIMSS) or the Programme for International Student Assessment (PISA) have received increasing attention. However, these programs have revealed that many countries – among which there are some of the world's leading economies – rank far behind their expectations. Hence, policy makers across the world have initiated measures to ensure and enhance educational quality in order to improve educational outcomes. In considering educational standards as one important measure to ensure educational quality, countries that had already worked with educational standards initiated their revisions; and countries that traditionally did not rely on educational standards also began to restructure their educational systems by devising and implementing educational standards. Altogether, a trend toward such standards as benchmarks for an educational system's efficiency can be observed (cf. DeBoer, 2011).

As educational standards are expected to ensure high-quality education and subsequently to maintain and increase competitiveness, science education standards across the world have one common overarching goal: scientific literacy. Science influences not only our world in an abstract, general way, but also our daily work and everyday experiences. Therefore, scientific literacy refers not only to the education of future scientists or engineers, but also to the education of citizens that can make informed decisions in a world permeated by science and technology. In this sense, most science education standards aim for what Roberts (2007) refers to as "scientific literacy – vision II." Despite this common overarching goal, science education standards vary considerably among countries with respect to what exactly learning outcomes should be in the light of this particular vision of scientific literacy. Some documents merely outline this vision of scientific literacy and leave it to the teacher to determine what exactly students should learn in order to be scientifically literate. This is the case, for example, with the Finnish Science Education Standards (2007). Other documents provide extensive lists of what content exactly students are expected to know, for example, the United States Science Education Standards (Valverde & Schmidt, 2000).

These differences have also led to different approaches regarding the assessment and development of educational quality. In countries where the teacher is responsible for the definition of learning outcomes, responsibility for the assessment of learning outcomes lies with the teacher as well (e.g., Lavonen, 2007). Countries where expected learning outcomes are defined through standard documents, often maintain external assessments of student learning outcomes (e.g., the United States, National Center for Education Statistics). Obviously, there will also be country-specific differences in how learning outcomes are fostered. In countries where educational standards have a long tradition, for example, teachers might more likely work towards these standards in their lessons than teachers in countries where standards have just been introduced. This raises the question of whether there is more that can be learned from a comparison of educational systems than just which one ranks higher in international large-scale assessments. Is there anything that can be learned from countries with a strong tradition in educational standards for countries that have just begun with the introduction of standards? Should standard documents be as precise as possible? Or should they leave room for interpretation by the teacher? Do national assessment programs push teachers toward training students for the test? Or can a combination of standard and assessment programs create room for teachers to find their own style of teaching while still ensuring high-quality education? And last but not least, how would instruction have to look like in order to create scientifically literate students?

This chapter attempts to summarize and subsequently discuss the individual symposium papers collected in this book in order to provide answers to the above questions regarding how to define, assess, and foster learning outcomes.

## 2 Defining Learning Outcomes

From a comparison of the different views brought together in this book, the notion of what the outcomes of science education should be seems to be very similar across countries. However, the genesis of this notion differs depending on a country's tradition in maintaining educational standards.

The **United States** has the longest tradition with respect to educational standards (Bernholt, Neumann & Nentwig, *this volume*, p. 15). Given the disappointing performance of students from the United States in large-scale assessments, the science education standards came under criticism for being too extensive and incoherent lists of content areas students should memorize (Valverde & Schmidt, 2000). As a solution, Duschl, Schweingruber, and Shouse (2007) recently suggested that standards should build on core concepts of science. Learning progressions should be developed based on empirical research in order to guide teachers in fostering students' understanding of the core concepts. In This book the chapter by Liu as well as that by Krajcik, Drago, Sutherland, and Merritt in this book provide an introduction to the idea of core concepts and learning progressions. Most notably, students are no longer obliged to acquire a large amount of factual knowledge. Instead, they are expected to develop an understanding of core concepts of science. This notion of core concepts does not only include concepts in a narrow sense, but also involves core skills such as scientific modeling (cf. Schwarz et al., 2009). Learning progressions are thought to describe how the understanding of core concepts or core skills can be developed by the teachers. They intend to describe levels of understanding based on empirical research, and they include information on instructional components which can foster students' progression from one level to the next (cf. Krajcik et al., *this volume*, p. 263). For the assessment of students' level of understanding, indicators need to be defined. This means that learning outcomes need to be specified for each level of understanding. In this context, Krajcik et al. (*this volume*) introduce the notion of learning performances which are supposed to describe what "students should accomplish with the content" (p. 268). Krajcik et al. (*this volume*) also stress the point that understanding of a core concept or skill does not only mean to have complex knowledge about it, but rather to be able to use this knowledge in a scientific way. In order to specify this kind of use, Krajcik et al. (*this volume*) introduce the notion of "scientific processes."

It is interesting that this movement toward a broader conception of learning outcomes – that moves away from listing specific content areas for students to know toward expecting students to use their knowledge in a meaningful way – is very similar to the notion of "competence" that has recently emerged in the **German-speaking countries**. Traditionally in these countries, educational systems worked in a more input-oriented way. Policy makers influenced the educational system through funding, teacher education, and curriculum development (for a more detailed description, see for example, Fensham, 2009). However, with the TIMSS and PISA reports at hand, policy makers saw a need for reforming the educational system and decided to move toward a more output-oriented system. At the beginning of this reform stood the introduction of educational standards (cf. Labudde, 2007; Schecker & Parchmann, 2007; Weiglhofer, 2007). These standards build on the notion of "competence" to describe learning outcomes. In this context, competence is defined as the cognitive and affective prerequisites in order to solve everyday problems (cf. Weinert, 2001). As such, competence represents a broader conception of knowledge including the skills as well as the motivation to solve particular problems as one may encounter in everyday life. Again, the idea basically was to emphasize that students should no longer only acquire factual knowledge but also a deeper understanding of this knowledge. As such, the general idea is very similar to the idea of what learning outcomes are considered in the new framework for science education in the United States: "As learners link ideas together in web-like fashion, they develop integrated understanding that enables them to access information effectively and to use it to solve complex problems" (Krajcik et al., *this volume*, p. 261).

Like learning progressions, competences are considered to be domain specific, that is, competences required in the domain of mathematics are different from those, for example, required in the domain "German as the first language." Following the introduction of educational standards, a new field of educational research has emerged in Germany. Competence models are developed and tested. These models create a framework which is thought to describe the knowledge and skills required to solve particular problems in the respective domain. Such a framework would allow for classifying problems according to the extent to which particular cognitive abilities and skills are needed in order to solve them.

In 2004, the *Institut zur Qualitätsentwicklung im Bildungswesen (IQB)* (Institute for the Development of Educational Quality) was founded. One major task of this institute was the development of assessment frameworks based on the educational standards as well as the planning and coordination of assessment programs in order to benchmark the educational standards. An overview of the (short) history of educational standards, the research on educational standards, and the process of standards setting is given in the chapter by Köller and Parchmann. Based on this, the chapter by Bernholt, Eggert, and Kulgemeyer discusses three research projects concerning the development of competence models in the field of science education. Each of these projects focuses on a different aspect of scientific competence as described by the German science education standards. In 2008, the IQB commissioned a group of science education researchers to create an assessment framework to guide the development of assessment items and to accompany the process of standards setting. This project is described in greater detail by Kremer, Fischer, Kauertz, Mayer, Sumfleth, and Walpuski (*this volume*). Whereas in the United States the new Framework for Science Education was submitted to public discussion very early, in Germany the project aimed at generating empirical data before going public. Although this well-intentioned decision aimed to maintain focus on empirically supported arguments instead of creating a rather normative discussion, it created resentment in the scientific community that led to extensive criticisms of both reasonable and unreasonable sorts. An overview of the criticisms is given in the chapter by Schecker.

Educational systems in the other European countries are characterized by a diversity, as each country has a different tradition regarding education and science education in particular. For one, there is a group of countries that was committed toward educational standards pretty much in the same way as that in the United States. This group includes, for example, the United Kingdom and Ireland. **The United Kingdom** has traditionally maintained a national curriculum. The latest revision focuses on the development of students' knowledge, skills, and understanding. The curriculum is structured through key stages and levels for each stage. However, there "is no obvious model of progression in learning underpinning the way in which subject content is specified by the national curriculum. Content seems more often to be placed at different levels on the basis of past practice, and practitioner wisdom" (Millar, Whitehouse & Abrahams, *this volume*, p. 395). The situation in Ireland seems to be similar. In his chapter on learning outcomes in **Ireland**, Kennedy focuses on science education at the tertiary level. According to Kennedy, learning outcomes are described as what students are expected to accomplish after completing the learning process. It seems that there is no description of overarching goals for the university level. Instead, learning outcomes are defined on a per-course base. As such, these statements can be considered to be very close to what Krajcik et al. (*this volume*) term "learning performances."

There also is a group of countries in Europe that have moved toward the introduction of educational standards in recent years. However, the history of standards varies between the countries. Ayas in his chapter describes the history of the national science curriculum in **Turkey**. This curriculum does not only include information about the general objectives (phrased similarly to those in Western countries) and content, but also provides statements that specifically state the students' gains as a result of school learning. According to Ayas, each of these statements completes the sentence "It is expected that in the related topic the students ..." (p. 442) embracing a verb such as "explain", "prepare", or "indicate." With respect to Bloom's Taxonomy (cf. Anderson et al., 2001), the learning outcomes cover the cognitive, affective, and psychomotor domains.

In the **Netherlands,** science education builds on a national curriculum. More specifically, as science is taught as three separate subjects (biology, chemistry, and physics), education in each of the subjects builds on a respective curriculum. Bertona in her chapter presents the case of the chemistry curriculum. This curriculum was recently found to be too content-oriented, focusing on isolated facts. As a consequence, a new curriculum has been developed, building on the idea of scientific literacy that will be introduced in 2012. This new curriculum specifies which knowledge and specific skills students are supposed to have acquired and which they are expected to be able to make use of in different contexts. As such, it aligns with the idea of competence without using the term explicitly.

In **France**, the curriculum details the intended learning outcomes (see Venturini & Tiberghien, *this volume*). Very similar to the tradition in the Netherlands or Germany, French teachers are autonomous with respect to the means for working toward the learning outcomes. In France, expected outcomes are also expressed in terms of competences. However, learning outcomes are phrased differently for the different grades in Middle School education:

> Learning outcomes from grade 7 to 9 are structured according to the hierarchical logic of domains of physics, their complexity increases steadily over grades and they constitute a coherent whole. This concerns knowledge as well as abilities. On the other hand, learning outcomes from grade 10 and 12 are structured according to themes and not according to the logic of physical domains. (Venturini & Tiberghien, *this volume*, p. 469).

The one country that has no tradition in educational standards and does not intend to introduce such standards is **Finland**. Still, within the Finnish educational system there is a very similar view on learning outcomes like those in the other European countries. In the National Core Curriculum for Basic Education (NCCBE), the general educational aims are described as well as subject-specific aims and respective core content. Lavonen, Krzywacki, and Koistinen in their chapter emphasize that content analyses have revealed how the goals phrased in the NCCBE are very similar to the notion of competences used by PISA (as well as in a particular number of other European countries such as Germany, France, or Switzerland). However, despite learning outcomes being defined as statements of what a learner is expected to know, understand, or be able to do, the authority – to foster these learning outcomes and even more importantly to assess students' achievement – lies with the teacher.

In the Asian-Pacific area, different approaches to standards and definitions of learning outcomes can be identified. **Taiwan** has traditionally maintained a national curriculum that might be seen as de facto standards. Also, Taiwan may be considered one of the early adopters of the idea of scientific literacy. It seems that Taiwan has always maintained a particular openness toward what is going on elsewhere and has constantly attempted to adopt ideas on how to develop the quality of the educational system as those ideas emerged across the world. In this course, Taiwan committed itself early to the idea of educational standards and respective assessment systems. This approach is tightly connected to the idea of scientific literacy as described by the PISA framework. As such, Taiwan adopted the notion of competences. Eight competences described in Taiwan's science standards draw a general picture of what Taiwanese students are expected to learn. However, as Chiu and Chen (*this volume*) state, little is known about specific learning outcomes are expected. That is the level of competence students are expected to obtain with respect to the eight specified competences. Chiu and Chen (*this volume*) suggest that learning outcomes may be categorized with respect to three dimensions: the knowledge dimension, the practice dimension, and the cognitive dimension. Altogether these dimensions are considered as a framework for describing what renders students competent. Australian educational policy, much like its German equivalent, was determined by the diversity of the Australian states. Only recently did **Australia** move from "an emphasis on learning objectives (i.e., 'inputs') to student learning outcomes (i.e., 'outputs')" (Pannizon, *this volume*, p. 343). As detailed by Panizzon in her chapter, learning outcomes are broadly conceived as indicators of what students have learned and what they are able to demonstrate cognitively, attitudinally, and/or behaviorally. Again this view has considerably been influenced by the idea of scientific literacy and the notion of scientific competence expressed in the PISA study.

In summary, there is a particular trend toward a common view on learning outcomes. Students are expected to be able to make use of what they learn at school instead of acquiring an all-embracing knowledge base. For science education, students are expected to acquire the necessary knowledge, skill, abilities, and what else it needs to solve particular problems or answer particular question about the scientific or technological nature of the world they live in. Comparing the different contributions in this book seems to indicate, however, that sometimes different terms are used and sometimes particular aspects of the described notion of learning outcomes are emphasized. In the United States, for example, the understanding of core concepts and the acquiring of core skills are at the very center of attention, whereas the German-speaking world uses the all-embracing term "competence". In the Netherlands, the context in which students learn has a great relevance for them, and in France the content is no longer specified when detailing learning outcomes in the upper level grades in Middle School Education. And there is another difference: the level of concreteness of the statements utilized to specify learning outcomes varies across countries. In Germany for example, much like in Finland, the competences are defined by rather abstract statements, whereas in the English-speaking world learning outcomes are to be concretized by learning performances. These are thought as more specific statements that can be operationalized in a test. A systematic comparison of the terms used in the different countries/regions brought together in this book is shown in Table

1. Apparently, "knowledge" and "skills" are the most frequently used terms to characterize the outcomes of student learning.

Table 1: Overview of Terms, Theoretical Constructs and Given Examples in the Different Chapters of this Book, Ordered by Countries/Regions of the Respective Authors.

| Country/Region | Term used<br>(Theoretical constructs)[1] | Example |
|---|---|---|
| Australia | Learning outcomes<br><br>(Content knowledge and understanding, inquiry skills and processes, attitudes, values, nature of science) | Not actually specified. |
| Finland | General goals<br><br>(Core tasks) | In grades 7–9, the core task of physics instruction in the seventh through ninth grades is to broaden the pupils' conception of the nature of physics. The instruction guides the pupil in thinking in a manner characteristic of science, in acquiring and using knowledge, and in evaluating the reliability and importance of knowledge in different life situations. |
| | Teaching intention<br><br>(Inquiry skills, content knowledge, attitude) | The pupils will learn in physics in grades 7–9 scientific skills, such as the formulation of questions and the perception of problems. |
| France | Learning outcomes<br><br>(Content, investigative processes, themes;<br>Knowledge, abilities, attitudes, competences) | Qualitatively interpreting the dispersion of white light by a prism. |
| Germany | Competence standards<br><br>(Weinert's notion of competence as cognitive abilities and motivational, volitional, and social readiness to solve problems in varying situations) | Students analyze phylogenetic relations as well as ecologically caused similarities in organisms by criterion-oriented comparisons. |
| Ireland | Learning outcomes<br><br>(Expectations of what a learner knows, understands and/or is able to demonstrate) | Recall genetics terminology: homozygous, heterozygous, phenotype, genotype, homologous chromosome pair, and so on. |

| | | |
|---|---|---|
| **Netherlands** | Attainment targets<br>*(Skills and knowledge; context-concept approach)* | The candidate is able to explain "selectivity" and "specificity" in relation to chemical reactions, and, if appropriate, demonstrate knowledge concerning catalysis, at least in the context of production of food, pharmaceuticals or transport of substances in the human body. |
| **Switzerland** | Competence<br>*(Weinert's notion of competence; combination of skills and domains)* | Students can perceive and observe basic phenomena with more than one sense. |
| **Taiwan** | Learning outcomes<br>*(Performances on knowledge, skills, argumentations and other related competencies)* | The foundation of scientific facts, information, and concepts held by students. |
| **Turkey** | General learning objectives<br>*(Scientific literacy)* | To enable students develop themselves so they become scientifically literate. |
| | Gained learning outcomes<br>*(Skills and abilities; concepts, skills and attitudes)* | It is expected that in relation to organs in the excretory system, the student shows the places of excretory system organs and structure on human body model and explains their roles briefly. |
| **USA** | Learning progression around core ideas<br>*(Practices, concepts, core ideas)* | Students create models of a gas at the molecular level showing how the gas takes the shape of its container. |
| **UK** | Intended learning outcomes<br>*(Topics, knowledge, understanding; knowledge, understanding, skills, abilities)* | In their study of science, the following should be covered: energy transfers can be measured and their efficiency calculated, which is important in considering the economic costs and environmental effects of energy use. |

[1] The terms, constructs, and examples are extracted from the respective chapters of this book; although most authors cited official national documents, there might be discrepancies in the nomenclature in some cases.

However, comparing these terms across the different countries/regions reveals the diversity when it comes to the meaning of these terms. For instance, "knowledge" and "skills" are used in some countries to refer to distinct areas of students' capabilities (e.g., in Australia and Finland), whereas other countries use these terms to describe two facets of a particular target performance (e.g., the Netherlands) or competence (e.g., Switzerland). The former interpretation of "knowledge" and "skills" as distinct areas does not specify the interrelation of these areas, but the latter interpretation of "knowledge" and "skills" does indicate that the central feature of student learning outcomes is the combination of these facets, because "only at the intersection of a skill and a domain is it possible for a student to achieve a competency" (Labudde, Nidegger, Adamina, & Gingis, *this volume*, p. 241). Irrespective of the theoretical implications of these differences, the presentation of "knowledge" and "skills" as either separate areas or as an amalgam within a curriculum has major implications for assessing student performance as well as for fostering student learning in classroom practice.

In addition to the diverse use of terms, the grain size of the related examples varies considerably. Whereas the examples from Switzerland (Labudde et al., *this volume*) and Taiwan (Chiu & Chen, *this volume*) are quite general, the examples from Ireland (Kennedy, *this volume*) or the Netherlands (Bertona, *this volume*) are very focused and concrete. The level of concreteness seems to reflect the amount of freedom and autonomy assigned to the individual teachers with regard to implementing the national curriculum in practice. Lavonen et al. (*this volume*) even claim that this might be a question of trust between teachers, policy-makers, and parents.

## 3  Assessing Learning Outcomes

Assessment systems follow countries' commitment to standards. Countries which traditionally maintained standards build on respective assessment systems in order to benchmark the standards. In the **United States** for example, the National Assessment of Education Progress program (NAEP) plays a very prominent role. However, given the move from content-driven standards toward the idea of core concepts and learning progressions, assessment systems needed to be refined too. Pellegrino's chapter – on the design of an assessment system that focused on students' achievement – raises two issues in carrying out assessments for K-12+ students:

1. Assessment needs to be integrated with curriculum and instruction; and all three have to build on existing research and models of teaching and learning.

2. Assessment should be conceptualized as reasoning from evidence, again based on empirical data and theoretical frameworks.

The first issue is addressed in the concept of learning progressions – developed on the basis of theoretical models and existing research on teaching and learning – that link curriculum, instruction, and assessment (see Krajcik et al., *this volume*). The second issue is addressed in greater detail in the chapter by Liu, who differentiates between two fundamental types of assessment:

1. Classroom assessment focusing on learners' actual level of understanding in order to inform instruction so that it can foster students' progression toward the next level.

2. Large-scale assessment to inform policy makers about students' overall progression with respect to the learning goals formulated in official documents.

Liu describes the process of developing an assessment instrument for a learning progression in great detail. He further discusses aspects of validity and reliability of assessment instruments as well as of the underlying learning progression – one aspect often neglected in the development of assessment instruments. Moreover, he focuses on the benchmarking of standards, that is, the process of defining qualitatively different performance levels.

Standards-setting is a process of particular relevance in the **German-speaking countries**, too. In Germany, for example, the development of an assessment framework and respective tasks in order to benchmark the newly introduced standards was one central part of the educational reform following the discussion of students' mediocre performance in TIMSS and PISA. In their chapter, Köller and Parchmann present an overview of how standards setting (i.e., benchmarking the standards) was achieved following the introduction of national educational standards in Germany. Kremer et al. (*this volume*) specify this process for the science subjects. Köller and Parchmann's chapter detail the theoretical model which, as suggested by Pellegrino (*this volume*), served as a guiding framework for the development of assessment instruments in order to benchmark the standards. Kremer et al. (*this volume*) further provide insights into the process of developing assessment items, as well as the first results from pilot testing the items. These items obviously require more than just factual knowledge to answer. It seems that with the shift from a focus on knowledge to one on competency (the construct used to describe learning outcomes), assessment instruments have evolved as well. This evolution takes into account the issues raised by Pellegrino (*this volume*). Based on models derived from theories of learning and from empirical research, a framework is developed which serves as the foundation for the development of assessment items. These items are used in order to obtain an empirical database for standards setting. Research aiming for a theoretical refinement of the assessment frameworks and subsequently the standards is presented by Bernholt, Eggert and Kulgemeyer (*this volume*). Their research investigated alternative models in order to better capture students' competence for better standards. None of these approaches, however, addresses the integration with curriculum and instruction, a point which is criticized by Schecker (*this volume*). Schecker also raises the point that ideally the development of educational standards should begin with the development of a theoretical model – development of assessment instruments (which should be validated against curriculum and instruction), and the collection of empirical data before defining standards – a process that has been carried out exactly as in Switzerland, where the formulation of standards was the final step of a large-scale assessment of student competences (Labudde et al., *this volume*).

Whereas the German-speaking countries in Europe share a somewhat common approach toward assessment, there is particular diversity among the other European countries. Millar, Whitehouse, and Abrahams (*this volume*), for example, take a look at the tradition of assessment systems in the **United Kingdom** and come to a critical conclusion:

> It would also be difficult to discern anything that could be termed a "theoretical model" or "perspective" on assessment underpinning the assessment practices that have been used. Practices are based on established practices, and on tacit views and ideas rather than explicit ones (p. 395).

However, Millar, Whitehouse, and Abrahams (*this volume*) also recognize progress. In the key stages 1 to 3 of the National Curriculum, students' progress is assessed by their teachers. In order to provide a foundation for such assessment, the Assessing Pupil Progress (APP) as a framework for teacher assessment has been developed. This framework differentiates five areas (assessment foci): (1) thinking scientifically; (2) understanding the applications and implication of science; (3) communicating and collaborating in science; (4) using investigative approaches; and (5) working critically with evidence. For each of these foci, eight performance levels are described. Test papers are provided by the authorities to be used by teachers – something which is also envisioned as part of the reform of the German educational system.

**Finland** has no tradition in central assessments. Instead, the responsibility for assessing students' progress with respect to the learning outcomes defined in the curriculum lies with the teacher. Whereas the general aims of science education are written from the teachers' point of view and include descriptions of teacher instruction in order to indicate what instruction should be like, the core curriculum also describes more specific objectives which serve as the basis for assessment through the teacher. The framework for assessment is based on the revised taxonomy of Bloom (Anderson et al., 2001) and differentiates two dimensions: knowledge and skills. The knowledge dimension comprises four types of knowledge (1) factual knowledge; (2) conceptual knowledge; (3) procedural knowledge; and (4) metacognitive knowledge and skills. The skills dimension embraces three cognitive processes: remember, understand, and apply and create (Lavonen et al., *this volume*, p. 488). In addition to the assessment through teachers, Finnish policy makers decided to organize a nationwide assessment of students' knowledge and skills. However, the intention is not to test the attainment of educational standards but to inform local authorities that "need assessment data for distributing educational resources and especially, for allocating support for low achieving schools" (Lavonen et al., *this volume*, p. 481).

In the **Netherlands**, central assessments and assessment through the teachers are not considered to serve two distinct purposes. Instead, both types of assessments are combined, as "the definitive grade of a specific subject in secondary school education is based for 50% on internal school exams and for 50% on external central exams." (Bertona, *this volume*, p. 437). Central exams take place at the end of secondary education. The internal exams are created by the teachers and take place at different times and occasions. It is interesting to note that because the Netherlands moves away from a content-oriented perspective to a perspective similar to the German notion of competence (i.e., the ability to use knowledge in different contexts), constructors of the central examination questions are not permitted to design items requiring knowledge not specified in the curriculum.

Two other countries or regions respectively with very elaborate assessment systems are Taiwan and Australia. In **Taiwan**, high-stakes national examinations play a central role in the screening process for high school students and the decision of their enrollment in senior high schools. Chiu and Chen (*this volume*) provide a thorough introduction to the national examinations with numerous examples of tasks utilized in the assessment. As the assessment concerns students' competence in contrast to their mere knowledge, the examination includes items on practices such as the ability to use tables and figures, and most items are context-based. The assessment system includes assessment in grades 4, 6, 9, and 12. And in addition to cross-sectional data, longitudinal data are obtained too, which is a rare in national assessments because of its costly nature.

Panizzon (*this volume*) provides an in-depth introduction to the **Australian** approach in assessing learning outcomes, which is not too different from what has been described for the other countries. Remarkable, however, is her point that although the shift toward scientific literacy as the overarching goal of education has led to diversification of the content areas in the curriculum, context-based teaching, and more authentic assessment tasks, national testing and a certain control-mania of policy makers has also led teachers to stick with a traditional way of teaching and assessing. Panizzon (*this volume*) makes a very valid point in this regard. It seems that not only in Australia but in most Western countries the success of scientific literacy has led to changes in the expected learning outcomes, curricula and central assessments. However, it also seems that in many countries the use of formative assessment is not at the center of the attention of teachers, nor is it at that of researchers and policy makers (cf. Ayas, *this volume*). This most likely is due to the fact that there is a lack of assessment instruments linked to the learning outcomes defined in the respective educational standards and a lack of instruments that teachers can easily use for formative assessment. Although new assessment instruments are developed in many countries by building on the new notion of learning outcomes, few of these instruments have been proven valid for formative assessment.

In summary, there is a particular shift in focus of assessment from the mere reproduction of factual knowledge to one of students' flexible usage of conceptual understanding, procedural skills, and attitudes in varying authentic situations. Triggered by this shift in focus, the value of factual knowledge decreases while the enhancement of applicable and transferable knowledge and skills increases. This tendency is consistent with the increasing acceptance of scientific literacy as the overall aim of science education (Roberts, 2007). In addition, curricula, teaching practice, and assessment are considered much more interrelated now. The alignment of all these three facets is a central building block in several national educational reforms, but such alignment seems to be one of the central challenges as well (cf. Pellegrino, *this volume*, p. 81). However, this trend does not seem to affect educational reforms in all the countries (cf. Millar et al., *this volume*). One considerable difference between the countries is the question of assessment authority. Some countries (e.g., Switzerland and Germany) are currently implementing national assessment systems to measure the outcomes of their national educational systems; other countries (e.g., the U.S. and the UK) that already have a long tradition concerning national assessments still make increasing use of this method of assessment. In contrast, the Finnish policy makers contend themselves with infrequent national and local monitoring based on samples, while leaving the appraisal of students' progress to the teachers. In between these extremes, a combination of national assessments and teacher-conducted tests is the basis for grading in the Netherlands (Bertona, *this volume*).

## 4  Fostering Learning Outcomes

As described in the preceding section, many countries, following the implementation or the revision of educational standards, are in the process of developing assessment systems, including respective frameworks and test items. Little is known, however, about the potential of this development for fostering student learning. What influence will these new approaches have on classroom practice? There seems to be a great diversity in the ways how teachers design instruction in order to foster student progress toward the intended learning outcomes within and between countries.

Krajcik et al. (*this volume*) describe what the instructional component of a learning progression can look like with the example of the Investigating and Questioning the World through Science and Technology (IQWST) curriculum. Although the IQWST curriculum was not originally based on a learning progression, it does align with the idea of learning progressions and curricular components built upon it. Therefore, the IQWST curriculum is designed around big ideas. In scope of the development, learning performances were specified for different levels of students' understanding of the big ideas. In a study where students' learning in the curriculum was investigated, the findings suggested that the curriculum indeed fosters students learning as intended. Bernholt, Eggert, and Kulgemeyer (*this volume*) envision that their work on the development of competency models can help teachers design learning environments and develop assessment systems. The authors also emphasize the need to find "effective ways to deal with competence orientation in classroom practice" (p. 193). Altogether it seems that in the German-speaking world there is a particular focus on creating standards-based assessments through developing respective assessment frameworks and new approaches to assessments. However, the whole focus lacks a systematic link with the curricula and instruction in particular – a point stressed by Schecker (*this volume*). Across the chapters in this volume, little is said about how new approaches of defining and assessing learning outcomes can foster learning outcomes.

Millar et al. (*this volume*) discuss the issue of "teaching to the test", as tests "become an important resource for teachers in preparing their teaching, and preparing students for their examinations" (p. 373). Obviously, in the UK, exams have become a more (or even the most) concrete definition of learning outcomes. However, teachers do not seem to use test results for formative assessment. This is a fact that Ayas (*this volume*) critically reflects, as it hinders assessment of learning outcomes to guide further instruction. In Finland, where assessment takes place in the individual schools and is the responsibility of the individual teachers, teachers, according to Lavonen et al. (*this volume*), reflect much more on teaching and learning in their classroom: "They can choose how to use different forms of assessment suitable for each situation, such as formative assessment of students' experimental work as well as summative assessment" (p. 481).

## 5 Discussion and Outlook

Despite the common aim to foster students' scientific literacy by improving science education, the approaches taken to define, assess, and foster learning outcomes vary considerably across the world. This is why a group of experts came together at a symposium at Strande near Kiel, Germany in order to discuss what can be learned from each other. For this purpose, each expert prepared a paper detailing his or her country's approaches to define, assess, and foster learning outcomes. This book presents the collection of these papers with the intent to identify possible answers to the key questions discussed at the symposium. The following are answers we have found regarding the question about how learning outcomes are defined:

1) There seems to be a consensus among most countries/regions across the world on a scientifically literate citizenship as the overarching goal of science education at school. Having a long tradition in some countries, scientific literacy as the overarching aim of education is adopted by more and more countries. This dissemination has been influenced considerably by the fact that the PISA framework builds on scientific literacy (e.g., Organization for Economic Co-operation and Development, 2010). Thus, as more and more countries introduce standards, such documents also build on the idea of scientific literacy.

2) Despite the consensus about scientific literacy as the overarching aim, definitions of learning outcomes as they can be found in standards documents are diverse among the countries/regions and sometimes even appear contradictory at first sight. Different terms, such as knowledge, skills, competences, understanding, and so on, are used to describe what students are expected to learn. Sometimes different terms denote the same accentuations, and sometimes the same terms connote different accentuations. This diversity becomes apparent from the different perspectives described in the chapters of this book. However, whereas the observed diversity in the details seems unnecessary and sometimes irritating, it also appears unavoidable, given the differences between national educational traditions as well as regional peculiarities.

3) Another difference appears in the grain size of expected learning outcomes. The educational authorities of some countries/regions contend themselves with rather general guidelines and leave the specification to local agencies or schools and their teachers. Other countries/regions rule in great detail, for example, what is expected of students to have learned at certain stages in their school education.

4) One similarity with respect to the definition of learning outcomes is a general trend away from mere knowledge of subject matter toward a deeper understanding and students' capacity to apply this knowledge in varying contexts. Again, the influence of PISA is obvious. The trend has been driven to different lengths in different countries/regions. Whereas some educational systems still rely on content-driven syllabi, in others the syllabi have already changed to less content-driven versions. Altogether, understanding as a learning outcome seems to receive growing support, that is, as a result of learning, students ought to be able to make reasonable use of their acquired knowledge.

5) The strongest divergence can be observed in the mode of implementation of standards as expected learning outcomes. In searching an empirical database first and setting standards on this ground, Switzerland has set an example that has not yet been followed by the other countries. The most common procedure still seems to be that educational authorities of some kind issue their expectations in official documents, which have been produced with more or less participation of other stakeholders in the field.

Looking at the diversity across nations, we beg the question of whether it would be worthwhile to internationally strive for a common set of definitions. At a first glance the answer is: probably not. The Bologna reform of the European tertiary level aims at achieving greater clarity in the descriptions of qualifications and at improving the efficiency and effectiveness of higher education. Accordingly, a huge effort is being made to achieve more coherence across institutions and national educational systems at university level. However, the implementation is heavily criticized by stakeholders on all levels of involvement. As there are by far more institutions and stakeholders involved on the primary and secondary levels, a similar approach does not seem to have good prospects. It is worth every effort, however, to take notice of each other's endeavors and to learn from each other. It seems to be more reasonable to strive for transparency than for assimilation. This includes the reflective use of particular terms as well as the explication of their interrelations and their relations to the overarching goals of scientific literacy. One example is the use of two terms that seem to be dominant in the current discussion in the countries concerned: "learning progressions" in the United States and "competences" in the German-speaking countries. While totally incompatible at first sight, the in-depth discussion at the symposium revealed an ample common ground. In both cases the focus goes beyond the acquisition of subject matter knowledge per se but encompasses – albeit with variations in detail – applicability and procedural skills. Both concepts also pertain to learning as a process: one defining the progression of learning, and the other preparing temporal development models of competences. Having an understanding of these commonalities opens the door for mutual learning.

Regarding the question of how learning outcomes are assessed, differences and congruencies can be observed. Obviously the type of assessment depends largely on the educational definition of standards and, perhaps even more so, on the political expectations of the authorities. The instruments for the assessment of knowledge acquisition appear to be available everywhere. Research instruments for measuring procedural skills seem to be still under construction. A common weakness appears to be the widespread neglect of school-based formative evaluation of the current level of learning, well-aligned to standards, as a diagnostic tool for teachers. Tentative attempts on this kind of formative evaluation have been reported, but the main focus everywhere seems to be on larger student samples, if not on whole populations.

The effects of standards and assessment approaches on classroom practice are, of course, manifold. Altogether one might conclude that the more specified and fine-grained the standards are, and the stricter the assessment is; the less pedagogical liberty will be left to teachers and the greater will be the temptation of narrowly teaching to the test. On the other side of the coin, the more open the definitions of learning outcomes are and the "softer" the assessment is, the less the guidance will be provided for teachers with lower aptitude. Which approach is perceived as more desirable will largely depend on teacher qualifications and hence on the quality of teacher training.

To conclude, this book provides the interested reader with pertinent answers to the question of how learning outcomes are defined across the world. The bottom line is: differently. However, there are similarities that give rise to the hope that a general description of what students are expected to learn at school, as envisioned by DeBoer (2011), is possible, although not in the short term. Regarding the assessment of learning outcomes, the fact that the same differences and similarities can be observed across countries/regions seems natural given that assessment frameworks somehow build on the definition of learning outcomes. However, one common trend may be observed, namely, that in line with a general trend of broader conceptions of learning outcomes beyond mere knowledge, assessment instruments are changing toward using a more holistic approach to assessing learning outcomes with respect to how students are supposed to make use of whatever they are supposed to learn at school. Finally, for all the countries/regions there is one common theme which is the lack of empirically validated teaching programs. It seems that little is known about how to work toward the learning outcomes, whatever they might be. This is where there are definitely more open questions than answers and where science education in the future will have to find answers. We hope we will be able to discuss them in the next symposium.

## References

Anderson, L. W., Krathwohl, D. R., Airasian, P. W., Cruikshank, K. A., Mayer, R. E., Pintrich, P. R., et al. (2001). *A Taxonomy for Learning, Teaching, and Assessing: A Revision of Bloom's Taxonomy of Educational Objectives.* New York: Longman.

DeBoer, G. E. (2011). The globalization of science education. *Journal of Research in Science Teaching, 48*(6), 567-591.

Duschl, R. A., Schweingruber, H. A., & Shouse, A. W. (2007). *Taking Science to School: Learning and Teaching Science in Grades K-8*. Washington, D.C.: National Academies Press.

Fensham, P. J. (2009). The link between policy and practice in science education: The role of research. *Science Education, 93*(6), 1076-1095.

Labudde, P. (2007). How to develop, implement and assess standards in science education? 12 challenges from a Swiss perspective. In D. Waddington, P. Nentwig, & S. Schanze (Eds.), *Making it Comparable: Standards in Science Education* (pp. 277-301). Münster: Waxmann.

Lavonen, J. (2007). National science education standards and assessment in Finland. In D. Waddington, P. Nentwig, & S. Schanze (Eds.), *Making it Comparable. Standards in Science Education* (pp. 101-126). Münster: Waxmann.

National Center for Education Statistics. *NAEP 2009 Year in Review*. Washington, DC. Available at: http://nces.ed.gov/nationsreportcard/pdf/about/2011471.pdf (Date of Access: October 1st, 2011).

Organization for Economic Co-operation and Development. (2010). *Education at a Glance 2010: OECD Indicators*. Paris, France: OECD Pub.

Roberts, D. (2007). Scientific literacy/science literacy. In S. Abell & N. G. Lederman (Eds.), *Handbook of Research on Science Education* (pp. 729-780). Mahwah, NJ: Lawrence Erlbaum Associates.

Schecker, H. & Parchmann, I. (2007). Standards and competence models – The German situation. In D. Waddington, P. Nentwig, & S. Schanze (Eds.), *Making it Comparable. Standards in Science Education* (pp. 147-164). Münster: Waxmann.

Schwarz, C. V., Reiser, B. J., Davis, E. A., Kenyon, L., Achér, A., Fortus, D., et al. (2009). Developing a learning progression for scientific modeling: Making scientific modeling accessible and meaningful for learners. *Journal of Research in Science Teaching, 46*(6), 632-654.

Valverde, G. & Schmidt, W. (2000). Greater expectations: Learning from other nations in the quest for 'world-class standards' in US school mathematics and science. *Journal of Curriculum Studies, 32*(5), 651-687.

Weiglhofer, H. (2007). Austria at the beginning of the way to standards in science. In D. Waddington, P. Nentwig, & S. Schanze (Eds.), *Making it Comparable. Standards in Science Education* (pp. 61-70). Münster: Waxmann.

Weinert, F. E. (2001). Concept of Competence: A Conceptual Clarification. In D. S. Rychen & L. H. Salganik (Eds.), *Defining and Selecting Key Competencies* (pp. 45-65). Göttingen: Hogrefe.